COGNITIVE–BEHAVIORAL INTERVENTIONS

Theory, Research, and Procedures

PERSONALITY AND PSYCHOPATHOLOGY
A Series of Monographs, Texts, and Treatises

David T. Lykken, Editor

1. The Anatomy of Achievement Motivation, *Heinz Heckhausen*. 1966°

2. Cues, Decisions, and Diagnoses: A Systems-Analytic Approach to the Diagnosis of Psychopathology, *Peter E. Nathan*. 1967°

3. Human Adaptation and Its Failures, *Leslie Phillips*. 1968°

4. Schizophrenia: Research and Theory, *William E. Broen, Jr*. 1968°

5. Fears and Phobias, *I. M. Marks*. 1969

6. Language of Emotion, *Joel R. Davitz*. 1969

7. Feelings and Emotions, *Magda Arnold*. 1970

8. Rhythms of Dialogue, *Joseph Jaffe* and *Stanley Feldstein*. 1970

9. Character Structure and Impulsiveness, *David Kipnis*. 1971

10. The Control of Aggression and Violence: Cognitive and Physiological Factors, *Jerome L. Singer* (Ed.). 1971

11. The Attraction Paradigm, *Donn Byrne*. 1971

12. Objective Personality Assessment: Changing Perspectives, *James N. Butcher* (Ed.). 1972

13. Schizophrenia and Genetics, *Irving I. Gottesman* and *James Shields*, 1972°

14. Imagery and Daydream Methods in Psychotherapy and Behavior Modification, *Jerome L. Singer*. 1974

15. Experimental Approaches to Psychopathology, *Mitchell L. Kietzman, Samuel Sutton*, and *Joseph Zubin* (Eds.). 1975

16. Coping and Defending: Processes of Self-Environment Organization, *Norma Haan*. 1977

17. The Scientific Analysis of Personality and Motivation, *R. B. Cattell* and *P. Kline*. 1977

18. The Determinants of Free Will: A Psychological Analysis of Responsible, Adjustive Behavior, *James A. Easterbrook*.

19. The Psychopath in Society, *Robert J. Smith*.

20. The Fears of Adolescents, *J. H. Bamber*.

21. Cognitive–Behavioral Interventions: Theory, Research, and Procedures, *Philip C. Kendall* and *Steven D. Hollon* (Eds.).

22. The Psychobiology of the Depressive Disorders: Implications for the Effects of Stress, *Richard A. Depue* (Ed.).

23. The Mental Health of Women, Marcia Guttentag, Susan Salasin, and Deborah Belle (Eds.).

24. Assessment Strategies for Cognitive–Behavioral Interventions, *Philip C. Kendall* and *Steven D. Hollon* (Eds.).

°Titles initiated during the series editorship of Brendan Maher.

COGNITIVE–BEHAVIORAL INTERVENTIONS

Theory, Research, and Procedures

Edited by

PHILIP C. KENDALL

STEVEN D. HOLLON
Department of Psychology
University of Minnesota
Minneapolis, Minnesota

ACADEMIC PRESS   New York   San Francisco   London   1979
A Subsidiary of Harcourt Brace Jovanovich, Publishers

ACADEMIC PRESS, INC.
111 Fifth Avenue, New York, New York 10003

United Kingdom Edition published by
ACADEMIC PRESS, INC. (LONDON) LTD.
24/28 Oval Road, London NW1 7DX

Library of Congress Cataloging in Publication Data

Main entry under title:

Cognitive-behavioral interventions.

   (Personality and psychopathology series)
   Includes bibliographies.
   1. Cognitive therapy. 2. Rational–emotive
psychotherapy. 3. Behavior therapy. I. Kendall,
Philip C. II. Hollon, Steven D. [DNLM: 1. Behavior
therapy. 2. Cognition. W1 PE861 / WM 425 P679]
RC489.C63C64   616.8'914   79–6940
ISBN 0–12–404480–8

For Philip C. Eichner, Robert A. Fachet, Lawrence C. Oleksiak, and all that is the concept of *Chaminade*

PCK

To my parents, Thomas and Vickie Hollon, who modeled well their marvelous delight in the process of inquiry

SDH

Contents

List of Contributors

Numbers in parentheses indicate the pages on which the authors' contributions begin.

Joan Asarnow (11), Department of Psychology, University of Waterloo, Waterloo, Ontario, Canada

Aaron T. Beck (153), Department of Psychiatry, University of Pennsylvania, Philadelphia, Pennsylvania 19104

Brian G. Danaher (389), Behavioral Sciences and Health Education, School of Public Health, University of California, Los Angeles, Los Angeles, California 90024

A. J. Finch, Jr. (37), Department of Psychology, Virginia Treatment Center for Children, Medical College of Virginia, Virginia Commonwealth University, Richmond, Virginia 23219

Myles Genest (287), Department of Psychology, University of Waterloo, Waterloo, Ontario, Canada

Marvin R. Goldfried (117), Department of Psychology, State University of New York at Stony Brook, Stony Brook, New York 11794

Steven D. Hollon (1, 153, 445), Department of Psychology, University of Minnesota, Minneapolis, Minnesota 55455

Philip C. Kendall (1, 37, 81, 445), Department of Psychology, University of Minnesota, Minneapolis, Minnesota 55455

Gloria Rakita Leon (357), Department of Psychology, University of Minnesota, Minneapolis, Minnesota 55455

Marsha M. Linehan (205), Department of Psychology, University of Washington, Seattle, Washington 98105

Verda L. Little (81), Department of Psychology, Virginia Commonwealth University, Richmond, Virginia 23284

Michael J. Mahoney (423), Department of Psychology, The Pennsylvania State University, University Park, Pennsylvania 16802

G. Alan Marlatt (319), Department of Psychology, University of Washington, Seattle, Washington 98105

Donald Meichenbaum (11), Department of Psychology, University of Waterloo, Waterloo, Ontario, Canada

Raymond W. Novaco (241), Program in Social Ecology, University of California, Irvine, Irvine, California 92717

Terry F. Pechacek (389), Laboratory of Physiological Hygiene, School of Public Health, University of Minnesota, Minneapolis, Minnesota 55455

Dennis C. Turk (287), Department of Psychology, Yale University, New Haven, Connecticut 06520

Preface

Cognitive–behavioral interventions represent a synthesis between opposing forces in the traditional and behavioral movements. Traditional psychotherapy has focused on the development of insight, but has been criticized for failing to directly manipulate those processes producing change and for lacking interest in the scientific evaluation of psychotherapy. Behavior therapy has emphasized systematic interventions and evaluation research, with the accurate specification of observable outcomes, but may have reduced its own effectiveness by ignoring those unobservable "mentalistic" processes so inexorably intertwined in any phenomena involving human beings. Cognitive–behavioral psychotherapy accepts these processes (e.g., belief systems, expectancies, attributions) as basic data, and seeks also to fashion interventions and assess their effectiveness on the basis of sound scientific principles. The cognitive–behavioral psychotherapist draws upon the phenomenological experience of the client-collaborator in the formulation of an intervention, and assesses change on the basis of both client report and external criteria.

The present volume surveys a variety of areas to which cognitive–behavioral strategies have been applied. The various contributors represent some of the major innovators in the field. Each has developed and systematically evaluated programs which apply sound empirically based procedures to cognitive and behavioral phenomena.

The opening chapter traces the short developmental history and describes the current professional environment of the cognitive–behavioral movement. The chapters that follow represent major contributions by the leading investigators across a number of areas of intervention. Each chapter describes a summary of research in the respective area, a description of the actual intervention procedures with supporting empirical data, and a consideration of the theoretical foundations and potential implications associated with the intervention.

The chapter contents vary across three dimensions. First, the interventions range from those that focus on the acquisition of new capacities to those that deal with the control and modification of existing processes. Second, several chapters focus on adult populations, several on child populations, and some on both. Finally, whereas a number of the chapters deal with problems that have been areas of traditional clinical concern, several others explore new and interesting applications for cognitive–behavioral interventions.

The content chapters open with a focus on various processes in children. Donald Meichenbaum and Joan Asarnow integrate a metacognitive developmental approach with cognitive–behavior modification and discuss the implications for children in the classroom. Next, Philip Kendall and A. J. Finch describe basic research and treatment evaluation data related to the cognitive and behavioral strategies for developing self-control in children. Verda Little and Philip Kendall review the areas of problem-solving, role-taking, and self-control training with delinquents.

The second major section, focusing primarily on adult problem populations, opens with Marvin Goldfried discussing anxiety reduction and the training of individuals to reevaluate potentially threatening events. Next, Steven Hollon and Aaron Beck describe interventions with depressed patients, followed by a description of assertion therapy by Marsha Linehan. Raymond Novaco then describes the cognitive regulation of anger and stress, followed by Dennis Turk and Myles Genest's discussion of the prevention and remediation of pain.

The third major section, focusing on habit problems, opens with Alan Marlatt providing an analysis of alcohol use and problem drinking. Gloria Leon next discusses the treatment of obesity and anorexia nervosa, while Terry Pechacek and Brian Danaher provide an analysis of the processes involved in quitting smoking. In the final content chapter, Michael Mahoney provides an account of how cognitive-behavioral processes are involved in a nonclinical area—the improvement of athletic performance.

The volume closes with an effort to explore the theoretical underpinnings of the range of cognitive–behavioral interventions. While sharing a common methodology, the field can be seen as heterogenous with respect to learning principles, underlying assumptions, and conceptual formulations. Our intent in this final chapter is not to promote any premature resolution, but rather, to stimulate theory-building by explicating some of the important areas of diversity.

This volume is directed toward both the clinician and the researcher. We have endeavored to furnish both sufficient literature review to stimulate continued inquiry and to provide practical "how to" material to facilitate systematic application. Our intent was to supply a volume which was both scholarly in style and applied in focus. The contributors are leaders in their field, and their work, we feel, is some of the most exciting and innovative in the discipline. From its inception, this work was targeted for the scientist and the practitioner interested in the newly emerging cognitive–behavioral approaches to intervention.

For their secretarial assistance in preparing this manuscript, we wish to thank Lydia Deavilo, Julie Williams, Joyce Montilino, and Norma Libson. Steven Norsted was most helpful with the indexing. We would also like to express our gratitude to those at Academic Press for their assistance, the University of Minnesota Department of Psychology for its support, and the Graduate School of the University of Minnesota for its financial support of our research. Last, though certainly not least, we would like to thank each of the contributors for being a part of this venture.

COGNITIVE–BEHAVIORAL INTERVENTIONS

Theory, Research, and Procedures

1

Cognitive–Behavioral Interventions: Overview and Current Status

PHILIP C. KENDALL
STEVEN D. HOLLON

INTRODUCTION

There are many approaches to the psychotherapy enterprise, and, at times, one wonders and speculates about the similarities and differences between the various treatment philosophies. Such a discussion has been evident concerning the territory of cognitive–behavioral interventions (Beck, 1970; Bergin, 1970; Ellis, 1973; Mahoney, 1977a; Meichenbaum, 1972a). Initially, the sentiments seemed to suggest that cognitive–behavioral approaches were "different," not identical to cognitive therapy (e.g., Beck, 1970) and not totally synonymous with rational–emotive therapy (e.g., Ellis, 1973). Although total equivalence with strict behavioral approaches was never suggested, cognitive–behavioral interventions are a rational amalgam of the two positions. It is not yet another new, exotic therapy. Rather, it is *a purposeful attempt to preserve the demonstrated efficiencies of behavior modification within a less doctrinaire context and to incorporate the cognitive activities of the client in the efforts to produce therapeutic change.*[1] The present volume brings together for the first time a collection of contributions that reflect the current status of the cognitive–behavioral approach. A careful reading of the text will no doubt result in realistic enthusiasm.

[1]Thanks are expressed to David Lykken.

1

Cognitive–Behavioral Interventions:
Theory, Research, and Procedures

REVOLUTION OR REACTION?

Cognitive–behavioral approaches to therapy are only partly the result of a revolution (Mahoney, 1977b) and are not entirely the outcome of a reactionary crusade (Williams, 1977). Rather, cognitive–behavioral interventions are the offsprings of bidirectional movements that have been dictated and directed by both empirical data and pragmatic necessities. The bidirectional movements involve behavior therapists' increasing concern with mediational therapeutic approaches and cognitive therapists' growing recognition of methodological behaviorism. Clearly, the efficacy of performance-based therapeutic procedures has been recognized, but it is only within the last half decade that cognitive–mediational processes have been integrated (Bandura, 1977; Meichenbaum, 1977) in the course of behavioral change. From the opposing direction, therapists who espoused the integrative effectiveness of cognitive psychotherapy have begun to accept the mandate for empirical evaluation and observable client improvement. Though perhaps more movement has been seen in behavior therapists' interest in cognitive phenomenon than in cognitive psychotherapists' empiricism, cognitive–behavioral interventions appear to be the infant offsprings of a paradoxical but successful marriage (Mahoney, 1977b; Meichenbaum, 1972a).

SCIENTIST–PRACTITIONER UNDERPINNINGS

Paul Meehl (1960) once noted that "The clinical psychologist has been able to assuage some of his therapeutic anxiety, and to refurbish his sometimes battered self-image, by keeping one foot planted on what seemed like comparatively solid ground, namely, psychodiagnosis [p. 19]." Most behavior therapy literature to date has found its basis in the solidity of learning theory and in the methods of an experimental–clinical science; many practicing behavior therapists have also been utilizing these approaches. Unfortunately, there are indications that the learning theory support for behavior therapy has been disappointing (Breger & McGaugh, 1965). However, a central component of behavior therapy is its experimental–clinical methodology, and it is this methodology that is likely to assuage current therapeutic anxieties.

Corresponding to the scientific mainstay of the behavior therapies, cognitive–behavioral interventions are emerging with empirical–clinical convictions (e.g., Goldfried, Linehan, & Smith, 1978; Kendall & Finch, 1978; Kendall & Wilcox, Note 1; Kendall, Williams, Pechacek, Graham, Shisslak, & Herzoff, 1979; Linehan, Goldfried, & Goldfried, Note 2; Meichenbaum, 1972b; Meichenbaum, Gilmore, & Fedoravicious, 1971; Novaco, 1975; Rush, Beck, Kovacs, & Hollon, 1977; Turk, 1977). The applied–experimental position of cognitive–behavior therapy should not imply that only cognitive psychology will offer meaningful insights or that the contributions of behavioral psychology will be eliminated. The current perspective can be characterized as one of openness, of listening to the data from a variety of informational sources and yet attentively guarding so as not to reverse our empirical advances. Such openness, like science itself, demands solid empirical analysis. The cognitive–behavioral approach seeks to study the clinical strategies that are the offshoots of social, developmental, and other areas of psychology while (using Meehl's phrase) "keeping one foot solidly planted" upon the principles of experimental–clinical psychology and social science research.

At the present time, the observer of the clinical–experimental psychologists who are involved in cognitive–behavioral interventions can recognize that these individuals are grounded in the scientific methods and that they share some, as Beck (1970) noted, common interests and basic philosophies. In addition, one may note that there are a number of "characteristics" that may be ascribed to the cognitive-behavioral approach. To this end, the reader is directed to the fundamentals of the cognitive–learning approach outlined by Mahoney (1977b). Yet, as Mahoney would also suggest, it may be somewhat premature to go any further in attempting to categorize the approach, to define its components, or to outline its methods. Such premature organization would only stagnate development and force researchers into somewhat unformulated molds. Avoiding such "school identification" is likely to further the multidimensional process advocated by Bergin (1970). For these reasons, our efforts here will consist more of an overview, and we shall restrict our description to general characteristics of cognitive–behavioral interventions in terms of the treatment target, the treatment approach, and the treatment evaluation. For purposes of perspective, the traditional behavior and the traditional cognitive approaches are included in our description.

As outlined in Table 1.1, the cognitive–behavioral approach is between the two more traditional extremes—the behavioral and the cognitive. It is a purposeful combination of the performance-oriented and the methodologically rigorous behavioral techniques with the treatment and evaluation of cognitive–mediational phenomena. Thus, internal as well as environmental variables are targets for treatment and are scientifically evaluated as contributors to behavior change. There are similarities across types of therapies, yet the cognitive–behavioral perspective would posit that using behavioral performance-based procedures and focusing upon both cognitive and behavioral problems would be superior to other therapeutic procedures because these undertakings are intentionally confronted in cognitive-behavioral modification rather than occurring serendipitously, as may be the case in other approaches. Although decidedly general, the overview in Table 1.1 gives some perspective to the emerging field of cognitive–behavioral therapy.

STREAMS OF INFLUENCE AND
SOURCES OF ACCEPTANCE

Within the relevant fields of psychology, there appear to be four relatively independent streams of influence that have affected the development of cognitive-

TABLE 1.1
General Characteristics of Cognitive–Behavioral Interventions

	Treatment target	Treatment approach	Treatment evaluation
BEHAVIORAL	Behavioral excesses or deficits	Behavioral "learning theory" interventions. Environmental manipulations (e.g., token economies, contingency management)	Observed changes in behavior with rigorous evaluation
	Behavioral excesses or deficits	Behavioral interventions. Skills training, information provision (e.g., modeling, role playing)	Observed changes in behavior with rigorous evaluation
COGNITIVE–BEHAVIORAL	Behavioral and cognitive excesses and deficits	Broadly conceived behavioral and cognitive methods	Observed changes in behavior and in cognition with methodological rigor
COGNITIVE	Cognitive excesses or deficits	Cognitive interventions with adjunctive behavioral procedures	Examination of cognitive and, to a lesser extent, of behavioral changes
	Cognitive excesses or deficits	Semantic interventions	Changes in cognitions, "integrative changes"; often, but not always, nonempirically evaluated

behavioral interventions. The palatability of these various endeavors has served as an initial basis for the apparent acceptance of this burgeoning approach.

The first influence stream posits that cognitions (i.e., thoughts) are subject to the same laws of learning as are overt behaviors (e.g., Cautela, 1967; Homme, 1965, Ullman, 1970). This position led to straightforward attempts to apply functional analytic assessment procedures and contingency-based intervention procedures to the modification of covert cognitive events. Some controversy exists regarding both the theoretical underpinnings and the empirical consequences of this approach (see Rachlin, 1977, with differing view points by Ellis, 1977, and Mahoney, 1977a). It may be simplistic to attempt to define cognitive–behavioral interventions in terms of hypothesized "mental" operations and covert conditioning models, yet efforts along these lines did provide an initial entry point for behaviorists into the cognitive arena.

The second influence stream is marked by the assertion that attitudes, beliefs, expectancies, attributions, and other cognitive activities are central to producing, predicting, and understanding psychopathological behavior and the effects of therapeutic intervention. Ellis's (1962) rational–emotive theory and Beck's (1963; 1976) cognitive theory have played important roles in generating acceptance of such cognitive phenomena. Early efforts at intervention focused on semantic techniques, for example, persuasion and reason, although later efforts have highlighted prospective hypothesis testing as a modal therapeutic paradigm. Efforts at empirical validation adhering to rigorous methodological standards of design and execution have further spurred interest (e.g., Meichenbaum et al., 1971; Rush et al., 1977; Trexler & Karst, 1972). Initially, this influence stream has largely grown out of the consulting room and has reflected a concern for phenomena that, although clinically relevant, have traditionally been difficult to isolate and to control.

Recent theoretical advances by recognized learning theorists, such as Kanfer's notions of self-regulation (Kanfer, 1970) and Bandura's theory of self-efficacy (Bandura, 1977), have furthered the process of casting covert cognitive processes into testable formulations that are easily integrated with behavioral paradigms. These developments constitute a third major influence stream, one springing from the experimental laboratory but concerned with the interface between covert and overt processes. Unlike the initial covert conditioning approach, these theories do not necessarily assume a direct correspondence between overt and covert events, although they do attempt to specify relationships between the respective domains.

Finally, a fourth influence stream has stemmed from the desirability and the apparent viability of combining cognitive treatment strategies with explicit behavioral contingency management in order to facilitate meaningful outcomes (e.g., self-instructional training via modeling with a response-cost contingency: Kendall & Finch, 1978; Kendall & Wilcox, Note 1). Such a strategy is analogous to systematically reinforcing an individual for engaging in the behaviors (e.g., evaluating beliefs, rehearsing self-statements) specified by cognitive theorists as likely to produce cognitive change. Generally speaking, then, incentive manipulations or manipulations of environmental contingencies can be used to facilitate a client's engagement in cognitive-restructuring or self-instructional training. Such an approach leaves open the possibility that the laws governing change in covert processes need not be isomorphic with the laws governing overt processes, while applying what are currently the most powerful respective change procedures separately.

Each of these streams of influence (and, perhaps, others) has contributed meaningfully to the shaping of cognitive–behavioral therapy, however incomplete at the present juncture. What does seem to emerge is a picture of greater flexibility in terms of models and approaches, without sacrifice of rigorous standards of assessment and evaluation. As Kazdin has commented (Note 3), cognitive–behavioral therapy is not a retreat to mentalism but is, instead, an attempt to include within behavior therapy terms that were once in the closet. No longer do theorists feel constrained to force all phenomena into either a cognitive or a behavioral model, nor do therapists feel constrained to limit themselves to one or another specific set of intervention procedures. The joint concern for theory and procedure within the context of an adherence to methodological behaviorism provides some protection against the dangers of unguided, unselective eclecticism.

The rapidity with which cognitive–behavioral influences have entered the mainstream of experimental–clinical psychology can be seen in an analysis of self-control. Although originally perceived as a venture into the lion's den (Kanfer & Karoly, 1972), many efforts were soon to follow (e.g., Goldfried & Merbaum, 1973; Mahoney & Thoresen, 1974; Thoresen & Mahoney, 1974). Yet, what were behaviorists doing discussing "self"-control? The self is as nonobservable as the mind, and numerous flags of caution were raised and waved. Now, just a few years later, self-control is no longer a flag (cue) for mentalism but, quite the contrary, a central focus of articles (e.g., Rehm, 1977), chapters (e.g., Mahoney & Arnkoff, 1978), and books (e.g., Stuart, 1977). We have learned a great deal as a result of our venture, and the way seems to have been paved for further advances.

Considering the following, a favorable future for cognitive–behavioral interventions is easy for us to predict. First, as hinted to by the present section heading, the streams of influence that evolved into cognitive–behavioral therapy will serve as a variety of sources for acceptance. That is, a number of different trends are coming together, and their commonality is recognized and fostered by the diverse interest groups. It is a joining of forces rather than a break for independence. Second, the cognitive–behavioral interventions are involved with clinically relevant target disorders while maintaining their commitment to scientific methods as the criteria for evaluation. This will, no doubt, foster acceptance. Last, with openness to a variety of sources of hypotheses and with the removal of several of the professional blinders, the cognitive–behavioral clinical researcher should, within methodological bounds, be capable of making noteworthy progress toward a more comprehensive understanding of human behavior.

In 1968, there was a symposium at the American Psychological Association Convention chaired by Marvin R. Goldfried that was entitled "Cognitive Processes in Behavior Modification." The participants, Gerald C. Davison, Thomas J.

D'Zurilla, Marvin R. Goldfried, Gordon L. Paul, and Stuart Valins, and the discussant, Louis Breger, discussed among other topics their growing dissatisfaction with the status of behavior therapy. The abstract for that symposium included the following:

> The predominant conceptualization of the "Behavior Therapies" as conditioning techniques involving little or no cognitive influence on behavior change is questioned. It is suggested that current procedures should be modified and new procedures developed to capitalize upon the human organism's unique capacity for cognitive control.

In 1974, Mahoney (1974) and Meichenbaum (1974), as separate participant-observers, noted that something was happening in behavior therapy. Indeed, a trend of interest has been recognized within behavior therapy and the broad framework of a cognitive psychology. This cognitive–behavioral trend is having an increasing impact.

Some 10 years after the early dissatisfactions and precisely 5 years after the recognition of "something going on," a number of authors have collaborated and contributed to this volume. The contents of this edition are indications that something has indeed happened and, with some promise and some caution, that much of the activity resulting from the cognitive–behavioral union will remain apparent in years to come.

REFERENCE NOTES

1. Kendall, P. C., & Wilcox, L. E. *A cognitive–behavioral treatment for impulsivity: Concrete versus conceptual labeling with nonself-controlled problem children.* Manuscript submitted for publication, 1979.
2. Linehan, M. M., Goldfried, M. R., & Goldfried, A. P. *Assertion therapy: Skill training or cognitive restructuring?* Manuscript submitted for publication, 1978.
3. Kazdin, A. E. Discussant's comments, *Clinical behaviorism: Past, present, and future.* Symposium presented at the meeting of the American Psychological Association, Toronto, 1978.

REFERENCES

Bandura, A. Self-efficacy: Toward a unifying theory of behavioral change. *Psychological Review,* 1977, *84,* 191–215.
Beck, A. T. Thinking and depression: I. Idiosyncratic content and cognitive distortions. *Archives of General Psychiatry,* 1963, *9.* 324–333.
Beck, A. T. Cognitive therapy: Nature and relation to behavior therapy. *Behavior Therapy,* 1970, *1,* 184–200.
Beck, A. T. *Cognitive therapy and the emotional disorders.* New York: International Universities Press, 1976.
Bergin, A. E. Cognitive therapy and behavior therapy: Foci for a multidimensional approach to treatment. *Behavior Therapy,* 1970, *1,* 205–212.
Breger, L., & McGaugh, J. L. Critique and reformulation of "learning theory" approaches to psychotherapy and neuroses. *Psychological Bulletin,* 1965, *63,* 338–358.
Cautela, J. R. Covert sensitization. *Psychological Reports,* 1967, *20,* 459–468.

Ellis, A. *Reason and emotion in psychotherapy.* New York: Stuart, 1962.

Ellis, A. Are cognitive behavior therapy and rational therapy synonymous? *Rational Living,* 1973, *8,* 8–11.

Ellis, A. Can we change thoughts by reinforcement? A reply to Howard Rachlin. *Behavior Therapy,* 1977, *8,* 666–672.

Goldfried, M. R., & Merbaum, M. (Eds.). *Behavior change through self-control.* New York: Holt, Rinehart & Winston, 1973.

Goldfried, M. R., Linehan, M. M., & Smith, J. L. Reduction of test anxiety through cognitive restructuring. *Journal of Consulting and Clinical Psychology,* 1978, *46,* 32–39.

Homme, L. E. Perspectives in psychology: XXIV. Control of coverants, the operants of the mind. *Psychological Record,* 1965, *15,* 501–511.

Kanfer, F. H. Self-regulation: Research issues and speculations. In C. Neuringer & J. L. Michael (Eds.), *Behavior modification in clinical Psychology.* New York: Appleton-Century-Crofts, 1970.

Kanfer, F. H., & Karoly, P. Self-control: A behavioristic excursion into the lion's den. *Behavior Therapy,* 1972, *3,* 398–416.

Kendall, P. C. & Finch, A. J., Jr. A cognitive–behavioral treatment for impulsivity: A group comparison study. *Journal of Consulting and Clinical Psychology,* 1978, *46,* 110–118.

Kendall, P. C., Williams, L., Pechacek, T. F., Graham, L. G., Shisslak, C. S., & Herzoff, N. Cognitive–behavioral and patient education interventions in cardiac catheterization procedures: The Palo Alto medical psychology project. *Journal of Consulting and Clinical Psychology,* 1979, *47,* 49–58.

Mahoney, M. J. *Cognition and behavior modification.* Cambridge, Massachusetts: Ballinger, 1974.

Mahoney, M. J. On the continuing resistance to thoughtful therapy. *Behavior Therapy,* 1977, *8,* 673–677. (a)

Mahoney, M. J. Reflections on the cognitive–learning trend in psychotherapy. *American Psychologist,* 1977, *32,* 5–13. (b)

Mahoney, M. J., & Thoresen, C. E. *Self-control: Power to the person.* Monterey, California: Brooks/Cole, 1974.

Mahoney, M. J., & Arnkoff, D. B. Cognitive and self-control therapies. In S. L. Garfield & A. E. Bergin (Eds.), *Handbook of psychotherapy and behavior change* (2nd ed.). New York: Wiley, 1978.

Meehl, P. E. The cognitive activity of the clinician. *American Psychologist,* 1960, *15,* 19–27.

Meichenbaum, D. H. Ways of modifying what clients say to themselves: A marriage of behavior therapies and rational-emotive therapy. *Rational Living,* 1972, *7,* 23–27. (a)

Meichenbaum, D. H. Cognitive modification of test anxious college students. *Journal of Consulting and Clinical Psychology,* 1972, *39,* 370–380. (b)

Meichenbaum, D. H. *Cognitive behavior modification.* Morristown, New Jersey: General Learning Press, 1974.

Meichenbaum, D. H. *Cognitive–behavior modification: An integrative approach.* New York: Plenum, 1977.

Meichenbaum, D. H., Gilmore, J. B., & Fedoravicious, A. Group insight versus group desensitization in treating speech anxiety. *Journal of Consulting and Clinical Psychology,* 1971, *36,* 410–421.

Novaco, R. W. *Anger Control: The development and evaluation of an experimental treatment.* Lexington, Massachusetts: Lexington Books, 1975.

Rachlin, H. Reinforcing and punishing thoughts. *Behavior Therapy,* 1977, *8,* 659–665.

Rehm, L. P. A self-control model of depression. *Behavior Therapy,* 1977, *8,* 787–804.

Rush, A. J., Beck, A. T., Kovacs, M., & Hollon, S. Comparative efficacy of cognitive therapy and pharmacotherapy in the treatment of depressed outpatients. *Cognitive Therapy and Research,* 1977, *1,* 17–38.

Stuart, R. B. *Behavioral self-management: Strategies, techniques, and outcome.* New York: Brunner/Mazel, 1977.

Thoresen, C. E., & Mahoney, M. J. *Behavioral self-control.* New York: Holt, Rinehart & Winston, 1974.

Trexler, L. D., & Karst, T. O. Rational–emotive therapy, placebo, and no treatment effects on public speaking anxiety. *Journal of Abnormal Psychology,* 1972, *79,* 60–67.

Turk, D. C. *A coping skills-training approach for the control of experimentally produced pain.* Unpublished doctoral dissertation, University of Waterloo, Waterloo, Ontario, Canada, 1977.

Ullmann, L. P. On cognitions and behavior therapy. *Behavior Therapy,* 1970, *1,* 201–204.

Williams, J. L. Implications of the rise of cognitive behaviorism. *American Psychologist,* 1977, *32,* 895–896.

2

Cognitive–Behavioral Modification and Metacognitive Development: Implications for the Classroom[1]

DONALD MEICHENBAUM
JOAN ASARNOW

INTRODUCTION

During a recent visit to a local school, the authors discovered that the principal had implemented a program that required the children to begin each morning with a 10- to 15-minute drill doing mathematical exercises. This was in addition to the regular daily mathematics lesson. The purpose of this morning activity was to have the children exercise their "faculties," wake up their minds, sharpen their cognitive skills, and so forth. These comments harken back to the days of faculty psychology, where the hope of educators was that the acquisition of logical and rigorous skills, such as Latin or geometry, would transfer to other content areas. Little transfer, however, seems to follow from such training, and one can question the pedagogical value of such daily exercises. Although we may take issue with the manner and content of such a faculty-based approach, we would argue that the principal was on the right track; he merely had the wrong content. His mistake was to focus on the content of learning instead of the processes of learning, the "what" instead of the "how" of learning. These distinctions will become more apparent as we develop our case.

The purpose of the present chapter is to review the related, but thus far unconnected, areas of cognitive–behavioral modification with children and metacognitive development, indicating the shared concerns of these two approaches. An examina-

---

[1]The authors are indebted to Ellen Ryan for her many helpful discussions and for her editorial perspicacity.

Cognitive–Behavioral Interventions:
Theory, Research, and Procedures

tion of the commonalities in these two approaches has implications for the business of teaching thinking to children. The present review has implications for the nature of the activities that the principal may employ to teach his pupils "how" to think.

COGNITIVE–BEHAVIORAL MODIFICATION WITH CHILDREN

There has been a recent shift in behavior therapy toward the use of more cognitively oriented interventions in the treatment of behavior disorders (Goldfried & Davison, 1976; Mahoney, 1974; Meichenbaum, 1977). Since the empirical and clinical data on cognitive–behavioral modification (*CBM*) with children has recently been reviewed (Craighead, Craighead-Wilcoxon, & Meyers, 1978; Karoly, 1977; Kendall, 1977; Meichenbaum, 1977, 1978), the present focus will be on the nature and limitations of the CBM outcome data and on how the technology of CBM has more recently been employed to teach academically based skills.

Impetus to Cognitive–Behavioral Modification with Children

Developmental research on a number of related problems has contributed to the burgeoning interest in CBM. One prominent research area has been the laboratory-based investigations of children's self-mediated cognitive strategies. For example, Mischel, Kanfer, and others have examined specific types of cognitive variables involved in children's ability to delay gratification.

A related influence on the development of CBM with children has been the work on verbal mediation, in which learning to use task-appropriate mediators is viewed as involving the separate phases of comprehension (Bem, 1971), production (Flavell, Beach, & Chinsky, 1966), and mediation (Reese, 1962). This verbal mediational "deficiency" literature suggests that a training program designed to improve task performance and engender self-control should provide explicit training in the comprehension of the task, the spontaneous production of mediators, and the use of such mediators to control nonverbal behavior.

Closely akin to the mediational literature has been a focus on the need for task analyses, or what Meichenbaum (1976) has called a cognitive–functional analysis of children's task performance. A cognitive–functional approach to psychological deficits emphasizes the role of the subject's cognitions (i.e., self-statements and images) in the behavioral repertoire. A functional analysis (in the operant sense of the term) of the subject's thinking processes is conducted, and a careful inventory is made of the subject's cognitive strategems as related to task parameters. Cameron (1976) and Meichenbaum (1977) have illustrated how one can go about answering the question: In what psychological processes must the successfully achieving individual engage, and in which of these is my subject failing?

Another major impetus to the work on CBM with children has been the developmental theorizing and research conducted by the Soviet psychologists Vygotsky (1962) and Luria (1961, 1969). These Soviet investigators have suggested that a child is socialized by means of internalizing the interpersonal instructions and communications of others. A stage model was proposed to describe the sequence by which children abbreviate and transform interpersonal instructions into covert intrapersonal speech, which in turn comes to guide and control the child's behavior. Although the Soviet model has been criticized (Bloor, 1977; Meichenbaum, 1975b; Wozniak, 1972), it has had a good deal of heuristic value in generating a training paradigm to teach children self-control, or the ability to think before they act.

Cognitive–Behavioral Modification with Children, Some Beginnings

In an attempt to combine the influences of developmental social learning literature, the work on mediational deficits and task analysis, and the Soviet work, Meichenbaum and Goodman (1971) developed a self-instructional training regimen that was composed of combinations of modeling, overt and covert rehearsal, prompts, feedback, and social reinforcement. A host of clinical suggestions as to how self-instructional training can be conducted with the children has been described elsewhere (Meichenbaum, 1977). The Meichenbaum and Goodman (1971) approach extended the work of Palkes and her colleagues (Palkes, Stewart, & Freedman, 1972; Palkes, Stewart, & Kahana, 1968). Each of the Palkes et al. studies was designed to enhance the self-control of impulsive and hyperactive children by teaching the children to "stop, look, and listen," to think before they act. The cognitive modeling and rehearsal procedures were designed to teach the children strategems of what to say to themselves prior to performing some task. Illustrative of the CBM self-instructional approach is a study by Douglas, Parry, Marton, and Garson (1976), who exposed children to a trainer who modeled the following strategems, which the child in turn would have an opportunity to try out:

> "I must stop and think before I begin." "What plans can I try?" "How would it work out if I did that?" "What shall I try next?" "Have I got it right so far?" "See I made a mistake there—I'll just erase it." "Now let's see, have I tried everything I can think of?" "I've done a pretty good job." [Douglas et al., 1976, p. 408].

A few observations should be offered before we consider the relative efficacy of such training. The general outline for conducting such think-aloud training programs has been to teach a variety of performance-relevant skills: (a) problem identification and definition or self-interrogation skills ("What is it I have to do?"); (b) focusing attention, and response guidance, which is usually the answer to the self-inquiry ("Now, carefully stop and repeat the instructions"); (c) self-reinforcement involving standard-setting and self-evaluation ("Good, I'm doing fine."); and (d) coping skills and error-correcting options ("That's okay. . . . Even if I make an error I can go slowly."). Such cognitive training is conducted across tasks, settings, and people (trainer, teacher, parent) in order to ensure that children do not develop task-specific response sets but, instead, develop generalized strategems.

Evidence for Efficacy

Although the initial results from these CBM studies with children are encouraging (see Meichenbaum, 1977), the evidence that CBM can foster generalized improvement has been equivocal. For example, in the initial Meichenbaum and Goodman (1971) study, improvement was evident on the experimental measures at a 4-week follow-up, but the treatment effects did not generalize to the classroom. The Palkes *et al.* (1968) study did not assess for generalization or follow-up, and the Palkes *et al.* (1972) study involved limited training and did not yield improvement at a 2-week follow-up. Studies, however, by Bornstein and Quevillon (1976), Varni and Henker (in press), and Kendall and Finch (1976, 1978) have obtained generalization of CBM to the classroom.

The results of two CBM studies with children are particularly noteworthy. In the Douglas *et al.* (1976) study the effects of modeling, self-verbalization, and self-reinforcement techniques on hyperactive boys was examined. The training period was much more extensive than other studies, covering a 3-month period in which the children were seen for two 1-hour sessions per week for a total of 24 sessions. In addition, 6 sessions were conducted with the child's teacher and 12 with the child's parents. The results indicated that, relative to an assessment control group, the children who received CBM treatment evidenced improvement on a variety of cognitive and motor tasks, such as listening, spelling, and oral comprehension tests, but they did *not* improve on the Connors' Teacher Rating Scale. Once again, evidence for generalization to the classroom as assessed by teacher ratings did not appear, although there was evidence of generalization across cognitive academically based tasks. In a related study, Camp, Blom, Hebert, and Van Doorninck (1977) employed a "think aloud" program to teach young, aggressive boys to develop answers to four basic questions: "What is my problem?" "What is my plan?" "Am I using my plan?" and "How did I do?" The CBM training yielded significant improvement relative to control groups on a variety of measures, including Porteus Maze, Matching Familiar Figures test, Wechsler Intelligence Scale for Children (WISC) peformance IQ, reading achievement, and classroom bheavior as evident by teacher ratings.

Two studies have also indicated the relative efficacy of CBM procedures with children. Watson and Hall (Note 1) have successfully employed self-control training (relaxation plus the Camp *et al.* "think aloud" program) on the treatment of hyperactive fifth- and sixth-grade boys. Relative to placebo-control training, improvement was evident not only on teacher's ratings (Connors abbreviated rating scale), but also generalized to reading comprehension scores. Barkley, Copeland, and Sivage (Note 2) also found that a self-control treatment program that involved self-instruction, self-monitoring, and self-reinforcement was effective in improving hyperactive children's behavior and attention to tasks, but the improvement did *not* extend to achievement scores. Both Watson and Hall and Barkley *et al.* comment on how readily classroom procedures can be modified to include self-instructional training.

In summary, as one surveys the CBM literature, the evidence for treatment efficacy with children who manifest self-control problems is promising. Evidence for treatment generalization, however, especially across response modes and settings, is less convincing and often equivocal. Perhaps more careful consideration must be directed at what we mean and expect when we seek generalization. It is our contention that the recent work on metacognitive development will help explicate the processes underlying generalization. Before examining the metacognitive literature, let us examine how the CBM technology of self-instructional training has recently been extended to academically based skills.

APPLICATION OF CBM TO ACADEMIC TASKS

Whereas the initial work on CBM with children focused on problems of self-control (e.g., impulsivity, hyperactivity, aggression, and cheating), more recent efforts have been directed at applying the CBM self-instructional approach to academically relevant tasks.

Operant Research Related to Cognitive–Behavioral Modification

In order that the self-instructional approach should not be seen as a totally novel or groundbreaking one, consider the following studies employing single-subject designs that were conducted within an operant framework. Each of the studies (Grimm, Bijou, & Parsons, 1978; Lovitt & Curtiss, 1968; Parsons, 1972) was concerned with the influence of self-verbalization on academic achievement. For example, Lovitt and Curtiss assessed the effect of having children verbalize an arithmetic problem before writing the answer, as opposed to simply writing the answer. The verbalization enhanced the child's performance. The studies by Parson and Grimm *et al.* combined self-verbalization with a strategy of breaking the problem into its component parts. Both studies noted significant improvement in performance when verbalization was added to the intervention. A study by Smith and Lovitt (1976) indicated that a teacher who verbalizes what she is doing in a mathematical problem enhanced the learning process. Leon and Pepe (Note 3) have successfully linked the operant and self-instructional training approaches in the classroom by teaching mathematical skills to learning-disabled and educationally mentally-handicapped 9- and 10-year-olds. The results indicated that both the self-instructional and the traditional remediation approaches were effective, but the self-instructional approach required less direct training time and was more generalizable to similar types of arithmetic problems.

A common element of these studies was to teach the child to self-verbalize and to break down the problems into component processes. Two examples will now be offered of how self-instructional training can be specifically employed in enhancing reading comprehension and serial recall.

Reading Comprehension: an Example

As an example, consider the Bommarito and Meichenbaum (Note 4) self-instructional study designed to enhance childrens' reading comprehension. The population consisted of a group of seventh- and eighth-grade readers who had comprehension or reading grade-levels that were 1 or more years below their academic grade and below their vocabulary level. The children seemed to have the basic prerequisite skills (e.g., decoding, knowledge of word families, knowledge of vocabulary) but, nonetheless, experienced comprehension problems. Recognizing that comprehension skills represent a set of complex processes that are not well-explicated, we conducted, with appropriate trepidation, a self-instructional training study designed to influence the childrens' organizational strategies. The children received six 45-minute individual self-instructional training sessions.

Some examples of the training procedure with the poor readers may be informative. The model for developing the self-instructional training program for the poor readers was the work of Gagné (1964). Gagné uses a task-analysis approach by beginning with a behavioral statement of the instructional objective. Then he asks what are the prerequisite behaviors the child must be capable of in order to perform the terminal behaviors. For each of these identified behaviors, the same question is asked, and a hierarchy of objectives is thereby generated. Gagné is proposing that an individual's acquisition of a complex behavior is dependent upon his prior acquisition of a succession of simpler behaviors. Thus, the instruction can be based on the cumulative learning process.

The self-instructional training approach followed a similar strategy, except that each step in the hierarchy was translated into self-statements and cognitive strategies that could be modeled by the trainer and rehearsed (initially aloud, and then covertly) by the child. The instructor models not only the task-relevant. problem-solving self-statements, but also coping self-statements that deal with frustration and failure.

In short, the child was shown (a) how to break down each task (e.g., reading comprehension) into manageable units; (b) how to determine the hierarchy of skills required to do the task; and (c) how to translate these skills into self-statements that can be rehearsed.

A major element of the training was the use of cognitive modeling, that is, the modeling of the cognitive strategies, critical thinking processes, and coping self-statements required for the task. The full instructional potential of modeling or observational learning is just beginning to be realized. Part of the impetus for this has been the growing realization that modeling or observational learning should *not* be equated with mimicry or exact matching or superficial imitation. Instead, the exposure to a modeling display permits the discrimination and organized covert storage of complex and integrated behavior chains that may then be retrieved to satisfy environmental demands.

The self-instructional training format most closely approximated a kind of Socratic dialogue, with the child helping by analyzing his or her own cognitions, contributing to the model package, reacting to the model, and the like. For example, the children helped in rule generation for doing such tasks as Cloze Exercises (i.e., sentences with words deleted that the children must fill in, giving the reasons for their choices). The trainer and then the child "tried on" the suggested rules. This interplay was enmeshed in a cognitive-modeling and overt and covert rehearsal format. Thus, the self-instructional training technique should be seen *not* as regimented or austere but, rather, as individually tailored and highly responsive to each child.

From a self-instructional framework, the question becomes: What should a poor reader say to himself or herself prior to, during, and following reading a passage in order to enhance understanding? What should he or she say to himself or herself when trying to answer questions about the story?

The content of the self-statements that were included in the self-instructional training paradigm recognized that a child's understanding and retention of a story depends not only on the information presented but also on the implications of that information in light of prior knowledge possessed by the child. As Bransford and Johnson (1972) state, subjects "do not simply interpret and store the memory of sentences per se. Rather, they create semantic products that are a joint function of input information and prior knowledge [p. 718]." Note that the present CBM strategy is not suggesting that good readers explicitly and consciously talk to themselves, but, instead, such cognitive acts have become automaticized in the manner that LaBerge and Samuels (1974) discuss in the automaticity process. Indeed, the ultimate objective of the self-instructional program is to approximate such proficiency. It is being suggested, though, that one way to have poor readers unlearn inefficient or faulty strategies and develop efficient reading skills is to deautomatize the reading act. Once the reading act is deautomatized, the child can be taught how to employ new cognitive strategies such that, with practice, these will in turn become automated.

By the last training session, after having built up to this phase by working on reading exercises, modeling, and self-instructional rehearsal, the poor reader's internal dialogue approximated the following modeled passage:

Well, I've learned three big things to keep in mind before I read a story and while I read it. One is to ask myself what the main idea of the story is. What is the story about? A second is to learn important details of the story as I go along. The order of the main events or their sequence is an especially important detail. A third is to know how the characters feel and why. So, get the main idea. Watch sequences. And learn how the characters feel and why.

While I'm reading I should pause now and then. I should think of what
I'm doing. And I should listen to what I'm saying to myself. Am I saying
the right things?
    Remember, don't worry about mistakes. Just try again. Keep cool,
calm, and relaxed. Be proud of yourself when you succeed. Have a blast!

Other self-statements to be emitted while answering the questions were also
included in the training package. Critical thinking and the acquisition of heuristic
principles to be applied to any reading materials were the focus of training. This
approach is consistent with the data reviewed by Wark (1968), who viewed reading
comprehension as implicit verbal behavior. He summarized several studies that
indicate that good readers apparently finish reading a passage and then categorize
and talk about that passage on a covert level. Good readers appear to say different,
more implied, meaningful things to themselves about what they have read then do
poor readers.

The results indicated that the self-instructional training group was significantly
different from a practice placebo group, who received exposure to all of the training
sessions and materials but did not receive self-instructional training, and also different relative to an assessment control group. The mean change scores for the
self-instructionally trained subjects on a reading comprehension test (i.e., Nelson
reading test) was 11.5 months with a range from 6 to 15 months; on a Cloze Exercise test the mean improvement was 13 months with a range from 11 to 19 months'
improvement. The Nelson and Cloze tests were given immediately after training.
The superiority of the self-instructional group relative to the two control groups was
maintained at a 1-month follow-up, as assessed by means of the Gates–McGinnitie
reading test.

A similar, cognitively based training approach to enhance reading comprehension
has been offered by Dansereau, Collins, McDonald, Dickhoff, Garland, and Holley
(Note 5) in which college students were given the mnemonic (MURDER) to employ
when reading. MURDER stands for get yourself in the *mood* for learning; read for
understanding; recall as much of the material as you can without looking; reprocess
the material in order to *digest* it using various meaning networks; *expand* and
deepen understanding by asking questions; and *review* your mistakes. The objective
of such a mnemonic is to engender rule-generative behavior. It is only one element
of the cognitively based learning-strategy curriculum outlined by Dansereau *et al.*
Other investigators who have found that a self-instructional approach can enhance
reading comprehension include Bower (1974), Egeland (1974), and Wozniak and
Neuchterlein (Note 6).

What Self-Instructions Do

Such self-instructional training may make it possible for students to do a kind of
thinking they could not, or would not, otherwise do. The subject's internal dialogue
is used as a tool for facilitating reading comprehension, accelerating problem-

solving ability, and fostering self-control. Meichenbaum (1974) has characterized such self-instructions as a form of "cognitive prosthesis" that could be employed to help overcome inadequate performance. More specifically, verbalizations on cognitive tasks may facilitate behavior in several ways. First, overt verbalizations may serve to organize information in the task or stimulus array and to assist the subject in generating alternatives regarding the solution. Second, verbalization may aid the subject in evaluating feedback by providing verbal mediators to distinguish relevant and irrelevant dimensions. Active rehearsal of hypotheses should facilitate the subject's retention in short-term storage and thereby reduce the memory load of the task. Self-instructional rehearsal may also enhance a positive task orientation, reinforce and help maintain task-relevant behaviors, and provide ways of coping with failure and self-reinforcing success.

Meichenbaum (1977) has theorized that self-instructions play a direct role in changing behavior, one analogous to that served by interpersonal instructions. In this context it is interesting to note that Gagné (1964) suggested that interpersonal instructions serve the following functions: (*a*) motivating the subject by eliciting an achievement set; (*b*) helping him identify the criterion performance and the salient parts of the stimulus situation; (*c*) aiding recall of relevant subordinate performance capabilities necessary to the task; and (*d*) changing thinking in terms of task-relevant hypotheses and controlling extraneous thoughts and behaviors. In this way, instructions provide the subject with a rule or principle by which he can mediate his behavior. The rule-generative aspects of self-statements are evident in the self-statements reported before for the training of hyperactive and hyperaggressive children and poor readers. It is interesting to analyze the self-statements employed by Camp *et al.*, Douglas *et al.*, and Meichenbaum and Goodman against Gagné's list of functions for interpersonal instructions. Also, see Chapter 3 by Kendall and Finch in the present volume.

Self-instructional training may help the subject to know exactly when and where to use what he has; that is, he may have some mediational skills but yet not think to apply them in appropriate occasions. To use a concept provided by Flavell *et al.* (1966), the genesis of internal speech, in its broadest sense, may entail a progressive "linguification" of more and more tasks and situations. Some suggestion that subjects require training in internalized "linguification" comes from the conclusion offered by Dykman, Ackerman, Clements, and Peters (1971), who state:

> We would have presumptive evidence of the importance of inner speech if it could be shown, for example, that inner-speech training decreases impulsivity, reaction time, or distractibility, or increases physiological reactivity. That is, one might train the child to talk to himself, but not aloud, possibly emphasizing inhibitory commands [p. 88].

The research we have been conducting over the last 10 years with a number of different clinical populations provides some of the evidence Dykman *et al.* sought (see Meichenbaum, 1977). Moreover, if one examines the host of remediational practices that have been suggested to be used with clinical populations, such as learning-disabled children (e.g., Vallett, 1969; Warner, 1973), it is interesting to note how often mediational or self-instructional training is implicit in such training packages. This analysis suggests that making the self-instructional aspects explicit will further enhance the efficacy of such remediational techniques.

Another Sampler, Memory Recall

The description of one further study from our lab will illustrate the elements that constitute a self-instructional training approach. In 1967, Keeney, Canizzo, and Flavell conducted a training study on serial recall with 5- and 6-year-olds. Keeney *et al.* examined the extent to which an induced rehearsal procedure that involved prompting children to rehearse would increase children's tendency to produce a rehearsal strategy on a serial-recall task. The Keeney *et al.* results, which are much cited, revealed that children who failed to rehearse spontaneously prior to training (*a*) could be induced to rehearse with brief training, and (*b*) abandoned the mediational strategy once the demand for strategy production was removed, even though the use of the strategy had previously resulted in improved performance. Such results have been interpreted as supporting a "production deficiency" hypothesis (Keeney *et al.*, 1967). According to this hypothesis, prior to mastering various mediational strategies, children go through a transitional period during which they have the basic ability to execute some target mediator effectively but lack the disposition to do so. The Keeney *et al.* study also questioned the possibility of the success of training (instructional manipulations) in altering the way children employ cognitive strategems. Later, we will question the adequacy of the production-deficiency model; but, for now, consider how the efficacy of an induced-rehearsal training paradigm can be enhanced by adding self-instructional components (i.e., cognitive modeling, self-verbalization, and task analysis).

The basic requirement of the serial recall task was that the child remember in a specific order a series of pictures of everyday objects. Asarnow and Meichenbaum (Note 7) assessed the relative efficacy of the Keeney *et al.* induced-rehearsal procedure versus the Meichenbaum and Goodman (1971) self-instructional procedure and versus a practice control group in enhancing kindergartners' serial recall. Table 2.1 summarizes the components in the respective treatments.

Once again, to convey a flavor of the self-instructional procedure, examples of the training protocol are offered. The objective of the training was to influence the children's tendency to rehearse during a 15-second delay period. A question-and-answer format was employed in the self-instructional training. At the outset of the training, the examiner supplied both questions and answers. As training progressed, the examiner supplied fewer questions, until the child was answering all questions and asking them as well. An example of the self-instructional dialogue that was modeled by the examiner and eventually employed by the subject was as follows:

> *Now what is it I have to do? I have to find a way to remember the order*
> *in which the pictures are pointed to. How can I do that? Hmm. I know I*
> *can keep saying the names of the pictures over and over again until it is*

TABLE 2.1
Summary of the Major Components Present in Each of the Three Training Conditions

	Training conditions[a]		
Components of training conditions	Practice	Rehearsal	Self-instructional training
A. Information conveyed to subject.			
1. There is a task-appropriate strategy. (Experimenter says there is a "best way" to remember the pictures.)	X	X	X
2. Rehearsal is a task-appropriate strategy. (Experimenter says "saying the names over and over again will help you remember.")		X	X
3. Information concerning the use of self-reinforcement and coping self-statements. (Experimenter models the sequence. "What is it now? I can't quite remember. I can remember if I think slowly and carefully. Dog, cat . . . dog, cat . . . , dog, cat, fish. That's it! Good.")			X
B. Practice.			
1. On task.	X	X	X
2. Rehearsing on task.	X[b]	X	X
3. Using self-reinforcement and coping self-statements.			X
4. Internalizing the instruction that rehearsal is a task-appropriate strategy. (Subject says "saying the names over and over again will help me remember.")			X
5. Internalizing the instructions on how to use rehearsal as a task-appropriate strategy. (Subject says "I can remember if I say the names over and over again in the same order as you (Experimenter) pointed to them, remembering which picture was first, second, and third, etc.")			X
6. Internalizing instructions on how to use self-reinforcement and coping self-statements. (Subject says "I can remember. . . . Think slowly and carefully. Dog, cat . . . dog, cat . . . dog, cat, fish. Good. I remembered.")			X
C. Elements of the atmosphere.			
1. Encouragement and support. (Experimenter says "Try your best. You can remember.")	X	X	X
2. Incentive, a prize. (Experimenter says "If you try your best you will get a prize.")	X	X	X
3. Feedback concerning the benefits of using a rehearsal strategy. (Experimenter says "See, saying the names over and over again helped you remember.")		X	X
4. Individualized instruction. (The difficulty level and amount of instruction provided by the experimenter for each training trial was determined by the subject's previous performance.)			X

[a] X = Component present.
[b] For subjects who begin rehearsing on task without the instruction to rehearse.

time to point to the pictures. Let me try it now. I have to remember three pictures. [Examiner pointed to the predetermined number of pictures and named each in turn.] That's right. . . . I just keep saying the names of the pictures in the right order. I won't forget the order of the pictures if I keep saying their names in the right order. [The examiner covered the pictures and continued to repeat the names of the pictures, saying good after each complete series.] Good. I knew I could do it. All you have to do is keep saying the names of the pictures—remembering which picture came first, second, etc.

Note that this example includes (*a*) questions concerning the nature and demands of the task; (*b*) answers to these questions, which describe the behaviors involved in the production of a rehearsal strategy; (*c*) answers to the questions, providing feedback concerning the value of employing a rehearsal strategy on the task; (*d*) rehearsal on the task; and (*e*) self-reinforcement. In addition, the examiner modeled the use of coping self-statements to be employed when encountering recall difficulties, for example:

Dog . . . what was next? Dog . . . I can't quite remember. I'll get it . . . Dog . . . let me see. . . . I can get it . . . just think nice and slowly . . . Dog . . . fish. That's it. Dog, fish, dog, fish. Good. I did it. Keep going. Dog, fish. Good. Dog, fish, dog, fish. I got it now.

This training sequence was individually tailored to the performance level and instructional needs of each child. Consequently, the difficulty level (number of items to be recalled) on each training trial was determined by the subject's performance on the previous trial. For example, if a child had difficulty rehearsing or showed inaccurate recall on a two-item trial, the subsequent trial involved the recall of two rather than of three items. The subjects in the practice and induced-rehearsal groups were yoked with a self-instructionally trained subject in order to control for training progress.

The results indicated that self-instructional training produced greater improvement and maintenance, as evidenced at a 1-week follow-up assessment, than either the Keeney *et al.* induced-rehearsal procedure or a practice control condition. The induced-rehearsal procedure once again resulted in improvement at an immediate posttest, but at the follow-up only the children who received the self-instructional training showed improved performance. In other words, the Keeney *et al.* (and Hagen, Hargrave, & Ross, 1973) results were replicated, indicating that inducing nonproducers to produce task-appropriate mediators results in only temporary gains. The Asarnow and Meichenbaum findings indicate that more stable gains can be achieved through self-instructional training.

Interestingly, children in the practice condition, who spontaneously but inconsistently rehearsed on the pretest, showed performance gains at both the posttest and the follow-up assessments. These children, who had already shown some tendency to rehearse, did not require the more extensive cognitive training in order to shift to a more mature mediational strategy. This result is consistent with findings by

Schleser, Meyers, and Cohen (Note 8), who found that the cognitive capacity of first- and second-grade school children, as assessed by performance on two Piagetian conservation tasks, interacted with the efficacy of self-instructional training. Preoperational children benefited most from the self-instructional training, whereas concrete operational children spontaneously employed different strategies to meet task demands, whether explicitly informed to do so or not. Thus, a consideration of the child's cognitive level and of the task-specific requirements would seem to influence the benefits to be derived from self-instructional procedures.

We recognize that the self-instructional training paradigm employed in both the reading study and the serial recall study are complex and multifaceted and, indeed, that other strategems (e.g., imagery) could have been used. Comparison, however, of the components of the self-instructional and induced-rehearsal procedures suggests that the success of the self-instructional procedure was due to one of, or to some combination of, the following factors:

1. Self-instructional training exposed the child to a general problem-solving strategy as well as to the task-specific rehearsal strategy.
2. Self-instructional training provided explicit feedback concerning the utility of employing a rehearsal strategy (see Borkowski, Levers, & Gruenenfelder, 1976; Kennedy & Miller, 1976).
3. Self-instructional training involved cognitive modeling.
4. Self-instructional training involved the child, using his own verbal commands to guide his behavior.
5. Self-instructional training was individually tailored.

It remains for future research to tease apart the relative contributions of these factors, as well as to assess the potential pedagogical value of teaching children to generate and to employ their own self-instructions across tasks and settings. This latter concern will be highlighted by the discussion of the work on metacognitive development.

Although the self-instructional training studies previously described have yielded positive results, not all attempts to use self-instructional training to teach academically based skills have met with success. Research by Burns, (1972), Higa (1975), Robertson and Keely (Note 9), and Robin, Armel, and O'Leary (1975) have provided equivocal results for the relative efficacy of self-instructional training in enhancing generalization. For example, Robin *et al.* successfully taught kindergartners identified as having handwriting problems to use self-instructions to improve their printing. However, the effects did not generalize to letters that had not been used in training. Kaufman and Hallahan (in press) argue that a potential problem mitigating positive effects in the Robin *et al.* study was that some children may not have needed much instruction in the first place.

Whatever the problems with these studies (see Meichenbaum, 1977), the concern is consistent with that offered in the brief review of the self-control studies, namely, the difficulty in obtaining generalization. The problem of generalization has been a major concern for the entire field of behavior therapy. No matter which behavior-modification technique is employed, be it operant conditioning, modeling, imagery rehearsal, etc., the evidence for generalization has not been overwhelming (e.g., Keeley, Shemberg, & Carbonell, 1976). The hope (and it is still only a hope) was that, as behavior therapy techniques were altered to incorporate cognitive factors, the likelihood of achieving generalization would increase. Although there is some evidence that this has been achieved (see Kendall & Finch, present volume; Mahoney, 1974; Meichenbaum, 1977), the evidence is *not* impressive, and, when pressed, we would argue that the evidence that generalization follows from CBM interventions is promissory at best. At the same time, we would argue that the absence of striking evidence for treatment generalization does not indicate that the efforts to "go cognitive" are misguided. Rather, we would argue that the way cognitive training has been conceptualized has been too simplistic. Some valuable guidelines for how CBM self-instructional training can be conducted comes from the work on metacognitive development.

METACOGNITIVE DEVELOPMENT

The purpose of this section is not to review the area of metacognitive development, but instead to draw parallels between this literature and the research on CBM. Since neither literature cites the other (except for the Borkowski and Cavanaugh, 1978 chapter), it is suggested that a fruitful dialogue should begin. The technology of CBM can be combined with the thoughtful analyses of cognitive processes undertaken by metacognitive researchers.

What is metacognitive development? Metacognitive development is the acquisition of knowledge and cognition about cognitive development (e.g., Brown, in press; Flavell, Note 11). To use Ann Brown's phrase, it is "knowing about knowing," or the subject's awareness of his own cognitive machinery and of the way this machinery operates. In terms of CBM, it is the self-communication one engages in, or the internal dialogue one emits before, during, and after performing a task. Most of the work in metacognitive development has focused on the development of metamemory. Research has also been conducted on metaattention (Miller & Bigi, Note 10) and metacommunication (Markman, in press).

Flavell and Wellman (1977) define metamemory as an individual's knowledge of anything germane to information storage and retrieval. Such memory-relevant knowledge is acquired throughout development. To illustrate the metacognitive approach, consider the work on metamemory, where certain types of knowledge about memory tasks (task variables) and memory strategies (strategy variables) are acquired at an earlier age than others. For example, even kindergartners know that a memory task is harder if it has a large number of items, whereas only older children know that a recall task is harder if one has to learn two sets of words that are easily confusable (Kreutzer, Leonard. & Flavell, 1975).

Flavell (Note 11) indicates that another important variable in metamemory is a person's knowledge about intrinsic and stable characteristics of self and others as a memorizer (person variables). For example, the data indicates that younger children are less aware or have less knowledge of their recall potential than older children. Moreover, metamemory and memory behavior are interlinked, such that one's memory behavior when confronted with a memory problem is determined in part by one's knowledge concerning what strategies are likely to be useful in the situation. Within this context, children are viewed as developing a sensitivity strategy, as noting which situations call for the use of memory and as learning when and how to prepare, when to retrieve, and how to plan to use a plan.

Metacognitive development is concerned with the nature of "intensive intellectual commerce" (Flavell, Note 11), the "executive processes" (Belmont & Butterfield, 1977), or what Gagné and Briggs (1974) call "cognitive strategies."

> A cognitive strategy is an internally organized skill that selects and guides the internal processes involved in defining and solving novel problems. In other words it is a skill by means of which the learner manages his own thinking behavior. . . . Cognitive strategies have as their objects the learner's own thought processes. Undoubtedly, the efficacy of an individual's cognitive strategies exerts a crucial effect upon the quality of his own thought [p. 29].

Cognitive strategies as described by Gagné and Briggs are similar to Skinner's (1968) self-management behaviors and Miller, Galanter, and Pribram's (1960) plans. Parenthetically, one can even characterize some of the CBM self-instructional training as a way of influencing the individual's TOTE systems à la Miller *et al.* (i.e., Test–Operate–Test–Exit), but that is getting ahead of ourselves.

Brown (in press) describes the metacognitive processes as including (*a*) prediction and planning, which precede problem-solving attempts; (*b*) checking and monitoring, which are subsequently performed to evaluate the outcome of these attempts; and (*c*) checking outcomes for internal consistency and against "common sense" criteria. In short, such processes as checking, planning, asking questions, self-testing, and monitoring ongoing attempts to solve problems are seen as central components of metacognitive development. To quote Brown, Campione, and Murphy (1977), metacognitive development refers to:

> The ability to stop and think before attempting a problem, to ask questions of oneself and others, to determine if one recognizes the problem, to check solutions against reality by asking not "is it right" but is it reasonable, to monitor attempts to learn to see if they are working or worth the effort [p. 3].

The similarity of Brown *et al.*'s description of the elements of metacognitive processes and the content of the self-statements that were employed by CBM therapists such as Camp, Douglas, and Meichenbaum is quite apparent.

The concern is with how one develops a training program to teach children to estimate task difficulty (and note that the task may be interpersonal as well as academic), to monitor and use a strategy, to adjust the strategy to task demands, and to make use of implicit and explicit information and feedback. How does one teach thinking, not so much *what* to think, but *how* to think? To quote once again Brown, Campione, and Barclay (Note 12):

> The aim of training is not to get children to perform more like adults on a single task, but to get them to think more like adults in a range of similar situations. If this is the desired goal, then why not train (*a*) generalization, or (*b*) skills which could conceivably be general

> enough to fit a variety of situations? We know of no studies where, far from attempting to
> train generalization, the experimenter has even hinted that this is the name of the game [p.
> 26].

If the name of the game is to teach generalized thinking (and note that some people have tried to play it before, for example, Covington, 1970 and Suchman 1961), then how shall we go about achieving this? The metacognitive and instructional literature on the maintenance and generalization of skills and strategies, especially with both retarded and normal children performing memory tasks, provides some valuable suggestions. Three fine papers by Borkowski and Cavanaugh (1978), Campione and Brown (1977), and Belmont and Butterfield (1977) are rich in their advice. The reader is encouraged to review these in detail, especially the Belmont and Butterfield paper. Let us summarize in point form the major issues, for they provide suggestions for CBM therapists, suggestions that, if followed, should enhance treatment maintenance and generalization.

1. Campione and Brown (1977), as well as Borkowski and Cavanaugh (1978), draw a distinction between maintenance (or durability) and generalization. Maintenance refers to the continued use of a previously trained strategy on a task identical to that used during training, with only the specific to-be-learned materials being changed. In contrast, generalization is examined by assessing the extent to which the subject uses a trained strategy on a task that differs from the training task. The generalization task may share common features and should require similar processes as those employed in training, but to demonstrate generalization the transfer task must require a modification in the specific form of the trained strategy. In order to determine if a specific task can be used as a means to assess maintenance or generalization, the investigator must be careful in specifying component processes required on the respective tasks. As Wood, Bruner, and Ross (1976) indicate, training or, to use their term, "tutoring," requires that the tutor must have at least two theoretical models: (*a*) a theory of the task or problem and how it may be completed, namely, a careful task analysis; and (*b*) a theory of the performance characteristics of the tutee. These issues have been discussed from a Piagetian viewpoint by Kuhn (1974).

A concern with issues of maintenance and generalization immediately focuses attention on the need for careful task analyses. Such task analyses, whether conducted intuitively (an armchair approach) or by means of a laboratory approach (à la Belmont & Butterfield, 1977), should provide the basis for selecting transfer tasks. To quote Belmont and Butterfield (1977):

> The investigator who would demonstrate transfer must thoroughly understand both the
> task he uses during training and the one he uses to test transfer.
> The child may very well understand that the transfer task requires use of his newly learned
> processes, but fail to engage the unshared processes on the second task that were not trained
> on the first. Without knowing precisely where the child's performance broke down, the
> investigator can hardly interpret a failure on the transfer test [p. 467].

The Belmont–Butterfield quote raises questions of how we should interpret what we should say to ourselves when we fail to obtain maintenance or generalization.

One possible class of self-statements we may emit may serve to denigrate the training ("I knew all this emphasis on cognitive training was misguided. Where are my reinforcers?"), or we might question the nature of the training, conducting a further task analysis of both the training and the transfer tasks. Attribution theory suggests that the investigator may be more disposed to attribute blame to something out there (a technique, a set of subjects) than to himself. For example, Belmont and Butterfield argue that the poor transfer performance of the subjects in the Keeney *et al.* study led to the proposition that the children had a deficit ("production deficiency"). Instead, one could suggest that the experimenter suffers from a deficit. It could be argued that the experimenter has shown an instructional deficit in nurturing the processes required to insure generalization. The Asarnow and Meichenbaum (Note 7) results, indicating that altering the nature of the training can lead to success in areas where training had previously failed, underscore Belmont and Butterfield's point. Turnure, Buium, and Thurlow (1976) have offered a similar argument for an "instructional deficiency" (i.e., the trainer failed to provide the child with efficient learning cues), in contrast to attributing a "production deficiency" to the child.

The first point to be garnered by CBM trainers from the research on metacognitive development is the important role of a component task analysis of the cognitive and behavioral processes involved in the training and transfer tasks. Before conducting a CBM training study, care must be taken to specify explicitly why certain tasks provide an assessment of maintenance and other tasks provide an assessment of generalization. It is only through this kind of analysis that the equivocal findings with respect to the generalization of CBM can be fully understood.

The use of overt verbalization in the CBM self-instructional procedure provides a means of assessing the effectiveness of training as well as the maintenance and generalization of strategies. The overt verbalization methodology provides a means for direct measurement of performance that Belmont and Butterfield (1977) call for.

2. The research on metacognitive development of retarded children has helped to specify the cognitive requirements for achieving generalization of some routine to a novel situation. To paraphrase Campione and Brown (Note 13), they offer the following requirements for generalization:

1. The subject needs to realize the need for a strategy.
2. The subject has to evaluate the task requirements and then has to select from an array of routines which one(s) might be appropriate.
3. Having selected one, the subject would have to execute the strategy and monitor its efficacy.
4. Such information (or feedback) would govern decisions about future actions [p. 23].

Meichenbaum (1977), from the vantage point of trying to develop a theory of change, has underscored many of the same processes, namely, the need for self-awareness, the role of deautomatizing a behavioral act, the role of problem-solving processes, and the like. The point to be highlighted is that similar constituent processes are being repeatedly identified as being central to the change (generalization) process.

One implication that follows from such analyses is that CBM training should be aimed at "executive" functions. As will be discussed later in the section on specific implications for the classroom, the objective of CBM training should be to train cognitive skills or executive routines that are transsituational. For example, Brown and Barclay (1976) have employed a "stop-check-and-study" routine to facilitate generalization in educable retarded children on a memory recall task, an ability that generalized to subsequent recall of prose passages (Brown *et al.*, Note 12).

In short, the work on metacognitive development, especially with retarded children, has suggested that a central aspect underlying inadequate performance is the child's general failure to be strategic, or, borrowing from Miller *et al.* (1960), the lack of a "plan to form a plan" (Campione & Brown, Note 13). The CBM work with children who have impulse- and academically based problems suggests that they also have problems in producing and implementing such plans. The model proposed by Campione and Brown (Note 13) for retarded children may not be population specific but, rather, may provide a useful model for examining inadequate performance in other populations. One implication of this line of reasoning is the need for strategy training or direct instruction in generalization. Borkowski and Cavanaugh (1978) indicate that the likelihood for maintenance and generalization are *increased* when training is conducted in depth, is prolonged, and includes feedback about the purpose and usefulness of strategies and when the selected generalization tests are conducive to the utilization of the acquired strategy. Thus, the inclusion of such practices as extended training, the fading of experimenter prompts, an increased demand for mental involvement in the task (e.g., mental transformation), training across settings, conditions, and persons, and feedback on the value of the strategy will *lessen* the likelihood of the child's following the to-be-taught strategy as a "blind-rule." For the objective of CBM is to provide children with knowledge or metastrategies of when and where a specific strategy will or will not work. Stokes and Baer (1977), from an operant perspective, have offered similar suggestions designed to enhance the generalization process, and Belmont (1978) has characterized the training of generalization as a means of teaching the individual the skill of self-programming.

Perhaps the best account of what is involved in training generalization or executive functioning has been offered by Borkowski and Cavanaugh (1978), who state:

> First, we need to identify several strategies each of which are operative in different learning situations. Second, we need to train children on several strategies, making sure that they know when and how to apply them. Third, we need to train the instructional package so that common elements between training and generalization contexts are evident, and distractors minimal. Fourth, we need to develop child-generated search routines, probably through the use of self-instructional procedures, that encourage the child to analyze a task, scan his or her available strategic repertoire, and match the demands of the task with an appropriate strategy and retrieval plan. Fifth, we need to instruct children in such a way that we utilize whatever skills they possess, in order to bring each child to an awareness of the advantage of executive monitoring and decision-making in solving problems. Finally, we may need to reinforce, in a very explicit way, successful executive functioning in order for it to come under the control of natural environmental contingencies, such as a child's good feelings about solving a difficult problem [p. 54].

IMPLICATIONS FOR THE CLASSROOM

The pronouncements about the need for teaching executive processes and the description of cognitive–behavioral procedures such as self-instructional training will have little impact upon educational practices unless specific implications and operational guidelines follow. The present section will only begin to explicate these implications and the needed guidelines. The intent of this section is to avoid the situation in which a principal (such as the one who was described in the introduction to this chapter) replaces a 10–15 minute morning arithmetic drill with a drill on training executive functioning or metaprocesses.

The first implication that may be drawn from the work on metacognitive development and CBM is that teachers need to be explicitly taught a metacognitive perspective. The ability to predict or to estimate task difficulty, to self-interrogate, self-test, or monitor the use of a strategy, to adjust the strategy to task demands, and to make use of implicit and explicit feedback must come to underlie the education of teachers. These executive abilities that require the selection, sequence, evaluation, and revision of cognitive strategies can be translated into sets of self-statements that are teachable. Flavell (Note 11) has offered the following description of the thoughts of a metacognitively sophisticated individual:

> Examine task features carefully. Is there a problem here that needs solving? Is the problem I just solved the one I initially intended to solve, or is it only a subproblem of the main problem or even an irrelevant problem? Keep track of post solution efforts, their outcomes, and the problem-relevant information they yielded. Remember to retrieve and apply this information when needed [p. 25].

By asking teachers to engage in the exercise of watching others teach, by reviewing their own curricula and so forth, they can begin to note the many opportunities available for engaging in such metacognitive processes or strategic thinking. Such teacher directives as "Check your work" or "Study your lesson," etc., will be seen as the occasion for the teacher to consider the metacognitive process involved and how the CBM technology can be applied to ensure that the children have the requisite component skills. The antidote for the circumscribed drill approach is an attempt to imbue the entire curriculum and educational environment with a concern for the "process," not just the "product," of learning.

A few brief examples of how this could be accomplished may illustrate the point. A number of CMB researchers (Camp *et al.*, 1977; Kendall & Finch, 1978; Meichenbaum & Goodman, 1971; Palkes *et al.*, 1968) have used play-like pictures to remind the child to use metaprocesses. Such metacognitive researchers as Brown (in press), Kestner and Borkowski (in press), and Turnure *et al.* (1976) have used oral game-like learning that relates to the children's personal interests as a means of teaching a self-interrogative strategy. (See Meichenbaum, 1977, for a discussion of how play and imagery can be used by tutors.)

Imbuing the environment with reminders to use metacognitive processes and the inclusion of more playful approaches are designed to remind both students and teachers that one objective of the educational process is for them to engage in active inferential constructive processes when listening to instructions or performing tasks. The objective is to have the children try to carry out the instructions mentally as they listen or to analyze the relationship between the stated directions and the behavioral goal. The goal is to have the child construct a mental representation of the "problem-as-solved" and to examine critically the relationship of the instructions to that representation.

But such skills as forming the mental representation of "problem-as-solved" must be explicitly trained. Consider a curriculum that required children to practice the production of metacognitive skills. We can conceive of academic tasks in which the teacher provided the children with a set of tasks, both academic and interpersonal, and the child's job was to identify, across the variety of tasks, what the problem is, *how* he or she will go about solving the task, where the likely pitfalls are, etc. In short, we would suggest that training should be focused on the production and evaluation of metacognitive skills. Children could be presented with a variety of tasks that require the production of "plans to produce plans." Teachers could give assignments and ask children to describe in detail how they are going to go about performing the assignment. Discussion could center on the process, not just the product, of the assignment. In short, the entire study-skill process could become the focus of education.

Some attempts along these lines have been made by CBM investigators employing problem-solving techniques in the classroom (see Meichenbaum, 1978, for a review of this literature). The focus of the CBM problem-solving approach has been on teaching children to become sensitive to interpersonal problems, to develop the ability to generate alternative solutions, and to understand means–end relationships and the effect of one's social acts on others. Children are taught the distinction between facts, choices, and solutions. A variety of teaching aids, such as verbal and behavioral videotapes, cartoon workbooks and poster–pictorial card activities are used to teach children to identify problems, to generate alternatives, to collect information, to recognize personal values, to make a decision, and then to review that decision at a later time. Inherent in such an approach is the need for a careful task-analysis by both the teacher and the student.

Modeling procedures, behavioral rehearsal, role playing, and other procedures provide useful ways of teaching such metaprocesses. The work by Sigal (Note 14) on the tutoring process, where he has examined the nature of teacher's questioning as means of fostering children's reflective or what he calls distancing behaviors, provides a useful model of how to nurture metacognitive processes.

Many other implications for the classroom could be offered, but perhaps the most important one that derives from the work on CBM and metacognitive development is that the training of cognitive strategies should focus directly and explicitly on the skills and tasks that are to be learned, and not on some presumed "underlying deficit." As Kaufman and Hallahan (in press), Ross (1976), and Vellutino, Steger, Moyer, Harding, and Niles (Note 15) have pointed out, training in skills that are unrelated to the ultimate goal of what is being taught, such as giving training in discriminating geometric shapes to a child who has difficulty in recognizing words, is unlikely to contribute to a remedial program. If we are going to teach metacognitive skills through the use of CBM techniques as well as by other means, then the suggestion is that we do so directly, on academically relevant material. From this perspective, the teacher's task is to provide the necessary instructional prompts (and this may include manipulating tasks, cognitive modeling, etc.) required to engender children's problem-solving behavior or metacognitive development.

CONCLUSION

A visit to the classroom will often turn up evidence of a teacher (or principal) talking to him- or herself. The intent of this chapter is to begin to influence the content of that internal dialogue in order that CBM and metacognitive skills will become part of the academic curriculum. For example, after being exposed to the CBM approach, one teacher, during a heated disciplinary interaction with a child in class, was observed to say aloud to herself the following (said in a fashion that would be overheard by the students): "Hold on, what is it about your behavior that is so upsetting? What is our problem?" and so forth. The children were being provided with a coping problem-solving model. Our principal's concern was with why so many teachers were now beginning to talk to themselves. We suggested that they might be practicing their arithmetic drills!

REFERENCE NOTES

1. Watson, D., & Hall, D. *Self-control of hyperactivity.* Unpublished manuscript, La Mesa–Spring Valley School District, San Diego, California, 1977.
2. Barkley, R., Copeland, A., & Sivage, C. *A self-control classroom for hyperactive and impulsive children.* Unpublished manuscript, Milwaukee Children's Hospital, 1978.
3. Leon, J., & Pepe, H. *Self-instructional training: Cognitive behavior modification as a resource room strategy.* Unpublished manuscript, University of New Mexico, 1978.
4. Bommarito, J., & Meichenbaum, D. *Enhancing reading comprehension by means of self-instructional training.* Manuscript in preparation, University of Waterloo, 1978.
5. Dansereau, D., Collins, K., McDonald, B., Dickhoff. J., Garland, J., & Holley, C. *Development and assessment of a cognitively based learning strategy curriculum.* Paper presented at the annual meeting of the American Educational Research Association, Toronto, 1978.
6. Wozniak, R., & Neuchterlein, P. *Reading improvement through verbally self-guided looking and listening* (summary report). Minneapolis: University of Minnesota, 1973.
7. Asarnow, J., & Meichenbaum, D. *Verbal rehearsal and serial recall: The mediational training of kindergarten children.* Unpublished manuscript, University of Waterloo, 1977.
8. Schleser, R., Meyers, A., & Cohen, R. *Cross task consistency as a function of cognitive level and instructional package.* Unpublished manuscript, Memphis State University, 1978.
9. Robertson, D., & Keeley, S. *Evaluation of a mediational training proeram for impulsive children by a multiple case study design.* Paper presented at American Psychological Association, 1974.
10. Miller, P., & Bigi, L. *Children's understanding of attention; or you know I can't hear you when the water's running.* Unpublished manuscript, University of Michigan, 1976.
11. Flavell, J. *Metacognitive development.* Paper presented at the NATO Advanced Study Institute on structural process theories of complex human behavior, Banff, Alberta, Canada, 1977.

12. Brown, A., Campione, J., & Barclay, C. *Training self-checking routines for estimating test readiness: Generalization from list learning to prose recall.* Unpublished manuscript, University of Illinois, 1978.
13. Campione, J., & Brown, A. *Toward a theory of intelligence: Contributions from research with retarded children.* Unpublished manuscript, University of Illinois, 1978.
14. Sigel, I. *Consciousness raising of individual competence in problem solving.* Paper presented at the third Vermont conference on the primary prevention of psychopathology. University of Vermont, 1977.
15. Vellutino, F., Steger, B., Moyer, S., Harding. C., & Niles, J. *Has the perceptual deficit hypothesis led us astray? An examination of current conceptualizations in the assessment and treatment of exceptional children.* Paper presented at Annual International Convention of the Council for Exceptional Children, New York, New York, April, 1974.

REFERENCES

Belmont, J. Individual differences in memory: The cases of normal and retarded development. In M. Greenberg & P. Morris (Eds.), *Aspects of memory.* London: Methuen, 1978.
Belmont, J., & Butterfield, E. The instructional approach to developmental cognitive research. In R. Kail & J. Hagen (Eds.), *Perspectives on the development of memory and cognition.* Hillsdale, New Jersey: Lawrence Erlbaum, 1977.
Bem, S. The role of comprehension in children's problem solving. *Developmental Psychology,* 1971, *2,* 351–359.
Bloor, D. The regulatory function of language: An analysis and contribution to the current controversy over the Soviet Theory. In J. Morton & J. Marshall (Eds.), *Psycholinguistics: Developmental and pathological.* Ithaca, New York: Cornell University Press, 1977.
Borkowski, J., & Cavanaugh, J. Maintenance and generalization of skills and strategies by the retarded. In N. Ellis (Ed.), *Handbook of mental deficiency: Psychological theory and research.* Second edition. Hillsdale, New Jersey: Lawrence Erlbaum, 1978.
Borkowski, J., Levers, G., & Gruenenfelder, T. Transfer of mediational strategies in children: The role of activity and awareness during strategy acquisition. *Child Development,* 1976, *47,* 779–786.
Bornstein, C., & Quevillon, R. The effects of self-instructional package on overactive boys. *Journal of Applied Behavior Analysis,* 1976, *9,* 179–188.
Bower, K. *Impulsivity and academic performance in learning and behavior disordered children.* Unpublished doctoral dissertation, University of Virginia, 1974.
Bransford, J., & Johnson, M. Contextual prerequisites for understanding: Some investigations of comprehension and recall. *Journal of Verbal Learning and Verbal Behavior,* 1972, *11,* 717–726.
Brown, A. Development, schooling and the acquisition of knowledge about knowledge. In R. Anderson, R. Spiro, & W. Montague (Eds.), *Schooling and the acquisition of knowledge.* Hillsdale, New Jersey: Lawrence Erlbaum, in press.
Brown. A., & Barclay, C. The effects of training specific mnemonies on the metamnemonic efficacy of retarded children. *Child Development,* 1976, *47,* 71–80.
Brown, A., Campione, J., & Murphy, M. Maintenance and generalization of trained metamnemonic awareness of educable retarded children. *Journal of Experimental Child Psychology,* 1977, *24,* 191–211.
Burns, H. *The effect of self-directed verbal commands on arithmetic performance and activity level of urban hyperpactive children.* Doctoral dissertation, Boston College, 1972. *Dissertation Abstracts International,* 1972, *33,* 1782B (Microfilm No. 72-22, 884).
Cameron, R. *Conceptual tempo and children's problem solving behavior: A developmental task analysis.* Unpublished doctoral dissertation, University of Illinois, 1976.
Camp, B., Blom, G., Hebert, F., & Van Doorninck, W. "Think aloud:" A program for developing

self-control in young aggressive boys. *Journal of Abnormal Child Psychology,* 1977, *5,* 157–169.

Campione, J., & Brown, A. Memory and metamemory development in educable retarded children. In R. Kail & J. Hagen (Eds.), *Perspectives on the development of memory and cognition.* Hillsdale, New Jersey: Lawrence Erlbaum, 1977.

Covington, M. The cognitive curriculum: A process-oriented approach to education. In J. Hellmuth (Ed.), *Cognitive studies, Vol. 1.* New York: Brunner/Mazel 1970.

Craighead, E., Craighead-Wilcoxin, L., & Meyers, A. New directions in behavior modification with children. In H. Hersen, R. Eisler, & P. Miller (Eds.), *Progress in behavior modification, Vol. 6.* New York: Academic Press, 1978.

Douglas, V., Parry, P., Marton, P., & Garson, C. Assessment of a cognitive training program for hyperactive children. *Journal of Abnormal Child Psychology,* 1976, *4,* 389–410.

Dykman, R., Ackerman, R., Clements, S., & Peters, J. Specific learning disabilities: An attentional deficit syndrome. In H. Myklebust (Ed.), *Progress in learning disabilities, Vol. 2.* New York: Grune & Stratton, 1971.

Egeland, B. Training impulsive children in the use of more efficient scanning techniques. *Child Development,* 1974, *45,* 165–171.

Flavell, J., Beach, D., & Chinsky, J. Spontaneous verbal rehearsal in a memory task as a function of age. *Child Development,* 1966, *37,* 283–299.

Flavell, J., & Wellman, H. Metamemory. In R. Kail & J. Hagen (Eds.), *Perspectives on the development of memory and cognition.* Hillsdale, New Jersey: Lawrence Erlbaum, 1977.

Gagné, R. Problem solving. In A. Melton (Ed.), *Categories of human learnings.* New York: Academic Press, 1964.

Gagné, R., & Briggs, L. *Principles of instructional design.* New York: Holt, Rinehart & Winston, 1974.

Goldfried, M., & Davison, G. *Clinical behavior therapy.* New York: Holt, Rinehart & Winston, 1976.

Grimm, J., Bijou, S., & Parsons, J. A problem-solving model for teaching remedial arithmetic to handicapped young children. *Journal of Abnormal Child Psychology,* 1978, *7,* 26–39.

Hagen, J., Hargrave, S., & Ross, W. Prompting and rehearsal in short-term memory. *Child Development,* 1973, *44,* 201–204.

Higa, W. *Self-instructional versus direct training in modifying children's impulsive behavior.* Unpublished doctoral dissertation, University of Hawaii, 1975.

Karoly, P. Behavioral self-management in children: Concepts, methods, issues and directions. In M. Hersen, R. Eisler, & P. Miller (Eds.), *Progress in behavior modification, Vol. 5.* New York: Academic Press, 1977.

Kaufman, J., & Hallahan, D. Learning disability and hyperactivity. In B. Lahey & A. Kazdin (Eds.), *Advances in child clinical psychology, Vol. 2.* New York: Plenum Press, in press.

Keeley, S., Shemberg, K., & Carbonell, J. Operant clinical intervention: Behavior management or legend? Where are the data? *Behavior Therapy,* 1976, *7,* 292–305.

Keeney, T., Cannizzo, S., & Flavell, J. Spontaneous and induced verbal rehearsal in a recall task. *Child Development,* 1967, *38,* 953–966.

Kendall, P. C., On the efficacious use of verbal self-instructional procedures with children. *Cognitive Therapy and Research,* 1977, *1,* 331–341.

Kendall, P. C., & Finch, A. J. A cognitive–behavioral treatment for impulse control: A case study. *Journal of Consulting and Clinical Psychology,* 1976, *44,* 852–857.

Kendall, P. C., & Finch. A. J. A cognitive–behavioral treatment for impulsivity: A group comparison study. *Journal of Consulting and Clinical Psychology,* 1978, *46,* 110–118.

Kennedy, B., & Miller, D. Persistent use of verbal rehearsal as a function of information about its value. *Child Development,* 1976, *47,* 566–569.

Kestner, J., & Borkowski, J. Children's maintenance and generalization of an interrogative learning strategy. *Child Development,* in press.

Kreutzer, M., Leonard, C., & Flavell, J. An interview study of children's knowledge about memory. *Monographs of the Society for Research in Child Development,* 1975, *40 (1,* Serial No. 159).

Kuhn, D. Inducing development experimentally: Comments on a research paradigm. *Developmental Psychology,* 1974, *10,* 592-600.

LaBerge, D., & Samuels, S. Toward a theory of automatic information processing in reaching. *Cognitive Psychology,* 1974, *6,* 293-323.

Lovitt, T., & Curtis, K. Effects of manipulating antecedent event on mathematic response rate. *Journal Applied Behavior Analysis,* 1968, *1,* 329-333.

Luria, A. *The role of speech in the regulation of normal and abnormal behaviors.* New York: Liveright, 1961.

Luria, A. Speech and formation of mental processes. In M. Cole & I. Maltzman (Eds.), *A handbook of contemporary Soviet psychology.* New York: Basic Books, 1969.

Mahoney, M. *Cognition and behavior modification.* Cambridge, Massachusetts: Ballinger Publishing Company, 1974.

Markman, E. Realizing that you don't understand: A preliminary investigation. *Child Development,* in press.

Meichenbaum, D. Self-instructional training: A cognitive prosthesis for the aged. *Human Development,* 1974, *17,* 273-280.

Meichenbaum, D. Enhancing creativity by modifying what subjects say to themselves. *American Educational Research Journal,* 1975, *12,* 129-145 (a).

Meichenbaum, D. Theoretical and treatment implications of developmental research on verbal control of behavior. *Canadian Psychological Review,* 1975, *16,* 22-27 (b).

Meichenbaum, D. Cognitive factors as determinants of learning disabilities: A cognitive functional approach. In R. Knights & D. Bakker (Eds.), *The neuropsychology of learning disorders: Theoretical approaches.* Baltimore, Maryland: University Park Press, 1976.

Meichenbaum, D. *Cognitive–behavior modification: An integrative approach.* New York: Plenum Press, 1977.

Meichenbaum, D. Teaching children self-control. In B. Lahey & A. Kazdin (Eds.), *Advances in child clinical psychology, Vol. 2.* New York: Plenum Press, 1978.

Meichenbaum, D., & Goodman, J. Training impulsive children to talk to themselves: A means of developing self-control. *Journal of Abnormal Psychology,* 1971, *77,* 115-126.

Miller, G., Galanter, E., & Pribram, K. *Plans and structure of behavior.* New York: Holt, 1960.

Palkes, H., Stewart, M., & Freedman, J. Improvement in maze performance on hyperactive boys as a function of verbal training procedures. *Journal of Special Education,* 1972, *5,* 337-342.

Palkes, H., Stewart, M., & Kahana, B. Porteus maze performance after training in self-directed verbal commands. *Child Development,* 1968, *39,* 817-826.

Parsons, J. The reciprocal modification of arithmetic behavior and program development. In G. Semb (Ed.), *Behavior analysis and education—1972.* Lawrence, Kansas: University of Kansas, 1972.

Reese, H. Verbal mediation as a function of age. *Psychological Bulletin,* 1962, *59,* 502-509.

Robin, A., Armel, S., & O'Leary, D. The effects of self-instruction on writing deficiency. *Behavior Therapy,* 1975, *6,* 178-187.

Ross, A. *Psychological aspects of learning disabilities and reading disorders.* New York: McGraw-Hill, 1976.

Skinner, B. F. *The technology of teaching.* New York: Appleton-Century-Crofts, 1968.

Smith, D., & Lovitt, T. Differential effects of reinforcement contingencies on arithmetic performance. *Journal of Learning Disabilities,* 1976, *9,* 21-29.

Stokes, T., & Baer, D. An implicit technology of generalization. *Journal of Applied Behavior Analysis,* 1977, *10,* 349-367.

Suchman, J. Inquiry training: Building skills for autonomous discovery. *Merrill–Palmer Quarterly in Behavior Development,* 1961, *7,* 147-169.

Turnure, J., Buium, N., & Thurlow, M. The effectiveness of interrogatives for promoting verbal elaboration productivity on young children. *Child Development,* 1976, *47,* 851-855.

Vallett, R. *Programming learning disabilities.* Palo Alto, California: Fearon Publications, 1969.

Varni, J., & Henker, B. A self-regulation approach to the treatment of the hyperactive child. *Behavior Therapy,* in press.

Vygotsky, L. *Thought and language.* New York: Wiley, 1962.

Wark, D. Reading comprehension as implicit verbal behavior. *17th yearbook of the National Reading conference,* 1968, 192–198.

Warner, J. *Learning disabilities: Activities for remediation.* Danville, Illinois: The Interstate Printers, 1973.

Wood, D., Bruner, J., & Ross, G. The role of tutoring in problem solving. *Journal of Child Psychology and Psychiatry,* 1976, *17,* 89–100.

Wozniak, R. Verbal regulation of motor behavior: Soviet research and non-Soviet replications. *Human Development,* 1972, *15,* 13–57.

3

Developing Nonimpulsive Behavior in Children: Cognitive–Behavioral Strategies for Self-Control

PHILIP C. KENDALL
A. J. FINCH, JR.

INTRODUCTION

The notion of impulsivity has been conceptualized as a cognitive style, an approach to a cognitive problem-solving task. Along with problem-solving differences in the display of impulsivity, research has evidenced behavioral correlates of the impulsive cognitive style. Thus, the conceptualization of impulsivity that we will be describing is one with both cognitive and behavioral components, and there are both cognitive and behavioral strategies that are specifically relevant for interventions designed to produce impulse control.

The importance of the study of impulsivity in children is evident in the fact that impulsive behavior, behavior lacking in self-control, is among the most common problems resulting in children being referred for mental health services. Although children in general are not known for their willingness or desire to spend time in the process of consideration, the problem is exacerbated when, for various reasons, the child's problem requires professional assistance. The problems are then usually described as behavior patterns that involve a lack of inhibitory control. Such problems can range from the more acting-out, aggressive absence of controls to the less aggressive, but more overactive, lack of attentional control. In many of these instances, the child's inability to exhibit self-control interferes with such daily activities as interpersonal interactions, classroom assignments, and general problem-solving.

This chapter has several major sections, each of which is seeking to fulfill one of several major aims. First, after presenting an overview of the conceptualization of

37

Cognitive–Behavioral Interventions:
Theory, Research, and Procedures

impulsivity, the theoretical underpinning of the cognitive–behavioral treatment and its theoretical ramifications will be discussed. This brief analysis seeks to present both the rationale for the particular treatment and a basis for further theoretical development. Second, the chapter provides a review of the literature on cognitive and behavioral characteristics of impulsivity in children. Studies from developmental psychology and child psychopathology will receive major attention, along with a brief consideration of several studies that have investigated self-control in children via a variety of different procedures. The goal in this section is to provide a familiarization with the status of the literature and to highlight the data that suggests specific deficits within impulsive children.

Last, several sections will examine the cognitive–behavioral treatment for impulsivity. Initially, we will review the literature on the treatment of impulsivity, with an emphasis on the variety of interventions and their relative successes. The proposed cognitive–behavioral treatment will be outlined, and specific "how-to" guidelines will be provided. Several studies that have evaluated the effectiveness of the cognitive–behavioral approach will then be reviewed, and the issues to be considered in clinical application will be described. It is our intention that these later sections provide the necessary information for the interested reader to initiate and evaluate the cognitive–behavioral treatment for impulsivity.

OVERVIEW OF THE CONCEPTUALIZATION OF IMPULSIVITY

Despite the fact that many of the childhood behavior problems are conceptualized as being indicative of a lack of impulse control, there has been only a limited amount of research interest in this area. Perhaps due to the lack of an operationalization, the analytic concept of impulse control did not generate meaningful empirical study. Instead, description and theory were of central concern. As operations for the assessment and study of various aspects of impulse-control emerged, researchers began more serious experimental investigations. For example, Mischel and his colleagues have developed a procedure for the study of the processes involved in a child's delay of gratification (see Mischel, 1974). In this program of research, the child's ability to impose a "delay" on gratification is studied using direct behavioral choice measures. Alternatives are provided to the subjects, and they must actually exercise a choice between rewards that vary in both delay time and value. The subject is usually placed in a situation in which a choice must be made between an immediate smaller reward or a larger but delayed reward.

More recently, Karoly and Kanfer (1974) and Karoly and Dirks (1977) have utilized a "scarecrow game" to study self-control in children. In these procedures a wooden figure that approximated a scarecrow was presented to the children, and the children were individually instructed to pretend to be like a scarecrow. "Can you hold your arms out straight just like him?" (Child imitates with arms.) "Good! Now, all you have to do to be a good scarecrow is stand here just like this one for as long as you can . . . [Karoly & Dirks, 1977 p. 400].'' These authors consider this task to be a type of "tolerance" analogue for self-control. Correspondingly, still other procedures present children with a favored toy but require that the child not play with it. The forbidden toy method has been employed by Fry (1975).

Our research program followed the paradigm associated with the cognitive dimensions of reflection–impulsivity (Kagan, 1966). This dimension describes differences among the problem-solving approaches of children. When a number of response alternatives are simultaneously available and uncertainty as to the correct response is high, impulsive children respond quickly, without a thorough evaluation of the various possibilities and, consequently, make many mistakes. However, reflective children demonstrate self-control by delaying a response until all alternatives have been considered carefully, and it is likely that their answer will be correct. The absence of self-control is seen in the impulsive children's responding without first delaying and evaluating the possible alternatives.

The instrument that we have used to assess impulsivity is the Matching Familiar Figures (MFF) test (Kagan, Rosman, Day, Albert, & Phillips, 1964). The MFF (see sample in Figure 3.1) is a 12-item, matching-to-sample task in which the child is shown a single picture of a familiar object and is instructed to select from an array of six variants the one picture that is identical to the stimulus picture. The examiner records the child's latency to the first response and the number of first-response errors. These latency and error scores are then separately rank-ordered and individually split at their respective medians. Children both above the median on the error score (high error rate) and below the median on the latency score (short latencies) are identified as impulsive. In contrast, children that are slow in terms of

Figure 3.1. Sample Matching Familiar Figures test item. (Reprinted by permission.)

latency to respond but are accurate in terms of a low error rate are considered reflective. Thus, the behavior that was displayed by the child and taken as indicating impulsiveness was that of fast and inaccurate responding. This approach uses cognitive task performance as the behavioral indicant of impulsiveness.

THEORETICAL PERSPECTIVES

Prior to our proposition of a cognitive–behavioral representation of the impulsivity–self-control dimension, an overview of other theoretical perspectives seems warranted. With intentional brevity, we will consider the impulsivity dimension from a temperment theory point of view and from a behavioral vantage point. Though the cognitive–behavioral position differs markedly from that of the temperament theorists, the behavioral analysis of impulsivity, when supplemented by a recognition of the necessity of cognitive training, appears to provide a conceptualization that is promising for theory, research, and clinical intervention.

Temperament Theory

Proponents of any number of different temperament theories of personality and personality development hold the position that some behavioral tendencies originate in inherited dispositions. Whereas many such theorists would not argue that certain aspects of personality are determined by the environment, they would insist that some others are genetically determined temperaments or, as others prefer, inborn dispositions. These dispositions are not specific traits but are broad personality types that transcend situational variation.

In a recent temperament theory of personality development proposed by Buss and Plomin (1975), there are four temperaments: activity, emotionality, sociability, and impulsivity. Our concern here is with impulsivity as a temperament. Buss and Plomin (1975) see impulsivity as a dimension that can range from impulsive to deliberate and that can be observed as quickness versus an inhibition of response. Further descriptions of impulsivity for Buss and Plomin is provided by Murray (1938):

> *Impulsion* is the tendency to respond quickly and without reflection. It is a rather course variable which includes: 1) short reaction time to social press, 2) quick intuitive behavior, 3) emotional driveness, 4) lack of forethought, 5) readiness to begin work without a carefully constructed plan. The subject is usually somewhat reckless, quick to move, quick to make up his mind, quick to voice his opinion. He often says the first thing that comes into his head, and does not always consider the future consequences of his conduct [p. 206].

The multidimensional nature of impulsiveness is evident in the characterization just given. There is reference to response inhibition, an absence of forethought, and a lack of persistence, to mention a few. Here, at least for basic description, temperament theorists appear to be concerned with a similar phenomena of behavior. However, it is clear that differences emerge in the analysis of the origins of this behavior pattern.

For Buss and Plomin (1975), "Impulsivity is the most troublesome of the four temperaments [p. 122]." If impulsivity were to meet their criteria for a temperament, it would have to be present in adults, show stability during childhood, and be shown to be related to inheritence. The last requirement, heritability, is most crucial. The evidence reviewed by Buss and Plomin indicates that there is not strong evidence for stability throughout development and that, although impulsiveness appears in adults, there are problems with the devices used to measure it in adults. Last, the authors conclude that "the genetic evidence for impulsivity is very weak [p. 139]." Furthermore, they note that impulsivity, as compared to the other temperaments, is most affected by the environment. These researchers are not the only investigators in this area, but from their work it would appear that a strong argument for the inheritance of impulsivity (not psychopathy) cannot be made at this time. Nevertheless, it is worthwhile to give a careful reading to this and other descriptive characterizations of impulsiveness by various personality theorists.

Behavioral Principles

Several theorists (Kanfer & Karoly, 1972; Skinner, 1953) propose primarily behavioral analyses of self-control. Focusing mostly on the self-control aspects of our impulsivity–self-control continuum, they state that responses (behaviors) to be changed are brought about by, and alterable by, variations in environmental variables. Self-controlling behaviors must be rewarded if they are expected to be more than transitory (see also Mahoney & Thoresen, 1974).

The process of self-regulation described by Kanfer and Karoly (1972) includes self-monitoring, self-evaluation, and self-reward. An individual who exhibits self-control initially monitors his/her own behavior, evaluates the performance against a criterion, and then provides him/herself with reward. Behavior therapists develop self-control in their clients by devising programs that focus upon self-monitoring, self-evaluation, and self-reward. Some programs, for example, have the client record the hours studied and, upon achieving a criterion, self-administor a reward. Many of these programs for self-control have been applied to behaviors that can be considered somewhat impulsive (e.g., overeating, smoking, or lack of studying).

A behavioral theory of *impulsiveness,* focusing primarily upon specious reward, has been proposed by Ainslie (1975). Impulsiveness is seen as the "choice" of something less rewarding when more rewarding alternatives are available but delayed. According to this analysis, impulsiveness is best accounted for by the decline of the effectiveness of reward that results from a delay in the reward. The effectiveness of the reward decreases as a function of delay, but this decrease is different for smaller–immediate versus larger–later rewards. To the extent that the larger reward is further delayed, the smaller-immediate reward (specious) is more appealing and is, consequently, chosen. Burns and Powers (1975) tested the "choice" model of self-control in children and found no support for it. Basically, the children chose the immediate reward almost exclusively, and the results were, consequently, quite dissimilar to earlier findings with pigeons. It should be mentioned, however, that

Burns and Powers analyzed the behavior of only two children, and further research is clearly needed.

The Ainslie (1975) analysis suggests that self-control can be established through one of several procedures. One method would be to rearrange reward contingencies so that the earlier alternative is never preferred, and another would be to constrain behavior so that the earlier alternative cannot be obtained when it is preferred. Finally, one could prevent the individual from obtaining cues about the availability of the specious alternatives. Giving the control to the individual, however, would require not only a rearrangement of reward contingencies but also a training in the means of evaluating alternatives, reaching decisions, and getting past the small immediate rewards.

A Cognitive–Behavioral Perspective

The procedures we will outline for the training of nonimpulsive behavior are considered to be an attempt to establish the child's self-control through special training that *combines* certain behavioral procedures with the process of cognitive training. Previous theoretical positions regarding the development of self-control have ranged from an emphasis on internal constitutional characteristics, such as will power, to a sole focus on the environmental variables that control behavior. The cognitive–behavioral viewpoint recognizes certain cognitive components of self-control as necessary and, correspondingly, places a necessary emphasis on behavioral aspects. But neither is sufficient. Recent advances in social learning theory in general (Bandura, 1977a) and in the more specific analysis of the phenomena of behavior change (Bandura, 1977b) emphasize the reciprocal nature of internal and external determinants of behavior. Indeed, the clinical potential for the use of cognitive processes and behavioral procedures is cogently presented by Bandura (1977b).

Accepting the position that there are some insufficiencies in a nonmediational analysis, a two-part definition of nonimpulsive behavior will be proposed. Recall for the moment that our impulsive children are fast and inaccurate responders. Are these children simply too quick—with their difficulty being a deficit in response inhibition that leaves them an insufficient period in which to perform more accurately? Or, do they lack the basic cognitive skills necessary to perform accurately on problem-solving tasks? Various data sources presented in this chapter suggest that children who behave impulsively have a dual dilemma: (*a*) they lack the capability of response inhibition (e.g., behavior appears automatic), and (*b*) they show deficits in cognitive problem-solving capacities. A proposed definition would then read as follows:

> *A child displays nonimpulsive (self-controlled) behavior when, prior to behaving, he/she engages in the cognitive evaluation of response alternatives and, having performed such reflection, is then capable of either engaging in the decided act or inhibiting the discarded possibilities* (Kendall & Wilcox, Note 1).

The necessity of the two-part definition is evident in an examination of the process of self-regulation proposed by Kanfer and Karoly (1972). As we pointed out earlier, this process has three phases: self-monitoring, self-evaluation, and self-reward. Although there are clearly behavioral components to each of these phases, there are also cognitive aspects that can serve to foster or to interfere with self-regulation. For instance, some individuals may be poor self-monitors (e.g., impulsives) and may require initial training in self-monitoring skills. Such efforts would rely heavily upon cognitive skills such as cue recognition, analysis of the situation, and, perhaps basic to the entire process, remembering to self-monitor. Perhaps the first step toward self-control is impulse control. The impulsive child is likely to initiate behavior without much forethought, and the aspect of the forethought that will be skipped is the self-monitoring. Kanfer and Karoly's (1972) analysis of self-regulation has much to offer those interested in developing self-control in children, and it is likely that its potential will be maximized when attention is directed to the cognitive skills that may be necessary for self-regulation to take place.

One of the major concerns of an operant approach to behavioral control was that the changes in behavior that were observed during training failed to generalize beyond the conditions under which the contingencies had been operative (Kazdin, 1975). One of the most important issues facing clinical researchers is the building of a methodology that will enhance the generalization of the treatment effects. Some initial evidence for the generalization of the cognitive–behavioral treatment for impulsivity (e.g., Kendall & Finch, 1976, 1978; Kendall & Wilcox, Note 2) has been positive, yet many questions remain, and more studies will be required before we have a complete understanding of how and when generalization takes place. Do the treatment effects transfer to other settings in the same manner as the treatment generalizes to other responses? Does the treatment procedure foster the child's ability to understand and incorporate rule-governed behavior? Perhaps if the child were to attribute the observed changes to him/herself, generalization would be a more likely result. The cognitive–behavioral treatment does place the child in a position of being responsible for change and thus should instill self-attributions for any observed changes. Whether or not these components of the intervention procedure contribute to the transfer of the treatment effects is an important empirical question.

STUDIES OF IMPULSIVITY

By way of introduction and in order to provide a solid basis for the characterization of impulsive children, we will be selectively reviewing several studies that have examined the behaviors of impulsive (and some reflective) children. Our selective but representative overview will specifically cover studies of children that are categorized along the reflection–impulsivity dimension, looking specifically at search-and-scan behavior, problem-solving behavior, and the relationship of the reflection–impulsivity dimension to other observed behaviors. A more comprehensive review of the reflective–impulsivity literature up to 1974 was provided by Messer (1976).

Search-and-Scan Behavior

The child's actual search-and-scan approach to the MFF task has been examined in several studies that have recorded the eye movements, the number of eye fixations, or the amount of viewing time for impulsive and reflective children. In one study, Siegelman (1969) devised an apparatus that required subjects to press a button to bring the standard and the alternatives into focus. Using such an apparatus allowed Siegelman to study the search-and-scan behavior of reflective and impulsive subjects. It was found that the impulsives looked less often and for a shorter duration at all the figures than did the reflectives. A related study by Drake (1970) employed a Mackworth eye camera apparatus to study visual information gathering. Impulsives were found to gather less information about the alternatives before responding than did the reflectives. The information gathering deficit was seen in fewer glances at each figure, the extent of the eye coverage of the figure, and the number of figure comparisons. Usui (1975) provides evidence from another culture (i.e., Japan) for the differences in search-and-scan behavior of impulsive and reflective children. In this study reflectives were found to increase the number of gazes as the number of variants increased, whereas impulsive children took fewer glances regardless of the number of variants. Messer (1976) summarizes this line of research by concluding that, in addition to spending less time viewing the stimuli, impulsives base their decisions on less information gathered in a less systematic fashion than do reflectives.

Problem-Solving Behavior

The problem-solving skills of impulsive and reflective children have been studied using a variety of tasks. Achenbach (1969) exposed impulsive and reflective children to a task that required the children to use analogical reasoning. Impulsive children were found to be more likely to answer with incorrect associations.

Problem-solving abilities of reflective and impulsive children were also studied using the 20-question task of Mosher and Hornsby (1966). This type of task is not unlike the game some families might play on a long car trip. For example, one passenger might say, ''I'm thinking of a famous person. Try to figure out who it is by asking questions that I can answer either ''yes'' or ''no.'' You are only allowed to ask 20 questions.'' One of the tasks that is presented to the child is an array of some 42 pictures including, for example, an apple, a fire hydrant, a book, a desk, an orange, etc. The objects that were pictured varied many ways but could be grouped into a number of categories (e.g., tools, red things, toys, things related to school, fruit). The object of the game was for the child to determine which picture the experimenter was thinking of by asking questions that could be answered "yes" or "no."

Ault (1973) and Denney (1973), using normal children, and Finch and Montgomery (1973), studying emotionally disturbed children, found that reflective children asked questions that employed a more advanced form of information-seeking behavior—e.g., questions that efficiently eliminated a number of possible answers simultaneously. For instance, the child might ask the question "Are you thinking of one of the fruits?" Such information-seeking behavior is an efficient problem-solving approach. In contrast, questions such as "Is it the orange?" are fast guesses that are inefficient, and these were employed more by impulsives. Though direct comparisons were not made, Finch and Montgomery (1973) suggest that the emotionally disturbed children in general may employ less mature information-seeking than do normal children.

Relationship to Other Behaviors

Montgomery and Finch (1975) studied typical classroom behaviors of impulsive and reflective emotionally disturbed children by having teachers complete ratings of locus of conflict on each child. Locus of conflict (Armentrout, 1971) ratings (based on Achenbach, 1966) are used to categorize a child's typical mode of conflict resolution. In internalization of conflict a child's impulses are highly controlled, and the conflict is between the impulses and their modulation. In externalization of conflict, impulses are freely discharged into the surrounding environment, and the conflict is between the behaviors of the child and the reactions they produce in others. To the extent that interpersonal conflicts of children resemble problem-solving tasks, a child's cognitive style should be expected to effect the ratings of locus of conflict. Therefore, Montgomery and Finch (1975) reasoned that a reflective cognitive style would play a major causative role in a child's ability to resist freely discharging impulses and to control their expression. On the other hand, an impulsive style would lead to the liberal discharge of impulses onto the environment without an evaluation of the potential consequences. Montgomery and Finch's (1975) results were consistent with the prediction and evidenced the importance of the relationship of cognitive impulsivity to certain behavioral patterns of discharging conflicts.

Parent ratings of behavior problems in emotionally disturbed boys indicated a similar relationship between cognitive impulsivity and patterns of behavior. Finch and Nelson (1976) made observations of impulsive and reflective emotionally disturbed children and gathered parent ratings. Impulsive boys were more likely than reflectives to blame others unfairly, threaten to injure themselves, hit and bully other children, and be excessively rough in play. On the other hand, the reflective emotionally disturbed boys were more reluctant to talk with adults outside the family. The relationship of impulsive behavior to the cognitive notion of impulsivity is supported by these studies of teacher and parent ratings of behavior.

An analysis of the persistence behavior of impulsive and reflective emotionally disturbed children (Finch, Kendall, Deardorff, Anderson, & Sitarz, 1975) indicated a significant relationship between response latency on the MFF and the duration of persistence on an extremely difficult task. Here, the impulsives were less likely to apply themselves in a persevering or industrious fashion.

An additional study contributed to the support of a relationship between cognitive style and behavior, but less directly than did those cited previously. In this study (Finch, Pezzuti, Montgomery, & Kemp, 1974), the academic achievement scores of impulsive and reflective emotionally disturbed children were analyzed. Since academic attainment involves a self-application to problem-solving tasks, a child's impulsivity was expected to affect his/her academic achievement. Perhaps because the performance of each of the children was consistently below grade-level, the hypothesized relationship between reflection–impulsivity and academic achievement was not found. Nevertheless, further inquiry proved informative. When the actual grade placements of the reflective and impulsive children were compared, there were significant differences. That is, although impulsive children had received similar achievement scores, they were being placed two grade levels behind their reflective counterparts. Since actual achievement did not differ, it seems reasonable to suggest that some classroom behavioral characteristics may account for the obtained differences.

Glenwick, Barocas, and Burka (1976) hypothesized that impulsivity has important consequences for classroom adjustment and a meaningful impact upon social relationships among children. In addition to MFF performance, these researchers gathered teacher and sociometric ratings. Though the relationships were not unequivocal, it was found that, when there was a significant relationship, the more impulsive the child, the more problems he/she was viewed by the teacher as having. Again in the sociometric data, when there was a significant relationship, the more impulsive child was seen as unpopular. Finally, Glenwick and Burka (1975) have reported that impulsivity in boys is related to a deficit in role-taking skills. These authors suggest that self-regulatory private speech may be the construct mediating both role-taking and nonimpulsive responding.

MODIFYING IMPULSIVITY

Considering the findings of the research on the various performances of impulsive children, it seems apparent that the more desirable behavior pattern would be one that is less impulsive. Considering also the generally detrimental impact that the behaviorally impulsive child has on parents and teachers, there appears to be mounting evidence to support the need for modifying a child's impulsivity and for developing a nonimpulsive, self-controlling pattern of behavior.

Numerous studies have investigated the modifiability of children's impulsive cognitive style. Most of the initial efforts focused on normal children of a variety of ages who were identified by the MFF as displaying the less-than-optimal impulsive task approach. As we shall consider in detail in a later section of this chapter, these initial studies provided the relevant information for the development of a clinically useful intervention program.

In this section of the chapter, we will cover a variety of the approaches used to modify impulsivity. These methods include imposed delay, modeling, effects of failure, search-and-scan strategies, reward contingencies, response-cost contingencies, and self-instructional training. Based upon these findings, a clinical intervention for the treatment of impulsivity within childhood psychopathology has been developed. This resulting cognitive–behavioral intervention will later be described in detail, as will the empirical evidence to support its clinical utility.

Imposed Delay

Aware of the negative effects of impulsivity, early researchers sought to study the effects of imposing an extended delay period before allowing the child to respond.

One of the earliest studies of the modification of impulsivity was conducted by Kagan, Pearson, and Welch (1966). These authors studied the value of an imposed delay and whether there would be a training advantage if the child were to perceive him/herself as similar to the trainer. The subjects of this study were first-grade children whose MFF performance indicated an impulsive cognitive style. Half of the subjects were persuaded that they shared some characteristics with the trainer whereas the others received no implication of similarity. The imposed delay conditions were given to both groups for each of the training tasks. For an inductive reasoning task, the trainer imposed a 10-second delay, and for both visual matching and haptic–visual tasks, a 15-second delay was imposed. Three 30-minute training sessions were employed, and the effects were assessed 6–8 weeks later. The observed outcome of the imposed delay included a significant increase in latency to respond for both training groups and an absence of the desired reduction in error rate. The manipulation of the child's perceived similarity to the trainer did not produce meaningful effects.

While examining the differences among the verbal behaviors of middle- and lower-class children, Schwebel (1966) also examined the effects of free and forced latency on the verbal tasks. In contrast to the middle-class children, who were not affected by the free–forced latency manipulation, the lower-class children were found to respond significantly faster during free latency. This impulsive responding also hampered verbal task performance. It should be noted, however, that Schwebel (1966) did not assess MFF behavior.

These studies, plus subsequent research by Heider (1971) and by Finch, Wilkinson, Nelson, and Montgomery (1975) using an imposed delay procedure as one of several interventions being evaluated, evidence the inability of an imposed delay to simultaneously increase the latencies *and* reduce the response errors of impulsive children.

Modeling

A great deal of the current psychological evidence tends to support the idea that much learned behavior can be acquired through the observation of another person. The majority of the clinical evidence demonstrates that such observation of a model affords the observer the opportunity to acquire new, therapeutically desirable response patterns (Bandura, 1969).

Assuming that the classroom teacher is a natural model for young children, Yando and Kagan (1968) examined the cognitive tempo of a group of teachers using the adult form of the MFF. Randomly selected children were tested with the MFF in the early fall and late spring to determine if exposure to an impulsive or reflective teacher model would affect the child's impulsive or reflective task performance. The teacher-models, as it turns out, were somewhat effective models, as evidenced by the significant increase in response latencies of the children with reflective teachers. However, the error scores of these children were not meaningfully different.

In a study specifically designed to assess the effects of observing experimental models, Debus (1970) assigned 100 impulsive first-grade children to 1 of 5 conditions. Four groups observed sixth-graders who were actually trained models. Experimental conditions consisted of (a) a reflective model; (b) an impulsive model; (c) a model who was impulsive for the first half and reflective for the second half; or (d) two models, one impulsive and one reflective. The fifth group was a control that did not view a model. The specific results of interest to our present analysis include the increased latencies in those subjects exposed to a reflective model and the lack of a significant decrease in the number of errors. A very similar study by Denney (1972) exposed impulsive children to videotaped reflective models and resulted in increased latencies. However, the models were again ineffective in decreasing the error rate.

Two studies that sought to modify impulsive responding via modeling and were able to both increase latencies and reduce errors were those conducted by Ridberg, Parke, and Hetherington (1971) and by Cohen and Przybycien (1974). In the Ridberg *et al.* (1971) study, the filmed models either displayed appropriate reflective scanning of the materials, verbalized a scanning method, or did a combination of the two. In general, the results indicated that exposure to a model altered both latencies and errors in the desired directions. Further division of the subjects according to IQ isolated the combined verbal cueing and scanning by the model as the most effective for the low-IQ subjects. These results are promising and suggest that modeling with appropriate verbal cues contributes meaningfully to a child's cognitive task approach.

Cohen and Przybycien (1974) used peer models to influence the impulsive behavior of fourth- and sixth-grade boys. The peers who served as models in this study also *verbalized* their task strategy. In addition, the peer models were chosen by the subjects, using sociometic methods. Thus, the subjects had chosen the peer to be trained to perform reflectively and to serve as the model. The results demonstrated that there were significant changes in the performed direction in both the latencies and errors on the MFF. The findings of several of the modeling studies are indicative of the potency of the effects of model behavior with verbal cues on the child's fast and inaccurate task performance. Plans for a program to develop nonimpulsive responding and self-control in children would profit from a recognition of the positive effects of modeling *and* verbal cueing.

The Effects of Failure Experiences

One aspect of the theoretical dynamics that have been hypothesized to underly the more desirable reflective cognitive style is fear of failure (Kagan & Kogan, 1970). This overconcern with making a mistake is thought to be absent in the impulsive child who does not attempt to avoid error at all cost. From this theoretical stance, one would hypothesize that an impulsive child's MFF performance should be more reflective following a failure experience.

Ward (1968) administered a modified version of the MFF and analyzed it to see if latencies would be longer on test items that immediately followed an incorrect response. In general, 70% of the subjects followed the hypothesized pattern, with a larger percentage of the impulsive children slowing down after making an error.

A more comprehensive study of the effects of failure was reported by Reali and Hall (1970). These authors administered a modified Design Recall Test (DRT) to 56 impulsive and 56 reflective third-grade boys. The DRT (12 sets were used) presents the child with a standard design and, once the standard is removed, requires the child to find the one of eight variants that is identical to the standard. Subject performance was recorded under four conditions. In one condition, the subjects received success on the first 6 trials and failure on the final 6. In another condition, failure on the first 6 trials was followed by success on trials 7–12. The third and fourth conditions received either all success trials or all failure trials, respectively. The central findings related to our present interests indicated that there were no differences in latencies for those impulsive children who experienced either all failure or all success trials. Also, there were no differences for impulsives (or reflectives) who experienced success–failure or failure–success trials. The apparent ineffectiveness of the failure trials condition suggests that the response of an impulsive child is not entirely the result of an absence of concern over errors.

A study by Messer (1970) was also designed to investigate the effects of failure on impulsive and reflective responding. In the main experiment, 131 third-grade impulsive and reflective children were assigned to a failure task, a success task, or a control condition. The manipulation of performance outcomes was based on an anagram task that was said to assess intellectual abilities. Although the impulsive subjects did behave in accordance with Messer's (1970) hypothesis, the differences only approached significance. Also, a greater percentage of the children in the control group than in the failure group showed minimal response latencies. Messer contends that the children in the control condition may have interpreted the second testing as evidence that they had performed poorly on the initial test.

When taken together, these studies provide little evidence for the hypothesized effects of failure experiences. Based upon these findings, Wilkinson (Note 3) concluded that there do not appear to be any therapeutically meaningful applications of failure experiences for the modification of impulsivity in children.

Response Contingencies

The use of response contingencies has a well-established track record with children (O'Leary & O'Leary, 1977). Yet there are a variety of contingencies that may be systematically applied. Taking into account the marked differences between impulsive and reflective children that have been outlined thus far, one might hypothesize that the individual differences in cognitive task approach would also be differentially responsive to variations in response contingencies. Two possible contingencies that could be applied would be reward and response-cost. When a child works for reward, the response contingency is usually such that one correct answer will earn one reward. When a child performs under conditions of response-cost, the child would be given a number of rewards in the beginning and lose one of the rewards in each instance in which a mistake is made.

Reward Contingencies

Briggs (1968) placed impulsive and reflective fourth-graders into one of three groups: trained to be impulsive, trained to be reflective, or not trained to be either. The supposed training task consisted of presenting complex geometric figures to the subjects as match-to-sample tasks from which they would earn reinforcements. Actually, none of the stimulus variants matched the standard, so that the experimenter could deliver reinforcements according to a predetermined design. The reinforcements (nonverbal) were red and green lights presented as performance feedback. Children in the increased latency condition produced both longer latencies and fewer errors.

The effects of two distinct types of reinforcements on the task behavior of impulsive fourth-grade boys were studied by Finney (1968). The rewards were symbolic tokens (grades) and concrete tokens (money). Though the use of the concrete tokens did increase response time, neither condition decreased error rate.

At this junction, the effects of reward-response contingencies on impulsive behavior is not particularly impressive. However, the entire class of response contingencies should not be discounted. As we shall see, other contingencies are more effective in producing the desired alteration of response time and accuracy.

In studies by Masarri and Schack (1972) and by Hemry (1973), evidence for the relative efficacy of certain contingencies began to emerge. Masarri and Schack (1972) compared the effects of positive social reinforcement versus social punishment on the discriminative learning performance of impulsive and reflective children. Results indicated that the social punishment condition was effective in reducing the number of errors made by subjects. Reflective subjects performed better under both conditions than did the impulsives, but the impulsive children in the punishment condition performed comparable to the reflective children in the positive condition. The hint of a differential responsiveness to response contingencies that emerges from this study will later receive additional support.

In a comparison of six contingency conditions (verbal reward, verbal punishment, verbal reward plus punishment, nonverbal reward, nonverbal punishment, nonverbal reward plus punishment), Hemry (1973) reported the performance of the impulsive and reflective children to be poorest under reward conditions and better under both punishment and punishment plus reward conditions. Since these later conditions were superior to reward contingencies and since there were no significant differences between the punishment condition alone and the punishment plus reward condition, one can question the effectiveness of a reward contingency alone in the modification of impulsiveness in children.

Response-Cost Contingencies

As noted earlier, a response-cost contingency initially requires giving the child a number of rewards (e.g., tokens, coins), with subsequent removal of a token or something desirable from the child for each occurrence of an incorrect behavior or response. In one study of the effects of incentive contingencies (Errickson, Wyne, & Routh, 1973), children who were identified as problems because of academic difficulties were given the MFF under two contingencies in a counterbalanced sequence. The two conditions were MFF using standard instructions and MFF with a response-cost contingency for errors. The children were found to be significantly less impulsive under the response-cost procedure. The reduction in impulsivity was seen in the significantly longer response latencies and in the significantly fewer response errors. When the response-cost procedure was given first in the sequence, subjects tended to maintain their relatively low error rates during the trials under the standard conditions. These findings suggest that a response-cost procedure is an effective incentive contingency for reducing response errors and for increasing response latencies (that is, for producing less impulsive behavior).

The findings of the Errickson *et al.* (1973) study demonstrate that desirable changes in behavior correspond to the enactment of response-cost conditions, but an important question remains—were the observed changes due to the contingent removal of the tokens for incorrect responding or to the reinforcing quality of having a larger number of tokens left after making fewer errors? In order to insure that the removal of the tokens is responsible for the desired effects, the effects of the response-cost contingency must be compared to the effect of a reinforcement condition. Such a study was conducted by Nelson, Finch, and Hooke (1975). In the Nelson *et al.* (1975) study, emotionally disturbed boys were initially administered the MFF under standard conditions. Two weeks later, subjects again took the MFF, but this time under conditions of reinforcement (receiving a chip for each correct response), response-cost (being given 12 chips and losing one for each mistake), or as a test–retest control. The overall outcome of the study indicated that both reinforcement and response-cost were effective in modifying the child's task performance but that there were differences for specific types of children. Emotionally

disturbed boys who had been identified as impulsive by their initial task performance were found to have made significantly fewer errors under response-cost than
under either the reinforcement or the control conditions. Reflectives, on the other
hand, made significantly fewer mistakes in the reinforcement condition when compared to the controls. These results support those of Errickson *et al.* (1973) and
demonstrate even more clearly that response-cost is an efficient contingency for
modifying impulsive behavior. In addition, other data to support the utility of the
response–cost contingency is available in studies by Messer (1970) and Hemry
(1973).

Research by Douglas and her colleagues (e.g., Firestone & Douglas, 1975; Parry
& Douglas, in press) has unveiled some unique qualities of the hyperactive child's
response to reinforcement contingencies. The performance of these children, it
appears, is more disrupted than that of normals by partial and noncontingent reinforcement. Also, positive reinforcement attracts the attention of hyperactive children, distracts them from their task, and orients them toward the rewarding adult.
Firestone and Douglas (1975) reported that a reward contingency led to a significant
increase in impulsive responding in hyperactive children. These effects suggest that
direct positive reinforcement is not the most desirable contingency management
procedure for these children.

In studying the role of punishment in the development of self-control, Cheyne
and Walters (1969, 1970) have focused on a specific type of self-control, a negative
self-control labeled *resistence-to-deviation*. The procedures that are basic to the
resistence-to-deviation studies entail a child's being individually presented with
pairs of toys and requiring the child to select one. For certain selections made by a
child, a loud buzzer, aversive but not seriously upsetting, was sounded contingently. Later, the children were left alone with toys including the punished toy, and
observers recorded the child's latency to touch the punished toy and the duration of
the interaction with the punished toy.

In studies that used varying intensities of the buzzer to vary the intensity of the
punishment (Cheyne & Walter, 1969), it has been shown that the overt resistance-
to-deviation is more affected by high-intensity punishment than by low-intensity
punishment. The timing of the punishment was varied by either enacting the loud
buzzer contingent upon the child's hand's approaching the previously punished toy
or waiting until 3 seconds after the child took the toy from the table. Results of this
manipulation of timing indicated that the early punishment was more effective than
late punishment, in terms of both latency and duration measures.

From a variety of research laboratories and across several methodologies and
tasks, evidence has been presented for the differential effects of various response
contingencies on the behavior of impulsive and hyperactive children. These differential effects indicate the potency of the response-cost method and suggest direct
implications for treatment procedures that employ incentive contingencies. Consider, for example, the child who is shown a "mathematics flash card" and is asked
"What is 7 times 12?" An impulsive child might blurt out "56-64 no, uh, 84!"
Under a contingency in which the child receives a reward for the correct answer, the

child's fast guessing would have been spuriously rewarded. Response-cost contingencies would prevent fast guessing (Kendall, 1976, 1977). The upshot is that *impulsive children appear to respond less quickly and more accurately when they are subjected to conditions under which they incur a loss for inappropriate responding.* Clinical intervention strategies that seek to reduce impulsivity should, in addition to social praise and encouragement, employ such response-cost contingencies for task performance.

Training in Search-and-Scan Strategies

Noting the specific deficits that impulsive children have when searching and scanning match-to-sample tasks (described in an earlier section of this chapter), attempts to modify cognitive impulsivity have employed training in more efficient search-and-scan strategies. Zelniker, Jeffrey, Ault, and Parsons (1972) administered a training task that required children to engage in a more thorough search and to develop a more systematic task strategy. Readministration of the MFF evidenced a decrease in errors, even in the absence of an increase in latency. In other studies that employ training in appropriate search-and-scan behavior (Egeland, 1974; Seggev, 1972), the children's posttraining behavior indicated increased latencies and decreased errors. Thus, training the impulsive child in an area in which there has been a demonstrated response deficit (task-oriented search-and-scan behavior) has much potential for therapeutic programming.

The relative strength of the strategy training procedures was examined in a study by Bender (1976) that compared the effects of strategy training with verbal self-instructions, strategy training alone, verbal self-instruction alone, and controls in modifying impulsive responding in children. Improvements on both the error and latency measures on an immediate posttest (MFF-like tasks) was evident for the group receiving the self-verbalization training. The immediate posttests also indicated that strategy training increased latency measures but did not affect the error rate. Though these findings did not hold on a posttreatment administration of the MFF itself, this study does suggest the value of self-instructional methods for treating impulsive children.

Self-Instructional Training

Children identified as having impulse-control problems have particular verbal-mediational deficits (suggested by the problem-solving studies described before) that can be directly treated with self-instructional training (Kendall, 1977). The self-instructional procedures have been discussed by Meichenbaum (1975, 1977) and will be described in more detail in a later part of the present chapter.

Verbal self-instructions have been studied for their role in developing verbal control of various behaviors in normal children (Bem, 1967; Birch, 1966; Meichenbaum & Goodman, 1969), in improving targeted classroom behaviors of problem children (Drummond, 1974, O'Leary, 1968; Monohan & O'Leary, 1971; Robin,

Armel, & O'Leary, 1975), and in prolonging a child's tolerance for resisting temptation (Hartig & Kanfer, 1973). Although the majority of studies appear to support the utility of verbal self-instructional training for the control of motor behavior, findings by Jarvis (1968) and by Miller, Shelton, and Flavell (1970) remind us of the incompleteness of our understanding.

In order to examine the efficacy of a cognitive self-verbalization treatment program in modifying nonverbal behavior, Meichenbaum and Goodman (1971) designed two studies with young impulsive children. In their first study, the cognitive training techniques had the trainer act as a model by performing a task while talking aloud. The subject then performed the task while the trainer instructed the subject aloud. Next, the subject was asked to perform the task again while instructing himself aloud. Subjects then whispered instructions to themselves and finally performed the task using covert self-instruction. The results indicated that a significant increase in latency but not a decrease in errors was found for the self-verbalization group relative to the controls.

In their second study, Meichenbaum and Goodman (1971) compared the usefulness of cognitive self-instructional training relative to a modeling and a control group in altering the attentional strategy of the impulsive child. In the modeling procedure, subjects were exposed to a model who verbalized self-instructions during task performance. Subjects who were in the cognitive self-instructional training condition were exposed to the same modeling behavior, but, in addition, they were trained to produce the self-instructions. Analysis of the results found that the cognitive self-instructional training and modeling both resulted in a significant increase in latencies but that only the self-instructional procedures resulted in a decrease in errors.

In a related study not directly obtaining measures on cognitive tempo, Palkes, Stewart, and Kahana (1968) employed self-directed verbal commands in order to train hyperactive boys in psychiatric treatment in self-control. Their results indicated that self-directed verbal commands were an effective technique in improving the Porteus Maze (Porteus, 1955) performance of these children. Additional support for the effectiveness of cognitive self-mediational training with hyperactive children is found in the study by Moore and Cole (Note 4).

A comprehensive analysis of a cognitive training program for hyperactive children was provided by Douglas, Parry, Marton, and Garson (1976). Hyperactive boys were trained via modeling, self-verbalization, and self-reinforcement techniques to use more effective and less impulsive strategies for approaching cognitive tasks, academic problems, and social situations. The findings of the Douglas et al. (1976) project provided supportive evidence for the effectiveness of cognitive training procedures with hyperactive children. More specifically, though some measures did not evidence desired changes, changes in both latency and error measures on the MFF, improvements on measures of reading ability, and beneficial changes on the Porteus Mazes test were evident following the training.

The importance of the actual verbalization of verbal instructions, as compared to silent readings of the self-directed commands, was demonstrated by Palkes, Stewart, and Freedman (1972). As in the earlier study by Palkes and her colleagues (Palkes, Stewart, & Kahana, 1968), the verbalization of self-instructions resulted in improved performance on the Porteus Mazes.

Bugental, Whalen, and Henker (1977) examined the effectiveness of two behavior-change approaches for hyperactive children in relation to the children's attributional style. These authors reasoned that the different approaches to treating hyperactivity should be more or less effective depending upon the matchup between the "style" of the treatment and the causal attributional systems of the children. Their hyperactive children received either instructions in self-controlling speech or contingent social reinforcement. Within each of these two groups, half were given Ritalin and half were unmedicated. The findings of the Bugental *et al.* (1977) study indicated that the self-instructional training improved Porteus Maze performance for children with causal attributions of personal control *and* for nonmedicated children. Although trends were noted, the social reinforcement procedure did not produce significant outcomes. Teacher ratings of classroom behavior did not indicate significant changes due to treatment. Thus, in addition to providing positive evidence for the value of self-controlling speech, it appears that an initial assessment of the child's attributional style may provide useful data to facilitate therapy by fostering treatment recommendations that match the child's attributional style.

Finch, Wilkinson, Nelson, & Montgomery (1975) sought to modify impulsive cognitive tempo in a group of emotionally disturbed boys. Impulsive boys were selected on the basis of their performance on the MFF and were assigned to one of three groups: cognitive training, imposed delay, and test–retest control. Subjects in the cognitive training group were seen individually for 6 half-hour treatment sessions over a 3-week period. In the first session, the experimenter performed one of the training tasks and talked to herself, giving specific step-by-step instructions and repeating them frequently. An error was deliberately made, and the examiner stated that she should have proceeded more slowly and should have been more careful. When the experimenter completed the task, the subject was asked to perform the task and to verbalize the self-instructions to himself. Further assistance was given in self-instructions if needed. During the last two sessions, subjects were instructed to continue using self-instructions but to do so covertly. The day following the sixth session, subjects were retested. The imposed-delay group had the same number of sessions, materials, and activities as the cognitive training group but did not receive training in verbal self-instructions. Rather, they were simply instructed to delay before responding. The results indicated that the cognitive verbal self-instructional training procedure resulted in a significant increase in latencies and a decrease in errors. In the imposed delay group, only an increase in latencies was obtained. Based upon these accumulated findings and on findings from other related studies (e.g., Camp, Blom, Herbert, & Van Doornenck, 1977; Patterson & Mischel, 1976), the verbal self-instructional procedures appear to offer considerable treatment potential in helping impulsive children to learn to delay their impulsive behaviors.

CLINICAL INTERVENTION PROCEDURES

The literature thus far reviewed speaks clearly to some of the specific deficits that are characteristic of impulsive children. In addition, each specific deficit carries with it valuable information for the formulation of a treatment program, and, as we have already seen, several investigators have studied the effects of different procedures to modify impulsivity in children. For the purposes of clinical intervention, our interests are in coordinating the various deficit information and in developing a multifaceted program for modifying impulsiveness in clinical populations. Briefly, let's review what we have stated thus far.

Impulsive children, those who respond quickly and make many errors in a situation of high response-uncertainty, display acting-out, conflict-externalizing behaviors. Despite equal academic achievement, they are placed several grades behind their reflective counterparts—perhaps due to classroom behavior. These children use inefficient search-and-scan strategies and a developmentally delayed process of information-seeking (suggesting a lack of verbal mediation). When response-consequence contingencies are manipulated, impulsive children apparently respond less impulsively under conditions of response cost than under direct reinforcement. Now, let us examine a treatment program that incorporates these known deficiencies and provides treatment components specifically relevant to the deficits.

The treatment program to be described is a cognitive–behavioral therapy. It includes cognitive training in the form of self-instructional training, appropriate search-and-scan behavior, and behavioral components, such as modeling of the efficient task behaviors and of the actual self-instructions, as well as the utilization of a response-cost contingency. The present cognitive–behavioral treatment does not attempt to treat dysfunctional cognitions. Rather, children that are identified as impulsive seem to *lack* cognitions in situations in which such thinking behavior would be very useful. These children appear to produce a behavioral response immediately and almost "automatically" following certain stimuli. The cognitive deficiency in these children is that they do not make efficient use of their cognitive capacities. Thus, our focus on cognition has been one in which we try to prevent automatic behavior and gradually induce thinking before responding. As two wise parents aptly put it, "You teach the kids to stop and think before they act."

The cognitive–behavioral treatment is also concerned with controlling the behavioral impulsiveness of the children. For instance, fast guessing and switching from one behavior to another are disruptive components of impulsivity in children. The excessive behaviors of these children are thought to be supressed by the response-cost procedure.

The treatment procedures rely heavily upon the principles of self-instructional training (Meichenbaum), upon those of modeling (Bandura), and upon a response-cost contingent on errors during the training tasks. For the purposes of illustration, we will employ psychoeducational training tasks, such as sequential recognition. Psychoeducational tasks are not the only possibility for training materials. Indeed, interpersonal tasks that require cooperation with peers or adults can serve as an excellent format for the intervention. The relative efficacy of various training materials is an important issue that requires further research study (Kendall, 1977).

In a sequential recognition task, a series of figures (beads or geometric designs) are presented in a sequential pattern, and the child is to decide the correct member of the alternatives by selecting which one would come next in the sequence. For example, one task might be, "Square-circle-circle-diamond-square-circle-circle-diamond-square. Which comes next in the sequence? Square, circle, or diamond?" Each child would then be given the cognitive-behavioral treatment in reference to this or similar cognitive training tasks (e.g., attention to detail, conceptual thinking, visual-motor reproduction). Each child works individually with one therapist for training sessions that last from 30 minutes to 1 hour. These sessions can be scheduled at various times, but we recommend two sessions per week for several weeks.

For this illustration, the cognitive training task will be instruction in maze performance. The verbal self-instructional procedures are implemented and practiced in the following sequence (modeled after Meichenbaum). First, the therapist performs the task while talking to himself outloud. At this time, the therapist is also modeling the appropriate behaviors that are associated with successful task performance (e.g., attention to the task, holding the pencil while visually scanning the material). The child is then asked to do one of the training tasks and to talk outloud, "saying as I did the plans that are going through your head while you do the maze." The therapist then performs additional mazes, still modeling task-approach behavior and still self-instructing, but at this point the self-instructions are more like whispers. The patient then performs some training tasks while whispering the self-instructions. Finally, the therapist and then the child would perform while using covert instructions (see also Table 3.1).

TABLE 3.1
Content and Sequence of Self-Instructional Procedures with Impulsive Children[a]

Content of self-instructions	Sequence of self-instructions
Problem definition: "Let's see, what am I supposed to do?"	The therapist models task performance and talks out loud while the child observes;
Problem approach: "Well, I should look this over and try to figure out how to get to the center of the maze."	The child performs the task, instructing himself out loud;
Focusing of attention: "I'd better look ahead so I don't get trapped."	The therapist models task performance while whispering the self-instructions, followed by
Coping statements: "Oh, that path isn't right. If I go that way, I'll get stuck. I'll just go back here and try another way."	The child's performing the task, whispering to himself;
Self-reinforcement: "Hey, not bad. I really did a good job!"	The therapist performs the task using covert self-instructions, with pauses and behavioral signs of thinking (e.g., stroking beard or chin, raising eyes toward the ceiling);
	The child performs the task using covert self-instructions.

[a] After Kendall, 1977; Kendall and Finch, 1978; Meichenbaum, 1975, 1977; and Meichenbaum and Goodman, 1971.

The content of the actual self-instructional procedures are step-by-step verbalizations that assist the child in performing the training task (see Table 3.1). These self-instructions include problem definition, problem approach, focusing of attention, coping statements, and self-reinforcement. The importance of the self-reinforcement component in modifying impulsivity in children has been demonstrated by Nelson and Birkimer (1978). Both the content and the sequence of the self-instructional procedures are independent of the tasks used in treatment. That is, one strength of the self-instructional method is that it can be tailored to different training tasks and to different verbal styles. In clinical procedures, the therapist should make sure that the child does not simply repeat the self-statement in a rote fashion but rehearses meaningful self-talk. At the start of each session, the therapist should inquire in order to ascertain if the child can recall the self-instructions. Here, a verbatim response is not as desirable as a response that, in the child's own words, indicates that he is mastering the material. At the end of each session, the therapist should encourage the child to use the self-statements outside of therapy and should ask the child to remember one such instance and to be prepared to describe it at the beginning of the following session.

The therapist's modeling of the appropriate behaviors necessary for successful task completion is an important component of the cognitive–behavioral treatment. The modeling procedure includes showing the child the proper strategy for using a wide variety of task-related behaviors. That is, the therapist models everything from sitting still and looking at the task to an analysis of the tasks and verbal use of the correct self-instructions. In addition, the therapist models an expectancy for success, an ability to cope with any possible mistakes, a desire to do well, and an acceptance of the result with appropriate self-reinforcement.

The response-cost component of the cognitive–behavioral treatment has been used with at least two different reward losses. In one instance, the loss of one of the five dimes was made contingent upon the inappropriate "switching" of behavior during individual therapy (Kendall & Finch, 1976). In studies that examined the effectiveness of the cognitive–behavioral treatment by comparing groups of children treated differently, each child was given 10 chips (Kendall & Finch, 1978) or 25 chips (Kendall & Wilcox, Note 2) that could be traded for items from a reward menu. The loss of one chip was contingent upon each error made during the cognitive–behavioral training sessions. It should also be mentioned that a cue card that reminded the child to "stop, listen, look, and think" was used. When applying response-cost, it is suggested that the therapist label the response-cost for the child by providing information as to why the token/chip was lost, point to the cue card to remind the child, and return to the overt self-instructions on the following task.[1]

[1]A more detailed delineation of the treatment procedures is available in a tentative therapy manual (Kendall and collaborators, Note 5). In this manual, the cognitive–behavioral treatment is described for each of 12 therapy sessions. The tasks that are employed in these sessions begin with psychoeducational materials, shift to interpersonal situations, and finally focus on personal problems. These graduated tasks are designed to facilitate the initial acquisition of the self-instructions and to aid in the development of generalization to extratherapy settings.

What should be more than apparent at this juncture is that the cognitive-behavioral treatment for impulsivity is a multifaceted program. Additionally, it should be obvious that each of the components has some demonstrated utility with impulsive children and that the treatment seeks to remedy deficiencies that are specific to this type of child.

EMPIRICAL SUPPORT FOR THE CLINICAL UTILITY OF THE COGNITIVE–BEHAVIORAL TREATMENT FOR IMPULSIVITY

One may be willing to accept, on rational grounds alone, the utility of the procedures that we have thus far outlined. However, meeting the more rigorous criteria of the methods of psychotherapy research provides the necessary conditions for further clinical utilization.

Two of the major obstacles interfering with the clinician's attempt to achieve a scientist–practitioner profession are the practitioners' claims of the lack of relevance of scientific research for their day-to-day concerns and the researcher's claims that practitioners do not make the effort to read and to apply their findings. Researchers read, analyze, and critique their own data, whereas practitioners generally do not read, or else read popularly distilled versions of the experimentalist's efforts. The popular versions are often presented so as to sound like a panacea—an occurrence that simply makes it easier for the experienced veteran to dismiss a new treatment method. Unfortunately, though the researcher is aware that the procedures must be tested on clinical samples, most of the experimental evaluations of therapy procedures are of the analogue variety.

The necessity of empirical–clinical evaluations within the area of self-control in children is captured in Karoly's (1977) characterization of the current status of the field:

> First it is probably a fair characterization of the field to assert that self-control training has: 1) been conducted mainly in laboratory settings, 2) employed nonclinical populations, 3) neglected individual differences and cognitive-development variables, 4) failed to apply systematic pretreatment assessment, 5) operated under the assumption of a general skills deficiency (as opposed to possible perceptual, decisional, or motivational deficiencies), 6) attempted to demonstrate the efficacy of a singular (or limited) intervention strategy, 7) focused on a narrow range of self-control responses (where the frequent use of quotation marks around terms like hyperactive, impulsive, overactive, distractible, learning disabled, delinquent, excitable, aggressive, and disruptive has served to absolve investigators of the responsibility for delineating topographic boundaries and for blasting the patient homogeneity myth), and 8) failed to pay sufficient attention to issues of maintenance and transfer. Self-management researchers will have their work cut out for them in the late 1970s. Of this there can be no doubt [p. 236].

Karoly's (1977) points are well-advised. Indeed, if an intervention is to receive clinical application, it must meet these issues. Fortunately, the cognitive behavioral treatment for impulsivity has undergone empirical clinical evaluations. Several studies of the treatment efficacy were conducted in a short-term psychiatric hospital for children and employed emotionally disturbed subjects who had been identified as cognitively impulsive. In addition, the cognitive–behavioral treatment is a multifaceted intervention, using several combined intervention strategies in order to achieve maximal effectiveness. Last, the evaluations used a multimethod assessment strategy as well as measures of transfer and maintenance of training. Thus, to the extent that the outcomes are supportive, it seems reasonable to conclude that these examinations of the cognitive-behavioral treatment have provided a basis for application to additional clinical populations.

Initially, Kendall and Finch (1976) reported on the results of a single-subject experimental evaluation of the clinical utility of the cognitive–behavioral treatment for impulsivity. The subject was a 9-year-old boy who had been described on previous psychological evaluations as uncooperative, aggressive, and feisty. The child was also labeled a behavior problem in the classroom and had been demoted just prior to the referral for outpatient service. During the initial interview the child was constantly moving about and hurried. He climbed in and out of his chair, talked rapidly about many topics, and changed the direction and purpose of his behavior without apparent reason. The child's initial performance on the MFF resulted in a mean latency of 4.59 seconds with 9 (of a possible 12) first-response errors. Given his age, this set of MFF scores would clearly place the child within the impulsive category.

In addition to the MFF scores, specific behaviors were targeted for intervention. The targeted behaviors were inappropriate and untimely "switches." Each switch consisted of a shift from one behavior to another when the first behavior was itself not yet complete. The frequency of switches of (a) topics of conversation; (b) games played with; and (c) rules of play were recorded during the baseline, treatment, generalization, and follow-up phases of the multiple-baseline design.

The application of the cognitive–behavioral treatment included the therapist's providing self-instructional training at the beginning of each therapy session. The therapist also displayed a cue card for the child. The card was 5×7 inches in size and stated "stop, listen, look, and think." Following the self-instructional training, the child was given five dimes that would be his to keep if he did not switch, for example, topics of conversation. The response-cost contingency was altered as each new target "switch" behavior was subjected to treatment.

The results of this single-subject investigation are presented in Figure 3.2. As can be seen, the baseline frequency of switching was relatively high. The success of the treatment procedure was evident in the changes in the target behaviors that occurred systematically following treatment installation. Results of the posttreatment administration of the MFF resulted in a mean latency of 18.73 seconds and five errors. This performance, when compared to the child's initial scores, was evidence of the desired change. In addition, these scores would no longer place the child in the impulsive category.

Two methods for assessing the transfer or generalization of the training were employed. The first method was to vary systematically components of the treatment

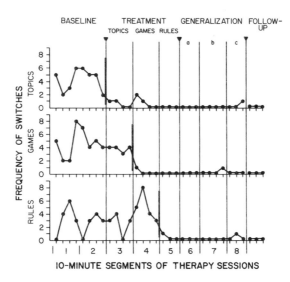

Figure 3.2. Frequency of switches in topics, games, and rules across 10-minute segments of therapy sessions as a function of treatment and generalization tests. (From P. C. Kendall and A. J. Finch, 1976. Copyright 1976 by the American Psychological Association. Reprinted by permission.)

(Kendall, Note 6). In Figure 3.2, the reader will see that there are three such assessments of generalization. Under generalization *a,* the therapy took place in a different room. The child was exposed to new walls, rugs, and bookshelves, as well as to an entirely different view out of the window. Generalization *b* altered the array of games presented during the therapy session. Prior to this test for transfer, the array of games in the therapy room had been held constant. The third generalization test, *c,* examined the child's behavior when a new and different therapist administered the program. The data presented in Figure 3.2 suggest that the generalization or transfer of the behavior changes were durable and widespread. The durable change in behavior that was observed when a different room, new toys, and a different therapist were involved in the program is strong evidence for generalization.

The second method used for the assessment of generalization was unobtrusive. That is, the child brought in an unsolicited report from his regular classroom teacher. On the reverse of the child's current classroom grades were a series of ratings on the child's study skills. From the dates that the report had previously been sent home, we could identify the teacher ratings that corresponded with the implementation of the treatment. In general, these reports indicated that the child had adopted more efficient study skills and that the child was working harder and participating more often.

Six months later, the child's MFF performance was again reflective, with a mean latency of 24.7 seconds and four errors. The total absence of switches observed at this time can be seen in Figure 3.2. It should be noted that the treatment did not continue during the period prior to follow-up assessment. The child was seen on occasion, once or twice a month, but the sessions were unstructured. Of course, the therapist could have served as an appropriate model for nonimpulsive behavior even during the sessions when training was not in effect.

The results of this experimental analysis suggest that the cognitive–behavioral program for training an impulsive, overactive child to verbally self-instruct using response-cost contingencies upon inappropriate behavior is an effective treatment procedure to reduce inappropriate behavioral switches and to alter an impulsive cognitive style. Of special interest at this time is the fact that the child was a referred client who was being treated in an outpatient psychiatric facility. Indeed, this is one clinical case that supports the clinical utility of the intervention procedures.

Bornstein and Quevillon (1976) provided additional support for the utility of a cognitive–behavioral procedure in their report of the treatment of three overactive preschool boys. These youngsters (age 4) were from lower- to middle-class settings and were enrolled in a Head Start program. The intervention approach used by Bornstein and Quevillon had both cognitive and behavioral components. The children received self-instructional training in the typical sequence and with the usual content (see Table 3.1), but the children also received candy contingent upon correct performance during training. The results of this intervention provided rather strong evidence, in that each child increased the amount of on-task behavior at the time that the training procedures went into effect. Also, treatment effects were maintained 22.5 weeks after the initiation of the study (see Figure 3.3). Although the Bornstein and Quevillon report does not include both self-instructions and response-cost, the use of the contingent reward for accuracy along with the self-instructional training clearly qualifies it as a cognitive–behavioral approach.

In order to further investigate the efficacy of the cognitive–behavioral treatment, Kendall and Finch (1978) conducted a group comparison investigation. These authors identified impulsive, emotionally disturbed children from among those children entering a psychiatric setting during an 8-month period. Those identified as impulsive were randomly assigned to either a treatment group or a control group. The treatment group received six sessions of verbal self-instructions via modeling and practice, with response-cost contingent upon errors during training. The children in the control group received similar exposure to the training tasks and similar experiences with the trainer, but without the specifics of the intervention. Multimethod assessment procedures were utilized. These assessments include two self-report measures (Impulse Control Categorization Instrument, ICCI, Matsushima, 1964; Impulsivity Scale, IS, Hirschfield revision [1965] of the Sutton–Smith & Rosenberg Scale, 1959), patient performance on the MFF, teaching ratings on an Impulsive Classroom Behavior Scale (ICBS, Weinreich, 1975) and the Locus of Conflict (LOC) Scale (Armentrout, 1971), and LOC ratings made by hospital staff on the unit where the child lived. These measures were taken at pretreatment, posttreatment, and at follow-up.

The results of the Kendall and Finch (1978) investigation indicated that the treated children performed significantly less impulsively on the MFF at posttreat-

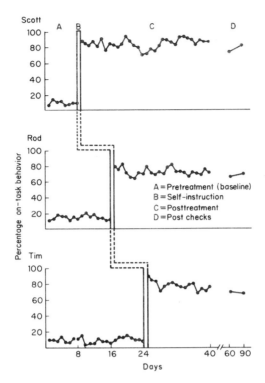

Figure 3.3. Daily percentage on-task behavior for Scott, Rod, and Tim across experimental conditions. (From P. H. Bornstein and R. P. Quevillon, *Journal of Applied Behavior Analysis*, 1976, *9*, 184. Copyright 1976 by The Society for the Experimental Analysis of Behavior.)

ment and at follow-up. These performance differences were evident on both the latency-to-respond measure (see Figure 3.4) and the error-rate measure (see Figure 3.5) of the MFF. In addition, the treated children were rated by their classroom teachers as significantly less impulsive in the classroom at posttreatment and at follow-up (see Figure 3.6). The self-report measures of impulsiveness (e.g., IS and ICCI) did not result in any significant changes due to treatment, nor did the teacher or staff LOC ratings. Nevertheless, the treated subjects did show a marked reduction in cognitive task performance (on the MFF) and in classroom behavior (on the ICBS). The positive changes on the ICBS are somewhat unclear due to the differences between the groups at the initial testing (a case of the ineffectiveness of random assignment). Interestingly, there was an observed tendency for degree of improvement observed in the classroom to be correlated with the number of response-cost occurrences that had taken place during treatment.

Following the report of the group comparison study by Kendall and Finch (1978), these authors conducted a series of supplemental analyses to examine the effects of the treatment on the verbal behavior and the hyperactivity ratings of the children. Since the cognitive–behavioral treatment focuses specifically upon the development

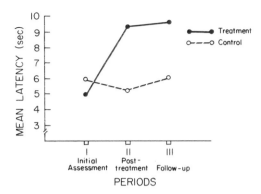

Figure 3.4. Mean latency in seconds for the treatment and control groups at the initial assessment, posttreatment, and follow-up periods. From Kendall, P. C. and Finch. A. J., A cognitive–behavioral treatment for impulsivity: A group comparison study. *Journal of Consulting and Clinical Psychology,* 1978, *46,* 110–118. Copyright 1978 by the American Psychological Association. Reprinted by permission.

of verbally mediated self-control (Kendall, 1977), one is necessarily led to the question of whether the treated child actually increases his or her effective use of language. Similarly, with the disturbing problems associated with hyperactivity in children, one is expected to inquire of the relationship of impulsivity to hyperactivity and of the potential utility of the cognitive–behavioral treatment to reduce ratings of hyperactivity. Such questions were evaluated by Kendall and Finch (Note 7). In this report, three studies were conducted.

In the analysis of verbal behavior, the tape-recorded verbalizations of nine treated impulsives, nine impulsive controls, and nine reflective children were examined. The tape recordings were collected during each child's performance of the MFF at the three measurement periods. The taped material was then coded into six verbal

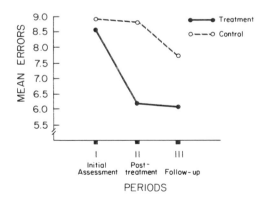

Figure 3.5. Mean errors for the treatment and control groups at the initial assessment, posttreatment, and follow-up periods. (From P. C. Kendall and A. J. Finch, 1978. Copyright 1978 by the American Psychological Association. Reprinted by permission.)

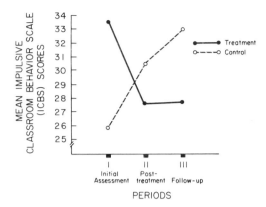

Figure 3.6. Mean Impulsive Classroom Behavior Scale (ICBS) scores for the treatment and control group at the initial assessment, posttreatment, and follow-up periods. (From P. C. Kendall and A. J. Finch, 1978. Copyright 1978 by the American Psychological Association. Reprinted by permission.)

codes. These codes were: task-related questions, statements of task difficulty, thinking out loud, verbalizing the answer, off-task verbalizations, and total on-task verbal behavior. When the treated impulsive children were compared to the impulsive controls, several of the verbal codes did not indicate significant differences. However, the total on-task verbal code did result in significant improvement for the treated children. That is, the treated impulsives increased their on-task verbalizations from pretreatment to posttreatment, with a drop-off at follow-up. The control group did not show meaningful changes across the three measurement periods.

A different question regarding verbal behavior was asked when verbalizations of the treated children were compared to those of the children that had originally been identified as reflective. Here, though we do not reveal changes that were due to treatment, we evaluate where the treated impulsives were at the end of treatment in relation to other, nonproblematic children. First, it was found that the impulsive children that had received treatment asked more task-related questions than the reflectives. Although several explanations could be entertained, it seems reasonable to imagine the treated children as having acquired some delay-before-responding skills and that these skills thus enabled the children to further inquire about the expectations of the task at hand. Second, the treated impulsives were found to have significantly reduced their off-task behavior in comparison to the reflectives. Indeed, the rate of off-task verbal behavior of the impulsives at follow-up was identical to the consistently low rate of the reflectives. Third, as in the comparison with impulsive controls, the treated children were found to have increased on-task verbal behavior when contrasted with the reflectives.

Problems are prevalent in any attempt to infer internalization of language. Nevertheless, the increases in on-task verbalizations and the reductions of off-task verbal behavior may be seen as suggestive evidence for the positive effects of the intervention.

The second study reported by Kendall and Finch (Note 7) examined the relationship between hyperactivity and the measures of impulsivity used in the Kendall and Finch group comparison study (1978). The results of these analyses indicated that ratings on a measure of hyperactivity (Connors, 1969) were related to only one measure of impulsiveness, the ICCI. The ICCI measures an aggressive, acting-out quality of impulsiveness and thus suggests that hyperactivity and impulsivity are related by an acting-out tendency. This suggestion is supported by other findings. For example, hyperactivity was related to externalization of conflict, as rated by both teachers and staff. It appears, then, that, among the emotionally disturbed children studied, impulsivity was relatively unrelated to the dimension of hyperactivity but that one aspect of impulsiveness, acting-out, was related meaningfully to hyperactivity.

In the third and final study reported by Kendall and Finch (Note 7) the five factors of the Conners rating scale (1969) were analyzed at pretreatment, posttreatment, and follow-up for the treated impulsive children versus the impulsive controls. The five factors of the Conners scale are *defiance–aggression, daydreaming–inattentive, anxious–fearful, hyperactivity,* and *health.* Only the defiance–aggression and the hyperactivity factor scores evidenced significant results. In both cases, the treated children received less pathological ratings, as compared to increasing ratings for the controls following treatment and at follow-up. Taken together, these results offer initial support for the cognitive–behavioral treatment.

Noting that Kendall and Finch (1978) failed to find changes in ratings of behavior made by dormitory staff, and in an attempt to provide an approximate replication, Furgerson (1977) attempted to combine the Kendall and Finch (1978) program with the "think aloud" program developed by Camp, Blom, Herbert, and Van Doornenck (1977). He reasoned that the increased emphasis on social behaviors in the Camp *et al.* program should facilitate generalization to the living units. Furgerson's study was conducted in the same psychiatric hospital as the Kendall and Finch report (1978). In addition to the ratings employed by Kendall and Finch, Furgerson (1977) also time-sampled under three separate conditions (unit, school, and gym) the physical, verbal, and total amounts of aggressive behavior. He found that upon the completion of nine training sessions (six as in Kendall & Finch, plus three as in Camp) there was improvement in teacher ratings of the children on the ICBS but that there were no changes in the frequency of aggressive behaviors. These findings, generalization to the classroom but not to the living unit, are consistent with those of Kendall and Finch (1978). Unfortunately, among other serious methodological problems, a number of the emotionally disturbed children in the Furgerson study were discharged from the hospital before the completion of follow-up assessment, and therefore only tentative conclusions about the generalization of the treatment effects can be drawn.

The present authors are aware that there have been unsuccessful attempts to achieve positive results with self-instructional procedures (e.g., Heath, 1978; Higa, 1973; Mash, Note 8; Weinreich, 1975). However, the cognitive–behavioral treatment includes a response-cost contingency[2] in addition to the self-instructional training and the importance of incentive manipulations provided concomitantly with self-instructions is among the speculations about the relative contributions of the various components of the cognitive–behavioral treatment (Kendall, 1977; Kendall, Note 9; Meichenbaum, in press). Nelson (1976) addressed this question in an analogue study in which cognitively impulsive children from a normal school system were used to compare the relative effects of the components of the cognitive–behavioral intervention. Some of the children in this study received self-instructional training, some received the response-cost contingency during training, and some received both self-instructions and response-cost training, and still others were in a test–retest control condition. In addition, one group that did not receive any training took the posttreatment administration of the MFF under conditions of response-cost. Children were retested within 3 days after training, and at follow-up periods 2½ and 6 weeks after training. The results of this investigation indicated that cognitive training in the form of verbal self-instructions produced significantly longer response latencies and significantly fewer errors, regardless of the presence or absence of the response-cost procedure. However, neither response latencies nor errors were significantly altered as a result of response-cost training, regardless of cognitive training. Although not significantly distinct from the others, the best procedure for significantly reducing impulsive responding was the combined self-instructions plus response-cost procedures.

Additional analyses reported by Nelson (1976) suggested that the response-cost condition was effective in increasing the time the child spent on the task but had no effect on the number of errors. Thus, perhaps the response-cost procedure increases task persistence but does not provide for the learning of task-relevant skills. The performance of the subjects who did not receive training but who took the posttest under conditions of response-cost lend some support to such a notion. That is, when response-cost was operative, the child tended to be more reflective, but, when not in effect (as in the two follow-ups), the number of errors was no different from that of the controls. In a sense, response-cost can be said to provide some motivational pressure to persist but, when applied alone, does not provide training in a problem-solving strategy. The cognitive self-instructional training may provide the skills that are responsible for improvements in task performance and, since there is evidence to suggest that verbalized responses alone increase persistence (e.g., Masters & Santrock, 1976), may also promote behavioral persistence.

However, recall that the Nelson (1976) study used normal impulsive children. The increased effectiveness of the combined approach may not be as readily apparent with normals as with disturbed children, since they may be said to have initially higher levels of motivation to perform well. The benefit of combining the self-

---

[2]This is *not* a response-cost only procedure. Response-cost is used for errors, but social praise is given for correct behavior. In addition, self-reward is an important component of the self-instructions that are taught.

instructional and response-cost procedures with clinical samples may be in the potential of response-cost to supress disruptive behaviors such as distractibility, excitability, or excessive motor behavior. This notion is an important issue that should be evaluated by future research in this area.

Also among speculations (Kendall, 1977) regarding the relative contribution of the various aspects of the cognitive–behavioral treatment to treatment efficacy was the relationship between the *quality* of self-instructions that the children are taught and potential treatment generalization. That is, there may be differential effects produced by training procedures that focus upon the specific training task (concrete labeling) as compared to an approach to training that applies to the specific instance of the training task at hand and is also appropriate for other tasks and in other situations (conceptual labeling). Corresponding to notions of metacognitive development (see Chapter 2 of this volume), the conceptual labeling–training procedures are thought to be more likely to produce generalization of the treatment effects.

In order to test this notion, Kendall and Wilcox (Note 2) used a randomized blocks procedure to assign 33 children (25 males, 8 females) to one of three groups, a conceptual treatment group, a concrete treatment group, and an attention–placebo control group. The children (mean age = 10 years 5 months) were non-self-controlled third to sixth graders who were referred by their teachers for being classroom behavior problems. All three groups of children received six 30–40-minute sessions twice a week for 3 weeks. Except for the cognitive–behavioral self-control training proper, subjects in all three groups were given identical task instructions and performance feedback (rewards for control subjects were yoked to a random-treatment subject). No criterion number of tasks were set; rather, all subjects worked for about 30 minutes, regardless of their progress. This procedure was employed to undermine the children's tendency to try to rush and finish all the tasks for each session (Kendall, 1977).

Although the treatment groups received conditions similar to controls, these subjects also received specific training in verbal self-instructions via modeling and a response-cost procedure contingent on errors during training. The self-instructions the subjects received, however, varied as a function of the treatment group to which they had assigned: The instructions learned by the "conceptual" group differed from those learned by the "concrete" group. Nevertheless, the major components of the self-control strategy (outlined in Table 3.1) presented to both treatment groups were similar.

For each component, the "concrete" instructions were worded so as to apply specifically only to the task at hand; the "conceptual" instructions, by contrast, were worded more globally and abstractly, in such a way that they could apply to a wide range of situations. The following are examples of the concrete and the conceptual self-instructions, coping statements, and response-cost labels used in the two treatment groups.

Concrete Self-Instructional Training

Problem Definition: I'm to find the picture that doesn't match.
Problem Approach: This one's a clock, this one's a clock.
Focusing of Attention: Look at the pictures.
Self-Reinforcement: The cup and saucer is different; (check answer sheet) I got it right. Good job!
Coping Statement: Oh, it's not the clock that's different, it's the teacup. I can pick out the correct one next time.
Labeling a response-cost: (done, obviously, by therapist) No, its not the clock, it's the teacup. You lose one chip for picking the clock.

Conceptual Self-Instructional Training

Problem Definition: My first step is to make sure I know what I'm supposed to do.
Problem Approach: Well, I should look at all the possibilities.
Focusing of Attention: I should think about only what I'm doing right now.
Self-Reinforcement: (checking the answer sheet) Hey, good job. I'm doing very well.
Coping Statement: Well, if I make a mistake I can remember to think more carefully next time, and then I'll do better.
Labeling a Response Cost: No, that's not the right answer. You lost one token for not taking your time and getting the correct answer.

In relation to each set of the psychoeducational tasks (used in the first four sessions), the verbal self-instructions were taught by graduating from overt to covert self-instructions. Therapists required the subjects to revert back to speaking the self-instructions out loud following an error. As the child became more and more proficient at using the instructions, the therapist answered fewer and fewer problems, though still answering occasional items to preserve a sense of cooperation and working-together within the treatment. Children were also given a visual aid in the form of a cue card that states, in pictures and words, "Stop, listen, look, and think" (after Palkes *et al.,* 1968).

In sessions five and six, the focus was on, respectively, interpersonal cooperation and play, and classroom and home behavior. The process of modeling, imitating, fading, and so forth was used differently in these sessions; that is, common problems were discussed in the light of the basic strategy of problem definition, problem approach, deliberate selection of a response, and self-reinforcement for effective behavior. Children were deliberately encouraged to use such self-instructional tactics in their classroom and interpersonal activities. Regarding the response-cost contingency, children were told that they could lose a chip for each mistake they made, either in failing to follow the procedures of self-instructional training or in giving the wrong answer to a problem. A variety of dependent measures were collected at pretreatment. posttreatment, and 1-month follow-up and used to examine the effects of treatment in the Kendall and Wilcox study (Note 2). Subject performance measures included the MFF (the three alternate forms developed by Egeland & Weinberg, 1976, were used for repeated measurements) and the Porteus Mazes (three alternate forms). Subject self-report was collected using the ICCI, and two ratings of classroom behavior were completed by teachers: the hyperactivity items of the Connors Teacher Rating Scale (1969) and the Kendall Self-Control Rating Scale (Kendall & Wilcox, Note 1). Given the need to be concerned with the generalization of the treatment effects, the Self-Control Rating Scale (SCRS) was developed for use in the assessment of self-control in extratherapy settings. The SCRS was found to show convergent validity with children's task performance on the MFF and Porteus Mazes and with behavioral observations, and discriminant validity by a very low and nonsignificant correlation with IQ. These correlations remained significant when mental and chronological age were partialed out. Also, increased self-control ratings were correlated with age. A second study reported by Kendall and Wilcox (Note 1) found differences on the SCRS, MFF latencies, and behavioral observations between children referred for self-control training and matched nonreferred children.

The results of the Kendall and Wilcox (Note 2) treatment outcome study are quite interesting. Although self-report data did not indicate change and several performance measures evidenced improvement for all subjects, blind teacher-ratings of both self-control and hyperactivity evidenced change due to treatment at posttreatment and at follow-up. The treatment effects were stronger for the conceptual labeling group than for the concrete labeling group on both self-control ratings (see Figure 3.7) and hyperactivity ratings. Thus, the use of conceptual labeling within the cognitive–behavioral treatment was found to facilitate generalization. In Figure 3.7 the teacher's SCRS ratings are plotted along with the mean SCRS score of 110 randomly selected children. As can be seen, the subjects in the study were initially quite lacking in teacher-rated self-control as compared to their classroom peers. At follow-up, however, although still at the upper end of one standard deviation above the mean, the conceptual labeling group evidenced significant improvement. These results are supportive of the efficacy of the cognitive–behavioral treatment and place the results in perspective regarding normal classroom behavior. Future research should extend the amount of training and examine the ability of the procedures to produce even greater improvements in self-control. Moreover, future research should examine the utility of the treatment procedures in modifying hyperactive children and facilitating their development of self-control.

The number of response-cost enactments during treatment in the Kendall and Wilcox study (Note 2) was not significantly related to measures of improvement. This finding is in contrast to the suggestive relationship between these variables reported by Kendall and Finch (1978). However, among other significant relation-

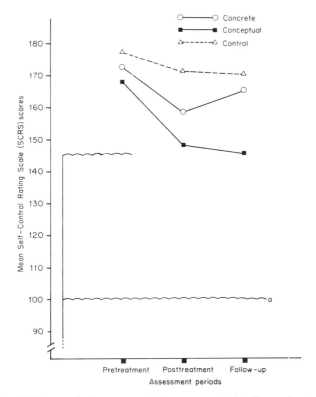

Figure 3.7. Mean SCRS scores for the concrete labeling, conceptual labeling, and control groups across the three assessment periods. SCRS = Self-Control Rating Scale. a = Mean SCRS score (99.3) of 110 randomly selected children (same grades and both sexes) extrapolated over time. The SD is 46.1. Thus, scores between 53.2 and 145.4 would be within 1 SD of the mean of the normative group. (From P. C. Kendall & L. E. Wilcox, Note 2.)

ships, Kendall and Wilcox (Note 2) did report that the therapists' ratings of a therapist–child relationship were significantly correlated with teacher ratings of improvement on the SCRS. An additional ancillary, but quite interesting, set of significant correlations were found between therapist empathy (Hogan, 1969) and several measures of improvement. The value of both empathy and a therapist–child relationship as contributors to the efficacy of the cognitive–behavioral treatment requires further experimental study.

ISSUES TO BE CONSIDERED IN CLINICAL APPLICATION

There are a number of practical issues that should be considered when one is deciding to implement the cognitive–behavioral intervention for impulsivity. These issues concern (a) the cognitive capacity of the children; (b) the structure of the training sessions; (c) the implementation of self-instructional training; and (d) the planning for the generalization of the treatment effects. Our discussion here will be brief, since some of these points are discussed in further detail elsewhere (Kendall, 1977).

Cognitive Capacity

In order to maximize the effectiveness of the intervention, the cognitive capacity of the child(ren) to be treated should be compatible with that required by the self-instructional training and by the training tasks. Decisions about a child's cognitive appropriateness may be fostered by an analysis of the child's level of cognitive development (Piaget, Bruner). An extreme example of an inappropriate use of self-instructional training would be the application of self-instructions to very retarded children. Less extreme, but perhaps more compelling, is the case of the low-IQ (or cognitively undeveloped) child who simply has difficulty in learning. However, with "slow" children, self-instructional training may prove quite effective when certain preliminaries are conducted. These preliminaries include, for example, initial training of the component skills of self-instruction (e.g., rote memorization of some clearcut, individual self-statements). Thus, at least one of the component skills—remembering the self-instruction—is taught before any behavior changes are expected. Depending upon the target behavior, there may be several other component skills that may also require pretraining before the cognitive–behavioral treatment can be expected to be effective. Considering the cognitive capacities of the subjects should prevent both difficulties in application and the potential for inappropriate dismissal of the procedures.

Moreover, modeling, as a performance component of the cognitive–behavioral procedures, is an important part of the training. Cognitive capacity plays a central role in the child's observational learning in that the child's capacity to process information governs how much he will benefit from observed experiences (Bandura, 1977a).

Lastly, though not unrelated to cognitive capacity, the age of the children should be considered prior to developing cognitive–behavioral interventions. It should also be noted that there is data to suggest that the MFF is not as meaningful a measure of reflectivity when it is used with preschoolers as when it is used with school-age children (Kagan & Messer, 1975; see also Block, Block, & Harrington, 1974, 1975).

Structure of the Training Sessions

When implementing the cognitive–behavioral procedures, the therapist should be concerned with the child's interest in and attention to the training tasks. What are some of the relevant methods for attaining and maintaining the child's interest? A favorable therapist–child relationship and interesting, age-appropriate training materials are certain to affect positively the child's attention-span. The child's desire to be in the treatment may have a potent, yet sometimes overlooked, incentive quality. Here, the scheduling of treatment sessions such that the child gets out of school or various tasks by participating in the treatment would certainly increase the desirability of treatment as perceived by the child.

There is also an implicit contingency involving the tasks used in training within the cognitive–behavioral procedures that should not be ignored. Do the children have to complete all those tasks that are brought to a treatment session? If so, they may perceive that they can leave when all the tasks are finished and therefore say to themselves, "Hurry-up!" The therapist can best prevent such an inappropriate perception by changing the completion criteria to something untimed. For instance, the therapist could say,

> *We are going to work on these tasks for 30 minutes (or however long is planned). Whether we finish all of these tasks or not doesn't matter. What's important is that we work for 30 minutes and that we do well on each task before we go on. After the 30 minutes you can turn in your tokens for a reward.*

At later stages of training, the therapist may then wish to teach the children how to deal effectively with externally placed time pressure.

Implementing the Self-Instructional Training

Several suggestions have been proposed by Meichenbaum (1977; in press) as important considerations to facilitate the implementation of self-instructional training. These suggestions (with some references added) include:

1. Using the child's own medium of play to initiate and model self-talk.
2. Using tasks that have a high "pull" for the use of sequential cognitive strategies.
3. Using peer teaching by having children cognitively model while performing for another child.
4. Moving through the program at the child's own rate and building up the package of self-statements to include self-talk of a problem-solving variety as well as coping and self-reinforcing elements.
5. Guarding against the child's using the self-statements in a mechanical, non-involved fashion.
6. Including a therapist who is animated and responsive to the child.
7. Learning to use the self-instructional training with low intensity responses.
8. Supplementing the training with imagery practice such as the "turtle technique" (Schneider & Robin, 1976).
9. Supplementing the self-instructional training with correspondence training (Risley, Note 10; Rogers-Warren & Baer, 1976).
10. Supplementing the self-instructional training with operant procedures such as

a response-cost system (Kendall & Finch, 1976, 1978; Kendall & Wilcox, Note 2; Nelson, 1976).

Attention to these points should further the clinical application of the self-instructional component of the cognitive–behavioral treatment.

Planning for Generalization

For many clinicians and researchers in the field, self-control training for children is perceived as an adjunct to behavioral management procedures to aid in the maintenance and generalization (transfer) of positive changes (Drabman, Spitalnik & O'Leary, 1973; Kazdin, 1975). Conceptually, since the cognitive–behavioral treatment seeks to develop verbally mediated self-control, the treatment should generalize to situations other than those of the training. Nevertheless, it would be insufficient to ascribe an ability to promote generalization to a therapy without purposefully examining it. Indeed, this research imperative led to the development of the SCRS (Kendall & Wilcox, Note 1) as a measure of self-control in extratherapy settings. Subsequent research pertaining to the generalization of the cognitive–behavioral treatment should address such important issues as the following: (a) The type of training tasks—will interpersonal tasks be more likely to generalize to social settings? (b) the type of self-instruction—will individualized self-statements foster transfer? (c) number of sessions—will an increase in training sessions increase the potential for generalization? (d) fading-out the therapy sessions—will immediate discontinuance be less transferable than a gradual fading out? (e) extra self-instructional training in self-reward—will generalization be promoted by refocusing the training to the building of self-reward skills and perceptions of self-efficacy? (f) multiple treatment settings—will providing the training in a variety of situations and settings increase transfer? and (g) individual difference variables—will an internal attributional style foster generalization? Research that addresses itself to these questions will provide valuable information for the modification and improvement of the cognitive–behavioral treatment for impulsivity.

ACKNOWLEDGMENTS

The authors wish to express their thanks to M. Sue Kendall for her valuable editorial comments.

REFERENCE NOTES

1. Kendall, P. C., & Wilcox, L. E. *Self-control in children: The development of a rating scale.* Manuscript submitted for publication, 1979.
2. Kendall, P. C., & Wilcox, L. E. *A cognitive–behavioral treatment for impulsivity: Concrete versus conceptual labeling with non-self-controlled problem children.* Manuscript submitted for publication, 1979.
3. Wilkinson, M. D. *Modification of an impulsive cognitive tempo.* Unpublished manuscript, Virginia Commonwealth University, 1975.

4. Moore, S. F., & Cole, S. D. *Cognitive self-mediation training with hyperkinetic children.* Unpublished manuscript, Rutgers University (Camden). 1977.
5. Kendall, P. C., with collaborators Bream, L., Herzog, K., Padawer, W., & Zupan, B. *Developing self-control in children: A manual of cognitive-behavioral strategies.* Unpublished manuscript, University of Minnesota, 1979.
6. Kendall, P. C. *Assessing generalization (transfer) and the single-subject strategies.* Manuscript submitted for publication, 1979.
7. Kendall, P. C., & Finch, A. J. *A cognitive-behavioral treatment for impulsivity: Analyses of verbal behavior and hyperactivity ratings.* Manuscript submitted for publication, 1979.
8. Mash, E. J. Personal communication, December, 1977.
9. Kendall, P. C. *Self-instructions with children: An analysis of the inconsistent evidence for treatment generalization.* Address presented to the Second National Conference on Cognitive Behavior Therapy Research, New York, October, 1978.
10. Risley, T. *The social context of self-control.* Paper presented at the Banff Conference on Behavior Modification, 1976.

REFERENCES

Achenbach, T. M. The classification of children's psychiatric symptoms: A factor analytic study. *Psychological Monographs,* 1966, *80* (6, Whole No. 615).

Achenbach, T. M. Cue learning, associative responding, and school performance in children. *Developmental psychology,* 1969, *1,* 717–725.

Ainslie, G. Specious reward: A behavioral theory of impulsiveness and impulse control. *Psychological Bulletin,* 1975, *82,* 463–496.

Armentrout, J. A. Parental child-rearing attitudes and preadolescents' problem behaviors. *Journal of Consulting and Clinical Psychology,* 1971, *37,* 278–285.

Ault, R. L. Problem-solving strategies of reflective, impulsive, fast–accurate, and slow–inaccurate children. *Child Development,* 1973, *44,* 259–266.

Bandura, A. *Principles of behavior modification.* New York: Holt, Rinehart and Winston, 1969.

Bandura, A. *Social learning theory.* Englewood Cliffs, New Jersey: Prentice-Hall, Inc., 1977. (a)

Bandura, A. Self-efficacy: Toward a unifying theory of behavioral change. *Psychological Review,* 1977, *84,* 191–215. (b)

Bem, S. Verbal self-control: The establishment of effective self-instruction. *Journal of Experimental Psychology,* 1967, *74,* 485–491.

Bender, N. N. Self-verbalization versus tutor verbalization in modifying impulsivity. *Journal of Educational Psychology,* 1976, *68,* 347–354.

Birch, D. Verbal control of nonverbal behavior. *Journal of Experimental Child Psychology,* 1966, *4,* 266–275.

Block, J., Block, J. H., & Harrington, D. M. Some misgivings about the Matching Familiar Figures Test as a measure of reflection–impulsivity. *Developmental Psychology,* 1974, *10,* 611–632.

Block, J., Block, J. H., & Harrington, D. M. Comment on the Kagan–Messer reply. *Developmental Psychology,* 1975, *11,* 249–252.

Bornstein, P. H. & Quevillon, R. P. The effects of a self-instructional package on overactive preschool boys. *Journal of Applied Behavior Analysis,* 1976, *9,* 179–188.

Briggs, C. H. *An experimental study of reflection–impulsivity in children.* Doctoral dissertation, University of Minnesota, 1966. *Dissertation Abstracts,* 1968, *28,* 3891-B. (University Microfilms No. 68-1610)

Bugental, D. B., Whalen, C. K. & Henker, B. Causal attributions of hyperactive children and motivational assumptions of two behavioral-change approaches: Evidence for an interactionist position. *Child Development,* 1977, *48,* 874–884.

Burns, D. J., & Powers, R. B. Choice and self-control in children: A test of Rachlin's model. *Bulletin of the Psychonomic Society,* 1975, *5,* 156–158.

Buss, A. H., & Plomin, R. *A temperment theory of personality development*. New York: John Wiley & Sons, 1975.

Camp, B., Blom, G., Herbert, F. & Van Doorninck, W. "Think aloud": A program for developing self-control in young aggressive boys. *Journal of Abnormal Child Psychology*, 1977, *5*, 157-169.

Cheyne, J. A., & Walters, R. H. Timing of punishment, intensity of punishment and cognition structure in resistance-to-deviation. *Journal of Experimental Child Psychology*, 1969, *7*, 231-244.

Cheyne, J. A., & Walters, R. H. Punishment and prohibitions: Some origins of self-control. In T. M. Newcomb (Ed.). *New directions in psychology, Vol. 4*. New York: Holt, Rinehart and Winston, 1970.

Cohen, S., & Przybycien, C. A. Some effects of sociometrically selected peer models on the cognitive styles of impulsive children. *Journal of Genetic Psychology*, 1974, *124*, 213-220.

Conners, C. K. A teacher rating scale for use in drug studies with children. *American Journal of Psychiatry*, 1969, *126*, 884-888.

Debus, R. L. Effects of brief observation of model behavior on conceptual tempo of impulsive children. *Developmental Psychology*, 1970, *2*, 22-32.

Denney, D. R. Modeling effects upon conceptual style and cognitive tempo. *Child Development*, 1972, *43*, 105-119.

Denney, D. R. Reflection and impulsivity as determinants of conceptual strategy. *Child Development*, 1973, *44*, 614-623.

Douglas, V. I., Parry, P., Marton, P., & Garson, C. Assessment of a cognitive training program for hyperactive children. *Journal of Abnormal Child Psychology*, 1976, *4*, 389-410.

Drabman, R. S., Spitalnik, R., & O'Leary, K. D. Teaching self-control to disruptive children. *Journal of Abnormal Psychology*, 1973, *82*, 10-16.

Drake, D. M. Perceptual correlates of impulsive and reflective behavior. *Developmental Psychology*, 1970, *2*, 202-214.

Drummond, D. *Self-instructional training: An approach to disruptive classroom behavior*. Unpublished doctoral dissertation, University of Oregon, 1974.

Egeland, B. Training impulsive children in the use of more efficient scanning techniques. *Child Development*, 1974, *45*, 165-171.

Egeland, B., & Weinberg, R. A. The Matching Familiar Figures test: A look at its psychometric credibility. *Child Development*, 1976, *47*, 483-491.

Errickson, E. A., Wyne, M. D., & Routh, D. K. A response-cost procedure for reduction of impulsive behavior of academically handicapped children. *Journal of Abnormal Child Psychology*, 1973, *1*, 350-357.

Finch, A. J. Jr., & Montgomery, L. E. Reflection–impulsivity and information seeking in emotionally disturbed children. *Journal of Abnormal Child Psychology*, 1973, *1*, 358-362.

Finch, A. J. Jr., Pezzuti, K. A., Montgomery, L. E., & Kemp, S. R. Reflection-impulsivity and academic attainment in emotionally disturbed children. *Journal of Abnormal Child Psychology*, 1974, *2*, 71-74.

Finch, A. J. Jr., Kendall, P. C., Deardorff, P. A., Anderson, J., & Sitarz, A. M. Reflection-impulsivity, locus of control, and persistence behavior in emotionally disturbed children. *Journal of Consulting and Clinical Psychology*, 1975, *43*, 748.

Finch, A. J. Jr., Wilkinson, M. D., Nelson, W. M., & Montgomery, L. E. Modification of an impulsive cognitive tempo in emotionally disturbed boys. *Journal of Abnormal Child Psychology*, 1975, *3*, 47-51.

Finch, A. J. Jr., & Nelson, W. M. Reflection–impulsivity and behavior problems in emotionally disturbed boys. *Journal of Genetic Psychology*, 1976, *128*, 271-274.

Finney, B. J. *The modification of conceptual tempo in disadvantaged boys*. Doctoral dissertation, Case Western Reserve University, 1968. *Dissertation Abstracts International*, 1970, *30*, 3782-A. (University Microfilms No. 70-5016)

Firestone, P., & Douglas, V. I. The effects of reward and punishment on reaction times and autonomic activity in hyperactive and normal children. *Journal of Abnormal Child Psychology,* 1975, *3,* 201–216.

Fry, P. S. Affect and resistance to temptation. *Developmental Psychology,* 1975, *11,* 466–472.

Furgerson, L. K. *A cognitive–behavioral treatment for impulsive–aggressive behavior in emotionally disturbed children.* Unpublished thesis, University of Richmond, 1977.

Glenwick, D. S., & Burka, A. A. Cognitive impulsivity and role-taking skills in elementary school children. *Perceptual and Motor Skills,* 1975, *41,* 547–552.

Glenwick, D. S., Barocas, R., & Burka, A. Some interpersonal correlates of cognitive impulsivity in fourth-graders. *Journal of School Psychology,* 1976, *14,* 212–221.

Hartig, M., & Kanfer, F. H. The role of verbal self-instruction in children's resistence to temptation. *Journal of Personality and Social Psychology,* 1973, *25,* 259–267.

Heath, B. L. *Application of verbal self-instructional training procedures to classroom behavior management.* Unpublished doctoral dissertation, University of Minnesota, 1978.

Heider, E. R. Information processing and the modification of an "impulsive conceptual tempo." *Child Development,* 1971, *42,* 1276–1281.

Hemry, F. P. Effect of reinforcement conditions on a discriminative learning task for impulsive vs. reflective children. *Child Development,* 1973, *44,* 657–660.

Higa, W. R. *Self-instructional versus direct training in modifying children's impulsive behavior.* Unpublished doctoral dissertation, University of Hawaii, 1973.

Hirschfield, P. P. Response set in impulsive children. *Journal of Genetic Psychology,* 1965, *107,* 117–126.

Hogan, R. Development of an empathy scale. *Journal of Consulting and Clinical Psychology,* 1969, *33,* 307–316.

Jarvis, P. E. Verbal control of sensory–motor performance: A test of Luria's hypothesis. *Human Development,* 1968, *11,* 172–183.

Kagan, J., Rosman, B. L., Day, D., Albert, J., & Phillips, W. Information processing in the child: Significance of analytic and reflective attitudes. *Psychological Monographs,* 1964, *78* (1, While No. 578).

Kagan, J. Reflection–impulsivity: The generality and dynamics of conceptual tempo. *Journal of Abnormal Psychology,* 1966, *71,* 17–24.

Kagan, J., Pearson, L., & Welch, L. Modifiability of an impulsive tempo. *Journal of Educational Psychology,* 1966, *57,* 359–365. (b)

Kagan, J. & Kogan, N. Individual variations in cognitive processes. In P. H. Mussen (Ed.), *Carmichael's manual of child psychology (3rd Ed.),* New York: Wiley, 1970.

Kagan, J., & Messer, S. B. A reply to "Some Misgivings about the Matching Familiar Figures Test as a Measure of Reflection–Impulsivity." *Developmental Psychology,* 1975, *11,* 244–248.

Kanfer, F. H., & Karoly, P. Self-control: A behavioristic excursion into the lion's den. *Behavior Therapy,* 1972, *3,* 398–416.

Karoly, P. Behavioral self-management in children: Concepts, methods, issues, and directions. In M. Hersen, R. Eisler, & P. Miller (Eds.), *Progress in behavior modification, Vol. 5.* New York: Academic Press, 1977.

Karoly, P., & Kanfer, F. H. Effects of prior contractual experiences on self-control in children. *Developmental Psychology,* 1974, *10,* 459–460.

Karoly, P., & Dirks, M. J. Developing self-control in pre-school children through correspondence training. *Behavior Therapy,* 1977, *8,* 398–405.

Kazdin, A. E. *Behavior modification in applied settings.* Homewood, Illinois: Dorsey Press, 1975.

Kendall, P. C. (Producer). *A cognitive–behavioral treatment for impulsivity.* Minneapolis, University of Minnesota, 1976. (Film)

Kendall, P. C. On the efficacious use of verbal self-instructional procedures with children. *Cognitive Therapy and Research,* 1977, *1,* 331–341.

Kendall, P. C., & Finch, A. J. Jr. A cognitive–behavioral treatment for impulse control: A case study. *Journal of Consulting and Clinical Psychology,* 1976, *44,* 852–857.

Kendall, P. C., & Finch, A. J. Jr. A cognitive–behavioral treatment for impulsivity: A group comparison study. *Journal of Consulting and Clinical Psychology, 1978, 46,* 110–118.

Mahoney, M. J., & Thoresen, C. E. *Self-control: Power to the person.* Belmont, California: Brooks/ Cole, 1974.

Massari, D. J., & Schack, M. L. Discrimination learning by reflective and impulsive children in a function of reinforcement schedule. *Developmental Psychology, 1972, 6,* 183.

Masters, J. C., & Santrock, J. W. Studies in the self-regulation of behavior: Effects of contingent cognitive and affective events. *Developmental Psychology, 1976, 12,* 334–348.

Matsushima, J. An instrument for classifying impulse control among boys. *Journal of Consulting Psychology, 1964, 28,* 87–90.

Meichenbaum, D. H., & Goodman, J. The developmental control by verbal operants. *Journal of Experimental Child Psychology, 1969, 7,* 533–565.

Meichenbaum, D. H., & Goodman, J. Training impulsive children to talk to themselves: A means of developing self-control. *Journal of Abnormal Psychology, 1971, 77,* 115–126.

Meichenbaum, D. Self-instructional methods. In F. Kanfer & A. Goldstein (Eds.), *Helping people change.* New York: Pergamon Press, 1975.

Meichenbaum, D. *Cognitive–behavior modification: An integrative approach.* New York: Plenum, 1977.

Meichenbaum, D. Teaching children self-control. In B. Lahey & A. Kazdin (Eds.), *Advances in child clinical psychology, Vol. 2.* New York: Plenum, in press.

Messer, S. The effect of anxiety over intellectual performance on reflection–impulsivity in children. *Child Development, 1970, 41,* 723–735.

Messer, S. B. Reflection–impulsivity: A review. *Psychological Bulletin, 1976, 83,* 1026–1052.

Miller, S. A., Shelton, J., & Flavell, J. H. A test of Luria's hypotheses concerning the development of verbal self-regulation. *Child Development, 1970, 41,* 651–665.

Mischel, W. Processes in delay of gratification. In L. Berkowitz (Ed.), *Advances in experimental social psychology, Vol. 7.* New York: Academic Press, 1974.

Monohan, J., & O'Leary, K. D. Effects of self-instruction on rule-breaking behavior. *Psychological Reports, 1971, 29,* 1059–1066.

Montgomery, L. E., & Finch, A. J. Jr. Reflection–impulsivity and locus of conflict in emotionally disturbed children. *Journal of Genetic Psychology, 1975, 126,* 89–91.

Mosher, F. A., & Hornsby, J. R. On asking questions. In J. S. Bruner, R. R. Olver, & P. M. Greenfield (Eds.), *Studies in cognitive growth.* New York: Wiley, 1966.

Murray, H. A. (and collaborators). *Explorations in personality.* New York: Oxford, 1938.

Nelson, W. M., Finch, A. J. Jr., & Hooke, J. F. Effects of reinforcement and response-cost on cognitive style in emotionally disturbed boys. *Journal of Abnormal Psychology, 1975, 84,* 426–428.

Nelson, W. M. *Cognitive–behavioral strategies in modifying an impulsive cognitive style.* Unpublished doctoral dissertation, Virginia Commonwealth University, 1976.

Nelson, W. J., & Birkimer, J. C. Role of self-instruction and self-reinforcement in the modification of impulsivity. *Journal of Consulting and Clinical Psychology, 1978, 46,* 183.

O'Leary, K. D. The effects of self-instruction on immoral behavior. *Journal of Experimental Child Psychology, 1968, 6,* 297–301.

O'Leary, K. D., & O'Leary, S. G. *Classroom management: The successful use of behavior modification (2nd Ed.).* New York: Pergamon Press, 1977.

Palkes, H., Stewart, M., & Kahana, B. Porteus Maze performance of hyperactive boys after training in self-directed verbal commands. *Child Development, 1968, 39,* 817–826.

Palkes, H., Stewart, M., & Freedman, J. Improvement in maze performance of hyperactive boys as a function of verbal-training procedures. *Journal of Special Education, 1972, 5,* 337–342.

Parry, P., & Douglas, V. I. The effect of reward on the performance of hyperactive children. *Journal of Abnormal Child Psychology,* in press.

Patterson, C., & Mischel, W. Effects of temptation-inhibiting and task-facilitating plans on self-control. *Journal of Personality and Social Psychology, 1976, 33,* 207–217.

Porteus, S. D. *The Maze test: Recent advances*. Palo Alto, California: Pacific Books, 1955.

Reali, N., & Hall, V. Effect of success and failure on the reflective and impulsive child. *Developmental Psychology, 1970, 3,* 392–402.

Ridberg, H. E., Parke, R. D., & Hetherington, E. M. Modification of impulsive and reflective cognitive styles through observation of film mediated models. *Developmental Psychology, 1971, 5,* 369–377.

Robin, A. L., Armel, S., & O'Leary, K. D. The effects of self-instruction on writing deficiencies. *Behavior Therapy, 1975, 6,* 178–187.

Rogers-Warren, A., & Baer, D. Correspondence between saying and doing: Teaching children to share and praise. *Journal of Applied Behavior Analysis, 1976, 9,* 335–354.

Schneider, M., & Robin, A. The turtle technique: A method for the self-control of impulsive behavior. In J. Krumboltz & C. Thoresen (Eds.), *Counseling methods*. New York: Holt, Rinehart and Winston, 1976.

Schwebel, A. Effects of impulsivity on performance of verbal tasks in middle- and lower-class children. *American Journal of Orthopsychiatry, 1966, 36,* 12–21.

Seggev, L. *Visual scanning training effects on impulsive children*. Doctoral dissertation, Syracuse University, 1972. *Dissertation Abstracts International, 1972, 33,* 429B-430B. (University Microfilms No. 72-20366)

Siegelman, E. Reflective and impulsive observing behavior. *Child Development, 1969, 40,* 1213–1222.

Skinner, B. F. *Science and human behavior*. New York: Macmillan, 1953.

Sutton-Smith, B., & Rosenberg, B. G. A scale to identify impulsive behavior in children. *Journal of Genetic Psychology, 1959, 95,* 211–216.

Usui, H. Psychological study of cognitive style (reflection–impulsivity): Analysis of visual search strategies of reflective and impulsive children. *Japanese Journal of Educational Psychology, 1975, 23,* 20–25.

Ward, W. C. Reflection–impulsivity in kindergarten children. *Child Development, 1968, 39,* 867–874.

Weinriech, R. J. *Inducing reflective thinking in impulsive, emotionally disturbed children*. Unpublished thesis, Virginia Commonwealth University, 1975.

Yando, R. M., & Kagan, J. The effect of teacher tempo on the child. *Child Development, 1968, 39,* 27–34.

Zelniker, T., Jeffrey, W. E., Ault, R., & Parsons, J. Analysis and modification of search strategies of impulsive and reflective children on the Matching Familiar Figures test. *Child Development, 1972, 43,* 321–335.

4

Cognitive–Behavioral Interventions with Delinquents: Problem Solving, Role-Taking, and Self-Control

VERDA L. LITTLE

PHILIP C. KENDALL

Delinquents are typically found to be a *heterogeneous* group when viewed from traditional psychiatric diagnoses, educational models, or psychosocial categories. And although behaviorally based classification systems have been shown to be reliable (e.g., Quay & Parsons, Note 1), the utility of such grouping of delinquents for treatment has not yet been demonstrated. Similarly, the more theoretically based schemes (e.g., Warren, 1971) for grouping this population have produced only variable treatment effects (Beker & Heyman, 1972).

A more fruitful method of categorizing and therapeutically intervening with this problematic population may lie in the purposeful focus on *specific problems* that are found to be common among large numbers of those who are labeled "delinquent." What deficits have been found to be present among delinquents, and what treatment techniques have proved to be efficacious in remediating these specific deficits?

This chapter will focus on three such specific areas: (*a*) Problem solving, a complex of abilities needed to solve interpersonal problems; (*b*) role-taking, a cognitive capacity to take the perspective of another person; and (*c*) self-control, a language-based internal mechanism for inhibiting impulses. Although each area will be reviewed separately, an attempt will be made to explore their possible relationships to each other. Evidence of its relevance for delinquency will be presented for each problem area, along with a description of measures used to assess the problem. Developmental issues will be discussed for each area as they pertain to normal development and provide a basis for treatment programming. Treatment approaches that are efficacious with children and adolescents will be described along with results of representative controlled studies that support their use. In addition, suggestions will be made for further research with delinquent populations.

81

It should be noted that the advent of behavior modification brought an important new tool to the field of delinquency. Token economies proliferated, and behavioral interventions were implemented with delinquents and predelinquents in institutions, in community settings, and in homes (see Khanna, 1974; Patterson, 1974; Reid & Patterson, 1976; Stumphauzer, 1973). A few studies compared the effectiveness of behavior modification with other treatment approaches (e.g., Jesness, 1975). In addressing the problems of delinquents from a cognitive–behavioral perspective, the authors do not discount the importance of the more behaviorally based programs. Many of these programs have shown positive results, and some of them have included cognitive elements similar to aspects of the programs to be described herein. Conversely, principles of operant psychology function within the cognitive–behavioral treatments reviewed in the following pages.

The upshot of this chapter is that there is evidence of important deficiencies in social cognition among delinquents and some data to suggest the efficacy of certain cognitive–behaviorally oriented treatments for remediating such deficits. Although delinquency has received only a modicum of attention from this cognitive–behavioral perspective, accumulating evidence from cognitive–behavioral interventions with a variety of other clinical disorders is encouraging (see Chapter 1, this volume). It is hoped that this chapter will foster additional cognitive–behavioral research with delinquents.

PROBLEM SOLVING

Reviews of research (e.g., Davis, 1966; Duncan, 1959; Simon & Newell, 1971) indicate that human problem solving has been investigated exclusively with *im*personal intellectual tasks, such as anagrams, puzzles, and water-jar, switch-light, and arithmetic tasks. As noted elsewhere (Allen, Chinsky, Larcen, Lochman, & Selinger, 1976), this type of task is not necessarily functionally related to *inter*personal problems that may arise in the course of everyday living. Furthermore, there is no evidence to support an assumption that impersonal and interpersonal problem-solving skills tap the same cognitive structures or that individuals who readily solve impersonal problems necessarily are similarly competent with social situations. In fact, low correlations between interpersonal cognitive problem-solving skills and measures of general intelligence and originality of thinking have been consistently found (Spivack, Platt, & Shure, 1976). In light of these findings, Spivack *et al.* declared: "The overall evidence would indicate that while skill in understanding certain aspects of social affairs is not totally independent of traditionally conceived intelligence, there remains good reason not to conceive of them as merely two facets of the same thing or manifestations of the same underlying processes [p. 12]."

The type of problem solving that is of concern in this chapter has to do with effective coping in social situations—interpersonal problem-solving. It can be said to represent more than basic intelligence as measured by IQ tests, and an attempt will be made to describe "what more" is represented.

Interpersonal Problem Solving and Normality

Evidence of the importance of an interpersonal problem-solving ability in successful coping with life comes from studies of both normal and nonnormal populations, and Jahoda (1953, 1958) has suggested that the capacity to problem solve in life situations is one criterion for defining positive mental health. Indeed, both longitudinal (Offer, 1969) and cross-sectional (Coelho, Hamburg, & Murphey, 1963) studies have documented the ability of normal adolescents to solve a wide variety of everyday problems. The latter authors found that normal college freshmen "were typically active in exploring problem-solving opportunities and used them in a way that reinforced their self-image as effective doers, working toward valued goals [p. 442]."

Likewise, the presence of interpersonal problem-solving deficits in nonnormal groups has consistently been reported in the literature, even when such deficits have been assessed by different approaches. For example, Freedman (Note 2) developed a set of typical interpersonal problem situations faced by high-school-aged males and administered the set to three samples of teenagers: A group of average high school students, a group of outstanding "superstar" high school students, and a third group of residents of state training schools for delinquents. Results indicated that the delinquent group was significantly poorer in providing effective solutions to the problem situations than either of the other two groups. These findings support the notion that legally defined problematic behavior in adolescence (i.e., delinquency) is, in part, a function of inadequate interpersonal problem-solving skills.

Interpersonal Cognitive Problem-Solving (ICPS) Skills

One of the most extensive projects attempting to link interpersonal problem-solving deficiencies to nonnormal behavior is that of Spivack, Platt, Shure, and their associates at the Hahnemann Medical College and Hospital in Philadelphia. These investigators have defined and measured a series of interpersonal cognitive problem-solving (ICPS) skills that have been shown to relate to social adjustment at various ages (Spivack, et al., 1976). Those skills found to be relevant for successful coping in social situations include: Sensitivity to interpersonal problems, tendency to link cause and effect spontaneously (causal thinking), readiness to view possible consequences of actions (consequential thinking), ability to generate solutions (alternative thinking), ability to conceptualize step-by-step means for reaching specific goals (means–ends thinking), and the ability to view situations from the perspective of other involved individuals (perspective taking).

There is evidence that these skills emerge at different ages, and whether they are demonstrated by a particular child in an interpersonal situation appears to relate to two factors: (*a*) The child may have a cognitive deficit in that he or she failed to learn the skills; or (*b*) The situation may arouse emotions that preclude using his or her typical social sensitivities and/or prevent free exploration of options. The role of the helping agent may be to improve the child's skills, reduce the emotional components that are interfering, or both (Spivack et al., 1976).

ICPS Skills Deficits in Adolescents

Much of the research conducted by the Hahnemann group has involved young children with an emphasis on primary prevention as well as remediation of deficits in ICPS skills among this age group (Shure & Spivack, 1978; Spivack & Shure, 1974). A few studies, however, have focused on adolescents. The populations that have been investigated include emotionally disturbed adolescent boys who were characterized as "impulsive" (Spivack & Levine, Note 3), male and female adolescent patients at a private psychiatric hospital (Platt, Spivack, Altman, Altman, & Peizer, 1974), and incarcerated heroin addicts aged 19–21 (Platt, Scura, & Hannon, 1973). In each case, when a nonnormal group was compared with a matched group of normals, those adolescents who were having adjustment problems were found to be deficient in three ICPS skills: means–ends thinking, alternative thinking, and perspective taking. The methods of measurement were:

1. Means–Ends Thinking

Each subject was given the beginning and end of a series of stories, each of which simulated a real-life problem to be solved, and was asked to fill in the middle to indicate how the character arrived at the stated outcome. Scoring considered the individual steps to reach the goal (means), awareness of possible obstacles, and awareness of the passage of time. Norms for various groups are available with the test manual (Platt & Spivack, Note 4).

2. Alternative Thinking

The subjects were asked to think of all the things a person could do to solve a series of four interpersonal problems. Scores were based upon the number of discrete and relevant solutions generated for each problem (Spivack et al., 1976).

3. Perspective Taking

Each subject was asked to make up a story about the picture on each of four Thematic Apperception Test (TAT) cards. Upon completion of the stories, the subjects again viewed the cards and retold the stories from the point of view of each of the characters in the pictures. Scoring was based on the subject's ability to coordinate the stories and to take into account the internal state of each character (Spivack et al., 1976).

In contrast with the three areas of deficiency just described, two other ICPS tests failed to differentiate between normal and nonnormal adolescents—measures of causal thinking and of sensitivity to interpersonal problems. The test of consequential thinking discriminated between groups in only one of the studies (Spivack & Levine, Note 3).

In regard to the timing of the normal development of ICPS skills, Spivack et al. (1976) reported that means–ends thinking is not found in preschool children but emerges in the "middle latency" years (i.e., between ages 9 and 12). In contrast, the ability to think of alternative solutions to interpersonal problems relates to social adjustment both in preschool years and in middle childhood, as well as in adolescence. Perspective taking has been found by other researchers to follow a well-delineated developmental sequence that, because of its apparent significance in the adjustment of adolescents, especially delinquents, will be detailed in a separate section of this chapter on role-taking. The notion that maladjusted adolescents are poor problem solvers in social situations thus has experimental as well as face validity. Unfortunately, the measures of specific problem solving skills devised by the Hahnemann group have been used only minimally with delinquents per se.

Treatment of ICPS Skills Deficits

A comprehensive training program for adolescents and adults with problem-solving deficits has been developed by the Hahnemann group. Their proposed program focuses on the *process* of solving problems rather than the *content* of problems, and practice of skills is emphasized. The 77-page Interpersonal Problem-Solving Group Therapy Manual (Platt, Spivack, & Swift, Note 5) presents detailed scripts for use by a group leader and basic materials for group exercises. Homework assignments also are provided for the students, who are given their own workbooks (Platt & Spivack, Note 6).

Although the program itself has not yet been evaluated, the authors do rely heavily on research from three areas. One is the findings of the Hahnemann research group, including that which was described earlier, and results of other studies with children and adults. The second source of material is a set of training exercises developed by Siegel and Spivack (Note 7) to treat chronic schizophrenics, a program that was based partially on D'Zurilla and Goldfried's (1971) five-stage approach to problem solving. The techniques included from Siegel and Spivack deal with finding new facts, making decisions, and presenting one's point of view.

A third body of knowledge used to develop the training program is the general psychological literature, from which a variety of specific tasks and techniques have been adapted. The techniques of modeling and group discussion that were used in the successful treatment of institutionalized delinquents (Sarason, 1968; Sarason & Ganzer, 1969, 1973) are used throughout treatment. Similar use is made of Meichenbaum and Cameron's (1973) technique of training patients to talk to themselves and McFall's (McFall & Lillesand, 1971; McFall & Marston, 1970) behavioral rehearsal techniques. Also incorporated in the training program are the following: Spohn and Wolk's (1963) discussion task, which improved the social participation of schizophrenics; modifications of the Matching Familiar Figures (MFF) task (Kagan, Rosman, Day, Albert, & Phillips, 1964); Draughton's (1973) technique of duplicating facial expressions; and Morton's (1955) use of the TAT.

The first half of the 19 units teaches a sequenced series of prerequisite skills deemed necessary for an individual to learn the specific problem-solving skills contained in the second half of the program. It can be seen from the description of program sources just given that the training is comprehensive. Given the explicitness of the instructions and the materials provided, the application of this program to a delinquent population should not be very difficult and is likely to prove informative. A useful first step would be the assessment of problem-solving skills to determine the extent of the specific deficits, as well as to provide a baseline for subsequent posttesting. Random assignment of delinquents with problem-solving deficits to treatment and control groups offers a simple research design, with analyses of variance used to determine differences between treatment and control groups in regard to posttreatment skills, behavioral adjustment, and/or recidivism to determine the utility of the program for the population studied. Although the Hahnemann problem-solving investigations are extensive and appear to offer an efficacious treatment package, additional approaches to problem-solving treatment are also promising.

D'Zurilla and Goldfried (1971) posit that the goals of problem solving and behavior modification are the same and that training in problem solving may be viewed as one of several behavior modification techniques for facilitating effective behavior. The five stages of problem solving they outline include (a) general orientation, or "set"; (b) problem definition and formulation; (c) generation of alternatives; (d) decision making; and (e) verification. The third stage, generation of alternatives, can be seen to represent the "alternative thinking" defined by the Hahnemann group. The fourth stage, decision making, may encompass "means-ends thinking," since one might logically assume that decisions would be based on a comparison of step-by-step plans for reaching certain goals. "Consequential thinking" also may be involved in this problem-solving model.

A test of the D'Zurilla and Goldfried (1971) model in combination with the communication models of Piaget (1972) and Gordon (1970) was conducted with mother–adolescent dyads (Robin, Kent, O'Leary, Foster, & Prinz, 1977). Treatment included a review of problem solving, discussion and role-playing of specific conflicts, self-monitoring of negative communication patterns and teaching of effective communication skills, social reinforcement, therapist feedback about performance, and discussion of the use of the skills at home. After five 1-hour sessions, mother–adolescent dyads demonstrated highly significant increases in problem-solving behavior, and a waiting list group showed little change. Unfortunately, self-report measures completed by mothers and adolescents indicated that treatment effects did not generalize to the home environment.

Treatment-outcome research specifically utilizing the D'Zurilla and Goldfried (1971) model of problem solving with delinquents has not yet been reported, but a study is currently underway at a state learning center for male delinquents (Bowman, Note 8). Rather than just teaching problem solving as a process, Bowman's approach also includes relaxation and verbal self-instructions. Treatment subjects will be compared with an attention control group who spend an equal amount of time with an adult who "actively listens" while they talk about their problems. Although its emphasis is on problem solving, the Bowman study will be concerned with the efficacy of a combination of cognitive–behavioral approaches to the treatment of delinquents.

An example of behavior therapy that appears to fit the problem-solving model involved a short-term behavioral intervention with delinquents and their families (Alexander & Parsons, 1973; Parsons & Alexander, 1973). Although the teaching of problem solving was not the specified objective, the treatment procedures can be fitted into the problem-solving paradigm without resorting to Procrustean violence. For example, the therapists "actively modeled, prompted, and reinforced in all family members: (a) clear communication of substance as well as feelings; and (b) clear presentation of 'demands' and alternative solutions; all leading to (c) negotiation, with each family member receiving some privilege for each responsibility assumed, to the point of compromise [Alexander & Parsons, 1973, p. 221]." In a later report of follow-up to their two treatment studies (Klein, Alexander, & Parsons, 1977), the problem-solving focus of treatment is more clearly stated: "The ultimate goal of the therapeutic process then becomes one of training the family in effective problem-solving techniques in order for the family unit to more adaptively meet the developmental changes occurring as children reach adolescence . . . [p. 471]." This short-term therapy was found to be superior to client-centered therapy, a psychodynamic family program, and a no-treatment control group. A 6–18 months follow-up indicated a significant reduction in recidivism for the delinquents in the training groups.

In treating the family unit rather than the individual delinquent, Alexander and Parsons hoped to reduce the incidence of delinquency among the siblings of delinquents as well as recidivism of the original delinquents. A 2½–3½ year follow-up indicated that they had done just that. The problem-solving intervention resulted in sibling court involvement one-third to one-half below that of the comparison groups, as well as a continued significantly lower rate of recidivism for the original problem adolescents. These results are particularly encouraging in view of the demonstrated long-range impact of treatment on the targeted delinquent and the apparent contribution to primary prevention of delinquency.

Within the framework of "behavioral contracting," Stuart and associates (Stuart, 1971; Stuart & Lott, 1972; Stuart, Tripodi, Jayaratne, & Camburn, 1976) have trained over 200 families of predelinquents and delinquents. Although their results are generally promising, one of their conclusions was that factors other than contracts themselves, such as the facilitation of communication or the process of negotiating the contracts, may be the real determinants of treatment outcome (Stuart & Lott, 1972). In the latest study (Stuart et al., 1976), the researchers suggested that contracting be conducted as part of "a more comprehensive intervention package that includes techniques aimed at modifying communication patterns within the family, academic skill-building at school, and improving peer experiences for the adolescent . . . [p. 260]." Another study of contingency contracting (Weathers & Liberman, 1975) failed to produce any systematic effects in six families of delinquent adolescents. Interestingly, this program included communication skills training and videotape feedback as well as contingency contracting. This was a multiple baseline study with no control group. The authors suggested that contracting be

viewed as a "supplementary aid" in a broader range of interventions with delinquents and stated, "In working with families that are decimated by divorce, crime,
drug abuse, and woefully inadequate communication and negotiation skills, the
introduction of a contingency contract is worth about as much as the paper it's
printed on [Weathers & Liberman, 1975]."

More positive results were obtained in a study with predelinquent adolescents and
their parents that focused on the negotiation process (Kifer, Lewis, Green, &
Phillips, 1974). The negotiation process was analyzed into component behaviors:
complete communication, which involved stating one's position and requesting the
other person to respond; identification of issues, which referred to statements that
explicitly identified the point of conflict; and suggestion of options, which appears
to be equivalent to D'Zurilla and Goldfried's (1971) "generation of alternatives"
and the Hahnemann group's "alternative thinking." Subjects received instructions,
practice, and feedback about hypothetical conflict situations. Only three parent–
child pairs were trained in this multiple baseline design. Results indicated an increase in the three component behaviors of the negotiation process as defined, as
well as in the percentage of agreements reached. Home observations revealed that
the increases were maintained in the natural environment, and eight of nine situations that were discussed after training by adolescent–parent pairs resulted in
agreements. Thus, it appears that teaching the process of problem solving can carry
over to the home environment, and this finding suggests that the method of obtaining follow-up data may be critical. Self reports from subjects in the Robin *et al.*
(1977) study described earlier failed to indicate generalization to the home of what
appeared to be a highly successful training program. Though one cannot deny that
generalization may *not* have occurred, the positive findings of Kifer *et al.* (1974)
suggest that researchers should be cognizant of possible critical differences between
follow-up data obtained by subject self report, especially adolescents and their
parents, and by observations of trained observers.

The work of Sarason and associates noted earlier (Sarason, 1968; Sarason &
Ganzer, 1969, 1973) involved institutionalized delinquents. Although the focus of
their research was on the differential effects of modeling and group discussion as
treatment methods, an examination of their successful treatment programs suggests
that the critical variable in the training may have been the teaching of problem-
solving skills. The sessions were presented to the boys as "learning opportunities
designed to enhance their ability to cope with situations that, for them, are problem
areas [Sarason, 1968, p. 262]." Both the modeling and the discussion treatment
groups resulted in positive change in attitudes and behavior greater than a no-
treatment group. In a second study (Sarason & Ganzer, 1973), boys "were given
examples of desirable and undesirable ways of coping with social, vocational, and
educational situations [p. 443]." This type of training appears to provide practice in
"alternative thinking" and possibly "consequential thinking." At any rate, both
modeling and structured discussion approaches had greater concurrent and long-
term positive effects than a no-treatment control group, with the treatment effects
not significantly differing between the two groups. It should be noted that the

treatment program in both of these studies included practice in role-taking, another area of deficiency found in nonnormal adolescents, but no effort was made to assess the effects of role-taking training per se.

Scopetta (1972) used a training procedure that included the playing of problem-solving skits by paraprofessional members of an institutional staff, role-playing of the situations by subjects who observed the skits, and group discussion. Delinquents who participated in this training showed significant reduction in antisocial behavior when compared with a problem-solving discussion-only group. Again, no measure of role-taking was included. Disappointing results were obtained when a similar training procedure was implemented with delinquents living in a group home (Thelen, Fry, Dollinger, & Paul, 1976). A major difference between the two studies was the use of a videotaped actor by Thelen *et al.* instead of live models, as in the Scopetta (1972) procedure. Subjects in the Thelen *et al.* program role-played the model's part after observing the videotape of the actor in various problematic interpersonal situations, viewed the original videotape again, and then role-played the situation for a second time. Behavior ratings of training subjects improved significantly from baseline during the period of training when group home situations were portrayed, but gains were not maintained when the training shifted to school situations or at the time of follow-up. Control subjects who observed lecture tapes emphasizing social skills showed no changes.

Summary and Discussion

There is evidence that successful coping with one's environment requires a set of interpersonal problem-solving skills that are not measured by traditional intelligence tests and that are different in important ways from those skills needed for the solving of impersonal problems. Furthermore, adolescents who exhibit deficits in interpersonal problem-solving skills are much more likely to appear in nonnormal groups—emotionally disturbed or delinquent—than in normal groups. Three specific cognitive deficits have been found: means–ends thinking, alternative thinking, and perspective taking. In regard to delinquents specifically, there is evidence that they are poor problem solvers in interpersonal situations. A number of promising treatment programs to remediate problem-solving deficits have been devised, but their application to delinquents has been limited. Results of the treatment efforts reviewed herein, however, suggest that this approach to treating delinquents may be efficacious. When families are available, teaching problem-solving skills to the entire family unit appears to offer the greatest payoff in terms of recidivism and prevention of sibling delinquency, although these results need replication. When only the individual delinquent youth is available, problem-solving treatment offers a promising adjunct to behavioral and/or traditional methods, and perhaps a viable alternative.

Some intriguing questions that arise from results of research in interpersonal problem solving relate to the significance of individual ICPS skills for adaptive coping and the relationship among the three skills found to be deficient in groups of nonnormal adolescents. For example, would focusing on remediation of one of these deficits rather than implementing a comprehensive training program result in significant changes in behavior? As to the relationship among ICPS skills, means–ends thinking and role-taking were found to load on the same factor in a factor analysis of adult problem-solving thinking (Platt & Spivack, 1973). This finding suggests that the ability to plan a sequence of events to solve a problem is involved in the ability to think about social situations from the standpoint of others in the situation. Platt *et al.* (1974) noted, "This is not surprising since seeing complex relationships among people and events as one develops a course of action is a necessary ingredient to developing a successful plan [p. 792]." Research findings suggest that role-taking ability may be critical for adjustment in adolescence and that remediation of role-taking deficits may facilitate positive behavior in delinquents. Thus, a relatively simple program focusing on one specific ICPS deficit has been shown to produce significant results. The section that follows will present the theoretical basis for role-taking as a cognitive function that mediates self-control, the normal course of development of role-taking skills, and some evidence for the utility of remediation of role-taking deficits in adolescents, particularly delinquents.

ROLE-TAKING

Half a century ago, Piaget (1926) described the young child as an unwitting prisoner of his own egocentric view of the world. Thus embedded in his own point of view, the child is unable to "decenter"—that is, to shift his attention from a single aspect of an object or an event in order to process simultaneously a number of important aspects. When one centers upon a given aspect of the perceptual field to the exclusion of other aspects, distortion occurs. This distortion can be partially corrected when focus is shifted from one part of the perceptual field to another, but mature thought occurs only when the individual is able to simultaneously decenter—that is, to consider a wide number of aspects of a situation at the same time.

Within Piaget's developmental framework, various levels of cognitive processes are differentiated in a lawful sequence, and the child becomes increasingly able to subordinate immediate sense impressions to thought in organizing information about the environment. For example, the very young child typically fails to report that the quantity of beads remains the same when they are poured from a tall, thin vase into a short, wide vase (Piaget, 1950). With increasing chronological age, however, comes an ability to subordinate the immediate perceptual input to a more abstract and internalized schema—in this case, both the height and the width of the vase. The older child thus is able to decenter, and he reports that the number of beads remains the same in this classic experiment of "conservation of quantity."

In the interpersonal sphere, the young child operates from his own individual perspective and remains ignorant of and unconcerned about differing perspectives of other people. This limited perspective is reflected in his communications, which typically fail to take into account the informational needs of the other person and, hence, have the flavor of a monologue. During the process of normal development, the child becomes aware that there *are* other points of view, and his communications increasingly reflect his cognizance of the perspective or role of the other. In addition, self-control develops as the child learns to relate his behavior to the needs of others. The development of role-taking ability thus releases the child from the prison of his own point of view and permits him to interact successfully in the social sphere. Although Piaget (1962a,b) called attention to the operation of the concepts of egocentrism and decentering in interpersonal behavior, the major thrust in that direction in both theory and research has come from other theorists and investigators.

In a relatively early work, Mead (1934) proposed that the ability to adopt alternative perspectives in regard to one's self is the very essence of social intelligence. He used the term *empathy* to refer to the capacity to "take the role of the other," and he suggested that practice at role-taking leads to social sensitivity and to the emergence of the self-concept and of self-control. Mead's concept of the "self" consists of the self as subject, or the "I," and the self as object, or the "me." The "me" is considered to be a representation of the "role of the other," that is, group values that are assimilated as one's own and that control the impulsive, spontaneous aspect of the self. In taking into account the possible reaction of another person to one's action, a person is then taking the role of the other and, as such, becomes aware of another aspect of himself.

A related theoretical notion is the nondevelopmental approach of Asch (1952). In his attempt to understand the relationship between individual behavior and social forces, Asch suggested the presence of a unique reciprocal relationship. His example of two boys jointly carrying a log illustrates his point. Asch noted that the boys are "fitting their actions to each other and to the object and are involved in a give-and-take requiring considerable sensitiveness [p. 173]." Anticipation of what the other will do in response to an intended action is necessary for effective interaction to occur, according to Asch, and adequate social interaction requires that the other's reciprocal role be represented in the psychological organization of each of the interacting individuals. Like Mead, Asch views the self as being simultaneously both the subject and the object of the experience.

Measures of Role-Taking

Taking his theory largely from Piaget, Flavell (Flavell, 1963, 1974; Flavell, Botkin, Fry, Wright, & Jarvis, 1968) devised methods for assessing role-taking ability that have been used extensively in research. The method that has seen most frequent use attempts to assess the accuracy of role-taking. In this task, the child is asked to tell a story from a set of seven cards containing pictures. Three of the cards are then removed, thus drastically altering the story, and the subject is asked to tell the story from the point of view of a person who has just entered the room and has seen only the four cards. The subject's problem is to suppress his previous perspective, derived from seeing all seven pictures, and to look at the four pictures naively.

Feffer (1959, 1967, 1970) assumed that the same processes are involved in both impersonal cognition and interpersonal cognition, and he stated that the cognitive representation of the role of the other in the self-organization is a prerequisite of effective social interaction. For example, a pervasive isolation between the roles of giving and taking within self-organization leads to a very real conservation problem. According to Feffer, the problem is how to give without diminishing one's self, or how to stop from taking too much. Feffer suggested that a mature cognitive structuring of the situation would represent the giving–taking relationship by a "network of schemas within self-organization in terms of which all possible variations of role and reciprocal can be generated and coordinated with one another [Feffer, 1970, p. 209]." Within such a structure, giving would result in another aspect of the self simultaneously receiving; in getting, another aspect of the self sacrifices. Interpersonal events, thus, are construed by Feffer as being composed of interacting participants who occupy such roles and reciprocals as giving–taking, asking–answering, and dominating–submitting.

In order to investigate his formulation of interpersonal behavior, Feffer (Feffer, 1959, 1960; Feffer & Jahelka, 1968) devised a measure of self-organization called the Role-Taking Task (RTT). This is a projective task using TAT cards in which the subject's role-taking is assessed from his skill in refocusing on his initial stories from the perspective of the other actors in the story. An adaptation of this measure has been used by the Hahnemann group in their investigations of "perspective-taking."

Following the cognitive–developmental tradition of Piaget, Chandler (1973; Note 9) examined egocentrism using a hybrid of the techniques of Flavell *et al.* (1968) and of Feffer (Feffer & Jahelka, 1968). In Chandler's task, the subject is presented with a sequence of cartoons depicting interpersonal episodes and is asked to tell the story from the point of view of a central character and then from the viewpoint of a late-arriving onlooker in the pictures. Role-taking ability is operationalized as the extent to which privileged information known to the subject is inappropriately ascribed to the bystander who could have no knowledge of the information. This task differs from Feffer's in that different perspectives are insured, and it simplifies the procedure of Flavell by including the bystander in the cartoons instead of having another person enter the room.

In addition to the instruments described above, a variety of other measures have been utilized to assess role-taking and "empathy" in children. And, as might be expected when different measures are used, the issue of construct validity has become critical in the developmental literature as variable research results have been reported. Disagreements among researchers have led to charges of "ersatz egocentrism" (Chandler & Greenspan, 1972), rejoinders (Borke, 1972), and a number of attempts to bring order out of the chaos (Feshbach, 1975; Hogan, 1975; Iannotti, 1975; Shantz, 1975a).

One of the points at issue is the extent to which a subject's response is *affective* rather than *cognitive*. Some experimental tasks appear to tap the child's ability to "share affectively" the feelings of another person, whereas other tasks focus on the "understanding or knowledge" of how another person feels. Whereas some researchers (e.g., Feshbach, 1975; Iannotti, 1975) have called for the use of measures that encompass both affective and cognitive elements of role-taking, others (e.g., Rotenberg, 1974) have attempted to explore differences between affective and cognitive role-taking. Rotenberg defined cognitive role-taking as the ability to predict the responses of another person in actual everyday situations, without being involved with the other person's feelings. The cognitive task was a guessing game in which each subject was asked standard questions about how his partner would respond in a number of social interactions. Affective role-taking was defined as "the behavioral disposition to relieve the distress of others [Rotenberg, 1974, p. 180]." The measure of affective role-taking disposition was the extent to which the subject reduced noxious noise to a partner, who was purportedly attached by earphones to an "awakening machine." Juvenile delinquents were found to be no different from nondelinquent agemates on cognitive role-taking, but they were significantly poorer than nondelinquents on affective role-taking. These results suggest that discrimination between affective and cognitive components of role-taking may be useful, especially in regard to delinquents.

Some other investigators who have attempted to define the construct of role-taking have focused on discriminating component skills that may be measured by widely used research indstruments. For example, Urberg and Docherty (1976) administered five role-taking tasks to preschoolers and found support for a hypothesis of a hierarchy of role-taking skills. These authors reported that different skills were required for different tasks. Selman and associates (Selman, 1971a,b, 1976; Selman & Byrne, 1974; Selman, Jaquette, & Lavin, 1977) have embarked on an extended investigation of "levels" of role-taking, including some longitudinal studies. These researchers have focused on the structure and content of children's social reasoning, and the tasks utilized typically involved the presentation of moral dilemmas similar to those devised by Kohlberg (1969; Selman *et al.,* 1977). Results of this research support the hierarchical nature of role-taking.

In general, there is some evidence to indicate that role-taking is multidimensional in nature and that differences among measures contribute to the variable research results that have been reported. When adolescents are of concern, it seems reasonable to utilize an instrument such as Chandler's (1973; Note 9), which apparently assesses higher-level role-taking skills (Borke, 1972; Kurdek, 1977; Urberg & Docherty, 1976). Alternatively, the work of Rotenberg (1974) suggests that it may be useful to attempt to separate affective and cognitive components of role-taking in research with delinquents.

Normal Development of Role-Taking Ability

Despite problems in defining the construct of role-taking, research results generally agree that role-taking ability is a function of age. Findings in this regard are consistent, although there are some disagreements about the particular age at which specific dimensions of role-taking appear. Flavell *et al.* (1968) indicated that the preschool child has not yet achieved the first step—an awareness of the existence of perspective. By the time of entry into school, however, the child is likely to have some understanding of perspective variation. Research with Feffer's (1959) RTT has revealed the following developmental pattern: At about age 6, there is a discontinuity between versions of the story—uncorrected decentering; between 7 or 8, a fluctuating form of coordination between perspectives is seen; and a synthesis of the different perspectives begins to become clearly evident at about 9 years of age (Feffer & Gourevitch, 1960). In a study designed to explore the lower limits of role-taking behavior (Urberg & Docherty, 1976), findings suggest that some dimensions of role-taking occur earlier than at age 6. Nevertheless, there is general agreement that profound changes in role-taking occur during the period of middle childhood, and by early and middle adolescence the individual's perspective-taking has developed to the point that the person can take the role of a third-person observer of himself and others in interaction, taking into account the feelings, thoughts, and intentions of all involved (Shantz, 1975b).

According to Piaget (1928), acquisition of role-taking skills or decentering is a maturational process that occurs as a result of active involvement with the environment and subsequent readjustments of cognitive structures. A necessary condition is held to be social exchanges, and Piaget emphasized the role of peers in this developmental process. "Discussion among equals" is a liberating force that enables a child to step outside of his own perspective, to become aware of contradictory points of view, and, finally, to reestablish equilibrium through resolution of competing views. Games with rules, verbal exchanges, and group actions all contribute to the demise of egocentrism. Flavell (1963) emphasized the influence of reinforcements, especially negative ones, from interactions with peers in the development of role-taking ability. In the course of conflict and arguments with other children, the child finds himself forced to reexamine his opinions and percepts in the light of those of others, and in the process gradually rids himself of cognitive egocentrism. Maccoby (1959) proposed that a child learns role-taking by practicing covertly the actions observed in adults with whom he interacts and who control the resources he needs. Such covert role-playing, according to Maccoby, is a way of learning "not only adult-like social actions directed toward others, but of learning reactions toward the self [p. 252]." Kerckhoff (1969) discussed a similar phenomenon, using the term *identification,* which he held is basically "a special case of role-taking–role-playing." Although Bandura (1969, 1971, 1977) has not addressed role-taking ability per se, his theoretical point of view and empirical findings in modeling studies support the acquisition of such ability through a social learning process.

According to Bandura (1976), most competencies are acquired and perfected by exposure to instructive example and reinforced practice. This line of thinking leads to the conclusion that role-taking ability, like other skills of living, is a learned phenomenon that occurs through interactions with the environment.

Role-Taking Ability and Normality

On the basis of Piaget's decentering formulations, one might hypothesize that the effectiveness of social interaction would be a function of the degree to which one is able to adopt more than one perspective at a time. This hypothesis was supported in a study with college students who were sorted into congruent dyads on the basis of their decentering scores on the RTT (Feffer & Suchotliff, 1966). In a password exercise in which each member of the dyad was required to communicate to his partner test words with one-word association clues, the higher-RTT-scoring dyads communicated words with fewer clues and more quickly than did the dyads composed of lower RTT performers.

As for comparisons of normal and nonnormal groups of children, Chandler (Chandler, Note 9; Chandler, Greenspan, & Barenboim, 1974) found marked developmental delays in role-taking ability among institutionalized emotionally disturbed children as compared with adjusted peers. Similar findings of the Hahnemann group (Platt *et al.*, 1974) have been noted in our earlier section on problem solving. Selman *et al.* (1977) reported that a clinic sample performed significantly lower than their public school peers on tasks assessing reasoning about interpersonal relations and the resolution of interpersonal problems, although there were no differences between groups on tasks of logico-physical reasoning. In addition, these authors reported that preliminary analyses of a 2-year follow-up indicated that the results were replicated.

Another area of abnormality in which children's role-taking ability has been examined is that of mental retardation. In a series of studies using Feffer's RTT, Affleck (1975a,b, 1976) found a direct association between role-taking ability and the interpersonal competencies of retarded children. In the latter study, retarded subjects who were higher in role-taking ability than their retarded peers were found to be more likely to use tactics that took into account the needs of the other person rather than simply make a request for the person to do something. It is important to note that, in some studies, role-taking ability does show a moderate correlation with intelligence. Yet, when IQ is held constant or partialed out, role-taking deficits continue to discriminate between normal and nonnormal children.

The deviant behavior and thinking of delinquents and psychopaths also have been attributed to role-taking deficiencies (Gough, 1948; Sarbin, 1954). Gough proposed that the psychopathic personality is pathologically deficient in role-playing ability, suggesting that such an assumption accommodates the already known facts about psychopathy. The notion that role-taking places a number of constraints on behavior was strongly stated:

> This role-taking ability provides a technique for self-understanding and self-control. Learned prohibitions ... may be observed by "telling one's self" not to behave in a certain way. ... Role-playing, or putting one's self in another's position, enables a person to predict the other's behavior. Finally, role-playing ability makes one sensitive in advance to the reactions of others; such prescience may then deter or modify the unexpressed action.[1]

In order to test his assumptions about role-taking deficiencies in psychopaths, Gough (1957) developed a socialization scale that is a part of the self-report, paper-and-pencil California Psychological Inventory. Gough (1960) reported a number of validation studies with this scale, which has been found to discriminate among various groups as to degree of socialization. In general, delinquent groups score further in the less-socialized direction than other groups, and the scale has been found to discriminate between delinquent and nondelinquent youths (see Megargee, 1972). More recently, Kendall, Deardorff, and Finch (1977) reported that the socialization scale not only successfully differentiated delinquents from nondelinquents but also discriminated first offenders from repeat offenders. The relationships of this scale to the more behavioral tasks that constitute the measures of role-taking described earlier, however, have not yet been examined.

Evidence that delinquents exhibit role-taking deficits on a behavioral task comes from studies that utilized the assessment technique of Chandler (1973; Note 9). This procedure requires the subject to set aside his own perspective and report only information that a late-arriving bystander could know about a situation. Chandler (1973) found significant differences between 45 chronically delinquent boys and 45 nondelinquent boys living in the same community, and he reported role-taking deficits in a "substantial proportion" of delinquents tested. Little (Note 10) administered Chandler's measure to 37 female delinquents in a state learning center and found role-taking deficits in 73% of the sample.

Although the research is limited, results appear relatively consistent—role-taking deficits are common among nonnormal groups of children. Such deficits have been found in emotionally disturbed and retarded children and in both institutionalized and noninstitutionalized delinquents. Even within groups of retarded children, role-taking deficits have been found to relate to interpersonal competencies. The questions that arise next are: How can role-taking deficits be remediated, and what behavioral effects can be anticipated from such remediation?

Remediation of Role-taking Deficits

Many interpersonal problem-solving programs (e.g., Allen *et al.*, 1976; Platt *et al.*, Note 5; Sarason, 1968; Sarason & Ganzer, 1969, 1973) make deliberate use of role playing as a training procedure, but role-taking ability per se has not been examined as a dependent variable in these programs. A recent exception is research with the problem-solving training program of Elardo and associates (Elardo & Cooper, 1977), which has been tested with elementary school children up to ages 9 and 10. Not only was role-taking and social competence shown to be positively

---

[1]From H. G. Gough, *American Journal of Sociology,* 1948, *53,* 363 (Chicago: The University of Chicago Press). Copyright © 1948 by The University of Chicago Press.

correlated (Elardo, Caldwell, & Webb, Note 11), but children in an experimental group who were taught problem solving and role-taking in their regular classrooms also gained in role-taking ability, problem-solving skills, and classroom adjustment (Elardo & Caldwell, Note 12). Flavell *et al.*'s (1968) measure was used to assess role-taking skills before and after treatment.

In a study dealing with hyperactive children (Douglas, Parry, Marton, & Garson, 1976), a multifaceted cognitive training program geared toward self-control included teaching problem-solving strategies, modeling, and training in self-verbalizations. Contingency management techniques were used when a child was especially unmanageable. A number of the self-verbalizations used for playing games or cooperating on a task with a peer seem to represent direct teaching of role-taking ability. For example, the trainer modeled thoughts such as, "I guess Tom wants to win as much as I do. He'll be unhappy if he loses too many times." (Douglas *et al.*, 1976, p. 395). One of the dependent measures on which change occurred was the MFF (Kagan *et al.*, 1964), a measure of cognitive impulsivity. Rather large improvements were found after training on both the latency and the error scores from the MFF, and these changes held up well at a 3-month follow-up. It is interesting to note, however, that children in the Douglas *et al.* (1976) program did not show improved classroom behavior as rated by their teachers. Role-taking ability per se was not assessed.

Allen *et al.* (1976) reported some positive results from their problem-solving training of elementary school children, but their findings led them to recommend greater use of role playing and behavioral rehearsal in order to enhance implementation of the problem-solving strategies that are taught. Role-taking skills were not measured. Although the children's problem-solving skills increased significantly, their behavior as assessed by teacher and peer ratings did not improve.

As was true for interpersonal problem solving, reports of the efficacy of role-taking training with delinquents have been minimal. Findings of research that has been reported, however, are highly promising. In a simple but innovative treatment project, Chandler (1973) assigned 45 chronically delinquent boys between the ages of 11 and 13 to one of three groups. Fifteen subjects were randomly assigned to an experimental treatment group in which they met one-half day a week for a 10-week period to participate in writing, performing, and videotape viewing of skits having to do with boys their ages. Another group of 15 spent the same amount of time in producing animated cartoons and documentary-style films about their neighborhood on 8-millimeter color film. The third group served as an assessment control. All subjects resided in the community rather than in an institution, although all were considered by court officials to be serious and chronic delinquents, and all had committed one or more crimes which would have been felonies if committed by an adult.

The experimental group that received role-taking training improved significantly more in role-taking ability than did the other two groups (Chandler, 1973). In addition, an 18-month follow-up of court contacts showed that the experimental training group committed about half as many known delinquencies as they had during the 18 months before training, a significantly greater improvement than for either of the other two groups. A later study with emotionally disturbed children in an institution (Chandler *et al.*, 1974) produced significant improvement in role-taking ability following similar remedial training, although attempts to assess effects on institutional adjustment produced only mixed findings.

Recent research by Little (Note 10) partially replicated and extended the work of Chandler (1973). Little randomly assigned 18 institutionalized females aged 13–16 (matched on the basis of role-taking deficits) to treatment and attention control groups that met twice a week for 3 weeks. The treatment groups improvised skits about the kinds of people they might encounter in everyday living, both adults and peers. Each skit had a part for every girl in a group of 5 or 6 girls. After the subjects selected the part they wanted to play, the skits were performed and videotaped. The group then watched the videotape, and each girl reported what it was like to play the role she had enacted. The procedure was then repeated until every girl had played every part. A new skit was then devised and played as before. The attention control group spent an equal amount of time in creating a videotaped documentary about the institution in which they resided. Control subjects were not allowed to appear on camera in an active role, in order to avoid possible overlap with treatment-group training procedures.

Role-taking errors were found to decrease significantly from pre- to posttesting for both treatment and control groups. Although the treatment group appeared to show the greater decrease, differences between groups were not significant. An attempt to use the institution's token economy as a measure of social adjustment and self-control was not successful, since no meaningful pattern of differential point totals was obtained. MFF scores failed to discriminate between groups, and no systematic relationship between MFF and role-taking scores was obtained for 30 subjects for whom data were complete.

The fact that both treatment and control subjects improved significantly in role-taking ability over the course of the study suggests the possibility that factors in the cooperative effort to make a videotaped documentary, or a period of residence in an institution, may have facilitated the acquisition of role-taking skills. In regard to the first possibility, Chandler's (1973) assessment-only control group and attention control group were not significantly different following the training period. In regard to possible effects of institutional living, researchers have found that first graders living in a kibbutz performed better on two measures of role-taking than did agemates living in the city (Nahir & Yussen, 1977), and it was hypothesized that greater peer interaction in the kibbutz contributed to improved role-taking. Fifth graders, however, showed significant differences on only one of the two measures. Hollos and Cowan (1973) found that 7–9-year-old Norwegian farm children performed more poorly on several role-taking tasks than agemates reared in villages and towns; they again attributed the differences to a social environment that provided the children with frequent peer contacts. In the Little (Note 10) study with institutionalized delinquents, an insufficient number of subjects, unfortunately, was available to form an assessment-only group that might have helped to clarify these issues.

Summary and Discussion

The extension of Piaget's theory and research to the development of cognitive processes as they operate in interpersonal situations has proved to be a fruitful approach to understanding social adjustment in children and adolescents. Reasonably reliable and valid measures of role-taking have been devised, and research has delineated a sequential, age-related process of development. There seems little doubt that egocentricity is abandoned as a result of social interaction and practice at taking the perspective of others in interpersonal situations. Furthermore, it is clear that deficiencies in role-taking appear in nonnormal groups of youngsters—emotionally disturbed, retarded, and delinquent.

There is evidence that role-taking ability can be taught to both children and adolescents within a problem-solving package or more simply in a program that provides opportunities for practice, modeling, and feedback, all of which appear to operate in the normal acquisition of role-taking skills. Delinquents have been successfully treated by both approaches, and one researcher (Chandler, 1973) who implemented fairly short-term role-taking training demonstrated reduction in court contacts over an 18-month period following treatment, as well as an immediate reduction in role-taking deficits. There is some evidence that institutional living may facilitate the acquisition of this social cognition skill, and further research to explore this possibility as well as the efficacy of training for deficient delinquents is highly recommended.

The precise relationship of problem solving and role-taking to self-control remains unclear, although it seems apparent that they are not unrelated. Delinquents are by definition poorly self-controlled, and the repetitive findings of deficits in problem-solving and role-taking ability among this population suggest that the lack of these cognitive skills has a powerful impact on the delinquent's ability to cope with his environment. In addition, the fact that remediation of problem-solving and role-taking deficits can lead to increased self-control supports their hypothesized role in self-controlling behavior. Theoretically, the relationship appears somewhat clearer. Spivack *et al.* (1976) stated: "Increased ability to problem-solve should enhance the capacity to wait or tolerate tension in a problem situation, as well as increase frustration tolerance when initial attempts to handle interpersonal problems fail [p. 170]." Both Mead (1934) and Gough (1948) stated strongly their view that role-taking serves the function of controlling impulsive aspects of one's self. The experimental evidence is not as clearcut.

Further specification of the exact relationship may lie in answering an intriguing question that arises from theory and research on problem solving and role-taking: What is the self-controlling mechanism that becomes available when a person learns to take the perspective of others involved in a social situation? A plausible answer may be that the person learns to emit (covertly) a self-statement such as "Wait, he seems to be upset by what is happening." If the emission of such covert self-controlling statements can be taught directly and have the desired effect on behavior, such treatment might be more quickly and easily implemented than a problem-solving or role-taking training procedure.

It is to the discussion of this possibility, the development of self control by verbal mechanisms, that we now turn. Developmental issues will be considered as they concern the normal acquisition of verbal self-control and as they suggest treatment strategies. Since little research has involved adolescents, results of treatment of children and preadolescents will be reviewed.

SELF-CONTROL

The demands of society for "self-control" increase inexorably as the child develops, and, by the time of adolescence, serious consequences often follow failure to measure up to these demands. For purposes of this discussion, self-control is viewed as the individual's governing of his own behavior to attain certain ends. In a cognitive–behavioral framework, this governing requires both the cognitive skills necessary to generate and evaluate alternatives (legislative) and the behavioral capacity to inhibit acting on the discarded alternatives and to engage in the selected option (executive) (Kendall & Wilcox, Note 13).

The position of the authors is that a child or adolescent will exhibit self-controlled behavior to the extent that he possesses a response repertoire that contains the necessary cognitive and behavioral skills and is motivated to use them in a particular situation. It is to the question of response repertoire that this discussion is largely directed, although the importance of motivation to use self-controlling responses is not minimized. The point is—if a delinquent lacks self-controlling mechanisms, addressing the problem of motivating him to control himself offers little promise of success. Thus, remediation of deficits should precede motivational issues, although the use of incentive motivation should be incorporated into procedures for training in self-control.

Normal Development of Self-Control

The neonate arrives on the scene with minimal control over himself and his existence. His arms flail wildly, his eyes fail to focus, his digestive tract empties automatically. The pattern of motor development unfolds in an orderly sequence, and both maturation and learning contribute to the development of motor control. McCandless (1961) stated that learning or practice is required for an infant to "organize maturational phenomena" so that previously impossible performances can be accomplished. It is in the second year of life that language begins to have an impact on behavior. And, as is true for motor control, both maturation and learning are involved in the acquisition of language as a controlling mechanism.

According to Mussen (1963), the verbal instructions of adults have no observable effect on motor behavior of infants only a few months of age. By the time a child is 1 or 2 years old, however, an adult's instructions produce orienting and investigatory responses in the child. And, by the time a child is 3 or 4, verbal instructions can release the action the child is already set to perform or can initiate some new action. Such instructions, however, cannot yet inhibit an action once started or shift the child from one action to another. The 3- or 4-year-old child normally can follow rather complicated instructions given by an adult, and it is at this age that the child is said to begin to regulate his own behavior on the basis of verbal self-instructions. As speech develops in richness and fluency, it comes to serve more of a regulatory function for the child. Between the ages of 4½ and 5½, the child's self-verbalizations shift from overt to covert (primarily internal) speech.

The process of development of verbal control of behavior thus seems to follow a standard developmental sequence. First, the initiation of motor behavior comes under control of adult verbal cues, and then the inhibition of responses is controlled by the speech of adults. Self-control emerges as the child learns to respond to his own verbal cues, first to initiate responses and then to inhibit them.

The relation of language to behavioral control has been of concern to psychologists for a number of years. Writing in 1924, Allport stated that human beings developed spoken language to control and direct their own behavior and to control the nonsocial environment, as well as for social control. An early experimental study (Waring, 1927) demonstrated the greater power of verbal cues than nonverbal cues over the motor behavior of children. Groups of children from 2 to 4 years of age were tested on a number of gross motor and discriminative skills. Control subjects were rewarded for correct performance with a smile and a nod, whereas experimental children received a word, "Benito," to indicate approval. Language approval was found to be significantly more effective in improving skills than nonlanguage approval. Waring reported that language approval had an immediate effect in improving learning and also carried over to other kinds of responses. She interpreted her findings as supporting her hypothesis of a strong linear relationship between early language habits and early habits of "conduct control."

Development of speech as a regulator of behavior has been extensively examined by Russian psychologists, and much of this work is reported in detail by Luria (1961). The apparatus typically used in these studies consists of a rubber bulb and a panel of sound and light stimuli that can be variably presented or patterned. The child's squeezes of the rubber bulb are recorded by an electrically driven event recorder to produce a record much like an EEG.

Luria (1961) and his colleagues first examined the "impellant" effects of adult speech, which may develop as early as the beginning of the child's second year, and related them to the inhibiting function of speech. For example, Luria noted that a child of 18 months will readily respond to verbal instructions such as "Give me your hands." Verbal instructions such as "Take off your socks," given while the child is putting them on, however, will fail to produce the desired response. Rather than getting compliance, such instructions tend to intensify the already started activity. When this phenomenon was explored with the Russian apparatus, similar results were found. Children who were asked to squeeze the bulb when the light came on and to stop when it went off showed extra-signal responding, a kind of motor spillover that produced continued squeezing. The introduction of a competing motor response such as "Squeeze the bulb when the light comes on and then place your hand on your knee" was successful in inhibiting the original action when the light went off. After practice with this set of instructions, children as young as 18 months were able to stop squeezing the bulb when given the previously ineffective verbal signal to squeeze only when the light is on. Luria attributed this result to the inhibitory influences produced by a preliminary conflict between two successive motor excitations. Thus, the diffuseness of the motor impulses is reduced by competing excitations, one of which inhibits the other. This motor control is necessary for adult verbal instructions to be effective in controlling the behavior of the child.

Luria and his associates then hypothesized that inhibition of motor responses might occur if the child received a distinct signal of the fulfillment of the task. Basing their thinking on the fact that neurophysiologists have pointed out that the regulation of action requires a system of afferent feedback, they changed the instructions to provide a signal to mark the end of the action. The child was told to press the bulb at the flash of light and thereby "put out the light." With this paradigm, 50% of children of 18 months–2 years and 75% of 2- to 3-year-olds produced clearcut motor responses. Removal of the feedback led in the overwhelming majority of the children to recovery of the original diffuseness of the motor reactions.

The next step in this program of research was to investigate the role of the child's own speech in the control of his behavior. Pairing of the child's verbalization of the word "Go" with the onset of the light was found to impede the organized motor reactions of the child of 2–2½ years. By 3–4 years of age, however, children strictly coordinated their verbal reactions with the light signal. The regulatory action of the external signal thus was replaced by the child's own verbal command. Luria also reported differences in development that are required for organized responding when the child is told to say, "Go, go" as compared with the instruction, "Press the bulb twice," when the light comes on. In the first case, two isolated impulses regulate the motor response. In the second, the regulatory influence can proceed only from the "significative" side of the self-instruction, which contains only a single, protracted, innervating signal—"I shall press twice." In children of 3 or 4, the verbal command of the child himself ("Go, go") was a successful regulator of the motor reactions, but the verbal command "I shall press twice" typically resulted in a single protracted movement. With the same age group, the child's spoken instruction, "Press," was found to produce distinct motor responses coordinated with the signal, whereas his verbal command, "Don't press," resulted in impulsive motor reactions. Only when the child was told to respond to the inhibitory signal "without uttering a single word" was inhibition of responses obtained. The act of speaking thus is seen to have a basic impulsive function that only later gives way to the semantic content or meaning of the words. Only then can speech serve as directive of behavior. Luria indicates that in normal development the regulatory function of speech is steadily transferred from the impulse side to the "analytic system of elective significative connections [Luria, 1961, p. 92]," and control shifts from the external to the internal speech of the child. This radical change is said to occur in the child at about the age of 4½–5½. Behavior becomes regulated by internally retained verbal rules, and the child responds to even complex instructions like "Press when the yellow light comes on and do not press in response to the blue light."

In summary, Luria's review of Russian research shows that early control of behavior occurs through competing motor responses and exteroceptive feedback. The impellant action of the child's speech recedes, and the leading role passes to the inhibiting functions. In the final stage, according to Luria (1961), "the external developed forms of speech become reduced, and the decisive influence is now exerted by that higher form of internal speech which constitutes an essential component both of thought and volitional action and whose objective study still remains the task of the rising generation of scientific psychologists [p. 95]."

In his theory of cognitive development, Piaget (1926) proposed a distinction between egocentric, or internal, speech and socialized speech. In egocentric speech there is no attempt by the child to adapt his speech to the needs of the listener, whereas in socialized speech there is a clear intention to communicate. Piaget held that egocentric speech disappeared as the child approached 7 years of age and his egocentrism declined. Vygotsky (1962) disagreed with Piaget's view of the fate of egocentric speech and stated that such speech simply "goes underground," or turns into inner speech, rather than disappearing. In an adult, according to Vygotsky, inner speech represents a person's "thinking for himself," and this process serves the same function for the adult that egocentric speech has for the child. Vygotsky hypothesized that inner speech develops and becomes stabilized at about the beginning of school age and that this occurrence is what produces the quick drop in egocentric speech observed at that stage. This view is consistent with that of Luria (1961) and other Russian investigators. In general, Russian research indicates that behavior that is learned with the use of language is acquired quickly, generalizes widely, and is highly stable. In stating the case for the importance of language, Mussen (1963) wrote, "Children over 5 years of age function and control their behavior primarily by means of verbal mediation; that is, by means of what American psychologists call mediated generalization or verbal mediation [p. 46]."

Research with a task similar to Luria's (Birch, Note 14) and with American children revealed an age-related developmental sequence of verbal inhibition of motor behavior similar to that found in Russian children. When told "press" to a green light and "don't press" to a red light, all children 5½ to 6½ years old reached the 90% criterion of success. In contrast, only 75% of 4½- to 5½-year-olds and 37.5% of 3½- to 4½-year-olds achieved criterion. The influence of learning on this apparently maturational phenomenon was examined by Bem (1967), who demonstrated that previously deficient 3-year-olds could be trained to make the required number of lever presses to match the number of light signals presented. The procedure used involved a sequence of verbal training, verbal fading, motor training, verbal–motor training, and verbal–motor fading. Bem suggested that some analogue of fading may be the "real world mechanism" by which speech becomes internal and verbal self-control is acquired.

The interaction between verbal and nonverbal behavior was examined within an operant framework by Lovaas (1961), who showed that aggressive nonverbal behavior could be increased in reinforcement of aggressive verbal behavior. Lovaas (1964) also demonstrated that verbal operants such as "fast" or "slow" can control both the rate of their own occurrence as well as latency, rate, and choice of manual responding. In discussing the development of verbal control of motor behavior, Lovaas suggested that such contributing factors as the imitation of parent's verbalizations, the reinforcement for acting congruently with one's statements, and the self-reinforcement from behaving according to one's plan or previous verbalizations.

In an extensive review of theories and reports of four studies of private speech (Kohlberg, Yaeger, & Hjertholm, 1968), the authors provided support for the cognitive developmental approach shared by Piaget and Vygotsky and lent credence to Vygotsky's hypothesis of what happens to speech—it becomes private. In the Kohlberg et al. (1968) studies, private speech was found to be common among 4–6-year-olds and to decline gradually thereafter. On the basis of theory and the findings of their studies, these authors (Kohlberg et al., 1968) hypothesized a hierarchy of private speech representing 7 different developmental levels. Only one of their categories constitutes self-guiding comments, and this category was placed at Level 5 in the sequence of development of private speech. The two later levels were called "inaudible muttering" and "silent inner speech."

In a study specifically addressed to examining the relative efficacy of the differential modes of delivery of verbalizations governing nonverbal behavior, Meichenbaum and Goodman (1969a) used a finger-tapping task with kindergarten and first-grade children. Findings reflected the expected developmental sequence. Kindergarten children's motor performance in response to cues "faster" or "slower" was similar to that of first-grade children when self-verbalizations were aloud, but whispered cues using only lip movements had little control over performance of kindergarten children. By contrast, the first-grade children performed better when the cues were covert rather than overt. On the basis of these results, the authors suggested that younger children should be encouraged to self-verbalize out loud and then gradually fade the cues to implicit speech.

There is considerable evidence to support the belief that self-control develops largely as a function of a child's development of language mechanisms and that such development follows an established, age-related sequence. Our discussion turns next to a description of the characteristics of children who have failed to develop private self-guiding speech and to some results of efforts to remediate their deficits.

Remediation of Deficits in Verbal Self-Control

The role of self-verbalizations in the control of behavior has been examined in relation to the characteristic response styles of children's cognitive behavior or conceptual tempo. For example, the dimension of reflection–impulsivity indicates the child's consistent tendency to reflect over alternative response possibilities before giving an answer, rather than responding impulsively. Unlike the area of role-taking in which measures abound, verbal self-control research has made major use of a single instrument—the MFF (Kagan *et al.,* 1964). This test requires subjects to select an appropriate match for a stimulus figure from among a selection of six similar figures, and latency to first response and errors are noted. Research with the MFF has shown that reflection–impulsivity is an important dimension of cognitive development with related behavioral concomitants (see Finch & Kendall, 1979; Messer, 1976). For example, impulsivity has been shown to be related to certain educational deficits and clinical syndromes. More impulsives are found among children diagnosed as hyperactive, brain damaged, epileptic, and mentally retarded. Impulsives tend to do less well in school and are poorer readers than are reflective children. The reflective child has been found to be better able to sustain attention, to be less aggressive, and to make more advanced moral judgments.

Results of a study specifically designed to explore the relationship between conceptual tempo and the verbal control of behavior (Meichenbaum & Goodman, 1969b) showed that the self-verbalizations of impulsive children of kindergarten age were less directive of actions than were those of reflectives. Whereas reflectives responded to the semantic aspects of their self-instructions by tapping several times to each utterance, the impulsive children used self-instructions in a motoric manner—that is, they tapped each time they uttered a word. This finding is reminiscent of Luria's discussion of the impellant power of words, a force that only later gives way to an inhibiting function when the meaning of words becomes overriding. Impulsives in the Meichenbaum and Goodman (1969b) study also responded to "don't push" with motor responses more frequently than did the reflectives. In addition, impulsive children showed significantly less verbal control of motor behavior under the covert condition of self-instruction (lip movements only) than did the reflective children, whereas overt self-instructions produced no difference in frequency of errors. The authors suggested that socialization factors play a vital role in the acquisition of speech-for-self and cognitive styles. This suggestion takes on added importance when one considers effects of socialization on delinquents.

A number of researchers have successfully altered the cognitive style of impulsivity by teaching children to use self-directed verbal commands (e.g., Kendall & Finch, 1976, 1978; Meichenbaum & Goodman, 1971; Palkes, Stewart, & Kahana, 1968). The procedure follows essentially the developmental sequence outlined by Luria (1961) and supported by later investigators. The child is instructed to pay attention to a model who talks aloud while performing a task, then whispers the instructions, and finally repeats the task while thinking the self-guiding words. The child then follows the same sequence of self-talk, thus practicing the verbal self-instruction (see Kendall, 1977).

An impulsive cognitive style also has been altered by modeling (Debus, 1970; Denney, 1972; Ridberg, Parke, & Hetherington, 1971; Yando & Kagan, 1968), without the structured practice of self-instructions. In one of the studies reported by Meichenbaum and Goodman (1971), a comparison of modeling with a combination of modeling and training in self-instruction was made. Results indicated that both conditions resulted in a significant increase in latencies to respond but that only the self-instructional training resulted also in a decrease in errors on the task. Similar support for the utility of self-instruction has been reported by Finch, Wilkinson, Nelson, and Montgomery (1975) with emotionally disturbed children.

Many of the attempts to teach self-verbalizations have involved the use of impersonal material as training tasks rather than interpersonal situations. Even so, some carryover of reduction in impulsivity in social settings such as behavior in the classroom has been noted (Kendall & Finch, 1976, 1978). In the previously mentioned (Douglas *et al.*, 1976) cognitive treatment of hyperactive children, however, improvement in classroom behavior did *not* occur even though a wide range of tasks and games was used in training. Treatment effects did generalize to reading, as trained subjects showed significant improvement on reading tests at a 3-month follow-up. Significant increases in latency and reductions in errors on the MFF also were maintained at follow-up.

On the basis of her research with aggressive boys, Camp (1977) postulated that maintaining response inhibition in both impersonal and interpersonal tasks may depend on an effective linguistic control system. According to her, difficulty in inhibiting aggressive behavior "could involve a weak or inconsistent response to covert commands as well as a high threshold for activating self-regulating verbalizations [Camp, 1977, p. 152]." Camp's treatment study (Camp, Blom, Hebert, & Van Doorninck, 1977), in which young aggressive boys were taught to "think aloud," found improvement on several measures and supported the notions that self-guiding covert speech is important to self-control in children and that self-verbalizations can be taught directly. Furthermore, such skill acquisition appears to affect behavior.

The evidence in regard to adolescents generally and to delinquents particularly is less clear. One recent study (Williams & Akamatsu, 1978) utilizing the Meichenbaum and Goodman (1971) self-guidance procedure with delinquents produced only mixed results. The children's form of the MFF was used for training, and the adult form was a dependent measure. Both a self-instructional training group and an attention-control group that practiced MFF items after being told to work slowly and carefully performed better than an assessment-only control group. Only the self-instructional group showed generalization of training effects to the WISC-R picture arrangement subtest, and the three groups did not differ on a delay of gratification measure. Williams and Akamatsu (1978) suggested that the two groups that practiced the MFF performed better than the assessment control group because of their exposure to "basic problem solving skills." This would not, however, explain why only the self-instructional training group showed generalization to another task. As noted earlier, verbal self-instruction is contained in some problem-solving programs (e.g., Bowman, Note 8) with delinquents, but the teaching of self-guiding speech as the major focus of treatment has been only minimally explored in this population.

The successful self-control treatment of an aggressive 16-year-old (McCullough, Huntsinger, & Nay, 1977) apparently included training in verbal mediation, although systematic instruction in self-verbalizations as used in the treatment of children (see Kendall, 1977) was not implemented. In an attempt to apply the McCullough *et al.* (1977) self-control treatment to delinquents, Huntsinger (Note 15) trained 12–16-year-old male residents of a state learning center. During four individual sessions over the period of 1 month, self-control treatment subjects learned to recognize both internal and external cues that accompanied their anger and were then taught to interrupt their behavioral sequence using thought-stopping, muscle relaxation, and breath control. Role playing and videotape feedback were used to teach these new ways of handling anger. Following this short-term training, no differences were found between self-control treatment subjects, a discussion-only group, and a nontreated control group on the dependent measures, which included aggressive behavior as reflected in the institution's token economy. It can be seen that this self-control treatment is reminiscent of some of the problem-solving programs described earlier, except that it focuses narrowly on the handling of anger. It is difficult to understand completely the negative results of this study, although the lack of a specific focus on self-instructional training and/or the brevity of the training may have been the significant factors. One should also consider the possible unreliability of the institution's token economy, since the Little (Note 10) study in a similar institution found no meaningful pattern of differential point totals from the token economy. The matter of reliable dependent measures of adjustment in institutions appears to be unresolved (Chandler *et al.*, 1974), although some success in obtaining reliable staff ratings of delinquents' behavior has been reported (e.g., Sarason & Ganzer, 1973) when a rating scale was used.

Summary and Discussion

The critical function of language in self-control has been suggested, and its sequential, age-related development has been outlined. Treatment of impulsive children by self-instructional methods that closely duplicate the normal process of development appears to offer an efficacious approach to remediation of at least some self-control deficits.

Although research findings with an adolescent population are sparse and mixed, successful treatment of adults with the same procedure (Meichenbaum & Cameron, 1973) suggests that adolescents may similarly benefit. From observation of the behavior of delinquents, one is led to speculate that, for many of these youngsters, words serve more of an impellant function than an inhibitory function as described by Luria (1961). Such a speculation, of course, remains to be investigated. Self-instructional training with adolescents may require the use of tasks with a higher interest level than those used with younger children, presentation to the subjects of an acceptable rationale for the training, or similar special adjustments in the training procedures that have been shown to be efficacious with younger children. Nevertheless, exploration of speech as a source of self-regulation for delinquents appears warranted on the basis of the theory and data presented herein. Implementation of a self-instructional treatment procedure is within reason in terms of time, energy, and cost, and the payoff is likely to be worth the effort.

FINAL COMMENTS

On the basis of both theory and research findings, a cognitive–behavioral approach to the treatment of delinquents appears to offer a promising adjunct to behavioral programs or an alternative to traditional methods of working with this problematic population. It is important to note, however, that this approach is recommended for the treatment of certain delinquents, not delinquency. One should not assume that all youngsters who are categorized as "delinquent" are deficient in the cognitive skills discussed. For example, 27% of the girls tested in a state learning center did *not* show role-taking deficits (Little, Note 10). This mitigates against the tendency to equate simplistically social egocentrism with delinquency. It may be, as Chandler (1973) noted, that role-taking deficits are more a measure of social ineptitude than of an antisocial orientation, since social egocentrism characterizes a broad spectrum of young people who have failed to make a successful adjustment in life. The consistent finding that cognitive deficits *do* occur in a large proportion of those labeled "delinquent," however, suggests that remedial programs should be implemented.

Although the emphasis in this chapter has been on remediation of deficits, one should not overlook the potential of these training programs for primary prevention of problems in social adjustment. Indeed, even at the preschool level, youngsters trained in ICPS skills were found to make better school adjustments than their agemates who were not trained (Shure & Spivack, 1978). It is possible that role-taking training in the fifth and sixth grades, when role-taking ability normally is mature, could prevent serious behavioral problems at home, in school, and with the law. Likewise, verbal self-instructional programs in the first grade, when covert self-guiding speech is present in normal children, might serve to decrease the behavior problems of children who otherwise may become labeled impulsive, hyperactive, aggressive, or delinquent. At any rate, it is highly recommended that research be conducted to determine further the possible effects of intervention before interpersonal difficulties become acute.

A question that emerges from the preceding review and discussion is: What is the best cognitive–behavioral treatment for delinquents? Obviously, the answer at this point can be no more than suggestive, and it is also obvious that the treatments are not independent. The comprehensive problem-solving training program of the Hahnemann group has not been tested with delinquents, although its content and procedures are based on research data. Other problem-solving approaches that have been implemented with delinquents also show promise. In addition, the more narrow focus on one component of problem solving, role-taking, also has produced positive changes in behavior of delinquents, although efforts at replication were not successful. An even narrower focus on the teaching of self-verbalizations as a mechanism for self-control has just begun to be tested on delinquents (with mixed results), but positive effects with other populations support such an approach. Theoretically, the treatment should be highly suitable for the poorly controlled delinquent. Further investigation of the efficacy of these programs for delinquents is indicated, however, before widespread treatment is implemented. Such research will be facilitated by the fact that measurable deficits are addressed and that treatments are precisely described. Given such a set of circumstances, treatment effects can be systematically assessed and programs implemented only when measured deficits are found in the population of concern. Such pinpointing of a specific need for treatment may serve also to make the best use of the limited funds and manpower that are typically available to those assigned responsibility for the care and rehabilitation of delinquents. Present evidence suggests that—whether one addresses the social inadequacies of delinquents at the level of interpersonal problem solving, role-taking, or verbal self-control—remediation of cognitive deficits may be indicated for a large proportion of this otherwise heterogeneous population.

ACKNOWLEDGMENT

The authors wish to thank David Pellegrini and Eugene S. Urbain for their valuable comments on an earlier version of this chapter.

REFERENCE NOTES

1. Quay, H. C., & Parsons, L. B. *The differential behavioral classification of the juvenile offender.* Laboratory report, Temple University, Philadelphia, Pennsylvania, 1971.
2. Freedman, B. J. *An analysis of social-behavioral skill deficits in delinquent and non-delinquent adolescent boys.* Unpublished manuscript, University of Wisconsin, 1974.
3. Spivack, G., & Levine, M. *Self-regulation in acting-out and normal adolescents* (Rep. M-4531). Washington, D.C.: National Institute of Health, 1963.
4. Platt, J. J., & Spivack, G. *Manual for the means–ends problem-solving procedure (MEPS).* Philadelphia: Hahnemann Medical College and Hospital, Department of Mental Health Sciences, January, 1975.
5. Platt, J. J., Spivack, G., & Swift, M. S. *Interpersonal problem-solving group therapy.* Philadelphia: Hahnemann Medical College and Hospital, Department of Mental Health Sciences, 1975.
6. Platt, J. J., & Spivack, G. *Workbook for training in interpersonal problem-solving thinking.* Philadelphia: Hahnemann Medical College and Hospital, Department of Mental Health Sciences, 1976.
7. Siegel, J. M., & Spivack, G. *Problem-solving therapy: The description of a new program for chronic schizophrenic patients.* Philadelphia: Hahnemann Medical College and Hospital, Department of Mental Health Sciences, 1973.
8. Bowman, P. C. *A cognitive-behavioral treatment program for impulsive youthful offenders.* Unpublished manuscript, Virginia Commonwealth University, 1978.
9. Chandler, M. J. *Egocentrism and childhood psychology: The development and application of measurement techniques.* Paper presented at the meeting of the Society for Research in Child Development, Minneapolis, April, 1971.
10. Little, V. L. *Developmental role-taking deficits in institutionalized juvenile delinquents.* Paper presented at the meeting of the Southeastern Psychological Association, Atlanta, March, 1978.
11. Elardo, P. T., Caldwell, B. M., & Webb, R. *An examination of the relationship between role-taking and social competence.* Paper presented at the Southeastern Conference on Human Development, Nashville, Tennessee, April, 1976.

12. Elardo, P. T., & Caldwell, B. M. *The effects of an experimental social development program on children in the middle childhood period.* Unpublished manuscript, University of Arkansas at Little Rock, 1976.

13. Kendall, P. C., & Wilcox, L. E. *Self-control in children: The development of a rating scale.* Manuscript submitted for publication, 1979.

14. Birch, D. *Some effects of the verbal system on the nonverbal behavior of preschool children.* Paper presented at the meeting of the Society for Research in Child Development, 1967.

15. Huntsinger, G. M. *Teaching self-control of verbal and physical aggression to juvenile delinquents.* Unpublished manuscript, Virginia Commonwealth University, 1976.

REFERENCES

Affleck, G. G. Role-taking ability and interpersonal conflict resolution among retarded young adults. *American Journal of Mental Deficiency,* 1975, *80,* 233–236. (a)

Affleck, G. G. Role-taking ability and the interpersonal competencies of retarded children. *American Journal of Mental Deficiency,* 1975, *80,* 312–316. (b)

Affleck, G. G. Role-taking ability and the interpersonal tactics of retarded children. *American Journal of Mental Deficiency,* 1976, *80,* 667–670.

Alexander, J. F., & Parsons, B. V. Short-term behavioral intervention with delinquent families: Impact on family process and recidivism. *Journal of Abnormal Psychology,* 1973, *81,* 219–225.

Allen, G. J., Chinsky, J. M., Larcen, S. W., Lochman, J. E., & Selinger, H. V. *Community psychology and the schools.* Hillsdale, New Jersey: Lawrence Erlbaum, 1976.

Allport, F. H. *Social psychology.* New York: Houghton Mifflin, 1924.

Asch, S. *Social psychology.* New York: Prentice-Hall, 1952.

Bandura, A. Social-learning theory of identificatory processes. In D. Goslin (Ed.), *Handbook of socialization theory and research.* Chicago: Rand McNally, 1969.

Bandura, A. Psychotherapy based upon modeling principles. In A. E. Bergin & S. L. Garfield (Eds.), *Handbook of psychotherapy and behavior change.* New York: Wiley, 1971.

Bandura, A. Effecting change through participant modeling. In J. D. Krumboltz & C. E. Thoresen (Eds.), *Counseling methods.* New York: Holt, Rinehart, & Winston, 1976.

Bandura, A. *Social learning theory.* Englewood Cliffs, New Jersey: Prentice-Hall, 1977.

Beker, J., & Heyman, D. S. A critical appraisal of the California differential treatment typology of adolescent offenders. *Criminology,* 1972, *10,* 3–59.

Bem, S. L. Verbal self-control: The establishment of effective self-instruction. *Journal of Experimental Psychology,* 1967, *74,* 485–491.

Borke, H. Chandler and Greenspan's "ersatz egocentrism": A rejoinder. *Developmental Psychology,* 1972, *7,* 107–109.

Camp, B. W. Verbal mediation in young aggressive boys. *Journal of Abnormal Psychology,* 1977, *86,* 145–153.

Camp, B. W., Blom, G. E., Hebert, F., & Van Doorninck, W. J. "Think aloud": A program for developing self-control in young aggressive boys. *Journal of Abnormal Child Psychology,* 1977, *5,* 157–169.

Chandler, M. J. Egocentrism and antisocial behavior: The assessment and training of social perspective-taking skills. *Developmental Psychology,* 1973, *9,* 326–332.

Chandler, M. J., & Greenspan, S. Ersatz egocentrism: A reply to H. Borke. *Developmental Psychology,* 1972, *7,* 104–106.

Chandler, M. J., Greenspan, S., & Barenboim, C. Assessment and training of role-taking and referential communication skills in institutionalized emotionally disturbed children. *Developmental Psychology,* 1974, *10,* 546–553.

Coelho, G. V., Hamburg, D. A., & Murphey, E. G. Coping strategies in a new learning environment. *Archives of General Psychiatry,* 1963, *9,* 433–443.

Davis, G. Current status of research and theory in human problem-solving. *Psychological Bulletin,* 1966, *66,* 36–54.

Debus, R. L. Effects of brief observation of model behavior on conceptual tempo of impulsive children. *Developmental Psychology,* 1970, *2,* 22–32.

Denney, D. R. Modeling effects upon conceptual style and cognitive tempo. *Child Development,* 1972, *43,* 105–119.

Douglas, V. I., Parry, P., Marton, P., & Garson, C. Assessment of a cognitive training program for hyperactive children. *Journal of Abnormal Child Psychology,* 1976, *4,* 389–410.

Draughton, M. Duplication of facial expressions: Conditions affecting task and possible clinical usefulness. *Journal of Personality,* 1973, *41,* 140–150.

Duncan, C. P. Recent research on human problem-solving. *Psychological Bulletin,* 1959, *56,* 397–429.

D'Zurilla, T. J., & Goldfried, M. R. Problem-solving and behavior modification. *Journal of Abnormal Psychology,* 1971, *78,* 107–126.

Elardo, P. T., & Cooper, M. *Project AWARE: A handbook for teachers.* Menlo Park, California: Addison-Wesley, 1977.

Feffer, M. H. The cognitive implications of role-taking behavior. *Journal of Personality,* 1959, *27,* 152–168.

Feffer, M. H. Cognitive aspects of role-taking in children. *Journal of Personality,* 1960, *28,* 383–396.

Feffer, M. Symptom expression as a form of primitive decentering. *Psychological Review,* 1967, *74,* 16–28.

Feffer, M. A developmental analysis of interpersonal behavior. *Psychological Review,* 1970, *77,* 197–214.

Feffer, M., & Gourevitch, V. Cognitive aspects of role-taking in children. *Journal of Personality,* 1960, *28,* 383–396.

Feffer, M., & Jahelka, M. Implications of the decentering concept for the structuring of projective content. *Journal of Consulting and Clinical Psychology,* 1968, *32,* 434–441.

Feffer, M., & Suchotliff, L. Decentering implications of social interaction. *Journal of Personality and Social Psychology,* 1966, *4,* 415–422.

Feshbach, N. D. Empathy in children: Some theoretical and empirical considerations. *The Counseling Psychologist,* 1975, *5,* 25–30.

Finch, A. J. Jr., & Kendall, P. C. Impulsive behavior: From research to treatment. In A. J. Finch, Jr. and P. C. Kendall (Eds.), *Clinical treatment and research in child psychopathology.* Hollingswood, New York: Spectrum Publications, 1979.

Finch, A. J., Jr., Wilkinson, M. D., Nelson, W. M. III, & Montgomery, L. E. Modification of an impulsive cognitive tempo in emotionally disturbed boys. *Journal of Abnormal Child Psychology,* 1975, *3,* 47–51.

Flavell, J. H. *The developmental psychology of Jean Piaget.* New York: Van Nostrand Reinhold Company, 1963.

Flavell, J. H. The development of inferences about others. In T. Mischel (Ed.), *Understanding other persons.* Oxford, England: Blackwell Basil, 1974.

Flavell, J. H., Botkin, P. T., Fry, C. L., Wright, J. W., & Jarvis, P. E. *The development of role-taking and communication skills in children.* New York: Wiley, 1968.

Gordon, T. *Parent effectiveness training.* New York: Wyden, 1970.

Gough, H. G. A sociological theory of psychopathy. *American Journal of Sociology,* 1948, *53,* 359–366.

Gough, H. G. *Manual for the California psychological inventory.* Palo Alto, California: Consulting Psychologists Press, 1957.

Gough, H. G. Theory and measurement of socialization. *Journal of Consulting Psychology,* 1960, *24,* 23–30.

Hogan, R. Empathy: A conceptual and psychometric analysis. *The Counseling Psychologist*, 1975, *5*, 14–18.

Hollos, M., & Cowan, P. A. Social isolation and cognitive development: Logical operations and role-taking abilities in three Norwegian social settings. *Child Development*, 1973, *44*, 630–641.

Iannotti, R. J. The nature and measurement of empathy in children. *The Counseling Psychologist*, 1975, *5*, 21–25.

Jahoda, M. The meaning of psychological health. *Social Casework*, 1953, *34*, 349–354.

Jahoda, M. *Current concepts of positive mental health*. New York: Basic Books, 1958.

Jesness, C. F. Comparative effectiveness of behavior modification and transactional analysis. *Journal of Consulting and Clinical Psychology*, 1975, *43*, 758–779.

Kagan, J., Rosman, B. L., Day, D., Albert, J., & Phillips, W. Information processing in the child: Significance of analytic and reflective attitudes. *Psychological Monographs*, 1964, *78*. (1, Whole No. 578)

Kendall, P. C. On the efficacious use of verbal self-instructional procedures with children. *Cognitive Therapy and Research*, 1977, *1*, 331–341.

Kendall, P. C., Deardorff, P. A., & Finch, A. J. Jr. Empathy and socialization in first and repeat juvenile offenders and normals. *Journal of Abnormal Child Psychology*, 1977, *5*, 93–97.

Kendall, P. C., & Finch, A. J. Jr. A cognitive–behavioral treatment of impulse control: A case study. *Journal of Consulting and Clinical Psychology*, 1976, *44*, 852–857.

Kendall, P. C., & Finch, A. J. Jr. A cognitive–behavioral treatment for impulsivity: A group comparison study. *Journal of Consulting and Clinical Psychology*, 1978, *46*, 110–118.

Kerckhoff, A. Early antecedents of role taking and role playing ability. *Merrill-Palmer Quarterly*, 1969, *15*, 229–247.

Khanna, J. L. (Ed.). *New treatment approaches to juvenile delinquency*. Springfield, Illinois: Charles C. Thomas, 1974.

Kifer, R. E., Lewis, M. A., Green, D. R., & Phillips, E. L. Training predelinquent youths and their parents to negotiate conflict situations. *Journal of Applied Behavior Analysis*, 1974, *7*, 357–364.

Klein, N. C., Alexander, J. F., & Parsons, B. V. Impact of family systems intervention on recidivism and sibling delinquency: A model of primary prevention and program evaluation. *Journal of Consulting and Clinical Psychology*, 1977, *45*, 469–474.

Kohlberg, L. Stage and sequence: The cognitive-developmental approach to socialization. In D. Goslin (Ed.), *Handbook of socialization theory and research*. Chicago: Rand McNally, 1969.

Kohlberg, L., Yaeger, J., & Hjertholm, E. Private speech: Four studies and a review of theories. *Child Development*, 1968, *39*, 691–736.

Kurdek, L. A. *Structural components and intellectual and behavioral correlates of cognitive perspective taking in first through fourth grade children*. Doctoral dissertation, University of Illinois at Chicago Circle, 1976. *Dissertation Abstracts International*, 1977, *37*, 3581B. (University Microfilms No. 77–541)

Lovaas, O. I. Interaction between verbal and nonverbal behavior. *Child Development*, 1961, *32*, 329–336.

Lovaas, O. I. Cue properties of words: The control of operant responding by rate and content of verbal operants. *Child Development*, 1964, *35*, 245–256.

Luria, A. R. *The role of speech in the regulation of normal and abnormal behavior*. New York: Liveright, 1961.

Maccoby, E. E. Role-taking in childhood and its consequences for social learning. *Child Development*, 1959, *30*, 239–252.

McCandless, B. R. *Children and adolescents—Behavior and development*. New York: Holt, Rinehart & Winston, 1961.

McCullough, J. P., Huntsinger, G. M., & Nay, W. R. Self-control treatment of aggression in a 16-year-old male. *Journal of Consulting and Clinical Psychology*, 1977, *45*, 322–331.

McFall, R. M., & Lillesand, D. B. Behavior rehearsal with modeling and coaching in assertion training. *Journal of Abnormal Psychology*, 1971, *77*, 313–323.

McFall, R. M., & Marston, A. R. An experimental investigation of behavior rehearsal in assertive training. *Journal of Abnormal Psychology*, 1970, *76*, 295–303.

Mead, G. H. *Mind, self, and society*. Chicago: University of Chicago Press, 1934.

Megargee, E. I. *The California Psychological Inventory handbook*. San Francisco: Jossey-Bass, 1972.

Meichenbaum, D., & Cameron, R. Training schizophrenics to talk to themselves: A means of developing attentional controls. *Behavior Therapy*, 1973, *4*, 515–534.

Meichenbaum, D., & Goodman, J. The developmental control of operant motor responding by verbal operants. *Journal of Experimental Child Psychology*, 1969, *7*, 553–565. (a)

Meichenbaum, D., & Goodman, J. Reflection–impulsivity and verbal control of motor behavior. *Child Development*, 1969, *40*, 785–797. (b)

Meichenbaum, D., & Goodman, J. Training impulsive children to talk to themselves: A means of developing self-control. *Journal of Abnormal Psychology*, 1971, *77*, 115–126.

Messer, S. B. Reflection–impulsivity: A review. *Psychological Bulletin*, 1976, *83*, 1026–1051.

Morton, R. B. An experiment in brief psychotherapy. *Psychological Monographs*, 1955, *69*. (Whole No. 386)

Mussen, P. H. *The psychological development of the child*. Englewood Cliffs, New Jersey: Prentice-Hall, 1963.

Nahir, H. T., & Yussen, S. R. The performance of kibbutz- and city-reared Israeli children on two role-taking tasks. *Developmental Psychology*, 1977, *13*, 450–455.

Offer, D. *The psychological world of the teen-ager*. New York: Basic Books, 1969.

Palkes, H., Stewart, M., & Kahana, B. Porteus Maze performance of hyperactive boys after training in self-directed verbal commands. *Child Development*, 1968, *39*, 817–826.

Parsons, B. V., & Alexander, J. F. Short-term family intervention: A therapy outcome study. *Journal of Consulting and Clinical Psychology*, 1973, *41*, 195–201.

Patterson, G. R. Interventions for boys with conduct problems: Multiple settings, treatments, and criteria. *Journal of Consulting and Clinical Psychology*, 1974, *42*, 471–481.

Piaget, G. W. Training patients to communicate. In A. A. Lazarus (Ed.), *Clinical behavior therapy*. New York: Brunner/Mazel, 1972.

Piaget, J. *The language and thought of the child*. New York: Harcourt, Brace, 1926.

Piaget, J. *Judgment and reasoning in the child*. New York: Harcourt, Brace, 1928.

Piaget, J. *The psychology of intelligence*. New York: Harcourt, Brace, 1950.

Piaget, J. *The moral judgment of the child*. New York: Collier Books, 1962. (a)

Piaget, J. *Plays, dreams and imitation in children*. New York: Norton, 1962. (b)

Platt, J. J., Scura, W., & Hannon, J. R. Problem-solving thinking of youthful incarcerated heroin addicts. *Journal of Community Psychology*, 1973, *1*, 278–281.

Platt, J. J., & Spivack, G. Studies in problem-solving thinking of psychiatric patients: Patient-control differences and factorial structure of problem-solving thinking. *Proceedings of the 81st Annual Convention of the American Psychological Association*, 1973, *8*, 461–462. (Summary)

Platt, J. J., Spivack, G., Altman, N., Altman, D., & Peizer, S. B. Adolescent problem-solving thinking. *Journal of Consulting and Clinical Psychology*, 1974, *42*, 787–793.

Reid, J. B., & Patterson, G. R. The modification of aggression and stealing behavior of boys in the home setting. In E. Ribes-Inesta & A. Bandura (Eds.), *Analysis of delinquency and aggression*. Hillsdale, New Jersey: Lawrence Erlbaum, 1976.

Ridberg, H. E., Parke, R. D., & Hetherington, M. Modification of impulsive and reflective cognitive styles through observation of film-mediated models. *Developmental Psychology*, 1971, *5*, 369–377.

Robin, A. L., Kent, R., O'Leary, K. D., Foster, S., & Prinz, R. An approach to teaching parents and adolescents problem-solving communication skills: A preliminary report. *Behavior Therapy*, 1977, *8*, 639–643.

Rotenberg, M. Conceptual and methodological notes in affective and cognitive role taking (sympathy and empathy): An illustrative experiment with delinquent and non-delinquent boys. *Journal of Genetic Psychology*, 1974, *125*, 177–185.

Sarason, I. G. Verbal learning, modeling, and juvenile delinquency. *American Psychologist*, 1968, *23*, 254–266.

Sarason, I. G., & Ganzer, V. J. Social influence techniques in clinical and community psychology. In C. D. Spielberger (Ed.), *Current topics in clinical and community psychology (Vol. 1)*. New York: Academic Press, 1969.

Sarason, I. G., & Ganzer, V. J. Modeling and group discussion in the rehabilitation of juvenile delinquents. *Journal of Counseling Psychology*, 1973, *20*, 442–449.

Sarbin, T. R. Role theory. In G. Lindzey (Ed.), *Handbook of social psychology, Vol. 1*. Cambridge, Massachusetts: Addison-Wesley, 1954.

Scopetta, M. A. *A comparison of modeling approaches to the rehabilitation of institutionalized male adolescent offenders implemented by paraprofessionals*. Doctoral dissertation, University of Miami, 1972. *Dissertation Abstracts International*, 1972, *33*, 2822B. (University Microfilms No. 72-31, 901)

Selman, R. L. The relation of role-taking to the development of moral judgment in children. *Child Development*, 1971, *42*, 79–91. (a)

Selman, R. L. Taking another's perspective: Role-taking development in early childhood. *Child Development*, 1971, *42*, 1721–1734. (b)

Selman, R. L. Toward a structural analysis of developing interpersonal relations concepts: Research with normal and disturbed preadolescent boys. In A. Pick (Ed.), *X Annual Minnesota Symposium on Child Psychology*. Minneapolis: University of Minnesota Press, 1976.

Selman, R. L., & Byrne, D. F. A structural developmental analysis of levels of role-taking in middle childhood. *Child Development*, 1974, *45*, 803–806.

Selman, R. L., Jaquette, D., & Lavin, D. R. Interpersonal awareness in children: Toward an integration of developmental and clinical child psychology. *American Journal of Orthopsychiatry*, 1977, *47*, 264–274.

Shantz, C. U. Empathy in relation to social cognitive development. *The Counseling Psychologist*, 1975, *5*, 18–21. (a)

Shantz, C. U. The development of social cognition. In E. M. Hetherington (Ed.), *Review of child development research, Vol. 5*. Chicago: University of Chicago Press, 1975. (b)

Shure, M. B., & Spivack, G. *Problem-solving techniques in childrearing*. San Francisco: Jossey-Bass, 1978.

Simon, H. A., & Newell, A. Human problem-solving: The state of the theory in 1970. *American Psychologist*, 1971, *26*, 145–159.

Spivack, G., Platt, J. J., & Shure, M. B. *The problem-solving approach to adjustment*. San Francisco: Jossey-Bass, 1976.

Spivack, G., & Shure, M. B. *Social adjustment of young children: A cognitive approach to solving real-life problems*. San Francisco: Jossey-Bass, 1974.

Spohn, H. E., & Wolk, W. Effect of group problem-solving experience upon social withdrawal in chronic schizophrenics. *Journal of Abnormal and Social Psychology*, 1963, *66*, 187–190.

Stuart, R. B. Behavioral contracting within families of delinquents. *Journal of Behavior Therapy and Experimental Psychiatry*, 1971, *2*, 1–11.

Stuart, R. B., & Lott, L. A. Jr. Behavioral contracting with delinquents: A cautionary note. *Journal of Behavior Therapy and Experimental Psychiatry*, 1972, *3*, 161–169.

Stuart, R. B., Tripodi, T., Jayaratne, S., & Camburn, D. An experiment in social engineering in serving the families of predelinquents. *Journal of Abnormal Child Psychology*, 1976, *4*, 243–261.

Stumphauzer, J. S. (Ed.) *Behavior therapy with delinquents*. Springfield, Illinois: Charles C. Thomas, 1973.

Thelen, M. H., Fry, R. A., Dollinger, S. J., & Paul, S. C. Use of videotaped models to improve the interpersonal adjustment of delinquents. *Journal of Consulting and Clinical Psychology*, 1976, *44*, 492.

Urberg, K. A., & Docherty, E. M. Development of role-taking skills in young children. *Developmental Psychology*, 1976, *12*, 198–203.

Vygotsky, L. S. *Thought and language*. Cambridge, Massachusetts: M.I.T. Press, 1962.

Waring, E. B. *The relation between early language habits and early habits of conduct control*. New York: Teachers College, Columbia University, 1927.

Warren, M. Q. Classification of offenders as an aid to efficient management and effective treatment. *Journal of Criminal Law, Criminology and Police Science*, 1971, *62*, 239–258.

Weathers, L., & Liberman, R. D. Contingency contracting with families of delinquent adolescents. *Behavior Therapy*, 1975, *6*, 356–366.

Williams, D. Y., & Akamatsu, T. J. Cognitive self-guidance training with juvenile delinquents: Applicability and generalization. *Cognitive Therapy and Research*, 1978, *2*, 285–288.

Yando, R. M., & Kagan, J. The effect of teacher tempo on the child. *Child Development*, 1968, *39*, 27–34.

5

Anxiety Reduction through Cognitive–Behavioral Intervention[1]

MARVIN R. GOLDFRIED

We shall not cease from exploration
And the end of all our exploring
Will be to arrive where we started
And know the place for the first.

—T. S. ELIOT

That an individual's cognitive set or attitude can have profound effects on his or her behavior and emotional reactions is hardly new to psychology. Numerous studies have clearly demonstrated that the way an individual perceives a situation, typically manipulated by experimental instructions, can alter that person's subsequent behavior. Extrapolating from these basic research findings as well as from a related body of literature on attitude formation, it is not unreasonable to assume that early social learning experiences lead individuals to develop generalized cognitive sets regarding various situations or social interactions in their lives and that these expectancies somehow mediate their emotional and behavioral reactions.

This chapter deals with the use of cognitive–behavioral procedures for anxiety reduction and focuses specifically on training individuals to reevaluate potentially

[1]Preparation of this chapter was supported in part by Grant MH24327 from the National Institute of Mental Health. Portions of this paper were adapted from M. R. Goldfried. The use of relaxation and cogtive relabeling as coping skills, in R. B. Stuart (Ed.), *Behavioral self-management: Strategies, techniques and outcomes,* New York: Brunner/Mazel, 1977. The author is grateful to Steven Beach, Marcia K. Johnson, Richard J. Landau, and Richard S. Lazarus, for their helpful comments on an earlier version of this chapter.

Cognitive–Behavioral Interventions:
Theory, Research, and Procedures

upsetting events so that they may be viewed within a more realistic perspective. We begin with a discussion of the theoretical and research foundations that underlie cognitive–behavioral approaches to anxiety reduction. The clinical implementation of one such approach, systematic rational restructuring, will then be described. In pointing to the relevance of such cognitive–behavioral procedures to various clinical problems, a review of the clinical outcome research on speech anxiety, test anxiety, interpersonal anxiety, and assertion problems will be presented. The chapter concludes with some speculations on the interplay between the cognitive and the behavioral aspects of the therapeutic intervention strategy and suggests some ways that cognitive psychology can offer a useful conceptual scheme for bridging the gap between cognitive behavior therapy and therapeutic approaches stemming from other theoretical orientations.

THEORETICAL AND RESEARCH FOUNDATIONS

It is of considerable interest to observe the trends in behavior therapy, especially the increasing receptivity to cognitive conceptualizations that currently characterizes the field. Behavior therapy initially resisted any allusion to cognitive metaphors; Breger and McGaugh's (1965) arguments against the narrowness of a learning theory orientation to therapy and deviant behavior were originally criticized by behavior therapists. Yet, in rereading their critique, many of their suggestions are most compelling, particularly when they observe that a peripheralist approach to learning theory is giving way to a more centralist orientation. No doubt, behavior therapists at the time lacked the appropriate "cognitive set" for incorporating such new information.

In describing how a cognitive restructuring procedure may be used clinically, it is only natural to turn to the writings of Albert Ellis (1962), who has long recognized the therapeutic significance of modifying inappropriate expectations and beliefs as a means of anxiety reduction. Illustrative of his basic orientation is the following premise:

> If . . . people essentially become emotionally disturbed because they unthinkingly accept certain illogical premises or irrational ideas, then there is a good reason to believe that they can be somehow persuaded or taught to think more logically and rationally and thereby to undermine their own disturbances.[2]

There are some interesting observations one may make with regard to this statement. Ellis clearly presented a viewpoint in 1962 that is consistent with a cognitive–behavioral orientation, one that has considerable relevance for self-management procedures (Goldfried & Merbaum, 1973). What is also interesting, is that, until very recently, Ellis' therapeutic approach was not incorporated into the mainstream of behavior therapy. In fact, Bandura's (1969) classic work, which emphasizes both the importance of cognitive processes and the issue of self-control,

---

[2]From "Reason and Emotion in Psychotherapy," by Dr. Albert Ellis, p. 191. Copyright © 1962 by the Institute of Rational Living, Inc. Published by arrangement with Lyle Stuart.

makes no reference at all to Ellis or to rational–emotive therapy. The difficulty in incorporating Ellis's approach into a behavioral orientation has in part been due, no doubt, to the lack of clear specificity of therapeutic procedures as well as to the absence of any empirical data base for its clinical effectiveness. The situation is clearly changing, and greater recognition has been paid to the implications that many of Ellis' concepts and procedures have for the field of cognitive behavior therapy (Beck, 1976; Goldfried & Davison, 1976; Goldfried, Decenteceo, & Weinberg, 1974; A. A. Lazarus, 1971; Mahoney, 1974; Meichenbaum, 1977).

Another contribution that is all too infrequently cited in the behavioral literature consists of the work of Richard S. Lazarus (1966). Lazarus and his colleagues have long argued for the important role that cognitive processes play in both the maintenance and the reduction of stress reactions. Several of his studies have demonstrated that threatening stimuli (e.g., stressful films) can be made less aversive to individuals by means of cognitive reappraisals. In theorizing about the relationship between cognitive processes and stress reactions, Lazarus has made the distinction between "primary" and "secondary" appraisal. Primary appraisal refers to the individual's labeling of a situation as being dangerous, whereas secondary appraisal refers to the use of cognitive processes in the attempt to cope with such stress. It should be added, however, that the two processes are not seen as being completely independent, in that what is initially judged as potentially stressful in part depends on the individual's available coping skills (Lazarus, 1966; Lazarus & Launier, 1978).

Lazarus's distinction between primary and secondary appraisal appears to parallel the assumptions associated with Ellis's viewpoint. Nonetheless, there are certain basic differences between the two orientations that are worth mentioning. Ellis maintains that anxiety is mediated by the individual's unrealistic appraisal of a situation, and that anxiety reduction may be brought about through a more realistic reevaluation, followed by attempts to confront the fearful situation. Lazarus, on the other hand, argues that an anxiety reaction is mediated by a perceived sense of threat, actual harm, or a difficult challenge, and that the secondary appraisal process used to cope with such perceived stress can involve a defensive distortion of the situation, a more realistic cognitive appraisal, or plans for direct action. Although most of the emphasis in Lazarus' (1966) conceptualization has been on attempts at coping with realistic sources of stress (e.g., illness, physical danger) by means of defensive distortion (e.g., denial, intellectualization), he has, nonetheless, recognized that an individual's perceived inability to cope with an environment viewed as hostile and dangerous may also mediate chronic levels of anxiety. Similarly, Lazarus has suggested that the "appraisal of threat means any cognitive maneuver in which the threat is reevaluated, whether it is based on a realistic interpretation of cues or distortion of reality through a cognitive tour de force [Lazarus, 1966, p. 267]." As such, Lazarus's conceptualization is the more comprehensive of the two (see Lazarus & Launier, 1978).

The inclusion of cognitive distortion as part of the coping process in part reflects the fact that much of Lazarus' work has focused on highly stressful situation, such as major life crises and films depicting physical mutilation. Under such conditions, individuals are more likely to react with coping attempts entailing avoidance or distortion (Lazarus, 1966). Perhaps an even more important reason for the different emphasis placed on the seemingly "maladaptive" nature of the coping process is that Lazarus' scheme has been *descriptive* of how individuals typically cope with stress, whereas Ellis's thinking has reflected a therapeutic approach that is *prescriptive* of more effective ways of coping. The need to provide links between the work done by Lazarus and others in the area of stress research and the current efforts within cognitive behavior therapy has been convincingly argued by Roskies and Lazarus (in press).

Regardless of the differences in the content of the cognitions believed to mediate and reduce anxiety, a common assumption is that the way individuals label or evaluate situations can affect their emotional reactions to those situations. That covert verbalization can elicit emotional reactions has been confirmed in a number of studies. One experimental test of the effect of self-verbalizations on mood states was carried out by Velten (1968). Subjects were asked to read self-referent statements that reflected elation ("This is great—I really do feel good."), depression ("I have too many bad things in my life."), or neutral feelings ("Utah is the beehive state."). Subjects' mood and behavior changed in a positive or negative direction as a function of the content of the statements they had read. These changes were measured by the subjects' verbal reports, as well as by indirect behavioral indicators of mood, such as writing speed, decision time, reaction time on a word association task, and spontaneous verbalizations. In a related study, Schill, Evans, Monroe, and Ramanaiah (Note 1) similarly found that rational self-statements facilitated, whereas irrational self-statements interferred with, performance on a mirror tracing task. Rimm and Litvak (1969) also investigated the effects of self-verbalizations on emotional arousal and found that affect-related statements elicited significantly greater emotional reactions (as indicated by breathing rate and depth) than did neutral sentences. May and Johnson (1973) and May (1977) similarly found that affectively-toned self-verbalizations resulted in increased heart rate and respiration. Changes in skin conductance have also been found when subjects are presented with verbal representations of situations previously labeled by them as troublesome, but not when they read statements of neutral, nonemotional content (Russell & Brandsma, 1974).

Although the results of the studies just cited offer support for the basic assumption that self-statements are capable of eliciting emotional responses, a recent report by Rogers and Craighead (1977) offers data that question the general conclusion that negative self-statements mediate emotional arousal. They found that physiological reactivity, as measured by skin conductance, was a function not only of the positive or negative nature of self-statements but also of the extent to which subjects believed such statements to be true of them. Specifically, no differences were found between positive and negative self-statements that had been rated as being either unequivocably true or clearly false for the individual. It was only for those instances in which the subjects believed the statements to be moderately relevant to them that Rogers and Craighead found physiological differences between negative and positive self-statement.

In addition to studies that deal with the influence of covert statements on emotional arousal, research is also needed to determine the consequences of individual variations in self-statements as they occur in the natural environment. Ellis (1962) hypothesizes that individuals' maladaptive emotional reactions are mediated by the nature of their beliefs or expectations about emotionally arousing situations. More specifically, Ellis maintains that certain individuals have a tendency to hold certain irrational beliefs. Among the various irrational ideas described by Ellis are the beliefs that it is essential to be loved and approved of by others and that one should achieve competence and perfection in all one's undertakings. According to Ellis, people who maintain these and other irrational beliefs tend to covertly verbalize their irrational ideas in the situations that produce overemotional responses. To the extent that individuals maintain expectancies that are not consistent with the real status of the world around them, they are more likely to experience disapointment and upset.

Goldfried and Sobocinski (1975) studied the relationship between irrational beliefs and emotional arousal in various types of situations. In a correlational study, significant positive relationships were found between the tendency to think irrationally, as measured by a paper-and-pencil test or irrational beliefs (Jones, Note 2), and measures of interpersonal anxiety, test anxiety, and speech anxiety. In a second experiment, Goldfried and Sobocinski focused on one specific irrational belief—the overriding importance of social approval—and investigated the likelihood of emotional arousal occurring among individuals who ascribe to this belief.

Two groups of subjects, scoring either high or low on the social approval belief, were asked to imagine themselves in several different situations. The first of these consisted of a neutral scene in which subjects were asked to visualize themselves in a bookstore, looking at several books on the shelves. Following this baseline scene, subjects were administered the Multiple Affect Adjective Checklist (Zuckerman & Lubin, 1965) to assess the extent to which they felt anxious, depressed, and angry. They were then asked to imagine themselves in five social situations in which they might conceivably perceive social rejection. One of these situations was as follows:

> One of your girlfriends has invited you to come to a party. Think of a girl you know. You get to her house and you walk through the door. You're standing there now at the door just inside her house. Look around you and you'll see a number of people—people whom you have not met before. And now your girlfriend is walking over to you. She says "hello," and she takes your coat. Try to see her face as vividly as you can. She takes your coat, and goes to put it away. You're standing there by yourself, and when she comes back out she walks over to some other people and starts talking to them. Try to stay in this situation, standing there by yourself, seeing your girlfriend talking to these people, and you're there alone looking around. Just notice how you feel in that situation [Goldfried & Sobocinski, p. 507].

Other situations included not being complimented on one's physical appearance, being excluded from a conversation, being alone on a Saturday night, and not receiving positive feedback during a job interview. The Adjective Checklist was administered at the completion of all five situations. Subjects were then presented with a therapeutic release situation in which they were asked to imagine themselves lying on the beach in the summertime without having any responsibilities or concerns. As is depicted graphically in Figures 5.1, 5.2, and 5.3, subjects who strongly

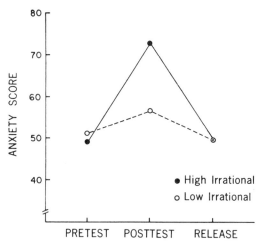

Figure 5.1. MAACL Anxiety rating at baseline, following the imaginal presentation of social rejection situations, and the therapeutic release situation for both high and low irrational conditions. (From Goldfried & Sobocinski, *Journal of Consulting and Clinical Psychology,* 1975, *43,* 508. Copyright 1975 by the American Psychological Association. Reprinted by permission.)

believed in the importance of receiving approval from others reported greater emotional arousal than did subjects for whom this belief was less salient. As can be seen in these figures, after imagining themselves in the therapeutic release situation, all subjects returned to their baseline scores.

Although these findings shed some light on the differential susceptibility to emotional arousal as a function of different types of beliefs, the exact nature of any irrational self-statements generated in response to the experimental conditions was not studied directly. Thus, it is impossible to determine whether or not the high irrationality subjects had a *greater tendency to perceive* the situations as entailing social rejection or whether the upset was primarily a function of the high irrationality subjects' *overgeneralization* of what was observed, such as telling themselves that their rejection in this particular situation is proof of their basic inadequacy as a person.

In a particularly interesting study in which a task analysis of assertive behavior was conducted, Schwartz and Gottman (1976) provide evidence that negative self-statements are associated with unassertive behavior. In comparing individuals who had been predetermined as being either assertive or nonassertive, Schwartz and Gottman found that the two groups could not be distinguished on the basis of their knowledge of what to say in certain assertion-related situations or on their ability to actually demonstrate an assertive response in hypothetical situations. They did differ, however, in their report of self-statements associated with their attempt at behaving assertively in a role-playing situation related to themselves. Specifically, unassertive subjects were found to have emitted fewer positive and more negative self-statements than highly assertive individuals. Conducting a within-condition

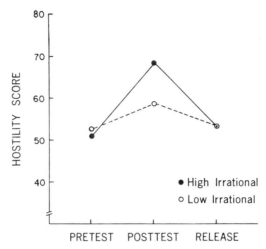

Figure 5.2. MAACL Hostility rating at baseline, following the imaginal presentation of social rejection situations, and the therapeutic release situation for both high and low irrational conditions. (From Goldfried & Sobocinski, 1975, p. 508. Copyright 1975 by the American Psychological Association. Reprinted by permission.)

analysis of the relationship between positive and negative self-statements, Schwartz and Gottman found that the internal dialogue of highly assertive individuals was primarily of a positive nature. For unassertive individuals, on the other hand, there

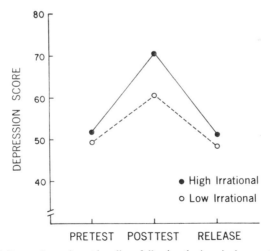

Figure 5.3. MAACL Depression rating at baseline, following the imaginal presentation of social rejection situations, and the therapeutic release situation for both high and low irrational conditions. (From Goldfried & Sobocinski, 1975, p. 508. Copyright 1975 by the American Psychological Association. Reprinted by permission.)

were no differences between positive and negative self-statements, reflecting what Schwartz and Gottman have called an "internal dialogue of conflict." It is also interesting to note that many of the negative self-statements typically reflected excessive concern that the subject had over the reaction of others (e.g., "I was worried about what the other person would think of me if I refused.") These findings have more recently been replicated by Pitcher (Note 3). Similarly, a study by Alden and Safran (1978) revealed that subjects who endorsed a series of irrational beliefs, as outlined by Ellis, also described themselves as being more unassertive and uncomfortable in assertion situations than subjects who tended to disagree with such beliefs, and, in fact, were found to be less assertive during a role-playing assessment.

Although the findings of several studies suggest that irrational self-statements may mediate anxiety, it should be noted that the research has focused exclusively on situations of a social-evaluative nature. It would be an overgeneralization to conclude that all forms of anxiety have their basis in irrational thinking. Indeed, some evidence by Sutton-Simon and Goldfried (1979) indicates that, although acrophobics engage in negative thinking while in height-related situations, such self-statements are unrelated to the rationality of their belief system.

The studies by Goldfried and Sobocinski (1975), Schwartz and Gottman (1976), Pitcher (Note 3), and Alden and Safran (1978) should also be interpreted in light of their correlational nature. It is possible to argue that heightened emotional arousal and unassertive behavior in social situations sensitizes an individual to certain irrational beliefs, rather than the reverse. However, findings from other research (May, 1977; May & Johnson, 1973; Rimm & Litvak, 1969; Russell & Brandsma, 1974; Velten, 1968) also support the contention that self-statements do have the potential for eliciting emotional reactions. Further support—albeit indirect—for the assumption that irrational beliefs precede emotional arousal in social situations comes from several clinical outcome studies that have demonstrated that various forms of social-evaluative anxiety may be alleviated by the direct modification of unrealistic self-statements. Before reviewing some of these studies, however, actual procedures for the clinical implementation of rational restructuring will be outlined.

CLINICAL IMPLEMENTATION OF
RATIONAL RESTRUCTURING

In both our professional and our personal lives, we have all had occasion to witness how cognitive restructuring can reduce anxiety. Within the therapeutic context, the therapist is often successful in helping clients to sort out their fears and concerns. The same is true of nonprofessional support systems, as in the case of concerned friends who help us to place upsetting events into a different perspective. However, the goal of cognitive restructuring, particularly when it is presented as a coping skill (Goldfried, in press), is to provide clients *themselves* with the ability to adopt a more reasonable perspective on potentially upsetting events.

As in the case of any intervention strategy, a given principle may be translated into a therapeutic technique in numerous ways. In the case of cognitive restructuring, the particular therapeutic procedures will vary, depending on one's theoretical orientation and the nature of the stressful situations in question (e.g., Beck, 1976; Ellis, 1962; Goldfried & Davison, 1976; A. A. Lazarus, 1971; Meichenbaum, 1977). Some of the similarities and differences among the currently available procedures are discussed by Meichenbaum (1977) and will not be repeated here. Suffice it to say that we do not as yet know which of any of our available intervention techniques is most effective.

A typical approach in persuading or teaching clients to think more reasonably has been characterized by heated arguments in which the therapist attempts to convince clients that unreasonable beliefs are responsible for their emotional reactions to problematic situations (Ellis, 1962). Often, the arguments reflect disagreement on several different issues that might be better dealt with in a more systematic and Socratic fashion. Systematic procedures for incorporating the basic tenets of Ellis' therapeutic approach within a more clearly defined social learning framework have been outlined in detail elsewhere (e.g., Goldfried, 1976; Goldfried & Davison, 1976; Goldfried, Decenteceo, & Weinberg, 1974; Goldfried & Goldfried, 1975) and will, therefore, only be touched upon briefly here. Specifically, the steps that are associated with what has been referred to as *systematic rational restructuring* will be reviewed.

Helping Clients Recognize That Self-Statements Mediate Emotional Arousal

The initial discussion leading to this acceptance is generally more theoretical than personal. The therapist's goal is to help clients recognize the general assumption that their emotional reactions can be directly influenced by labels, expectations, and self-statements. Because of the overlearned nature of many expectations and beliefs, it should be emphasized that many of such assumptions occur more or less automatically, rather than being carefully thought out. Thus, it is important that clients accept the premise that, even though they may not deliberately *tell themselves* certain things prior to or during emotionally upsetting situations, they nonetheless react disproportionately *as if* they view the situation in a given way. When presented in a simple and objective manner, it is rare to find clients who cannot accept this basic premise.

Helping Clients See the Irrationality of Certain Beliefs

Once the clients have agreed that their emotional reactions can be mediated by thoughts and self-statements, it is important to have them acknowledge the irrational or unrealistic nature of a series of beliefs that individuals frequently hold. The two beliefs that most typically appear in clinical cases are (*a*) the expectation that it is essential to receive approval and love from others in order to have any feelings of self-worth; and (*b*) the notion that perfection is required in all accomplishments in order to see oneself as anything but a failure.

Instead of trying verbally to convince clients that these thoughts are irrational, the social psychological literature suggests that the therapist could more effectively promote attitude change by having the clients *themselves* offer arguments to support the irrationality of these beliefs (Janis & King, 1954; King & Janis, 1956). Thus, the therapist can play devil's advocate, giving clients the task of providing as many reasons as possible to convince the seemingly irrational therapist that his or her views are untenable. The ultimate objective of this step is to prompt clients not only to agree that certain beliefs are irrational but also to generate specific reasons for the unreasonableness of these views (e.g., "If other people disagree with you, that doesn't mean they dislike you."). During the fourth phase of the treatment procedure, these reasons may be personalized (e.g., changing "you" to "me") and used as coping self-statements. At this point, however, everything is discussed on an objective basis; by minimizing personal involvement, it makes it easier for the client to generate believable counterarguments.

Helping Clinets Understand That Unrealistic Self-Statements Mediate Their Own Maladaptive Emotions

Following the second step, some clients spontaneously acknowledge that they can see where certain irrational assumptions are particularly relevant to their own emotional reactions. In other cases, it may be necessary to explore systematically various emotionally arousing situations of the clients' current life in an attempt to investigate and enhance their awareness of the irrational expectations influencing their anxiety. By gradually and systematically guiding clients through this third phase, the typical conclusion reached by them is that what they need to learn is how to stop thinking irrationally in certain situations. The situations reviewed in this phase can be arranged in a hierarchy, as in desensitization.

Helping Clients to Modify Their Unrealistic Self-Statements

Up until this point, much of what has gone on during the clinical interaction has been intellectual and theoretical. In much the same way that relaxation skills are not particularly effective in reducing anxiety if they are not *used* by the individual in potentially upsetting situations (e.g., Goldfried & Trier, 1974), so thinking rationally probably has minimal therapeutic impact if it is not employed when clients are experiencing anxiety. Although many individuals can put upsetting events into realistic perspective at a later point in time, the purpose of this, the most crucial phase in the therapeutic procedure, involves using the clients' hindsight ability to enable them to reevaluate situations rationally *before or during* the situations themselves. A convenient way for providing clients with practice in using rational reevaluation as a coping mechanism is via imaginal presentations of anxiety-arousing scenes. In many respects, it parallels self-control desensitization (Goldfried, 1971) in that clients maintain the image while attempting to cope. Clients may be instructed to "think aloud" so that the therapist can prompt and otherwise assist them in evaluating and modifying unrealistic assumptions.

A technique that has been found to be most useful clinically in assisting clients to ferret out unrealistic assumptions associated with anxiety-arousing situations involves the use of incomplete sentences. Specifically, the therapist can prompt the client at appropriate times during hierarchy presentation with such phrases as "If I stumbled over a word during this speech I'd be upset because...." and "If people noticed I made a mistake it would bother me because...." In completing these sentences, clients are often better able to recognize, and then to reevaluate, their unrealistic expectations in anxiety-related situations. In addition to using this technique for imaginal rehearsal in the consultation session, clients are urged to apply this procedure in real-life situations.

RESULTS OF CLINICAL OUTCOME RESEARCH

Until very recently, most of the empirical support for the effectiveness of rational–emotive therapy has been based on clinical case-reports (Ellis, 1962). Within the past several years, however, the positive findings of several controlled-outcome studies have added stronger evidence for the clinical utility of this approach. A comprehensive review of the literature may be found in Ellis and Grieger (1977). The review that follows specifically covers the clinical research on three target problems: speech, test, and interpersonal anxiety.

Speech Anxiety

In one of the earliest well-controlled studies on the use of a cognitively oriented approach to the reduction of speech anxiety, Meichenbaum, Gilmore, and Fedoravicious (1971) studied the effectiveness of systematic desensitization, rational–emotive therapy, and a combined desensitization and rational–emotive package, utilizing both attention placebo and waiting-list control groups. All therapy was carried out in groups, and rational–emotive therapy primarily consisted of discussions of the irrational self-statements that typically occur in a number of anxiety-provoking interpersonal situations, including public speaking. On the basis of behavioral and subjective estimates of anxiety during an actual speech-giving situation, the authors found that rational–emotive therapy and systematic densensitization were comparably effective and better than either of the control conditions. These improvement effects were maintained at a 3-month follow-up. They also noted that the combined treatment procedure was somewhat less effective than either systematic desensitization or rational–emotive therapy alone, possibly because, in combination, neither of the two procedures could be fully implemented within the eight-session treatment. From a post hoc analysis, Meichenbaum *et al.* also present some particularly intriguing data suggesting that systematic desensitization may be more effective in cases of circumscribed speech anxiety, whereas rational–emotive therapy seems to produce greater change when anxiety in public speaking situations is part of a larger network of social–evaluative anxiety.

Trexler and Karst (1972) have similarly used rational–emotive therapy in the group treatment of speech anxiety and have compared its effectiveness with attention placebo and waiting-list controls. Participants in the rational–emotive condition discussed the ways in which irrational ideas contributed to their feelings of anxiety in speech-giving and in other interpersonal situations. Although the findings indicated that rational–emotive therapy resulted in improvement on some measures (the Personal Report of Confidence As a Speaker and the Irrational Beliefs Test), other measures (behavioral indicators of anxiety during a speech) failed to show improvement. This is in contrast to the results of Meichenbaum *et al.*, who found improvement on virtually all of their measures of speech anxiety. A number of factors could explain these discrepant findings, including the fact that Meichenbaum *et al.* used more experienced therapists and conducted the treatment over eight, as opposed to four, sessions. In addition, because the actual rational–emotive procedures employed in both studies are described in only general terms, it is difficult to determine the extent to which the treatments themselves may have differed in these two reports.

The relative effectiveness of systematic rational restructuring and self-control desensitization (Goldfried, 1971) was investigated by Casas (Note 4). Casas used the standard dependent variables employed in outcome research in this area, such as giving a speech before a live audience, subjective measures of anxiety, physiological measures, and a variety of questionnaires. Anxiety reduction was found to be comparable for both treatment groups but not significantly different from a waiting-list control, a finding that might very well be attributed to the brevity of the treatment (four group sessions over a 2-week period). One interesting post hoc finding that emerged, however, was that, within the rational restructuring group, subjects who scored high on the Fear of Negative Evaluation Scale improved significantly more than those whose scores were low. That this interaction was not obtained within the other two conditions suggests that rational restructuring may be particularly appropriate in instances in which speech-anxious individuals manifest excessive concern over the opinions of others.

The post hoc findings of Casas, which are consistent with the post hoc results reported by Meichenbaum *et al.* (1971), were followed up in a study by Fremouw and Zitter (1978). In comparing the relative effectiveness of cognitive restructuring plus relaxation training versus skills training, Fremouw and Zitter divided their speech-anxious subjects into high and low socially anxious groups. The former treatment package consisted of training subjects in the use of relaxation as a coping skill and replacing negative self-statements (e.g., "I will sound stupid.") with coping statements (e.g., "I can only improve."). The skills training condition involved modeling, behavior rehearsal, and videotaped feedback of performance in practice speech-giving situations. Their results indicate that both treatment procedures—carried out in five group sessions—were effective in reducing speech anxiety when compared with waiting list and placebo controls. Although skills training was comparably effective for high and low socially anxious groups, non-significant trends indicated greater superiority of cognitive restructuring–relaxation training for high as compared with low socially anxious subjects. It would be important to replicate this study, providing subjects more than five sessions to learn the cognitive restructuring and coping relaxation skills.

In another outcome study combining cognitive restructuring and coping relaxation in the treatment of speech anxiety, Weissberg (1977) compared systematic desensitizations, desensitization plus coping imagery (i.e., involving slow, deep breathing and the use of task-relevant self-statements during hierarchy presentation), and cognitive modification (i.e., coping by means of deep breathing, task-relevant self-statements, and realistic, anxiety-inhibiting statements). The findings of this study revealed no consistent superiority of any treatment procedure, although there were some "trends" that suggest the greater effectiveness of the cognitive-modification procedure. As in the case of the Fremouw and Zitter study, however, the three weekly 2-hour group sessions may simply have been too brief to have adequately tested the effectiveness of the intervention procedures.

In an interesting study to determine the feasibility of using peers as therapists, Fremouw and Harmatz (1975) studied the effectiveness of a treatment package that combined the use of both rational self-statements and relaxation as coping skills, together with training in public speaking. The four conditions that were compared consisted of helpers (who worked with another speech anxious subject), helpees (who were trained by the helpers), latent helpers (who received the same training as the helpers, but worked with subjects only after posttesting), and waiting-list control subjects. The dependent measures included a speech in front of a live audience, and various paper-and-pencil measures of anxiety. The results indicated that both the helper and the helpee groups showed comparably significant improvement that was maintained at follow-up. Although the latent helpers also improved, the change was not as clear-cut at posttest. However, after they worked with the waiting-list subject, latent-helper improvement matched up to that obtained by the helper and the helpee conditions. These findings suggest that, even though the latent helpers had the coping skills in their repertoire, these skills were not as effective until they were given adequate opportunity to apply them.

In general, the outcome findings, when taken together, indicate that training subjects to reevaluate realistically their performance in public-speaking situations can be an effective procedure for reducing speech anxiety. Whether it is more effective than systematic desensitization or other intervention procedures continues to remain an open question, although there is reason to believe that cognitive restructuring may be particularly suited to public-speaking anxiety that is less situation-specific and more reflective of social-evaluative anxiety. However, this hypothesis is in need of further testing and would require outcome research that provides treatment over a longer time-period than has typically been the case.

Test Anxiety

Based on the assumption that test anxiety may be composed of both "worry" and "emotionality" components (Liebert & Morris, 1967; Mandler & Watson, 1966; Marlett & Watson, 1968; Morris & Liebert, 1970), Meichenbaum (1972) developed an eight-session group treatment package involving cognitive restructuring and a modified systematic desensitization. Specifically, test-anxious subjects were given relaxation training, discussed potential irrational thoughts underlying test anxiety, and then were provided with imaginal practice in coping with anxiety in test-related situations by means of relaxation and self-instructions to focus on only the test itself. Compared with traditional systematic desensitization, this cognitive-modification treatment package produced greater pre–post reductions in test anxiety, as determined by subjective anxiety, performance in an analog test situation, and grade-point average.

A recent study by Goldfried, Linehan, and Smith (1978) investigated the effects of rational restructuring alone in the reduction of test anxiety. To overcome the difficulties typically associated with obtaining a sufficiently large number of participants in outcome research, this study was first done at Stony Brook and was then replicated at Catholic University. The objectives of this research strategy were to increase the participant pool, to enhance the generalizability of the findings, and to demonstrate that collaborative outcome research is possible (cf. Bergin & Strupp, 1970). The same assessment procedures were used in both settings, and, to insure standardization of treatment, therapy manuals were utilized and tape recordings of pilot therapy groups were exchanged by the two therapists as cross-checks on consistency of the therapy program. The subjects, undergraduates who responded to various announcements describing the test-anxiety program, were assigned to rational restructuring, prolonged exposure, or a waiting-list control. The two treatment conditions consisted of six group-therapy sessions.

In the rational restructuring conditions, the subjects were exposed to a 15-item standardized hierarchy based on a preliminary analysis of their scores on the Suinn Test Anxiety Behavior Scale (Suinn, 1969). Prior to the actual implementation of rational restructuring, the therapist served as a model in which he or she imagined being in a test situation while "thinking aloud," demonstrating the process of rational reevaluation. Each hierarchy item was then presented for a total of four 1-minute exposures during which subjects were asked to "remain" imaginally in the scene, to tune into their self-defeating thoughts (e.g., "I'm going to fail this test, and then everyone's going to think I'm stupid."), and to attempt to reevaluate their reactions more realistically (e.g., "Chances are I probably won't fail. And even if I do, people probably won't think I'm stupid. And even if they do, that doesn't mean that I *am* stupid."). Following each trial, subjects recorded their thoughts and feelings on a special in-session record form and discussed their experiences during the imaginal situations as a group after the fourth trial presentation.

The prolonged-exposure condition served as a control for exposure to the test-anxiety hierarchy items as well as to any nonspecific factors associated with receiving treatment. The rationale presented to the subjects in this condition emphasized the importance of habituation and extinction in the reduction of anxiety. The same hierarchy was used for subjects in the rational restructuring and prolonged-exposure conditions. Subjects in this condition, however, were instructed only to focus on their emotional reactions during each of the four 1-minute exposures. Following the final presentation of each item, a group discussion was carried out so that group members could share their experiences.

The data analysis revealed a consistent pattern: On the basis of various questionnaire measures of test anxiety (e.g., S-R Inventory of Anxiousness, Suinn Test Anxiety Behavior scale), greater pre–post anxiety reduction was found for subjects in the rational restructuring condition, followed by those having undergone prolonged exposure of the same hierarchy items, with no changes emerging on the pre- and posttesting for a waiting-list control. These findings were maintained at follow-up. Furthermore, only subjects in the rational restructuring condition reported a decrease in subjective anxiety when placed in an analogue test-taking situation. Although the rational restructuring procedure was generally found to be superior to prolonged exposure, it is of considerable interest that exposure alone also produced significant anxiety reduction. We have observed this same finding in the case of speech anxiety (Goldfried & Goldfried, 1977), which further adds to the finding of a number of other studies (e.g., Aponte & Aponte, 1971; Barrett, 1969; Calef & MacLean, 1970; D'Zurilla, Wilson, & Nelson, 1973; Malleson, 1959; McGlynn, 1973; Mylar & Clement, 1972; Raimy, 1975; Wilson & Davison, 1971) that suggest that prolonged exposure is a viable therapeutic manipulation—although not as effective as exposure together with some active coping procedure.

The Goldfried et al. (1978) findings raise the question of whether the simple presence of a cognitive restructuring component, and not the combined cognitive and relaxation aspects of the treatment, might in itself have been responsible for the anxiety reduction found by Meichenbaum (1972). This question was investigated directly by Osarchuk (Note 5) in an outcome study evaluating the relative effectiveness of rational restructuring and of self-control desensitization in the treatment of test anxiety.

Subjects for Osarchuk's study were selected from college-student volunteers who responded to announcements describing a "Test Anxiety Program." The therapy was carried out in group settings over a 6-week period. The four treatment procedures consisted of self-control desensitization, rational restructuring, self-control desensitization plus rational restructuring, and prolonged exposure. The self-control desensitization procedure was based on the guidelines outlined by Goldfried (1971), and the hierarchy was the same as that used in the study by Goldfried et al. (1978); all four treatment groups used this same hierarchy. The subjects assigned to rational restructuring, instead of imagining themselves in each of these situations and relaxing, were taught to reevaluate realistically the test-taking situation. The combined desensitization and rational restructuring procedure involved training in the use of both relaxation and rational restructuring. These subjects were given practice in relaxing away their experienced anxiety and then placing the test-taking situation into a more realistic perspective. Subjects in the prolonged exposure condition were told that therapy would help them habituate to test-taking situations and that they would learn to bring about extinction by focusing on their anxiety while remaining in the situation. They received imaginal exposure to the hierarchy items and were instructed in the use of focused attention on their feelings of tension. The pretest, posttest, and 2-month follow-up assessment batteries were the same as those employed in the Goldfried *et al.* (1978) study. Although no differences among conditions were found in the analogue test-taking situations, various subjective measures revealed that self-control desensitization, rational restructuring, and combined desensitization and rational restructuring were equally effective but superior to the prolonged exposure. That these differences were due to the nature of the treatment procedures themselves is supported by the finding that the credibility of therapy and the confidence and ability of therapists were rated comparably across the four conditions.

Results somewhat discrepant from these were obtained by Holroyd (1976), who similarly attempted to dismantle the cognitive and relaxation components of Meichenbaum's (1972) cognitive-modification treatment package for test anxiety. The four conditions, each of which was carried out over seven group sessions, consisted of cognitive therapy (getting subjects to reevaluate rationally anxiety-arousing self-statements and then to focus on the task at hand), group desensitization, a combined cognitive therapy and desensitization, and an attention placebo control. On the basis of serveral measures (e.g., performance and anxiety in an analogue testing situation, grade-point average), the cognitive-therapy procedure was found to be more effective than the other methods. The relative inferiority of the combined treatment package parallels the findings noted by Meichenbaum *et al.* (1971) in the case of speech anxiety.

An important distinction between the Osarchuk and Holroyd studies consists of the framework within which the desensitization and cognitive procedures were presented to subjects. Although Osarchuk provided all subjects with a coping orientation (i.e., they were going to learn a procedure for actively and independently reducing their anxiety), Holroyd provided this orientation *only* to subjects undergoing cognitive therapy. Subjects in the desensitization condition were provided with the standard rationale. In a relevant factorial study on the relationship between treatment procedure and therapeutic orientation, May (Note 6) found cognitive and relaxation procedures to be comparably effective in the group treatment of test anxiety. However, subjects provided with a coping orientation to the therapeutic intervention improved more than subjects for whom the therapy was described within more of a passive framework. These same findings were obtained by Denney and Rupert (1977).

Taken together, the research on test anxiety suggests that a combined therapy program using both cognitive procedures and self-control desensitization is no more effective than a therapeutic intervention program that deals primarily with either of these two components separately. The finding by Meichenbaum (1972) that a combined treatment package was more effective than desensitization may have been more a function of the "coping" emphasis inherent in his treatment package than a function of the fact that it contained relaxation and cognitive components. Holroyd's finding that a cognitive approach was superior to desensitization must be similarly interpreted in light of the coping emphasis given to subjects in this condition.

Interpersonal Anxiety

The relevance of rational restructuring for interpersonal anxiety is frequently observed within clinical settings, where clients' complaints of anxiety in social situations are often accompanied by excessive concern about the reactions of others. Studies of socially anxious individuals have found them to be more concerned over the evaluation of others, more desirous of avoiding disapproval, and more likely to perceive feedback from others as being negative (Smith, 1972; Smith & Sarason, 1975). As noted earlier, empirical support for the contention that unrealistic self-statements may mediate various forms of social-evaluative anxiety comes from Goldfried and Sobocinski (1975), who found that the tendency to hold irrational beliefs was positively correlated with paper-and-pencil measures of social anxiety. Goldfried and Sobocinski further found that individuals who unrealistically expected approval from others experienced greater emotional upset when imagining themselves in social situations that might be interpreted as involving rejection by others than did individuals who had fewer such expectations.

Considering this evidence, an approach to anxiety reduction that teaches clients to reevaluate realistically the consequences of their behavior in various situations would seem to be particularly relevant when anxiety primarily centers around social-evaluative interactions. This point received peripheral support from the post hoc findings of Meichenbaum *et al.* (1971) that rational–emotive therapy was more effective than desensitization when clients' speech anxiety was accompanied by anxiety in other interpersonal situations and of Casas (Note 4), who observed rational restructuring to be more effective for speech-anxious individuals who were excessively concerned over the opinions of others.

One of the earliest studies to focus directly on the effectiveness of rational–emotive therapy in the treatment of interpersonal anxiety was conducted by DiLoreto (1971). Using undergraduates who volunteered for a program on the reduction of interpersonal anxiety, rational–emotive therapy was compared with systematic desensitization, client-centered therapy, an attention-placebo discussion group, and a waiting-list control. Each of the therapy conditions was conducted within a group setting and carried out over a 9-week period. DiLoreto also studied the

interaction between type of client and effectiveness of treatment by assigning introverts and extroverts to each of the five conditions. On the basis of a variety of
measures (e.g., questionnaire measures of social anxiety, behavioral signs of anxiety during an actual social interaction, as well as questionnaire measures of general
anxiety), the results indicated that the three-treatment procedures produced significantly greater reductions in anxiety than either the placebo or the waiting-list controls. In general, however, the desensitization procedure was superior to the other
two. Although systematic desensitization was comparably effective for extroverts
and for introverts, the rational–emotive therapy was found to be effective for only
the introverted, but not the extroverted, subjects. When one looks only at the results
for introverts, rational–emotive therapy turns out to be just as effective as the
desensitization. Although there are, undoubtedly, a number of ways to interpret
these data (e.g., introverted subjects may be more susceptible to attitude change
than extroverted individuals), a close inspection of DiLoreto's data reveals that
introverted subjects were more anxious interpersonally. This is a particularly relevant consideration, especially in light of the subject population used in the study.
That is, out of a class of 600 undergraduates, no less than 100 qualified as being
"socially anxious." In looking at the data for only the more anxious subjects, then,
the rational–emotive condition produced just as much change as did desensitization.

A further test of the effectiveness of cognitive therapy for interpersonal anxiety
(Kanter & Goldfried, 1979) also evaluated the possibility that individuals experiencing high levels of anxiety might encounter difficulties in applying a cognitive
restructuring procedure. In clinical contexts, highly anxious clients frequently report that they are "too anxious to think straight." This is consistent with the
experimental evidence indicating that subjects typically find it difficult to use complex mental processes when experiencing high levels of anxiety (Gaudry & Spielberger, 1971; Lazarus, 1966; Spielberger, 1966). Highly anxious subjects might,
therefore, require preliminary relaxation training before rational restructuring could
prove to be effective, whereas a treatment package involving both relaxation and
rational restructuring should be no more effective than rational restructuring alone in
the case of individuals for whom social anxiety was less severe.

The study employed a 2 × 4 design in which anxiety level (high versus moderate)
was crossed with treatment procedure (rational restructuring, self-control desensitization, rational restructuring plus self-control desensitization, or waiting-list control). The distinction between high versus moderate anxiety level was based on a
median split of the scores obtained on the Social Avoidance and Distress scale
(Watson & Friend, 1969). The participants in this study were community residents
who responded to newspaper announcements of a therapy program focusing on the
reduction of interpersonal anxiety. The therapy was carried out in a group setting
over seven weekly sessions of approximately 1½ hours each.

The results of the Kanter and Goldfried study indicated that each of the three
therapeutic procedures resulted in significant decrements in anxiety at posttesting;
these decrements were either maintained or improved upon at follow-up. Although
rational restructuring, desensitization, and the combined treatment were effective in

reducing anxiety, the overall pattern of the findings indicated that they were not equally effective. Between-group comparisons at posttesting revealed that rational restructuring was more effective than desensitization in reducing state anxiety, trait anxiety, and irrational beliefs. When compared with waiting-list controls, rational restructuring was also significantly more effective on a greater number of variables than was desensitization. Rational restructuring also produced significant within-group improvement on many more variables than did desensitization. Finally, there was a greater tendency for rational restructuring to result in generalization of anxiety reduction to nonsocial situations. Some of these findings are presented graphically in Figure 5.4. It should be emphasized that these results were based primarily on the self-report measures of anxiety; the findings for the behavioral signs of anxiety and for pulse rate failed to differentiate among conditions.

It is unlikely that the superiority of rational restructuring was attributable to differential expectation of success or demand characteristics associated with the different treatment conditions. Participants in each of the four conditions were initially comparable with regard to their expectancy for improvement, and the rationale presented for each of the three treatment procedures did not differentially alter this expectancy.

Contrary to expectation, no interaction was obtained between anxiety level and effectiveness of treatment procedure. There are several possible reasons for this finding. To begin with, the pretest anxiety scores for participants tended to be high

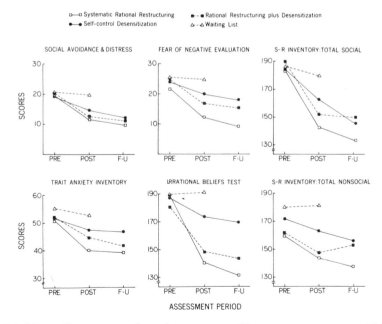

Figure 5.4. Mean self-report scores for each treatment condition at pretest, posttest, and follow-up assessments. (From Kanter and Goldfried, 1979.)

relative to what has been reported in previous outcome studies (e.g., DiLoreto, 1971; Meichenbaum *et al.*, 1971). Although this may indicate that they were similar to those typically found in an actual clinical setting, the nature of this population may have inadvertently precluded meaningful classification of individuals into two distinct levels of anxiety. Another possibility is that the hierarchical presentation of increasingly more anxiety-provoking items may have undermined the disrupting effects of anxiety level. Still another explanation might lie in the use of the Social Avoidance and Distress scale (Watson & Friend, 1969) to designate anxiety level, since this scale may be assessing pervasiveness of anxiety rather than absolute level of anxiety. That is, participants who score high on this scale may be reporting that they experience anxiety in a number of different situations, quite independent of the amount of anxiety experienced in any one.

In light of the results obtained by DiLoreto (1971), it is somewhat surprising that desensitization was not more effective in reducing social anxiety. The discrepant findings may best be interpreted in light of some of the differences between DiLoreto's research and the Kanter and Goldfried study. To begin with, the desensitization procedure used by Kanter and Goldfried was presented within a self-control framework in which participants were instructed to use anxiety as a signal to relax during continued scene visualization. In contrast, DiLoreto employed desensitization as originally outlined by Wolpe (1958). However, this difference cannot adequately explain the discrepancy, since data from other outcome research indicate that the self-control variation of desensitization is equal to, if not more effective than, standard desensitization (Goldfried, 1977). A second major difference between the two studies involves the nature of the subject population employed. DiLoreto used a population of undergraduates who were not nearly as socially anxious as the community residents that comprised the Kanter and Goldfried sample. That pretreatment anxiety level may be an important factor in the effectiveness of a cognitive intervention procedure was noted by Meichenbaum *et al.* (1971), Casas (Note 4), and even DiLoreto (1971) himself. The fact that Kanter and Goldfried's participants were more socially anxious than those in DiLoreto's study, then, may very well have accounted for the superiority of rational restructuring over desensitization. Although this interpretation is, seemingly, a direct contradiction of the original expectation that high levels of anxiety would interfer with the effectiveness of rational restructuring, the hypothesis was based on the debilitating effects of high states of anxiety on cognitive processes. As already suggested, however, by using the Social Avoidance and Distress Scale as the measure of anxiety, Kanter and Goldfried may have inadvertently been assessing pervasiveness or "trait" anxiety rather than intensity or "state" anxiety (Cattell & Scheier, 1960).

Another form of interpersonal anxiety that has been the target of cognitive restructuring procedures consists of unassertive behavior. Although the absence of assertive behavior has traditionally been construed in the behavior therapy literature as reflecting a skill deficit—that is, the appropriate behaviors do not exist within the individual's response repertoire—there is abundant anecdotal evidence that clients frequently show dramatic increases in assertive behavior after having carefully considered the consequences of engaging in such behavior (Goldfried & Davison, 1976; Lange & Jakubowski, 1976). In these instances, the clients' assertion problems appear to be maintained by an unrealistic concern over the possible reactions of others (e.g., disapproval) and not by an actual inability to emit the assertive response itself. If this clinical observation is, in fact, true, then a lack of assertive behavior may be more appropriately construed as a reflection of social-evaluative anxiety than as a behavioral deficit.

This hypothesis was directly investigated by Linehan, Goldfried, and Goldfried (1979), who also addressed the issue of whether sex of the therapist plays an important role in the effectiveness of assertion training with women. Although the argument is often informally made that female clients are more likely to show therapeutic progress with female as opposed to male therapists, there has been little evidence to date that directly bears on this question. In light of the large number of community residents involved in this study ($N = 79$), it was carried out in sequential waves, and also at both Catholic University and Stony Brook. A 2×5 factorial design was employed, in which sex of therapist (female versus male) was crossed with treatment procedure (behavior rehearsal, rational restructuring, behavioral rehearsal plus rational restructuring, attention placebo, and waiting-list control). The participants in the study, all of whom were women over the age of 21, were respondents to announcements advertising an Assertion Training Program.

Each client in the treatment conditions was seen for a total of eight individual therapy sessions. A total of eight different therapists (four male and four female) who were either advanced clinical psychology graduate students or postdoctoral fellows were used. Detailed therapy manuals were drawn up for each procedure, and consistency in implementing the procedures across therapists was maintained by means of training tapes, role playing, and detailed supervision of sessions. The behavior rehearsal, rational restructuring, and behavior rehearsal plus rational restructuring procedures employed the same hypothetical assertion situations for training purposes and made use of therapist modeling, coaching, feedback, and between-session homework assignments. The primary focus within the behavior rehearsal condition consisted of training in various behavioral components of assertiveness, such as adequate eye contact, content of assertive responses, and verbal style. In the rational restructuring condition, the training focused solely on learning to anticipate more rationally the consequences of an assertive response, and not on the behavior itself. In the combined behavior rehearsal plus rational restructuring condition, participants were taught to reevaluate rationally the possible consequences of assertion and then to practice the actual assertive response. The attention-placebo condition was based on a modified version of client-centered therapy and consisted of reflection of feeling, clarification, and questioning, thereby controlling for any nonspecific factors (i.e., nonspecific vis-à-vis the behavioral procedures) associated with receiving treatment. All waiting-list subjects received group assertion training (employing a combination of the already named procedures) following the completion of the posttesting. The assessment procedures employed an extended interaction role-playing measure, a quasi-unobtrusive situation test of assertiveness (i.e., having to assert oneself to a confederate interferring with the subjects' performance on a task), and a questionnaire battery containing self-report measures of assertiveness.

Although the interpretation of results is complicated somewhat by the number and type of outcome measures used as well as by the variety of comparisons possible, certain conclusions are, nonetheless, clear. In general, it was found that a combined intervention procedure employing both behavior rehearsal and rational restructuring was the most effective in increasing assertive behavior and in reducing the emotional discomfort associated with such interactions. Participants in the behavior-rehearsal procedure showed greater gains on measures of overt assertion when compared with these in conditions not having a behavior rehearsal component. Rational restructuring alone, in which clients were taught to reevaluate more realistically the consequences of behaving assertively but were not trained in what to say or in how to say it, resulted in improvement comparable to those found from behavior rehearsal on the basis of a questionnaire measure of assertiveness. Participants in rational restructuring were also able to persist as long as clients in those conditions employing behavior rehearsal when confronted with an extended interaction role-playing test. Although the content of their responses was not as assertive as the other two behavioral interventions, it was superior to both control groups.

The finding that combined behavior rehearsal and rational restructuring was the most effective procedure is particularly interesting, especially in light of the past research using a combined treatment package of cognitive restructuring and desensitization that has failed to demonstrate the efficacy of such interventions (Holroyd, 1976; Meichenbaum et al., 1971). This finding may be due to the duration and detailed nature of the treatment (i.e., eight individual sessions with specific between-session homework assignments) and/or to the particular nature of the target problem in question; Lange and Jakubowski (1976) and Wolfe and Fodor (1975) have suggested that training in both rational thinking and behavioral skills is required for facilitating assertive behavior.

Another major finding was that sex of therapist was not a significant factor in facilitating assertiveness among the female participants. No differences were found between male and female therapists on any measure, nor was there any interaction between sex of therapist and sex of the other person in the assertion situations comprising the dependent measures. Although these findings are clear and unequivocal, care must be taken as to how they are interpreted. For example, it would be an overgeneralization to view these findings as evidence for the absence of any differential effects of sex of therapist in actual clinical settings. Those who have written about biases that may be associated with sex of therapist in working with female clients (e.g., Barrett, Berg, Eaton, & Pomeroy, 1974; Chesler, 1972) have suggested that the therapist's values and theoretical orientation come into play particularly when selecting the overall goals for therapy and deciding on the specific intervention procedures. Inasmuch as the concept of assertiveness reflects values that are congruent with the changing role of women, one can argue that therapist bias would have little effect on the outcome of assertion training. Within the context of the study in question, potential bias may have been undercut by virtue of a built-in agreement between client and therapist that the goal was to facilitate assertive behavior. In the case of the behaviorally oriented procedures, the specific behaviors that were used to operationally define assertiveness were directly written into the therapy training manuals. What might be concluded, then, is that within a predetermined assertion therapy program, particularly where the guidelines and number of sessions are clearly specified, sex of therapist plays no role in differentially facilitating behavior change.

In designing the treatment packages for this study, Linehan *et al.* were mindful of the possibility that increased assertiveness might not uniformly result in positive reinforcement from others. In light of societal prejudices that tend to discourage assertive behavior in women, Linehan *et al.* took extra care in preparing their clients for possible negative reactions to their newfound assertive behavior pattern. Thus, some of the situations used in the training, as well as some used for the dependent measures, involved receiving verbal criticism from another individual following the client's assertive response. Not only does it appear that the interventions were successful in maintaining change, but clients in the rational restructuring and behavior rehearsal conditions also actually reported increasing their assertive behavior between the end of treatment and the follow-up.

In concluding the discussion of this particular study, a point needs to be made about the use of role playing as an assessment procedure in assertion-therapy research. As noted by Goldfried and Linehan (1977), the use of a role-playing test in assertion training studies—where one of the essential components of the treatment program typically includes role-playing for purposes of behavior rehearsal—should cause us to question seriously the possibility that subjects are simply being taught to perform more adequately during the assessment. Although the Linehan *et al.* study revealed that essentially the same findings were obtained on role-playing situations that were not used as part of the therapy, the very close parallel between behavior rehearsal and those assertion components scored during role-playing assessment causes us to question the generalizability of the findings. The need for this caution became strikingly apparent during posttesting. Participants in the treatment conditions employing behavior rehearsal had been provided with a set of written guidelines pointing out that appropriately assertive interactions involved maintenance of good eye contact, absence of apologetic remarks, appropriate loudness of response, and other essential components typically associated with assertive behavior. During the posttest assessment, several participants were observed studying these guidelines while waiting for the role-playing test! It should be noted, however, that several participants in each of the three behavioral treatment conditions also reported that they frequently referred to their coaching aids when attempting to engage in assertive behavior in their natural environments. In fact, several participants in the rational restructuring condition told their therapists that, between sessions, they frequently recited to themselves their memorized lists of "rational" self-statements (e.g., "I can still feel good about myself even though someone else is annoyed at me."). The influence of these written guidelines in producing assertive behavior in both the natural environment and the role-play test remains an unanswered question.

In a related study on assertion training with women, Wolfe and Fodor (1977) compared a skill-acquisition program entailing modelling and behavior rehearsal with a procedure that additionally made use of rational–emotive therapy. Although the skill acquisition and acquisition plus rational–emotive therapy programs produced comparable improvements on a role-playing assessment measure, each of these procedures was significantly better than either consciousness-raising or waiting-list control. Interestingly enough, however, only the condition incorporating rational–emotive therapy resulted in significant decrements in subjective anxiety during the role-playing assessment.

Other recent studies have similarly supported the clinical effectiveness of the use of rational self-statements in reducing unassertive behavior. Thorpe (1975) pitted rational therapy against behavior rehearsal, desensitization, and placebo conditions in the treatment of unassertive behavior. He found that training subjects to reevaluate rationally the consequences of their assertive behavior was as effective as skill-training procedures. Similar findings were obtained in studies by Alden, Safran, and Waldman (in press) and by Carmody (1978). An additional interesting finding by Thorpe was that the self-instruction procedure was more effective than desensitization, which is consistant with the results obtained by Kanter and Goldfried (1979) for social anxiety. In a study on the maintenance of the effects of assertion training, Martorano, Nietzel, and Melnick (Note 7) compared rational restructuring and a covert modeling procedure that taught participants how to deal with noncompliance to their assertive response. Consistent with the results of Linehan *et al.* (1979), both conditions resulted in comparable improvement on self-report measures of assertiveness, although covert modeling proved to be more effective on the role-playing assessment procedures. At a follow-up assessment involving an unobtrusive phone call, participants in both conditions were found to be comparably assertive. Finally, a study by Glass, Gottman, and Shmurak (1976) with heterosexually shy college males found that a treatment procedure emphasizing the use of rational self-statements was significantly more effective in improving heterosexual interaction than was an intervention procedure emphasizing skill training.

It may be concluded that social-evaluative anxiety can be effectively reduced by an intervention procedure that trains clients to reevaluate realistically their behavior in social situations. Evidence also exists that such a procedure is more effective than is desensitization. Furthermore, training individuals to reevaluate rationally the potential consequences of behaving assertively may, at times, be just as effective as skill training procedures, although a combination of both procedures is likely to be most beneficial. The results of the various outcome studies comparing the effectiveness of skill training and cognitive techniques of facilitating assertive behavior cast serious doubt on the contention that unassertive behavior is best construed as a skill deficit. This conclusion is consistent with the results of Schwartz and Gottman (1976), who found that most unassertive subjects knew what to say in certain situations but were inhibited from emitting this response themselves when placed in a situation calling for assertive behavior. Schwartz and Gottman also report data that this inhibition may be the result of negative self-statements typically reflecting concern over the reaction of others. In light of this and of the available outcome studies on assertion training, it may be more appropriate to view unassertive behavior, at least in part, as being a function of social-evaluative anxiety and amenable to cognitive intervention procedures designed to reduce this form of anxiety.

COGNITION AND EXPERIENCE

It has often been maintained that an understanding of the development, structure, and function of cognitive processes is ultimately based on the study of language (e.g., Staats, 1972, 1975). Language may function in various ways, whether it be as a means of labeling stimuli, of understanding one's associations to such labels, or of aiding an individual in overt action (Staats, 1975). Certainly, when one considers how very much the therapeutic enterprise is based on the interchange of language between therapist and client, it becomes strikingly evident that linguistic and communication analyses require far more attention than it has heretofore received in the behavior therapy literature.

Most of what has been discussed throughout this chapter is based on the assumption that an individual's internal dialogue or self-statements mediate motional arousal. Although there exists some indirect empirical support for this premise, it is not at all unusual to encounter individuals within clinical settings who have great difficulty in describing the internal dialogue that may be mediating their upset in any given situation. Such observations may certainly call into question the validity of the assumption that cognitive variables are associated with emotional arousal. A more plausible interpretation, however, is that individuals often lack the ability to provide accurate introspective information on their cognitive processes (Nisbett & Wilson, 1977). It is of interest to note that psychoanalysts such as Kubie (1934) have suggested that people may be unable to report fully on their cognitions because of the well-learned associations between thoughts, emotion, and behavior.

Our knowledge of the complex interplay between cognition and overt behavior is certainly far from complete. However, if we ever hope to develop the field of cognitive behavior therapy, it is crucial that we have a more complete understanding of the interrelationship between cognition and experience. And, although the study of language may provide us with useful information, it would be a mistake to assume that language and cognition can be equated. Menzel and Johnson (1976) have suggested that language and the communication process are reflective of basic cognitive structures that can be studied more directly. The section that follows describes some of the research in experimental cognitive psychology and offers some speculations that hopefully may point to potentially fruitful directions for future clinical and research efforts.

The Need for Experiential Referents

In attempting to understand the meaning of any given word or utterance, we need to know something about its referent. Much of what we encounter as miscommunication in everyday life can be traced to two or more individuals using the same words but intending different referents. This is clearly illustrated when another person attempts to teach you a physical skill. In learning to ski, for example, the instructor is forever directing the student to "bend the knees." Anyone who has ever struggled through the process of learning to ski will recall repeating such instructions covertly, bending one's knees, but having little success. After much practice, however, a day arrives when you bend the knees in just the right way, experience the sense of control, and then remark "Oh! Bend the *knees!*" Once having had a different and, in this case, more appropriate experience, the sentence takes on a completely different meaning.

A study by Bransford and Johnson (1972) has dramatically demonstrated how prior knowledge can provide the necessary experiential referent for language comprehension and recall. They presented subjects with a passage containing words having familiar lexical meanings. However, half of the subjects saw a picture offering an appropriate referent beforehand, whereas the remaining subjects did not have the opportunity to see the picture. The passage was as follows:

> If the balloons popped, the sound wouldn't be able to carry since everything would be too far away from the correct floor. A closed window would also prevent the sound from carrying, since most buildings tend to be well-insulated. Since the whole operation depends on a steady flow of electricity, a break in the middle of the wire would also cause problems. Of course, the fellow could shout, but the human voice is not loud enough to carry that far. An additional problem is that a string could break on the instrument. Then there could be no accompaniment to the message. It is clear that the best situation would involve less distance. Then there would be fewer potential problems. With face to face contact, the least number of things could go wrong [p. 719].

After having seen this passage, it should come as no surprise to the reader that subjects not given the referent beforehand had greater difficulty in both comprehension and recall. Having had the opportunity to see the picture beforehand—the picture itself is reproduced as Figure 5.5, on page 148 of this volume—clearly made the task easier. And seeing the picture after having looked at the seemingly incomprehensible passage should provide the reader with a rapid clarification of its meaning—as in the "bend the knees" example. This phenomenon is often seen clinically, when clients report sudden shifts or clarifications in belief systems, referred to by Mahoney (1974) as the "cognitive click."

Repeating certain utterances under conditions when individuals "believe" or "do not believe" what they are saying, or when the contrast between stating something one "understands" versus merely repeating words with no real comprehension, is strikingly similar to the differentiation between "emotional" and "intellectual" insight or understanding as described by psychoanalytic writers. Consistent with the illustrations noted, Dollard and Miller (1950) have suggested that emotional insight can be provided to clients only if they have the experiential referent for the labels offered by the therapist. They state:

> The patient himself must have the emotional experience and must correctly label it. If the patient has only a collection of sentences not tied to emotional or instrumental responses, little immediate therapeutic effect may be anticipated, though some dealyed effects may occasionally occur. If the patient is so frightened that he cannot listen, interpretation will have small effect. The therapist's interpretations must be timely, that is, must occur when the patient can listen and when the emotional response to be labeled is actually occurring [pp. 304–305].

The examples cited provide instances in which the individual does not comprehend the utterance until exposed to the experiential referent (i.e., the feeling of bending one's knees in a given way, or visual exposure to the picture). However, there may be instances in which an individual has already encountered the relevant experience some time in the past, with the cognitive click occurring once that person is able to retrieve the event from long-term memory. In understanding the process in such cases, the distinction made between *episodic* and *semantic* memory is particularly relevant (Tulving, 1972). According to Tulving, episodic memory refers to the pool of realtively discreet or isolated past events that are not tied to any cognitive structure. Semantic memory, on the other hand, deals with more "meaningful" information, in the sense that the events are integrated or coded into a larger associative network. Because there are fewer associative cues to enable the individual to retrieve experiences stored in episodic memory, such events are less likely to be recalled and used as referents for comprehension. In such instances, one can explain the shift from an intellectual to an emotional understanding of an utterance as involving the retrieval of the needed referent from episodic memory, and its subsequent shift in "meaning" when it becomes integrated into the larger cognitive structure associated with memory.

The clinical implications of such a conceptualization would suggest that the client needs to be provided with learning experiences prior to the use of language or labels that require such experiential referents for their meaning and comprehension. Or, if such experiences have occurred in the past but are stored in episodic memory and are consequently not "being used" to gain a more accurate perception of current situations, steps may need to be taken to integrate such experiences into semantic memory in such a way that the existing conceptual categories become somewhat realigned. One wonders about the extent to which this latter guideline parallels what psychoanalysts have meant when they indicate that the therapist must be careful in the "timing" of interpretations, offering them only at the time when the patient appears ready to accept and to "understand" certain isolated and seemingly irrelevant past events.

Another study by Bransford and Johnson (1973) has shown how slights shifts in *context* can create striking changes in the meaning of an event. Consider the following passage:

> The man stood before the mirror and combed his hair. He checked his face carefully for any places he might have missed shaving and then put on the conservative tie he had decided

to wear. At breakfast, he studied the newspaper carefully and, over coffee, discussed the possibility of buying a new washing machine with his wife. Then he made several phone calls. As he was leaving the house he thought about the fact that his children would probably want to go to that private camp again this summer. When the car didn't start, he got out, slammed the door and walked down to the bus stop in a very angry mood. Now he would be late [p. 415].

If the reader would now reconsider the passage, but this time adding "the *unemployed* man stood before the mirror...," the meaning of the communication would, indeed, be different. As noted by Bransford and Johnson, change occurs not only in the understanding of what events took place but also in one's inferences about why they did. Consider now still a different meaning that emerges when the passage begins with "the *stockbroker* stood before the mirror...."

The role of context in the communication of meaning has some very important clinical implications. The ability of the therapist to understand or to "empathize" with what a client described depends greatly on a shared pool of experiences that can provide the appropriate context within which the communication takes place. Baer and Stolz (1978) have discussed the difficulty that *est* graduates have in describing the changes they have experienced to non-*est* friends. They suggest that the language used by *est* graduates to describe their changes has connotative meanings based on having gone through certain experiences (cf. bending the knees in a given way), and is not readily comprehended by those not having shared such experiences. Indeed, Baer and Stolz suggest that one of the main effects of *est* may be to provide the individual with a shift in epistemology, in that life events are now viewed within a different context.

Meaning and the Internal Dialogue

It has already been acknowledged that the clinical assessment of a client's "internal dialogue" is not as straightfoward as it might seem. One reason why we may expect to have difficulty in assessing a person's cognitive processes by direct introspection is that we assume that the individual is reacting to specific and easily delineated stimuli. However, there are data to indicate that people react emotionally to classes of stimuli as well as to specific events (Proctor & Malloy, 1971; Staats, 1975). Inasmuch as those stimuli to which we frequently respond in real-life situations are indeed complex, our emotional reactions may be to only certain elements of this stimulus complex that in themselves can be part of a larger, and perhaps less obvious, conceptual class. Hence, we frequently speak of interpersonal events as reflecting "hidden agendas" or in some ways being "symbolic" of something else. Because referents (objects, persons, events) have a multitude of features, the meaning of any verbal or nonverbal communication can only become clear when we also know the broader context (e.g., past interpersonal events) in which it is being used (cf. Olson, 1970).

Despite clients' difficulties in reporting what they are "telling themselves" in any given situation, they frequently will acknowledge that they are behaving "as if'' they are saying certain things to themselves. Perhaps our difficulties in assessing these cognitive mediators have been a function of our incorrect conceptualization of the nature of the "internal dialogue." Rather than assuming that an individual is emitting one or more coherent self-statements, it might be more appropriate to view such covert events as involving affective associations, comprising the *connotative meanings* assigned to events or objects (Osgood, Suci, & Tannenbaum, 1957). Indeed, one of the major characteristics of human memory is its associative nature; associations are involved both in the meaning assigned to concepts and in the retrieval of information (Bower, 1975).

As noted earlier, a procedure that has been found to be useful clinically in the implementation of systematic rational restructuring has involved the use of an associative task. Thus, instead of asking clients what they may be "saying to themselves" that contributes to their upset in given situations, the therapist assists clients in ferreting out the relevant cognitive mediators by having them complete such sentences as "Making a mistake in front of my friends would upset me because...," or "If this other person disagrees with me that means...." Clinical work with such a technique has been most fruitful in that it appears to help individuals to recognize more readily, and subsequently to reevaluate, the implicit meaning they assign to given situations in their lives. The similarity to Jung's early research (Jung, 1910) on the use of word associations to determine the idiosyncratically perceived significance of certain words is particularly striking. There is also a parallel to the clinical work of psychoanalysts, who have long recognized the need for gathering information on the associative meaning that individuals attribute to given events and people. Thus, Kubie (1952) has recommended the use of free-association techniques under standardized conditions for evaluating an individual's "thinking profile" and any changes resulting from therapeutic intervention.

An assessment instrument that may very well appeal to cognitive behavior therapists and psychoanalysts alike is the *semantic differential,* which is an associative scaling technique originally developed by Osgood *et al.* (1957) from a learning-theory base for the purpose of assessing connotative or affective meaning that people assign to objects, other individuals, or events. Although there have been occasional usages of the semantic differential to measure changes in meaning resulting from therapeutic intervention (e.g., Endler, 1961; Hekmat & Vanian, 1971), there nonetheless remains great potential for the use of such a procedure in placing interpersonal events of individuals in semantic space with regard to evaluation, potency, and activity. Alternatively, one may use *multidimensional scaling* methods. Such procedures not only have the potential for assessing semantic distance, but can also shed light on the characteristic features that individuals use in classifying things as being semantically similar (Rips, Shoben, & Smith, 1973). The ability to assess the connotative similarities and differences among problematic events and individuals in a client's life, noting how they compare with nonproblematic events and individuals, may very well provide us with the information required to affect therapeutic change. The implications for assessing dysfunctional marital interactions are particularly striking, as a way of evaluating how each partner perceives (or misperceives) the communication from one's spouse, and the relevant hidden agendas to which each may be responding.

Still another possible way of assessing semantic structure and the nature of faulty classificatory processes might make use of the methodology devised by Collins and Quillian (1969) for the measurement of category size. With this procedure, subjects are presented with a series of sentences in which specific objects are said to be part of more general classes of objects (e.g., "A canary is a bird," "A penguin is a bird," "An ostrich is a bird.") Depending on the number of similar features shared by the specific example and what the subject considers to be the prototype of the category (e.g., the "typical" bird), the reaction time in identifying these statements as being true will vary. As one might predict, "A canary is a bird" is more rapidly identified as being true than is "An ostrich is a bird." If modified for clinical use, such a procedure may prove to be helpful in assessing the cognitive structure of clients by having them classify specific problematic events (e.g., making a mistake, forgetting someone's name, being criticized) into more general anxiety-arousing semantic categories (e.g., Being an Unworthy Person).

Just as the meaning of a communication at times requires the differentiation of the intended referent from alternate referents that might conceivably be the object of the communication (Olson, 1970), so might such discrimination be helpful in facilitating change in cognitions, affect, and behavior. Perhaps one may more readily learn to ski if the instructor would take the time to point out to the novice the correct *and* incorrect ways of bending one's knees. In therapy, it might be more beneficial for us to assist clients in the appropriate use of labels that they apply to events, others, and themselves by pointing out the similarities and differences to other events or people to whom such labels might be applied. Thus, when a client employs the connotative label of "bad," it might be important to specify those other events or individuals that might also be labeled as being "bad," as well as those considered "good." Landau (Note 8), in describing how phobias may be understood within an information-processing model, has made some similar observations in pointing out how semantic structure associated with phobic objects may best be altered. He suggests that, at the same time the therapist is assisting a client to reassess the aversive characteristics of a phobic object (e.g., the dog's fangs), it might also be useful additionally to help the client to become more aware of the positive attributes involved (e.g., the handsome coat).

No doubt, there are numerous other procedures and principles from experimental cognitive psychology that can have important implications for assessment and for therapeutic intervention (see Bower, 1978; Lang, 1977). With the growing interest in cognitive variables among behavior therapists, further extrapolations are likely to be forthcoming. Inasmuch as concepts from cognitive psychology are also currently being used by psychoanalytically oriented writers to explain various clinical phenomena (e.g., Horowitz, 1976), experimental cognitive psychology may very well offer us a common language for bridging the gap between psychoanalytic and cognitive–behavioral approaches to intervention.

CONCLUSION

The present chapter has reviewed some of the theoretical and research foundations, clinical procedures, and outcome data associated with the use of rational restructuring as a skill for coping with anxiety. The results of a variety of studies suggest that training in the realistic reevaluation of anxiety-producing situations is an effective clinical procedure for actively coping with anxiety. However, there seem to be limits to the effectiveness of this approach to anxiety reduction, and some findings point to the possibility that there may be an interaction between target problem and therapeutic procedure. Although the precise nature of this interaction is far from clear, available evidence suggests that training in realistic thinking may be more appropriate in cases of pervasive anxiety, or in instances in which the anxiety is mediated by concerns regarding the evaluation of others. In the case of social anxiety, including lack of interpersonal assertiveness, training clients to reevaluate realistically the consequences of their behavior seems to be more effective than the use of relaxation skills and, depending on the outcome measure used, just as successful as an approach promoting the acquisition of more effective overt behaviors. In the case of more focal target problems, such as anxiety that is specific to public speaking and test-taking situations, both relaxation and rational restructuring seem to be comparably effective.

Further investigation into the nature of the interaction between treatment procedure and target behavior is clearly in order. Bandura (1969) has suggested that techniques for the reduction of anxiety should differ depending on whether the emotional response is directly evoked by conditioned aversive stimuli or is maintained by self-generated symbolic activities. Davidson and Schwartz (1976) have similarly argued that self-regulatory coping procedures in the treatment of anxiety are likely to vary depending upon whether the anxiety is composed of cognitive or of somantic components. The likelihood that important interactions exist with the maintenance and reduction of other emotional responses should be investigated as well; Beck's (1976) work on coping with depression and Novaco's (1975) research on the control of anger represent important beginnings in this direction.

The conceptualization of maladaptive cognitions within the broader context of cognitive psychology and semantics has the potential of providing us with a more thorough understanding of the cognitive structure that may be mediating emotional arousal. This might not only assist us in obtaining a more adequate definition of the ''situation'' or ''stimulus'' to which a person may be reacting, but also can provide a means by which we might better understand those cognitive processes contributing to the functional similarity of various events and the resulting cross-situational consistency we often see in various maladaptive emotional reactions. Finally, the use of more general principles of cognitive psychology to understand the interplay between cognition and experience may also help to bring cognitive behavior therapy into closer alignment with other therapeutic orientations that for years have clinically witnessed phenomena similar to those discussed throughout this chapter.

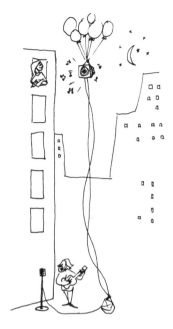

Figure 5.5. Picture used to provide appropriate referent in the Bransford and Johnson (1972) study.

REFERENCE NOTES

1. Schill, T., Evans, R., Monroe, S., & Ramanaiah, N. V. *The effects of self-verbalizations on performance: A test of the rational–emotive position.* Unpublished manuscript, Southern Illinois University at Carbondale, 1976.
2. Jones, R. G. *A factored measure of Ellis' irrational belief system, with personality and maladjustment correlates.* Unpublished doctoral dissertation, Texas Technological College, 1968.
3. Pitcher, S. W. *Variability in assertive behavior: Subject and situational factors.* Paper presented at the Twelfth Annual Convention of the Association for the Advancement of Behavior Therapy, December, 1978.
4. Casas, J. M. *A comparison of two mediational self-control techniques for the treatment of speech anxiety.* Unpublished doctoral dissertation, Stanford University, 1975.
5. Osarchuk, M. *A comparison of a cognitive, a behavior therapy and a cognitive plus behavior therapy treatment of test anxious college students.* Unpublished doctoral dissertation, Adelphi University, 1974.
6. May, R. L. *The treatment of test anxiety by cognitive modification: An examination of treatment components.* Unpublished doctoral dissertation, University of Kansas, 1975.
7. Martorano, R. D., Nietzel, M. T., & Melnick, J. *A comparision of covert modeling with reply training and systematic rational restructuring as treatments for unassertiveness.* Unpublished manuscript, University of Kentucky, 1977.
8. Landau, R. J. *A semantic-feature model of phobias.* Unpublished manuscript, State University of New York at Stony Brook, 1977.

REFERENCES

Alden, L., & Safran, J. Irrational beliefs and nonassertive behavior. *Cognitive Therapy and Research,* 1978, *4,* 357–364.

Alden, L., Safran, J., & Weidman, R. A comparison of cognitive and skills training strategies in the treatment of unassertive clients. *Behavior Therapy,* in press.

Aponte, J. F., & Aponte, C. E. Group preprogrammed systematic desensitization in alleviating test anxiety in college students. *Journal of Abnormal Psychology,* 1971, *77,* 282–289.

Baer, D. M., & Stolz, S. B. A description of the Erhard Seminars Training (*est*) in the terms of behavior analysis. *Behaviorism,* 1978, *6,* 45–70.

Bandura, A. *Principles of behavior modification.* New York: Holt, Rinehart, and Winston, 1969.

Barrett, C. L. Systematic desensitization versus implosive therapy. *Journal of Abnormal Psychology,* 1969, *74,* 587–592.

Barrett, C. J., Berg, P. I., Eaton, E. M., and Pomeroy, E. L. Implications of women's liberation and the future of psychotherapy. *Psychotherapy: Theory, Research and Practice,* 1974, *11,* 11–15.

Beck, A. T. *Cognitive therapy and the emotional disorders.* New York International Universities Press, 1976.

Bergin, A. E., & Strupp, H. H. New directions in psychotherapy research. *Journal of Abnormal Psychology,* 1970, *76,* 13–26.

Bower, G. H. Cognitive psychology: An introduction. In W. K. Estes (Ed.), *Handbook of learning and cognitive processes. Vol. I: Introduction to concepts and issues.* Hillsdale, New Jersey: Lawrence Erlbaum Associates, 1975.

Bower, G. H. Contacts of cognitive psychology with social learning theory. *Cognitive Therapy and Research,* 1978, *2,* 123–146.

Bransford, J. D., & Johnson, M. K. Contextual prerequisites for understanding: Some investigations of comprehension and recall. *Journal of Verbal Learning and Verbal Behavior,* 1972, *11,* 717–726.

Bransford, J. D., & Johnson, M. K. Considerations of some problems of comprehension. In W. G. Chase (Ed.), *Visual information processing.* New York: Academic Press, 1973.

Breger, L., & McGaugh, J. L. Critique and reformation of "learning theory" approaches to psychotherapy and neurosis. *Psychological Bulletin,* 1965, *63,* 338–358.

Calef, R. A., & MacLean, G. D. A comparison of reciprocal inhibition and reactive inhibition therapies in the treatment of speech anxiety. *Behavior therapy,* 1970, *1,* 51–58.

Carmody, T. P. Rational–emotive, self-instructional, and behavioral assertion training: Facilitating maintenance. *Cognitive Therapy and Research,* 1978, *2,* 241–253.

Cattell, R. B., & Scheier, I. H. Stimuli related to stress, neuroticism, excitation, and anxiety response patterns. *Journal of Abnormal and Social Psychology,* 1960, *60,* 195–204.

Chesler, P. *Women and madness.* Garden City, New York: Doubleday, 1972.

Collins, A. M., & Quillian, M. R. Retrieval time from semantic memory. *Journal of Verbal Learning and Verbal Behavior,* 1969, *8,* 240–247.

Davidson, R. J., & Schwartz, G. E. The psychobiology of relaxation and related states: A multi-process theory. In D. I. Mostovsky (Ed.), *Behavior control and the modification of physiological activity.* Englewood Cliffs, New Jersey: Prentice-Hall, 1976.

Denney, D. R., & Rupert, P. A. Desensitization and self-control in the treatment of test anxiety. *Journal of Counseling Psychology,* 1977, *4,* 272–280.

DiLoreto, A. O. *Comparative psychotherapy: An experimental analysis.* Chicago: Aldine-Atherton Inc., 1971.

Dollard, J., & Miller, N. E. *Personality and psychotherapy.* New York: McGraw-Hill, 1950.

D'Zurilla, T. J., Wilson, G. T., & Nelson, R. A preliminary study of the effectiveness of graduated prolonged exposure in the treatment of irrational fears. *Behavior Therapy,* 1973, *4,* 672–685.

Ellis, A. *Reason and emotion in psychotherapy.* New York: Lyle Stuart, 1962.

Ellis, A., & Grieger, R. (Eds.) *Handbook of rational–emotive therapy*. New York: Springer, 1977.

Endler, N. S. Changes in meaning during psychotherapy as measured by the semantic differential. *Journal of Counseling Psychology, 1961, 8,* 105–111.

Fremouw, W. J., & Harmatz, M. G. A helper model for behavioral treatment of speech anxiety. *Journal of Consulting and Clinical Psychology, 1975, 43,* 652–660.

Fremouw, W. J., & Zitter, R. E. A Comparison of skills training and cognitive restructuring-relaxation for the treatment of speech anxiety. *Behavior Therapy, 1978, 9,* 248–259.

Gaudry, E., & Spielberger, C. D. *Anxiety and educational achievement.* New York: Wiley, 1971.

Glass, C. R., Gottman, J. M., & Shmurak, S. H. Response acquisition and cognitive self-statement modification approaches to dating skills training. *Journal of Counseling Psychology, 1976, 23,* 520–526.

Goldfried, M. R. Systematic desensitization as training in self-control. *Journal of Consulting and Clinical Psychology, 1971, 37,* 228–234.

Goldfried, M. R. *Behavioral management of anxiety: A clinician's guide.* Audiocassettee tape-T44A. New York: BioMonitoring Applications, 1976.

Goldfried, M. R. The use of relaxation and cognitive relabeling as coping skills. In R. B. Stuart (Ed.), *Behavioral self-management: Strategies, techniques, and outcomes.* New York: Brunner/ Mazel, 1977.

Goldfried, M. R. Psychotherapy as coping skills training. In M. J. Mahoney (Ed.), *Psychotherapy process: Current issues and future directions.* New York: Plenum, in press.

Goldfried, M. R., & Davison, G. C. *Clinical behavior therapy.* New York: Holt, Rinehart, & Winston, 1976.

Goldfried, M. R., Decenteceo. E. T., & Weinberg, L. Systematic rational restructuring as a self-control technique. *Behavior Therapy, 1974, 5,* 247–254.

Goldfried, M. R., & Goldfried, A. P. Cognitive change methods. In F. H. Kanfer & A. P. Goldstein (Eds.), *Helping people change.* New York: Pergamon Press, 1975.

Goldfried, M. R., & Goldfried, A. P. Importance of hierarchy content in the self-control of anxiety. *Journal of Consulting and Clinical Psychology, 1977, 45,* 124–134.

Goldfried, M. R., & Linehan, M. M. Basic issues in behavioral assessment. In A. R. Ciminero, K. S. Calhoun, & H. E. Adams (Eds.), *Handbook of behavioral assessment.* New York: John Wiley & Sons, 1977.

Goldfried, M. R., Linehan, M. M., & Smith, J. L. The reduction of test anxiety through rational restructuring. *Journal of Consulting and Clinical Psychology, 1978, 46,* 32–39.

Goldfried, M. R., & Merbaum, M. (Eds.) *Behavior change through self-control.* New York: Holt, Rinehart, and Winston, 1973.

Goldfried, M. R., & Sobocinski, D. The effect of irrational beliefs on emotional arousal. *Journal of Consulting and Clinical Psychology, 1975, 43,* 504–510.

Goldfried, M. R., & Trier, C. S. Effectiveness of relaxation as an active coping skill. *Journal of Abnormal Psychology, 1974, 83,* 348–355.

Hekmat, H., & Vanian, D. Behavior modification through covert semantic desensitization. *Journal of Consulting and Clinical Psychology, 1971, 36,* 248–251.

Holroyd, K. A. Cognition and desensitization in the group treatment of test anxiety. *Journal of Consulting and Clinical Psychology, 1976, 44,* 991–1001.

Horowitz, M. J. *Stress response syndrome.* New York: Jason Aronson, 1976.

Janis, I. L., & King, B. T. The influence of role playing on opinion change. *Journal of Abnormal and Social Psychology, 1954, 49,* 211–218.

Jung, C. G. The association method. *American Journal of Psychology, 1910, 21,* 219–269.

Kanter, N. J., & Goldfried, M. R. Relative effectiveness of rational restructuring and self-control desensitization for the reduction of interpersonal anxiety. *Behavior Therapy, 1979, in press.*

King, B. T., & Janis, I. L. Comparison of the effectiveness of improvised versus non-improvised role-playing in producing opinion change. *Human Relations, 1956, 9,* 177–186.

Kubie, L. S. Problems and technique of psychoanalytic validation and progress. In E. Pumpian-Mindlin (Ed.), *Psychoanalysis as science*. Stanford, California: Stanford University Press, 1952.

Kubie, L. S. Relation of the conditioned reflex to psychoanalytic technic. *Archives of Neurology and Psychiatry*, 1934, *32*, 1137–1142.

Lang, P. J. Imagery in therapy: An information processing analysis of fear. *Behavior Therapy*, 1977, *8*, 862–886.

Lange, A. J., and Jakubowski, P. *Responsible assertive behavior: Cognitive/behavioral procedures for trainers*. Champaign, Illinois: Research Press, 1976.

Lazarus, A. A. *Behavior therapy and beyond*. New York: McGraw-Hill, 1971.

Lazarus, R. S. *Psychological stress and the coping process*. New York: McGraw-Hill, 1966.

Lazarus, R. S., & Launier, R. Stress-related transactions between person and environment. In L. A. Pervin & M. Lewis (Eds.), *Perspectives in interactional psychology*. New York: Plenum, 1978.

Liebert, R. M., & Morris, L. W. Cognitive and emotional components of test anxiety: A distinction and some initial data. *Psychological Reports*, 1967, *20*, 975–978.

Linehan, M. M., Goldfried, M. R., & Goldfried, A. P. Assertion training: Skill training or cognitive restructuring. *Behavior Therapy*, 1979, in press.

Mahoney, M. J. *Cognition and behavior modification*. Cambridge: Ballinger, 1974.

Malleson, N. Panic and phobia: A possible method of treatment. *Lancet*, 1959, *1*, 225–227.

Mandler, G., & Watson, D. Anxiety and the interruption of behavior. In C. D. Spielberger (Ed.), *Anxiety and behavior*. New York: Academic Press, 1966.

Marlett, N., & Watson, D. Test anxiety and immediate or delayed feedback in a test-like avoidance task. *Journal of Personality and Social Psychology*, 1968, *8*, 200–203.

May, J. R. Psychophysiology of self-regulated phobic thoughts. *Behavior Therapy*, 1977, *8*, 150–159.

May, J. R., & Johnson, H. J. Physiological activity to internally elicited arousal and inhibitory thoughts. *Journal of Abnormal Psychology*, 1973, *82*, 239–245.

McGlynn, F. D. Graded imagination and relaxation as components of experimental desensitization. *The Journal of Nervous and Mental Disease*, 1973, *156*, 377–385.

Meichenbaum, D. H. Cognitive modification of test anxious college students. *Journal of Consulting and Clinical Psychology*, 1972, *39*, 370–380.

Meichenbaum, D. H. *Cognitive behavior modification*. New York: Plenum, 1977.

Meichenbaum, D. H., Gilmore, J. B., & Fedoravicious, A. Group insight versus group desensitization in treating speech anxiety. *Journal of Consulting and Clinical Psychology*, 1971, *36*, 410–421.

Menzel, E. W., & Johnson, M. K. Communication and cognitive organization in humans and other animals. *Annals of the New York Academy of Sciences*, 1976, *280*, 131–142.

Morris, L. W., & Liebert, R. M. Relationship of cognitive and emotional components of test anxiety to physiological arousal and academic performance. *Journal of Consulting and Clinical Psychology*, 1970, *35*, 332–337.

Mylar, J. L., & Clement, P. W. Prediction and comparison of outcome in systematic desensitization and implosion. *Behaviour Research and Therapy*, 1972, *10*, 235–246.

Nisbett, R. E., & Wilson, T. D. Telling more than we can know: Verbal reports on mental processes. *Psychological Review*, 1977, *84*, 231–259.

Novaco, R. *Anger control: The development and evaluation of an experimental treatment*. Lexington, Massachusetts: Lexington Books, 1975.

Olson, D. R. Language and thought: Aspects of a cognitive theory of semantics. *Psychological Review*, 1970, *77*, 257–273.

Osgood, C. E., Suci, G. J., & Tannenbaum, P. H. *The measurement of meaning*. Urbana, Illinois: University of Illinois Press, 1957.

Proctor. S., & Malloy, T. E. Cognitive control of conditioned emotional responses: An extension of behavior therapy to include the experimental psychology of cognition. *Behavior Therapy*, 1971, *2*, 294–306.

Raimy, V. *Misunderstandings of the self.* San Francisco: Jossey-Bass, 1975.

Rimm, D. C., & Litvak, S. B. Self-verbalization and emotional arousal. *Journal of Abnormal Psychology,* 1969, *32,* 565–574.

Rips, L. J., Shoben, E. J., & Smith, E. E. Semantic distance and the verification of semantic relations. *Journal of Verbal Learning and Verbal Behavior,* 1973, *12,* 1–20.

Rogers, T., & Craighead, W. E. Physiological responses to self-statements: The effects of statement valence and discrepancy. *Cognitive Therapy and Research,* 1977, *1,* 99–118.

Roskies, E., & Lazarus, R. S. Coping theory and the teaching of coping skills. In P. Davidson (Ed.), *Behavioral medicine: Changing life styles.* New York: Brunner/Mazel, in press.

Russell, P. L., & Brandsma, J. M. A theoretical and empirical integration of the rational–emotive and classical conditioning theories. *Journal of Consulting and Clinical Psychology,* 1974, *42,* 389–397.

Schwartz, R., & Gottman, J. Toward a task analysis of assertive behavior. *Journal of Consulting and Clinical Psychology,* 1976, *44,* 910–920.

Smith, R. E. Social anxiety as a moderator variable in the attitude similarity–attraction relationship. *Journal of Experimental Research in Personality,* 1972, *6,* 22–28.

Smith, R. E., & Sarason, I. G. Social anxiety and the evaluation of negative interpersonal feedback. *Journal of Consulting and Clinical Psychology,* 1975, *43,* 429.

Speilberger, C. D. (Ed.) *Anxiety and behavior.* New York: Academic Press, 1966.

Staats, A. W. Language behavior therapy: A derivative of social behaviorism. *Behavior Therapy,* 1972, *3,* 165–192.

Staats, A. W. *Social behaviorism.* Homewood, Illinois: Dorsey Press, 1975.

Suinn. R. M. The stabs, a measure of test anxiety for behavior therapy: Normative data. *Behaviour Research and Therapy,* 1969, *7,* 335–339.

Sutton-Simon, K., & Goldfried, M. R. Faulty thinking in two types of anxiety. *Cognitive Therapy and Research,* 1979, *3,* 193–203.

Thorpe, G. L. Desensitization, behavior rehearsal, self-instructional training and placebo effects on assertive-refusal behavior. *European Journal of Behavioural Analysis and Modification,* 1975, *1,* 30–44.

Trexler, L. D., & Karst, T. O. Rational–emotive therapy, placebo, and no-treatment effects on public-speaking anxiety. *Journal of Abnormal Psychology,* 1972, *79,* 60–67.

Tulving, E. Episodic and semantic memory. In E. Tulving & W. Donaldson (Eds.), *Organization of memory.* New York: Academic Press, 1972.

Velten, E. Jr. A laboratory task for induction of mood states. *Behaviour Research and Therapy,* 1968, *6,* 473–482.

Watson, D., & Friend, R. Measurement of social-evaluative anxiety. *Journal of Consulting and Clinical Psychology,* 1969, *33,* 448–457.

Weissberg, M. A comparison of direct and vicarious treatments of speech anxiety: Desensitization, desensitization with coping imagery, and cognitive modification. *Behavior Therapy,* 1977, *8,* 606–620.

Wilson, G. T., & Davison, G. C. Processes of fear reduction in systematic desensitization: Animal studies. *Psychological Bulletin,* 1971, *76,* 1–14.

Wolfe, J. L., & Fodor, I. G. A cognitive/behavioral approach to modifying assertive behavior in women. *The Counseling Psychologist,* 1975, *5,* 45–52.

Wolfe, J. L., & Fodor, I. G. Modifying assertive behavior in women: A comparison of three approaches. *Behavior Therapy,* 1977, *8,* 567–574.

Wolpe, J. *Psychotherapy by reciprocal inhibition.* Stanford: Stanford University Press, 1958.

Zuckerman, M., & Lubin, B. *Manual for the Multiple Affect Adjective Checklist.* San Diego: Educational and Industrial Testing Service, 1965.

6

Cognitive Therapy of Depression[1]

STEVEN D. HOLLON
AARON T. BECK

INTRODUCTION

> *It would appear that no matter what interpersonal factors mobilize depressive behaviors, once the latter reach the melancholic stage, they become biologically autonomous and become relatively refractory to psychotherapeutic intervention.*
>
> —Akiskal and McKinney, 1975, p. 293.

Depression is one of the oldest recognized disturbances of psychological life. It is also one of the most prevalent. It has been estimated that 1 person in 10 will experience one or more major affective episodes during his lifetime (Task Force on Nomenclature and Statistics, American Psychiatric Association, Note 1). As a clinical syndrome, depression is marked by *change:* Previously gratifying activities seem to lose their appeal; active, striving individuals become torn by doubt and indecision; and interest and involvement turn to apathy and withdrawal. In the extreme, hope can yield to pathological despair and can culminate in self-destruction. The link between depression and suicide has been so pronounced that suicide has been called the mortality of depressive mental illness (Silverman, 1968).

At times, depressions may appear to be triggered by external events—the loss of a

---

[1]Throughout this chapter, the term *cognitive therapy* will refer to a specific approach to the treatment of depression based on cognitive theory and utilizing both cognitive and behavioral techniques (Beck, 1964, 1967, 1970). Approaches relying solely on semantic or persuasive techniques will be referred to as *cognitive–semantic* or *strictly cognitive* approaches.

Cognitive–Behavioral Interventions:
Theory, Research, and Procedures

loved one or a major financial or vocational reversal. At other times, depressions may appear to overrun an individual with no apparent precipitant. Etiological theories have been diverse, ranging from speculations concerning biochemical deficiencies and hereditary–constitutional deficits through speculations concerning internal psychological factors or subtle disruptions in patterns of commerce between the organisms and the environment. Despite the diversity in etiological theories, the observed clinical syndrome has generally been described in strikingly consistent terms. Traditionally considered to be a disorder of affect, most descriptions also specify changes in cognitive, behavioral, motivational, and vegetative components. In their effort to integrate these diverse etiological models with this consistent clinical syndrome, Akiskal and McKinney (1975) proposed that any of a variety of factors might trigger a common psychobiological process. Once triggered, this process takes on a life of its own. This "final common pathway" model was presumed to act primarily through a biochemical mechanism and, as indicated in the opening quote, to be relatively unresponsive to psychosocial interventions.

At the time that Akiskal and McKinney's monograph was prepared, their pessimistic evaluation of psychosocial interventions appeared amply justified by the available literature. Particularly telling was the general inefficacy of traditional psychotherapy approaches when compared to pharmaco- or somatic therapies (Hollon & Beck, 1978). As late as 1970, there existed no published study in which any type of psychotherapy had been shown to be more effective than either alternative treatments or no treatment conditions in any controlled comparison with a homogenously defined sample of depressives.

This general statement no longer holds. Converging lines of research from basic experimental psychology and descriptive psychopathology have led to the articulation of cognitive and behavioral theories of depression. These theories, in turn, have stimulated the development of novel and, apparently, powerful methods of intervention. A cognitive theory of depression posits that depression is, in part, a consequence of pervasive, negative misconstructions of objective experiences (Beck, 1963, 1967, 1976). Depressed individuals are seen as exhibiting what Beck (1967) has labeled the negative cognitive triad; they regard *themselves* as deprived, defeated, or diseased, *their worlds* as full of roadblocks to their obtaining even minimal satisfaction, and *their futures* as devoid of any hope of gratification and promising only pain and frustration.

Cognitive therapy is a cognitive–behavioral approach to treatment designed to identify, evaluate, and change these maladaptive belief systems and dysfunctional styles of information processing (Beck, 1964, 1967, 1970). Clients[2] are trained to distinguish fact from belief and to test the latter, much as a scientist would evaluate a hypothesis. Cognitive theory argues that the depressive syndrome involves interactive behavioral, biochemical, affective, and cognitive systems; change in the

---

[2]Throughout this chapter, the term *client* is used in lieu of the term patient, simply for purposes of consistency. This usage should not be interpreted as suggesting that the depressions discussed are in any way less severe than those typically considered in the pharmacological literature.

cognitive system is seen as producing change across the syndrome as a whole. Unlike Akiskal and McKinney, we would argue that cognitive–behavioral strategies may prove to be uniquely effective interventions in ameliorating even severe depressions.

To what extent can depression be conceptualized as a cognitive phenomenon? How can cognitive behavioral theories be translated into specific clinical procedures? How do cognitive–behavioral approaches to therapy compare with existing interventions?

In this chapter, we will first describe cognitive theory and supporting evidence, contrasting this approach to alternative models. Second, the literature concerning therapy efficacy will be reviewed. Specific attention will be paid to the results of a major comparative study between cognitive therapy and pharmacotherapy (Rush, Beck, Kovacs, & Hollon, 1977). The third and final section will present clinical procedures involved in the practice of cognitive therapy, accompanied by clinical examples.

THEORIES OF DEPRESSION

Overview

Cognitive theory can be compared with three other major theoretical approaches: biochemical, dynamic, and behavioral. A basic distinction needs to be made between theories of etiology and theories of intervention. Whereas each of the major theoretical formulations has given rise to a variety of related intervention strategies, there need be no necessary congruence between the factors that trigger a disorder and the factors that alleviate it. Theory can serve as a powerful guide in the search for effective interventions, but no amount of evidence confined to the efficacy of an intervention, no matter how compelling, can be considered supportive of the initial etiological theory.

An overview of the various major theoretical approaches to depression is presented in Table 6.1. In keeping with the desire to separate consideration of etiology from intervention, Table 6.1 is divided into theories of etiology (theory), theories of intervention (process), and procedures of intervention (procedures). This latter distinction follows Bandura's (1977a) observation that one set of processes may mediate change (e.g., cognitive) whereas a different set of procedures (e.g., behavioral) may most effectively alter those processes.

Four Major Theories

Cognitive Theory

Cognitive theory posits that depression is the consequence of a negative cognitive set. Depressed individuals are seen as evidencing Beck's negative cognitive triad:

TABLE 6.1
Therapy

Approach	Theory	Process	Procedure
Biological:	Biochemical imbalance	Restoration of normal physiolocial processes	Pharmacotherapy and/or somatic therapies
Dynamic:	Anger directed against the self following real or symbolic loss	Insight into unconscious conflict and cathartic discharge of affect	1. Supportive: Amelioration of aggravating unconscious conflicts 2. Depth: Resolution of unconscious conflicts
Behavioral:			
Affective	Anxiety inhibits potentially gratifying behaviors	Reduction of conditioned anxiety	Systematic desensitization or alternative counter-conditioning procedures
Operant	Deficit in reinforcement or excess in punishment	Increase occurrence of reinforcement (decrease punishment)	1. Direct contingency management by therapist 2. Skills training
Self-control	Deficit in self-reinforcement or excess self-punishment	Increase administration of self-reinforcement (decrease self-punishment)	Skills training in (a) self-monitoring; (b) self-evaluation; and (c) self-reinforcement
Cognitive:	Maladaptive beliefs and distorted information processing	Change beliefs and alter information processing distortions	1. Cognitive therapy: Inductive reasoning, empirical examination of beliefs, training in (a) self-monitoring; (b) cognitive hypothesis testing; and (c) cognitive restructuring 2. RET: Deductive reasoning and persuasion

negative beliefs regarding themselves, their world, and their future. Systematic distortions in information processing are seen as maintaining belief in the validity of these views despite contradictory environmental evidence. Examples of such distortions include:

1. *Selective abstraction* (a stimulus set); forming a conclusion regarding a particular event on the basis of an isolated detail, while ignoring contradictory and more salient evidence

2. *Arbitrary inference* (a response set); drawing a conclusion in the absence of evidence

3. *Overgeneralization* (a response set); extracting a belief or rule on the basis of a particular event and applying that concept in an unjustifiable fashion to other dissimilar situations.

4. *Magnification* (a response set); the overestimation of the significance or magnitude of undesirable consequent events.

5. *All-or-none thinking* (a response set); the tendency to think in absolute terms.

Cognitive theory suggests that these dysfunctional beliefs and distorted information processing styles serve both to depress mood and to lead to behavioral passivity. If one were as impoverished and the future as bleak as believed by depressed individuals, then their sadness and apathy would seem both logical and attuned to reality. Cognitive theory argues that it is aberrant thinking that leads predictably and inexorably to what may seem to an outside observer to be unexplainable dysphoria and self-defeating passivity.

Furthermore, there appears to be a gross change in the cognitive organization in depression, characterized by a limitation in the number, content, and formal qualities of the cognitive-response categories, particularly in reference to the clients' self-concept and personal expectations. The response categories (schemes) tend to be global, rigid, and negatively toned (Beck, 1964). The activation and prepotency of these crude categories disrupt normal information processing and account for the cognitive distortions. The clients' inferences regarding external stimuli are seen as being molded predominately by these negative cognitive schemes.

What evidence exists to support such a theory? The first requirement of any such theory is that the presumably causal phenomenon co-vary with the phenomenon under scrutiny. Several studies (Beck & Hurvich, 1959; Beck & Ward, 1961; Hauri, 1976) have indicated differences between depressives and nondepressives in terms of manifest dream content, with depressives reporting themes of personal loss and failure. Similarly, depressives were found to identify more often with the victimized, rather than the victimizing, identical twin on a pictoral projective device (Beck, 1961). Weintraub, Segal, and Beck (1974) found that the tendency to endorse negatively distorted outcomes on a multiple-choice measure of expectancy correlated significantly with ratings of negative affect. Furthermore, although not analyzed by more powerful cross-lagged panel procedures, 4 of 10 correlations over time from cognition to affect (correlations between cognition at time X and affect at a later time) were significant, whereas only 1 of 10 comparable affect to cognition correlations over time proved significant. Hammen and Krantz (1976) similarly found that depressed female college students were significantly more likely than were matched controls to endorse a negatively distorted interpretation of various hypothetical situations. Vatz, Winig, and Beck (Note 2), working with a clinically depressed sample, found ratings of sadness correlated with self-ratings of pessimism ($r = .56$) and of negative self-concept ($r = .79$).

Nelson (1977) reported significant correlations between the Beck Depression Inventory (BDI) (Beck, Ward, Mendelson, Mock, & Erbaugh, 1961), a self-report measure of syndrome depression, and various depressogenic attitude clusters on the Jones Irrational Belief Test (IBT) (Jones, 1968), a true–false inventory designed to assess belief in the types of irrational beliefs considered by Ellis (1962) to be causes of emotional distress. Although correlations were described as only moderate, the IBT was devised as a measure of belief related to general maladjustment, not specifically depression. Hollon and Kendall (Note 3) have developed an Automatic Thoughts Questionnaire (ATQ) as a measure of experienced cognitive content. Items were derived by asking individuals to report cognitions associated with depressive experiences and were cross-validated on a separate sample of psychometrically identified depressed college students. Results indicated that the 30 negative cognitions on the ATQ were endorsed as occurring significantly more often by depressed than by nondepressed subjects. Weissman and Beck (Note 4) have developed a Dysfunctional Attitudes Scale (DAS), similar in format to Jones' IBT but focused specifically on beliefs relevant to depression. Such attitudes may well represent relationships assumed to operate in the world, even if they rarely occur in any individual's train of thought.

Depressives appear to differ from nondepressives in terms of *what* they think; they also appear to differ in terms of *how* they process information. In a major reformulation of the learned helplessness model of depression,[3] Abramson, Seligman, and Teasdale (1978) have argued that a tendency to attribute negative outcomes to global, stable, internal factors may be central to depression. Klein, Fencil-Morse, and Seligman (1976), Kuiper (1978), and Risley (1978) have found that depressives are particularly likely to attribute negative outcomes (e.g., failure) to internal factors (e.g., personal incompetence).

Alloy and Abramson (1979) noted differences between depressed and nondepressed subjects in terms of perceived personal control over outcomes. Curiously, the actual distortion of real contingencies occurred for the nondepressives. Normals consistently overestimated the degree of control they could exercise over outcomes. Since perceived control (the capacity to make desired outcomes occur) may be intimately related to engaging in voluntary behaviors, such findings may point to instances when thinking may be accurate but dysfunctional.

DeMonbreum and Craighead (1977), Wener and Rehm (1975), and Nelson and Craighead (1977) have found that depressed subjects underestimate the amount of reinforcement received relative to nondepressives. Such findings suggest the operation of distorting cognitive activity in apparent nonresponsiveness to reinforcement.

Seligman and colleagues (Klein & Seligman, 1976; Miller & Seligman, 1973, 1975) have noted differences between depressed and nondepressed subjects in terms of expectancy formation and change in expectations as a function of prior outcomes on chance and skill tasks. Specifically, depressed subjects were found not to alter expectations regarding subsequent performance on the skill task on the basis of feedback regarding previous trials. Abramson, Garber, Edwards, and Seligman (1978) extended these observations to a rigorously diagnosed inpatient, unipolar depressed sample. Neither matched schizophrenic nor depressed schizophrenic controls evidenced the phenomenon, a finding suggesting that this insensitivity to

---

[3]The learned helplessness theory of depression (Seligman, 1975) states that depression is a consequence of exposure to noncontingent events. In essence, individuals exposed to situations that are essentially uncontrollable are seen as developing the belief that outcomes occur independently of their actions. This expectation is then inappropriately generalized to situations that are, in reality, controllable. Learned helplessness has always involved a major cognitive component; with the reformulation cited, cognitive factors are accorded an even greater, more varied function.

outcomes is characteristic of nosological depression only, rather than a general feature of psychopathology or syndrome depression associated with other types of disorders. Failures to replicate the phenomenon in depressed alcoholics (O'Leary, Donovan, Krueger, & Cysewske, 1978) or mixed psychiatric inpatients high on syndrome depression (Smolen, 1978) may further suggest that the expectancy-shift deficit on skill tasks is specific to nosological depression.

Differences in cognitive processes may well prove highly sensitive to situation-by-actor interactions. Garber and Hollon (Note 5) found that, although depressed college students evidenced little outcome-relevant change in performance expectations when they were engaged, themselves, in performing on a skill task, the expectations that they generated for *other* individuals performing on that same task were identical to those generated by nondepressives. The authors suggested that the expectancy-shift phenomenon did not represent a generalized belief in uncontrollability or a deficit in information processing that generalized across performers, but, rather, the phenomenon appeared to represent a specific cognitive distortion regarding only one's *own* performance on tasks requiring skilled performance.

Several studies have indicated that memory functions differ between depressives and nondepressives. Lishman (1972) and Lloyd and Lishman (1975) have found that depressed subjects were more likely to recall negative events than were nondepressives. Isen, Shalker, Clark, and Karp (1978) found that induced negative mood similarly led to increases in recall of negatively toned materials. Although the nature of the mechanism involved remains unclear, Isen *et al.* speculate that a negative feedback loop may exist between cognitive content and mood; negative thoughts or events trigger negative mood states that cue the retrieval of dysphoric memories, which further depress mood, accentuating a downward cycle.

Documenting the existence of differences in cognitive content and processes between depressed and nondepressed subjects does not, of course, mean that such differences are causal to depression. Any hypotheses regarding the etiology of clinical depression would require evidence linking shifts in cognitive content and processes to subsequent changes in affective, behavioral, motivational, and vegetative components of the depressive syndrome.

A variety of studies have used cognitive induction procedures to induce negative mood states. Velten (1968) had subjects read presumably depressing, elating, or neutral statements. Subjects reading the negative statements reported increases in dysphoric affect. Similar dysphoric mood inductions were reported by Coleman (1975), Strickland, Hale, and Anderson (1975), Hale and Strickland (1976), and Natale (1977a,b). Teasdale and Bancroft (1977) found that instructions to "think sad thoughts" led to increased dysphoric mood and physiological concomitants in clinical depressives. Moore, Underwood, and Rosenhan (1973) and Masters, Barden, and Ford (1979) have used negative fantasies to induce dysphoric affect in schoolchildren, and Averill (1969) induced dysphoric affect by having subjects view a "sad" movie.

Similarly, such cognitive inductions appear related to physiological changes consistent with the relevant mood-state. Changes in physiological process have been found following covert rehearsal of affectively valenced self-referential statements

(May & Johnson, 1973; Rimm & Litvak, 1969; Russell & Brandsma, 1974). Shaw (Note 6) found that visualizing depressive fantasies led to reduced arousal as measured by galvanic skin response, a finding consistent with studies documenting lower indices of arousal for depressed versus nondepressed psychiatric patients (Lader & Noble, 1975).

These data appear to indicate that specific cognitions can indeed induce affective and correlated physiological states. One important qualification appears necessary. In a recent replication of the initial Velten study, Rogers and Craighead (1977) instructed subjects to rate degree of belief (subjective validity) in the covert statements. Physiological as well as affective measures indicated that changes were associated with both the specific act of ideating and belief in the validity of the content ideated, not the act of ideating alone. These data appear to indicate that models that treat cognitions as covert "behaviors" may be inadequate, since such models focus solely on the reported occurrence of covert events rather than on more subjective aspects, such as belief and meaning. Similarly, efforts at intervention that emphasize repetition of covert self-statements may have limited impact if those covert self-statements are not seen as being accurate.

The second major tenet of cognitive theory is that cognitive factors influence behavioral performance and motivational factors. Several studies have found that increases in expectations following successful task performance were associated with subsequent increases in performance levels (Klein & Seligman, 1976; Loeb, Beck, & Diggory, 1971; Miller & Seligman, 1973). Seligman and colleagues (Hiroto & Seligman, 1975; Klein & Seligman, 1976; Miller & Seligman, 1975) have demonstrated the converse effect, in which the experience of noncontingent failure appears to produce subsequent deficits on performance measures.

Miller's (1975) review of the evidence for psychological deficits in depression led him to conclude that deficits exist in performance between depressives and nondepressives across a wide variety of tasks. In general, these deficits appear attributable to either cognitive (negative expectations, low self-confidence) or motivational (noninterest in outcome) factors. Friedman (1964) has similarly argued that apparent evidence for psychomotor retardation in depression was largely explicable in terms of cognitive variables, such as indecision and negative expectations for success prior to task initiation. He observed that depressives did not differ from nondepressives on a series of performance tasks once they were encouraged to begin working.

Taken together, all of the studies cited appear to indicate that depressives (*a*) differ from nondepressives in terms of manifest cognitive content; and (*b*) differ from nondepressives in terms of cognitive processing in such critical areas as attributions for success and failure, perception of control, perception of reinforcement, expectation of success and/or reinforcement, recall of information, and search for information. Difficulties in these domains might well be expected to interfere with relatively more normal processes of reinforcement. Specifically, it does not appear that depressives are either totally impervious to reinforcement or absolutely unmotivated to achieve success, but it does appear that elements of a negative cognitive set interfere with these goal-directed processes. Similarly, there appears to be support for both major tenets of cognitive theory: (*a*) Thinking (or, perhaps more precisely, thinking and believing) negative thoughts can lead to negative affect; whereas (*b*) negative cognitive sets appear to interfere with the performance of voluntary, especially skilled, behaviors.

Biochemical Theories

Current biological theories generally focus on presumed imbalances in biogenic amines, such as norepinepherine (Schildkraut, 1965), or indoleamines, such as serotonin (Coppen, 1967; Glassman, 1969). Both substances serve as neurotransmitters in the brain, conducting impulses from one nerve to another across the synaptic cleft between the nerves. These specific neurotransmitters appear concentrated in the limbic system, which appears to be a center for the mediation of various motivational systems. Schildkraut's initial formulation of the amine hypothesis suggested that deficits in norepinepherine are associated with depression, whereas excesses are associated with mania. Subsequent models have become increasingly complex but retain this general form. Indoleamine theories have followed the same general form as the norepinepherine models. Related alternate models have been proposed, including imbalances in hormonal regulatory systems and instability in electrolyte balances.

Supporting evidence for the biochemical theories in humans comes from at least four sources: (*a*) correlational studies relating biochemical processes to levels of depression; (*b*) genetic studies that appear to indicate hereditary factors in at least some types of affective disorders; (*c*) biochemical induction studies; and (*d*) pharmacological treatment studies. Studies relating to treatment will be considered in more detail later (see Section III, B, 1). For now, it is sufficient to note that evidence that an intervention reduces an existing phenomenon does not in any way support the theory of induction from which it may have been derived (or, in the case of the biochemical theories, which may have been derived from it).

None of the remaining three lines of evidence can, as yet, be considered conclusive. Although differences between depressed and nondepressed samples in biochemical processes have been demonstrated frequently, these differences are generally based on examinations of metabolites of the various neurotransmitters. In addition to being difficult to assay, relationships between metabolite levels and actual levels of neurotransmitters at the synapses vary markedly across individuals, situations, and states.

Most critical, of course, is the correlational nature of such designs; it is not possible to determine whether changes in brain physiology produce depression, depression produced changes in brain physiology, or some third variable produces changes in both. It has been shown, for example, that manipulations in levels of environmental stressors (e.g., control, predictability) are followed by changes in neurotransmitters in infrahuman species (Weiss, Stone, & Harrell, 1970).

Similarly, whereas a series of relatively well-controlled studies have implicated hereditary factors in bipolar affective disorders (those individuals showing manic or both manic and depressive episodes) and, perhaps, a very restricted subset of unipolar depressives, defined by three or more episodes of depression requiring hospitalization (Angst, 1966; Angst & Perris, 1972; Bertleson, Harvald, & Hauge, 1977; Perris, 1968), comparable studies involving nonpsychotic, nonbipolar depressives generally show little evidence of genetic transmission (Price, 1968; Stenstedt, 1966).[4] Since these latter affective disorders comprise perhaps 80% of all affective disorders of clinical significance, care must be used in assessing the generality of genetic factors in etiology.

Pharmacological induction evidence derives primarily from the observation that reserpine, a substance that depletes levels of norepinepherine and serotonin, induces depressions in about 10–15% of those individuals to whom it is administered. However, recent reevaluation of these data cautions that these figures approximate the incidence of affective disorders in the general population and that the bulk of the individuals in whom depressions appear to be induced have had prior histories of depression (Mendels & Frazier, 1974). Attempts to induce depression by means of other chemical agents known to deplete brain amines have been largely unsuccessful despite their capacity to reduce amine metabolite levels below those found to occur in clinically depressed individuals (Mendels & Frazier, 1974). Although speculating that some one or more of the biochemical theories will eventually prove most satisfactory, Mendels and Frazier conclude that none of the existing theories can be considered adequate at this time.

Dynamic–Motivational Theory

Dynamic theories of depression have traditionally focused on the role of retroflected anger—anger turned against the self following a real or symbolic loss (Abraham, 1949; Freud, 1917). Modeled after realistic loss or grief situations, depression is seen as a consequence of the turning against the self (actually the incorporated other) of the anger precipitated by symbolic loss or rejection. The individual is largely unaware of his or her hatred, which, being unacceptable, remains outside of consciousness. Depression, self-depreciation, and anxiety result from a mysterious "alchemy" generated by the retroflected anger that can neither be dismissed nor be expressed by the client. Freud (1917) formulated this mechanism in the following terms:

> If one listens patiently to a melancholic's many and various self-accusations, one cannot in the end avoid the impression that often the most violent of them are hardly at all applicable to the patient....We perceive that the self-reproaches are reproaches against a love object which have been shifted away from it onto the patient's own ego [p.248].

[4]It is not clear exactly what implications evidence of important genetic factors have for either theories of etiology or theories of intervention. As Beck (1967) has noted, such evidence only specifies genetic transmission, not the mechanism by which the phenotype is manifested. Similarly, evidence for genetic transmission need not preclude psychosocial interventions; available evidence points toward important genetic factors in the etiology on nonpsychotic anxiety states (Slater & Cowie, 1971). Yet, such states have proven at least as amenable to psychosocial interventions as to pharmacological ones (Hollon & Beck, 1978).

Although dynamic theory has had a profound impact on theory and practice, supporting evidence has been equivocal at best. As previously cited, studies of manifest dream content have revealed a preponderance of themes of loss and failure, rather than anger and hostility (Beck & Hurvich, 1959; Beck & Ward, 1961; Hauri, 1976). Examination of the content of free-association fantasies during analysis similarly failed to indicate excessive covert hostility but did indicate many themes of personal incompetence and failure (Beck, 1963). Identification on a series of projective stimuli was with the victim, rather than with the aggressor (Beck, 1961). Dream, free association, and projective identification themes were chosen because such materials are precisely where unconscious fantasies might be expected to be manifested. Beck concluded that the data could be more parsimoniously interpreted as reflecting a *belief* in personal incompetence rather than any converted internalized anger.

Since the alchemy hypothesis regards depression as the product of unconscious anger, levels of overt anger and overt depression might be expected to be inversely correlated, whereas increases in the overt expression of anger should co-vary with clinical improvement. Friedman (1970) found the exact opposite relationships to hold; measures of overt hostility and "covert" hostility (e.g., guilt, resentment, and internalized anger) were positively intercorrelated with one another and negatively correlated with improvement.

Paykel, Weissman, Prusoff, and Tonks (1971) have questioned traditional notions that depressives evidence less overt hostility than do nondepressives. Although depressives may evidence little hostility with such high-status figures as professional caregivers (Weissman & Paykel, 1974), anger is often intense and overtly expressed in relationships with immediate family members (Weissman, Klerman, & Paykel, 1971).

Forrest and Hokanson (1975) have demonstrated a behavioral preference for, and physiological arousal reduction following, what appears to be "masochistic" self-shock in a two-person interaction situation. Given the option of responding to another subject's response with shock delivery, self-shock of lesser strength, or a friendly signal, depressed college students both chose the self-shock option and evidenced arousal reduction, usually interpreted as an indication of perceived relative personal safety. However, both response preference and physiological arousal reduction were modifiable for both depressed and nondepressed subjects. Forrest and Hokanson arranged response contingencies such that the previously nonpreferred responses, aggressive countershock for the depressives and "masochistic" self-shock for the nondepressives, became differentially reinforced, invariably eliciting a "friendly" counterresponse from the other subject. Over 90 trials, both depressed and nondepressed groups shifted behavioral preference and physiological arousal reduction to the differentially reinforced response. The authors interpreted these data as indicating that masochistic behavior, traditionally regarded as a consequence of retroflected aggression, may actually be maintained by differential reinforcement, with mild levels of self-injurious behaviors that effectively prevent stronger levels of punisment from others becoming established. The adoption of nonaggressive strategies (in this instance, self-injurious behaviors) was interpreted within the context of a general social-learning theory, as were findings that similar strategies were adopted (with comparable physiological concomitants) by females when interacting with males (Hokanson, Willers, & Koropsak, 1968), by blacks when interacting with whites, and by college students when interacting with college professors (Hokanson, Burgess, & Cohen, 1963). Combined with the Weissman *et al.* findings, these studies suggest that anger and aggression may not be mysteriously "absent" in depression, resurfacing as masochism. Rather, the expression of such affects and behaviors may be regulated by instrumental considerations and perceived environmental contingencies.

Finally, the results of success–failure manipulations raise further challenges to the retroflected anger model. Consistent with this model, depressives are often assumed to have a "need to fail," a motivational process leading to avoidance of reinforcement, behavioral passivity, and sabotage of therapeutic efforts. Although performance deficits have frequently been observed (Miller, 1975), such deficits appear most closely related to subjective uncertainty and negative expectations, rather than motivational or physiological deficits (Beck, Feshbach, & Legg, 1962; Friedman, 1964). Clear and unambiguous feedback signalling success led to an increase in motivation, optimism, performance, and mood in two studies (Klein & Seligman, 1976, Loeb, Beck, & Diggory, 1971), a finding more consistent with a "negative expectation" model than a "need to fail" model.

Overall, the congruence of fantasy and conscious themes, the correlation between the expression of anger and depression and the inverse correlation between expression of anger and improvement, the modulation of masochistic and aggressive behaviors in response to perceived status deficits and expected outcomes, and the benign response to success all appear incompatible with the retroflected anger model. These findings are compatible with a cognitive perspective, one in which depressives view themselves as incompetent and at the mercy of relatively more powerful external forces.

Behavioral Theories

Behavioral theories can be divided into roughly three main groups. These groups include affect-mediated (or classical), outcome-mediated (or operant), and cognitive-mediated (or self-control) approaches.

The affect-mediated theories (Wolpe, 1971; Wolpe & Lazarus, 1966) focus on the role of classically conditioned anxiety; since certain stimuli come to elicit conditioned emotional responses, individuals avoid encountering those stimuli. When those stimuli are also cues for major potential sources of gratification (e.g., members of the opposite sex, job interviews, competitive interactions), the individual is effectively barred from major sources of satisfaction. Wolpe also suggests that excessive levels of anxiety may be directly transformed into depression, a formulation reminiscent of the psychoanalytic "alchemy" hypothesis of "actual neurosis." There appears to have been little systematic testing of this formulation.

Outcome-mediated, or operant, paradigms focus directly on the quality and rate of environmental events. Ferster (1973, 1974) speculated that depression might be produced by any of three situations:

1. Low rates of reinforcement
2. High rates of punishment
3. The removal of discriminative stimuli for response-reinforcer sequences.

Lewinsohn (1973, 1974, 1975a) has developed a major line of research focusing on the role of low rates of response-contingent reinforcement as a critical factor in depression. Whereas a major loss, such as the death of a spouse or the loss of a job, provides an obvious instance of change in the reinforcement potential of the environment, many depressions appear to be unprecipitated. Lewinsohn has focused on general deficits in social skills as a partial explanation of this phenomenon. Depressed individuals presumably lack the necessary skills to obtain gratifications from others and are thus rendered vulnerable to small fluctuations in external reinforcements.

Studies by Lewinsohn and colleagues (Lewinsohn & Graf, 1973; Lewinsohn & Libet, 1972; MacPhillamy & Lewinsohn, 1974) have documented inverse correlations between reported levels of positive events and self-related mood. However, these correlational findings do not establish any causal link between events and mood. In the Lewinsohn and Libet study, time-lagged correlations between pleasant activities and mood were examined for evidence of causality; the pattern of results was as compatible with either a negative-mood-reduces-reinforceable-behavior or a third-variable-causal-interpretation as with Lewinsohn's preferred reduced-reinforcement-leads-to-negative-mood model.

Similarly, studies involving observations of interpersonal behaviors indicate that depressives elicit less reinforcement from others and appear to exhibit lower levels of social skills (Lewinsohn & Shaffer, 1971; Lewinsohn, Weinstein, & Alper, 1970; Libet & Lewinsohn, 1973). These findings are typically regarded as supportive of the notion that deficit in social skills is a causal factor in depression. However, these studies were conducted with individuals who were currently depressed. Such a design is correlational in nature. It is entirely possible that the observed deficits in social skills are components, rather than causes, of the depressive syndrome. In contrast, Schrader, Craighead, & Schrader (1978) found depressives equally as skilled as nondepressives in an analog interaction situation. These authors suggested that social-skill deficits may reflect the suppression of the performance of existing skilled behaviors in interpersonal interactions, rather than deficits in the acquisition of such skills that predate the onset of the depression.

Direct tests of Lewinsohn's theory have also been equivocal (Blaney, 1977). Hammen and Glass (1975) induced depressed and nondepressed college students to increase activities according to prearranged behavioral schedules. No increase in mood was evident, despite an apparent increase in presumably reinforcing activities. Lewinsohn (1975b) argued that the authors failed to ascertain whether the specific activities prescribed were indeed potentially reinforcing for the subjects, but such an argument is relatively uncompelling.

Rehm (1977) has proposed a model of depression based on deficits in self-control. Drawing on Kanfer's (1970) concept of operations based on prior reinforcement history overriding current external contingencies, Rehm postulates deficits in self-monitoring, self-evaluation, and self-reinforcement behaviors. With regard to self-monitoring, depressives are said to (a) attend selectively to negative events and (b) attend selectively to immediate rather than to delayed outcomes. Self-evaluative behaviors are said to be maladaptive in terms of (c) failing to make internal attributions of causality and (d) setting excessively stringent criteria for self-evaluation. Self-reinforcement deficits are characterized by (e) low rates of self-reinforcement behaviors and (f) high rates of self-punitive behavior.

Selective attention to negative events appears to be compatible with either a cognitive or a self-control behavioral analysis, whereas only correlational questionnaire evidence (Rehm & Plakosh, 1975) was provided to support the notion of differential attention to immediate versus delayed outcomes. Consideration of self-evaluation processes appears largely to involve a translation of cognitive processes into behavioral terms. Two studies (Roth, Rehm, & Rozensky, Note 7; Rozensky, Rehm, Pry, & Roth, Note 8) indicated that depressives administer self-punishment more frequently than nondepressives, whereas depressives administered fewer self-reinforcements in the first, but not the second, study. Punishment and reinforcement were self-administered following correct or incorrect responses on a word-recognition task.

Rehm's self-control model attempts to deal with many of the same processes specified in cognitive theory. In comparing the self-control and cognitive models, Rehm states that "the self-control model deals with the same phenomena in a way that specifies the distortion processes in operational terms and places them in a theoretical context with other factors in depression.... The self-control model postulates specific relationships among covert cognitive processes and the overt symptomatology seen in depression. [Rehm, 1977, p. 800]." We would argue that the self-control model adds little to existing cognitive models and consists, at best, of a semantic rewording of cognitive theory into behavioral terminology. Nevertheless, such an effort may facilitate research into the behavioral and cognitive antecedants of the various phenomena of interest. Clearly, the self-control model can be said to be the most cognitive of the behavioral approaches.

From a cognitive perspective, the major criticism of behavioral theories of depression is that they underestimate the role of idiosyncratic content and individual differences in information processing, processes that may have major implications for both etiology and intervention. The roles of cognitive factors are receiving increased attention in the formulation of basic learning theories (Bandura, 1977a; Bolles, 1972; Grings, 1973; Kanfer, 1970). This same shift in theoretical formulations appears to be occurring as well in relation to behavioral models of depression.

Summary

Cognitive, biochemical, and behavioral theories each seem buttressed by supporting correlational evidence. There appears to be little support for the more traditional dynamic–motivational approach. Furthermore, there appears to be some evidence for both the cognitive and the biochemical models as etiological theories and, perhaps, some support as well for the behavioral theories.

It seems quite likely that the various components of the depressive syndrome will prove mutually interactive over time. As Akiskal and McKinney suggested, it may be possible to enter the system from any of several directions to trigger the full syndrome. Cognitively mediated etiologies will, we believe, prove particularly important, both within most individuals and across the greatest number of individuals. Biochemically mediated factors may prove prepotent for some individuals (particularly the bipolar and, perhaps, a small subset of the unipolar depressives). Behavioral formulations are certainly not incompatible with cognitive formulations; only the strictly behavioral formulations appear inadequate to account for some of the findings from experimental and descriptive clinical studies. There appears to be considerable support for a cognitive theory of depression as a model for a large percentage of the clinically significant depressions.

SYSTEMS OF INTERVENTIONS

Theories of Intervention

Both the biochemical and the various psychosocial theories of depression have been associated with one or more programs of intervention. Major examples of these various interventions were listed in the "Process" column in Table 6.1. Biochemical theories have been associated with both pharmacological and somatic interventions. Dynamic-motivational theories have given rise to a variety of approaches, ranging from supportive approaches designed to protect the individual from their alleged "need to suffer" and presumed self-sabotage (Appel, 1944; Ayd, 1961; Campbell, 1953) to depth approaches designed to promote insight into the motivational abnormalities and personality flaws presumed to underlie vulnerability to depression (Adler, 1961; Gero, 1936). Attempts to provide symptom relief via the expression of hostility have also been utilized. Intervention procedures typically involve semantic interchanges designed to provide affective catharsis and to promote insight into motivational processes.

Affect-mediated behavioral approaches have largely focused on the diminution of anxiety (Lazarus, 1968; Wolpe & Lazarus, 1966). Treatment procedures involve standard behavioral techniques used to decondition anxiety: systematic desensitization, counterconditioning, flooding, and implosive therapies.

Operant behavioral approaches generally focus on increasing the amount of obtained reinforcement. Two major approaches can be distinguished: direct contingency management procedures (e.g., token economies, systematic reward for appropriate behaviors and/or extinction of "depressive" behaviors, or making therapist time contingent upon engagement in various prescribed activities) and skills training designed to facilitate securing available reinforcements from the environment (e.g., training in social skills, training in self-monitoring or functional analyses).

Self-control behavioral approaches (Rehm, 1977) have focused on increasing rates of self-rewarding behaviors and/or decreasing rates of self-punitive behaviors. Specific procedures involve both direct contingency manipulation and skills-training in self-monitoring, self-evaluation, and self-reinforcement.

Some of the target phenomena of self-control models involve cognitive processes (e.g., self-evaluations) treated as "covert" behaviors. This approach predates the self-control model, dating at least to Homme (1965). Homme considered cognitive events (thoughts) as being essentially unobservable operant behaviors, subject to the same laws as other, observable behaviors. This behavioral approach to cognition therapy led to cognitive events being subjected directly to contingency management procedures (Jackson, 1972; Johnson, 1971). Whereas it seems unlikely that covert cognitive events invariably follow the same principles as voluntary behaviors (e.g., if thinking about unpleasant events is aversive, why wouldn't such thought be rapidly suppressed?), efforts to apply topographical and functional analyses to both cognitive and behavioral events appear laudable.

Cognitive therapy (Beck, 1964, 1970) can best be classified as a cognitive-behavioral intervention strategy. Although the primary targets of both behavioral and cognitive modification strategies are the beliefs and cognitive processes presumed to underlie depression, considerable use is made of a variety of behavioral techniques. Specifically, training in self-monitoring, behavioral rehearsal, role playing, and conducting functional analyses outside of the treatment setting is provided. Little use is made of direct contingency management techniques. Novel treatment components involve cognitive self-monitoring and reevaluation techniques, quite similar to cognitive restructuring strategies described by Goldfried (see Chapter 5, this volume). Also unique to cognitive therapy is the degree of integration of cognitive and behavioral techniques; behavioral assignments are specifically designed to test various beliefs rather than simply to get the client moving, whereas cognitive techniques are often used to offset the difficulties depressives have in instituting behavioral homework assignments.

Rational–emotive therapy shares a basic adherence to cognitive theory but emphasizes a greater reliance on semantic and persuasive techniques than does cognitive therapy. Furthermore, the specific approach has been traditionally structured as a deductive debate; the therapist knows in advance what types of irrational beliefs the client holds and frequently relies on verbal persuasion to produce changes in beliefs. In cognitive therapy, inductive processes are used to examine self- and therapist-monitored data, and explicit experiments are devised to test the validity of the client's (or the therapist's) beliefs.

Given the diversity in theories of depression and in associated theories and procedures of intervention, which, if any, of the approaches can be said to be effective intervention strategies? In the following section, the comparative outcome literature involving the various approaches will be reviewed.

Controlled Outcome Studies

Depression has traditionally been considered to be a self-limiting disorder. Controlled comparisons between randomly assigned groups appear to be a minimal criterion for demonstrating treatment efficacy. Single-subject designs have been utilized relatively infrequently; one must be able to count on a return of the target phenomenon during reversal phases in order to demonstrate treatment efficacy, and this is sometimes problematic. Since depression is also traditionally considered an episodic disorder, prevention of relapse following treatment termination may prove equally important to reduction of acute symptomatology.

Pharmacological Approaches

A large body of literature exists documenting the efficacy of a variety of pharmacological agents. Chief among these agents are the tricyclic antidepressants (imipramine, amitriptyline, desipramine, and nortriptyline), the monoamine oxidase inhibitors (phenelzine, isocarboxazid, nialamide, tranylcypromine, and iproniazid), and, more recently, lithium. Morris and Beck (1974) reviewed 146 double-blind, placebo-controlled studies conducted through 1972, finding tricyclics superior to placebo in 61 of 93 group comparisons and various monoamine oxidase inhibitors superior to placebo in 8 of 13 comparisons. In no instance was placebo found superior to active medication. Lithium, banned in this country until the last decade, has drawn increasing interest, primarily as an antimanic and prophylactic agent. A recent review by an American Psychiatric Association Task Force (1975) concluded, on the basis of controlled, double-blind studies, that lithium is clearly superior to placebo in reducing acute manic episodes and in preventing either manic or depressive relapses in bipolar affective patients. Lithium's usefulness as a prophylactic for nonbipolar depressives is far less certain. For both nonbipolar and bipolar patients, tricyclic antidepressants appear most effective in reducing acute depressive symptoms.

Despite their widespread usage and the impressive number of studies in which average response rates for drugs exceeded those for placebo, the magnitude, generality, stability, and safety of the drugs can be questioned. With regard to magnitude, most drug–placebo comparisons are conducted over a brief several-week period and reported in terms of relative group averages on various outcome measures. For example, Klerman, DiMascio, Weissman, Prusoff, and Paykel (1974) defined a "significant clinical improvement" as a 50% reduction in initial symptomatology over a 4-week active medication period. However, it is not clear how adequate such a reduction is in absolute terms. Furthermore, it is not clear that symptom reduction continues unabated throughout the time that an individual remains on medication. Although maximum drug–placebo differences usually emerge between 2 and 10 weeks of treatment, the natural course of the average depressive episode usually lasts from 24 to 56 weeks (Robins & Guze, 1969). Whereas drugs are clearly associated with relative reductions in symptom levels, they may not produce remission in absolute terms.

Drug efficacy can also be questioned with regard to generality. Small but important subsets of depressives cannot tolerate various medications due to the occurrence of noxious side effects. More important numerically is the apparent difficulty encountered in achieving compliance with medication regimes. Shaw (Note 9) has reviewed controlled-drug studies and has found an average dropout rate from the active medication cells of about 30%. Comparable figures for controlled psychotherapy studies averaged only about 10%. Although compliance can probably be improved by more careful attention to therapist–client relationship factors, at least some portion of the drug terminators may be responding to nuisance side-effects and/or perceived lack of improvement. Although determining the precise reasons for treatment termination is always difficult, it is likely that estimates of drug response are inflated by the exclusion of nonresponding dropouts from drug-response calculations.

Treatment stability refers to the maintenance of symptom reduction following the termination of active treatment. Current practice is turning increasingly toward maintaining depressed patients (both nonbipolar and bipolar) on medication on a permanent basis, much as diabetics are maintained on insulin (Davis, 1976; Paykel, Klerman, DiMascio, Weissman, & Prusoff, 1973; Schou, 1976). Although an estimated 55% of all index cases will have no subsequent episodes (Robins & Guze, 1969), depression has traditionally been considered an episodic phenomenon. In the Boston–New Haven project (Klerman *et al.,* 1974), 36% of the drug responders offered no treatment during follow-up relapsed within 8 months of drug termination. Independent of any questions regarding treatment efficacy, it is apparent that active medication produces few, if any, effects that last beyond treatment termination.

Finally, it is ironic that the tricyclic antidepressants have one of the lowest active dosage to lethal dosage ratios of any of the psychotropic medications, if abused. Although not all depressives are suicidal, many are. Availability of means is a key factor in suicide attempts. Although potential lethality would not preclude the use of medications, it should spur efforts to develop alternative approaches to treatment.

Traditional–Dynamic Intervention

Traditional and dynamic interventions have fared poorly in controlled comparisons with either nonspecific control conditions or the pharmacotherapies. Four studies have compared traditional dynamic interventions with pharmacotherapy. Daneman (1961) found that combining dynamically oriented individual supportive psychotherapy with imipramine did not appear to improve on remission rates generated by imipramine alone. Similarly, neither dynamically oriented group psychotherapy (Covi, Lipman, Derogatis, Smith, & Pattison, 1974) nor traditional marital therapy (Friedman, 1975) appreciably increased improvement rates when combined with tricyclics over those obtained by tricyclics alone. Furthermore, neither ''active'' psychotherapy exceeded improvement rates associated with combined nonspecific, pill–placebo control groups in either study. Klerman, Weissman, and colleagues (Klerman *et al.*, 1974; Weissman, Klerman, Paykel, Prusoff, & Hanson, 1974) similarly found no appreciable effect of social casework therapy on the prevention of relapse; combined psychotherapy–pharmacotherapy treatment neither improved on drug-only maintenance rates nor exceeded pill–placebo or nontreatment maintanance effects.

In the Friedman and the Klerman–Weissman *et al.* studies, the specific types of ''traditional psychotherapy'' were associated with a positive treatment response, although not in terms of depressive symptomatology. Friedman found that couples receiving marital therapy rated their marriages as improved, and Klerman-Weissman *et al.* found that individuals receiving interpersonally oriented social casework therapy rated their relationships as more satisfying. It seems fair to conclude that marital therapy and social casework therapy may be effective for some problems when applied by experienced therapists to clinically depressed (or, in the Klerman-Weissman, *et al* studies, previously clinically depressed) clients, but it also seems fair to conclude that such approaches are specifically *ineffective in ameliorating depression per se or in preventing subsequent relapse.*

Behavioral Interventions

The affect-mediated behavioral approaches have generally been evaluated by methodologically inadequate single-case studies. Beutler (1973) utilized implosive therapy with a female inpatient, and Badri (1967), Sammons (Note 10), and Wanderer (1972) utilized combinations of systematic desensitization and assertive training with depressed clients in separate case-studies. Shapiro, Neufeld, and Post (1962) combined desensitization with rational–emotive therapy in the treatment of a depressed inpatient. In each of these studies, clinical outcome was reported to be favorable. Despite being interpreted by the various authors as being supportive of both the respective theoretical formulations and intervention efficacies, in each case design inadequacies such as absence of control groups or treatment reversals and failures to control auxiliary treatment precluded drawing such conclusions.

Hannie and Adams (1974) provided a controlled comparison between flooding, nonspecific supportive group therapy and a no-treatment (milieu only) control involving depressed female inpatients. Subjects were chosen if they evidenced *both* depression and anxiety. Treatment in the flooding condition consisted of nine individual sessions over 3 weeks, during which anxiety-eliciting stimuli were imagined as vividly as possible until anxiety had spontaneously diminished. Subjects in the flooding cell reported significantly lower scores on the Multiple Affect Adjective Checklist (MAACL) (Zuckerman & Lubin, 1965) than did subjects in the two control conditions. Differences were noted on selected items from the Mental Status

Schedule (Spitzer, Burdick, & Hardesty, 1964) between the flooding and nonspecific conditions, but neither group differed from the no-treatment milieu/control.

Although these results offer some support for the clinical efficacy of flooding, it should be noted that all patients selected were both depressed and anxious. Since the major outcome measures were composite ratings assessing both syndromes, it is not possible to determine whether the treatment directly influenced depression or functioned solely by reducing syndrome anxiety. These data cannot be clearly interpreted as demonstrating any impact of flooding on depression *per se*.

Programs that seek first to provoke, then to reinforce the expression of anger, generally referred to as Anti-Depressive Programs (ADPs), appear best classified as affect-mediated behavioral interventions, since the treatment rationales are couched in behavioral terms. Nonetheless, such programs evidence ties to a dynamic alchemy theory in terms of the hypothesized role of anger in the intervention. ADP's focus on locking depressed inpatients in a room and forcing them to work on repetitive, meaningless tasks with no positive feedback regarding performance. Eventually, the patient rebels against the procedure, generally becomes angry, and refuses to continue. At that point, the patient is released from the work room and is praised effusively for asserting him/herself.

Initial tests have indicated generally positive outcomes (Barnes, 1977; Patterson, Taulbee, Golsom, Horner, & Wright; Note 11, Taulbee & Wright, 1971a,b), but, in each case, have involved only comparisons between unequal groups. It should be noted that ADPs involve several components: provocation to the point of anger, assertion of personal (or basic human) rights, and subsequent release from the "treatment" situation. If the ADPs do indeed demonstrate any efficacy in adequately controlled studies, treatment efficacy could be attributed to any of a variety of factors. Not the least of these factors is the potential role of success; available experimental literature indicates that personal efficacy has positive effects on depression (Klein & Seligman, 1976; Loeb *et al.,* 1971). Before concluding that the provocation of anger is a necessary component of the treatment package, controlled studies must determine whether comparable effects can be generated simply by enabling the client to be effective in controlling the environment.

Operant approaches have been evaluated in two separate single-subject designs. Reisinger (1972) used a token economy system to reinforce smiling behaviors in a male inpatient depressive. Although demonstrating experimental control over smiling in an ABA design, there was no evidence that treatment effects generalized to any other components of the depressive syndrome.

Hersen, Eisler, Alford, and Agras (1973) utilized a token economy to modify work, occupational therapy, responsibility, and personal hygiene behaviors in three neurotically depressed male inpatients. Again, experimental control over the target behaviors was demonstrated via an ABA design. Furthermore, contingency-related increases and decreases were paralleled by changes in nurses' ratings of the patients on the Behavioral Rating Scale (BRS) (Williams, Barlow, & Agras, 1972), which assesses rates of talking, smiling, and motor activity. Even though the BRS had been found to correlate with syndrome depression measures in the Williams *et al.* study, the ratings served as the sole outcome measure in the Hersen *et al.* design. It remains unclear whether the token system reduced syndrome depression per se or only increased rates of motor activity.

Although neither the Reisinger nor the Hersen *et al.* study adequately documented treatment efficacy relative to syndrome depression, both studies did demonstrate behavioral responsivity to reinforcement contingencies on the part of the depressed patients. Finding depressed inpatients responsive to clear-cut, concrete contingencies is compatible with either behavioral or cognitive formulations but is difficult to accommodate within either biochemical (which emphasizes a generalized anhedonia) or psychodynamic (which emphasize a need to suffer or retroflected hostility) formulations.

McLean, Ogston, and Grauer (1973) provided one of the few adequately controlled group comparisons supporting the efficacy of primarily behavioral techniques. Twenty couples were identified in which one spouse could be said to exhibit an incapacitating but nonpsychotic depression. The couples were randomly assigned to either 8 weeks of social learning therapy or were referred back to the initial referral source for conventional treatments. The exact nature of the treatments received by the comparison group was determined by the referral source but included traditional psychotherapy, couples counseling, or medication for the various patients. Social-learning therapy consisted of 8 weekly sessions involving training in social-learning principles, utilization of spouse feedback boxes (in which different colored lights indicated whether an interaction was seen as friendly or hostile), and the use of reciprocal behavioral contracting. Change scores on the Depression Adjectives Checklist (DACL) (Lubin, 1967), a measure of dysphoric affect, and summed scores on ratings of five behavioral target problems indicated greater positive changes for the social-learning treatment group at posttreatment and at a 3-month follow-up.

Treatment efficacy appears to have been adequately demonstrated in this study. However, the use of only a single depression-relevant measure, especially one that measures only one component affect of the full syndrome, makes it difficult to evaluate the magnitude of change obtained in clinical terms or to compare the results with those obtained in other studies.

Lewinsohn and colleagues have provided several demonstrations of their behavioral approach to depression in either single case (Lewinsohn & Atwood, 1969; Lewinsohn & Shaffer, 1971; Lewinsohn & Shaw, 1969; Lewinsohn *et al.* 1970) or analogue designs (Robinson & Lewinsohn, 1973a,b) but have not provided any adequately controlled single-subject or groups design evaluations of treatment efficacy. Although treatment interventions targeted either at identifying potential reinforcers and increasing the frequency of their occurrence or at isolating and modifying deficits in social skills behaviors (Lewinsohn & Shaw, 1969; Lewinsohn *et al.*, 1970) have been associated with positive changes, the design limitations mentioned previously generally preclude clearly attributing those changes to the treatment procedures.

Behavioral approaches modeled, at least in part, on Lewinsohn's program have met with, at best, limited success in three controlled comparisons. Two of the three studies (Shaw, 1977; Taylor & Marshall, 1977) involved comparisons with cognitive therapy and will be described below. In the third, Padfield (1976) found differences between groups on only one of four measures, the Grinker Interview Checklist (Grinker, Miller, Sabshin, Nunn, & Nunnally, 1961), in a comparison of individual behavioral therapy with nondirective therapy in a sample of female depressed outpatients. That single significant difference favored the nondirective therapy. Treatment extended over 12 weeks and involved a clinical sample, making the general absence of overall group differences particularly noteworthy.

Cognitive–Behavioral Interventions

Taylor and Marshall (1977) found a combined cognitive–behavioral intervention superior to a strictly cognitive modification procedure (involving only rational and semantic intervention procedures), a strictly behavioral procedure, and a waiting-list control over a 6-week treatment course. The cognitive modification procedure and the behavior modification procedure did not differ from one another in terms of outcome but were both superior to the waiting-list control. Subjects in the study were college student volunteers, and therapists were relatively inexperienced professionals in training. Outcome measures included the Beck Depression Inventory (BDI) and the D-30 (Dempsey, 1964), a 30-item subscale of the depression scale from the Minnesota Multiphasic Inventory (MMPI).

Treatment results from the Taylor and Marshall study, along with the results of the other published studies that involved controlled comparisons and provided mean scores on the depression measures, are graphed in Figure 6.1.[5] Scores are presented on three measures: the BDI, the MMPI-D, and the Hamilton Rating Scale for Depression (HRS-D) (Hamilton, 1960), a clinician rating scale, in order to facilitate comparisons across studies using comparable measures.

As can be seen in Figure 6.1, the Taylor and Marshall findings were closely paralleled by findings from Shaw (1977). College students applying for treatment at a University Counseling Center were randomly assigned to behavioral, cognitive-behavioral, or nondirective treatment or a waiting-list control condition. The behavioral treatment was modeled after Lewinsohn's program, and the cognitive-behavioral approach was modeled after Beck's cognitive therapy.

Unlike the Taylor and Marshall study in which clients were seen in individual sessions, Shaw conducted treatment in groups, with each of the respective treatment-types meeting as a separate group over a 4-week active treatment period. All therapy was conducted by the author. Outcome was assessed by means of self-report on the Beck Depression Inventory (BDI) and clinician-rating on the

---

[5]The Padfield (1976) and McLean, Ogston, & Grauer (1973) studies were excluded, since results were presented only as change scores not suitable for graphic presentation. The Hannie and Adams study (1974) was excluded because of the confounding of anxiety and depression in terms of both measures and interventions.

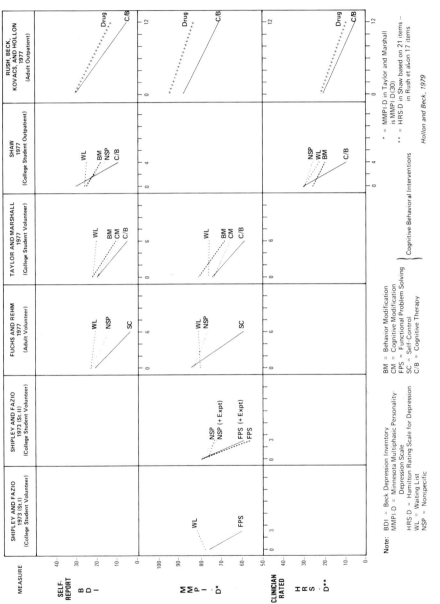

Figure 6.1. Pre–post group means in studies comparing cognitive–behavioral with alternative treatments.

Note: BDI = Beck Depression Inventory
       MMPI-D = Minnesota Multiphasic Personality-
                Depression Scale
       HRS-D = Hamilton Rating Scale for Depression
       WL = Waiting List
       NSP = Nonspecific

       BM = Behavior Modification
       CM = Cognitive Modification
       FPS = Functional Problem Solving
       SC = Self-Control
       C/B = Cognitive Therapy

       Cognitive-Behavioral Interventions

       * = MMPI-D in Taylor and Marshall
           is MMPI-D (30)
       ** = HRS-D in Shaw based on 21 items –
            in Rush et al.on 17 items

                               Hollon and Beck, 1979

175

Hamilton Rating Scale for Depression (HRS-D). Ratings on the HRS-D were made from videotaped interviews and were judged by clinicians blind both to treatment condition and to assessment point (pre-, post-, or follow-up).

Subjects in cognitive therapy evidenced greater improvement on both measures than did all other groups. The behavior therapy and nondirective therapy groups both showed improvement relative to the waiting-list controls but did not differ from one another. Differences between the active treatment groups were maintained at a 1-month follow-up; the group means between the cognitive therapy and behavior therapy groups were no longer significantly different, but no significant change in scores from posttreatment to follow-up was apparent for either group.

As in the Padfield study, behavior therapy and a nonspecific control group did not differ, whereas, as in the Marshall and Taylor comparison, the cognitive–behavioral intervention evidenced greater improvement than did the behavioral treatment alone. These findings, combined with the relative comparability of the solely cognitive and solely behavioral procedures, suggest that the combination of cognitive and behavioral procedures may prove uniquely effective.

Four other studies (Fuchs & Rehm, 1977; Rehm, Fuchs, Roth, Kornblith, & Roman, Note 12; Shipley & Fazio, 1973), all involving approaches similar in many ways to Beck's cognitive therapy, appear to buttress these conclusions. Shipley and Fazio (1973) conducted two studies, both involving college-student volunteers. In Study I, subjects were assigned to either *functional problem solving (FPS:* An intervention similar to cognitive therapy, consisting of correcting errors in discrimination or misinterpretations of situations and errors in selecting behavioral responses) or a waiting-list control. Pretreatment to posttreatment comparisons over the 3-week treatment period demonstrated significantly greater improvement for the functional problem solving subjects.

This finding was essentially replicated in a second study involving a similar volunteer population. In this study, functional problem solving was compared with a nonspecific treatment control. In addition, half of the subjects in each condition were given an expectational manipulation, being told that their specific treatment condition was expected to be superior. Since subjects were randomly distributed across the 2 × 2 design (treatment by expectation), both functional problem solving cells can be considered independent replications.

As shown in Figure 6.1, both problem-solving treatment cells evidenced greater improvement on the MMPI-D than did either nonspecific control condition. No differences were apparent as a function of the expectancy manipulation.

Fuchs and Rehm (1977) and Rehm *et al.* (Note 12) have evaluated the efficacy of a treatment approach based on Rehm's (1977) self-control model of depression. In both studies, subjects were depressed female volunteers from the community who responded to newspaper advertisements. In the Fuchs and Rehm study, subjects were randomly assigned to either self-control, nonspecific control, or waiting-list conditions. All treatment was conducted in a group format over a 6-week period by relatively inexperienced therapists. Treatment efficacy was evaluated by means of both the BDI and the MMPI-D. As shown in Figure 6.1, subjects in the self-control treatment group evidenced greater improvement on both measures than those in either of the control conditions, and subjects in the nonspecific control evidenced greater change than those in waiting-list control. A 1-month follow-up indicated that improvements were maintained after treatment termination.

In the Rehm *et al.* study (Note 12), the female volunteers were assigned to either self-control or social-skills training. Treatment in both conditions was conducted in group formats on a weekly basis over a 6-week period. Although both groups showed significant improvement, subjects in the self-control condition showed greater change on syndrome depression.

These findings, combined with the results from the group comparisons reported earlier, appear to indicate that combined cognitive–behavioral (or cognitively oriented behavioral) interventions may prove superior to strictly cognitive–semantic or strictly behavioral interventions and are certainly superior to nonspecific or waiting-list controls. It should be noted that only the Padfield and the Shaw samples involved clients who had sought treatment, rather than subjects participating in a study (Shipley & Fazio, 1973) or volunteers responding to advertised treatment opportunities (Fuchs & Rehm, 19787; Rehm, Note 12; Taylor and Marshall, 1977). It seems appropriate to include Rehm's self-control procedures as cognitively oriented behavioral strategies, since at least the self-evaluative component of the treatment package is targeted at basically cognitive processes. Basic operational differences do exist, however, between Rehm's approach, conceptualized within a behavioral self-control paradigm, and Beck's cognitive therapy (see the following section, *Cognitive Therapy Procedures*). In addition to exploring the potential efficacy of the self-control approach in a bona fide clinical population, controlled comparisons of self-control procedures with Beck's cognitive therapy would be quite valuable.

Referring to Figure 6.1, it can be seen that, despite the potential for variation across the samples used in the different studies, the pattern of comparisons within the studies shows a striking consistency across measures. Waiting-list controls across four studies (Fuchs & Rehm, 1977; Shaw, 1977; Shipley & Fazio, 1973, Study 1; Taylor & Marshall, 1977) showed little or no change and, in some cases, even increased slightly. In no instance did any waiting-list control show significant pre–post interval changes. Nonspecific or nondirective therapy control treatments evidenced small degrees of improvement in the Shipley and Fazio (Study II), Shaw, and Fuchs and Rehm studies. Pre–posttreatment improvements were generally slight even where significant, and posttreatment differences were generally superior to waiting-list controls. Cognitive modification practiced as a semantic intervention only was equivalent to strict behavior modifiction, with neither differing appreciably from the nonspecific treatment comparison in the Shaw study. In each instance and on each measure, the various cognitive–behavioral combinations (cognitive therapy—Taylor and Marshall, Shaw; self-control therapy—Fuchs and Rehm; and functional problem solving—Shipley and Fazio, Studies I and II) evidenced the greatest improvement.

One additional study exists in which a strictly cognitive intervention did not prove superior to a strictly behavioral intervention, although both proved superior to treatment controls. Hodgson and Urban (Note 13), working with volunteer college students, assigned subjects to 3 weeks of interpersonal perception training (based loosely on cognitive theory), interpersonal skills training, a nonspecific control group, or a waiting-list control. All subjects were seen in a group-therapy format. Multivariate assessment on the DACL and the Self-Rating Depression Scale (SDS) (Zung, 1965) indicated that both active treatment groups improved significantly more than did the no-treatment control but did not differ from one another. Such a finding argues for the comparability of strictly cognitive to strictly behavioral therapy. Inspection of the descriptions provided of the actual therapeutic procedures utilized suggests that the cognitive intervention bore little resemblance to recommended cognitive–behavioral procedures in Beck's cognitive therapy (Beck, Rush, Shaw, & Emery, 1979, or see the following section, *Cognitive Therapy Procedures*). Subjects in the interpersonal perception training group were provided with a cognitive treatment rationale and then led through a series of group process interactions that focused on ''distortions in interpersonal perception.'' One of the sessions, for example, was devoted to having subjects imagine that they and other group members were animals. Subjects then discussed apparent differences in their respective perceptions. Such procedures seem far removed from efforts to carefully analyze and alter functional relationships between cognition, behavior, and affect in the clients' everyday environments by means of both cognitive and behavioral techniques.

What of combined cognitive–behavioral interventions with *bona fide* clinical populations? Of the studies reviewed so far, only Shaw's comparison, in which cognitive therapy proved superior to behavior therapy, the Hannie and Adams, the McLean, *et al.*, and the Padfield comparisons involved clients initiating a request for psychological interventions. Although populations selected by Rehm and his colleagues were drawn from community volunteers and may be quite similar to typical outpatient clinical populations, such generalizability simply cannot be assumed. Furthermore, in the bulk of the comparisons, at least those discussed so far, suicidal subjects were routinely screened out of the treatment samples. For these reasons, generalizability to clinical populations cannot be assumed.

Several studies have been conducted involving cognitive therapy (utilizing both behavioral and cognitive techniques) with clinical populations. Rush, Khatami, and Beck (1975) treated three outpatient depressives with cognitive therapy. Although decreases in reported syndrome depression on the BDI were consistent with treatment efficacy, the lack of experimental controls precluded attributing improvement to the specific intervention. Schmickley (1976) had 11 depressed outpatients treated with cognitive therapy in a Community Mental Center in an ABA reversal design. As a group, the patients improved with four 1-hour sessions over a 2-week interval but evidenced return of symptoms with the cessation of treatment. Schmickley interpreted these findings as being consistent with treatment efficacy, but, again, the nature of the design precluded drawing any rigorous conclusions. An initial drop in symptom levels immediately after beginning a formal treatment phase is not unusual in depressed populations and is frequently followed by a subsequent return of increased symptom-levels early in treatment. Single-subject and multiple baseline across subjects designs must be rigorously designed to avoid confounding treatment effects with the natural course of depressive symptoms during formal treatment.

Rush *et al.* (1977) compared individual cognitive therapy with pharmacotherapy in the treatment of outpatient depressives. All patients were screened in accordance with the Feighner diagnostic criteria (Feighner, Robins, Guze, Woodruff, Winokur, & Muñoz, 1972) in order to select a sample of primary, nonbipolar, nonpsychotic depressives with no indication of schizophrenia, bipolar affective illness, alcohol or drug addiction, other major neurosis, sociopathy, organic brain syndrome, or mental retardation. All subjects with a prior history of nonresponse to tricyclic antidepressants were also excluded.[6] All subjects were required to have minimum scores of 20 on the BDI and 14 on the first 17 items of the HRS-D in order to be included in the sample.

Clients assigned to cognitive therapy received a maximum of 20 sessions over a 12-week treatment interval. Pharmacotherapy involved once-weekly sessions over the same 12-week period. Treatment visits in this modality lasted an average of 20 minutes and involved nonspecific supportive contact and careful monitoring of medication dosage and side effects. The medication involved was imipramine hydrochloride, with a starting dosage of 75 mg increased to a maximum of 250 mg per day.

Over the 12-week active treatment period, both treatments were associated with significant reductions in symptomatology as assessed by the BDI, MMPI-D, and HRS-D, but the clients treated with cognitive therapy showed significantly greater improvement than those treated with antidepressant medications. Follow-up at 3 and 6 months indicated that improvement was maintained over time, although significantly more of the drug-treated clients sought additional treatment during the follow-up period. Follow-up at 1 year indicated continued differences between the groups at that point (Kovacs, Beck, Rush, & Hollon, Note 14).

Overall, these findings provide strong evidence for the efficacy of cognitive therapy in the treatment of outpatient, nonbipolar depressives. Although the pharmacotherapy appeared as effective as might have been expected, cognitive therapy evidenced a significantly greater level of clinical efficacy, both in terms of reduction of acute symptomatology and in terms of prevention of relapse. Becker and Schuckit (1978) have argued that the sample selected was so chronically depressed that it provided an unfair comparison for effective pharmacological treatment, but reanalysis of the data separating acute from chronic depressives indicated that the bulk of the differential response came from the acute depressives. The more chronically depressed subjects seemed to respond about equally to the two treatment modalities (Rush, Hollon, Beck, & Kovacs, 1978).

Clearly, these results require replication. The efficacy of the antidepressants is so firmly established that multiple trials with comparable outcomes would be required before claims for treatment superiority would be justified. For now, it is important

---

[6]This procedure, standard in many drug trials, risks biasing the sample in favor of the drugs (see Hollon & Beck, 1978).

to note that a cognitive–behavioral intervention, as represented by cognitive therapy, has been shown to be superior to pharmacotherapy in terms of both reducing acute symptomatology and preventing subsequent relapse in at least one study. Combined with apparent lack of efficacy of the traditional approaches relative to pharmacotherapy and with the apparent superiority of combined cognitive–behavioral approaches over strictly behavioral or strictly semantic cognitive approaches, these findings appear to make a strong case for the clinical efficacy of cognitive–behavioral interventions.

Summary

Combined cognitive–behavioral interventions appear to be particularly efficacious treatment strategies in depression, whether operationalized in terms of Becks's cognitive therapy, Rehm's more behaviorally oriented self-control model, or various other combined programs. Neither strictly behavioral nor strictly cognitive procedures appear to be as effective, although either typically prove superior to waiting-list or no-treatment controls. Traditional approaches to psychotherapy appear generally to be ineffective. Pharmacological and somatic approaches remain the standards against which the various psychosocial approaches should be compared; efforts should be directed at improving on evident drug-treatment response rates. To date, only the cognitive–behavioral combination (Beck's cognitive therapy) has demonstrated any apparent superiority over drugs.

There appear, then, to be theoretical reasons for considering the role of cognition in depression, procedural advantages to considering the role of cognition in change, and strong practical reasons for incorporating such procedures in clinical practice. In the following section, the various steps involved in the implementation of cognitive therapy will be presented.

COGNITIVE THERAPY PROCEDURES

General Considerations

Cognitive therapy consists of the systematic application of empirical procedures to the cognitive, behavioral, and affective processes of the depressed client (see Beck *et al.*, 1979, for a detailed summary of treatment procedures). The practice of cognitive therapy can be compared to the conduct of any scientific inquiry. Beliefs, assumptions, and expectations are treated as "hypotheses" to be tested. Emphasis is placed on formulating rigorous tests and on utilizing sound methodological principles to evaluate these hypotheses.

The basic strategy that underlies interaction between client and therapist is one of *collaborative empiricism*. Client and therapist serve as active collaborators in the identification of problem areas and in the design and execution of tests of the various beliefs. The data generated by these tests, rather than therapist credibility or authority, are relied upon to provide understanding and to produce change. The client is not persuaded to change by the therapist; rather, the evidence generated by the client in unbiased experiments is allowed to speak for itself.

Working with depressed clients usually requires considerable activity on the part of the therapist. Even though collaborative empiricism serves as a guide to the therapeutic interaction, early sessions typically require considerable structuring, encouragement, and guidance on the part of the therapist.

Cognitive therapy is generally conducted within a *time-limited* framework. The most extensive treatment manual currently available (Beck *et al.,* 1979) outlines a 20-session treatment program. The 20-session program, administered over a 12-week period, was associated with full clinical remission in 83% of the moderately to severely depressed outpatients treated in the Rush *et al.* study. Similarly, Shaw and Hollon (Note 15) have found comparable results with a 12-week treatment course using a single 2-hour session once weekly in a group treatment format.

Given the remitting nature of most depressive episodes, time-limited treatment would seem to be particularly desirable. There is some evidence that the frequency of sessions, rather than the length of time in treatment, may be of particular importance. Clients treated in individual cognitive therapy once weekly over 20 sessions did less well than clients treated twice weekly for up to 20 sessions over only 12 weeks (Rush, Beck, Kovacs, Khatami, Fitzgibbons, & Wolman, Note 16). Similarly, Morris (1975) found comparable improvement with 6 sessions over 3 weeks as with 6 sessions over 6 weeks.

It is generally helpful to begin the initial session with some standardized measure of the severity of the client's depression, for example, the BDI, and to provide the client with a brief description of cognitive therapy. *Coping with Depression* (Beck & Greenberg, 1974) is a brief six-page pamphlet that describes common symptoms, basic cognitive theory in depression, and major treatment techniques. Instructing the client to read this pamphlet serves as a useful teaching device and often elicits concerns regarding the nature of treatment. It is always important to assess the client's expectation prior to initiating therapy, since depressed clients often hold pessimistic views that, if left unattended to, could interfere with their carrying out the initial homework assignments.

Specific Techniques

Self-Monitoring Skills

In addition to standardized depression assessment devices, it is usually advantageous to have the client initiate systematic self-monitoring of relevant phenomena from the first session on. Mood, ongoing events, pleasant activities, and mastery behaviors are frequently rated categories, although considerable flexibility can be employed where indicated. For example, one client who viewed her problems as stemming from fatigue related to some as yet undiagnosed physical ailment was instructed to self-monitor subjective energy levels. At the next session it was appar-

TABLE 6.2
Weekly Self-Monitoring Record from a Depressed Male[a]

	Monday 1/16	Tuesday 1/17	Wednesday 1/18	Thursday 1/12	Friday 1/13	Saturday 1/14	Sunday 1/15
9–10	Did dishes (40), breakfast	Drove to class, eat (50)	Meeting with sales agent (50)	Therapy session (25 P)	Up–out to dentist, nauseous (25)	Up early (60), to work, working with J. (M)	Sleep
10–11	Went to bookstore (45 P)	Sculpture class (55 M)	Meetings (55)	Mail out brochures, eat (50 M,M)	Dentist, toast at diner	Apply hardwall, finish wall (65 P)	Sleep
11–12	Filled gas, read paper (45)	Sculpture class (55 M)	Meeting (55)	Make business calls (M, P)	Home, read magazine (25)	Off to store (60 P)	Read paper (25)
12–1	Looked at mail, real estate ads (45)	Looked at boots at stores (40), guilty	Fill car, buy paper (55)	Read mail (60), phone calls (45), coffee (30)	Call models, truck relay out (25)	Work on alarm system (55 P)	Read magazine (30)
1–2	Went to work (40)	Went to work (50)	Make calls (45)	Work at lumber yard (35)	Replace relay (40 P,M)	Come home read mail, talk to J. (45)	Read magazine, eat (30)

2–3	Cut end rows (45 P)	Talked with boss (50)	Go to work (45)	Lumber yard and hardware store (25)	Work on sculpture, (50 P) still nauseous	Eat lunch (30) wash dishes	Watch tube (30)
3–4	Painted end rows (50 P,M)	Head for home (45)	Install fixtures (30)	Repair tires (25)	Off to work (50)	Clean home (30)	Watch tube (30)
4–5	Installed grill plates (60 P,M)	Leave for night class (45)	Home to eat (35)	Replace tiles, & clean up (25)	Patching wall, and clean up (50)	Clean home (25), wash clothes, relax	Watch tube (30), eat
5–6	Installed grill plates and mike (60 P)	Sculpture class (50 P)	Go to movie (45)	Clean up, head for home (25)	Work on wall, to store (50 P)	Relax, make drinks dinner (25)	Watch tube (30)
6–7	Come home (50)	Sculpture (50)	Movie (45 P)	Eat, watch tube (25)	Home to eat (25), read magazine	Eat, talk, drink wine (35)	Watch tube (30), read
7–8	Eat dinner, (45) talk to J.	Head home, talk to J. (50)	Movie (35), fight with J.	Watch tube, called therapist (25)	Talk to J. (25), out for ice cream	Relax, talk (35)	Took bath (30–45)
8–12	Watch tube (45), made molds (60 P,M)	Work on sculpture (50)	Coffee out (45), then home	Watch tube, talk to J. (20)	Back home (35), tooth still hurts	Relax, talk (35)	Read magazine bed, 10:30 (35)

*a*Note: M = Mastery Behavior

P = Pleasure

(0–100) = Current mood, 0 is the worst you've ever felt, 100 is the best you've ever felt.

ent that she suffered from a curious type of fatigue that improved whenever she engaged in physical activity. Table 6.2 presents a set of ratings provided by a typical client during the first week of therapy. Mood was rated on a 100-point scale, with 0 representing "the worst you've ever felt in your whole life" and 100 representing "the best you've ever felt in your whole life." Ratings of pleasant events, mastery behaviors, or other ratings can also be put on this 100-point metric or, as is more often the case, simply noted in a frequency-count fashion.

As can be seen in Table 6.2, the client evidenced rather striking patterns of mood fluctuations, even within the course of a single day. These data can serve as the basis for both behavioral and cognitive interventions, as will be discussed later. For example, the variability observed was used to question the client's initial assertion that his depression was a continuous, unbroken phenomenon. Similarly, the client had entered therapy expressing the conviction that his dysphoria was, in part, a function of his disliked, presumably unpromising, work situation. However, it was apparent that his actual mood was higher when at work that at most other points during the week. Weekends, which he typically left unstructured, were often the periods of lowest absolute mood.

Timing of the ratings may also prove to be important. Hollon and Evans (Note 17) have observed that, for depressed college students, self-ratings of mood were noticeably lower when made retrospectively at the end of the day than when made on an hourly basis throughout the day. Clients often have difficulty maintaining hourly self-monitoring records, lapsing into retrospective recording. These data suggest that mood ratings made on such a basis may be particularly vulnerable to negative distortions in recall.

Behavioral Techniques

A variety of techniques involve the systematic alteration of the client's ongoing behavior. Bandura (1977b) has argued for a differentiation between the processes involved in change, which he considers to be largely cognitive, and the procedures most likely to produce change, seen as being largely enactive. Without denying the power of behavioral procedures, we prefer not to leave the processes of learning and inference in enactive situations to the vagaries of subjective interpretation. Rather, behavioral techniques are chosen and implemented so as to maximize the probability of participation and to enhance the potential for disconfirmation of previously held beliefs. In short, behavioral procedures are always implemented in conjunction with cognitive–symbolic techniques. Patients are encouraged to generate predictions or to explicate beliefs and, then, to evaluate them in the light of their own performance.

The explicit *disconfirmation* of stated beliefs by means of direct, self-monitored experiences following from the client's own activities is followed by a discussion of the contingencies involved and the conclusions that can be drawn. Such a procedure, involving both enactive and cognitive–symbolic components, is seen as the optimal paradigm for generating cognitive change and for maximizing the generality of the behavioral procedures. Instead of simply "getting the client moving," such a combination increases the probability of the client's being able to challenge successfully anticipated nongratification or fantasized incompetence in future situations. Similarly, rather than simply mobilizing the client in the face of negative expectations, the client is trained to evaluate systematically such predictions, putting the beliefs to an unbiased test, eventually learning that it is the negative expectations that are inaccurate.

A variety of specific behavioral tasks have been utilized in cognitive therapy. Several of these procedures, specifically, graded task assignments, activity scheduling, pleasurable event scheduling, and "M and P" therapy, will be briefly outlined.

Graded Task Assignment.   Several studies have indicated that the experience of producing desired outcomes can raise mood (Loeb *et al.,* 1971), increase optimism and self-esteem (Loeb, Beck, Diggory, & Tuthill, Note 18; Loeb *et al.,* 1964), and improve performance on subsequent tasks (Klein & Seligman, 1976) for depressed subjects.

Graded task assignments serve to order the sequence in which tasks are attempted, from least demanding to most demanding, so as to maximize the individual's probability of initiating and completing any given sequence. Several components are important. First, the task is divided into smaller subtasks. For example, the process of writing a resumé can be broken into the following steps: getting a pen, getting paper, placing the paper on the table, turning on the light, pulling up a chair, sitting in the chair, starting with descriptive information such as name, address, etc. As each step is completed, it can be checked off on a list of relevant steps involved in task completion. Such a procedure ensures that the most concrete, easily achievable steps are attempted first, facilitating task initiation. Equally important, the client produces a visible record of behavioral accomplishments with which to challenge beliefs regarding personal incompetence. By the time he or she has reached the more demanding, generally more abstract components of the task, a considerable string of "successes" has been generated. When a formal, step-by-step task analysis is performed in advance, either during the therapy session or by the client before entering the performance situation, the client is assured of having a discrete, concrete *plan* to follow. Separating planning from implementation has the effect of reducing the number of tasks confronting the client at any point in time. Rather than being confronted with the need to decide what to do next as well as to do it, the client must now only implement a decided-upon behavior. Available data indicate that apparent psychomotor retardation may be more a function of indecisiveness at behavioral choice-points than any inability to perform discrete behaviors (Friedman, 1964, Miller, 1975). In general, the capacity to generate small successes appears to be associated with an increase in observed motivation; small successes appear to have the effect of priming-the-pump for initiating items further along on the hierarchy. Finally, the process allows the formal collection of beliefs or predictions generated prior to task initiation. These cognitions can be a rich source of data regarding belief systems that can be worked on with the more formal cognitive techniques documented in the following.

The outcomes obtained when using graded task assignment procedures can also be compared to the outcomes obtained when tasks are handled in an unstructured, global way to illustrate (*a*) the efficacy of structure, ordering in terms of increasing subtask difficulty and "priming" with small successes; and (*b*) the role of negative expectations in undercutting motivation and in suppressing competencies.

Activity Scheduling.   Activity scheduling involves planning the client's days in a systematic fashion. The client and therapist simply schedule, on an hour-by-hour basis, activities for the client to engage in between sessions. Such a procedure appears to reduce passivity and to decrease the amount of time spent in rumination.

The client's reaction to the process is always of critical importance. Some clients may feel overwhelmed, others insulted, others concerned that they are boring the therapist or appear immature or helpless, etc. Idiosyncratic responses to activity scheduling or to its implemantation can be important both because they may inter- fere with carrying out the agreed-upon activities and because they may provide particularly relevant cues to underlying belief systems. As always, consideration of the cognitive aspects of the various behavioral procedures not only enhances the probability of the procedures being put into effect but also provides material for insuring the subsequent generalization of the principles involved.

One interesting variation on activity scheduling is *selective scheduling*. Fre- quently, mildly to moderately depressed clients can use their self-monitoring to identify particular times when they are most prone to behavioral passivity and depressogenic rumination. Patients evidencing marked diurnal variation may find that they need actively to schedule only their mornings (or evenings, for those showing decreases in mood in the evening). One client who experienced marked early morning dysphoria would sit down the evening before and plan, in consider- able detail, the routine he would follow. The next morning, he would simply run through the routine, checking off each item as he went. The patient described the procedure as "planning my work, then working my plan."

Yet another client, after averaging his self-monitored mood states over the days of the week, noted that two days were particularly discrepant from the rest. On the average, Sundays were accompanied by the lowest mood ratings, Mondays by the highest. Somewhat surprised, he reviewed his recorded activities and found that he spent the bulk of his time Sunday doing little, even recreational, but did tend to ruminate about the fantasized rigors of the week ahead. On the basis of his self- generated data, he began scheduling purely recreational activities on Sundays, activities that got him out of the house and provided a source of distraction from his tendency to ruminate.

As noted, behavioral deficits in depression may reflect indecisiveness and response-initiation deficits at choice points, rather than psychomotor retardation, as classically defined (Friedman, 1964; Miller, 1975). Athough the actual mecha- nisms involved remain a matter of considerable theoretical controversy, the efficacy of separating the need to decide what to do next from the process of doing appears to have a beneficial effect. Whether this separation proves useful in working with all types of depressions or only with some varieties is also open to question. However, the issue can best be resolved by empirical trials, rather than by simply generalizing on the basis of theory. What is apparent is that, for at least a great many depressed clients, the process of actively scheduling desired behaviors can serve as a powerful therapeutic tool.

Scheduling Pleasurable Activities.   Patients may experience little pleasure for at least two reasons. First, they may have lost the capacity to derive satisfaction from their experiences. Anhedonia, or the inability to experience pleasure, can be conceptualized as a consequence of either behavioral or physiological processes (Costello, 1972), dynamic processes (Freud, 1917), or cognitive processes (Beck, 1967, 1976; Hollon & Evans, Note 17). Second, clients may experience little pleasure simply by not engaging in those activities that are most likely to produce pleasurable consequences (Beck *et al.*, 1979; Lewinsohn, 1974, 1976). In the latter instance, activities most likely to be rewarding can be "prescribed." For example, a favorite food, favorite hobby, previously gratifying activity, etc., can all be assigned as "homework." It is important not to accept the prediction of a depressed client as an unalterable fact, particularly when it involves the anticipation of nongratification. Depressed clients frequently report experiencing pleasure *once they have engaged in a task* that they had not anticipated would be enjoyable. It is generally easier to induce the client to engage in an activity designed as a test: "I don't know whether or not you'll find this pleasurable, but we can set it up as an experiment, where you do it and monitor your mood throughout," rather than to present such activity as an assignment or requirement. Such a procedure gets the client into the situation without requiring that the client and therapist resolve, in advance, who generates the most accurate predictions. Few activities are less useful than arguing with a client over the accuracy of any given belief. In fact, the therapist should point out that even negative results provide valuable feedback.

Potentially reinforcing activities can be identified in a variety of ways. Clients can often report activities that were previously experienced as pleasant, particularly when the therapist asks the question in terms of "What used to feel good, that doesn't anymore?" Similarly, clients can often respond informatively to the probe "What would you do if you didn't feel so bad?" Client-generated self-monitoring records can often provide an additional source of data, with instances of rated pleasurable events or elevations in mood indicating relevant activities. This procedure is a major component of Rehm's self-control approach to depression (Rehm, 1977). Lewinsohn and colleagues (Lewinsohn & Graf, 1973; Lewinsohn & Libet, 1972; MacPhillamy & Lewinsohn, Note 19) have constructed a 320-item Pleasant Events Schedule (PES) that can serve as a useful device for defining a set of potentially pleasurable activities. Rehm (1977) has emphasized the potential utility of increasing the probability of desirable behaviors by making the delivery of potentially reinforcing, freely available stimuli contingent upon the completion of those desirable behaviors.

Encouraging the client to record anticipatory thoughts regarding the scheduled pleasurable events, along with their subsequent reactions to these events, can provide especially useful information. Not infrequently, clients discover that much of their dysphoria was either anticipatory or based on self-fulfilling prophecy. The tendency to discredit experiences after they occur, a largely cognitive process, can also sometimes be identified. Thus, one patient, after engaging in an activity, enjoying it at the moment and recording it as being pleasurable at that moment, found herself thinking later "That was only one good moment, it's really nothing in relation to all the pain that I'm experiencing.'' By the time of her next session, she reported not having experienced any pleasure, a report at variance with her own records. If subjective recall had been relied upon, the experience would have been interpreted as an instance of apparent anhedonia.

Mastery and Pleasure (M and P) Technique.   Activities, whether scheduled or unscheduled, can be rated on several dimensions. For depressed clients, two particularly relevant dimensions involve degree of mastery and degree of pleasure. In Table 6.2, examples are provided of dichotomous ratings of mastery and of pleasant events. *Mastery* can be defined as engaging in any task that initially seemed difficult or in which you had to overcome an initial sense of inertia or doubt in order to complete. *Pleasure* can be defined as any sense of subjective positiveness or any any sense of relief from feelings of dysphoria. Definitions here can be quite important; depressed clients frequently disqualify small accomplishments or small pleasure by equating them with the absence of accomplishment or the absence of any pleasure. Since most trial-and-error learning is based upon small, incremental changes, such discrediting can undermine the recognition of potentially useful interventions. M & P techniques, broadly defined, may include the scheduling of potential mastery activities. Furthermore, it may encompass efforts to define mastery and pleasure as continuous phenomena rather than as all-or-none events. By focusing attention on these two important areas, it is possible to determine whether the client really does experience a deficit in the frequency of either or whether reported deficits are more closely linked to failures in identification or subsequent derogation of these classes of experience. Such data can then provide the basis for appropriate interventions, either in terms of increasing the frequency or salience, altering the evaluation, or preventing the subsequent negative reevaluation of these events.

Cognitive Techniques (Introspective)

A variety of procedures can be utilized to facilitate the process of cognitive change. As noted, change in cognitions can occur either in terms of process (the actual occurrence of automatic negative thoughts) or in terms of content, the meaning applied by the individual. Content can further be subdivided into *automatic thoughts,* sometimes reported as verbal ruminations, fantasies, daydreams, images, etc., the spontaneous train of thought that appears accessible to report, and the *silent assumptions,* beliefs *inferred* on the basis of patterns or consistencies observed in the client's reported cognitions and/or reactions to events. These silent assumptions correspond most closely to the irrational beliefs discussed by Ellis (1962). In our experience, clients rarely report thinking in terms of logical syllogisms (for instance, ''Unless I am loved all of the time by all people...''). Rather, they report automatic thoughts such as ''I am a loser,'' or ''It's hopeless,'' or ''Nothing ever works out.'' The Automatic Thoughts Questionnaire (Hollon & Kendall, Note 3) was designed to assess raw cognitions, whereas the Dysfunctional Attitudes Scale (Weissman & Beck, Note 4) was designed to assess attitudes specific to depression. Both of these instruments are available to assess the cognitive phenomenon of depressed clients.

The various cognitive techniques are based upon the basic principles of cognitive theory: (*a*) that cognitions can influence subsequent behavior and affect; and (*b*) that *beliefs* are best treated as inferences regarding the nature of the world, rather than as *facts* about the world. The cognitive procedures seek to (*a*) facilitate the identification of the operation of self-statements; (*b*) help the client learn to "distance" him or herself from the certainty with which the particular belief is held; and (*c*) promote the systematic evaluation of the accuracy of those beliefs.

Identifying Automatic Thoughts.   Any of a variety of techniques can be used to collect inferences that people make. Most, of course, depend on self-report. The therapist can monitor the verbal production of the client, noting inferences as they are expressed, and can elicit statements likely to contain such inferences. For example, it is often useful to ask for predictions regarding the outcome of any planned activity, including expectations about the course of therapy itself. Similarly, the therapist can ask for retrospective assessments of situations or concurrent judgments and beliefs. Where both client and therapist have shared an experience, such information may become particularly revealing by highlighting discrepancies in interpretation.

Clients can monitor their automatic thoughts in a variety of ways. Specific times can be set aside to record cognitions (either graphically or on audiotape), or records can be kept in a more or less continous fashion. The occurrence of marked changes in mood can be used to signal periods when self-monitoring can be particularly revealing. The actual structure of the record can vary; free-form diaries may prove more satisfying to some clients, whereas structure response columns may prove more useful to others. The use of NCR (no carbon required) paper is particularly advantageous (Shelton & Ackerman, 1974). The NCR paper permits both therapist and client to retain, with a minimum of trouble, full records of all cognitions recorded (or, any self-monitoring). This procedure provides an especially detailed set of "process notes" for both to work with between sessions. Records provided by the client to the therapist can further be shared with colleagues, students, or colleagues in training. Such a procedure is beneficial to the client, by virtue of increasing the number of therapists "working" on his or her belief systems and, in our experience, a superb means of preparing a potential therapist for doing cognitive therapy.

Evaluating Thought Content.   The heart of cognitive therapy involves examining the validity of beliefs on a moment-to-moment basis. The first, critical step involves the client's ability to "distance" him or herself from the content of the belief. First discussed by Beck (1970), distancing involves recognizing that any belief is, at best, only a hypothesis, not a fact. A variety of strategies can be utilized to facilitate this process; discussions and practice during therapy, similies (e.g., one client, a former college professor, learned to treat himself *as if* he were an unhappy student; he would attend to automatic thoughts regarding his own inadequacy, the unfairness of the world, or his lack of a meaningful future, without accepting in advance that they were true, just as he used to do in his dealings with students), or the routinization of standardized cognitions to serve as reminders (e.g., "That's a prediction,'' or ''That's a belief, not a fact.''). The capacity to distance in the face of strong emotional arousal is often extremely difficult to master and, at present, only poorly understood. At present, repetition, practice, and a gradual emphasis on generalization appear to be at least adequate procedures.

Once a belief or set of beliefs has been recognized, it can be subjected to critical scrutiny. The client can be trained to ask several standard questions to facilitate the hypothesis-testing process. Chief among them are:

1. ''What's my evidence?''
2. ''Is there any other way of looking at that?''
3. ''Even if it is true, is it as bad as it seems?''

These questions are, certainly, not exhaustive. The basic paradigm is one of subjecting the automatic thoughts to critical scrutiny. This hypothesis-testing process can be applied during verbal interaction between the therapist and client, between sessions ''in the head'' of the client, or as a formal, written process. Table 6.3 provides a sample of the testing process, applied in the ''triple column'' format. The client records the nature of the situation in the first column. In the second column, the client notes the emotional reaction and rates the degree of intensity on a 0- to 100-point scale. In the third column, the client records the automatic thoughts or beliefs identified in the situation, rating them for degree of belief on the same 100-point metric. In column four, the client actually examines the validity of the identified beliefs in column three. The client lists ''rational responses,'' guided by the standard questions listed. It is helpful to have the client rate the degree of belief in the ''rational responses'' on the same 100-point metric. Finally, the fifth column is used to rerate the degree of emotion and the degree of belief in the original automatic thoughts. This procedure frequently demonstrates to the client how the correction of inaccurate negative ideas improves mood and, thus, provides an immediate reward.

Several additional points can be important. Patients often report experiencing ''clusters'' of automatic negative thoughts, rather than any single thought in isolation. Although it is probably useful to deal with as many types of thoughts as possible, it is important to focus on at least one thought long enough to work it through. Second, clients will often attempt to answer one automatic thought with another automatic thought. For example, one client responded to a thought about her own inadequacy with the thought ''That's a stupid thing to believe.'' Furthermore, clients may neglect to carefully explore a cognition or may not succeed in determining what are, for them, persuasive counterarguments or evidences. The ratings of the plausibility of the responses in column four can provide a useful guide in such instances.

One client found himself having increasing difficulty in challenging recognized automatic thoughts, despite having experienced success earlier in therapy. On examining his records, he discovered that the greatest change had occurred in the care with which he evaluated the specific automatic thoughts. Rather than reviewing evidence specific to each thought, he was applying standard responses in a rote

TABLE 6.3
Evaluating Automatic Negative Thoughts: Client's Record

Daily Record of Dysfunctional Thoughts

Date	Situation	Emotion(s)	Automatic Thought(s)	Rational Response	Outcome
	Describe: 1. Actual event leading to un-pleasant emotion, or 2. Stream of thoughts, daydream, or recollection, leading to un-pleasant emotion.	1. Specify sad–anxious, etc. 2. Rate degree of emotion, 1–100%.	1. Write automatic thought(s) that preceded emotion(s). 2. Rate belief in automatic thought(s), 0–100%.	1. Write rational response to auto-matic thought(s). 2. Rate belief in rational response, 0–100%.	1. Rerate belief in automatic thought(s), 0–100%. 2. Specify and rate subsequent emotions, 0–100%.
2/5	Not getting filing and lots of other stuff done.	Anxious–Sad–Angry 85%	A failure again, I can never get my work done. I'm no good. 85%	I have gotten filing and other work done in the past, but usually in smaller bites, not all at once. 80%	1. 45% 2. Anxious–Sad 50%
2/7	Sitting and idly looking thru some old books. 6:30 AM	Depressed 75%	Feeling guilty because I'm not doing work. I'm going to slip back into funk if I'm not careful. 70%	After 12 hours of high-energy work yesterday (phone work, building, filing, letter, therapy, driving) I think its OK to relax from 5:30 AM to 6:30 AM the following day 95%	1. 10% 2. Joyful, Exuberant 95%
	(Example of misapplication: Applies "Rational Response" in rote fashion without examining belief—note the lack of rated belief in the "Rational Response" and the lack of subsequent effect in belief and emotion in "Outcome.")				
2/9	I can't handle it any more, too much in the past to undo, lack of setting prior-ities, misuse of time, plus the present seems untenable	Depressed 80%	No options—either direct job in my specialty or nothing at all	The present does not predict the future 20%	1. 95% 2. Depressed 95%

"Explanation: When you experience an unpleasant emotion, note the situation that seemed to stimulate the emotion. (If the emotion occurred while you were thinking, daydreaming, etc., please note this.) Then note the automatic thought associated with the emotion. Record the degree to which you believe this thought: 0% = not at all; 100% = completely. In rating degree of emotion: 1 = a trace; 100 = the most intense possible.

fashion, such as "That's a prediction." or "There's no evidence for that belief." The inadequacy of his hypothesis testing was reflected both in the reduced plausibility ratings given the responses in column four and in the overall brevity of those written responses (see Example 3 in Table 6.3).

Prospective Hypothesis Testing. Even though clients frequently derive considerable benefit from reviewing evidence from their own past experience, there are also times when it is advantageous to test a belief in a prospective fashion. Guided by the principle of collaborative empiricism, client and therapist can design a study to test a particular belief. For example, one client expressed the belief that there was something wrong with him if he "didn't like his job." After some discussion, it was decided to poll the clerical and clinical staff at the treatment center. The client who conducted the actual poll discovered that most of the people polled reported working primarily for the money, not for love of job. The client discovered that his attitudes were more or less the same as a number of people whom he had considered to be far happier and better adjusted than he. Similarly, another client tested the belief that, when depressed, he couldn't complete a task involving patience and judgment. He chose to file all the personal papers that had accumulated over a several-month period and estimated that the task would take several days to complete, if it could be completed at all. To his surprise, he found that, by applying the principles discussed under the behavioral techniques section and by challenging his negative predictions as he went along, he was able, in the course of a single afternoon, to finish a task he had put off for months.

Identifying Underlying Assumptions. As the individual develops a repertoire of behavioral and cognitive tools with which to counteract the various depressive phenomena, the focus of attention begins to shift away from dealing with specific target symptoms and beliefs and toward the identification of the underlying assumptions that appear to organize the belief systems of the client. As noted, the process of identification depends largely on inductive reasoning. The therapist can formulate hypotheses regarding the client's beliefs; but, since these are, at best, educated guesses, they require rigorous prospective testing.

Two major differences can be distinguished between cognitive therapy (Beck, 1963) and rational–emotive therapy (Ellis, 1962) in terms of the ways in which these underlying assumptions are approached. In cognitive therapy, the process of identification is largely inductive, at least with respect to the individual client. Even though the therapist begins early in treatment to try to generate and to test hypotheses regarding potential assumptions, the evidence for and testing of these hypotheses is closely tied to the monitored cognitive and behavioral data presented by the client. Thus, client and therapist work collaboratively to attempt to identify attitudes or beliefs that run through the client's life. In rational–emotive therapy, the process is one of deduction. Efforts are made to demonstrate to the client that he or she does hold to one or more of the identified universe of irrational beliefs.

The second major area of difference involves how efforts at change are pursued. In cognitive therapy, change in relatively enduring belief systems is sought in an empirical fashion; as hypothesized underlying assumptions are identified, efforts are made to generate predictions, consistent with these assumptions, that can be subjected to empirical test. These tests may take the form of a review of existing evidence or the prospective generation of controlled observations. In rational-emotive therapy, persuasive arguments are offered by the therapist in an effort to change belief.

One client, for example, described himself as a "bad person" with regularity across a variety of situations: vocational, familial, marital, social, etc. On exploration, it became apparent that most of the situations shared certain common features. All involved some valued objective that was neglected, for instance, completing a job resumé, calling an invalid mother, honoring a promise to his wife, or writing a letter to a friend. In each case, the individual would berate himself, begin a cognitive search for an "explanation" as to why he didn't complete the valued task, and, when failing to find a good reason, would berate himself even more. After some discussion, the following sequence of beliefs emerged:

1. Some things are valuable to me.
2. Things that are highly valued should be done.
3. If I don't do things that should be done, there must be something wrong with me. I must be a "bad person."
4. If I am a "bad person," no one will love me, and I will not get what I want.

It is important to note that the first belief in the sequence was a relatively straightforward description; beginning with the second belief, potentially counterproductive beliefs came into play. Furthermore, even though the chain could be reconstructed, the patient was initially only aware of thinking about the specific label "bad person." He could readily report the second belief, regarding it as a general truism that applied to everyone, and, when he stopped to think about what it meant when he labeled himself a "bad person," was able to volunteer that it had something to do with being irresponsible. But the final link in the chain, that good things do not happen to "bad people," was something that he rarely formulated in exactly those terms, although he could readily generate specific examples of "bad things" that would happen to "bad people."

Efforts at change focused on each level of belief. However, generalizable change was maximized by the client's realization that affectionate relationships and vocational successes depended upon many variables, only some of which were related to his own conscientiousness and diligence.

"Alternative Technique" Intervention for Suicide.   This particular technique appears to be particularly useful in working with clients expressing suicidal ruminations. Alternative therapy involves reconceptualizing what formerly appeared to be an insolvable problem in new, more flexible terms. Such a reformulation increases the probability that solutions can be found. Basically, alternative therapy involves focusing attention on the second of the three challenges to fixed beliefs, "Is there another way of looking at this?" Depressed clients frequently focus on a single aspect of their lives or a single interpretation of that aspect and may have genuine difficulty in conceptualizing other ways of examining an issue. Thus, when working with a suicidal client, rather than attempt to provide solutions for the problem as defined by the client, the therapist pays attention to looking for more flexible ways of conceptualizing the basic issues. Thus, rather than attempt to arrive at a solution for the question "How do I survive if my husband/wife leaves me? That would be unbearable," the basic premise that life would be unbearable without that individual can be examined. For example, one client, after indicating that she could not tolerate the thought of living without her current lover, was asked to examine the premise that life was devoid of pleasure if she was alone. Even based on her own prior experience, she was readily able to generate examples of times before she was in a relationship when she was quite pleased with herself. By focusing so intently on how to prevent being rejected, she had uncritically accepted the premise that life following a rejection would be intolerable. By changing the focus of attention, the therapist was able to assist the client to look at the overall situation much more flexibly, a maneuver that both facilitated subsequent problem solving and helped to resolve the immediate suicidal crisis. The emphasis is not on denying the importance of the desired outcome or on trying to convince the client that things are not so bleak as they seem. Rather, the therapist's role is simply to promote a more flexible and expanded review of the entire situation.

Termination

Throughout treatment, preparation is made for eventual termination. Several strategies can facilitate a sense of self-reliance and minimize dependence while solidifying learning. First, the very nature of a time-limited contract ensures frequent consideration of termination. Second, once the client obtains reasonable symptomatic relief, the frequency of sessions can be reduced from 2 or more per week to 1 per week. This change can be presented explicitly as a test of the client's capacity to function independent of therapy. We have found that clients often exhibit distress in anticipation of the change but typically handle the reduction of contact quite well. Third, relapses during treatment can be turned to good clinical advantage; a smooth course of improvement can be more readily attributed to nontreatment factors than multiple reductions of symptom levels. Planned therapeutic relapses can sometimes facilitate this learning process. Most important, clients leave treatment trained in specific self-help skills, a training accompanied by complete and detailed sets of records. Treatment techniques are presented as a set of skills that can be applied whenever needed, much as one takes a shower when dusty, rather than as a "curative" process designed to make the individual invulnerable to subsequent depressions. Client reports from systematic follow-ups indicate that they do indeed utilize the component cognitive and behavioral skills when needed. Such a strategy appears to be associated with an overall reduction in relapse following treatment termination.

SUMMARY

It appears that cognitive therapy, a combination of cognitive and behavioral techniques based on a cognitive theory of depression, may be a particularly effective intervention in the treatment of nonpsychotic, nonbipolar depression. Studies with samples ranging from analogue to clinical populations have documented treatment efficacy relative to alterative approaches. To date, only cognitive therapy has been shown to be more effective than pharmacotherapy in a clinical population.

Several questions of interest can be raised. Since both cognitive therapy and pharmacotherapy appear to generate strong rates of clinical improvement, what would be the consequence of combining the two approaches? Similarly, how effective might other cognitive–behavioral approaches, for instance, Rehm's self-control therapy, prove in comparative trials with cognitive therapy and/or pharmacotherapy? Direct comparisons between cognitive therapy and self-control therapy, along with consideration of their respective mechanisms of action, appear indicated.

The issue of appropriate populations also needs to be addressed more comprehensively. Studies to date have excluded bipolar or psychotic subjects, largely on the basis of clinical lore. At this time, there simply is no evidence regarding the potential efficacy of a cognitive–behavioral approach with these populations. Traditional approaches to psychotherapy have generally been considered to be ineffective with such clients; however, the empirical evidence suggests that traditional approaches have generally been ineffective with any kind of depressed clients.

Theoretically, efforts to base cognitive models more firmly in experimental cognitive psychology are clearly needed. The interchange between behavior therapists and behavior theorists has been useful to the former; similar efforts regarding cognitive processes and the interface between cognitive and behavioral processes as they relate to depression would appear to be particularly rich areas for further study.

At this point, it seems fair to conclude that cognitive variables play a role in the etiology of at least some depressions and that consideration of both cognitive and behavioral factors in depression appears to lead to particularly effective treatment interventions. In terms of both theory and therapy, a cognitive–behavioral approach appears to offer significant advantages over alternative formulations.

REFERENCE NOTES

1. Task Force on Nomenclature and Statistics, American Psychiatric Association. *Diagnostic and statistical manual of mental disorders* (3rd ed., draft version of April 15, 1977). (Available from Task Force on Nomenclature and Statistics, American Psychiatric Association, 722 West 168 Street, New York, New York.)
2. Vatz, K. A., Winig, H. R., & Beck, A. T. *Pessimism and a sense of future time constriction as cognitive disorders in depression.* Unpublished manuscript, University of Pennsylvania, 1969.
3. Hollon, S. D., & Kendall, P. C. *Cognitive self-statements in depression: Development of an Automatic Thoughts Questionnaire.* Unpublished manuscript, University of Minnesota, 1978.

4. Weissman, A. N., & Beck, A. T. *Development and validation of the Dysfunctional Attitude Scale: A preliminary investigation.* Paper presented at the Annual Meeting of the American Educational Research Association, Toronto, Ontario, 1978.
5. Garber, J., & Hollon, S. D. *Universal versus personal helplessness in depression: Belief in uncontrollability or incompetence?* Unpublished manuscript, University of Pennsylvania, 1977.
6. Shaw, B. F. *Subjective and physiological responses to depression inducing stimuli.* Paper presented at the Annual Meeting of the Canadian Psychological Association, Victoria, British Columbia, 1972.
7. Roth, D., Rehm, L. P., & Rozensky, R. A. *Depression and self-reinforcement.* Unpublished manuscript, University of Pittsburgh, 1974.
8. Rozensky, R. A., Rehm, L. P., Pry, G., & Roth, D. *Depression and self-reinforcement behavior in hospital patients.* Unpublished manuscript, University of Pittsburgh, 1974.
9. Shaw, B. F. *Drug trials in depression: An analysis of premature termination rates.* Unpublished manuscript, University of Pennsylvania, 1977.
10. Sammons, R. A. *Systematic resensitization in the treatment of depression.* Paper presented at the meeting of the Association for the Advancement of Behavior Therapy, Chicago, November, 1974.
11. Patterson, W. E., Taulbee, E. S., Golsom, J. C., Horner, R. F., & Wright, H. W. *Preliminary report: Comparison of two forms of milieu therapy in the treatment of depression.* Unpublished manuscript, Veterans Administration Hospital, Tuscaloosa, Alabama, 1968.
12. Rehm, L. P., Fuchs, C., Roth, D., Kornblith, S., & Roman, J. *Self-control and social skills training in the modification of depression.* Unpublished manuscript, University of Pittsburgh, 1975.
13. Hodgson, J. W., & Urban, H. B. *A comparison of interpersonal training programs in the treatment of depressive states.* Unpublished manuscript, Pennsylvania State University, 1975.
14. Kovacs, M., Beck, A. T., Rush, A. J., & Hollon, S. D. *Comparative efficacy of cognitive therapy and pharmacotherapy in the treatment of depressed outpatients: A 12-month follow-up.* Unpublished manuscript, University of Pittsburgh, 1978.
15. Shaw, B. F., & Hollon, S. D. *Cognitive therapy in a group format with depressed patients.* Unpublished manuscript, University of Western Ontario, 1977.
16. Rush, A. J., Beck, A. T., Kovacs, M., Khatami, M., Fitzgibbons, R., & Wolman, T. *Comparison of cognitive and pharmacotherapy in depressed outpatients: A preliminary report.* Paper presented at meeting of the Society for Psychotherapy Research, Boston, Massachussetts, 1975.
17. Hollon, S. D., & Evans, M. *Self-monitoring of mood in depression: When is what you saw what you got?* Unpublished manuscript, University of Minnesota, 1978.
18. Loeb, A., Beck, A. T., Diggory, J. C., & Tuthill, R. *The effects of success and failure on mood, motivation, and performance as a function of predetermined level of depression.* Unpublished manuscript, University of Pennsylvania, 1966.
19. MacPhillamy, D., & Lewinsohn, P. M. *The pleasant events schedule.* Unpublished manuscript, University of Oregon, 1971.

REFERENCES

Abraham, K. Notes on the psycho-analytical investigation and treatment of manic-depressive insanity and allied conditions. In *Selected papers of Karl Abraham.* London: Hogarth Press, 1949.
Abramson, L. Y., Garber, J., Edwards, N. B., & Seligman, M. E. P. Expectancy changes in depression and schizophrenia. *Journal of Abnormal Psychology,* 1978, *87,* 102–109.
Abramson, L. Y., Seligman, M. E. P., & Teasdale, J. D. Learned helplessness in humans: Critique and reformulation. *Journal of Abnormal Psychology.* 1978, *87,* 49–74.
Adler, K. Depression in the light of individual psychiatry. *Journal of Individual Psychology,* 1961, *17,* 56–67.

Akiskal, H. S., & McKinney, W. T. Overview of recent research in depression: Ten conceptual models. *Archives of General Psychiatry*, 1975, *32*, 285-305.

Alloy, L. B., & Abramson, L. Y. Judgement of contingency in depressed and nondepressed students: Sadder but not wiser. *Journal of Experimental Psychology: General*, in press.

American Psychiatric Association Task Force. The current status of lithium therapy: Report of an APA Task Force. *American Journal of Psychiatry*, 1975, *132*, 997-1001.

Angst, J. Sur ätiologie und nosologie endogenen depressiven psychosen. *Monographs of Neurological Psychiatry*, 1966, *112*, 1-118.

Angst, J., & Perris, C. The nosology of endogeneous depression: A comparison of the findings of two studies. *International Journal of Mental Health*, 1972, *1*, 145-158.

Appel, K. E. Psychiatric therapy. In J. Hunt (Ed.), *Personality and the behavior disorder (Vol. II)*. New York: Ronald Press, 1944, 1107-1163.

Averill, J. R. Autonomic response patterns during sadness and mirth. *Psychophysiology*, 1969, *5*, 399-414.

Ayd, F. J. Jr. *Recognizing the depressed patient*. New York: Grune & Stratton, 1961.

Badri, M. B. A new technique for the systematic desensitization of pervasive anxiety and phobic reactions. *Journal of Psychology*, 1967, *65*, 201-208.

Bandura, A. Self-efficacy: Toward a unifying theory of behavioral change. *Psychological Review*, 1977, *84*, 191-215. (a)

Bandura, A. *Social learning theory*. Englewood Cliffs, New Jersey: Prentice-Hall, 1977. (b)

Barnes, M. R. Effects of antidepressive program on verbal behavior. *Journal of Clinical Psychology*, 1977, *33*, 545-549.

Beck, A. T. A systematic investigation of depression. *Comprehensive Psychiatry*, 1961, *2*, 163-170.

Beck, A. T. Thinking and depression: I. Idiosyncratic content and cognitive distortions. *Archives of General Psychiatry*, 1963, *9*, 324-333.

Beck, A. T. Thinking and depression: II. Theory and Therapy. *Archives of General Psychiatry*, 1964, *10*, 561-571.

Beck, A. T. *Depression: Clinical, experimental, and theoretical aspects*. New York: Harper & Row, 1967.

Beck, A. T. Cognitive therapy: Nature and relation to behavior therapy. *Behavior Therapy*, 1970, *1*, 184-200.

Beck, A. T. *Cognitive theory and the emotional disorders*. New York: International Universities Press, 1976.

Beck, A. T., Feshbach, S., & Legg, D. The clinical utility of the digit symbol test. *Journal of Consulting Psychology*, 1962, *26*, 263-268.

Beck, A. T., & Greenberg, R. L. *Coping with depression*. New York: Institute for Rational Living, 1974.

Beck, A. T., & Hurvich, M. S. Psychological correlates of depression. 1. Frequency of "masochistic" dream content in a private practice sample. *Psychosomatic Medicine*, 1959, *21*, 50-55.

Beck, A. T., Rush, A. J., Shaw, B. F., & Emery, G. *Cognitive therapy of depression: A treatment manual*. New York: Guilford, 1979.

Beck, A. T., & Ward, C. H. Dreams of depressed patients: Characteristic themes in manifest content. *Archives of General Psychiatry*, 1961, *5*, 462-467.

Beck, A. T., Ward, C. H., Mendelson, M., Mock, J. E., & Erbaugh, J. K. An inventory for measuring depression. *Archives of General Psychology*, 1961, *4*, 561-571.

Becker, J., & Schuckit, M. A. The comparative efficacy of cognitive therapy and pharmacotherapy in the treatment of depressions. *Cognitive Therapy and Research*, 1978, *2*, 193-198.

Bertelsen, A., Harvald, B., & Hauge, M. A Danish twin study of manic-depressive disorders. *British Journal of Psychiatry*, 1977, *130*, 330-351.

Beutler, L. E. A self-directed approach to the treatment of a complex neurosis with implosive therapy. *Journal of Clinical Psychology*, 1973, *29*, 106-108.

Blaney, P. H. Contemporary theories of depression: Critique and comparison. *Journal of Abnormal Psychology*, 1977, *86*, 203–223.

Bolles, R. C. Reinforcement, expectancy, and learning. *Psychological Reviews*, 1972, *79*, 394–409.

Campbell, J. D. *Manic-depressive disease*. Philadelphia: Lippincott, 1953.

Coleman, R. E. Manipulation of self-esteem as a determinant of mood of elated and depressed women. *Journal of Abnormal Psychology*, 1975, *84*, 693–700.

Coppen, A. The biochemistry of affective disorders. *British Journal of Psychiatry*, 1967, *113*, 1237–1264.

Costello, C. G. Depression: Loss of reinforcers or loss of reinforcer effectiveness? *Behavior Therapy*, 1972, *3*, 240–247.

Covi, L., Lipman, R. S., Derogatis, L. R., Smith, J. E., & Pattison, J. H. Drugs and group psychotherapy in neurotic depression. *American Journal of Psychiatry*, 1974, *131*, 191–197.

Daneman, E. A. Imipramine in office management of depressive reactions (a double-blind study). *Diseases of the Nervous System*, 1961, *22*, 213–217.

Davis, J. M. Overview: Maintenance therapy in psychiatry: II. Affective disorders. *American Journal of Psychiatry*, 1976, *133*, 1–14.

DeMonbreum, B. G., & Craighead, W. E. Distortion of perception and recall of positive and neutral feedback in depression. *Cognitive Therapy and Research*, 1977, *1*, 311–330.

Dempsey, P. An unidimensional depression scale for the MMPI. *Journal of Consulting Psychology*, 1964, *28*, 364–370.

Ellis, A. *Reason and emotion in psychotherapy*. New York: Stuart, 1962.

Feighner, J. P., Robins, E., Guze, S. B., Woodruff, R. A., Winokur, G., & Muñoz, R. Diagnostic criteria for use in psychiatric research. *Archives of General Psychiatry*, 1972, *26*, 57–63.

Ferster, C. B. A functional analysis of depression. *American Psychologist*, 1973, *28*, 857–870.

Ferster, C. B. Behavioral approaches to depression. In R. J. Friedman & M. M. Katz (Eds.), *The psychology of depression: Contemporary theory and research*. Washington, D.C.: Winston/Wiley, 1974.

Forrest, M. S., & Hokanson, J. E. Depression and autonomic arousal reduction accompanying self-punitive behavior. *Journal of Abnormal Psychology*, 1975, *84*, 346–357.

Freud, S. (1917) Mourning and melancholia. In J. Strachey (Ed.), *The standard edition (Vol. 14)*. London: Hogarth Press, 1957.

Friedman, A. S. Minimal effect of severe depression on cognitive functioning. *Journal of Abnormal and Social Psychology*, 1964, *69*, 237–243.

Friedman, A. S. Hostility factors and clinical improvement in depressed patients. *Archives of General Psychiatry*, 1970, *23*, 524–537.

Friedman, A. S. Interaction of drug therapy with marital therapy in depressed patients. *Archives of General Psychiatry*, 1975, *32*, 619–637.

Fuchs, C. Z., & Rehm, L. P. A self-control behavior therapy program for depression. *Journal of Consulting and Clinical Psychology*, 1977, *45*, 206–215.

Gero, G. The construction of depression. *International Journal of Psychoanalysis*, 1936, *17*, 423–461.

Glassman, A. Indoleamines and affective disorders. *Psychosomatic Medicine*, 1969, *31*, 107–120.

Grings, W. W. Cognitive factors in electrodermal conditioning. *Psychological Bulletin*, 1973, *79*, 200–210.

Grinker, R. R., Miller, J., Sabshin, M., Nunn, J., & Nunnally, J. D. *The phenomena of depression*. New York: Hoeber, 1961.

Hale, W. D., & Strickland, B. R. Induction of mood states and their effect on cognitive and social behaviors. *Journal of Consulting and Clinical Psychology*, 1976, *44*, 155.

Hamilton, M. A rating scale for depression. *Journal of Neurology, Neurosurgery, and Psychiatry*, 1960, *23*, 56–62.

Hammen, C. L., & Glass, D. R. Depression, activity, and evaluation of reinforcement. *Journal of Abnormal Psychology*, 1975, *84*, 718–721.

Hammen, C. L., & Krantz, S. Effect of success and failure on depressive cognitions. *Journal of Abnormal Psychology*, 1976, *85*, 577–586.

Hannie, T. J., & Adams, H. E. Modification of agitated depression by flooding: A preliminary study. *Journal of Behavior Therapy and Experimental Psychiatry*, 1974, *5*, 161-166.

Hauri, P. Dreams in patients remitted from reactive depression. *Journal of Abnormal Psychology*, 1976, *85*, 1-10.

Hersen, M., Eisler, D., Alford, G., & Agras, W. S. Effects of token economy on neurotic depression: An experimental analysis. *Behavior Therapy*, 1973, *4*, 392-397.

Hiroto, D. S., & Seligman, M. E. P. Generality of learned helplessness in man. *Journal of Personality and Social Psychology*, 1975, *31*, 311-327.

Hokanson, J. E., Burgess, M. M., & Cohen, M. The effects of displaced aggression on systolic blood pressure. *Journal of Abnormal and Social Psychology*, 1963, *67*, 214-218.

Hokanson, J. E., Willers, K. R., & Koropsak, E. Modification of autonomic responses during aggressive interchange. *Journal of Personality*, 1968, *36*, 386-404.

Hollon, S. D., & Beck, A. T. Psychotherapy and drug therapy: Comparisons and combinations. In S. L. Garfield & A. E. Bergin (Eds.), *The handbook of psychotherapy and behavior change (2nd ed.)*. New York: Wiley, in press.

Homme, L. E. Perspectives in psychology. XXIV. Control of coverants, the operants of the mind. *Psychological Record*, 1965, *15*, 501-511.

Isen, A. M., Shalker, T. E., Clark, M., & Karp, L. Affect, accessibility of material in memory, and behavior: A cognitive loop? *Journal of Personality and Social Psychology*, 1978, *36*, 1-12.

Jackson, B. Treatment of depression by self-reinforcement. *Behavior Therapy*, 1972, *3*, 298-307.

Johnson, W. G. Some applications of Homme's coverant control therapy: Two case reports. *Behavior Therapy*, 1971, *2*, 240-248.

Jones, R. G. *A factored measure of Ellis' irrational belief system*. Wichita, Kansas: Test Systems, Inc., 1968.

Kanfer, F. H. Self-regulation: Research issues and speculations. In C. Neuringer & J. L. Michael (Eds.), *Behavior modification in clinical psychology*. New York: Appleton-Century-Crofts, 1970.

Klein, D. C., Fencil-Morse, E., & Seligman, M. E. P. Learned helplessness, depression, and the attribution of failure. *Journal of Personality and Social Psychology*, 1976, *33*, 508-516.

Klein, D. C., & Seligman, M. E. P. Reversal of performance deficits and perceptual deficits in learned helplessness and depression. *Journal of Abnormal Psychology*, 1976, *85*, 11-26.

Klerman, G. L., DiMascio, A., Weissman, M., Prusoff, B., & Paykel, E. Treatment of depression by drugs and psychotherapy. *American Journal of Psychiatry*, 1974, *131*, 186-191.

Kuiper, N. A. Depression and causal attributions for success and failure. *Journal of Personality and Social Psychology*, 1978, *36*, 236-246.

Lader, M., & Noble, P. The affective disorders. In. P. H. Venables & M. J. Christie (Eds.), *Research in psychophysiology*. New York: Wiley, 1975.

Lazarus, A. Learning theory and the treatment of depression. *Behaviour Research and Therapy*, 1968, *6*, 83-89.

Lewinsohn, P. M. Clinical and Theoretical aspects of depression. In K. S. Calhoun, H. E. Adams, & K. M. Mitchell (Eds.), *Innovative treatment methods in psychotherapy*. New York: Wiley, 1973.

Lewinsohn, P. M. A behavioral approach to depression. In R. M. Friedman & M. M. Katz (Eds.), *The psychology of depression: Contemporary theory and research*. Washington, D.C.: Winston/Wiley, 1974.

Lewinsohn, P. M. The behavioral study and treatment of depression. In M. Hersen, R. Eisler, & P. Miller (Eds.), *Progress in behavior modification*. New York: Academic Press, 1975. (a)

Lewinsohn, P. M. Engagement in pleasant activities and depression level. *Journal of Abnormal Psychology*, 1975, *84*, 729-731. (b)

Lewinsohn, P. M. Activity schedules in the treatment of depression. In J. D. Krumboltz & C. E. Thoresen (Eds.), *Counseling methods*. New York: Holt, Rinehart, and Winston, 1976.

Lewinsohn, P. M., & Atwood, G. E. Depression: A clinical-research approach. *Psychotherapy: Theory, Research and Practice*, 1969, *6*, 166-171.

Lewinsohn, P. M., & Graf, M. Pleasant activities and depression. *Journal of Consulting and Clinical Psychology*, 1973, *41*, 261-268.

Lewinsohn, P. M., & Libet, J. Pleasant events, activity schedules, and depressions. *Journal of Abnormal Psychology*, 1972, *79*, 291–295.

Lewinsohn, P. M., & MacPhillamy, D. J. The relationship between age and engagement in pleasant activities. *Journal of Gerontology*, 1974, *29*, 290–294.

Lewinsohn, P. M., & Shaffer, M. The use of home observations as an integral part of the treatment of depression: Preliminary report and case studies. *Journal of Consulting and Clinical Psychology*, 1971, *37*, 87–94.

Lewinsohn, P. M., & Shaw, D. A. Feedback about interpersonal behavior as an agent of behavior change: A case study in the treatment of depression. *Psychotherapy and Psychosomatics*, 1969, *17*, 82–88.

Lewinsohn, P. M., Weinstein, M. S., & Alper, T. A behavioral approach to the group treatment of depressed persons: Methodological contributions. *Journal of Clinical Psychology*, 1970, *26*, 525–532.

Libet, J. M., & Lewinsohn, P. M. Concept of social skill with special reference to the behavior of depressed persons. *Journal of Consulting and Clinical Psychology*, 1973, *40*, 304–312.

Lishman, W. A. Selective factors in memory: II. Affective disorders. *Psychological Medicine*, 1972, *2*, 248–253.

Lloyd, G. G., & Lishman, W. A. Effect of depression on the speed of recall of pleasant and unpleasant experiences. *Psychological Medicine*, 1975, *5*, 173–180.

Loeb, A., Beck, A. T., & Diggory, J. Differential effects of success and failure on depressed and nondepressed patients. *Journal of Nervous and Mental Disease*, 1971, *152*, 106–114.

Loeb, A., Feshback, S., Beck, A. T., & Wolf, A. Some effects of reward upon the social perception and motivation of psychiatric patients varying in depression. *Journal of Abnormal and Social Psychology*, 1964, *68*, 609–616.

Lubin, B. *Manual for the Depression Adjective Check Lists.* San Diego: Educational and Industrial Testing Service, 1967.

MacPhillamy, D. J., & Lewinsohn, P. M. Depression as a function of levels of desired and obtained pleasure. *Journal of Abnormal Psychology*, 1974, *83*, 651–657.

Masters, J. C., Barden, R. C., & Ford, M. E. Affective states, expressive behavior and learning in children. *Journal of Personality and Social Psychology*, 1979, *37*, 380–390.

May, J. R., & Johnson, H. J. Physiological activity to internally elicited arousal and inhibitory thoughts. *Journal of Abnormal Psychology*, 1973, *82*, 239–245.

McLean, P. D., Ogston, K., & Grauer, L. A behavioral approach to the treatment of depression. *Journal of Behavior Therapy and Experimental Psychiatry*, 1973, *4*, 323–330.

Mendels, J., & Frazer, A. Brain biogenic amine depletion and mood. *Archives of General Psychiatry*, 1974, *30*, 447–451.

Miller, W. R. Psychological deficit in depression. *Psychological Bulletin*, 1975, *82*, 238–260.

Miller, W. R., & Seligman, M. E. P. Depression and the perception of reinforcement. *Journal of Abnormal Psychology*, 1973, *82*, 62–73.

Miller, W. R., & Seligman, M. E. P. Depression and learned helplessness in man. *Journal of Abnormal Psychology*, 1975, *84*, 228–238.

Moore, B. S., Underwood, B., & Rosehan, D. L. Affect and altruism. *Developmental Psychology*, 1973, *8*, 99–104.

Morris, J. B., & Beck, A. T. The efficiency of anti-depressant drugs: A review of research (1958–1972). *Archives of General Psychiatry*, 1974, *30*, 667–674.

Morris, N. E. A group of self-instruction method for the treatment of depressed outpatients. Unpublished doctoral dissertation, University of Toronto, 1975.

Natale, M. Effects of induced elation–depression on speech in the initial interview. *Journal of Consulting and Clinical Psychology*, 1977, *45*, 45–52. (a)

Natale, M. Induction of mood states and their effect on gaze behavior. *Journal of Consulting and Clinical Psychology*, 1977, *45*, 717–723. (b)

Nelson, R. E. Irrational beliefs in depression. *Journal of Consulting and Clinical Psychology,* 1977, *45,* 1190-1191.

Nelson, R. E., & Craighead, W. E. Selective recall of positive and negative feedback, self-control behaviors, and depression. *Journal of Abnormal Psychology,* 1977, *86,* 379-388.

O'Leary, M. R., Donovan, D. M., Krueger, K. J., & Cysewski, B. Depression and perception of reinforcement: Lack of differences in expectancy change among alcoholics. *Journal of Abnormal Psychology,* 1978, *87,* 110-112.

Padfield, M. The comparative effects of two counseling approaches on the intensity of depression among rural woman of low socieconomic status. *Journal of Counseling Psychology,* 1976, *23,* 209-214.

Paykel, E. S., Klerman, G. L., DiMascio, A., Weissman, M. M., & Prusoff, B. A. Maintenance antidepressants, psychotherapy, symptoms, and social function. In J. O. Cole, A. M. Freedman, & A. J. Friedhoff (Eds.), *Psychopathology and psychopharmacology.* Baltimore, Maryland: Johns Hopkins University Press, 1973.

Paykel, E. S., Weissman, M. M., Prusoff, B. A., & Tonks, C. M. Dimensions of social adjustment in depressed women. *Journal of Nervous and Mental Disease,* 1971, *152,* 158-172.

Perris, C. Genetic transmission of depressive psychoses. *Acta Psychiatrica Scandinavica,* 1968, *42* (supplement no. 203), 45-52.

Price, J. The genetics of depressive behaviour. In A. J. Coppen & A. Walk (Eds.), *Recent developments in affective disorders. British Journal of Psychiatry, Special Publication No. 2,* Ashford, Kent, 1968.

Rehm, L. P. A self-control model of depression. *Behavior Therapy,* 1977, *8,* 787-804.

Rehm, L. P., & Plakosh, P. Preference for immediate reinforcement in depression. *Journal of Behavior Therapy and Experimental Psychiatry,* 1975, *6,* 101-103.

Reisinger, J. J. The treatment of "anxiety-depression" via positive reinforcement and response cost. *Journal of Applied Behavioral Analysis,* 1972, *5,* 125-130.

Rimm, D. C., & Litvak, S. B. Self-verbalization and emotional arousal. *Journal of Abnormal Psychology,* 1969, *74,* 181-187.

Risley, R. Depression and distortion in the attribution of causality. *Journal of Abnormal Psychology,* 1978, *87,* 32-48.

Robins, E., & Guze, S. B. Classification of affective disorders: The primary-secondary, the endogenous-reactive, and the neurotic-psychotic concepts. In T. A. Williams, M. M. Katz, & J. A. Shields (Eds.), *Recent advances in the psychobiology of the depressive illnesses.* Chevy Chase, Maryland: U.S. Department of Health, Education and Welfare, 1969.

Robinson, J. C., & Lewinsohn, P. M. Behavior modification of speech characteristics in a chronically depressed man. *Behavior Therapy,* 1973, *4,* 150-152. (a)

Robinson, J. C., & Lewinsohn, P. M. Experimental analysis of a technique based on the Premack Principal changing verbal behavior of depressed individuals *Psychological Reports,* 1973, *32,* 199-210. (b)

Rogers, T., & Craighead, W. E. Physiological responses to self-statements: The effects of statement valence and discrepancy. *Cognitive Therapy and Research,* 1977, *1,* 99-120.

Rush, A. J., Beck, A. T., Kovacs, M., & Hollon, S. D. Comparative efficacy of cognitive therapy versus pharmacotherapy in outpatient depressives. *Cognitive Therapy and Research,* 1977, *1,* 17-37.

Rush, A. J., Hollon, S. D., Beck, A. T., & Kovacs, M. Depression: Must pharmacotherapy fail for cognitive therapy to succeed? *Cognitive Therapy and Research,* 1978, *2,* 199-206.

Rush, A. J., Khatami, M., & Beck, A. T. Cognitive and behavior therapy in chronic depression. *Behavior Therapy,* 1975, *6,* 398-404.

Russell, P. L., & Brandsma, J. M. A theoretical and empirical investigation of the rational-emotive and classical conditioning theories. *Journal of Consulting and Clinical Psychology,* 1974, *42,* 389-397.

Schildkraut, J. J. The catecholamine hypothesis of affective disorders. *American Journal of Psychiatry,* 1965, *122,* 509–522.

Schmickley, V. G. *The effects of cognitive–behavior modification upon depressed outpatients.* Unpublished doctoral dissertation, Michigan State University, 1976.

Schou, M. Prophylactic and maintenance therapy in recurrent affective disorder. In D. M. Gallant & G. M. Simpson (Eds.), *Depression: Behavioral, biochemical, diagnostic and treatment concepts.* New York: Spectrum Publications, 1976.

Schrader, S. L., Craighead, W. E., & Schrader, R. M. Reinforcement patterns in depression. *Behavior Therapy,* 1978, *9,* 1–14.

Seligman, M. E. P. *Helplessness.* San Francisco: Freeman, 1975.

Shapiro, M. B., Neufeld, I. L., & Post, F. Note: Experimental study of depressive illness. *Psychological Report,* 1962, *10,* 590.

Shaw, B. F. Comparison of cognitive therapy and behavior therapy in the treatment of depression. *Journal of Consulting and Clinical Psychology,* 1977, *45,* 543–551.

Shelton, J. L., & Ackerman, M. J. *Homework in counseling and psychotherapy.* Springfield, Illinois: Charles C. Thomas, 1974.

Shipley, C. R., & Fazio, A. F. Pilot study of a treatment for psychological depression. *Journal of Abnormal Psychology,* 1973, *82,* 372–376.

Silverman, C. *The epidemiology of depression.* Baltimore, Maryland: Johns Hopkins University Press, 1968.

Slater, E., & Cowie, V. *The genetics of mental disorders.* London: Oxford Universities Press, 1971.

Smolen, R. C. Expectancies, mood, and performance of depressed and nondepressed psychiatric inpatients on chance and skill tasks. *Journal of Abnormal Psychology,* 1978, *87,* 91–101.

Spitzer, R. L., Burdock, E. I., & Hardesty, A. S. *Mental Status Schedule.* New York: Biometrics Research, 1964.

Stenstedt, A. Genetics of neurotic depression. *Acta Psychiatrica Scandinavica,* 1966, *42,* 392–409.

Strickland, B. R., Hale, W. D., & Anderson, L. K. Effect of induced mood states on activity and self-reported affect. *Journal of Consulting and Clinical Psychology,* 1975, *43,* 587.

Taulbee, E. S., & Wright, H. W. Attitude therapy: A behavior modification program in a psychiatric hospital. In H. C. Rickard (Ed.), *Behavioral interventions in human problems.* New York: Macmillan, 1971. (a)

Taulbee, E. S., & Wright, H. W. A psychosocial-behavioral model for therapeutic intervention. In C. D. Spielberger (Ed.), *Current topics in clinical and community psychology (Vol. 3).* New York: Academic Press, 1971. (b)

Taylor, F. G., & Marshall, W. L. Experimental analysis of a cognitive-behavioral therapy for depression. *Cognitive Therapy and Research,* 1977, *1,* 59–72.

Teasdale, J. D., & Bancroft, J. Manipulation of thought content as a determinant of mood and corrugator electromyographic activity in depressed patients. *Journal of Abnormal Psychology,* 1977, *86,* 235–241.

Velten, E. A laboratory task for induction of mood states. *Behavior Research and Therapy,* 1968, *6,* 473–482.

Wanderer, Z. W. Existential depression treated by desensitization of phobias: Strategy and transcript. *Journal of Behavioral Therapy and Experimental Psychiatry,* 1972, *3,* 11–116.

Weintraub, M., Segal, R. M., & Beck, A. T. An investigation of cognition and affect in the depressive experience of normal men. *Journal of Consulting and Clinical Psychology,* 1974, *42,* 911.

Weiss, J. M., Stone, E. A., & Harrell, N. Coping behavior and brain norepinephrine in rats. *Journal of Comparative and Physiological Psychology,* 1970, *72,* 153–160.

Weissman, M. M., Klerman, G. L., & Paykel, E. S. Clinical evaluation of hostility in depression. *American Journal of Psychiatry,* 1971, *128,* 261–266.

Weissman, M. M., Klerman, G. L., Paykel, E. S., Prusoff, B., & Hanson, B. Treatment effects on the social adjustment of depressed patients. *Archives of General Psychiatry,* 1974, *30,* 771–778.

Weissman, M. M., & Paykel, E. S. *The depressed woman: A study of social relationships*. Chicago, Illinois: University of Chicago Press, 1974.

Wener, A. E., & Rehm, L. P. Depressive affect: A test of behavioral hypotheses. *Journal of Abnormal Psychology*, 1975, *84*, 221–227.

Williams, J. G., Barlow, D. H., & Agras, W. S. Behavioral measurement of severe depression. *Archives of General Psychiatry*, 1972, *72*, 330–337.

Wolpe, J. Neurotic depression: Experimental analog, clinical syndromes and treatment. *American Journal of Psychotherapy*, 1971, *25*, 362–368.

Wolpe, J., & Lazarus, A. A. *Behavior therapy techniques*. New York: Pergamon Press, 1966.

Zuckerman, M., & Lubin, B. *Manual for the Multiple Affective Adjective Check List*. San Diego: Educational and Industrial Testing Service, 1965.

Zung, W. W. A self-rating depression scale. *Archives of General Psychiatry*, 1965, *12*, 63–70.

7

Structured Cognitive–Behavioral Treatment of Assertion Problems

MARSHA M. LINEHAN

INTRODUCTION

Although procedures for encouraging assertive behavior have been in existence for some time (Salter, 1949), it was not until the early 1970s that assertion training became prominent in the clinical and research literature (Heimberg, Montgomery, Madsen, & Heimberg, 1977; Rich & Schroeder, 1976). Since that time, an increasing array of assertion training programs have been offered to the general public, popular articles and books (Bower & Bower, 1976; Cheek, 1976), have been published, and training seminars and books for therapists, group leaders, and facilitators (Lange & Jakubowski, 1976) have multiplied. The rise in the popularity of assertion training among the general public has been accompanied by a corresponding increase in the number of clinical problems for which some variant of assertion training is applied. For example, Heimberg et al. (1977) list obsessive-compulsive disorders, maladaptive interpersonal behaviors, aggressive and explosive behaviors, and chronic psychiatric problems as responsive to assertion training. Richie (Note 1) suggests assertion training for the following: depression and low self-esteem, social isolation and shyness, marital dysfunction, sexual communication, parent–child conflict, children's school adjustment problems, employment problems, labor–management disputes, career development and management training, management of problems with overeating, smoking, drug addiction, and alcoholism, and antisocial and aggressive behaviors. In addition, assertion training has been recommended to assist disadvantaged groups, including the elderly (Corby, 1975), blacks (Cheek, 1976), and women (Wolfe & Fodor, 1977); it has been applied to such diverse problems as chronic urinary retention (Barnard,

205

Cognitive–Behavioral Interventions:
Theory, Research, and Procedures

Flesher, & Steinbrook, 1966), hallucinatory and delusional behavior (Nydegger, 1972), and frigidity (Goldstein, 1971). It is not unusual to see assertion training programs being advertised to the public as relevant to career choice problems, low self-esteem, identity problems and personal growth (especially for women), and a host of other problems in living. One gets the impression that much of the public, and perhaps some professional service providers, believe that almost any problem in living can be ameliorated by one panacean procedure. The empirical support for such a belief is weak.

The expansion in the popularity and breadth of application of assertion training has led to enormous terminological obfuscation with respect to the label "assertion training." The label is at times used to apply to the target behaviors of the training (i.e., assertive behaviors), whereas at other times the label refers to the procedures of accomplishing the training (e.g., response practice,[1] modeling) that, in the research literature, have been most often used in teaching assertion. A related problem has to do with the range of target behaviors subsumed under the construct of assertion. As more and more clinical applications of assertion training are reported, the range of behaviors has expanded such that the term *assertion* seems at times to be synonymous with the more general construct of *social skills*.

The term *assertion* denotes a behavioral *target* for assertion training. Unfortunately, in the popular press and, to a large extent, in the psychological literature, it is often assumed that *assertion training* is synonymous with *procedures* historically associated with the treatment of the nonassertive individual. For example, Heimberg *et al.* (1977) in their review of assertion research observe that experimental studies have been concentrated in three areas, one of which involves "studies comparing the effectiveness of assertion training to that of *other behavior therapy methods.* The principal target behaviors have been *assertive behavior, general social skills,* and *heterosexual anxiety* [italics added, p. 958]." This quote makes it obvious that the authors are identifying the label "assertion training" with a set of procedures and not with the target behaviors to be learned. Most often, the assumption is that assertion training is synonymous with a behavior rehearsal treatment package (Rimm, Hill, Brown, & Stuart, 1974). In a review of the uses and misuses of the terms *behavior therapy* and *cognitive therapy,* Ledwidge (1978) repeatedly refers to assertiveness training as a behavior therapy (rather than a cognitive therapy) technique!

Even if one acknowledges that there are several alternative methods for assertion training, the label is almost always associated with therapeutic procedures that fall under the general rubric of behavior therapy. Rich and Schroeder (1976), for example, although noting that assertion training does not refer to a unique or well-defined set of procedures, nevertheless state that assertion training consists of *behavioral*

---

[1]As noted by Rich and Schroeder (1976), the inconsistency in "brand names" applied to response-practice procedures has led to a proliferation of terms (e.g., behavior rehearsal, role-playing) to describe similar or identical procedures. Although the author agrees with Rich and Schroeder's suggestion that response practice is perhaps the most accurate label, the terms are used interchangeably throughout this chapter.

training procedures. It should be clear, however, that, if the label is associated with the therapeutic goal rather than the therapeutic method, this association is not necessary. For example, it is not inconceivable that a psychoanalyst would consider an increase in a client's assertive behaviors as a sign of improvement. When this is the case, that increased assertive behavior is one of the goals of psychoanalysis, it would seem appropriate to label the method of therapy (i.e., psychoanalysis) a method of assertion training. The same would hold true for any method of therapy utilized in full or in part to bring about changes in the client's assertive behavior. The implication of this usage of the label is that the method chosen for assertion training is a function of the therapist's own opinions about the factors underlying the etiology and maintenance of assertive behaviors.

MODELS OF ASSERTION TRAINING

Although there are many theories about the etiology and maintenance of nonassertive behavior, most behavioral assertion training packages seem to be based on one or more of three general models. These models are: the skill-deficit model, the response-inhibition model, and the faulty-discrimination model. A fourth model, which is generally held by the client and is usually not shared by the therapist, is the rational-choice model. The skill deficit model assumes that unassertive individuals have a behavioral skill deficiency; that is, the relevant assertive skills are absent from their behavioral repertoire. The response-inhibition model assumes that the person has the requisite skills but is inhibited from behaving assertively. There are two major hypotheses about the determinants of inhibition. The first hypothesis is that the inhibition is due to conditioned anxiety responses; the second is that inhibition is due to maladaptive beliefs, self-statements, and expectations. The faulty discrimination model also assumes that the individual has the requisite skills, but, in addition, assumes that if unassertive individuals knew *how* to use these skills in particular situations they would behave in an assertive manner (i.e., the response would not be inhibited by anxiety or problematic beliefs). According to this model, unassertive persons do not discriminate accurately as to when an assertive response would be appropriate and effective and when not; thus, it is extinguished in all situations. The fourth model simply assumes that the unassertive person has perfectly valid reasons for choosing not to behave assertively; the person has the skills, is not inhibited, knows when an assertive response is likely to be effective, and, for a wide variety of possible reasons, chooses to behave in a nonassertive manner. What follows is a fuller description of each of these models, together with a discussion of their applications and, where available, the supporting research.

Skill-Deficit Model

The skill-deficit model posits that the requisite assertive behaviors are not present in the unassertive person's behavioral repertoire. Although a given individual may have the requisite component response capabilities (e.g., necessary vocabulary words, posture), it is assumed that the person has not learned to combine and to sequence the components to produce an assertive response. Following this conceptualization, the primary goal of assertion training is to teach the client the requisite skills. Most of the early research on assertion training was based on a skill deficit model. Many of these studies consisted of analogue experiments concerned with the effective procedural components of assertion training (e.g., Hersen, Eisler, & Miller, 1973; McFall & Twentyman, 1973), although several studies were carried out using a multiprocedure method designed to test the effectiveness of entire skill-training packages (Galassi, Galassi, & Litz, 1974; Rathus, 1972, 1973b). Procedures that have been effectively used in skill training include modeling (Eisler, Hersen, & Miller, 1973; Friedman, 1971; Goldstein, Martens, Hubben, Van Belle, Schaff, Wiersma, & Goldhart, 1973; Kazdin, 1974; McFall & Lillesand, 1971), instructions (Hersen, Eisler, Miller, Johnson, & Pinkston, 1973; McFall & Twentyman, 1973), in-session response practice (Lazarus, 1966; McFall & Marston, 1970; McFall & Twentyman, 1973), and feedback (Galassi, Galassi, & Litz, 1974; Hersen *et al.*, 1973; McFall & Twentyman, 1973). Unfortunately, much of this research has been done with either a student population or schizophrenic inpatients, and, thus, the generalizability of the results to an outpatient, nonstudent population is still to be determined. In addition, self-evaluation, self-regulated reinforcement, therapist reinforcement, and *in vivo* practice have typically been included in multi-procedure packages (Galassi, Galassi, & Litz, 1974; Rathus, 1973b; Richie, Note 2). The relative value of each of these additional procedures, however, has not been empirically assessed.

An analysis of the skill-training literature indicates clearly that the skills presumed to be absent are most often the verbal and nonverbal motor behavioral sequences that constitute an effective assertive response. A broad definition of skill, however, would include not only the specific motor action under consideration but also the cognitive capabilities (e.g., accurate perception and coding of the situation, knowledge of response outcomes) needed to decide when and how to engage in the action, as well as the arousal management capability needed to maintain physiological and affective responses at an optimum level. For instance, Welford (1976) suggests that skills should be thought of as ways of using capacities in relation to environmental demands.

This wider approach to assertion skill definition assumes a tripartite model of personality and behavioral functioning. As pointed out by Staats (1963, 1975) and reiterated by Lang (1971), Cone (1977), and others (most recently discussed by Wolpe [1978]), behavior may be usefully regarded as occurring in one (or a combination) of three response systems: the motor system, the cognitive system, and the physiological system. Although the notion that cognitions should be considered as behaviors is controversial (Ledwidge, 1978), the recognition of the three systems is helpful in developing behavioral treatment strategies for assertion problems. Within the assertion-skill acquisition literature, comparatively little attention has been paid to cognitive skill deficits, although presumably most programs involving coaching and feedback, especially if *in vivo* response practice is encouraged, have paid some attention to these areas. In a similar manner, skill-training programs not only ignore arousal management skills but also usually assume that an absence of arousal management (usually in the form of anxiety in assertive situations) is a *consequence* of motor skill deficits ("You are anxious because you do not know what to do."). An alternate hypotheses is that, at least with some individuals, high physiological arousal interferes with the production of adequate response sequences in assertive situations. What is suggested here is that a broad-band approach is needed in describing assertion skills. Not only should a range of component verbal and non-verbal motor capabilities be considered (e.g., eye contact, refusal behaviors), but cognitive assertive capabilities (e.g., accurate perception of assertive response consequences) as well as physiological arousal management capabilities (e.g., relaxed respiration in assertive situations) should also be included in any list of relevant components or skills.

The inclusion of both the cognitive system and the physiological system in a skills paradigm is consistent with the work of Meichenbaum (1977), who argues that cognitions must be seen as general coping skills that a client can use in preparing for and coping with stressful situations, and is also in agreement with the work of Goldfried (1971, 1977), who has proposed a coping skills approach to relaxation training (see Chapter 5, this volume). Although some research has been done to describe the verbal and nonverbal motor components of assertion skill (Eisler, Hersen, & Miller, 1973), little research has been done to delineate those cognitive and physiological component responses essential for the appropriate performance of assertive behaviors.

Response Inhibition Model

Anxiety Inhibition

An alternate model of unassertive behavior assumes that the person may, in fact, have the behavioral skills but is *inhibited* from behaving assertively. The anxiety hypothesis states that this inhibition is due to conditioned social-evaluative anxiety. Thus, many investigators have included various measures of anxiety in assertion situations among their dependent variables (Kazdin, 1973, 1975; McFall & Lillesand, 1971; McFall & Marston, 1970; McFall & Twentyman, 1973). Although the results have been mixed, there usually is a reduction in anxiety associated with increased assertiveness, even when it was not the primary focus of the intervention.

Few studies have been done in which the primary focus of the intervention was a direct modification of anxiety responses to assertive situations. Weinman, Gelbart, Wallace, and Post (1972) employed systematic desensitization with a group of male schizophrenics along a dimension of appropriate assertive behavior. Although they found no significant effects of the therapy on assertive behavior, this could have been a function of the population they used. Thorpe (1975) found that systematic desensitization was effective in increasing assertive behavior but less so than either therapies aimed at skill acquisition or at modification of cognitive self-instructions.

Trower, Yardley, Bryant, and Shaw (1978) compared systematic desensitization with a skills-acquisition training package for two types of clients: those assessed as socially unskilled and those assessed as socially phobic and presumably inhibited by anxiety. They predicted that socially phobic clients would show greater behavioral change after desensitization, whereas socially unskilled clients would show greater change after the skills-acquisition training. Their hypotheses received only minimal support. There was no difference between treatments for the socially phobic clients and only a slight superiority of skills-acquisition training over desensitization for the socially unskilled client. Unfortunately (for the purposes of the present chapter), differences in assertion per se as a function of the two treatments is not possible to ascertain from the Trower *et al.* study. Neither group improved on assertion measures with either treatment. Since skills-acquisition training packages, similar to the ones used, have been shown to be effective in a wide variety of other investigations, one must suppose that there was a problem in the treatment or the assessment in the Trower *et al.* study, at least with respect to the area of assertion difficulties.

Belief-Mediated Inhibition

The contention that unassertive behavior may be mediated by an individual's unrealistic beliefs is supported by anecdotal clinical evidence that clients often show dramatic increases in assertive behavior after having carefully considered the consequences of engaging in such activities (Goldfried & Davison, 1976; Lange & Jakubowski, 1976). In these instances, the client's assertion problems appear to be maintained by unrealistic fears over the possible reaction of others (e.g., disapproval), and not by an actual inability to emit the assertive response itself. A recent study by Schwartz and Gottman (1976) offers evidence to support this clinical observation. Furthermore, Jakubowski-Spector (1973) has emphasized the role played by cultural beliefs and expectations in inhibiting assertive behavior among women in particular.

Within the past few years, outcome studies have started to support the effectiveness of therapies based on the modification of beliefs and expectations as an approach to reducing social-evaluative anxiety (Goldfried, Linehan, & Smith, 1978; Kanter & Goldfried, Note 3; Meichenbaum, Gilmore, & Fedoravicious, 1971; Trexler & Karst, 1972). In general, the rationale underlying this approach assumes that the way individuals evaluate situations determines their emotional responses to these events. Specifically, it is assumed that one's unrealistic beliefs and negative self-statements result in maladaptive emotional responses. Research findings supporting these assumptions are summarized by Goldfried (1977), Mahoney (1974), and Meichenbaum (1977). From this vantage point, the aim of therapy is to modify unrealistic beliefs and to train the client to differentiate realistically dangerous situations from those in which danger does not, in fact, exist. This intervention strategy is most closely associated with the rational–emotive therapeutic approach advocated by Ellis (1962).

To date, few studies have been carried out to test the effectiveness of a therapy designed to facilitate assertive behavior by modifying unrealistic beliefs and expectations. Wolfe and Fodor (1977) compared a behavior-rehearsal approach with a combined behavior-rehearsal rational–emotive treatment. Although the rational-emotive component did not increase assertive behavior, it did lead to significantly less anxiety in assertive situations. Thorpe (1975) pitted rational therapy against behavior rehearsal, desensitization, and placebo conditions in the treatment of unassertive behavior and found that training subjects to alter their beliefs and self-statements about assertion was as effective as skill-training procedures. In a related area, an outcome study by Glass, Gottman, & Shumurak (1976) with heterosexually shy college males found that a treatment procedure emphasizing the use of rational self-statements was significantly more effective in improving heterosexual interaction than an intervention procedure emphasizing skill training.

An analysis of cognitive procedures used to increase assertive skills indicates that the treatment strategy may be effective in at least two ways. First, to the extent that maladaptive beliefs and expectations mediate emotional responses, the changing of these beliefs may be effective in reducing anxiety responses to assertive situations. Since these anxiety responses may be functionally related to either the inhibition of assertive responses or the avoidance of assertive situations, reduction should produce an increase in assertive behavior. A second way that the therapy may work is in changing the client's rules about when assertive behavior is called for, when it is acceptable. To the extent that the therapy is effective in changing the behavioral norms and rules under which the client operates, the treatment may be effective in increasing assertion. Although the rationale for most cognitive assertion therapies is that the change in beliefs will reduce inhibiting social-evaluative anxiety (e.g., Wolfe & Fodor, 1977), the presence of assertion anxiety is not a necessary assumption to explain the efficacy of the treatment.

Faulty Discrimination Model

Unlike the inhibition model, which assumes that the individual knows how to act but is inhibited, the faulty discrimination model assumes that the unassertive person does not know how to match specific actions with specific situations. As noted by Rich and Schroeder (1976), unassertive behavior may be due to a failure on the part of the person to discriminate adequately the situations in which a given response, already in his or her repertoire, is likely to be effective. Thus, although individuals may possess an array of potentially effective assertive responses, they may fail to act or may act inappropriately. The faulty discrimination model would lead to a therapy aimed at teaching the client to discriminate which situations call for which behaviors.

Both the skill-deficit model and the belief-mediated inhibition model assume that the individual may not have discrimination skills. Thus, in most response acquisition programs, the coaching and instructions focus, at least in part, on when to apply the specific behaviors being taught. Even if such training is not explicit, the discrimination principles are at least partially conveyed by the specific behaviors taught (e.g., modeled, reinforced) as appropriate in specific situations. Therapies based on the belief-mediated inhibition model assume that a major factor in an individual's nonassertive behavior is faulty discrimination (i.e., faulty beliefs about which behaviors are appropriate and/or effective in various situations). For example, in their book on cognitive–behavioral assertion training, Lange and Jakubowski (1976) include three discrimination mistakes (mistaking firm assertion for aggression, mistaking nonassertion for politeness, mistaking nonassertion for being helpful) in their list of five major reasons for nonassertive behavior. To a large extent, treatments aimed at changing beliefs focus on teaching clients how to discriminate realistic from unrealistic expectations about the consequences of their own behavior.

Rational Choice Model

An underlying belief of many assertion trainers seems to be that if an individual behaves nonassertively in a situation in which most people would behave assertively, there is something wrong. The person does not know how to respond, he or she is inhibited (either by anxiety or faulty beliefs), or the person is not able to choose an appropriate response for the particular situation. It often seems that, in the behavioral literature, if it's assertive, it's good! Frequently, however, when questioned, clients will state that they do not want to respond assertively. If questioned further, the client can quite often give cogent and rational reasons for such a decision. Religious beliefs, intense caring for the other individual, fatigue, high probability of punishment, or lack of concern about the outcome of the situations are but a few of the reasons clients may have for nonassertive behavior. Unfortunately, therapists may be tempted to discard such reasons as rationalizations on the part of the client. However, if the client and therapist hold the model that the client may rationally decide against assertive behavior, then the treatment concern should be to help the unassertive person discriminate when the decision to forego assertion is freely chosen and when the absence of assertive behavior is due to other factors. Discussion can be helpful in these cases, and it would seem critical that the therapist listen to the client's reasons with an open mind. However, it is often impossible to determine whether or not the client is actually free to choose in a particular situation. The phrase "freedom to choose" is used here to mean that the client has the capability for appropriate assertion and is not inhibited by uncontrollable internal factors (e.g., anxiety, unrealistic beliefs). One way of determining if the client has freedom of choice in a specific situation is to assess the client's assertion skills and/or inhibitions in a range of different but comparable situations. If the client is assertive in other situations, the therapist may decide to accept the client's reasons for choosing nonassertion. If deficits or inhibitions exist, the therapist might give the client assertion training across a broad band of situations and then discuss again the original decision. Often, clients spontaneously begin behaving assertively in situations in which they had previously given elaborate reasons to justify nonassertive behavior; however, in other cases, clients maintain their previous nonassertive behavior in certain situations.

STRUCTURED COGNITIVE–BEHAVIORAL
TREATMENT OF ASSERTION PROBLEMS

As noted in the discussion of the four models of unassertive behavior, the performance of assertive behavior in appropriate situations seems to depend on the individual's having the necessary motor and cognitive repertoires. In addition, given the possible inhibiting and disruptive effects of anxiety responses, the individual needs to have skills in managing physiological arousal. Thus, three behavioral target-systems or content areas must be addressed in any assertion training program: verbal and nonverbal motor skills, cognitive skills, and arousal management skills.

A wide range of therapeutic procedures have been used by behavior therapists to help clients increase their assertive behavior. Rich and Schroeder (1976) suggest that procedures used in assertion training programs can be organized into five functional categories: response-acquisition operations, response-reproduction operations, response-shaping and strengthening operations, cognitive-restructuring operations, and response-transfer operations. Given that Rich and Schroeder themselves made a cogent argument for not confusing the training procedures with the targets of the training, it is not clear why they included cognitive-restructuring operations as a separate category. The category includes both general verbal attempts on the part of the therapist to influence the client's cognitions, attitudes, and expectancies, (e.g., presentation of the therapy rationale) and specific training procedures aimed at changing the client's covert verbalization and cognitive sets related to nonassertive behavior (e.g., rational–emotive procedures). Their inclusion of Loo's (1971) projected consequences method, which consists of several procedures already included under other categories (e.g., modeling, response practice), indicates clearly that Rich and Schroeder are defining assertive behaviors in the narrow sense of overt verbal and nonverbal motor skills. The newer assertion-training methods that attempt to improve the cognitive components of the client's assertive skills apparently necessitated the creation of a new category.

In addition, Rich and Schroeder failed to include a category that would easily encompass several procedures suggested in the literature as potentially effective in reducing noncognitive factors inhibiting assertive behavior (e.g., biofeedback). Thus, there seems to be a need for a category to incorporate those procedures aimed at response disinhibition. These procedures would include both those aimed at changing the environment as well as those aimed at changing behaviors functionally related to assertive responses. In the latter case, many of the procedures used may fit adequately under one or more of the other four categories (e.g., if a client needs to learn to relax, one might use the response-reproduction operation of response practice, a method also used in teaching assertion skills).

The assertion-training procedures considered by Rich and Schroeder as well as others that might be used to reduce assertion inhibitions can be fitted into a modified list of Rich and Schroeder's categories, excluding the cognitive restructuring operations category and adding a response-disinhibition operations category. The therapeutic procedures include pretreatment assessment as therapy, desensitization, meditation, and environmental restructuring procedures (response disinhibition); task overview, instructions, and modeling (response-acquisition); therapist feedback and coaching, therapist reinforcement, self-evaluation, and self-regulated reinforcement (response-shaping and strengthening); and self-instructions and *in vivo* response practice (response transfer).

In order to clarify the relationship between therapeutic procedures available for use in assertion training and the targeted behavioral systems in which assertion skills are required for effective assertive performance, a three-dimensional representative grid, similar to the one used by Cone (1977) to illustrate methods of behavioral assessment, can be constructed. The grid is illustrated in Figure 7.1. Since the research suggests that performance of assertive behaviors may be situationally determined (Eisler, Hersen, Miller, & Blanchard, 1975; Linehan and Glasser, Note 4), universes of generalization are included as the third dimension. Although studies by Eisler *et al.,* (1975), Linehan & Glasser (Note 4), and Linehan & Seifert (Note 5) suggest that sex and familiarity of the other person in the situation are relevant situational parameters, specific situational universes of generalization have not been included in the grid. Not enough research has been done to specify adequately normative parameters; in the individual case, an idiographic assessment is needed to complete the grid.

What follows is, first, a description of the training procedures identified on the grid, together with suggestions on how these procedures might be applied to training in each of the three behavioral target systems. Second is a description of specific content and guidelines that could be used in a structured cognitive–behavioral

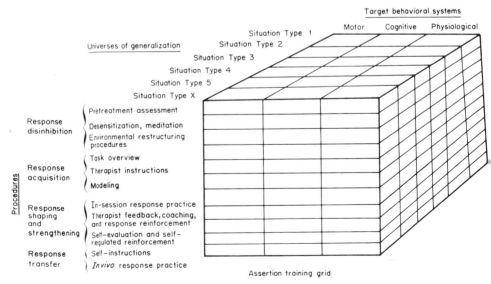

Figure 7.1. Assertion training grid.

approach to assertion training. Finally, there is a summary of a large-scale clinical outcome study done by the author, Marvin Goldfried, and Anita Goldfried (Linehan, Goldfried, & Goldfried, in press) comparing the effectiveness of the combined cognitive–behavioral approach to treatments aimed at either direct training of verbal and nonverbal motor skills or at cognitive restructuring skills.

Procedures for Assertion Training

The following procedures include those used by the author and associates in previous research studies on assertion training and some procedures from our work here in the psychology clinic at the University of Washington. Not every procedure is appropriate for use with all clients; decisions on which procedures are likely to be effective must be based on a comprehensive behavioral analysis done with the individual client. In general, the procedures described are independent of the target system to which they can be applied. In theory, each procedure listed could be applied to the cognitive system, to the overt motor system, or to the physiological system; in actuality, some of the procedures may be appropriate to only one or two target systems. Examples of the application of a specific procedure to a particular target system should not, however, lead to the assumption that the procedure would be ineffective if applied to other target systems. The separation of behavioral targets from therapy procedures will, it is hoped, serve to expand the use of procedures with demonstrated effectiveness in one system to other systems in which they may be equally effective.

Pretreatment Assessment As Therapy[2]

Assessment is often overlooked as a therapeutic method. Although the major function of any assessment procedure is to analyze the client's strengths and deficits and to provide direction for therapy, the therapeutic nature of the assessment itself is seldom recognized and utilized. The initial contact with the client in the form of an assessment interview begins the process of establishing a good therapeutic relationship that is often critical in obtaining the client's cooperation and in reducing fears and beliefs that might inhibit progress (Linehan, 1977). Assessment can be regarded as a complex interaction between the client and the therapist during which they agree upon a common conceptualization or way to view the problems the client presents. Frequently, this involves the client's looking at these problems in a new way, which can be therapeutic in and of itself (Meichenbaum, 1975).

Two kinds of clients are potential candidates for assertion training: those who recognize that they have an assertive problem and seek help for it and those who present various other problems that the therapist determines would be helped by assertion training. With both kinds of clients, the assessment interview presents an

---

[2]Since the assertion training procedures described have been most frequently used by us with a clinical population and, thus, are often part of a larger, multifaceted therapy program, the terms *therapist* and *trainer* and *therapy* and *training* are used interchangeably in describing our program.

opportunity for them to reconceptualize their problems. The assessment procedure, particularly one with an emphasis on behavioral analysis and consequent pinpointing of behavioral targets and controlling variables, can lead to an increase in the client's expectations regarding the possibility of improvement, a change that is, in itself, therapeutic (Goldstein, 1962). In many cases in which the client views himself or herself as "going crazy," "losing control," or "a terrible person" because of submissive or aggressive behavior, uncontrollable anxiety in assertive situations, indecisiveness, or other assertion problems, a behavioral explanation may bring tremendous relief and consequent behavior change. With those clients whose presenting problem seems, on the surface, to be far removed from the area of assertion, a reconceptualization of the problem in terms of an absence of assertive behaviors may, at times, be helpful in motivating the client to change. This is especially true when as assertion problem appears less intractable to the client than does the original problem. The assessment interview is the first step in orienting the client toward acceptance of specific procedures and techniques as useful in overcoming his or her problems.

The importance of assessment as a method of therapy, that is, the beginning of change, is not limited, however, to clinical behavioral-assessment procedures. Every time a client is subjected to a particular assessment technique, whether it be behavioral analysis, psychometric test, or questions about the client's early childhood, the client is given information about the way the therapist conceptualizes the problem, and, subsequently, the client's perception changes. If a client reports a drinking problem and the therapist administers a TAT and Rorschach, the client's expectations regarding the therapist's conceptualization of the problem, as well as expectations for the kinds of treatment, are very different than if the therapist has the client role play saying "no" to an offer of a drink. The assessment interview then must be regarded as the beginning of the therapeutic intervention, a legitimate method of therapy, more than a tool to determine a client's deficits. The questions that need to be addressed by the therapist whenever an assessment is administered are, How does the client view the problem and his/her behaviors after such an assessment? and How will this perception affect the client's progress in therapy?

Desensitization, Biofeedback, and Meditation

Excessively high physiological arousal interferes both with cognitive processing and with the production of complex motor sequences (Welford, 1976). Therefore, if during the assessment process it is determined that the client is deficient in physiological arousal management skills when approaching, or in, an assertive situation, the therapist must institute procedures designed to increase the client's skill in reducing the unwanted arousal. There are a wide range of procedures designed to focus specifically on teaching clients to control their physiological responses. Among the most popular are systematic desensitization and a self-control variation of desensitization proposed by Goldfried (1971), both of which are intended to teach the client to relax. In addition, biofeedback procedures and procedures designed to teach general meditation skills are gaining in acceptance (Benson, 1975; Marlatt & Marques, 1977). Although the research literature suggests that systematic desensitization used in isolation as an assertion-training procedure is not as effective as other methods (Thorpe, 1975), there are no well-controlled studies that examine whether the inclusion of desensitization would increase the effectiveness of other treatment packages for socially anxious clients. To date, no research has been done to examine the efficacy of biofeedback or meditation as procedures in assertion training. It would seem, however, that some method of direct training in arousal management would be necessary for those clients in whom the level of arousal is so high that other procedures that might reduce arousal (e.g., cognitive restructuring procedures, behavioral rehearsal methods) cannot even be attempted.

Environmental Restructuring Procedures

In examining the assertion-training literature, one is left with the impression that all nonassertive behavior is due to some deficiency in the client. Almost no attention is given to the possibility that the client may be interacting in an environment that does not reward assertive responses. There are at least three different approaches the therapist can take when a punishing environment is the problem:

1. The therapist can actively intervene in the client's environment in an attempt to restructure the response consequences.
2. The therapist can teach the client how to modify the environment (including leaving it if necessary and possible) such that the contingencies will change.
3. The therapist can teach the client how to resist the effects of nonreward or punishment and persist with assertive behaviors in the hope of achieving more long-range goals.

Restructuring the environment is the treatment of choice for institutionalized persons and children. Restructuring the environment is particularly useful in the case of an adult whose significant other person(s) is both responsible for ignoring or punishing assertive responses and willing to cooperate with the therapist.

With the exception of a few studies done with psychiatric patients, where the natural environment was restructured to reinforce differentially the patient's assertive behavior (Blanchard & Hersen, 1976), direct environmental intervention as a method of increasing assertive behaviors has not been reported. Similarly, little attention has been paid to the second alternative, teaching clients how they might go about changing their own environment so that rewards for assertive behaviors will be forthcoming. Although many of the performance guidelines for effective assertive behavior are, presumably, designed to increase one's chances of being effective in assertion situations and, thus, rewarded, these strategies are not designed to modify the client's environment so that future rewards for assertive behavior will be easier to obtain. An exception to this is the work of Bower and Bower (1976), in which they describe a comprehensive approach to modifying one's immediate environment, including changing the rate at which relevant individuals are positively responsive to assertive behaviors. Although there is as yet no data on the clinical effectiveness of their assertion training book, we have found it useful to give to clients in conjunction with teaching them environmental change skills.

In many cases, the very real possibility that persons might have to leave their immediate environment if they wish to increase their assertive behaviors must also be examined. This would seem to be an especially relevant possibility when the client is being punished by an unyielding spouse and divorce may be the only alternative or when assertive behaviors are being punished in a work situation in which a job change might be a solution to the problem. The third alternative, teaching the client to resist the effects of the nonreward or punishment, seems to be one of the goals of many of the cognitive assertion training programs, especially those designed for women; several of the cognitive approaches explicitly teach the belief that disapproval is not a catastrophe. If the environment cannot be immediately changed and if, in addition, it is not feasible to leave the environment, the only alternative to behaving nonassertively is for the person to learn to persist in the face of a meager reinforcement schedule.

Task Overview

In an indirect way, the assessment interview introduces the conceptual model the therapist plans to use in dealing with the client's problems. The orientation or task overview of therapy presents directly and deliberately to the client precise information about what has to be learned (e.g., relaxation skills, cognitive restructuring), as well as the clarification of the conceptual model (e.g., skill deficit, faulty discrimination) within which the learning will take place. Many apparent failures to learn are due to failure to understand what has to be learned, rather than to problems with acquisition or memory (King, 1948; Seymour, 1954). Thus, for the client, the overview serves the function of clarifying the task. Comprehension of the task is improved if information on particular aspects is given before practice begins; full comprehension can be ensured only if there is precise information about what has to be learned (Welford, 1976). Other failures in assertion treatment may be due to an inadequate clarification of the conceptual model or rationale underlying the treatment. The importance of the treatment rationale in affecting therapeutic gain has been demonstrated by Rosen (1974) in his studies on desensitization.

Therapist Instructions

Instructions are verbal guidelines describing the response components to be learned. They can vary from general guidelines ("Be sure and state clearly the message." "When restructuring your thinking, be sure and check out the probability that the dire consequences will occur." "Relax your muscles.") to very specific suggestions as to what the client should do ("Inhale deeply and then exhale." "Don't clench fists." "Don't hit or pound on things.") or think ("The fact that I say no to someone does not make me a selfish person."). As can be seen by the examples, instructions can be used in the modification of responses across each of the three behavioral target systems. In addition, we generally give the clients a set of written handouts that summarize the instructions given in the therapy session.

Modeling

Modeling can be provided by the therapist, audiotapes, videotapes, films, or imaginary models. The procedure involves providing the client with examples of appropriate alternative responses. In the area of verbal and nonverbal motor skills, the therapist, playing the part of the person attempting assertive behavior, can role-play situations with the client, or they can watch and discuss available tapes and/or films. The advantage of a therapist model, as opposed to tapes or filmed models, is that the situations can be tailored to fit the client's needs. However, the burden on the therapist is somewhat greater in that the role-playing requires the therapist, often on short notice, to be able to produce a competent response in what is frequently an unfamiliar situation. Immediately following the modeling, it is important to discuss the behaviors modeled to be sure that the client is observing the relevant responses. Kazdin (1974) has suggested the use of imaginary models to increase the production of assertive behaviors. Although this technique might be useful in disinhibiting a response (Bandura, 1969), it may not be effective in actually teaching a novel response. When the target behavioral repertoire is the cognitive system, the therapist might verbally model coping self-statements, self-instructions, or how to restructure problematic expectations and beliefs. In essence, the therapist is verbalizing more useful ways for the client to think in assertive situations.

In addition to in-session behavioral modeling of the requisite assertive skills, it is often useful to have clients observe the behavior of competent persons in their own environment. The behaviors that they observe can then be discussed and practiced in sessions for eventual use back in their environment. We frequently provide written models for how to apply some of the therapeutic procedures. For example, one can give the client written examples of self-monitoring diaries to use as a guideline in recording their *in vivo* practice.

In-session Response Practice

In-session response practice, usually called *behavior rehearsal* or *role-playing,* is the procedure most closely identified with assertion training. The procedure simply involves having the client practice the responses to be learned in simulated situations. Any assertion skill, whether a verbal or nonverbal motor response, a cognitive response, or a physiological response, can be practiced. The practice can be either overt or covert. If overt, the therapist usually describes the situation to the client and then, in the case of motor-skill training, role-plays with the client. If the physiological system is the target, the therapist might ask the client to practice relaxing during the role play. Densensitization procedures, which include in-session relaxation practice, might also be employed.

In the teaching of cognitive assertive skills, clients may be asked to verbalize several assertive self-statements. In the specific case of the cognitive restructuring method, clients first examine and verbalize any maladaptive beliefs, rules, and possible expectancies elicited by the situation and then restructure these beliefs verbally by generating more adaptive coping statements, rules, etc. An alternative to having clients verbalize coping statements is to have them write the statements down after each practice trial. The advantage of using a verbal method at the beginning of treatment is that the therapist can give immediate feedback and coaching, which often is needed by the clients in learning the procedure. In later stages, the written method may be preferable in that it allows clients to improve independently their own performance over several trails. There are at present no data indicating which procedure is preferable. Covert response practice, in which the client practices the requisite response in imagination, is also effective in assertion training (Kazdin, 1974; McFall & Lillesand, 1971) and may be more effective than overt methods for teaching more complex cognitive skills (Bandura, 1969). Covert methods are also useful when the client refuses to engage in overt rehearsal. Frequently, after a few sessions of covert practice, the client will agree to practice the responses overtly.

Therapist, Feedback, Coaching, and Response Reinforcement

Therapist feedback, coaching, and reinforcement follow both in-session response practice and the client's verbal or written description of *in vivo* efforts to practice the assertive skills. In response feedback, clients are usually given an explicit description of their performance. On occasion, we have used a biofeedback technique to give clients explicit feedback on muscular tension while they imagine themselves engaging in assertive behaviors. If the responses are not recorded (written or audio- or videotaped), the therapist must closely attend to the client's behavior and, at the same time, select those responses on which the client should be given feedback. At the beginning of therapy, when the client may do little that appears competent, the therapist is usually well-advised to give feedback on a limited number of response components. For example, although the therapist may point out all of the competent response components, only one or two of the responses needing improvement should be mentioned. Feedback on more may lead to stimulus overload and/or discouragement about the rate of progress. Thus, a response-shaping paradigm is used with feedback, coaching, and reinforcement designed to encourage successive approximations to the goal of effective assertive performance.

Coaching involves telling the client how a response is discrepant from the criterion and how it might be improved (e.g., "You were stuttering; try to be more fluent." "You didn't restrucuture your belief—If I say 'no' to him he will never want to see me again—to a more realistic expectation that, although he may not like it, he probably will keep dating you. Next time, try to assess the probabilities of the dire consequences occurring."). Therapist reinforcement usually takes the form of verbal praise and acknowledgment. Although the importance of reinforcement in shaping and strengthening behavioral responses is widely accepted, it is interesting that very little research has been done examining the role of reinforcement in the development of assertive behaviors. Even in analogue studies, in which the training is accomplished via tape recorders, both the title of the research and the assessment instructions generally indicate to the subject that assertive responses will be reinforced. Clinical practice suggests that with some clients the "permission" and approval of the therapist might, at times, be all that is needed for changes in assertive responding. Certainly, all assertion-training programs include some form of reinforcement.

Self-Evaluation and Self-Regulated Reinforcement

In self-evaluation, clients evaluate their own performance against the performance criterion previously learned. Overt motor behavior is evaluated on the basis of the rules and principles for effective verbal and nonverbal assertive responses that have been given to the client during the response-acquisition stage. Except when biofeedback procedures are used, physiological responses are almost always self-evaluated. Criterion is usually set by the client and is dependent on the client's own standards for comfort. When the target behaviors are perceptual coding, discrimination skills, or capabilities in generating coping self-statements, the criterion is usually not as explicitly stated. In the cognitive restructuring therapies (e.g., rational–emotive therapy, rational restructuring), the criterion for evaluating adaptive cognitive responses often seems to be whether or not the person subsequently feels more comfortable or acts more assertively. It would be useful to have available lists of explicit cognitive guidelines that have been empirically developed. The work of Schwartz and Gottman (1976) in describing differences in self-statements between assertive and nonassertive individuals might be useful in beginning to develop such guidelines.

In order to strengthen further the assertive responses, clients are also taught to reward themselves for assertive behavior. Although the notion of self-reinforcement is controversial (Cantania, 1975), the data suggest that self-regulated reinforcement is an effective method of increasing performance (Bandura, 1976). In many cases, however, it is necessary also to teach the client principles of self-regulated reinforcement, and, frequently, it is necessary to shape the client's self-reinforcement behavior through modeling and external reinforcement. We generally ask the client to evaluate and reward his/her own assertive behavior before the therapist gives feedback, coaching, and reinforcement. In this manner, the therapist can use the same procedures to teach assertion skills *per se* as well as to improve the self-evaluation and self-reward skills of the client.

Self-Instructions

This method involves teaching clients to verbalize to themselves one or more principles of assertion skill before they attempt to behave assertively. For example, the client may verbalize a set of self-instructions relevant to motor performance ("Remember, be firm."), cognitive responses ("OK, assess the probabilities of his getting angry; he probably won't."), or physiological responses ("Let go; relax my hands; breathe slow."). This method is similar to Meichenbaum's self-instructional treatment (Meichenbaum, 1977) and is intended not only to help the clients guide their own behavior in the initial stages of therapy but also as a method of teaching general rules to facilitate response transfer and maintenance after treatment ends.

In Vivo Response Practice

Although few analogue studies of assertion training employ *in vivo* response practice as a component procedure (e.g., McFall & Twentyman, 1973), most clinical studies do incorporate homework assignments as an important part of the training (Galassi, Galassi, & Litz, 1974; Rathus, 1973b). Clients are generally instructed to monitor situations in which assertive behavior might be appropriate, observe their motor, cognitive, and/or physiological response to the situation, and note the consequences that the behavior produces. In our training, we generally ask clients to record the situation, note their anxiety and anger level both during and after the situation, describe their verbal and nonverbal performance, their maladaptive thoughts, and the restructured adaptive thoughts, and then evaluate their performance. Clients are also asked to record behaviors done well (which can include responses across all three systems) and those needing improvement. A modification of this assignment, suggested by Richie (Note 1), is to instruct the clients also to give themselves "reward points" (from 1 to 100) for their performance. The client then adds up the points at the end of each week. Sometimes the summing of the points itself is reinforcing; however, a client could also exchange the points for more tangible rewards. Since we ask clients to write extensively on each homework practice, we assign only five *in vivo* practices to be brought to sessions per week, although the client is encouraged to practice whenever the occasion arises.

Contents for the Cognitive and Overt-Motor Target Behavioral Systems

What follows is a description of the content of a structured cognitive–behavioral assertion therapy that we developed as part of a study comparing treatments based on the motor-skill deficit model, the belief-mediated inhibition model, and a combined cognitive–behavioral treatment strategy (Linehan *et al.,* in press). The areas described included content within both the verbal and nonverbal motor system as well as the cognitive-response system. The clinician, however, is always treating an individual person, not a behavioral-response system. Thus, although the content described in the following has been categorized as primarily motor or cognitive, it should be noted that one cannot manipulate one response system in isolation from the other systems. For the most part, the procedures just described have an effect on more than one target system. For example, verbal instructions were used to effect changes in motor behaviors. This procedure is effective, however, because it modifies the client's cognitive system (i.e., knowledge about what constitutes an effective response). In a reciprocal manner, changes in motor behavior (e.g., increased refusal behavior in a situation in which, previously, the person aquiesced to unreasonable requests) can result in changed cognitions. For example, expectancies for negative response outcomes may be modified in light of actual positive outcomes that the client experiences. Although, with a particular client, the assertion trainer may want to use procedures aimed at direct training of physiological arousal management skills (e.g., systematic densensitization), those procedures have been covered adequately elsewhere and are not included here.

Cognitive–Behavioral Task Overview

Several content areas must be discussed with the client before assertive response-acquisition procedures can be initiated. First, the client and therapist must agree on a general definition of what assertive behavior involves and when it is appropriate; there is considerable ambiguity about just what the term involves. Although we use the definition ''standing up for rights and expressing opinions and preferences in a direct way without anxiety or undue guilt,'' there are many alternate definitions that would be just as useful in the individual case. Second, it is important to discriminate assertive behavior from submissive and aggressive behaviors. Besides clarifying the nature of what needs to be learned, this discrimination also serves to reduce fears that assertion training will result in aggressive behavior; clients with aggression problems can be reassured that the aim of therapy is not to make them passive in the face of attempts to violate their legitimate rights. Third, it is useful to discuss with the client the various models of unassertive behaviors, relating each model to the specifics of the individual client's problems. Generally, we have stressed the role of both maladaptive emotional responses (usually anxiety and/or anger) and verbal and nonverbal motor deficits in both submissive and aggressive behaviors. Since in our experience we have found it difficult at the beginning of therapy to concentrate on teaching the client cognitive skills for reducing the maladaptive emotional responses while at the same time teaching the motor skills, we usually focus first on teaching cognitive restructuring skills and then incorporate the training of verbal and nonverbal motor skills. Thus, in the task overview we also include a discussion of the rationale for dealing with emotional control before learning other behavioral skills. A portion of our therapist manual, describing content areas that we cover, is presented in Table 7.1. Usually, the astute clinician can elicit most of this information *from* the client rather than presenting it didactically *to* the client.

The Cognitive System: Cognitive Restructuring Training

Our method for cognitive restructuring training is quite structured and is based on the method of *systematic rational restructuring* proposed by Goldfried, Decenteceo, and Weinberg (1974). The primary goals of the *task overview* procedure, with respect to cognitive restructuring, are to explain the belief-mediated inhibition model in some detail (''Anxiety and anger stem from one's interpretation or evaluation of situations.'') and to help the client see the relevance of unrealistic and self-defeating beliefs and evaluations in mediating his/her own emotional upset. The

TABLE 7.1
Therapy Manual Excerpt: Task Overview for Cognitive–Behavioral Assertion Training

I. *The role of anxiety and behavioral deficit in submissive behavior*
   A. Submissive behavior is usually the result of two factors working together: *anxiety* and *lack of skills*.
   B. The ability to assert yourself effectively is a *complex skill* composed of two parts: First, it is necessary that you have learned how to perform the required behavior, and, second, you need to have learned in which situations and in which way the performance of the behavior is appropriate and useful for you. Although you may have many of the skills (e.g., such as how to say the word "no"), many people have never learned how or when to stand up for themselves and to express their opinions and preferences.
   C. The most difficult situations are those in which there is the possibility of negative consequences, because these situations usually lead to anxiety.
   D. Effects of anxiety: disorganization of thinking and behavior.
   E. Effects of lack of skills or faulty application: often anxiety; combined, they lead to a vicious circle in which the more anxious you get, the less you know what to say and the less you know about what to say and how, the more anxious you get.
   F. What is needed is both to reduce the anxiety by learning to control your fears and also training to learn how to act assertively.

II. *The role of anger and behavioral deficit in aggressive behavior*
   A. Often the unassertive person feels angry a lot of the time.
   B. When you finally get so angry as to do or to say something, you may *overshoot* and become aggressive.
   C. Sometimes this is due to lack of skills in expressing anger, and, often, it leads to indirect hostility–sarcasm.
   D. Frequently one feels guilt and hurt later.
   E. Others often respond by attacking or by disliking.
   F. Effects of anger: disruption of thinking and behavior.
   G. Effect of lack of skill or faulty application: often a belief that you can't improve the problem situation, a belief that can cause frustration and anger; combined, they lead to a vicious circle in which the more angry you get, the less able you are to come up with an effective solution to the problem and the less able you are to solve the problem, the more angry you get.

III. *Rationale for dealing with emotions first*
   A. Due to the disruptive aspects of both anxiety and anger on thinking and behavior, there is a need to learn to control emotional responses before learning skills.
   B. Object of therapy is to teach you the skills of emotional control or coping so that you can act effectively and say and do what you want in any particular situation.
   C. Want to learn to distinguish between realistic caring (e.g., may not express an opinion because you know the other person is very sensitive) and unrealistic anxiety (e.g., not expressing an opinion because you are afraid others will think you are stupid).
   D. Need to distinguish between anger on the one hand and intense caring about what happens to you or others on the other; between anger and not wanting or liking something.

technique used to enhance this awareness involves having the client actively generate realistic counterarguments to a series of very general unrealistic beliefs presented in a hypothetical and somewhat extreme form by the therapist. Several themes adapted from Ellis (1962) have worked well in our experience ("Everyone has to love me or I am a worthless person." "If something bad happens in my life, it will be a catastrophe and my life will be ruined forever."). However, the therapist also needs to listen closely to clients' descriptions of their own assertion problems to gather ideas about other maladaptive beliefs or rules that are likely to be mediating behavior in assertive situations. Once the client accepts the self-defeating nature of unrealistic beliefs, the therapist helps the client relate these beliefs to his/her own assertion problems.

An example of this procedure might be as follows. The therapist presents the belief, ''If anyone is ever hurt or angry with a person, that person must feel responsible and guilty and, indeed, is a bad and evil person.'' and asks if the client agress. If the client disagrees, the therapist questions the disagreement and pushes the client to defend his/her disagreement. If, as sometimes happens, the client agrees with the proposition, the therapist can restate the proposition in an even more extreme form, for example, ''So, if a person is just walking down the street, minding his own business, and a stranger comes up to him and starts accusing him of all sorts of wrongdoings, the person should feel guilty and terrible for causing the stranger to get upset?'' or the therapist can restate the belief in terms of the consequences of the belief for the therapist, for example, ''So, if one of my clients ever gets angry with me, no matter what I have done and no matter what their problem is, I am responsible and am, therefore, a bad and evil person.'' Almost always, the client will disagree with one of these restatements of the proposition.[3] After several minutes of playing the devil's advocate, the therapist then summarizes the more adaptive belief. In this example, a summary might be ''It would be nice if other people did not get angry or hurt by what I say or do, but I cannot predict or control others' emotions; their anger does not make them right and me wrong.'' The therapist and the client then discuss how the self-defeating belief has mediated the client's anxiety, inhibiting assertive behaviors in various situations. The agreement with the more adaptive belief that the therapist elicits at this stage of therapy can be used by the therapist during the course of therapy whenever the client restates the self-defeating belief (''But I thought you said . . . ?''). As noted by Goldfried *et al.* (1974), this technique is similar to the attitude-change procedures developed by Freedman and Fraser (1966) and, thus, is a modified ''foot-in-the-door'' technique.

Once the clients accept the belief-mediated model and see the relevance of maladaptive beliefs to their own nonassertive behavior, the therapist can begin procedures designed to help them utilize a more adaptive set of beliefs in assertive situations. Generally, we stress to the client that, rather than acquiring a new set of beliefs, they are learning to use a set of beliefs already held (when calmly considering the matter) in a new set of situations, namely, those that call for assertive behaviors. The procedures used include *instructions* on how to restructure problematic beliefs (see Tables 7.2 and 7.3 for a summary of the general guidelines and

---

[3]If, after pointing out to the client the consequences of his/her belief system, the client still fundamentally holds self-defeating beliefs (e.g., a person's basic value and worth is a function of the approval of other people), cognitive restructuring therapy, at least with respect to those beliefs, should not be done. Although this view is controversial, it seems to this author that further efforts to change the client's beliefs are an attempt to use the power of the therapist's role to change a client's values so that they will be more similar to those held by the therapist. Such efforts raise serious ethical questions.

TABLE 7.2
Instructional Aids and Related Handout for Cognitive–Behavioral Assertion Training: No. 1

Guidelines for cognitive restructuring

1. Determine the fear
   What dire consequences am I expecting? (What is the worst thing that can happen to me if I stand up for my rights in this situation? What's so upsetting about that?)
2. Assess the probabilities
   How likely is it that the worst will happen? (How likely is it that my friend will never want to see me again if I don't agree to do this favor?)
3. Evaluate the "catastrophe"
   What would happen if the dire consequences occurred? (Would my life be over, not worth living, if someone is inconvenienced by me?)
4. Identify the rules
   What assumptions and beliefs are governing my feelings in this situation? (Should I please everybody? Is it necessary that everyone like me? Am I expecting the world to be fair? Should people be the way I would like them to be just because I want it? Any other "shoulds"?)

suggestions we give on how to restructure). Also, we often *model* for the client a whole progression of thoughts to demonstrate how one might restructure a set of maladaptive beliefs. For example, the therapist might sit back and, with eyes closed, say the following:

> *I'm imagining that I am in a store and the clerk has given me the wrong change. As she turns to help the next person, I'm noticing she owes me $.35 more. A lot of people are in line behind me. Hmmm, I want to ask for the correct change, but I'm beginning to feel anxious about doing it. What am I thinking? Well, the clerk will probably get angry and everybody else will be mad that I am making them wait. I'll really feel like a fool. I'm really being selfish. I should be more considerate. Besides, I don't need the money.*
>
> *Hey, wait a minute, I can restructure that! The clerk probably won't be angry, and even if she is, it's not a catastrophe. I have a right to get the correct change, and, if other people waiting in line are upset, it's unfortunate, but it doesn't have to be my problem. There is no reason why I shouldn't ask for my change. I'm still an OK person.*

The client is also provided with *in-session practice* of cognitive restructuring by means of hierarchically presented imaginal situations during which the client searches for the rules and beliefs mediating his/her response and, if necessary, restructures the belief. Before each restructuring practice, the client is encouraged to verbalize one of more restructuring principles or adaptive beliefs that can guide the restructuring (*self-instructions*). After each practice sequence, the therapist and client discuss the clients' restructuring; client *self-evaluation* and *self-regulated reinforcement* is encouraged; and the therapist gives *feedback, coaching,* and *response reinforcement* when appropriate. Clients are also assigned *in vivo* practice of

TABLE 7.3

Instructional Aids and Related Handout for Cognitive–Behavioral Assertion Training: No. 2

Suggested assertive beliefs[a]

1. I am under no obligation to say "yes" to people simply because they ask a favor of me.
2. There is no law in the sky that says other people's opinions are more valid than mine.
3. If I say "no" to someone and they get angry, that does not mean that I should have said "yes."
4. I have a right to assert myself even though I may inconvenience others.
5. The fact that other people might not be assertive doesn't mean that I shouldn't be.
6. I can still feel good about myself even though someone else is annoyed with me.
7. Standing up for myself over "small" things can be just as important to me as "big" things are to others.
8. The fact that I say "no" to someone does not make me a selfish person.
9. If someone doesn't do something I ask them to do, that doesn't mean I shouldn't have asked them in the first place.
10. I have a right to disagree with other people, even though they feel strongly about their own opinion.
11. Just because I have already agreed to do something doesn't mean I can't change my mind and say "no."
12. I have a right to tell others when the way they are acting is annoying or upsetting to me and to give them suggestions for different ways of behaving.
13. Saying "no" to a friend probably won't make her dislike me forever.
14. People I care about might be disappointed when I don't do things that they want me to do, but that is not a catastrophe.
15. If I have to always do things I don't want to do just to get someone to like me, then I have to wonder if their liking me is critical to my well-being.
16. Other people don't have magical abilities to know what I want if I don't tell them.
17. The fact that some people are inconsiderate and obnoxious is a pain in the ass, but there is no reason why they shouldn't be that way.
18. I have a right to enjoy what I am doing and to ask others to stop doing things that interfere with my enjoyment.
19. I may want to please people I care about, but I don't have to please them all the time.
20. Give, give, giving is not the be-all and end-all of life. I am an important person in this world, too.
21. If I refuse to do a favor for someone, that doesn't mean I don't like them. They will probably understand that, too.
22. I do not have to make myself responsible for solving others' problems and for making them happy.
23. I have a right to intimidate others by my mere presence. I don't have to try to look weak, stupid, or ineffectual just so people won't be threatened by me.
24. I can choose not to assert myself, and I can still feel good about myself.

[a]*Note:* We break the above-suggested beliefs into four separate lists and give them out over several sessions.

cognitive restructuring whenever they experience problematic emotional responses between sessions. We ask them also to try cognitive restructuring in assertive situations. During subsequent sessions, the homeworks are discussed.

The Overt–Motor System: Verbal and Nonverbal Skill Training

After several sessions of cognitive restructuring training, the client is usually ready to begin learning specific motor behaviors to use in assertive situations. At

TABLE 7.4

Instructional Aids and Related Handout for Cognitive–Behavioral Assertion Training: No. 3

Principles of assertive behavior[a]

Guidelines for effective delivery: My appearance
Nonverbal behavior: How do I look?

_____ Eye contact?   1. Keep good eye contact; look at person I'm talking to instead of down at the floor or off to the side. Lean forward slightly.

_____ Relaxed posture?   2. Try to keep my body relaxed, not rigid or tense. Breathing deeply may help to relax me.

_____ Still?   3. Don't fidget and move around excessively, wring hands, change feet, etc.

_____ No fists or pounding?   4. Don't clench fists, hit, or pound on things. If I get angry, express it directly instead of indirectly by clenching fists, etc.

_____ Serious?   5. Act serious; avoid laughing or inappropriate smiling when someone is trying to jeopardize my rights.

Tone of voice: How do I sound?

_____ Firm?   1. Speak in a definitive and firm voice as if I really mean what I say.

_____ No whining?   2. No whining, pleading, or apologetic voice.

_____ No stammering?   3. No stammering, undue hesitance, mumbling, or extraneous words (e.g., er, ah, mmm.).

_____ No sarcasm or hostitlity?   4. No sarcasm, hostility, or yelling. If I am angry, express it directly rather than indirectly by a hostile, sarcastic, or "cold" voice.

_____ Calm?   5. When I am talking to someone who is speaking rapidly in a loud voice, keep my voice low and speak slowly.

_____ Steady?   6. Maintain my voice at a steady volume. When my voice becomes lower at the end of a request or refusal, I may sound as if I am unsure.

Guidelines for effective content: What I say
Nonthreatening situations: Dealing with everyday situations

_____ Comments concise?   1. Keep what I say concise and to the point; say what I want directly instead of beating around the bush.

_____ Message clear?   2. Be sure and state clearly the message I want the other person to hear, instead of expecting them to infer it from other things I say.

_____ Statement of wishes?   3. Try to use phrases "I want," "I don't want," instead of "I need," "You should," or "I can't," perhaps one statement of why.

_____ No apologetic behavior?   4. Perhaps give one factual reason, but not apologetic behavior or long-winded excuses.

_____ No "shoulds"?   5. No "shoulds" or inappropriate demands; don't tell others what they "should" do, feel, want, etc.

(continued)

TABLE 7.4 (continued)

Principles of assertive behavior[a]	
_____ No threats or attacks?	6. When angry, express it directly rather than by attacking or threatening.
Threatening situations: Dealing with people who are jeopardizing my rights	
_____ Request first?	1. Request first! Sometimes simply asking, in a direct way, for what I want is effective and all that is necessary.
_____ Be persistent?	2. If another person attacks, threatens, ignores me, or tries to change the subject, I can continue to state clearly, concisely, and in a firm voice what I want; ignore any destructive comments the other person makes.
_____ Process statements?	3. If persistence doesn't work, I can make a statement about what is happening between me and the person, but no imputing of motives (e.g., "You don't seem to be hearing what I am saying," not "You just don't want to listen to me.").
_____ Statement of feeling?	4. I can express my feelings of discomfort in the situation (e.g., "I'm starting to feel angry about this.").
_____ Statement of consequences?	5. In a case where a person refuses to listen to my wishes and it is important to me, I can state the consequences of his behavior (e.g., what I will do), but no exaggerated or vindictive threats.
_____ Insist?	6. If the person ignores my rights in the situation after repeated requests, I can insist or, in effect, demand that my rights be maintained; no demands before requesting.
_____ Reward?	7. Remember to reward people who respond positively to me when I am behaving assertively.

[a] _Note:_ To avoid overloading the client, we break these principles into four separate lists and give them to clients as we cover each section in therapy.

this point, we begin integrating training in verbal content, nonverbal behaviors, and strategies of assertive behavior into the overall program. The same procedures used to teach cognitive restructuring are used in teaching motor skills. Instructions, modeling, therapist feedback, coaching, and response reinforcement are based on the Principles of Assertive Behavior described in Table 7.4. Additional principles, relevant to the individual case, are often formulated and are usually based on client or therapist observations of the assertive behaviors most likely to be reinforced in the client's own environment. In-session practice is accomplished by the therapist and the client role playing a set of hierarchically presented assertion situations. During each role-play, the therapist can vary the difficulty of the situation, for example, by structuring the responses to the client so that the client either has to persist for increasingly longer periods of time or is faced with criticism. As with the teaching of cognitive restructuring, the client is given homework assignments, in this case, to practice *in vivo* the assertive behaviors learned in session. Clients are taught to guide their own behavior using the Principles of Assertive Behavior as *self-instructions*. After both in-session and *in vivo* practices, clients are asked to self-evaluate and self-reinforce their own behaviors.

Once the client has acquired a few assertive motor skills, we ask him to practice integrating the cognitive restructuring skills with the motor skills in both their in-session and their *in vivo* practice. An example of a self-monitoring form that integrates the two types of skills is presented in Table 7.5. Since one of our therapy goals is that the client learn to regulate his/her own behavior, at least in the content area of the therapy, we gradually fade out the therapist instructions, modeling, feedback, coaching, and response reinforcement, as well as the in-session practice. As the responses become more automatic in assertive situations, the self-instructions, self-evaluation, and self-reinforcement often drop out also. At this point, it is expected that the assertive behaviors will be maintained by *in vivo* practice followed by environmentally regulated reinforcement; that is, the behaviors work for the client.

Clinical Effectiveness of a Structured Cognitive–Behavioral Assertion Program

In order to evaluate the clinical effectiveness of the cognitive–behavioral assertion training program, we (Linehan, Goldfried, & Goldfried, in press) conducted a large-scale outcome study and compared it with both a treatment that focused on direct training of verbal and nonverbal motor skills and also a treatment program to teach cognitive restructuring skills. Thus, we were able to compare the relative effectiveness of treatment based on a skill-deficit model with one based on a belief-mediated inhibition model and to compare both with a treatment based on a combination of the two models.

Method

Seventy-nine unassertive women who came from communities near Stony Brook, New York, and Washington, D.C., participated in the study. The mean age of the women was 34.2, and there was a mix of both married and single women, as well as women working fulltime outside the home, parttime outside the home, and fulltime at home. In addition, we attempted to approximate, as closely as possible, a clinical population by rejecting women as possible candidates for participation in the research (though not in the therapy) who scored above zero on the Rathus Assertion Inventory (Rathus, 1973a) or below the midrange on the Assertion Difficulty Inventory (an inventory developed specifically for this study). The therapist consisted of four male and four female clinical psychology graduate students (six) and postdoctoral interns (two). Each therapist saw an equal number of clients in each treatment.

TABLE 7.5
Self-Monitoring Form for Cognitive–Behavioral Assertion Training

Record of attempts to act assertively and to overcome anxiety and anger in daily situations

Name _____

Date _____

Describe situation:

Beginning Subjective Anger Points (SAPS) _____   Anxiety (SUDS) _____
                                        (0–100)   (0–100)

Self-defeating thoughts:

Reevaluation:

What I did:

Done well:

Needing work:

Ending Subjective Anger Points (SAPS) _____   Anxiety (SUDS) _____
                                     (0–100)   (0–100)

Were you pleased with your performance? _____
                                        $(1-5)^a$

^{a}1 = no, not at all; 2 = yes, a little; 3 = yes, somewhat good; 4 = yes, quite a bit; 5 = very much so at this time.

Participants were randomly assigned to one of three behavioral-treatment groups (motor skill training, cognitive restructuring, combined motor-skill cognitive-restructuring) and two control groups (relationship therapy and waiting list). Participants in each treatment and in the relationship control were seen weekly for eight individual sessions of 45 minutes each. The three behavioral treatments were highly structured, and the format for each group was similar: Treatment components included coaching, modeling, self-instructions, rehearsal (of assertive behavior, cognitive restructuring, or both), self-evaluation, feedback, and *in vivo* practice. Therapy sessions consisted of practicing motor skills, cognitive restructuring, or a combination of both in 12 predetermined training situations. The situations were arranged in a hierarchy of increasing difficulty over the eight sessions. There were four training trials per situation. Before the first trial, the therapist modeled self-statements as well as the response to be learned, be it a verbal–nonverbal motor skill, restructuring, or a combination of both. During the modeling, the therapist interacted with a tape-recorded partner. The format for each trial followed a four-step sequence: (*a*) the therapist read a one-line statement of the situation, and the client verbalized one or more self-instructions; (*b*) the situation was read in detail, and the client practiced either acting assertively, cognitively reevaluating the situation, or a combination of both; (*c*) the participant evaluated her behavior, anxiety level, or both; and (*d*) the therapist gave the client feedback. Modeling was faded out over the course of the therapy. Guidelines (for cognitive restructuring, effective assertive behavior, or both) developed for each treatment were given to participants.

Measures to assess treatment outcome included participant questionnaires, a peer questionnaire, a behavioral role-play test, and a contrived situational test. Participants were administered the Rathus Assertiveness Inventory, the Assertion Difficulty Inventory, the S-R Inventory of Anxiousness (Endler, Hunt, & Rosenstein, 1962) and the S-R Inventory of Hostility (Endler and Hunt, 1968) as pre- and posttest measures. The situations used in the two S-R inventories as well as the Assertion Difficulty Inventory are described in what follows. In addition to completing the questionnaires, each participant gave the name of a person who knew her well and could evaluate her assertive behavior at posttest by completing a questionnaire. Open-ended questions requested such information as whether changes were observed and the effect of such changes on the relationship.

An extended interaction behavioral role-playing test was administered at pre- and posttest. A trained male–female assessment team delivered role-play lines verbatim to participants from predetermined scripts. Following a response of the participant, the assessors delivered an additional predetermined prompt, up to five prompts, or until the participant gave in or stopped responding. For example, when the participant role-played a customer who is returning a defective item, the assessor would continue to respond with prompts, all variations of the theme "I'm sorry, I can't help you without a sales slip." The role-play interactions were tape recorded, and the order of male versus female assessor was varied across the six situations.

The major dependent variables were (*a*) assertion content; (*b*) speech dysfluencies; (*c*) loudness–affect; (*d*) eye gazing; (*e*) number of responses per interaction;

and (*f*) subjective reports of anxiety, guilt, and anger obtained after each of the role-play situations. Assertion content was rated on a five-point scale from transcriptions of the audiotapes (1 = No response, give up, irrelevant or incomplete responses, to 5 = unqualified or direct assertion). Speech dysfluencies were scored by counting the number of stammers, blockages, etc. that participants made during each response (adapted from Mahl, 1959). The loudness–affect quality of the response was rated from audiotapes (1 = barely audible response to 5 = volume strong, affect does not detract from assertiveness). For these three measures, two separate scores were computed for each situation: a first-response-only score and an average situation score obtained by averaging across all responses for that interaction. Duration of eye gazing (i.e., looking at the face of the role-playing partner) was timed by the unoccupied assessor, and a percentage score was obtained by dividing by the total time of the interaction. Number of responses was obtained by counting the number of prompts delivered by the experimenter. Following each role-play situation, participants estimated on a scale of 0 (low) to 100 (high) how much anxiety, guilt, and anger they had experienced during the role-play.

Finally, a contrived situational test was administer at pre- and posttest. While participants were trying to complete a questionnaire in an adjoining room, a female confederate, following a predetermined script, set up six interactions that interfered with the participant's efforts, so that the participant was required either to initiate assertive behavior or to exhibit refusal behavior. Following the participant's initiation or refusal response, the confederate delivered up to four prompts (refusals or repeated requests) until the participant stopped responding or gave in. The entire situation was tape recorded, and the dependent variables consisted of assertion content per interaction and number of responses per interaction. Assertion content and number of prompts were scored as in the behavioral role-play test.

Results

Results of the participant questionnaire battery, with the exception of the S–R Inventory of Anxiousness, showed the order of adjusted posttest means, from most to least improved, to be consistent across all measures: (*a*) motor skills plus cognitive restructuring; (*b*) and (*c*) cognitive restructuring or motor skills in varying order; (*d*) relationship control; and (*e*) waiting list. The order of means of the S–R Inventory of Anxiousness, from most to least improved, was cognitive restructuring, motor skills plus cognitive restructuring, motor skills, relationship, and waiting-list control. Results indicate a significant improvement across all questionnaire measures, with the exception of the S–R Inventory of Hostility, for the four contact conditions. There were no significant pre–post differences on S–R Inventory of Hostility for the motor skills and the relationship groups, nor were there significant within-group differences on any measure for the waiting-list control.

On the behavioral role-playing test, all three behavioral treatments were equally successful at enabling participants to attempt (and persist at attempting) an assertive response in the situation. However, the two treatments that focused on direct training of verbal and nonverbal motor responses were more effective in improving the assertion quality of the response. Since behavioral role-playing tests in most outcome research on assertion training have required a single response, separate analyses were carried out for the first response only on the extended interaction test. Participants in each of the three behavioral groups were rated as significantly more assertive on their first responses than those in relationship therapy or waiting-list control conditions. There were no significant treatment effects for speech dysfluencies or the loudness–affect variable. Separate analyses were carried out for role-play test situations in which no therapeutic training had been provided. On untrained items, motor skills participants as well as motor skills plus cognitive restructuring participants showed significant improvement when compared with waiting-list and relationship treatment on assertion content, eye gazing, and total number of responses. Motor skills participants were better than cognitive restructuring participants on assertion content.

The contrived situational test represents an attempt to come somewhat closer to naturalist interaction than does role-playing assessment. It was used for posttesting only and was scored for assertive content of first response to each interaction, assertive content across all responses, and the total number of responses per interaction. The order of adjusted means from the most to least assertive was the same on all three measures: (a) motor skills; (b) motor skills plus cognitive restructuring; (c) cognitive restructuring; (d) relationship; and (e) the waiting-list control group. Although both the motor skills plus cognitive restructuring and motor skills alone groups did not differ from each other, each of these two conditions was superior to both the relationship and the waiting-list control groups on the basis of assertion content across responses and total number of responses.

On the peer questionnaire, peers were asked to evaluate whether the participant seemed easier or more difficult to get along with, or the same, over the previous 2 months. Results indicated that, when compared with participants in the relationship and waiting-list control groups, clients in the three behavioral treatment groups were more likely to be seen as *easier* to get along with. In summary, across all types of measures, there is some support for concluding that a combined cognitive restructuring plus motor skills training approach is superior to a program aimed at either the cognitive system (cognitive restructuring) or the overt–motor system (motor skills training). Unfortunately, the study does not answer the question of whether the combined program's superiority is due to its applicability to a wider range of individuals as opposed to a greater effectiveness with each person.

This study is unusual in that, in contrast to the large volume of studies applying cognitive–behavioral techniques to a student population, it demonstrates the usefulness of a structured cognitive–behavior treatment program with a population similar to adult outpatients. The ability to generalize the results of this study is also enhanced by its cross-setting collaborative nature; care was taken to ensure comparability of treatment procedures and outcome measures. In addition, eight therapists, both male and female, conducted the treatment programs. The absence of differences in the findings between the two settings as well as across the eight therapists indicates the validity of results beyond the idiosyncracies of a single location, client population, or set of therapists. Since all the participants in this study were women, the results cannot automatically be assumed to apply to a male population as well. However, one might anticipate that the results would be similar with a group of unassertive males.

ASSESSMENT OF ASSERTION: A CONSTRUCT IN SEARCH OF A DEFINITION

Successful therapy of any kind is intimately tied to the clinical assessment on which the treatment is based. In considering assertion training, the therapist is generally interested in measuring those behavioral referents that fall under the general construct of assertion. The assessment of any behavioral construct, however, is directly tied to the definition of the construct. As noted by MacDonald (in press), imprecision in construct definition necessarily results in imprecision in assessment. Unfortunately, the construct *assertion* is characterized by a great deal of conceptual ambiguity (Linehan & Egan, in press). An analysis of published definitions of assertion, items included in inventories measuring assertion, and content areas included in assertion training programs indicate that almost any positively valued interpersonal behavior is likely to be labeled as assertive (Goldfried & Linehan, 1977). Definitions of assertion are almost as diverse as the authors giving them and range from those that are relatively precise and restrictive to those that are general and inclusive. For example, MacDonald (in press) empirically generated a definition of assertion that included the open expressions of preferences, by words or actions, in a manner that causes others to take them into account and any act that maintains one's rights. Wolpe (1973) defines assertion as the "proper expression of any emotion other than anxiety towards another person [p. 81]." (It is not clear why Wolpe excludes the expression of anxiety.) In contrast, Alberti and Emmons (1974) offer a very broad definition of assertion that includes a general category of any "behavior which enables a person to act in his (sic) own best interests [p. 2]."

An examination of the content of behavioral role-play tests of assertion reveals a pattern of wide variation in response classes included. For example, McFall and his associates (McFall & Lillesand, 1971; McFall & Marston, 1970; McFall & Twentyman, 1973) seem to limit use of the term *assertion* to the ability to refuse unjust demands; Eisler, Miller, and Hersen, (1973) add standing up for rights and expression of feelings; Galassi and Galassi (1976) include these three and, in addition, include the response class of making requests. There seems to be little agreement as to which response classes should be included under the construct "assertion." Analyses of the self-report inventories used to assess assertion has not clarified the issue. Galassi and Galassi (Note 6) found 9 factors in the College Self-Expression Inventory; Gambrill and Richey (1975) found 11 factors in their assertion inventory; Gay, Hollandsworth, and Galassi (1975) discovered 14 factors in the Adult Self-Expression Scale. Although several authors (e.g., Gambrill & Richey, 1975; Hall, 1977) have suggested that this multidimensionality is a function of the situational specificity of assertive behaviors, an examination of the dimensions obtained by the factor analyses suggests that several different response categories, in addition to situational categories, are included under the single construct of "assertion" (Goldfried & Linehan, 1977).

Since definitions of a construct are arbitrary, arguments about the "true" meaning of assertion are pointless. However, excessive multidimensionality in the definitions and measurement of assertion creates difficulties for the assertion trainer. First, if response classes that are trained and assessed vary across studies, it is not known whether or not procedures that are effective for increasing one class of assertive responses will necessarily be effective for increasing other classes of responses that are also labeled as assertive. For example, although a procedure may be effective for teaching a very simple response class (e.g., refusal behavior), it may not be effective in teaching a complex skill (e.g., demanding one's rights when discriminated against by one's boss). A second disadvantage is that multidimensionality in construct definition and assessment (where the dimensional scores are summed to give a total score) can obscure behavior–behavior relationships. Often, positive correlations are assumed even when they are absent. This faulty assumption can lead to the neglect of training in content areas needed by the client.

A second area in which the definitions of assertion vary is in the inclusion and exclusion of the three response systems (motor, cognition, and physiological). For example, some definitions include only motor behavior (see MacDonald, earlier), whereas others suggest that the concept of assertion includes the absence of undue anxiety (Alberti & Emmons, 1974). Many of the self-report inventories are probably measuring responses across all three of the systems. For example, the Gambrill and Richey (1975) inventory asks how often the person engages in specific behaviors (motor) and also how comfortable the person is when engaging in the motor behaviors. The term "comfortable" could refer to either physiological arousal (e.g., anxiety) or cognitions (e.g., approval or disapproval of one's own behavior). Other investigators use the term uncomfortable (e.g., McFall & Lillesand, 1971) or similar response-system ambiguous terms such as "difficulty" (e.g., Galassi, DeLeo, Galassi, & Bastien, 1974; Linehan *et al.*, in press).

The measurement scores that one obtains with the aforementioned instruments, therefore, are not particularly useful to the behavioral therapist in constructing an adequate and individualized treatment program. The exception is the Gambrill and Richey inventory, which does give a score indicating how often the client engages in assertive activities, comfort in these situations, and a list of behaviors that the client would like to improve. The therapist must use other assessment methods to determine the source of the discomfort. Specific information about assertion-skill deficits within each of the three response systems is also needed before training can begin. Interviews, self-monitoring, imaginal procedures, behavioral role-play tests, and *in vivo* observations can be used singly or in combination to obtain much of this information; physiological measures can also be obtained during these procedures.

It is only through comprehensive assessment that an assertion training program can be designed so that the behavioral targets are relevant to the client's needs. The cognitive–behavioral treatment presented in this chapter, therefore, will almost certainly require modification for the individual client. Other procedures may be added, and procedures described may be dropped; content areas can vary, and guidelines may be adjusted to suit the idiosyncratic environment of the client. Essentially, assertive behavior must be regarded as a complex response to the specific demands of the client's environment. All three response systems—motor, cognitive, and physiological—are activated in the performance of assertive behavior; to restrict assessment, training, and evaluation to one or two systems is to seriously limit the utility of the training. Assertion therapists and trainers, therefore, have a responsibility to their clients to design and implement a program that is as thorough as it is responsible to the client's individual needs.

ACKNOWLEDGMENTS

This chapter would not have been completed without the help of Kelly Egan. She edited, rewrote, respelled, and coaxed these pages to completion. I thank her. Appreciation is also expressed to Jamye MacDermott for her willingness to put in long hours on her own time to type the manuscript.

REFERENCE NOTES

1. Richie, C. A. *How to conduct an assertion training group: A workshop manual for trainers.* Unpublished manuscript, University of Washington, 1977.
2. Richie, C. A. *Utilizing self-reinforcement in group assertion training for women: Implications for immediate and long-term change.* Paper presented at the meeting of the Association for Advancement of Behavior Therapy, San Francisco, December, 1975.
3. Kanter, N. J., & Goldfried, M. R. *Relative effectiveness of rational restructuring and self-control desensitization for the reduction of interpersonal anxiety.* Unpublished manuscript, State University of New York at Stony Brook, 1976.
4. Linehan, M. M., & Glasser, J. *Effects of situational context on reported difficulty of assertive behavior.* Unpublished manuscript, The Catholic University of America, 1976.
5. Linehan, M. M., & Seifert, R. *How appropriate is assertive behavior? Real and perceived sex differences.* Manuscript submitted for publication, 1978.
6. Galassi, J. P., & Galassi, M. D. *A factor analysis of a measure of assertiveness.* Unpublished manuscript, West Virginia University, 1973.

REFERENCES

Alberti, R. E., & Emmons, M. L. *Your perfect right.* San Luis Obispo, California: Impact, 1974.
Bandura, A. *Principles of behavior modification.* New York: Holt, Rinehart, & Winston, 1969.
Bandura, A. Self-reinforcement: Theoretical and methodological considerations. *Behaviorism,* 1976, *4,* 135–155.
Barnard, G. W., Flesher, C. K., & Steinbrook, R. M. The treatment of urinary retention by aversive stimulus cessation and assertive training. *Behavior Research and Therapy,* 1966, *4,* 232–236.
Benson, H. *The relaxation response.* New York: Morrow, 1975.
Blanchard, E. B., & Hersen, M. Behavioral treatment of hysterical neurosis: Symptom substitution and symptom return reconsidered. *Psychiatry,* 1976, *39,* 118–129.

Bower, S. A., & Bower, G. H. *Asserting yourself: A practical guide for positive change.* Reading, Maine: Addison-Welsey, 1976.

Cantania, C. A. The myth of self-reinforcement. *Behaviorism,* 1975, *3,* 192–199.

Cheek, D. K. *Assertive black . . . puzzled white.* San Luis Obispo, California: Impact, 1976.

Cone, J. D. The relevance of reliability and validity for behavioral assessment. *Behavior Therapy,* 1977, *3,* 411–426.

Corby, N. Assertion training with aged populations. *The Counseling Psychologist,* 1975, *5,* 69–74.

Eisler, R. M., Hersen, M., & Miller, P. M. Effects of modeling on components of assertive behavior. *Journal of Behavior Therapy and Experimental Psychiatry,* 1973, *4,* 1–6.

Eisler, R. M., Hersen, M., Miller, P. M., & Blanchard, E. B. Situational determinants of assertive behavior. *Journal of Consulting and Clinical Psychology,* 1975, *43,* 330–340.

Eisler, R. M., Miller, P. M., & Hersen, M. Components of assertive behavior. *Journal of Clinical Psychology,* 1973, *29,* 295–299.

Ellis, A. *Reason and emotion in psychotherapy.* New York: Lyle Stuart, 1962.

Endler, N. S., & Hunt, J. McV. S–R Inventories of Hostility and comparison of the proportion of variance from persons, responses, and situations for hostility and anxiousness. *Journal of Personality and Social Psychology,* 1968, *9,* 309–315.

Endler, N. S., Hunt, J. McV., & Rosenstein, A. J. An S–R Inventory of Anxiousness. *Psychological Monograph,* 1962, *76* (17; whole no. 536).

Freedman, V. L., & Fraser, S. C. Compliance without pressure: The foot-in-the-door technique. *Journal of Personality and Social Psychology,* 1966, *4,* 195–202.

Friedman, P. H. The effects of modeling and role-playing on assertive behavior. In R. D. Rubin, H. Fensterheim, A. A. Lazarus, & C. M. Franks (Eds.), *Advances in behavior therapy.* New York: Academic Press, 1971.

Galassi, J. P., DeLeo, J. S., Galassi. M. D., & Bastien, S. The College Self-Expression Scale: A measure of assertiveness. *Behavior Therapy,* 1974, *5,* 165–171.

Galassi, M. D., & Galassi, J. P. The effects of role-playing variations on the assessment of assertive behavior. *Behavior Therapy,* 1976, *7,* 343–347.

Galassi, J. P., Galassi, M. D., & Litz, M. C. Assertive training in groups using video feedback. *Journal of Counseling Psychology,* 1974, *21,* 390–394.

Gambrill, E. D., & Richey, L. A. An assertion inventory for use in assessment and research. *Behavior Therapy,* 1975, *6,* 550–561.

Gay, M. L., Hollandsworth, J. G., & Galassi, J. P. An assertiveness inventory for adults. *Journal of Counseling Psychology,* 1975, *22,* 340–344.

Glass, C. R., Gottman, J. M., & Shumaurak, S. H. Response acquisition and cognitive self-statements modification approaches to dating skills training. *Journal of Counseling Psychology,* 1976, *23,* 520–526.

Goldfried, M. Systematic desensitization as training in self-control. *Journal of Consulting and Clinical Psychology,* 1971, *37,* 228–234.

Goldfried, M. R. The use of relaxation and cognitive relabeling as coping skills. In R. B. Stuart (Ed.), *Behavioral self management,* New York: Brunner/Mazel, 1977.

Goldfried, M. R., & Davison, G. C. *Clinical behavior therapy.* New York: Holt, Rinehart, & Winston. 1976.

Goldfried, M. R., Decenteceo, E. T., & Wienberg, L. Systematic rational restructuring as a self-control technique. *Behavior Therapy,* 1974, *5,* 247–254.

Goldfried, M. R., & Linehan, M. M. Basic issues in behavioral assessment. In A. R. Ciminero, K. S. Calhoun, & H. E. Adams (Eds.), *Handbook of behavioral assessment.* New York: Wiley-Interscience, 1977.

Goldfried, M. R., Linehan, M. M., & Smith, V. L. The reduction of test anxiety through rational restructuring. *Journal of Consulting and Clinical Psychology,* 1978, *46,* 32–39.

Goldstein, A. P. *Therapist–patient expectancies in psychotherapy.* New York: Pergamon Press, 1962.

Goldstein, A. Case conference: Conflict in a case of frigidity. *Behavior Therapy and Experimental Psychiatry,* 1971, *2,* 51–59.

Goldstein, A. P., Martens, J., Hubben, J., Vanbelle, H. A., Schaff, W., Wiersma, H., & Goldhart, A. The use of modeling to increase independent behavior. *Behavior Research and Therapy*, 1973, *11*, 31–42.

Hall, J. R. Assessment of assertiveness. In P. McReynolds (Ed.), *Advances in Psychological Assessment, Vol. 4*. San Francisco: Jossey-Bass, 1977.

Heimberg, R. G., Montgomery, D., Madsen, C. H., & Heimberg, J. S. Assertion training: A review of the literature. *Behavior Therapy*, 1977, *8*, 953–971.

Hersen, M., Eisler, R. M., & Miller, P. M. Development of assertive responses: Clinical, measurement, and research considerations. *Behavior Research and Therapy*, 1973, *11*, 505–521.

Hersen, M., Eisler, R., Miller, P., Johnson, M., & Pinkston, S. Effects of practice, instructions, and modeling on components of assertive behavior. *Behavior Research and Therapy*, 1973, *11*, 443–451.

Jakubowski-Spector, P. Facilitating the growth of women through assertive training. *The Counseling Psychologist*, 1973, *4*, 75–86.

Kazdin, A. E. Covert modeling and the reduction of avoidance behavior. *Journal of Abnormal Psychology*, 1973, *81*, 87–95.

Kazdin, A. E. Effects of covert modeling and model reinforcement on assertive behavior. *Journal of Abnormal Psychology*, 1974, *83*, 240–252.

Kazdin, A. E. Covert modeling, imagery assessment, and assertive behavior. *Journal of Consulting and Clinical Psychology*, 1975, *43*, 716–724.

King, P. H. M. Task perception and interpersonal relations in industrial training. *Human Relations*, 1948, *1*, 373–412.

Lang, P. J. The application of psychophysiological methods to the study of psychotherapy and behavior modification. In A. E. Bergin & S. L. Garfield (Eds.), *Handbook of Psychotherapy and Behavior Change*. New York: John Wiley, 1971.

Lange, A. J., & Jakubowski, P. *Responsible assertive behavior: Cognitive/behavior procedures for trainers*. Champaign, Illinois: Research Press, 1976.

Lazarus, A. A. Behavior rehearsal vs. non-directive therapy vs. advice in effective behavior change. *Behavior Research and Therapy*, 1966, *4*, 209–212.

Ledwidge, B. Cognitive behavior modification: A step in the wrong direction? *Psychological Bulletin*, 1978, *85*(2), 353–375.

Linehan, M. M. Behavioral interviews. In J. D. Cone & R. P. Hawkins (Eds.), *Behavioral assessment: New directions in clinical psychology*. New York, New York: Brunner/Mazel, 1977.

Linehan, M. M., & Egan, K. J. Assertion training for women. In A. S. Bellack & M. Hersen (Eds.), *Research and practice in social skills training*. New York: Plenum Press, in press.

Linehan, M. M., Goldfried, M. R., & Goldfried, A. P. Assertion therapy: Skill training or cognitive restructuring. *Behavior Therapy*, in press.

Loo, R. M. Y. *The effects of projected consequences and overt behavioral rehearsal on assertive behavior*. Unpublished doctoral dissertation, University of Illinois, 1971.

MacDonald, M. L. Measuring assertion: A model and a method. *Behavior Therapy*, in press.

Mahl, G. F. Exploring states by content analysis. In I. D. Pool (Ed.), *Trends in content analysis*. Urbana Illinois Press, 1959.

Mahoney, M. J. *Cognition and behavior modification*. Cambridge: Ballinger, 1974.

Marlatt, G. A., & Marques, J. K. Meditation, self-control, and alcohol use. In Richard B. Stuart (Ed.), *Behavioral self-management*. New York: Brunner/Mazel, Inc., 1977.

Meichenbaum, D. H. *Cognitive behavior modification*. New York: Plenum, 1977.

Meichenbaum, D. Self-instructional methods. In F. Kanfer & A. Goldstein (Eds.), *Helping people change*. New York: Pergamon Press, 1975.

Meichenbaum, D. H., Gilmore, H. B., & Fedoravicious, A. Group insight versus group desensitization in treating speech anxiety. *Journal of Consulting and Clinical Psychology*, 1971, *36*, 410–421.

McFall, R. M., & Lillesand, D. B. Behavior rehearsal with modeling and coaching in assertion training. *Journal of Abnormal Psychology*, 1971, *77*, 313–323.

McFall, R. M., & Marston, A. An experimental investigation of behavioral rehearsal in assertive training. *Journal of Abnormal Psychology,* 1970, *76,* 295–303.

McFall, R. M., & Twentyman, C. T. Four experiments on the relative contributions of rehearsal, modeling, and coaching assertion training. *Journal of Abnormal Psychology,* 1973, *81,* 199–218.

Nydegger, R. V. The elimination of hallucinatory and delusional behavior by verbal conditioning and assertive training. *Journal of Behavior Therapy and Experimental Psychiatry,* 1972, *3,* 225–227.

Rathus, S. A. An experimental investigation of assertion training in a group setting. *Journal of Behavior Therapy and Experimental Psychiatry,* 1972, *3,* 81–86.

Rathus, S. A. A 30-item schedule for assessing assertive behavior. *Behavior Therapy,* 1973, *4,* 398–406. (a)

Rathus, S. A. Instigation of assertion behavior through videotape-mediated assertive models and directed practice. *Behavior Research and Therapy,* 1973, *11,* 57–65. (b)

Rich, A. R., & Schroeder, H. E. Research issues in assertiveness training. *Psychological Bulletin,* 1976, *83,* 1081–1096.

Rimm, D., Hill, G., Brown, N., & Stuart, J. Group-assertive training in treatment of expression of inappropriate anger. *Psychological Reports,* 1974, *34,* 791–798.

Rosen, G. M. Therapy set: Its effects on subjects' involvement in systematic desensitization and treatment outcome. *Journal of Abnormal Psychology,* 1974, *83,* 291–300.

Salter, A. *Conditioned reflex therapy.* New York: Creative Age, 1949.

Schwartz, R. M., & Gottman, J. M. Toward a task analysis of assertive behavior. *Journal of Consulting and Clinical Psychology,* 1976, *44,* 910–920.

Seymour, W. D. *Industrial training for manual operations.* London: Pitman, 1954.

Staats, A. W. *Complex human behavior.* New York: Holt, Rinehart, & Winston, 1963.

Staats, A. W. *Social behaviorism.* Homewood, Illinois: The Dorsey Press, 1975.

Thorpe, G. L. Desensitization, behavioral rehearsal, self-instructional training, and placebo effects on assertive-refusal behavior. *European Journal of Behavioral Analysis and Modification,* 1975, *1,* 30–44.

Trexler, L. D., & Karst, T. O. Rational–emotive therapy, placebo, and no-treatment effects on public speaking anxiety. *Journal of Abnormal Psychology,* 1972, *79,* 60–67.

Trower, P., Yardley, K., Bryant, B. M., & Shaw, P. The treatment of social failure: A comparison of anxiety-reduction and skill-acquisition procedures on two social problems. *Behavior Modification,* 1978, *2,* 41–60.

Weinman, B., Gelbart, P., Wallace, M., & Post, M. Inducing assertive behavior in chronic schizophrenics: A comparison of socioenvironmental, desensitization, and relaxation therapies. *Journal of Consulting and Clinical Psychology,* 1972, *39,* 246–253.

Welford, A. T. *Skilled performance: Perceptual and motor skills.* Glenview, Illinois: Scott, Foresman and Company, 1976.

Wolfe, J. L., & Fodor, I. G. A comparison of three approaches to modifying assertive behavior in women. *Behavior Therapy,* 1977, *8,* 567–574.

Wolpe, J. *The practice of behavior therapy.* New York: Pergamon Press, 1973.

Wolpe, J. Cognition and causation in human behavior and its therapy. *American Psychologist,* 1978, *33,* 437–446.

The Cognitive Regulation of
Anger and Stress

RAYMOND W. NOVACO

INTRODUCTION

The interrelationships between cognition, emotion, behavior, and the environment have begun to intrigue cognitive–behavioral interventionists. Contemporary interest in the cognitive determinants of emotional state and in environment-behavior relationships has stimulated a growing body of theory and research that is of direct relevance to models of therapeutic intervention. Although the developing array of cognitive approaches to clinical disorders has an ancestry of behavioral techniques based on learning theory, it is incumbent on the newer formulations to articulate theoretical models that specify their conceptual framework and permit scrutiny of their propositions. Put another way, it is too easy and dangerous to become preoccupied with developing treatment procedures and to ignore or avoid the task of conceptual specification.

Anger and its therapeutic regulation are the concerns of this chapter. The approach that will be adopted consists of viewing anger as an affective stress reaction that has important cognitive and behavioral determinants. The general theoretical model is one of human stress, and a more specific and corresponding model of anger will also be developed. This effort is likely to be characterized more by ambition than by refinement, yet it is my conviction that it is a necessary step for the progress of therapeutic interventions for anger problems.

ANGER AND HUMAN EXPERIENCE

The arousal of anger has salient manifestations and consequences. When anger occurs, blood pressure increases, muscles tighten, respiration quickens, a frown

241

Cognitive–Behavioral Interventions:
Theory, Research, and Procedures

forms on the face, and one is inclined toward agressive ideation. These effects are often troublesome, particularly when the arousal of anger prompts impulsive aggressive actions. Although anger has been consistently found to increase the probability of aggression (Rule & Nesdale, 1976), nonspecialists too readily associate anger with aggression. Consequently, anger is commonly viewed in negative terms. Elsewhere (Novaco, 1976a), I have described the adaptive as well as the maladaptive functions of anger as it affects behavior.

Anger is a strong emotion that has been associated with the baser qualities of humans. Averill (1974) has argued that prior to the eighteenth century it was common to speak of emotions as "passions" by which the individual was "gripped," "seized," or "torn." Anger is, perhaps, the prototype in such views. Becoming angry seems to signify that one is out of control—being driven by uncivilized forces that ultimately must be checked. This view of anger as a passion that takes control of the personality is rooted in ancient philosophical beliefs, such as those of Aristotle.[1] Furthermore, early philosophers such as Aristotle and the Stoic Marcus Aurelius, disassociated the arousal of anger from the intellectual faculties.[2] This view of anger and of other emotions as passions continued with the writings of the seventeenth-century subjectivist Descartes,[3] who also believed that anger was almost always accompanied by the desire to aggress. Anger arousal, in these ancient views, was not accompanied by reason.

The association between anger and aggression engenders the belief that anger is negative or harmful because it is expected to result in harmdoing. Journalistic reports of persons consumed by fits of rage and who perform violent acts are frequently encountered in reading the daily paper, particularly in tabloids with affinities for sensational stories. Such accounts often portray incidents in which the anger reaction was elicited by a minor provocation. For example, an Associated Press story (February 2, 1978), "Enraged Man Kills Boy," described the homicidal behavior of a man who became enraged when his parked car was struck by a frisbee. Because of the anger–aggression association, the potential positive functions of anger are easily overlooked. People who directly witness the expression of anger often respond to this emotion with fear or with counterattack.

Although anger does have positive functions and does not always result in aggressive behavior, an important feature of anger arousal is its relationship to stress.

[1]Examining problems of volition in his famous *Ethica Nicomachea,* Aristotle stated, "For choice is not common to irrational creatures as well, but appetite and anger are.... Still less is it anger; for acts due to anger are thought to be less than any other objects of choice [Ross, 1963, section 1111, 10–19]." Aristotle also wrote in his *Physiognomica* that "when we are mastered by a fit of temper we become more obstinate and totally intractable; we grow headstrong and violent and do whatever our temper impels us to do [Ross, 1963, section 809, 35]."

[2]"For he who is excited by anger seems to turn away from reason with a certain pain and unconscious contraction [Aurelius, 1925, p. 146]."

[3]In his treatise on "The Passions of the Soul," Descartes wrote: "Anger is also a species of hatred or aversion which we have towards those who have done some evil to or have tried to injure not any chance person but more particularly ourselves. Thus it has the same content as indignation.... But it is incomparably more violent than these three other passions, because the desire to repel harmful things and to revenge oneself, is the most pertinent of all desires [Haldane & Ross, 1931, p. 420]."

Within the present framework, anger is viewed as an affective stress reaction. That is, it is construed as an emotional response to perceived environmental demands that has adverse implications for health and behavior. These concepts will receive further explication later. A central idea pertinent to clinical concerns is that chronic anger in response to aversive events can have deleterious consequences that go considerably beyond the experience of an unpleasant emotional state.

The presentation of this view of anger will follow a development of the concept of stress. The model of anger that will be proposed can be seen as a particular aspect of a more general model of human stress. Similarly, the therapeutic procedures for anger management that will be described are to be understood as a particular form of a more general therapeutic approach that is called *stress inoculation*. Thus, the conceptual formulations of anger and of its regulations are specific exemplifications of more general theoretical schemes. Although the therapeutic approach called *stress inoculation*, to be described subsequently, was not deduced from the theoretical framework, it is, nonetheless, based upon the conceptual scheme and is intended to be consistent with its propositions.

The chapter will first delineate the various conceptions of human stress that are prominent in contemporary literature. Although there are biological and sociological models of stress that have considerable following, the emphasis will be upon psychological models, since it is this orientation that characterizes the anger concepts. Particular attention will be given to cognitive mediators of stress because cognitive factors occupy a central role in the proposed model of anger.

THEORETICAL MODELS AND RESEARCH ON HUMAN STRESS

Recent research in the behavioral sciences has demonstrated that the prevalence of physical illnesses, mental disorders, depressed mood, and social disorganization are in part a function of identifiable variations in the physical and social environment (e.g., Aakster, 1974; Brenner, 1973; Dohrenwend & Dohrenwend, 1974; Glass, 1977; Johns, 1974; Kiritz & Moos, 1974; Levine & Scotch, 1970; Lipowski, 1973; Reeder, Schrama, & Dirken, 1973). Stressful circumstances long have been thought to affect mental and emotional functioning, whether the stress was engendered by discrete traumatic events or by prolonged exposure to adverse psychological conditions. However, it has been only recently that stressors at various levels of the environment have been investigated systematically for their effects on nonspecific physiological responses and on specific diseases. Environmental presses in the form of specific aversive stimuli (e.g., noise), behavioral constraints (e.g., crowding), organizational demands (e.g., work pressure), and cultural forces (e.g., role prescriptions) have been shown to exert adverse effects on the well-being of individuals and of communities.

The study of human stress is, necessarily, a task that involves multiple levels of analysis (Lazarus, 1966). The topic of stress has emerged as a rubric under which a wide variety of adaptation-related phenomena has been investigated. At times, this heterogeneity has prompted the suggestion that usage of the concept of stress be discontinued in favor of subordinate concepts that are more restricted in scope, such as threat, arousal, conflict, or anxiety. However, the viability of this argument for more limited concepts diminishes as one goes beyond the psychological level of analysis and recognizes the range of environmental forces that impact on humans and the extent of deleterious effects that can result from exposure to such forces.

Stress can be understood as a state of imbalance between environmental demands and the response capabilities of the person or system to cope with these demands (McGrath, 1970; Mechanic, 1968). The relative ratio of demands to resources can be thought to mark the condition of stress.

The term *stress* is an engineering metaphor, and the analogy has been in part responsible for inexact usage of the concept. In engineering, stress refers to an external force that, when applied to a physical structure, produces a strain on the structure. The resultant strain is a function of both the magnitude of the stress and the properties of the structure. Unfortunately, in the behavioral sciences, ''stress'' has been used equivocally to refer both to an agent and to a result (cf. Selye, 1975). In the present analysis, it refers to neither; vis-à-vis the engineering analogy, the present usage of ''stress'' more closely parallels the engineering concept of strain, since it refers to a condition of the organism or system.

Stress is construed here as a hypothetical state that is induced by environmental forces and is manifested by reactions at various physiological, behavioral, and social levels. The term *stressor* denotes the external force experienced by the organism. Stressors are aversive events or elements in various environmental fields that disturb the organism's equilibrium, interfere with its performance, or even threaten its survival. Stressors can be viewed as environmental demands.[4] Consistent with intervening variable logic (Spence, 1944), the observable consequences of the hypothetical condition (stress) are denoted by the term *stress reaction*. Stress reactions are the adverse health and behavioral consequences of the failure to cope with environmental demands. Thus, ''stress'' as a hypothetical construct is defined by the functional relationships between antecedent events and their adverse consequences.

Stress can be best understood in terms of *transactions* between persons and environments (Lazarus & Launier, 1978). A dynamic view of stress as involving such transactions requires an examination of demand–coping processes that occur over time. What may appear to be beneficial in the short run (e.g., competitive drive and high job involvement leading to job advancement) may prove harmful in the future (e.g.. myocardial infarction). Conversely, circumstances that, for example, engender unpleasant emotional arousal may then induce coping activities that result in long-term benefit, as when unhappiness leads one to terminate a floundering relationship or when anxiety impels one to conquer a challenging task.

Stress, as a description of a hypothetical condition, should be thought to exist in

---

[4]The term *environmental stressor* is frequently encountered in the literature pertaining to the physical environment's effects on behavior. It is advocated here that use of this expression be discontinued because of its redundancy. From where does a stressor originate except from an environment? The expression gives the illusion of saying more than it actually does say.

varying degrees of severity. The degree of severity is a function of various response parameters, such as the frequency, intensity, duration, and form of the stress reaction. The more negatively valenced the response is on such parameters, the more reliable is the description of the state of affairs as being one of stress.

Existing theoretical models for the study of stress have a common interest in how environmental demands impact on health and behavior. However, these various approaches, which follow disciplinary lines in their analyses, differ with regard to their point of focus in the delineation of environment–behavior relationships.

The pioneering work of Hans Selye (1956, 1973, 1976) has been recognized universally. His research began with investigations of toxins as noxious agents and the study of inflammation as the prototype stress response. Selye's view is that stress is a *nonspecific response* that is a common residual of all specific reactions to evocative agents. According to this view, the syndrome of reactions to particular stressors may be particular to the noxious agent and conditioning may shape the reactivity of particular organs, but all syndromes are thought to have common physiological components—these being adrenal cortex enlargement, shrinkage of lymphatic structures, and gastrointestinal disturbances.[5]

The approach to stress exemplified by Selye is predominantly *response focused*. Selye is principally concerned with the biological reactions of the organism in response to whatever demands present themselves. The nature of stress is construed in terms of the tricomponent biological response cluster and the tristage General Adaptation Syndrome. In his model, the process of adaptation is marked by three discrete states: (*a*) an alarm reaction characterized by involuntary adjustments of the body to restore equilibrium—typically, activation of the autonomic nervous system and adrenal discharge; (*b*) a stage of resistance marked by constructive metabolism and a return to equilibrium; and (*c*) a stage of exhaustion that ensues if the stressor persists and that represents the collapse of the adaptive mechanism. Thus, the adrenal, lymphatic, and intestinal changes constitute the *spatial* dimension of Selye's concept, and the three-stage GAS represents the *temporal* dimension.

Selye's view of stress as a response indeed departed from the then-existing perspective of physiological research that, consistent with the work of Cannon, viewed stress with a stimulus focus. Physiological investigations still commonly view stress in terms of external forces that impact the organism, such as "heat stress," "noise stress," or "gravitational stress."

Those who study stress from a social perspective also adopt an approach that is *situation* or *stimulus focused*. They are primarily interested in the social circumstances that induce health, behavioral, and organizational impairments. The specific nature of the resultant impairment is of less interest than the social events or environmental attributes that give rise to those impairments. Although investigators in this area have studied broad social conditions and particular social environments, such as occupational settings, at the forefront of this line of research on social stress

---

[5]Selye's nonspecificity thesis has been sharply criticized by Mason (1975), who has argued that uncontrolled factors in physiological research, such as emotional arousal, may be responsible for the ubiquitous reactions observed by Selye. As an endocrinologist, Mason also questioned the evidence base that hormonal responses are nonspecific to any demand.

has been the body of work on stressful life events (Dohrenwend, 1978; Dohrenwend & Dohrenwend, 1974). This paradigm construes stressors as discrete life events that, when experienced in sufficient quantity, result in adverse effects on psychological and physical well-being.[6] The role of mediational processes has been deemphasized, as also is the fact that life events are often the product of the person's behavior.

Psychological approaches to stress give considerable attention to mediational processes and have an *interaction focus*. That is, they are concerned with the interchange between person and environment. Their experimental investigations concentrate on the intervening factors that mediate the relationship between stressors and stress outcomes. A multitude of stress-inducing circumstances have been examined and many kinds of stress reactions have been measured, but the predominant concern has been with regard to the cognitive, personality, and social psychological factors that accentuate or ameliorate stress effects.

Psychological formulations of stress (Appley & Trumbull, 1967; Cofer & Appley, 1964; Lazarus, 1966; McGrath, 1970) emphasize the role of mediational processes. That is, particular external events or conditions that might be classified as stressors are not viewed as having uniform effects across individuals, and particular individuals may be more vulnerable to exposure to certain environmental demands. Common to these approaches is the assumption that the perceived environmental demands and the individual's perception of threat must be determined in order to calibrate potential adverse effect.[7]

---

[6]The pioneering work in this area was performed by Homes and Rahe (1967), whose Social Readjustment Rating Scale and its variations have been used in an extensive array of epidemiological studies (e.g., Coddington, 1972; Dohrenwend, 1973; Gersten, Langer, Eisenberg, & Orzeck, 1974; Theorell & Rahe, 1971). These studies have confirmed the hypothesized relationship between life events and stress outcomes. The number and severity of stressful events have been found to have a strong positive correlation with psychophysiological symptoms for samples of households (Dohrenwend, 1973; Markush & Favero, 1974; Myers, Lindenthal, & Pepper, 1971), and convergent findings have been obtained for smaller homogeneous populations, such as college students, naval personnel, and hospital patients (Rahe, Mahan, Arthur, & Gunderson, 1970; Spilken & Jacobs, 1971; Wyler, Masuda, & Holmes, 1971).

[7]The psychological approach to stress is often limited by the boundary conditions of experimental laboratory methodology. Psychological models have been concerned primarily with reactions to stressors that can be manipulated experimentally, and the standard body of procedures has well-known liabilities with respect to subject samples. Moreover, the stress situations used in laboratory investigations are not the sort that impinge on people over extended periods of time and result in social pathogies. Such is the recognized trade-off between internal and external validity. Yet, additional limitations of psychological laboratory investigations are associated with the customary procedural paradigms of such experimentation that follow from stimulus–response frameworks. That is, subjects are routinely exposed to some stimulus condition intended to induce a state of affairs that is hypothesized to result in certain response outcomes. When those outcomes occur, the experiment is terminated, thus restricting the time frame of the analysis and, importantly, precluding the examination of interactive processes between the subjects and the environmental conditions over time. Discontent with traditional procedural paradigms has prompted the advocacy of alternative approaches. Lazarus and Launier (1978) have suggested the use of idiographic methods for the study of stress as a transactional concept, and Stokols (1978) has proposed the concept of *environmental optimization* to characterize the exchanges between person and environment that mark the process of adaptation to environmental demands.

Nearly all theoretical models are bound to particular disciplinary analyses. As Scott and Howard (1970) have noted, theoretical models of stress are "field-specific." That is, they can only be applied to a limited range of environmental fields to which the individual is exposed. However, the phenomena of stress transcend the boundaries or levels of analyses of particular disciplines, and, consequently, the descriptive and explanatory language of any individual discipline is insufficient for an understanding of stress. Even though a comprehensive understanding of stress will require the convergent efforts of multidisciplinary investigation, the study of stress is not likely to escape disciplinary prescriptions, since methodologies are rooted in disciplinary domain. Research methodologies are formulated for their applicability to phenomena at a particular level of analysis.

COGNITIVE MEDIATORS OF STRESS

The body of research on human stress permits the generalization that the effects of environmental demands upon individuals are not uniform. Exposure to aversive stimulation and to the subtle presses of various environments has differential consequences for those who are thus subjected. Personality factors, such as the coronary-prone behavior pattern (Glass, 1977), and social conditions, such as group membership, may attentuate or exacerbate the functional value of particular stressors.

Psychological approaches to the study of stress have emphasized the role of cognitive processes. Psychological views of stress (Appley & Trumbull, 1967; McGrath, 1970) have construed stress as resulting from perceived environmental demands being disproportionately greater than perceived resources for coping. Analyses of the cognitive mediation of stress responses have often utilized the concept of *control*. However, there are semantic difficulties with the usage of this concept.

Control over stress has had three conceptualizations: (*a*) "personal control" by Averill (1973), who specified three forms of control (behavioral, cognitive, and decisional) that might mitigate stress effects; (*b*) "perceived control" best exemplified in the work of Glass and Singer (1972), who found that the adverse after-effects of exposure to noise and to other psychosocial stressors were attenuated by perceptions of controllability; and (*c*) "locus of control" the extensively researched personality variable of Rotter's (1966) social learning theory that has been found to mediate stress effects (Auerbach, Kendall, Cuttler, & Levitt, 1976; Lefcourt, 1966, 1973).

Describing the cognitive mediation of stress in terms of control results in confusion if the term "control" is intended to specify some class of cognitive processes. Control can be best understood to describe a *relationship* between person and environmental events, whether they be internal or external. It is inexact to use the term "control" to describe a class of cognitive activities. An additional disadvantage of the control concept is that it fails to capture the temporal aspects of person-environment transactions. Better candidates for generic terms are available from existing psychological literature. It is proposed here that the two basic classes of cognitive processes pertinent to an analysis of psychological stress are *expectations* and *appraisals*.

With respect to the experience of environmental demands, individuals hold anticipations or expectations of the demand itself and of their performance in response to it. In a temporary sequence, this is the first stage of cognitive activity. When the demand occurs and following its occurrence, it is appraised or interpreted. Similarly, persons appraise their performance in response to the demand.

In the most extensively developed and influential formulation of psychological stress, Lazarus (1966, 1967) proposed a theoretical model that consisted of an integration of the concepts of threat, appraisal, and coping. In this model, threat is defined not only in terms of a noxious or harmful stimulus configuration but also with respect to the person's appraisal of the threat circumstances. Coping refers to the activation of behavior designed to deal with threat. Lazarus differentiated two levels of appraisal—"primary appraisal," which pertains to the judgment or perception of the severity of threat, and "secondary appraisal,"[8] which pertains to the person's judgment regarding the consequences of available coping strategies. Despite the considerable research on human stress that has come forth since the first statement of his theoretical model, Lazarus has not significantly altered his concept of appraisal; however, he has placed greater emphasis on coping as a crucial factor in understanding human stress (cf. Lazarus & Launier, 1978).

The concept of appraisal was first used with regard to emotion by Arnold (1960), who used this concept in conjunction with the specification of neurological and biochemical mechanisms (a system of relays that she called the "estimative system") involved with the experience of emotional states and the impulse to action. Systematic laboratory research conducted by Lazarus and his colleagues provided a firm foundation for this term as a major concept in the area of stress. This body of research is painstakingly set forth in Lazarus (1966), and briefer reviews have also been published (Lazarus, 1967). Importantly, other investigators have corroborated the basic findings of Lazarus and his colleagues. Recently, Rogers and Mewborn (1976), conducting a study on fear pertaining to disease and injury, found that the appraised severity of the threatened event and the belief in the efficacy of coping responses were the only significant regression analysis coefficients in predicting intentions to adopt recommended health practices. Their findings can be interpreted as support for the primary and secondary appraisal concepts.

More frequently, investigators have sought to study Lazarus's concept of *reappraisal*, particularly defensive reappraisal (e.g., denial and intellectualization). Reappraisal was viewed by Lazarus as the principal means of coping with threat when

---

[8]In Lazarus's model, the difference between primary and secondary appraisal is the object of the appraisal and not a temporal matter. Nor does "secondary" mean less important. Lazarus has, however, had second thoughts on his choice of the term *secondary,* perhaps having better chosen *appraisal of coping resources* (Lazarus & Launier, 1978).

direct action is not possible. The conceptual basis for the ideas regarding defensive reappraisal was the psychodynamic notion of ego-defense, and the initial experiment by Speisman, Lazarus, Mordkoff, and Davison (1964) manipulated soundtrack passages for a subincision film so that conditions of trauma, denial, and intellectualization were created. Relatively recent investigations by Holmes and Houston (1974) on threat of shock, Neufeld (1975) with exposure to gory scenes, and Geen, Stonner, and Kelly (1974) regarding violent scenes have extended the work performed by Lazarus and his colleagues (Lazarus & Alfert, 1964; Lazarus, Opton, Nomikos, & Ranklin, 1965; Nomikos, Opton, Averill, & Lazarus, 1968; Speisman *et al.*, 1964).

As mentioned earlier, usage of the concept of control has blurred distinctions that can be made in the classification of cognitive mediational processes. Certain exemplifications of the concept of control, such as those of Averill (1973), can be understood as instances of appraisal, to the extent that they refer to evaluation of the meaning of environmental demands. Other exemplifications of control, namely, those of Glass and Singer (1972) and of Rotter (1966), can be conceptualized in terms of expectation. The Glass and Singer (1972) controllability manipulations can be viewed as having influenced an *expectancy for personal efficacy*. That is, control over a stressor can be understood in terms of a subjective probability to exert influence or obtain reinforcement in a situation in which one is exposed to an environmental demand. This expectation for efficacy may pertain to the regulation of the stressor itself, of the conditions of one's exposure to it, or of one's psychological and physiological responses to the exposure. The other instance of control terminology pertaining to stress, that of "locus of control," nicely fits the proposed scheme, since locus of control precisely is an expectancy construct.

A recent theoretical analysis by Bandura (1977) postulates that efficacy expectations determine the initiation, degree, and persistence of coping efforts. Bandura differentiates efficacy and outcome expectations—the former pertains to beliefs about personal mastery, whereas the latter pertains to judgments concerning the outcomes of particular courses of action that the individual may or may not expect to be able to execute. Bandura has specified the dimensions on which efficacy expectations may vary (i.e., magnitude, generality, and strength), as well as their various sources (i.e., performance accomplishments, vicarious experience, verbal persuasion, and emotional arousal). He has argued that efficacy expectations account for the effects of various psychological treatments and has supported his theory concerning this cognitive mechanism by experimental analysis (Bandura & Adams, 1977; Bandura, Adams & Beyer, 1977).

Expectancy has been and continues to be an important construct in the description, explanation, and prediction of behavior. The most notable of early expectancy theorists, Rotter (1954) formulated a theory of behavior in which behavior potential is specified as being a function of expectancy and of reinforcement value. Rotter's "locus of control" concept is a form of expectation—specifically, a generalized expectation for control over reinforcement. The concept is dimensionalized in terms of internality–externality. Internal control refers to the perception or expectation that positive and/or negative events are a consequence of one's own behavior and are, thus, under personal control. External control refers to the perception or expectation that events are independent of one's own behavior and are, therefore, beyond personal control (Lefcourt, 1966). The locus of control concept is now sufficiently familiar to most readers so as to not require further description. However, it is too frequently the case that investigators have ignored the systematic status of this construct in conducting experiments in which locus of control is used as a blocking factor. As Rotter (1975) has reacted, the misunderstandings and misuses of this construct have in part resulted from neglecting reinforcement value and the psychological situation as important factors in the prediction of behavior. In Rotter's theory, the situational expectancy is a function of both a specific expectancy and a generalized expectancy, the latter of which is modfied by previous experience in the situation. Locus of control is one kind of generalized expectancy. As experience in the situation increases, the relative contribution of the generalized expectation decreases relative to the specific expectation. These distinctions regarding the locus of control concept, in addition to those noted by Bandura (1977) (i.e., that locus of control pertains primarily to action–outcome contingencies), must be kept in mind when various perspectives on control and expectation are being considered.

Recent theoretical developments in both the clinical and the stress literatures have focused on another kind of expectation, namely, *learned helplessness*. Originally identified as a mechanism to account for the behavior of dogs whose instrumental learning was impaired by prior exposure to inescapable aversive stimulation (Overmeier & Seligman, 1967; Seligman & Maier, 1967), the task performance impairments were subsequently discovered to occur with humans as well (Hiroto, 1974; Thornton & Jacobs, 1971). The concept of helplessness is basically the learned expectation that one's behavior is noninstrumental in achieving desired outcomes—or that reinforcement is independent of the organism's responses. Experimentally, helplessness is typically engendered by exposing subjects to an uncontrollable aversive situation that they can neither escape nor solve (Hiroto & Seligman, 1975). Then, performance on a subsequent task involving controllable aversive stimulation is examined. Subjects exposed to helplessness pretreatments have generally been found to have debilitated performance on the subsequent tasks (Hiroto & Seligman, 1975; Seligman, 1975). Locus of control has been found to mediate the effects of helplessness pretreatments on a nonproblem-solving task as externals were found to have greater deficits in performance (Cohen, Rothbart, & Phillips, 1976).

The helplessness construct has recently been used to account for clinical depression. The hypothesis was first put forth by Miller and Seligman (1973, 1975) and elaborated by Seligman (1975). The thesis that the helplessness paradigm is a model for the etiology of depression received wide attention, as evidenced by the appearance of an special issue of the *Journal of Abnormal Psychology* (February, 1978) that was devoted entirely to this topic. The body of articles in that issue gives the helplessness thesis a rigorous examination and includes a reformulation of the theory (Abramson, Seligman, & Teasdale, 1978), as well as critical evaluations (e.g., Buchwald, Coyne, & Cole, 1978; Costello, 1978; Depue & Monroe, 1978).

Expectation, conceived in a variety of ways, has been a widely recognized determinant of behavior and emotion. Although there may be specific exemplifications in the form of perceived control, predictability, locus of control, or helplessness, the essence of these variously labeled cognitive activities is some subjective probability about events and one's responses to them. Thus, expectation can usefully be designated in conjunction with appraisal as the cognitive determinants of stress responses.

A MODEL OF HUMAN STRESS

Human stress is here conceived in transactional terms (Lazarus, 1966; Lazarus & Launier, 1978). That is, stress is a concept used to refer to transactions between the person and the environment, thus implying continual feedback processes. As Lazarus has noted, the psychological laboratory analysis of variance models have distinct limitations for the study of stress in that they comfortably curtail analysis to the concept of interaction but fail to get at phenomena the essence of which is the interplay of person and environment variables. We must come to terms with the "reciprocity of causation" (Lazarus & Launier, 1978).

The proposed model of stress is depicted in Figure 8.1. The model incorporates the various aspects of stress phenomena that have been discussed previously. Cognitive processes are identified in two locations—first, in the form of expectations that

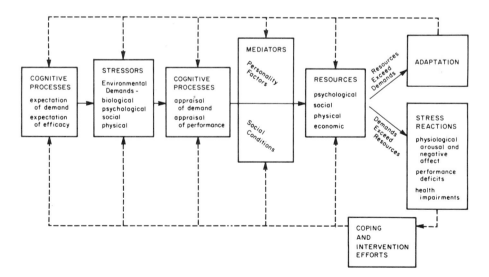

Figure 8.1. A psychological model of human stress.

occur prior to the exposure to environmental demands (stressors) and, second, in the form of appraisals that accompany and/or follow the demands. The complexity of the depicted scheme may, indeed, weigh against its value. There are clearly more components specified than there are data points for substantiation. However, the model is offered here as a heuristic scheme rather than as an explanatory device.[9]

The exposure to and experience of the environmental demands is thought to be mediated by indentifiable personality factors and social conditions. Such factors and conditions are not thought to be independent of the cognitive processes but, in fact, may be intimately linked with them. Oppressive social conditions may be linked to low expectations of efficacy and to the appraisal of demands as severely threatening.

A good example of the interrelationship between personality and cognition in stress research is the work on the Type A behavior pattern that has been construed by Glass (1977) as a style of coping with stress—more specifically, as a characteristic way of attempting to achieve control over aversive stimulation. The time urgency, inordinate achievement striving, and generalized hostility observed among Pattern A individuals can be expected to result in high expectations of accomplishments and hostile appraisals of persons or conditions that thwart personal achievement. Behavior patterns have also been found to mediate the experience of naturalistic stressors. Research on traffic congestion by the author and his colleagues has found that the dimensions of the coronary-prone behavior pattern and various expectations are significant mediators of the stress reactions induced by impedance conditions of commuting (Novaco, Stokols, Campbell, & Stokols, in press; Stokols, Novaco, Stokols, & Campbell, 1978).

When the enacted resources exceed the perceived demands, adaptation can be thought to occur. When the perceived demands exceed the enacted resources, stress reactions can then be observed to occur in varying degrees of severity. Various forms of coping responses or intervention efforts may be initiated to achieve adaptation. These attempts at coping may be directed at any one or several of the components in the process.

This chain of events is meant to be portrayed as a dynamic sequence of interchanges, although this may not be satisfactorily conveyed pictorially in Figure 8.1. The phenomena represented in the various boxes are not to be understood as occurring in tandem or as a static process that follows a fixed sequence. I am attempting to describe a process that occurs transactionally over time.

A COGNITIVE MODEL FOR ANGER AROUSAL

The arousal of anger is here viewed as an affective stress reaction. That is, anger arousal is a response to perceived environmental demands—most commonly, aversive psychosocial events. Anger is construed as involving both physiological and

---

[9]The author is indebted to Jerome E. Singer for his comments on the complexity problems.

cognitive determinants (Konečni, 1975b; Novaco, 1975; Schachter & Singer, 1962). Consistent with Konečni's (1975b) analysis, anger is thought to consist of a combination of physiological arousal and a cognitive labeling of that arousal as anger. The cognitive label need not be precisely that of "anger" but may be a term that is semantically proximate, such as "annoyed," "irritated," "enraged," "provoked," etc.

As discussed earlier, stress reactions vary on a number of parameters of severity. The determination of anger as a clinical problem can similarly be evaluated in terms of its frequency, intensity, duration, mode of expression, and effects on performance, health, and personal relationships. The severity of anger as a stress reaction depends upon the activation of coping efforts and the long-term health and psychological costs that result. Coping efforts may successfully resolve the provoking circumstances. However, seemingly beneficial personal and social consequences of one's anger may be relatively small or short-lived. The extent to which anger has enduring negative effects on the self or others as a result of instigating aggressive activities, disrupting performance, contributing to health problems, or causing impairment to valued social relationships reflects its severity as a stress reaction.

Anger has cognitive determinants, correlates, and consequences. Consistent with the analysis of stress, anger is determined by expectations and appraisals. Provocation experiences are mediated by the expectations that one has regarding events and one's response to them, as well as by the appraisal of their meaning during and following their experience. Expectations and appraisals are interrelated. Expectations, as subjective probabilities about events, are based on previous appraisals of related circumstances. Appraisals are a function of the expectations one holds regarding oneself and others.

These cognitive factors have a mutually influenced relationship to anger. That is, becoming angry has feedback effects such that future expectations and appraisals

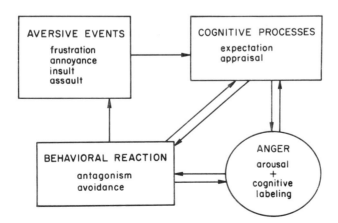

Figure 8.2.   Determinants of anger arousal.

are a function of the experienced anger arousal. Pertinent to therapeutic interventions, the absence or minimization of anger in conjunction with previously provoking circumstances may lead to changes in cognitive structuring that will prevent future anger and encourage adaptive behavior.

Anger arousal is a significant antecendent of aggression (Rule & Nesdale, 1976), but anger is not necessary for the occurrence of aggression. However, the relationship between anger and aggression is thought to be one of bidirectional causality, as postulated by Konečni (1975a). That is, the level of anger influences the level of aggression and vice versa. Although aggressive behavior can be a function of conditions other than those specified here (e.g., reinforcement contingencies, modeling influences, or pain), the central idea depicted in Figure 8.2 is that external aversive events have no direct relationship to anger arousal. Provocation is always mediated by the processes of appraisal and expectation. This proposed cognitive mediation of provocation requires further elaboration.

The Appraisal of Provocation

Anger arousal results from particular appraisals of aversive events. External circumstances provoke anger only as mediated by their meaning to the individual. The Roman period Stoic philosophers Marcus Aurelius and Epictetus espoused such views in the first and second centuries.

> Art thou angry with him whose arm-pits stink? Art thou angry with him whose mouth smells foul? What good will this anger do thee? He has such a mouth, he has such armpits: It is necessary that such an emanation must come from such things [Aurelius, 1925, p. 187].

> It is not men's acts which disturb us, for those acts have their foundation in men's ruling principles, but it is our own opinions which disturb us [Aurelius, 1925, p. 281].

> Why then are we angry? Because we admire the goods of which these men rob us. For, mark you, stop admiring your clothes, and you are not angry at the man who steals them; stop admiring your wife's beauty, and you are not angry at her adulterer [Epictetus, 1961, p. 125].

Although one might quarrel with the wisdom of some of the just given prescriptions, the general principles that can be abstracted from the ideas evangelically set forth by these ancient philosophers suit the perspective of the cognitive psychologist. The advocacy of the Stoics was for men to become impervious to perturbations—by means of will and reason to become autonomous from circumstances that were beyond their control (Hadas, 1961).

For William James and for the Danish physiologist, Carl Lange, emotions were mental states resulting from the perception or consciousness of physiological manifestations that had been excited by external events. Emotion was the feeling of bodily changes. However, James did note that anger had cognitive determinants, when he stated, "One may get angrier in thinking over one's insult than at the moment of receiving it... [1890, p. 443]."

G. Stanley Hall (1899), who hoped to advance the study of anger beyond the foundation of the James–Lange theory, wrote an extensive linguistic and conceptual analysis of anger distilled from previous work and reported the results of a large-scale survey (over 2000 returns) that was intended to shift the psychological analysis of anger from philosophical to empirical inquiry. Although lacking a general abstraction, Hall's reported material is rich with accounts of anger as determined by personal appraisals of provoking circumstances.

In 1918, R. F. Richardson published on monograph on anger that was based on introspective experimentation with 10 subjects. Richardson's analysis emphasizes appraisal processes in the stimulation of anger.

> It is well known that there is little constancy in the outside situation, associated with the emotion of anger. What one will take as an insult, another will regard as a joke. With the same individual, what will at one time excite anger, will at another be scarcely noticed. We commonly say, referring to some incident, 'There was nothing for him to be angry about,' and the statement may be correct if the outside situation is viewed as the stimulus to the emotion [1918, p. 11].

> Anger does not arise when the subject is rigidly attending to the damage, but only when he begins to feel the damage as humiliating, irritating or as contrary to justice [1918, p. 58].

The interests of experimental psychology in observable events resulted in a preference for the study of aggressive behavior over the emotion of anger. The volume of research on aggression, which began with the publication of the classic monograph by Dollard, Doob, Miller, Mowrer, and Sears (1939), consistently ignored anger in the specification of the functional relationships between provocation events, accompanying circumstances, and harmdoing actions. Although the authors of the frustration–aggression monograph rarely, if at all, used the term *anger* in the postulation and elaboration of their thesis on aggression (they used the term *instigation*), they did specify the role of cognitive elements in the instigation process. Dollard *et al.* attempted to stay close to a strict behavioral analysis, yet they recognized that inferential states determined the instigation to aggression. An instigation was a (hypothetical) condition aroused by a frustration, and its intensity was held to be strongest toward the *perceived* source of the frustration.

A major reformulation of the frustration–aggression hypothesis occurred with the work of Berkowitz (1958, 1962, 1964). Pertinent to the present analysis of anger and appraisal, Berkowitz (1962) proposed that *anger* and *interpretation* mediated the frustration–aggression relationship—that is, they were hypothesized "to intervene between the objective situation and the individual's reaction to it [1962, p. 46]." Berkowitz used "anger" in lieu of "instigation to aggression" and argued that it would be profitable now to consider this emotional state as the mediating condition. He felt that the neglect of the emotional state of anger was a notable omission of the formulation by Dollard *et al.* The presence of anger, coupled with an aggressive cue associated with the anger instigation, was thought by Berkowitz to determine aggressive reactions.

Earlier research by Pastore (1952) and Cohen (1955) had shown that the experience of frustration did not uniformly provoke aggression but that "arbitrariness" of frustrations was an important mediating factor. In view of this research and of other work that differentiated among kinds of frustrations, Berkowitz (1962) stated that the interpretation of the frustrating circumstances was the other major omission in the formulation by the Yale scholars.

Although Berkowitz (1962) argued for greater focus on anger as the emotional-response mediator of frustration–aggression relationships, relatively little attention was given to anger in the remainder of his important book, and his subsequent empirical and theoretical work was primarily concerned with the symbolic operation of aggressive cues. The appraisal of provocation circumstances has been central to his analysis of aggressive behavior.

The model of aggression adopted by Feshbach (1964, 1970) specifies a mediating response-drive stimulus as an intervening variable. This intervening condition, postulated as a Hullian $_rD_s$ factor, was held by Feshbach as that which motivates aggressive behavior. He referred to this factor as aggressive drive, which was facilitated by anger. Whereas Feshbach's model does distinguish anger from aggressive drive, his model incorporates cognitive factors with regard to the elicitation of both anger and aggressive drive. He suggested that ego threat is a particularly potent elicitor of hostility and that it serves as a means of distinguishing frustration from attack (Feshbach, 1970). Furthermore, he stated that cognitive distinctions regarding potentially frustrating conditions can be traced developmentally, noting that the concept of intentionality emerges at about the 8-year-old level. The Stanford-Binet intelligence test includes comprehension items pertaining to the perception of intent, and, in fact, respondents are asked to describe how they would respond to an injury, the infliction of which should be appraised as unintentional. Concerning child development, Feshbach (1970) writes "The child, then, is exposed to a number of socializing influences which foster discrimination among types of frustrations and determine the matching of aggressive and non-aggressive responses to these discriminations [p. 203]." For Feshbach, the elicitation and the reduction of anger and aggression are cognitively mediated processes.

In Bandura's (1973) social learning theory of aggression, cognitive appraisal mechanisms have an important role in the arousal of anger. He adopts a general arousal model that asserts that, under various conditions that dispose people to behave aggressively, nearly any source of emotional arousal increases the probability of aggression. Anger is, thus, a facilitating condition for aggession. Pertinent to the notion of appraisal, Bandura emphasizes the cognitive capacity of humans for self-arousal. That is, he notes that anger arousal can be generated internally by rumination about provoking incidents and that this process is susceptible to change brought about by cognitive reinterpretation of perceived insults and annoyances. He illustrates, "consider the example of a person who becomes angered by an apparent social slight only to discover that the invitation to the social function has arrived in the next mail. He is likely to show an immediate drop in anger arousal and aggressiveness . . . [p. 57]." Although Bandura does recognize appraisal processes as determinants of anger and aggression, his more central emphasis on cognitive mediation is with respect to the anticipated consequences of behavior.

The theories of Berkowitz, Feshbach, and Bandura respectfully assign anger arousal to response energizing, response motivating, and response activating functions, but, in each case, anger is viewed as an emotional state that facilitates aggression, rather than as a necessary condition. Importantly, for each of these aggression theorists, anger arousal occurs by virtue of the appraisal of provoking circumstances. Beck (1976), in his work on emotional disorders, also identified appraisal as a central mediator. He states, "The common factor for arousal of anger is the individual's appraisal of an assault on his domain, including his values, moral code, and protective rules [p. 71]."

Ample research has demonstrated that the appraisal of provocation (the behavior of another person toward oneself or others that is experienced as aversive) influences the magnitude of aggressive behavior. Aggression has been found to increase with antagonistic appraisals and to decrease with syntonic appraisals.

Perhaps the best example of antagonistic appraisal is the perceived intentionality of aggression by another. The competitive reaction-time task developed for experimental purposes by Taylor provided a means for evaluating aggressive intent influences. His research found that the perceived aggressive intent of one's opponent in adminstering aversive consequences for defeat elevated aggressive responding by the subject (Epstein & Taylor, 1967; Taylor, 1967). A number of subsequent investigations have corroborated this finding (Greenwell & Dengerink, 1973; Nickel, 1974; O'Leary & Dengerenk, 1973; Shantz & Voydanoff, 1973).

Related to the perception of aggressive intent is the appraisal of aversive events in terms of threats to self-esteem. Early personality research had shown that high self-esteem subjects respond with less aggression to provocations (Rosenbaum & deCharms, 1960; Veldman & Worchel, 1961; Worchel, 1960). More recently, Green and Murray (1973) found that high self-disclosure followed by personal threat engendered by critical commentaries was a strong elicitor of anger and aggression. Low self-esteem has been identified by Toch (1969) as a key determinant of anger arousal and assault in exchanges between police and criminals.

The perception of someone as deserving of punishment has been found to increase the magnitude of aggressive responses to provocation in studies on the justification for aggression (Berkowitz & Rawlings, 1963; Brock & Buss, 1964; Meyer, 1972) and on the dehumanization of the victim (Bandura, Underwood, & Fromson, 1975). Furthermore, when perceived physiological arousal is attributed to the aversive behavior of another, increases in anger and aggression have been observed to occur (Geen, Rakosky, & Pigg, 1972).

The feedback between provocation, arousal, cognition, and aggression is exemplified in several studies on sexual arousal and aggression. Sexual arousal, in conjunction with provocation, can either facilitate or inhibit aggressive behavior, depending on the magnitude and sequences of the erotic arousal and the cognitive circumstances attending the opportunity to aggress (Baron, 1974; Baron & Bell, 1977; Donnerstein, Donnerstein, & Evans, 1975; Jaffe, Malamuth, Feingold, & Feshbach, 1974; Malamuth, Feshbach, & Jaffe, in press; Zillman, 1971; Zillman & Sapolsky, 1977).

Although various appraisal processes have been shown to heighten anger and aggression, other forms of appraisal have had demonstrated effects in the diminution of aggression. Among the most important of these concerns the cognitive reinterpretation of the provoking experience. Cognitive reinterpretation or restructuring has aggression-reducing influences (Frodi, 1973; Green & Murray, 1973; Kaufmann & Feshbach, 1963; Mallick & McCandless, 1966). Zillman, Bryant, Cantor, and Day (1975) also found that information concerning mitigating circumstances reduced aggressive retaliation, but this occurred only under conditions of moderate arousal. When very high arousal was induced by following provocation with a strenuous task, aggression levels were not significantly lowered by the additional information. Reduced arousal, as indexed by galvanic skin response, has also been obtained in conjunction with the observation of aggressive film scenes by inducing the observers to appraise the film as fictional (Geen & Rakosky, 1973).

Expectations as Mediators of Provocation

The experimental attention given to expectation as a determinant of aggression and anger has been comparatively less than that given to appraisal processes. However, much of the experimental work on frustration–aggression is interpretable in terms of expectation. That is, interferences with goal-directed behavior are easily viewed as thwartings of outcome expectancies that induce arousal and associated behavioral reactions. Dollard *et al.* (1939) not only discussed frustration in terms of expected rewards, but they also understood the inhibition of aggression in terms of expected (''anticipated'') punishments. Pastore (1952), in his efforts to reformulate the frustration–aggression hypothesis, suggested that arbitrary frustrations involved the frustration of an expectancy.

Worchel (1974) found that thwartings of expectancies led to greater aggression than did frustrations that were random, with even more aggression being manifested when behavioral freedoms were eliminated. Whereas a number of investigations have examined the effect of different types of frustration on aggression (e.g., Buss, 1963; Hokanson & Burgess, 1962), Bandura (1973) has argued that the blocking of goal-directed behavior is a less powerful determinant of aggression than are other social-learning variables (i.e., insult, modeling, prior aggressive training, and the instrumentality of aggressive acts). He suggests that when thwarting instigates aggression it is the implied insult that is the key factor, rather than interference with goal-directed activity. Bandura views the functional value of thwarting vis-à-vis aggression in terms of the intensification of performance. That is, the delay or omission of anticipated rewards generates aversive arousal that energizes behavior, the nature of which is determined by social learning. Bandura's (1973) social-learning approach to aggression places relatively stronger emphasis on expectation than on appraisals of aversive events, as he views the stimulus control of aggression to be extensively determined by the anticipated consequences of behavior. His cognitive perspective is quite compatible with the present analysis of expectation as a cognitive determinant of anger arousal.

In the aggression literature, expectations have not been investigated with *anger* as the primary subject matter. The focus of existing research has been on how expectations moderate the manifestation of aggression that is often energized by anger arousal. The investigations concerned with expectations principally have been of two varieties: (*a*) those concerned with the performance of aggression in accord with the values of observers; and (*b*) studies that have examined the inhibition of aggression either due to expected retaliation or to expectations related to sex roles. Borden (1975) reported that the inferred or explicit values of observers influence aggressive responding by virtue of the expectations of approval held by the person having an opportunity to aggress. A number of studies concerned with modeling effects can also be interpreted in a similar manner (e.g., Baron, 1971; Baron & Kepner, 1970). With regard to the inhibition of aggression, recent experimental work has shown that, as Dollard *et al.* (1939) hypothesized, aggressive behavior is inhibited by expectations of retaliation (Albert, 1973; Dengerink & Levendusky, 1972; Dertke, Penner, Hawkins, & Suarez, 1973). However, Baron (1974) did find that, when the instrumentality of aggression is high, this inhibition is weakened.

Sex-role expectation has been suggested as an explanation for the observed differences in the expression of aggression toward males and females. It has generally been found that, when the sex of instigator and/or target of aggression has been varied, both men and women behave less aggressively toward women than toward men (Frodi, Macaulay, & Thome, 1977). In their review of sex differences in aggression, Frodi *et al.* concluded that "sex role expectations, in interaction with the behavior encountered, play a significant part in determining men's and women's aggressiveness [1977, p. 643]." In addition, when females have been found to increase aggression over experimental trials toward male instigators, the escalation has been thought to result from violation of social expectations regarding male behavior toward females (Taylor & Epstein, 1967).

In the present model, expectations are viewed as determinants of anger by virtue of several psychological circumstances that involve the combination of induced arousal and the presence of contextual cues that lead to the experience or labeling of the arousal as anger. When one's experience is discrepant from expectations, arousal accompanies the disturbance in equilibrium, as the person seeks to adjust to the demands of the situation. Expectations for desired outcomes that do not occur result in aversive arousal that is experienced as anger as a function of contextual cues that signify thwarting or antagonism. The magnitude of the discrepancy between obtained outcomes and expected outcomes will influence the level of arousal. When the discrepancy is negatively valenced, the probability for anger is increased as the person may attempt to account for the disturbance in equilibrium in terms of external factors that have antagonistic properties. Here, appraisal processes come into play as the person seeks to account for the arousal induced by the discrepancy between the obtained and the expected.

Another way in which expectations influence anger arousal is with regard to the anticipation of aversive events. When one expects an antagonistic experience and when the prepotent appraisals of the events in question are anger-inducing, the expectation of annoyance can lead to selective perception of situational cues in such a way that anger more readily occurs. When one confronts an antagonist, certain words and gestures can have a greater salience than they otherwise might, and anger occurs in conjunction with one's appraisal of them as insulting, thwarting, or annoying.

A third way in which expectations lead to anger is when anger arousal is expected to be instrumental in achieving desired outcomes. In this case, anger may be an adaptive emotional response to a conflict as it energizes problem-solving behavior. However, at times, anger occurs because one has unnecessarily low expectations for resolving conflict by nonantagonistic means and attempts to achieve control over the aversive experience through anger and aggression.

The discussion just given has delineated the ways in which appraisals and expectations are viewed as determinants of anger. Important for the clinical interventions, these cognitive factors are thought to be given representation in language form through the person's private speech. Internal sentences or self-statements reflect expectations and appraisals. Private speech as self-stimulation can both elicit and sustain anger arousal.

Private speech can act as a self-arousal mechanism when anger is elicited regarding past events, as the person is reminded of previous provocation or reinterprets past occurrences with anger-engendering appraisals. When conflict is ongoing, antagonistic self-statements may inflame anger by focusing attention on aversive characteristics of persons or situations, thus increasing the salience of cues associated with anger. In addition, anger arousal can be maintained or prolonged by ruminative self-statements that temporally extend attention to the provocation circumstances.

At present, the relationship between private speech and provocation is hypothetical. Early learning-theory formulations of psychotherapy (Dollard & Miller, 1950) emphasized the role of thought and language as cue-producing responses that affect emotional arousal. However, the effects of self-statements on emotional state have just begun to be explored, largely due to the influence of Ellis (1973) and Meichenbaum (1974). An extensive account of the mechanisms of private speech and of its role as self-instruction can be found in Meichenbaum (1977).

Although no research has been reported on the association of anger and private speech, a number of studies have found that arousal and anxiety states are influenced by self-verbalization. Rimm and Litvak (1969), in testing several propositions of Rational Emotive Therapy (Ellis, 1962), found that affectively loaded sentences increased respiration rate and depth. Using similar procedures, Schwartz (1971) and May and Johnson (1973) have shown that internally elicited thoughts to stimulus words having stressful content influence autonomic system responses. Russell and Brandsma (1974) obtained galvanic-skin-response effects for anxiety-arousing sentences, although an effort at replication (Rogers & Craighead, 1977) was not successful.

The therapeutic techniques for the regulation of anger that are described in this chapter use self-instruction as a central cognitive intervention. However, it is not necessary for their implementation to assume that anger is *generated* by self-statements. In fact, this assumption has not been made (Novaco, 1975). With regard to the treatment model, it has only been hypothesized that the use of therapeutically designed self-instructions can serve as a means to *regulate* anger. Nonetheless, basic research is needed to delineate the relationship between anger and self-verbalization, and the present model of anger-arousal does hypothesize that a relationship exists. Experimental efforts are being made by the author on this topic, particularly with regard to how the content of private speech influences anger after provocation has occurred.

CLINICAL INTERVENTIONS FOR ANGER AND AGGRESSION

Aggressive behavior and problems associated with chronic anger are beginning to receive the attention that they deserve in the clinical literature. As one might intuit from the previous discussion, considerably more is known about these problems than has been extended to applied settings.

Interventions for problems of anger, aggression, and violence have consisted of psychodynamic, behavioral, cognitive–behavioral, surgical, and psychophar-macological procedures. Although the procedure of choice will probably vary with the nature of the clinical setting, the behavioral approaches appear to be in greatest favor.

Early Treatment Approaches

The earliest clinical account of the treatment of anger was reported by Witmer (1908) of an 11-year-old boy who had been subject to "outbursts of uncontrollable and unreasoning anger" and to "mean moods." Witmer adopted an educational approach to therapy in his treatment of children, and his procedure was characterized by problem-solving methods.

Two psychoanalysts, Fritz Redl and David Wineman (1951, 1952), offered in the early 1950s an extensive presentation of a treatment mode for aggression-related problems in their books, *Children Who Hate* and *Controls from Within*. Their analysis of aggression problems is in terms of a *control system* component of personality, "by which is meant those parts of the personality which have the function and the power to decide just which of a given number of desires or strivings will or will not be permitted to reach the level of behavioral action, and in which form [Redl & Wineman, 1951, p. 71]." They analogize the control-system concept to the dam and locks on a water reservoir, consistent with the hydraulic model of personality espoused by psychoanalysts.

The "repair job" consists first of determining whether the problem is due to impulsivity or an upsurge of aggressive forces (water force) of an abnormal quantity or to the controls the function of which is to screen and check impulses before they are allowed expression (regulatory machinery).

The work of Redl and Wineman can be characterized as ego psychology. That is, they are primarily concerned with the ego functions of personality and with the operations of the *reality principle*. Even though their analyses and portrayals are couched in psychoanalytic language, which has well-known shortcomings for its diffuseness, they do nonetheless identify factors that are not so distant from the kinds of things deemed important to cognitive–behavioral theorists. For example, their interest in cognitive functions of the ego pertains not just to contact with the outside world in terms of its physical and social dimensions ("sizing up reality"); they also discuss "internalized" cognitive functions, referring to the appraisal of the urges of the id and the value demands of the superego.

The Redl and Wineman books are based on their observations in their Detroit Group Project and its residential facilities, Pioneer House and summer camp. In *Children Who Hate* they described the control-breakdown processes, and in *Controls from Within* they offer their treatment techniques for the ego disturbances of the extremely aggressive child. For them, the achievement of behavioral control is accomplished by *internalization* of control mechanisms. Such mechanisms are developed therapeutically by techniques of *ego support*—these techniques pertain to (*a*) environmental design; (*b*) activity programs and structures; (*c*) behavior management strategies; and (*d*) conflict resolution processes. Their procedures were designed for implementation in a residential facility for children with conduct problems.

Behavioral Interventions: Operant Conditioning

The most systematic approach to the treatment of aggressive behavior within any framework is that of Gerald Patterson at the University of Oregon. His research during the past 10 years has been an outstanding demonstration of behaviorism as applied to the understanding and modification of aggression. Patterson's approach is behavioral in the strict sense in that he confines his theoretical analyses to observable events, focusing on their functional relationships, and his treatment regimes consist of the manipulation of the setting events and reinforcement contingencies that are believed to control behavior. His work on aggression has predominantly involved the study of children, particularly boys with conduct problems.

Patterson's work on aggression began with a monograph on assertive behavior in children that traced the development of assertion–aggression in two nursery school groups over two semesters (Patterson, Littman, & Bricker, 1967). In this monograph, aggression was construed as a high-amplitude response that is a subclass of a broader category of assertive behaviors that have as a common characteristic the fact that they coerce or demand a reaction from the environment (i.e., force a *particular set* of consequences from the social environment). Aggression was viewed as the outcome of specialized socialization processes. The thrust of this monograph was to outline the acquisition process for producing such behaviors in children. Their report focused on the child's interaction in his peer group, and it was assumed that the reactions of other children provide the reinforcing contingencies for the shaping of aggressive behaviors. They proposed a two-stage model: The first stage concerns the acquisition process and follows operant conditioning principles, and the second stage specifies emotional states as conditions that elicit the previously acquired instrumental responses and identifies reinforcement for high-amplitude aggressive acts. The basic finding of Patterson *et al.* (1967) was that children initially low on rates of aggression were conditioned by peers to accelerate to high levels of aggression and that this acceleration was a function of the frequency of victimization and successful counteract.

A series of published and unpublished studies followed this seminal investigation. In these subsequent projects, Patterson and his colleagues developed procedures for the description of aggressive interactions and for clinical intervention. This required extensive observation in home settings in order to establish base rates for deviant and prosocial behaviors and for the contingencies effected by parents. Efforts were also made to modify the behavior of aggressive boys in school classrooms by manipulating the social environment to reinforce the problem child for attending to academic material (Patterson, Cobb, & Ray, 1972).

Soon thereafter, Patterson sensed that interventions aimed at the direct training of the aggressive child were less effective than programs designed to train parents, teachers, and peers. A parent training procedure was developed (Patterson, Cobb, & Ray, 1972) that involves several components: a programmed text on child management techniques that parents are required to learn, training in the observation and recording of behavior, and the execution of behavior modification techniques.

The research reports of Patterson and his colleagues (Patterson, Cobb, & Ray, 1972; Patterson, Ray, & Shaw, 1968; Patterson & Reid, 1973) presented the results of the investigations concerning the treatment program. The first study, involving five boys, showed a 65–72% reduction of deviant behavior from baseline to termination and persistence of treatment effects for three or four boys on follow-up. This involved a mean treatment of 22.8 hours of therapy time per family. The second study (actually conducted in 1969) involved 13 boys from 6 to 13 years of age who were showing extreme aggression when referred. Improvement was found for 9 of 13, whereby reductions from baseline were greater than or equal to 30%. A follow-up 6–12 months later found persistence of change for eight of nine boys. The mean treatment time was 25.7 hours per family. The third study concerned 11 families with extremely aggressive boys, and, for 9 of 11 cases, reductions greater than or equal to 30% from baseline were demonstrated. The mean treatment time was 31.7 hours per family.

Subsequently, Patterson (1974) reported the outcome of a clinical intervention with 27 boys having conduct problems. Behavior in the home and in the classroom was examined. The intervention was found to substantially reduce deviant behavior in the home and to increase appropriate behavior in the classroom. Although his report received criticism by Kent (1976), a reanalysis of disputed findings by Reid and Patterson (1976) maintained that treatment effects were indeed obtained and did persist.

Behavioral Interventions: Classical Conditioning

Whereas the work of Patterson and his colleagues follows the Skinnerian tradition of an operant analysis of behavior, the behavior therapy approach of Wolpe and Lazarus (1966), which is based on a Pavlovian or classical conditioning model, has stimulated the use of systematic desensitization and assertion training techniques in the treatment of aggression. Although it is the case that assertion techniques are most commonly applied to persons who have difficulty in expressing anger in social situations, some recent reports have emerged that examine the application of these techniques with persons who are aggressive. The logic here is that people frequently are aggressive because they have not learned appropriate alternative responses. Assertive training is intended to provide a socially effective alternative to aggression. At times, authors have construed assertion as intermediate between passivity and aggression.

Rimm, Hill, Brown, and Stuart (1974) described and evaluated the use of group assertive training for anger problems as applied to 13 male student subjects. Seven received treatment and six were placebo controls. Treatment was administered in six sessions over a 3-week period. The procedures and analyses of this investigation are not rigorous, but the authors did report reductions in anger as measured by self-rating. Galassi and Galassi (in press) attempted to modify aggressive behavior through assertive training, but they were unsuccessful.

Systematic desensitization approaches to the remediation of anger have most commonly made use of relaxation counterconditioning. Rimm, deGroot, Boord, Reiman, and Dillow (1971) compared desensitization, placebo, and nontreatment groups with regard to the treatment of anger associated with automobile driving and obtained significantly greater reductions in anger self-ratings and GSR reactivity to hierarchy items for the desensitization condition than for the comparison groups. Effectiveness of desensitization treatment of anger was also reported by Herrell (1971) in the case of a young soldier who became excessively angry when given orders and by Evans (1971) in the case of a 22-year-old male with problems of aggression. Hearn and Evans (1972) developed a logic for the use of reciprocal inhibition therapy for anger and obtained reductions in anger for a student-nurse sample on various self-ratings for both treated and untreated stimulus items. A 6-month follow-up on the experimental and control groups found that treatment effects had been maintained (Evans & Hearn, 1973).

An attempt to differentiate various ingredients of desensitization treatment with respect to anger was made by O'Donnell and Worell (1973). These investigators examined desensitization with motor relaxation, desensitization with cognitive relaxation, no relaxation, and no treatment conditions as applied to white males whose anger was aroused by racial stimuli. Reductions in anger were obtained for both desensitization groups relative to the control conditions across several measures, although the group receiving cognitive relaxations alone actually increased on systolic and diastolic blood pressure, concurrent with reporting significantly lower anger to the stimulus items. The authors also reported finding that those subjects for whom desensitization was most effective were those who were partitioned as initially lower in anger on the pretreatment arousal procedure.

An interesting alternative to relaxation counterconditioning in the treatment of anger by systematic desensitization was reported by Smith (1973). He described the successful use of humor that was introduced into the hierarchy items for a 22-year-old female when muscle relaxation proved ineffective in inhibiting intense anger that occurred in response to the behavior of her son. Smith conjectured that the treatment effects were due, at least in part, to the modification of cognitive mediational processes. This client had stated that the humor hierarchy enabled her "to view the anger situations from a new perspective [1973, p. 580]." Of course, the present author would hypothesize that this is precisely the reason that the treatment effects were obtained, rather than being due to a counterconditioning of humor to anger stimuli.

THE STRESS INOCULATION MODEL

A coping-skills therapy that is called *stress inoculation* has been developed for clinical problems pertaining to anxiety, anger, and pain. The stress-inoculation concept was originally proposed as an approach applied to problems of anxiety (Meichenbaum, 1975; Meichenbaum & Cameron, Note 1). Subsequent conceptualization and research extended the stress inoculation model to anger (Novaco, 1977a,b) and to pain (Turk, 1976; see also Chapter 9, this volume). Stress inoculation has further been proposed as a preventive strategy (Meichenbaum & Novaco, 1978). As a coping-skills therapy, this approach is concerned with developing a client's competence to respond to stressful events so that disturbing emotions are reduced and behavioral adaptation is achieved. The therapeutic approach incorporates three treatment phases: cognitive preparation, skill acquisition, and application training.

The theoretical framework for the general model can be found in Meichenbaum (1977). The review by Mahoney and Arnkoff (1977) discussed this approach vis-à-vis the range of other cognitive and self-control therapies. Although the present chapter will focus on its application to anger problems, two other experimental analyses of stress inoculation training have appeared, one concerned with anxiety (Hussian & Lawrence, 1978) and the other with pain (Horan, Hackett, Buchanan, Stone, & Demchik-Stone, 1977).

Hussian and Lawrence (1978) studied the comparative effectiveness of generalized stress inoculation training, test-specific stress inoculation training, discussion control, and waiting-list control treatments as applied to a sample of test-anxious students. Their investigation found both treatment groups to improve significantly over controls across several dependent measures. The test-specific condition was found to result in greater therapeutic gain. Although this study was methodologically sound and the results were carefully analyzed, the authors do not seem to have conceptualized stress inoculation as anything more than training in coping self-statements. Within the perspective of the present model, it is not clear what the generalized and test-specific conditions were intended to operationalize. Furthermore, their experiment failed to operationalize adequately the third phase (application training of the treatment model).

A component analysis of stress inoculation as applied to pain was reported by Horan *et al.* (1977). They attempted to determine the "active ingredients" of the treatment approach. To do so they implemented five treatment conditions: no treatment, nonspecific treatment, coping skills training, exposure, and stress inoculation. The nonspecific treatment was intended to operationalize the education component, and the exposure condition was meant to test the application practice component. The authors found that the coping-skills training improved subject's ability to deal with pain, but no effects were found for education or for practice. This was not surprising, since, although the coping-skills component was nicely implemented, the educational phase and the application phase were quite inadequately operationalized. The stress-inoculation package did result in improvement on direct measures of pain tolerance (cold pressor), but generalization to another pain condition (pressure algometer) was not found. Since the treatment was conducted in a single session, the absence of generalization effects is to be expected.

The stress inoculation approach to anger management aims to impart anger-control skills that are of three basic forms: (*a*) preventive; (*b*) regulatory; and (*c*) executional. The general goals are to prevent anger from occurring when it is maladaptive, to enable the client to regulate arousal and its concommitant cognitions when provocation occurs, and to provide the person with the behavioral skills needed to manage the provocation experience. *The therapeutic strategy does not attempt to inculcate suppression of anger,* as one might think from a superficial acquaintance with an approach advocating the self-control of anger. This should be apparent from the author's view of anger as having positive functions (cf. Novaco, 1976a). Far from emotion suppression, the therapy attempts to minimize the maladaptive effects of anger and to maximize the adaptive functions. However, it is also assumed that anger, as a chronic problem for someone, occurs with undesirable frequency, intensity, and duration. Consequently, the therapeutic task is not only to help the client to learn to recognize anger and to express it adaptively (as would be the focus of psychodynamic practitioners) but also to prevent anger from occurring in many circumstances and to regulate the level of arousal so that effecting coping behavior can be executed.

The term *inoculation* is a medical metaphor. It refers to a process of exposing the client to manageable quantities of stressors that arouse, but do not overwhelm, the client's defenses. In conjunction with this exposure, the client is taught a variety of cognitive and behavioral coping skills intended to provide a means of managing the stress experience. The three stages of the treatment process are described below.

Cognitive Preparation

The value of cognitive structuring with respect to the arousal and regulation of anger has been developed in the preceding in terms of the processes of appraisal and expectation. The beneficial effect of cognitive preparation for impending stress has become an accepted proposition in various areas of applied psychology. Haggard (1949) advised in his work on stress associated with undersea warfare: "A person is able to act realistically and effectively in a stressful situation only if he knows the nature and seriousness of the threat, knows what to do, and is able to do it [p. 209]." Other research on the stress conditions of combat have emphasized the role of cognitive preparation in the attenuation of stress reactions (Bourne, 1969, 1970).

The idea of cognitive preparation as a means of facilitating coping with stress marked the early work of Janis (1958) in the study of hospitalized patients. His work and that of other investigators (Andrew, 1970; Cassell, 1965; Egbert, Battit, Welch, & Bartlett, 1964; Kendall, Williams, Pechacek, Graham, Shisslak, & Herzoff, 1979; Langer, Janis, & Wolfer, 1975) have shown that cognitive interventions for the distress of surgery have led to better adjustment during surgery, shorter time to discharge, and reduction in the use of medication. Personality variables, such as repression-sensitization, trait anxiety, and coping style, can mediate the intervention effects (Andrew, 1970; Auerbach *et al.* 1976; Diskin, Goldstein, & Grencik, 1977; Goldstein, 1973). Significant for the present therapeutic model, Langer *et al.* (1975) demonstrated that a cognitive intervention consisting of reappraisal, calming self-talk, and selective attention effectively reduced both pre- and postoperative stress.

The anger-control components of the cognitive preparation phase consist of (*a*) education about anger arousal and its determinants; (*b*) identification of the circumstances that trigger anger; (*c*) discriminating the adaptive and maladaptive occurrences of anger; and (*d*) introducing the anger-management techniques as coping strategies to handle conflict and stress. As a cognitive self-control therapy, my approach to the treatment of anger assumes that personal knowledge about one's anger patterns facilitates the capacity to regular anger arousal. This requires the combination of conceptual background and information derived from self-monitoring. Effective self-management is dependent upon awareness of the properties of external events that elicit anger, as well as the internal processes, both cognitive and affective, that determine and accompany this emotion.

These objectives are achieved by means of two clinical supplements developed by the author, these being a client instructional manual and an anger diary. The client manual is written in simple language and explains the nature of anger and its various causes. It also describes what can be done to regulate anger and thereby clues the client to the prospective therapeutic process. Among the assets of the client manual are that it engages the client in a self-help process, that it provides for a shared language system between client and therapist, and that it reduces the amount of time spent didactically in therapy sessions. The anger diary is simply a means of charting the frequency and intensity of anger experiences, as well as obtaining self-ratings on coping performance.

Skill Acquisition

This phase involves the learning of cognitive and behavioral coping skills. The basic process consists of recognition of the determinants and manifestations of anger, the suggestion of alternative coping activities, modeling of the coping techniques by the therapist, and a rehearsal of what to do by the client.

At the cognitive level, the client is helped to modify appraisals and expectations concerning the provocation circumstances. This is similar to the notion of alternative construction advocated by Kelly (1955) and to the efforts that would be made in Rational Emotive Therapy to modify the exaggerated importance often attached to events (Ellis, 1973, 1977). The fundamental idea is to promote flexibility in the cognitive structuring of a situation that previously has elicited anger.

The appraisal of aversive events as personal affronts or ego threats is challenged by the therapist, and alternative appraisals are suggested. Learning how "not to take things personally" becomes a key focus of the therapeutic process. In this regard, efforts are made to induce the client to shift from an ego orientation to a task orientation when aversive events are experienced. The readiness to view circumstances as insults or personal thwartings must be short-circuited. In contrast, the client is encouraged to adopt a task orientation whereby one attends to what must be done to resolve the conflict or to achieve desired goals and thus strives to implement a behavioral strategy to produce those outcomes.

As delineated earlier, anger can result from inordinately high expectations of oneself and others. The exaggerated importance ascribed to events that result in anger can be modified by adjusting expectations. The high minimal goal-levels that doom the client to frustration and annoyance are identified, and the value of moderated expectations is stressed. In this vein, clients are encouraged to cultivate their sense of humor. Humor has been found to reduce aggression-related arousal (Singer, 1968), and its value in mitigating anger was demonstrated by Smith (1973), as was seen earlier. These mitigational effects may be due to attentional-shift or distracting properties of the humor stimuli (Baron, 1978). Whatever the reason, humor is an excellent mechanism for not taking oneself and one's predicament too seriously. As such, it is an antidote for a key cause of proneness to provocation.

A most important vehicle for obtaining and maintaining these desired changes in appraisal and expectation is the use of self-instruction (Meichenbaum, 1974). Private speech puts these cognitive processes in language form, and it can provide the cues to guide further adaptive coping. However, because private speech is thought here to give language representation to appraisals and expectations, the simple utterance of self-verbalizations that resemble coping self-statements is not expected to have anger-control value. Quite possibly, the making of self-statements having surface structure of "coping" or "control" (e.g., "Don't take it personally." "He didn't mean to do it." "Don't get upset, now.") can foment anger when the self-verbalization is incongruent with the actual appraisal of the experience. Thus, for a given individual, if self-instruction is intended to facilitate anger control, the self-verbalizations must either follow from a syntonic appraisal of the circumstances or at least be compatible with alternative syntonic appraisals that are prepotent for the subject.

The cognitive control of anger by means of private speech is implemented by viewing provocation experiences in terms of a sequence of stages. This technique is intended to partition a demanding task into more manageable units. It also provides a framework for casting the various self-instructions. The stages consist of (*a*) preparing for a provocation; (*b*) impact and confrontation; (*c*) coping with arousal; (*d*) subsequent reflection; (*e*) conflict unresolved; and (*f*) conflict resolved. Examples of the self-instructions used in these various stages can be found in Table 8.1.

The preparation stage provides the opportunity to adjust expectations of both the psychosocial demand and one's efficacy in response to the demand. It also helps to establish a cognitive set that will encourage benign or syntonic appraisals of anticipated problems. To be sure, not all provocation can be anticipated. Many annoyances are quite spontaneous. However, persons who are prone to provocation and who have chronic anger problems do become angry in routine circumstances

TABLE 8.1
Self-Instructions for the Regulation of Anger

Preparing for a provocation

This could be a rough situation, but I know how to deal with it.
I can work out a plan to handle this. Easy does it.
Remember, stick to the issues and don't take it personally.
There won't be any need for an argument. I know what to do.

Impact and confrontation

As long as I keep my cool, *I'm* in control of the situation.
You don't need to prove yourself. Don't make more out of this than you have to.
There is no point in getting mad. Think of what you have to do.
Look for positives and don't jump to conclusions.

Coping with arousal

My muscles are getting tight. Relax and slow things down.
Time to take a deep breath. Let's take the issue point by point.
My anger is a signal of what I need to do. Time for problem solving.
He probably wants me to get angry, but I'm going to deal with it constructively.

Subsequent reflection

Conflict unresolved
Forget about the aggravation. Thinking about it only makes you upset.
Try to shake it off. Don't let it interfere with your job.
Remember relaxation. It's a lot better than anger.
Don't take it personally. It's probably not so serious.

Conflict resolved
I handled that one pretty well. That's doing a good job.
I could have gotten more upset than it was worth.
My pride can get me into trouble, but I'm doing better at this all the time.
I actually got through that without getting angry.

with particular antagonists. Both the situations and the annoyers are indeed predictable, as one can learn from careful self-monitoring.

The second stage pertains to the immediate experience of the provocation, and the self-instructions here are designed to promote the adoption of a problem-solving response mode. Stages three and four allow for the possible failure of the self-regulation efforts. Rather than have agitation escalate as the client reverts to former styles of responding, the person is taught to use the awareness of anger arousal as a further signal or cue to initiate other coping efforts. When the situation terminates unfavorably, self-instructions provide a means of mitigating self-arousal from ruminations. In sum, private speech that is shaped by the therapeutic process functions as an instructional cue that guides the clients' thoughts, feelings, and behavior in the direction of effective coping.[10]

A variety of behavioral skills are imparted to the client to facilitate anger regulation and the management of provocation circumstances. The general goals of the behavioral interventions are to provide skills for responses that are incompatible with anger, for increased competence in interpersonal communication, and for problem-solving. To the extent that one behaves in a moderated, task-oriented manner in response to provocation, a reciprocal influence can be exerted on level of anger. Syntonic responses to conflict not only minimize interpersonal agitation that elevates arousal but also avoid generating the cues that are associated with anger and aggression. Research has shown that beneficient responses to provocation can result in reductions of physiological arousal when positive reactions from others can be expected (Hokanson, Willers, & Koropsak, 1968).

A basic behavioral component of the therapy is relaxation training. A number of investigations reviewed earlier have shown that relaxation counterconditioning is a useful means of treating anger. The Jacobsen (1938) procedures of systematically tensing and relaxing sets of muscles are the advised technique, since they enable the client to identify internal cues associated with tension and to learn relaxation as an alternative response. Less resistance to relaxation induction is encountered with the use of the Jacobsen procedures than with a cognitive relaxation (i.e., whereby the client simply attends to various somatic regions and attempts to relax them through suggestion). Since angry people are usually tense, the Jacobsen procedures tell them to do what they are already doing. It might also be recalled that O'Donnell and Worell (1973) found that the desensitization of anger accomplished through muscle relaxation was more effective than relaxation induced cognitively.

Although the relaxation-training techniques are employed in a counterconditioning procedure for anger-eliciting situations, the therapeutic objective is to inculcate a sense of self-control rather than to develop a response that will physiologically inhibit anger. Anger has been defined here as a combination of physiological

---

[10]Witmer (1908) described an incident in the treatment of an 11-year-old boy that reports the effective use by the boy of self-instruction. This boy in residential care, who was subject to "outbursts of uncontrollable and unreasoning anger," protested about having to wash his hands at mealtime and threatened not to return to the table. He did return, and later said to the clinician present, "I nearly got mad, but I just said to myself, 'I will control my temper' [p. 178]."

arousal plus cognitive labeling, and progressive relaxation has been shown to decrease physiological arousal (Jacobsen, 1938; Paul, 1969; Paul & Trimble, 1970; Redmond, Gaylor, McDonald, & Shapiro, 1974). However, anger is primarily determined by cognitive factors, among which are expectations of efficacy and appraisal of resources for coping. Thus, the training of relaxation skills is intended to impart the expectation that one can master troublesome situations and internal states. Following Goldfried (1971), the relaxation techniques are viewed as training in self-control.

The therapeutic model stipulates that anger is an emotional response to stressful demands, which signals that problem-solving strategies need to be implemented. Through extensive self-monitoring of anger reactions, the client is taught to recognize anger from both internal and external cues. The early recognition of anger allows for the initiation of self-regulation efforts at points in the provocation sequence at which there is a higher probability of achieving control. That is, if one is not tuned to the arousal state until after the provocation is well under way, the chances of achieving regulation are correspondingly reduced. Anger arousal must become an explicit cue to cope with, rather than be a diffuse part of, an antagonistic experience.

Effective coping requires skills in verbal communication and in problem solving. Impulse delay is also essential. People who have problems with anger are quick to respond to aversive events. The client must be taught to pause between impulse and action, however, not as a ''count to ten'' effort (which can result in ''blast off,'' that is, an explosive outburst of suppressed emotion), but to engage in alternative constructions of the events and to be mindful of what outcomes are desired during the interposed delay. Anger becomes a cue for the task-oriented response set that prevents aggressive overreactions and the escalation of arousal by self-stimulation.

It has been noted that persons having aggression problems are often lacking in verbal skills (Bandura, 1973). In a most thorough investigation, Camp (1977) found that young aggressive boys have ineffective linguistic control skills, particularly at the level of covert mediation. Competence in verbal communication is essential to the control of anger during provocative interchanges. Green and Murray (1973) found that the expression of feeling and cognitive reinterpretation reduced hostility. A number of studies have shown that nonaggressive communication results in lowered arousal and antagonism (Hokanson *et al.*, 1968; Kaufman & Feshbach, 1963). Hence, clients are taught how to express negative sentiment in nonantagonistic ways that are respectful of the rights of others. The procedures of assertion training are of considerable value in this regard (e.g., Lange & Jacobowski, 1976).

The essence of problem solving with respect to provocation management is to focus on issues and objectives and to engage in behavior that is instrumental in achieved desired outcomes. This is what is meant by the expression *task-oriented*. Efforts are made to teach clients to respond to provocation as a problem that calls for a solution, rather than a threat that calls for an attack.

Various components of the problem-solving process were articulated by D'Zurilla & Goldfield (1971), who construed the process in terms of (*a*) general orientation;

(*b*) problem definition; (*c*) generation of alternatives; (*d*) decision making based on anticipated consequences; and (*e*) verification. Their perspective is quite consistent with the approach advocated here with respect to anger. The experimental work performed by Spivack and his associates (Platt & Spivack, 1972, 1974; Shure & Spivack, 1972; Spivack, Platt, & Shure, 1976; Spivack & Shure, 1974) has found that disturbed populations (young children, adolescents, and adult psychiatric patients) have deficits in problem-solving thinking in terms of the ability to conceptualize solutions and means–end relationships. Atrops (1978) found that for a hospitalized anger population alternative thinking and means–end problem solving can be significantly influenced by the author's treatment approach to anger control.

Application Training

Skills-training approaches have emphasized the value of practice (D'Zurilla & Goldfried, 1971; Meichenbaum, 1975; Suinn & Richardson, 1971). Whereas the skill-acquisition phase involves the introduction, modeling, and rehearsal of coping techniques, the practice phase allows the client to test the acquired proficiencies by applying the anger-control methods to provocations that are regulated by the therapist. The competence emphasis of the treatment model necessitates a thorough examination of performance capabilities.

In contrast to pain and many anxiety problems (nonsocial phobias) that are elicited by physical stimuli, anger is more difficult to generate for clinical testing purposes by the actual problem conditions. To a significant extent, one must rely on simulations of provocation.[11] The application phase of the anger-management approach is conducted by means of imaginal and role-play inductions of anger. Although these are simulation procedures, they can be quite provoking, as attested by significant elevations in physiological arousal in laboratory evaluations (Novaco, 1975). Although the role-play procedure is the more powerful anger-induction method, the author has obtained blood-pressure elevations of 100 mm for many nonclinical subjects in response to imaginal provocation scenes.

The content of the test provocations is presented sequentially in hierarchical form. Early in the treatment process, the therapist constructs with the client a hierarchy of anger situations that the client is *likely to encounter* in his personal life. The coping skills that have been rehearsed with the therapist are then applied to these situation scenarios, graduating from the mildest to the most arousing provocations. It is suggested that each situation be attempted first imaginally then in role play. This sequential process enables both the therapist and the client to gauge the degree of attained improvement.[12]

[11]One might compare the arousal induction procedures used by Novaco (1975) for anger with those used by Turk (1976) for pain for an illustration of this point. Whereas pain can be generated by a physical simulus, such as the cold pressor test, anger requires more elaborate procedures of social interaction.

[12]A more extended account of the treatment procedures can be found in the therapist and client manuals that are available from the author.

Although simulated provocations are used for their ease in regulation in the treatment sessions, application training should not be restricted to them. The clients should be encouraged to test their coping skills with actual provocation circumstances, as gradually directed by the therapist. This can be arranged and gauged through the information obtained in the anger-diary entry ratings, which are reviewed at the start of each session. As indicated earlier, persons have chronic anger problems are aroused to anger in circumstances that are quite routine. Hence, the therapist can identify those situations in which the client should attempt to apply the coping skills such that the probability of success is maximized.

EXPERIMENTAL EVALUATION OF THE TREATMENT APPROACH

The present approach is distinguished from other behavioral therapy alternatives for anger by its emphasis on cognitive factors and by the attempt to provide a general theoretical framework for anger.[13] The treatment method, although not deducible from the theoretical scheme, is, nontheless, based on the articulated conception of anger as an affective stress-reaction having cognitive processes as central determinants. The model specifies a number of testable propositions regarding anger arousal and anger regulation that, it is hoped, will receive experimental attention.

In the initial treatment project (Novaco, 1975, 1976b), the comparative effectiveness of cognitive coping and of relaxation training were examined separately and in combination. The project examined the extent to which cognitive processes and relaxation techniques could be therapeutically used to regulate the experience and expression of anger for 34 persons who were both self-identified and assessed as having serious anger-control problems. The treatment program consisted of an experimental combination of cognitive self-control and relaxation procedures aimed at increasing personal competence in managing provocations and in regulating the arousal of anger. Component treatments were incorporated into the experimental design in order to permit a comparative evaluation.

The substance of the treatment program was derived from a functional analysis of the role of anger in human behavior and from a set of hypothetical principles for anger management derived from the research literature on aggression and on behavior therapy. The propositions served as heuristic statements of conditions that would, hypothetically, facilitate the management of anger. The propositions were integrated with the functional analysis of anger and involved the therapeutic arrangement of variables affecting competence in the regulation of anger and the

---

[13]Patterson's work on *aggression* has, of course, been conducted with an explicit theoretical framework. An account of the theory of coercion that directs his understanding of the development of aggressive behavior can be found in Patterson (1976).

constructive response to provocations. From this formulation of factors and strategies for anger control, four treatment conditions were constructed: (*a*) the primary treatment, which combined cognitive and relaxation controls; (*b*) a cognitive treatment condition; (*c*) a relaxation training condition; and (*d*) an attention-control condition. Each was conducted over a period of six sessions.

The experimental treatments were evaluated in a pre- and posttreatment design by anger-inventory assessment, by laboratory provocations in imaginal, role play, and direct experience modes using self-report and physiological indices, and by anger-diary ratings. The anger inventory was a self-report instrument developed by the author and has since been refined. It consists of 80 descriptions of provocation incidents for which the respondent rates anger that he/she would experience on a five-point scale. The laboratory provocation procedures were also constructed for this project and consisted of two provocation instances for both the imaginal and the role-play modes and for both the pre- and the posttreatment procedures. A direct encounter provocation was also used in the posttreatment series. The dependent variables consisted of self-report ratings of anger, changes in systolic and diastolic blood pressure, the number of galvanic skin responses, and ratings of coping behaviors for the provocation incidents. Throughout the treatment phase, participants kept a diary of their real-life anger experiences and rated their personal anger incidents on a seven-point scale. The series of assessments and treatment involved 12 visits of approximately 45 minutes each.

It was predicted that (*a*) the combined treatment condition would result in the greatest improvement on all dependent variables when compared to all other treatment groups; (*b*) all three treatment conditions would each differ significantly from the attention control condition; (*c*) the cognitive treatment alone would be superior to relaxation training alone in the reduction of anger for the inventory and for the role play and direct provocation conditions; and (*d*) relaxation training alone would result in a greater reduction in anger than the cognitive treatment for the imaginal provocation condition.

Across the multiple indices and procedures used in the project, it was found that the combined treatment condition had a very significant and generalized effect in reducing anger and in increasing anger management when compared to the attention control condition. The effects of the combined treatment were significantly different from the attention-control condition for the anger inventory, all measures except two for both the imaginal and the direct provocation procedures, and for five measures in the role-play mode. The means for the anger-diary ratings reflected the differential improvement hypothesized for the treatment groups, but this measure was not judged to be rigorous enough to justify further analysis.

Although less effective than the combined treatment, the cognitive treatment condition showed significant improvement over the controls. There were significant differences in favor of the cognitive group for the inventory and for nearly half of the anger measures across provocation modes. It was, therefore, concluded that the cognitive treatment resulted in a definite and generalized improvement in anger management. Compared to the combined treatment, the cognitive-treatment condition was most often not statistically different, as only six contrasts reached significance. However, the combined treatment was consistently the more improved group on the basis of the magnitude of the means.

The relaxation-training condition differed from controls across anger measures for the imaginal provocations but not for the inventory or for the other provocation modes. The results for the imaginal provocations thus demonstrated a good transfer of training for the relaxation group, but the effects were limited in their generalizability. The comparison of relaxation training with the combined treatment found only one dependent variable contrast in the imaginal condition in which the combined treatment group was more improved. However, there was a significant difference in favor of the combined treatment for the inventory, and nearly half of the anger measures in the role play and direct provocation modes resulted in significant contrasts, thus indicating the combined treatment to be superior.

There were surprisingly few significant differences between the cognitive and the relaxation group, although the magnitude of the means was often in favor of the cognitive condition. Since the relaxation-treatment group differed more often from the combined treatment in the less improved direction and less often from controls in the more improved direction than did the cognitive treatment group, it was concluded that the cognitive treatment alone resulted in greater improvement than did the relaxation treatment alone.

Following this encouraging beginning, the treatment approach to anger was re-conceptualized in terms of the stress inoculation model that was initially proposed by Meichenbaum and Cameron (Note 1). The stress-inoculation approach for anger problems was first applied in a community psychology intervention regarding the training of law enforcement officers who routinely must manage an assortment of provocation and conflict situations (Novaco, 1977b). The success of this consultation project, which has implictions for prevention (cf. Meichenbaum & Novaco, 1978), encouraged a reformulation of the clinical treatment approach.

The revised approach was then evaluated clinically in a case study of a hospitalized patient with severe anger problems (Novaco, 1977a). This patient was seen in therapy three times per week for 3.5 weeks in the hospital, during which time staff ratings of his behavior showed progressive improvement on anger dimensions and convergent evidence was obtained on self-monitored ratings of his behavior on weekend leaves from the hospital. Following discharge, he was seen biweekly for a 2-month period, and, in this interval, the frequency of anger reactions and his ability to manage provocative incidents showed continued improvement. In a follow-up on this case 1 year after discharge, the patient reported being "98% normal" and being pleased with his adjustment. Two years after discharge, he has reported a lower frequency of anger than at termination.

Subsequently, an experimental evaluation was conducted (Novaco, Note 2) of the therapist training procedure in a consultation project with experienced probation officers. A group of participants were trained in the treatment method over a period of 10 sessions and were compared to an untrained control group. The project participants each had at least 4 years of experience in probation counseling, and the groups were matched on educational and professional background. Half of each group had masters' degrees in counseling or social work. The weekly training sessions were evaluated by the project participants who in these weekly ratings expressed a high degree of satisfaction with the training experience. After the training procedure was completed, the experimental group and control groups were given a case history to analyze and for which they were to plan a course of treatment. The trained counselors were found to be significantly higher in performance with respect to both problem assessment and treatment plan. Two months after the completion of training, the groups were compared for their performance on a role-play test intake interview for an adolescent with anger problems. The results for the interview performance showed significant differences between groups, as the trained counselors received superior ratings on interviewer poise, effectiveness in reaching an understanding of the problem, and rapport with the client. The ratings were obtained from the interviewee and from independent raters of the taped interview, all of whom were blind to the fact that half of the counselors were untrained in the treatment method.

Several recent investigations have used the author's treatment procedures in the evaluation of therapy for anger. Schrader, Long, Panzer, Gillet, and Kornblath (Note 3) reported the results of applying the anger-control package to six adolescents having a history of verbal and physical abuse. Using a multiple baseline design, they found sizeable decreases in target behaviors for five of their six subjects during the treatment phase. The treatment gains were maintained for all but one of the subjects on follow-up. Schrader *et al.* thus provide an important demonstration of the effectiveness of the treatment program for a difficult clinical population.

Also, two doctoral dissertations under the author's supervision have been conducted that pertain to the treatment interventions. Crain (1977) investigated the effects of self-instructional therapy for anger among groups of anger expressors and anger suppressors. He also designed, as a comparison condition, a "focused awareness" treatment based on principles of Gestalt therapy. In contrast with the focus-awareness treatment on four of five dependent measures and with a control condition on two of five measures, the self-instructional therapy resulted in lower levels of expressed, experienced, or anticipated anger for the group of anger-expressor clients. The self-instruction condition generally also resulted in lower anger for the anger-suppressor group.

A more complete implementation of the author's treatment procedures was performed by Atrops (1978), who investigated the effects of cognitive interventions for anger and their combination with social skills training for institutionalized subjects in a hospital for the criminally insane. Forty-three subjects, pretested and screened for anger problems, were treated in five therapy conditions: (*a*) combined cognitive treatment and social skills training; (*b*) cognitive treatment alone; (*c*) social skills training alone; (*d*) attention control; and (*e*) no treatment. Excluding the no treatment group, a 2 × 2 experimental design was used to evaluate the relative contributions of the cognitive and social skills interventions. The principal dependent measures consisted of videotape ratings of performance in response to the role-play provocation with a live confederate, self-reports of positive and negative self-statements, relevant and irrelevant means on measures of alternative thinking and problem solving, and ratings of ward behavior. Whereas the treatment condition of social skills training alone showed very little improvement over control conditions, the cognitive intervention resulted in significant improvements in alternative thinking and problem solving. Significant cognitive main effects were also found for voice articulation and modulation on posttest role-play performance. Planned comparisons among the treatment conditions found that the combined treatment exhibited the greatest improvement in role-play provocation performance as measured by various voice, posture, and movement indexes, as well as by verbal content. This research by Atrops, which was carefully performed, has demonstrated the usefulness of the cognitive–behavioral approach to anger problems with a very different client population, and it has shown the potency of the cognitive interventions.

SUMMARY AND CONCLUSIONS

An effort has been made to delineate a conceptual foundation for therapeutic intervention for anger problems. This was undertaken with the conviction that cognitive–behavioral interventionists must face the task of conceptual specification. If cognitive factors are viewed as determinants of clinical disorders, it is imperative that we develop theoretical schemes that articulate the nature and operation of these cognitions.

The present chapter has cast the stress inoculation approach to anger within a more general framework of the cognitive mediation of human stress. The processes of expectation and appraisal have been identified as the principal cognitive mediators of stress and anger. Although the analysis is far from complete, the experimental literature on anger and aggression was used to support this proposition. Future research on anger should be directed at the cognitive mediation hypothesis, particularly with regard to the expectation factor, which has received relatively less empirical attention than has the appraisal of provocation.

The stress-inoculation model with its three-stage procedure readily lends itself to experimental analysis. The empirical support for this approach to the treatment of anger is only beginning to be found, and it is hoped that research will be energetically pursued on this promising means of treatment for such serious and pervasive clinical problems.

REFERENCE NOTES

1. Meichenbaum, D., & Cameron, R. *Stress inoculation: A skills training approach to anxiety management.* Unpublished manuscript, University of Waterloo, 1973.
2. Novaco, R. W. *Cognitive determinants of anger disorders: Theoretical and therapeutic directions.* Paper presented at the 83rd Annual Convention of the American Psychological Association, Toronto, 1978.

3. Schrader, C., Long, J., Panzer, C., Gillet, D., & Kornblath, R. *An anger control package for adolescent drug abusers.* Paper presented at the 11th Annual convention of the Association for the Advancement of Behavior Therapy, Atlanta, 1977.

REFERENCES

Aakster, C. W. Psycho-social stress and health disturbances. *Social Science and Medicine,* 1974, *8,* 77–90.

Abramson, L., Seligman, M., & Teasdale, J. Learned helplessness in humans: Critique and reformulation. *Journal of Abnormal Psychology,* 1978, *87,* 49–74.

Albert, R. Effects of attributions made by a victim on retaliation and transmission of aggression. *Proceedings of the 81st Annual Convention of the American Psychological Association, Montreal, Canada.* 1973, *8,* 119–120.

Andrew, J. M. Recovery from surgery with and without preparatory instruction, for three coping styles. *Journal of Personality and Social Psychology,* 1970, *15,* 223–226.

Appley, M., & Trumbull, R. *Psychological stress.* New York: Appleton-Century-Crofts, 1967.

Arnold, M. B. *Emotion and personality.* New York: Columbia University Press, 1960.

Atrops, M. *Behavioral plus cognitive skills for coping with provocation in male offenders.* Unpublished doctoral dissertation, Fuller Theological Seminary, 1978.

Auerbach, S. M., Kendall, P. C., Cuttler, H. F., & Levitt, N. R. Anxiety, locus of control, type of preparatory information, and adjustment to dental surgery. *Journal of Consulting and Clinical Psychology,* 1976, *44,* 809–818.

Aurelius, M. A. *The mediations of Marcus Aurelius Antoninus* (Translation by G. Long). New York: A. L. Bunt Company, 1925.

Averill, J. R. Personal control over aversive stimuli and its relationship to stress. *Psychological Bulletin,* 1973, *80,* 286–303.

Averill, J. R. An analysis of psychosocial symbolism and its influence on theories of emotion. *Journal for the Theory of Social Behavior,* 1974, *4,* 147–190.

Bandura, A. *Aggression: A social learning analysis.* Englewood Cliffs, New Jersey: Prentice-Hall, 1973.

Bandura, A. Self-efficacy: Toward a unifying theory of behavior change. *Psychological Review,* 1977, 191–215.

Bandura, A., & Adams, N. E. Analysis of self-efficacy theory of behavioral change. *Cognitive Therapy and Research,* 1977, *1,* 287–310.

Bandura, A., Adams, N. E., & Beyer, J. Cognitive processes mediating behavior change. *Journal of Personality and Social Psychology,* 1977, *35,* 125–139.

Bandura, A., Underwood, B., & Fromson, M. E. Disinhibition of aggression through diffusion of responsibility and dehumanization of victims. *Journal of Research in Personality,* 1975, *9,* 253–269.

Baron, R. Reducing the influence of an aggressive model: The restraining effects of discrepant modeling cues. *Journal of Personality and Social Psychology,* 1971, *20,* 240–245.

Baron, R. The aggression-inhibiting influence of heightened sexual arousal. *Journal of Personality and Social Psychology,* 1974, *30,* 318–322.

Baron, R. Aggression-inhibiting influence of sexual humor. *Journal of Personality and Social Psychology,* 1978, *36,* 189–197.

Baron, R., & Bell, P. A. Sexual arousal and aggression by males: Effects of type of erotic stimuli and prior provocation. *Journal of Personality and Social Psychology,* 1977, *35,* 79–87.

Baron, R., & Kepner, C. R. Model's behavior and attraction toward the model as determinants of adult aggressive behavior. *Journal of Personality and Social Psychology,* 1970, *14,* 335–344.

Beck, A. T. *Cognitive therapy and the emotional disorders.* New York: International Universities Press, 1976.

Berkowitz, L. The expression and reduction of hostility. *Psychological Bulletin,* 1958, *55,* 257–283.

Berkowitz, L. *Aggression: A social psychological analysis.* New York: McGraw-Hill, 1962.

Berkowitz, L. Aggressive cues in aggessive behavior and hostility catharsis. *Psychological Review,* 1964, *71,* 104–122.

Berkowitz, L. Some determinants of impulsive aggression: Role of mediated association with reinforcement for aggression. *Psychological Review,* 1974, *81,* 165–176.

Berkowitz, L., & Rawlings, E. Effects of film violence on inhibition against subsequent aggression. *Journal of Abnormal and Social Psychology,* 1963, *66,* 405–412.

Borden, R. J. Witnessed aggression: Influence on an observer's sex and values on aggressive responding. *Journal of Personality and Social Psychology,* 1975, *31,* 567–573.

Bourne, P. G. *The psychology and physiology of stress.* New York: Academic Press, 1969.

Bourne, P. G. *Men, stress, and Vietnam.* Boston: Little, Brown, & Company, 1970.

Brenner, M. H. *Mental illness and the economy.* Cambridge, Massachusetts: Harvard University Press, 1973.

Brock, T. C., & Buss, A. Effects of justification for aggression and communication with the victim on post aggressive dissonance. *Journal of Abnormal and Social Psychology,* 1964, *68,* 403–412.

Buchwald, A., Coyne, J., & Cole, C. A critical evaluation of the learned helplessness model of depression. *Journal of Abnormal Psychology,* 1978, *87,* 180–193.

Buss, A. Physical aggression in relation to different frustrations. *Journal of Abnormal and Social Psychology,* 1963, *67,* 1–7.

Camp, B. W. Verbal mediation in young aggressive boys. *Journal of Abnormal Psychology,* 1977, *86,* 145–153.

Cannon, W. B. *Bodily changes in pain, hunger, fear, and rage.* New York: Appleton, 1915.

Cassell, S. Effect of brief puppet therapy upon the emotional responses of children undergoing cardiac catherization. *Journal of Counseling Psychology,* 1965, *29,* 1–8.

Coddington, R. D. The significance of life events as etiological factors in the diseases of children, II. A study of a normal population. *Journal of Psychosomatic Research,* 1972, *16,* 205–213.

Cofer, C. N., & Appley, M. H. *Motivation: Theory and research.* New York: Wiley, 1964.

Cohen, A. R. Social norms, arbitrariness of frustration, and status of the agent of frustration in the frustration–aggression hypothesis. *Journal of Abnormal and Social Psychology,* 1955, *51,* 222–226.

Cohen, S., Rothbart, M., & Phillips, S. Locus of control and the generality of learned helplessness in humans. *Journal of Personality and Social Psychology,* 1976, *34,* 1049–1056.

Costello, C. A critical review of Seligman's laboratory experiments on learned helplessness and depression in humans. *Journal of Abnormal Psychology,* 1978, *87,* 21–36.

Crain, D. *Awareness and the modification of anger problems.* Unpublished doctoral dissertation, University of California, Los Angeles, 1977.

Dengerink, H. A., & Levendusky, P. G. Effects of massive rehabilitation and balance of power on aggression. *Journal of Experimental Research in Personality,* 1972, *6,* 230–236.

Depue, R., & Monroe, S. Learned helplessness in the perspective of the depressive disorders: Conceptual and definitional issues. *Journal of Abnormal Psychology,* 1978, *87,* 3–20.

Dertke, M. G., Penner, L. A., Hawkins, H. L., & Suarez, C. The inhibitory effects of an observer on instrumental aggression. *Bulletin of The Psychonomic Society,* 1973, *1,* 112–114.

Diskin, S. D., Goldstein, M. J., & Grencik, J. M. Coping patterns of law enforcement officers in simulated and naturalistic stress. *American Journal of Community Psychology,* 1977, *5,* 59–74.

Dohrenwend, B. S. Social status and stressful life events. *Journal of Personality and Social Psychology,* 1973, *28,* 225–235.

Dohrenwend, B. S. Social stress and community psychology. *American Journal of Community Psychology,* 1978, *6,* 1–14.

Dohrenwend, B. S., & Dohrenwend, B. P. (Eds.) *Stressful life events: Their nature and effects*. New York: Wiley, 1974.

Dollard, J., Doob, L., Miller, N., Mowrer, O., & Sears, R. *Frustration and aggression*. New Haven: Yale University Press, 1939.

Dollard, J., & Miller, N. E. *Personality and psychotherapy: An analysis in terms of learning, thinking, and culture*. New York: McGraw-Hill, 1950.

Donnerstein, E., Donnerstein, M., & Evans, R. Erotic stimuli and aggression: Facilitation or inhibition. *Journal of Personality and Social Psychology*, 1975, *32*, 237–244.

D'Zurilla, T., & Goldfried, M. Problem solving and behavior modification. *Journal of Abnormal Psychology*, 1971, *78*, 107–126.

Egbert, L. D., Battit, G. E., Welch, C. E., & Bartlett, M. K. Reduction of post-operative pain by encouragement and instruction of patients. *New England Journal of Medicine*, 1964, *270*, 825–827.

Ellis, A. *Reason and emotion in psychotherapy*. New York: Lyle Stuart Inc., 1962.

Ellis, A. *Humanistic psychology: The rational emotive approach*. New York: Julian Press, 1973.

Ellis, A. *How to live with and without anger*. New York: Reader's Digest Press, 1977.

Epictetus. *The discourses as reported by Arrian, Vol. 1*. (Translation by W. A. Oldfather) Cambridge, Massachusetts: Harvard University Press, 1961.

Epstein, S., & Taylor, S. P. Instigation to aggression as a function of degree of defeat and perceived aggressive intent of opponent. *Journal of Personality*, 1967, *35*, 265–289.

Evans, D. R. Specific aggression, arousal, and reciprocal inhibition therapy. *Western Psychologist*, 1971, *1*, 125–130.

Evans, D. R., & Hearn, M. T. Anger and systematic desensitization: A follow-up. *Psychological Reports*, 1973, *32*, 569–570.

Feshbach, H. S. The functions of aggression and the regulation of aggressive drive. *Psychological Review*, 1964, *71*, 257–272.

Feshbach, S. Aggression. In P. H. Mussen (Ed.), *Carmichael's manual of child psychology, Vol. II*. New York: Wiley, 1970.

Frodi, A. Alternatives to aggressive behavior for the reduction of hostility. *Goteborg Psychological Reports*, 1973, *3* (abstract only).

Frodi, A., Macaulay, J., & Thome, P. R. Are woman always less aggressive than men? A review of the experimental literature. *Psychological Bulletin*, 1977, *84*, 634–660.

Galassi, J., & Galassi, M. Modifying assertive and aggressive behavior through assertion training: A preliminary investigation. *Journal of College Student Personnel*, in press.

Geen, R., & Rakosky, J. Interpretations of observed aggression and their effects GSR. *Journal of Experimental Research in Personality*, 1973, *6*, 289–292.

Geen, R., Rakosky, J., & Pigg, R. Awareness of arousal and its relation to aggression. *British Journal of Social and Clinical Psychology*, 1972, *11*, 115–121.

Geen, R., Stonner, D., & Kelly, D. R. Aggression anxiety and cognitive appraisal of aggression-threat stimuli. *Journal of Personality and Social Psychology*, 1974, *29*, 196–200.

Gersten, J. C., Langner, T. S., Eisenberg, J. G., & Orzeck, L. Child behavior and life events: Undesirable change or change per se? In B. S. Dohrenwend & B. P. Dohrenwend (Eds.), *Stressful life events: Their nature and effects*. New York: John Wiley & Sons, 1974.

Glass, D. C. Behavior patterns, stress, and coronary disease. Hillsdale, New Jersey: Lawrence Erlbaum Associates, 1977.

Glass, D., & Singer, J. *Urban stress: Experiments on noise and social stressors*. New York: Academic Press, 1972.

Goldfried, M. Systematic desensitization as training in self-control. *Journal of Counseling and Clinical Psychology*, 1971, *37*, 228–234.

Goldstein, M. J. Individual differences in response to stress. *American Journal of Community Psychology*, 1973, *1*, 113–137.

Green, R., & Murray, E. Instigation to aggression as a function of self-disclosure and threat to self-esteem. *Journal of Consulting and Clinical Psychology*, 1973, *40*, 440–443.

Greenwell, J., & Dengerink, H. A. The role of perceived versus actual attack in human physical aggression. *Journal of Personality and Social Psychology*, 1973, *26*, 66–71.

Hadas, M. *Essential works of stoicism*. New York: Bantam Books, 1961.

Haggard, E. Psychological causes and results of stress. In D. Lindsley (Ed.), *Human factors in undersea warfare*. Washington: National Research Council Press, 1949.

Haldane, E. S., & Ross, G. (Ed.) *The philosophical works of Descartes, Vol. 1*. Cambridge: Cambridge University Press, 1931.

Hall, G. S. A study of anger. *American Journal of Psychology*, 1899, *10*, 516–591.

Hearn, M. T., & Evans, D. R. Anger and reciprocal inhibition therapy. *Psychological Reports*, 1972, *30*, 943–948.

Herrell, J. M. *Use of systematic desensitization to eliminate inappropriate anger*. Proceedings of the 79th Annual Convention of the American Psychological Association. Washington, D.C.: American Psychological Association, 1971, 431–432.

Hiroto, D. S. Locus of control and learned helplessness. *Journal of Experimental Psychology*, 1974, *102*, 187–193.

Hiroto, D. S., & Seligman, M. P. Generality of learned helplessness in man. *Journal of Personality and Social Psychology*, 1975, *31*, 311–327.

Hokanson, J. E., & Burgess, M. The effects of three types of aggression on vascular processes. *Journal of Abnormal and Social Psychology*, 1962, *64*, 446–449.

Hokanson, J. E., Willers, K. R., & Koropsak, E. The modifications of autonomic responses during aggressive interchange. *Journal of Personality*, 1968, *36*, 386–404.

Holmes, D. S., & Houston, B. K. Effectiveness of situation redefinition and affective isolation in coping with stress. *Journal of Personality and Social Psychology*, 1974, *29*, 212–218.

Holmes, T. S., & Rahe, R. E. The social readjustment rating scale. *Journal of Psychosomatic Research*, 1967, *11*, 213–218.

Horan, J. J., Hackett, G., Buchanan, J. D., Stone, C. I., & Demchik-Stone, D. Coping with pain: A component analysis of stress inoculation. *Cognitive Therapy and Research*, 1977, *1*, 211–222.

Hussian, R. A., & Lawrence, P. S. The reduction of test, state, and trait anxiety by test-specific and generalized stress inoculation training. *Cognitive Therapy and Research*, 1978, *2*, 25–38.

Jacobsen, E. *Progressive relaxation*. Chicago: University of Chicago Press, 1938.

Jaffe, Y., Malamuth, N., Feingold, J., & Feshbach, S. Sexual arousal and behavioral aggression. *Journal of Personality and Social Psychology*, 1974, *30*, 759–764.

Janis, I. *Psychological stress*. New York: Wiley, 1958.

Johns, M. W. Stress and coronary heart disease. In A. T. Welford (Ed.), *Man under stress*. New York: John Wiley and Sons, 1974.

Kaufman, H., & Feshbach, S. The influence of anti-aggressive communications upon the response to provocation. *Journal of Personality*, 1963, *31*, 428–444.

Kelly, G. *The psychology of personal constructs (Vols. 1 and 2)*. New York: Norton, 1955.

Kendall, P. C., Williams, L., Pechacek, T., Graham, L., Shisslak, C., & Herzoff, N. Cognitive–behavioral and patient education interventions in cardiac catherization procedures: The Palo Alto Medical Psychology Project. *Journal of Consulting and Clinical Psychology*, 1979, *47*, 49–58.

Kent, R. A methodological critique of "Interventions for Boys with Conduct Problems." *Journal of Consulting and Clinical Psychology*, 1976, *44*, 297–299.

Kiritz, S., & Moos, R. Physiological effects of the social environment. *Psychosomatic Medicine*, 1974, *36*, 96–114.

Konečni, V. J. Annoyance, type and duration of post-annoyance activity and aggression: The "cathartic effect." *Journal of Experimental Psychology*, 1975, *104*, 76–102. (a)

Konečni, V. J. The mediation of aggressive behavior: Arousal level versus anger and cognitive labeling. *Journal of Personality and Social Psychology*, 1975, *32*, 706–712. (b)

Lange, A., & Jakubowski, P. *Responsible assertive behavior*. Champaign, Illinois: Research Press, 1976.

Langer, E. L., Janis, I. L., & Wolfer, J. A. Reduction of psychological stress in surgical patients. *Journal of Experimental Social Psychology*, 1975, *11*, 155–165.

Lazarus, R. S. *Psychological stress and the coping process.* New York: McGraw-Hill, 1966.

Lazarus, R. S. Cognitive and personality factors underlying threat and coping. In M. H. Appley & R. Trumbull (Eds.), *Psychological stress.* New York: Appleton-Century-Crofts, 1967.

Lazarus, R. S., & Alfert, E. The short-circuiting of threat. *Journal of Abnormal and Social Psychology,* 1964, *69,* 195–205.

Lazarus, R. S., & Launier, R. Stress-related transactions between person and environment. In L. A. Pervin and M. Lewis (Eds.), *Perspectives in interactional psychology.* New York: Plenum Press, 1978, pp. 287–327.

Lazarus, R., Opton, E. M., Nomikos, M. S., & Rankin, N. O. The principle of short-circuiting of threat: Further evidence. *Journal of Personality,* 1965, *33,* 622–635.

Lefcourt, H. Internal versus external control of reinforcement: A review. *Psychological Bulletin,* 1966, *65,* 206–220.

Lefcourt, H. M. The function of the illusions of control and freedom. *American Psychologist,* 1973, *28,* 417–425.

Levine, S., & Scotch, N. A. (Eds.) *Social stress.* Chicago: Adline Publishing Company, 1970.

Lipowski, Z. J. Affluence, information inputs, and health. *Social Science and Medicine,* 1973, *7,* 517–529.

Mahoney, M., & Arnkoff, D. Cognitive and self-control therapies. In S. L. Garfield & A. E. Bergin (Eds.), *Handbook of psychotherapy and behavior change (2nd Ed.).* New York: Wiley, 1977.

Malamuth, N., Feshbach, S., & Jaffe, Y. Sexual arousal and aggression: Recent experiments and theoretical issues. *Journal of Social Issues,* in press.

Mallick, S. K., & McCandless, B. R. A study of catharsis of aggression. *Journal of Personality and Social Psychology,* 1966, *4,* 591–596.

Mandler, G. *Mind and emotion.* New York: John Wiley & Sons, 1975.

Markush, R. E., & Favero, R. V. Epidemiologic assessment of stressful life events, depressed mood, and psychophysiological symptoms: A preliminary report. In B. S. Dohrenwend & B. P. Dohrenwend (Eds.), *Stressful life events: Their nature & effects.* New York: John Wiley & Sons, 1974.

Mason, J. A historical view of the stress field. *Journal of Human Stress,* 1975, *1,* 6–12 and 22–36.

May, J. R., & Johnson, H. J. Physiological activity to internally elicited arousal and inhibitory thoughts. *Journal of Abnormal Psychology,* 1973, *82,* 239–245.

McGrath, J. C. *Social and psychological factors in stress.* New York: Holt, Rinehart, & Winston, 1970.

Mechanic, D. *Medical sociology: A selective view.* New York: Free Press, 1968.

Meichenbaum, D. *Cognitive behavior modification.* Morristown, New Jersey: General Learning Press, 1974.

Meichenbaum, D. A self-instructional approach to stress management: A proposal for stress inoculation training. In C. Spielberger & I. Sarason (Eds.), *Stress and Anxiety, Vol. 2.* New York: Wiley, 1975.

Meichenbaum, D. *Cognitive behavior modification.* New York: Plenum Press, 1977.

Meichenbaum, D., & Novaco, R. W. Stress inoculation: A preventative approach. In C. Spielberger & I. Sarason (Eds.), *Stress and Anxiety (Vol. 5).* New York: Halstead Press, 1978.

Meyer, T. Effects of viewing justified and unjustified film violence on aggressive behavior. Journal of Personality and Social Psychology, 1972, *22,* 21–29.

Miller, W. R., & Seligman, M. Depression and the perception of reinforcement. *Journal of Abnormal Psychology,* 1973, *82,* 62–73.

Miller, W. R., & Seligman, M. F. Depression and learned helplessness in man. *Journal of Abnormal Psychology,* 1975, *84*(3), 228–238.

Myers, J. K., Lindenthal, J. J., & Pepper, M. P. Life events and psychiatric impairment. *Journal of Nervous and Mental Disease,* 1971, *152,* 149–157.

Neufeld, R. W. Effect of cognitive appraisal on d' and response bias to experimental stress. *Journal of Personality and Social Psychology,* 1975, *31,* 735–743.

Nickel, T. The attribution of intention as a critical factor in the relation between frustration and aggression. *Journal of Personality,* 1974, *42,* 482–492.

Nomikos, M. S., Opton, E., Averill, J., & Lazarus, R. S. Surprise versus suspense in the production of stress reaction. *Journal of Personality and Social Psychology*, 1968, *8*, 204–208.

Novaco, R. W. *Anger control: The development and evaluation of an experimental treatment.* Lexington, Massachusetts: D. C. Heath, Lexington Books, 1975.

Novaco, R. W. The function and regulation of the arousal of anger. *American Journal of Psychiatry*, 1976, *133*, 1124–1128. (a)

Novaco, R. W. Treatment of chronic anger through cognitive and relaxation controls. *Journal of Consulting and Clinical Psychology*, 1976, *44*, 681. (b)

Novaco, R. W. Stress inoculation: A cognitive therapy for anger and its application to a case of depression. *Journal of Consulting and Clinical Psychology*, 1977, *45*, 600–608. (a)

Novaco, R. W. A stress inoculation approach to anger management in the training of law enforcement officers. *American Journal of Community Psychology*, 1977, *5*, 327–346. (b)

Novaco, R. W. Anger and coping with stress. In J. Foreyt & D. Rathjen (Eds.), *Cognitive behavior therapy: Therapy, research, and practice.* New York: Plenum Press, 1978.

Novaco, R., Stokols, D., Campbell, J., & Stokols, J. Transportation, stress, and community psychology. *American Journal of Community Psychology*, in press.

O'Donnell, C. R., & Worell, L. Motor and cognitive relaxation in the desensitization of anger. *Behavior Research and Therapy*, 1973, *11*, 473–481.

O'Leary, M. R., & Dengerink, H. A. Aggression as a function of the intensity and pattern of attack. *Journal of Research in Personality*, 1973, *7*, 61–70.

Overmier, J. P., & Seligman, M. P. Effects of inescapable shock on subsequent escape and avoidance responding. *Journal of Comparative and Physiological Psychology*, 1967, *63*, 28–33.

Pastore, N. The role of arbitrariness in the frustration–aggression hypothesis. *Journal of Abnormal and Social Psychology*, 1952, *47*, 728–731.

Patterson, G. R. Intervention for boys with conduct problems: Multiple settings, treatments, and criteria. *Journal of Consulting and Clinical Psychology*, 1974, *42*, 471–481.

Patterson, G. R. The aggressive child: Victim and architect of a coercive system. In L. A. Hamerlynck, E. J. Mash, & L. C. Handy (Eds.), *Behavior modification and families I: Theory and research. II: Applications and developments.* New York: Brunner/Mazel, 1976.

Patterson, G. R., Cobb, J. A., & Ray, R. S. Direct interventions in the classroom: A set of procedures for the aggressive child. In F. W. Clark, D. R. Evans, & L. A. Hamerlynck (Eds.), *Implementing behavior programs for schools and clinics.* Champaign, Illinois: Research Press, 1972.

Patterson, G. R., Littman, R. A., & Bricker, W. Assertive behavior in children: A step toward a theory of aggression. *Monographs of the Society for Research in Child Development*, 1967, *32*(5).

Patterson, G. R., Ray, R. S., & Shaw, D. A. Direct intervention in the families of deviant children. *Oregon Research Institute Research Bulletin*, 1968, *8*(9).

Patterson, G. R., & Reid, J. B. Intervention for families of aggressive boys: A replication study. *Behavior Research and Therapy*, 1973, *11*, 1–12.

Paul, G. L. Physiological effects of relaxation training and hypnotic suggestion. *Journal of Abnormal Psychology*, 1969, *74*, 425–437.

Paul, G. L., & Trimble, R. W. Recorded vs. "live" relaxation and hypnotic suggestion: Comparative effectiveness for reducing physiological arousal and inhibiting stress response. *Behavior Therapy*, 1970, *1*, 285–302.

Platt, J. J., & Spivack, G. Problem-solving thinking of psychiatric patients. *Journal of Consulting and Clinical Psychology*, 1972, *39*, 148–151.

Platt, J. J., & Spivack, G. Means of solving real-life problems: I. Psychiatric patients versus controls, and cross-cultural comparisons of normal females. *Journal of Community Psychology*, 1974, *2*, 45–48.

Rahe, R. H., Mahan, J. R., Arthur, R. J., & Gunderson, E. K. The epidemiology of illness in naval environments. *Military Medicine*, 1970, *35*, 443–452.

Redl, F., & Wineman, D. *Children who hate.* New York: The Free Press, 1951.

Redl, F., & Wineman, D. *Controls from within: Techniques for the treatment of the aggressive child.* New York: The Free Press, 1952.

Redmond, D. P., Gaylor, M. S., McDonald, R. H., & Shapiro, A. P. Blood pressure and heart rate response to verbal instruction and relaxation in hypertension. *Psychosomatic Medicine*, 1974, *36*, 285-297.

Reeder, L. G., Schrama, P. G., & Dirken, J. M. Stress and cardiovascular health: An international cooperative study: 1. *Social Science and Medicine*, 1973, *7*(8), 573-584.

Reid, J. B., & Patterson, G. R. Follow-up analyses of a behavioral treatment program for boys with conduct problems: A reply to Kent. *Journal of Consulting and Clinical Psychology*, 1976, *44*, 297-307.

Richardson, R. F. *The psychology and pedagogy of anger*. Baltimore: Warwick and York, Inc., 1918.

Rimm, D. C., deGroot, J. C., Boord. P., Reiman, J., & Dillow, P. V. Systematic desensitization of an anger response. *Behavior Research and Therapy*, 1971, *9*, 273-280.

Rimm, D. C., Hill, G. A., Brown, N. H., & Stuart, J. E. Group-assertive training in treatment of expression of inappropriate anger. *Psychological Reports*, 1974, *34*, 791-798.

Rimm, D. C., & Litvak, S. B. Self-verbalization and emotional arousal. *Journal of Abnormal Psychology*, 1969, *74*, 181-187.

Rogers, T., & Craighead, W. E. Physiological response to self-statements: The effects of statement valence and discrepancy. *Cognitive Therapy and Research*, 1977, *1*, 99-120.

Rogers, R. W., & Mewborn, E. R. Fear appeals and attitude change: Effects of a threat's noxiousness, probability of occurrence, and the efficacy of coping responses. *Journal of Personality and Social Psychology*, 1976, *34*, 54-61.

Rosenbaum, M. E., & deCharms, R. Direct and vicarious reduction of hostilities. *Journal of Abnormal and Social Psychology*, 1960, *60*, 105-111.

Ross, W. D. (Ed.) *The works of Aristotle, Vol. IX*. Oxford: Oxford University Press, 1963.

Rotter, J. *Social learning and clinical psychology*. Englewood Cliffs, New Jersey: Prentice-Hall, 1954.

Rotter, J. Generalized expectancies of internal versus external control of reinforcement. *Psychological Monographs*, 1966, *80*(Whole No. 609).

Rotter, J. Some problems and misconceptions related to the construct of internal versus external control of reinforcement. *Journal of Consulting and Clinical Psychology*, 1975, *43*, 56-67.

Rule, B., & Nesdale, A. Emotional arousal and aggressive behavior. *Psychological Bulletin*, 1976, *83*, 851-863.

Russell, P. L., & Brandsma, J. M. A theoretical and empirical integration of the rational–emotive and classical conditioning theories. *Journal of Consulting and Clinical Psychology*, 1974, *42*, 389-397.

Schachter, S., & Singer, J. E. Cognitive, social, and physiological determinants of emotional state. *Psychological Review*, 1962, *69*, 379-399.

Schwartz, G. E. Cardiac responses to self-induced thoughts. *Psychophysiology*, 1971, *8*, 462-467.

Scott, R., & Howard, A. Models of stress. In S. Levine & N. A. Scotch (Eds.), *Social stress*. Chicago: Aldine, 1970.

Seligman, M. *Helplessness: On depression, development, and death*. San Francisco: W. H. Freeman & Co., 1975.

Seligman, M., & Maier, S. F. Failure to escape traumatic shock. *Journal of Experimental Psychology*, 1967, *74*, 1-9.

Selye, H. *The stress of life*. New York: McGraw-Hill, 1956.

Selye, H. The evolution of the stress concept. *American Scientist*, 1973, *61*, 692-699.

Selye, H. Confusion and controversy in the stress field. *Journal of Human Stress*, 1975, *1*. 37-44.

Selye, H. *The stress of life (2nd Ed.)*. New York: McGraw-Hill, 1976.

Shantz, D. W., & Voydanoff, D. A. Situational effects of retaliatory aggression at three age levels. *Child Development*, 1973, *44*, 149-153.

Shure, M. B., & Spivack, G. Means–ends thinking, adjustment and social class among elementary school-aged children. *Journal of Consulting and Clinical Psychology*, 1972, *38*, 348-353.

Singer, D. L. Aggression arousal, hostile humor, and catharsis. *Journal Of Personality* and *Social Psychology Monograph Supplement*, 1968, *8*(1; Part 2).

Smith, R. E. The use of humor in the counter conditioning of an anger response. *Behavior Therapy*, 1973, *4*, 576–580.

Spence, K. The nature of theory construction in contemporary psychology. *Psychological Review*, 1944, *51*, 47–68.

Speisman, J., Lazarus, R., Mordkoff, A., & Davison, L. Experimental reduction of stress based on ego-defense theory. *Journal of Abnormal Social Psychology*, 1964, *68*, 367–380.

Spilken, A. Z., & Jacobs, H. A. Predictions of illness behavior from measures of life crises, manifest distress, and maladaptive coping. *Psychosomatic Medicine*, 1971, *33*, 251–254.

Spivack, G., Platt, J., & Shure, M. *The problem-solving approach to adjustment*. San Francisco: Jossey-Bass Publishers, 1976.

Spivack, G., & Shure, M. B. *Social adjustments of young children: A cognitive approach to solving real-life problems*. San Francisco: Jossey-Bass Publishers, 1974.

Stokols, D. Environmental psychology. *Annual Review of Psychology*, 1978, *29*, 253–295.

Stokols, D., Novaco, R. W., Stokols, J., & Campbell, J. Traffic congestion, Type-A behavior, and stress. *Journal of Applied Psychology*, 1978, *63*, 467–480.

Suinn, R., & Richardson, F. Anxiety management training: A non-specific behavior therapy program for anxiety control. *Behavior Therapy*, 1971, *2*, 498–510.

Taylor, S. P. Aggressive behavior and physiological arousal as a function of provocation and the tendency to inhibit aggression. *Journal of Personality*, 1967, *35*, 297–310.

Taylor, S. P., & Epstein, S. Aggression as a function of the interaction of the sex of the aggressor and the sex of the victim. *Journal of Personality*, 1967, *35*, 474–486.

Theorell, T., & Rahe, R. H. Psychosocial factors and myocardial infarction: An inpatient study in Sweden. *Journal of Psychosomatic Research*, 1971, *15*, 25–31.

Thornton, J. W., & Jacobs, P. D. Learned helplessness in human subjects. *Journal of Experimental Psychology*, 1971, *87*, 367–372.

Toch, H. *Violent men*. Chicago: Aldine Publishing Co., 1969.

Turk, D. *An expanded skills training approach for the treatment of experimentally induced pain*. Unpublished doctoral dissertation. University of Waterloo, 1976.

Veldman, D., & Worchel, P. Defensiveness and self-acceptance in the management of hostility. *Journal of Abnormal and Social Psychology*, 1961, *63*, 319–325.

Witmer, L. The treatment and cure of a case of mental and moral deficiency. *The Psychological Clinic*, 1908, *2*, 153–179.

Wolpe, J., & Lazarus, A. *Behavior therapy techniques*. Oxford: Pergamon Press, 1966.

Worchel, P. Status restoration and the reduction of hostility. *Journal of Abnormal and Social Psychology*, 1960, *63*, 443–445.

Worchel, S. The effects of three types of arbitrary thwarting on the instigation to aggression. *Journal of Personality*, 1974, *42*, 300–318.

Wyler, A., Masuda, M., & Holmes, T. Magnitude of life events and seriousness of illness. *Psychosomatic Medicine*, 1971, *33*, 115–122.

Zillman, D. Excitation transfer in communication-mediated aggressive behavior. *Journal of Experimental Social Psychology*, 1971, *7*, 419–434.

Zillman, D., Bryant, J., Cantor, J. R., & Day, K. D. Irrelevance of mitigating circumstances in retaliatory behavior at high levels of excitation. *Journal of Research in Personality*, 1975, *9*, 292–293.

Zillman, D., & Sapolsky, B. S. What mediates the effect of mild erotica on annoyance and hostile behavior in males. *Journal of Personality and Social Psychology*, 1977, *35*, 587–596.

Regulation of Pain: The Application of Cognitive and Behavioral Techniques for Prevention and Remediation

DENNIS C. TURK

MYLES GENEST

Pain has traditionally been treated primarily by medical and surgical means. In recent years, other means of treatment have been given more serious attention: A variety of cognitive, behavioral, and combined interventions have been proposed and used in conjunction with the more established methods. The approaches to be reviewed are not intended to replace more traditional medical and surgical treatments for pain but represent adjunctive approaches that enhance the clinician's armamentarium.

This chapter is organized into three main sections. First, to provide some rationale for the potential utility of the various cognitive and behavioral strategies, a brief overview of the pain phenomenon will be provided. The second section will elaborate the variety of preventative and remedial regimens that have been employed. This section will examine the relative efficacy of the different intervention strategies for both acute and chronic pain, as well as for aversive medical procedures. The third section will include a summary and some concluding comments regarding common features of the various treatments, with suggestions for enhancing the utility of cognitive–behavioral interventions.

PERVASIVENESS AND COMPLEXITY OF THE PAIN PHENOMENON

Since his earliest days, man has been concerned with avoiding or relieving nociceptive stimulation. Perhaps the first recorded references to remedies for pain is included in the Egyptian papyri. For example, in the Ebers papyrus (circa 1550 BC),

287

Cognitive–Behavioral Interventions:
Theory, Research, and Procedures

reference is made to the prescription of opium by Isis for Ra's headache (Bonica, 1953).

In our quest for attenuation of pain, we have submitted ourselves to such pernicious and often ineffective procedures as purging, puking, poisoning, puncturing, cutting, cupping, blistering, bleeding, leeching, heating, freezing, sweating, trepanning, and shocking. The pharmacopia has included practically every known organic and inorganic substance. Patients have chewed, imbibed, sucked, or suffered treatment with crocodile dung, teeth of swine, hooves of asses, spermatic fluid of frogs, eunuch fat, fly specks, lozenges of dried vipers, powder of precious stones, oils derived from ants, earthworms, and spiders, plus bricks, feathers, hair, human perspiration, and moss scraped from the skull of a victim of violent death (Shapiro, 1963).

Let us consider the treatment that Charles II of England endured at the hands of the best physicians of his day. A pint of blood was extracted from his right arm and a half-pint from his left shoulder. This was followed by an emetic, two physics, and an enema comprising 15 substances. Next, his head was shaved and a blister raised. Following in rapid succession, more emetics, sneezing powder, bleedings, soothing potions, a plaster of pitch, and pidgeon dung was smeared on his feet. Potions containing 10 different substances, chiefly herbs, as well as 40 drops of extract of human skull, were swallowed. Finally, application of bezoar stones (gallstones from sheep and goats) was prescribed. Following this extensive treatment, the king died (Haggard, 1929). Whether the cause of death was attributable to a medical condition or iatrogenic complications is unclear. Although we may be appalled by such treatments, therapeutic interventions hardly less esoteric (e.g., acupuncture, transcutaneous electrical stimulation, ultrasound) are frequently employed today in the quest to control pain.

No medical symptom is more ubiquitous than pain. Chapman (1973) noted that it was not uncommon for patients seen at the University of Washington Pain Clinic to have experienced as many as 20–25 operations, with some spending over $25,000 in health services. Surgeons have shown great ingenuity in designing operations to relieve intractable pain. Almost every site along the nervous system from the periphery (sympathectomies and rhizotomies) along the spinal cord (percutaneous cordotomies) to the brain (thalamotomies and prefrontal lobotomies) has been attacked. Although the operations may be brilliantly performed and may be technically successful, pain frequently recurs (Hilgard & Hilgard, 1975). It has recently been estimated (Toomey, Ghia, Mao, & Gregg, 1977) that no more than 50% of chronic pain patients have adequate amelioration of pain as a function of purely somatogenic treatments. To date, none of the conventional medical and surgical approaches has resulted in adequate or permanent regulation of pain.

In addition to the expenditure in human suffering, pain is extremely costly for society in regard to disability payments and medical services. Bonica (1974) estimated that pain costs Americans $5–10 billion annually. This estimation does not include the $900 million spent on over-the-counter pills, powders, and soothing salves. The regulation of pain continues to provide a challenge for health professionals.

One explanation for the inadequacy of conventional regimens to regulate pain consistently and definitively is related to an assumption underlying these treatments. The sensory input triggering a pain response is often referred to as a noxious stimulus. From this respondent view of pain, the antecedent noxious stimulus produces a pain response almost as a reflex. Actually, there is little neurological evidence of noxious stimuli. Each stimulus merely generates a wave of energy, an action *potential* along certain nerve routes. What makes volleys of stimuli noxious is the way each person perceives and appraises them.

An alternative to the traditional medical "specificity" model of pain has been offered by Melzack and Wall (1965, 1970)—the gate control theory. From this conceptualization, pain perception and response are viewed as complex phenomena resulting from the interaction of sensory–discriminative, motivational–affective, and cognitive–evaluative components, or "contributory causes." Although the posited physiological and anatomical bases for the gate control theory are speculative, having received some criticism (e.g., Kerr, 1975; Nathan, 1976), the multidimensional perspective has received considerable support (e.g., Hilgard & Hilgard, 1975; Tursky, 1976).

Melzack and Wall's component model of pain has focused attention on the idea that pain is not a function of any particular system alone; rather, each specialized portion of the entire nervous system contributes to the pain experience. The failure to take this into account can explain the frequent frustration encountered in treating patients with surgery, anesthetic blocks, or other measures designed to block the so-called pain pathways.

Melzack and Casey (1968) suggested that "the surgical and pharmacological attacks on pain might well profit by redirecting thinking toward the neglected and almost forgotten contribution of motivational and cognitive processes. Pain can be treated not only by trying to cut down sensory input by anesthetic blocks, surgical intervention and the like but also by influencing the motivational and cognitive factors as well [p. 435]."

Although factors contributing to the perception of pain are quite diverse, the complexity of the phenomenon should not deter us from searching for better ways to achieve regulation. The remainder of this chapter examines many innovative intervention strategies designed to assuage pain and suffering.

COGNITIVE, BEHAVIORAL, AND COMBINED
COGNITIVE–BEHAVIORAL INTERVENTIONS

A great number of treatment programs has been developed for a variety of pain syndromes and aversive medical procedures. Some order is provided to this array of approaches by two distinguishing dimensions (although there is some overlap within each): (*a*) duration of the nociceptive stimulation (acute or chronic); and (*b*) focus of treatment (prevention or remediation).

We will attempt to be comprehensive without being exhaustive. No discussion of laboratory-produced pain will be included, since this literature has recently been extensively reviewed (Turk, 1978b, in press). We will also exclude examination of hypnotic approaches in pain regulation. Comprehensive texts in this area are readily available (see Hilgard & Hilgard, 1975, for a recent review). Thus, the present chapter will focus on the application of cognitive, behavioral, and combined cognitive–behavioral interventions with clinical populations.

Acute Pain and Discomfort

As noted before, conventional medical treatments assume that pain is a specific sensation, with the intensity of pain proportional to the nociceptive sensory input or to the extent of tissue damage. The assumption of a simple one-to-one relationship between a stimulus and a sensation—one pain, one cause—has led to the expectancy that, if the cause of the pain is eliminated, the pain itself should vanish. This strategy does work well enough in some situations, such as anesthetization of the patient (blocking conscious awareness of nociceptive stimulation) during major surgery. However, in other situations in which acute pain and distress are likely to be perceived, it is necessary for the patient to be alert and cooperative (e.g., cardiac catheterization, gastrointestinal endoscopic examinations, debridement of burns). In many situations of intense nociceptive stimulation, potent analgesics may be unable totally to block perception of stimulation (e.g., treatments for burns, Fagerhaugh, 1974; migraine headaches, Wolff, 1943). Beecher (1959) noted that morphine, the most potent analgesic, is effective in only about 70% of the cases in which it is used. It also appears that morphine, when it is effective, may actually be reducing anxiety, fear, worry, and other emotions that are usually intermingled with pain (Beecher, 1966). Although the patient who has received the morphine may still experience nociceptive sensations, the reduction in associated anxiety may lead him to report that the pain is reduced (Barber, 1959; Beecher, 1959; Cattell, 1943; Hill, Kornetsky, Flanary, & Wikler, 1952a,b). This data has led Beecher (1966) to advocate the increased use of tranquilizers rather than potent narcotics to relieve suffering. Finally, in some acute situations, administration of powerful analgesics may have deleterious effects. For example, some concern has been expressed with regard to the effects of analgesics upon both the mother and the fetus during childbirth (Fiajalkowski, 1969). In such situations, cognitive and behavioral interventions may be of particular value.

Preventative Interventions

Both the gate-control conceptualization of pain and more general theories of adaptive coping (e.g., Janis, 1958; Lazarus, 1966) suggest that cognitive factors contribute to an appraisal of threat, which, in turn, influences the perception of and response to pain. Techniques designed to modify the individual's appraisal of situations from threatening to more benign have been employed as preventative intervention strategies in a number of situations.

Anxiety may be viewed as a result of an individual's appraisal of a situation as threatening. As such, anxiety is perhaps the most consistently identified psychological mediator of the pain experience (Barber, 1959; Cattell, 1943; Dick-Read, 1959; Hill et al., 1952a,b). It appears that, when a patient becomes very anxious or fearful while receiving nociceptive stimulation, there is a tendency to report that the pain is more intense. On the other hand, when a patient remains relaxed and does not become anxious about the situation and the intense stimulation, the tendency is to report that the pain is less acute. In fact, some investigators have suggested that reducing anxiety, in and of itself, would be sufficient to attenuate the perception of pain (e.g., Beecher, 1966; Shor, 1962).

The appraisal of threat may be influenced by providing information related to (a) the physical properties or objective characteristics of the procedures to be undertaken; (b) the sensations that might be experienced as a result of the stressor; and (c) overt and covert strategies designed to facilitate coping with the stressor. Let us review some of the studies that have attempted to reduce anxiety by providing patients with each of these forms of preparatory communication.

Procedural Information.   The most common approach to altering cognitive appraisal has been to provide information about the objective aspects of the impending event. Typically, patients have been informed about the onset, duration, likelihood, intensity, or other procedural details of a forthcoming situation (e.g., Andrew, 1970; DeLong, 1971; Johnson, 1973; Johnson, Morrissey, & Leventhal, 1973; Johnson & Rice, 1974; Melamed & Siegel, 1975; Vernon & Bailey, 1972; Vernon & Bigelow, 1974; Williams, Jones, Workoven, & Williams, 1975).

Johnson et al. (1973), for example, provided a group of patients who were to undergo a gastrointestinal endoscopic examination with a description of the procedures to be employed. The preparatory communication described the various stages of the examination: the clinic where the examination would be performed; throat swabbing to achieve local anesthesia; intravenous puncture; passage of a flexible fiberoptic tube 12 mm in diameter and 90 cm long, to be retained for 30 to 90 minutes; the patient's position on the examination table; lighting of the examination room; and pumping of air into the stomach. Explanations of the purposes of these activities, a description of the photographic technique, as well as a statement about the skill and experience of the medical team, were all provided. Finally, patients were provided with photographs showing the equipment to be employed and the examination room. We will consider the relative efficacy of this information shortly.

In general, investigations of *procedural-oriented* preparatory communications have failed to demonstrate unequivocally their utility. Johnson and her colleagues (Fuller, Endress, & Johnson, 1977; Johnson, 1975) argued that the failure of this approach may be attributed to the fact that little attention has been given to qualitative characteristics of the information supplied. In particular, Johnson (1975) suggested that *sensory-oriented* information based on the subjective experiences that typically accompany an aversive event should be included.

Sensory Information.   Several investigations (e.g., Johnson, 1973; Johnson, Morrissey, & Leventhal, 1973; Johnson & Rice, 1974; Skipper & Leonard, 1968) have demonstrated the efficacy of providing preparatory messages regarding sensory aspects of the impending event. Sensory information typically emphasizes the specific sensations that the patient is likely to experience during the procedures— what might be seen, felt, tasted, or heard. Information provided to surgery patients in a study by Johnson, Rice, Fuller, and Endress (1977) illustrates the content of typical sensory messages. Patients receiving the sensory information were advised that preoperative medication would make them sleepy, lightheaded, and relaxed. Postoperative sensations in the incision were described as "tenderness, sensitiveness, pressure, pulling, or burning." Other sensations described were dryness of the mouth, tiredness after physical effort, and pulling and pinching when stitches were removed.

In the Johnson *et al.* (1973) endoscopic examination study discussed previously, a group of patients receiving a sensory message was compared to the procedural information group. Patients in the sensory message group, like the procedural information group, received a description of each of the steps of the examination. In addition, for the sensory group the message included information about what sensations would be experienced, for example, a needle stick, drowsiness, the lighting in the room, a sensation of fullness in the stomach when air was pumped into it, and so on. Both groups required less medication to produce sedation than did control patients. However, the patients who heard the sensory information showed less tension during tube passage and less restlessness during the examination and tended to have less heart-rate acceleration during the examination than either the group receiving only procedural information or the control group. We should note that the sensory information group actually received *both* the procedural *and* the sensory information. It is difficult to prevent the provision of some form of procedural information in medical settings, since this is considered to be an important component of good medical practice.

In controlled laboratory studies in which it is much easier to manipulate independently the type and quantity of information, the role of sensory versus procedural information is somewhat equivocal. Whereas Johnson (1973) reported on the merit of sensory as compared to procedural information, Staub and Kellett (1972) indicated that neither form of information was sufficient to enhance tolerance relative to a control group. The combination of *both* procedural *and* sensory information was, however, an effective technique for pain control.

Returning to surgery patients, Johnson *et al.* (1977) noted that, although sensory and procedural information did prove to be effective with cholecystectomy patients, this was not the case with herniorrhaphy patients. Thus, the presentation of some form of preparatory information is more complex than it may at first seem. The lack of generality across patient populations should sensitize us to intricate and subtle factors that deserve consideration.

In another study with surgery patients, Langer, Janis, and Wolfer (1975) exposed one group of patients to information about probable sensations of pain and discomfort, together with reassurances about the high quality of the medical care they would receive. Langer *et al.* reported that patients receiving the realistic sensory information evidenced more anticipatory stress than did a group of patients who received no information about sensations to be expected. The information was also *not* found to have a positive effect on reaction to the surgery or speed of recovery. These results suggest that we might profitably examine individual differences in coping style (Andrew, 1970; Auerbach, Kendall, Cuttler, & Levitt, 1976; Cohen & Lazarus, 1973; DeLong, 1971).

It appears that individuals who rely on denial (avoiders) when confronted with anxiety-provoking stimuli respond poorly when confronted with information pertaining to surgery (Andrew, 1970; DeLong, 1971) and show better relative adjustment when not exposed to such input (Cohen & Lazarus, 1973). Conversely, individuals who tend to be sensitized to stressful stimuli (copers) adjust relatively well when exposed to specific information about surgery (Andrew, 1970; DeLong, 1971) but poorly when not given such information (Cohen & Lazarus, 1973). Individuals toward the middle of this continuum of deniers and sensitizers, as well as those who tend to report intermediate levels of preoperative anxiety, recover relatively well regardless of whether or not they received any preparatory information.

Auerbach *et al.* (1976) report a similar interaction when they compared recovery from dental surgery and the locus of control construct (Rotter, 1966). "Internals," who are characterized as perceiving themselves as having personal control over the reinforcement they obtain as a consequence of their behavior, adjusted poorly in surgery when given *general,* marginally relevant information; however, they demonstrated good adjustment in recovery when provided with *specific* information regarding procedures and sensations they might experience. The reverse was true for individuals characterized as "externals," who are said to perceive their reinforcement as determined by factors outside of their personal control.

Coping Strategy Information. Up to this point, we have examined preparatory messages that function to alert patients of what to expect regarding sensations and procedures. In addition, one can provide patients with information concerning behaviors that can directly affect their situation. Although a person may have no alternative but to endure such aversive diagnostic procedures as were described, one may nevertheless be able to alter the *impact* of the aversive stimuli. Leventhal and his colleagues (Leventhal, Singer, & Jones, 1965; Leventhal & Watts, 1966) suggested that behavioral preparation, that is, detailed instructions on how and when to act and on prior rehearsal of specific action, are necessary to sustain control over threat.

Behavioral coping techniques include relaxation, the performance of deep breathing, coughing, leg exercises, turning, and ambulation. Of course, the appropriate behaviors will vary with the noxious event that is to be endured (Egbert, Battit, Welch, Bartletts, 1964; Fuller *et al.*, 1977; Johnson & Leventhal, 1974; Johnson *et al.*, 1977; Lindeman, 1972; Lindeman & Van Aernam, 1971; Schmitt & Wooldridge, 1973; Wolfer & Visintainer, 1975). In these studies, behavioral coping strategies in conjunction with some form of information regarding what to expect generally have increased individuals' abilities to cope with noxious situations.

Another study using the endoscopic situation described previously (Johnson & Leventhal, 1974) illustrates the provision of instructions concerning behavioral coping strategies. The authors provided one group of patients with preparatory information about the procedures to be employed and sensations that might be experienced, as well as specific instructions for rapid mouth breathing and panting to reduce gagging during throat swabbing. The patients were also provided with specific instructions on how to act while the tube was being inserted: swallowing motions with the chin down and mouth open. Patients were encouraged to practice these behaviors following the instructions.

To summarize the groups in the Johnson and Leventhal (1974) study, all subjects were provided with specific procedural information that included: (*a*) the fact that they would receive premedications in their rooms and what the effects would be; (*b*) the area of the hospital where the examination would be conducted; (*c*) the fact that their throats would be made numb by "painting" with medicine; (*d*) that they would receive a drug in an arm vein that would make them sleepy but leave them awake; (*e*) that the tube was the thickness of a thumb; and (*f*) patients usually did not find the examinations difficult. The group receiving the sensory-description information was presented with a tape message and a booklet of photographs describing each phase of the examination and sensations that might be experienced (e.g., needle stick, drowsiness, sensation of fullness, etc.). The group receiving the behavioral instructions were supplied with information regarding rapid mouth breathing and panting to reduce gagging during throat swabbing, instructions on how to act while the tube was being inserted, and practice in these behaviors. No photographs accompanied the taped messages describing the behavioral control techniques. Each of these two sets of information (i.e., procedural-sensory and procedural-behavioral) was manipulated independently and in combined format. Johnson and Leventhal (1974) reported that the combined sensory-procedural plus behavioral-instruction treatment was more effective than either given separately both in decreasing emotional behavior and in enhancing cooperation during the endoscopic examination. Each component separately proved to be better than the procedural information alone.

Similar results were obtained by Egbert *et al.* (1964) with surgery patients. Patients received information regarding physical relaxation, deep breathing exercises, and body maneuvers designed to make movement more comfortable during the postoperative period. This group was also provided with information about the procedures to be employed and the expected sensations. This cognitive–behavioral information group was compared with a group furnished with only procedural information. The patients receiving the combined treatment required smaller quantities of narcotics following surgery and were discharged earlier than the procedure-alone group. The procedure-alone group was consistently inferior at managing postoperative pain.

Another area in which preventative interventions have been implemented is childbirth (Bing, 1967; Chabon, 1966; Chertok, 1959; Doering & Entwisle, 1975; Wright, 1964). Perhaps the earliest consideration of this population was by Dick-Read (1959), who postulated that pain in childbirth was a function of anxiety and tension in an anxiety–tension–pain cycle. Dick-Read suggested that the reduction of anxiety by appropriate information and relaxation exercises would break the cycle and thereby "eliminate" pain in the labor and delivery process. Wright (1964) examined the antenatal preparation literature and identified 33 varieties of training. Common features underlying almost all of these include: information about labor and birth provided prior to delivery, some type of relaxation procedures, patterned breathing, and support from attendants during the deliver process.

In a typical study of prepared childbirth, Doering and Entwisle (1975) examined 279 women who received either no preparation, information but no specific behavioral coping techniques, or prepared childbirth, including both preparatory information and behavioral coping strategies (e.g., relaxation and controlled breathing). The data revealed a strong positive association between a mother's prior preparation and (a) her attitude toward her baby; and (b) a significant reduction in the amount of analgesic medication administered. No difference in attitude or in medication use was noted between the no-information and the procedural-sensory-information groups.

We must be cautious in drawing conclusions from such studies and from dependent measures like attitude and medication administered. It is quite possible that certain types of women not only seek such training but also in general tend to view childbirth more positively. Administration of analgesic medication may not be an accurate index of pain experienced, for there may be implicit demands placed on the mother to refuse medication. It is also quite possible that physicians and childbirth coaches may be more reluctant to offer medication to patients who have received antenatal training. We should note that the prepared childbirth approaches have not received unanimous support (e.g., Davenport-Slack & Boylan, 1974; Javert & Hardy, 1951), and efficacy may be related to factors other than training, such as menstrual difficulties (Tanzer, 1968). Even with these cautions, the voluminous literature on prepared childbirth generally documents the value of such combined cognitive–behavioral approaches (e.g., Chertok, 1959, 1969; Enkin, Smith, Derner, & Emmett, 1972; Huttel, Mitchel, Fisher, & Meyer, 1972; Tanzer, 1968; Velvovsky, Platanov, Ploticher, & Shugon, 1960).

Combined Approaches.   Some of the combined cognitive–behavioral control approaches with patients undergoing stressful medical procedures were discussed earlier (e.g., Johnson & Leventhal, 1974), when we examined the effects of different sorts of preparatory information. Several other comprehensive approaches merit our attention.

In a recent study, Kendall and his colleagues (Kendall, Williams, Pechacek,

Graham, Shisslak, & Herzoff, 1979) examined the relative efficacy of a regimen composed of cognitive and behavioral control strategies as compared to a patient education group (including procedural information), an attention placebo intervention group, and a no-treatment control group. The patients were all to undergo a particularly stressful cardiac catheterization procedure involving the insertion, into a vein in the groin of a small catheter that then advances into the heart. Through the catheters, physicians measure blood pressure in the heart chambers as well as visualize the main pumping chambers of the heart and of the coronary arteries.

The combined cognitive–behavioral treatment group in the Kendall *et al.* (1979) study were exposed to a series of procedures focused upon labeling the stress, identifying stress-related cues, discussing cognitive coping, reinforcing cognitive coping styles, cognitive rehearsal, and experimenter performing as a coping model. (The experimenter modeled not only coping strategies employed but also negative thoughts and aversive arousal and ways of coping with these as well as with the discomfort; for a discussion of coping versus mastery models, see Meichenbaum, 1973.) One point that deserves emphasis in the Kendall *et al.* approach is the encouragement and reinforcement of the patients' *own* cognitive coping strategies. No cognitive coping strategies were imposed upon the patients. The results of this study support the utility of such a comprehensive approach. The cognitive-behavioral treatment group demonstrated the highest rating of adjustment (rated by physicians and technicians) and the lowest levels of self-reported anxiety.

In the Langer *et al.* (1975) study of surgery patients described earlier, one group of subjects was provided with a combined treatment designed to reduce stress and to augment postsurgical recovery. Subjects in the combined group were trained to reappraise anxiety-provoking cues and events through presentation of a conceptualization of stress, by analogy to other stress situations, and by alteration of maladaptive internal monologues. Training in the use of attention-diverting cognitive-coping strategies was also included, as was sensory and procedural information. Subjects receiving this training were compared to groups receiving only procedural and sensory information, the combined treatment with the exclusion of the preparatory information, and no intervention. Both combined groups (with and without sensory information) demonstrated less pre- and postoperative stress than did the preparatory information alone group. The combined groups also requested less analgesic medication and fewer sedatives than either of the other two groups. We should, nevertheless, be cautious in our interpretations and generalizations, for the issue of control is quite complex, as was reviewed by Averill (1973).

The results we have reviewed underscore the complexity of preparatory communications and support the need for the development of differential forms of preparation. Not only must the individual's coping style be considered but also the amount and temporal spacing of advance information, the mode of presentation (e.g., audiotape, videotape, written format, or dialogue with significant other), as well as the content of the information. The hypothesis that information about sensations that might be experienced and procedures to be employed will result in reductions of distress and more adaptive recovery has received only equivocal support and has not been firmly established. The combination of such cognitive with behavioral techniques appears to be a more promising approach. Caution should be exercised before making generalizations to *all* contexts for *all* individuals. An appropriate set of questions to be considered is: What type of information, presented in what manner, when, by whom, in which situation, will reduce stress for which individuals? If these questions can be answered appropriately, it may be possible to intervene selectively with suitable communications designed to facilitate reappraisal of the situation as more benign, fostering more adaptive coping. The rather hackneyed plea for additional research must be made again.

Remedial Interventions

Up to this point, all of the studies reviewed have included the presentation of some form of information, either about the procedures to be employed, sensations that might be experienced, and/or cognitive and behavioral coping techniques prior to the onset of the nociceptive stimulation. Much less attention has been given to the use of cognitive and behavioral interventions as remedial strategies in acute situations, that is, situations of relatively brief nociceptive stimulation. Fagerhaugh (1974) described the operation of a burn unit in which information about procedures, sensations, and coping strategies was left to be presented informally by patients farther along in the course of recovery. She described the various types of coping strategies that patients recommended to each other. Although this informal patient support seems useful, it is unsystematic. Careful interviewing of patients leaving the ward, soliciting information about coping strategies employed would be most useful in the development of a more systematic approach to fostering adaptive coping. This area is conspicuous in its lack of investigation.

Chronic Pain and Discomfort

Chronic pain is characterized by long histories of unsuccessful treatments that may involve multiple surgeries and prescriptions for analgesic medication. The problem is often compounded by the presence of strong arousal, anxiety, depression, and disturbed interpersonal relations. Sternbach (1974) has labeled one subset of chronic pain patients as "low-back-pain losers." The defining characteristics of this group include complaint of back pain for over 6 months, inability to work, support by social security, welfare, or disability payments, and continued seeking of medical or surgical relief despite previous surgeries. For this review, we will operationally define chronic pain as being present if the patient has complained of pain for over 6 months.

Preventative Interventions

A wealth of data has been collected in the area of preventative intervention with chronic muscle-contraction and vascular headaches. Cognitive and behavioral interventions have focused upon prevention of the onset of headaches, rather than upon remediation of the headache once present.

Phenomenologically, a muscle-contraction (tension, nervous, psychogenic) headache is characterized by sensations of tightness and persistent band-like pain located bilaterally in the occipital and/or forehead region. A migraine headache is experienced as an aching, throbbing, unilateral pain often coincident with the pulse beat. Physicians tend to believe that the majority of headaches do not result from organic pathology but, rather, from stressful stimulation in combination with predisposing psychological and physiological characteristics. If this is the case, we might expect that employing various cognitive and behavioral techniques to reduce stressful stimulation would result in a reduction in the incidence of headaches.

A substantial body of literature has been compiled describing the relative efficacy of biofeedback techniques that use instrumentation to provide patients with information about changes in bodily functioning of which a person is usually not aware. The principles of biofeedback training are based upon laws of operant learning. First, the body function to be brought under control is defined and monitored with sufficient accuracy and sensitivity to detect reliably moment-to-moment changes in functioning. These changes are translated into some information that can be fed back to the patient immediately, usually in the form of visual signals or auditory tones. It is critical that the patient be motivated to learn to master these functions and to transfer the newly acquired skills into his natural environment.

Electromyogram (EMG) biofeedback has been successfully used to treat muscle-contraction headaches. In the first published investigation (Budzynski, Stoyva, & Adler, 1970), biofeedback was employed to train five patients suffering from muscle-contraction headaches to attain "deep levels of relaxation." The training was facilitated by providing the patients with a tone with a frequency proportional to the integrated EMG activity in the frontalis muscle. There was a steady decline in headache activity and EMG over the training period. Tension headaches were eliminated in two patients and were reduced markedly in another. For the other two patients, headaches returned shortly after the end of training. Reinstitution of home relaxation practice for both patients and additional feedback sessions for one led to cessation of headaches.

In a better-controlled study, Budzynski and his colleagues (Budzynski, Stoyva, Adler, & Mullaney, 1973) used three experimental conditions: frontalis EMG feedback, false feedback, and no feedback. Patients in the EMG feedback and false feedback groups received 16 sessions of biofeedback training followed by a 3-month follow-up. Only the group receiving the EMG feedback showed a consistent decline in headache activity, drug usage, and EMG levels.

Alpha feedback has also been used to treat muscle-contraction headaches. McKenzie, Ehrisman, Montgomery, and Barnes (1974) reported data on six chronic headache sufferers, all of whom benefited from 10 sessions of biofeedback training of alpha-frequency electroencephalograms (EEG). Concomitant neck and forehead EMGs were also recorded. Alpha production was readily produced across all patients and was correlated with a decrease in the frequency of headaches. Four patients displayed a reduction in at least one of the EMG measures, one patient showed no change, and another manifested an increase in the forehead measure.

All of the biofeedback studies reviewed required patients to practice the relaxation skills they acquired at home, usually twice a day. Most also suggested that the patients employ the skills whenever they noticed they were becoming tense, and in particularly stressful situations. Thus, these studies tend to confound the actual feedback training with relaxation skills.

Epstein, Hersen, and Hemphill (1974) reported on a single case with longstanding history of tension headaches that was treated with EMG feedback in a controlled single-subject experiment. In the first phases of this study, only EMG feedback was used as the mode of therapeutic intervention, with no home practice in relaxation. Using an ABAB design, both headache activity and session EMG activity were reduced during experimental phases and returned during the baseline. Further EMG feedback-training during outpatient follow-up also showed decreases in headache levels with a return of headaches to baseline. Institution of home practice in relaxation without further feedback led to a marked reduction in headache frequency. This case study isolated home practice as crucial to permanent reduction in headaches. We might question whether the EMG or alpha training employed in other studies was necessary or sufficient for producing a reduction in the incidence of headache activity.

In two studies (Cox, Freundlich, & Meyer, 1975; Haynes, Griffin, Mooney, & Parise, 1975), tension headache patients who received biofeedback training were compared with headache patients who received only relaxation training. In both of these studies, the patients receiving the biofeedback training reported significant reductions in headache activity; however, the relaxation training groups also reported significant reductions in the incidence of headaches, with no significant difference between the groups. In still another study, Tasto and Hinkle (1973) were able to demonstrate that relaxation by itself was successful in treating six patients suffering muscle-contraction headaches.

In a recent study, Holroyd, Andrasik, and Westbrook (1977) employed a combined therapeutic intervention that focused on altering maladaptive cognitive responses that were assumed to mediate the occurrence of muscle-contraction headaches. Patients were provided with a rationale for treatment, emphasizing the function of specifiable maladaptive cognitions in the creation of subsequent disturbing emotional and behavioral responses (based on Beck, 1976, and Meichenbaum, 1976). Patients were encouraged to attribute their headaches to relatively specific cognitive self-statements rather than to external or to complex internal dispositions. Lists of stressful situations were constructed, and patients were taught to focus on (a) the cues that trigger tension and anxiety; (b) how she responded when anxious; (c) thoughts prior to becoming tense and following such an episode; and (d) the way in which these cognitions contributed to the tension headaches. Following this sequence, patients were instructed to interrupt deliberately the sequence preceding their emotional response at the earliest possible point and to engage in cognitive control techniques incompatible with further stress and tension (e.g., cognitive reappraisal, attention deployment, fantasy).

This cognitive control regimen was employed with 10 tension headache patients, who were compared to patients receiving either biofeedback or no specific treatment. Training consisted of eight biweekly sessions, with a 15-week follow-up. At the termination of treatment and at follow-up, only the cognitive control group demonstrated substantial improvement in frequency, duration, and intensity of headaches. Interestingly, only the biofeedback group demonstrated significant reductions in electromyographic activity.

The Cox *et al.* (1975), Haynes, Moseley, and McGowen (1975), and Holroyd *et al.* (1977) studies tend to temper the current enthusiasm for biofeedback procedures with muscle-contraction headache patients. These data do not support the supposition that the training in reducing frontalis EMG or in production of alpha is necessary or sufficient to reduce the incidence of headache activity. The failure to find any relationship between EMG activity and tension headache activity in these studies raises questions about the etiological significance of the physiological variable, frontalis EMG (see also Epstein & Abel, 1977).

Although in general these behavioral and cognitive approaches (i.e., coping–stress training, relaxation, and biofeedback training) do seem to be able to reduce the incidence of headache activity, it is as yet unclear why they do. Perhaps, learning EMG-reduction fosters a sense of control, or, perhaps, increased relaxation through daily activities reduces prolonged muscle contraction. Other plausible explanations can be offered, for example, recognizing early headache onset may lead to a ''short-circuiting'' of muscle tension before it crystalizes into a headache, and focusing on physiological activity may distract attention from stressful events. Determination of the necessary and sufficient components of such interventions awaits additional empirical research. This does not diminish the utility of employing such interventions with patients who suffer from chronic headache conditions but underscores the number of components that may contribute to the effectiveness.

Biofeedback methodology has been employed to treat migraine as well as muscle-contraction headache. Sargent, Green, and Walters (1973) hypothesized that a voluntary increase in finger temperature is correlated with an increase in blood flow to the peripheral regions, with a concurrent decrease of blood flow to the cranial region. Since an increase in cranial blood flow is characteristic of migraine headaches, the authors combined finger temperature biofeedback with autogenic training in order to treat the condition. Autogenic training (Schultz & Luthe, 1959) involves the simultaneous regulation of mental and somatic functioning by mediating on passive activities (e.g., ''My mind is calm and quiet.''). On the basis of self-reports of the amount of analgesic medication used and frequency and intensity of headaches, plus independent clinical ratings, 74% of the patients were rated by the authors as having benefited from the biofeedback training. Similar results employing autogenic training and finger-temperature feedback have been reported by Mitch, McGrady, and Iannone (1976) and by Turin and Johnson (1976). In none of these studies did the investigators report finger temperature before or after training. Therefore, we cannot tell whether the temperature was lower than normal before treatment of migraine patients, whether it rose significantly during training, or whether a rise was maintained after treatment. The Sargent *et al.* (1973) and Mitch *et al.* (1976) studies do not permit us to evaluate the contribution of the biofeedback training separately from the autogenic training, nor can we determine the contribution of the practice of relaxation at home. Turin and Johnson (1976) did examine the contribution of the autogenic phases and concluded that they were not essential for the reduction of headache activity.

In a recent study, Kewman (1977) trained one group of migraine headache patients to raise their finger temperatures and a second group of patients to lower finger temperature, whereas a third group received no temperature training but self-monitored and recorded headache activity. Interestingly, all three groups showed significant decreases in headache activity. Obviously, the reduction in headache activity can not be attributed solely to the specific effects of temperature biofeedback training.

In another study, Andreychuk and Skriver (1975) compared biofeedback for handwarming, biofeedback for alpha enhancement, and self-hypnosis. All three of the treatment groups showed significant reductions in incidence of migraine headaches, with no significant differences between the groups. The Andreychuk and Skriver (1975) and Kewman (1977) studies advance the question of whether or not the biofeedback training is necessary for reducing migraine headache activity. It is also unclear why such variable physiological systems should be equally effective.

The emphasis of the biofeedback attacks on migraine have been aimed at maladaptive physiological functioning. We might stop at this point and consider some comments made 35 years ago by Wolff (1943). "The patient...must appreciate that anything out of a bottle can offer no more than transient help [in migraine]...the long term aim should be to help the individual understand the basis of his tension, the factors in his life that aggravate it, and aid him in resolving his conflicts [Wolff, 1943]." The efficacy of biofeedback training, assuming it produces some level of awareness of maladaptive physiological functioning, could benefit from Wolff's cogent comments. We might paraphrase Wolff and suggest that anything that comes from a machine will produce transient effects unless we also address treatment to life situations and to psychological variables. Indeed, some investigators have designed therapeutic interventions directed at both maladaptive life-style and physiological symptomatology.

Mitchell and Mitchell (1971) demonstrated that behavioral treatment programs that concentrate on several aspects of the migraine patient's life-style are more effective than programs that concentrate solely on the headache symptom. In the first of two experiments, Mitchell and Mitchell found that significantly greater relief from headache was achieved by a group that received a combination of muscle relaxation, desensitization, and assertive therapy than by a group that received training in muscle relaxation only. The second experiment found that the combined therapy was more effective than was systematic desensitization. In both experiments, relaxation training and systematic desensitization had negligible effects on headache frequency.

More recently, Mitchell and White (1977) employed a cognitive–behavioral therapeutic regimen with a migraine population. In this study, a sequential "dismantling'' strategy was employed (Romanczyk, Tracey, Wilson, & Thorpe, 1973). The complete cognitive–behavioral package was separated into four components, and the effect of each was assessed. Subsets of the initial group of patients received one, two, three, or all four of the components. That is, all patients began at the same point, receiving the first component of the treatment package. A subset of the initial group returned for the addition of the second component, a subset of this group returned for the presentation of the third, and, finally, a subset of these returned for the fourth and last phase of the treatment. In this manner, the contribution of each phase of the package can be assessed.

The four components employed by Mitchell and White consisted of: (a) self-recording of the frequency of migraine episodes; (b) self-monitoring of antecedent stress cues; (c) physical and mental relaxation and self-desensitization; and (d) 13 additional cognitive and behavioral control strategies (e.g., thought stopping, imaginal modeling, rational thinking). patients were treated in groups such that 12 patients received the self-recording component, 9 the self-recording and self-monitoring, 6 the self-recording, self-monitoring, physical and mental relaxation, and self-desensitization; and, finally, 3 received all four components. Patient contact was only once per component, with 12 weeks intervening between components. The majority of the training was conducted by a series of tapes that the patients listened to and practiced at home. After the 60 weeks of training (only four personal contacts between patients and trainer for the combined training group), a 3-month follow-up was conducted.

Mitchell and White (1977) reported that neither the self-recording nor self-monitoring produced substantive reductions in migraine episodes. Significant reduction in migraine frequency was displayed by both the groups that received three components; however, the group that received all four components significantly decreased migraine attacks at 60 weeks and at the 3-month follow-up relative to the group receiving one, two, or three components.

These studies suggest that training in cognitive and behavioral control strategies can help individuals to modify and to adapt more effectively to their environment. These treatments attempt to have patients reappraise situations previously perceived as unmanageable, tension producing, and beyond their control. The approach of Mitchell and his colleagues is designed to prevent or to short-circuit the development and onset of the headache, rather than specifically to cope with headaches once they have developed. In the Mitchell studies and the Holroyd et al. study described earlier, we can note the use of cognitive and behavioral-control strategies solely as preventive approaches. The point to note here is that, with many pain populations, a worthwhile goal of treatment is not only to teach techniques for enduring the noxious stimulation but also to foster approaches to altering environments that exacerbate the experience of pain.

The treatment employed by Mitchell and White (1977) is exciting, given the relative efficacy and cost-effectiveness of the approach. Patients were seen in groups and, at most, for four sessions with the trainer; the majority of the training was incorporated into a series of tapes. The automation of such packages deserves further attention if such therapeutic regimens are to be utilized by a variety of health providers who are unlikely to expend inordinate amounts of time with a small number of patients (e.g., Khatami & Rush, 1976).

Many of the combined approaches include not only cognitive and behavioral control but also decisional control—a choice among alternative actions (Averill, 1973). This might be contrasted with approaches that impose specific cognitive and behavioral coping strategies upon *all* patients.

Taken together, the clinical studies employing multifaceted cognitive–behavioral control strategies provide substantial evidence supporting the efficacy of such combined therapeutic regimens. Given the frequent lack of control groups and of single-case and small-group designs, this conclusion should be treated as somewhat tentative. However, the results are definitely encouraging, especially when compared to the equivocal results of the specific information approaches employed in many studies. Identifying the necessary and sufficient components of these combined approaches would seem to be the next step to take.

Remedial Interventions

The last area we will consider is the application of cognitive and behavioral interventions in chronic pain conditions.

The *sine qua non* of pain is that the patient somehow signifies to his world that he has a pain problem. The conventional view of pain described previously considers pain in stimulus–response terms. It is a respondent view of pain in which an antecedent stimulus elicits pain behavior. Pain has also been viewed from an operant-conditioning perspective. Operants are behaviors that are potentially subject to voluntary control. Operants are capable of being elicited by antecedent stimuli and are subject to influences by consequences. That is to say, when an operant is followed systematically by a reinforcing consequence, that operant will tend to increase; it will occur more frequently. When an operant that previously had been receiving systematic positive reinforcement is no longer followed by that reinforcement, its rate will subsequently diminish and perhaps be totally extinguished. The practical effect is that a person may display some operant behaviors because operants are being systematically reinforced, *not* because they are elicited by antecedent stimuli.

The operant approach to pain does not deal directly with pain *per se*, which is regarded as a private, subjective experience not lending itself to objective measurement or control. Rather, it focuses on an individual's maladaptive "pain behvior," such as decreased activity in areas of work, sex, and social endeavors, complaining, crying, and so forth, as the target of diagnosis and treatment.

The operant conditioning method of managing patients with chronic pain includes (*a*) identification and elimination of positive reinforcement of pain behavior; (*b*) increase in physical activity; and (*c*) gradual decrease in and eventual elimination of intake of analgesic and other drugs. To influence behavior through operant conditioning, the health professional must (*a*) identify the behaviors to be be produced, increased, maintained, eliminated, and diminished; (b) determine what kinds of reinforcement are likely to be effective for the individual; and (c) regulate the occurrences of reinforcement of the behaviors to be influenced.

The foremost proponents of the operant-conditioning approach to managing pain have been Fordyce and his colleagues (Fordyce, 1973, 1974, 1976; Fordyce, Fowler, Lehmann, DeLateur, Sand, & Trieschmann, 1973). For all the fervor generated for this operant conditioning approach by Fordyce and his colleagues, they have provided relatively little (albeit impressive) data.

In a study that illustrates this approach, Fordyce et al. (1968) systematically manipulated medication, attention, and rest as positive reinforcement for nonpain behavior in a 37-year-old female with an 18-year history of debilitating back pain. The operant treatment consisted of (a) providing medication on a time-contingent rather than a pain-contingent basis (i.e., at specific time intervals and not because the patient experienced and/or complained or pain); (b) providing social reinforcement (staff attention and praise) for nonpain behaviors, for example, increased ward activity, and extinguishing pain behavior such as moaning, grimacing, and inactivity; (c) providing social reinforcement for increased walking; and (d) providing programmed rest-periods as a reward for increased involvement in occupational therapy. From the report of Fordyce et al., we can note that no control procedures were followed.

Fordyce and his colleagues have published one larger-scale study (Fordyce et al., 1973) that deserves careful scrutiny. In this study, 36 chronic pain patients, who were referred to the Pain Clinic at the University of Washington over a 5-year period (1967–1971), were treated by the operant conditioning approach. Patients received from 4 to 12 weeks of inpatient treatment (mean = 7.7 weeks) and from 0 to 24 weeks of outpatient treatment (regular schedule in physical and occupational therapy). Thirty-one of the patients were followed up from 5 to 175 weeks (mean = 76.17 weeks) following termination of treatment. In addition to the inpatient and outpatient treatments, whenever possible the spouses of the patients received individual counseling in ignoring pain behavior and in reinforcing nonpain behavior.

The results reported note that the patients indicated significantly less pain at follow-up, less interference with daily activities, reductions in medication intake, and reductions in the amount of time spent reclining due to pain.

A number of concerns may be raised regarding the evidence for the efficacy of the operant approach as employed by Fordyce et al. (1973). No control procedures were employed; the length of the treatments varied for each of the patients, as well as the length of time to follow-up. Before inclusion in the program, each patient was interviewed by a psychiatrist, a psychologist, and a social worker. No information is provided concerning how many patients were rejected and for what reasons. It is possible that the 36 selected were a biased population, in which case generalization from this group might be questioned. The follow-up data was collected by questionnaire, with patients asked to report retrospectively how much pain they had experienced prior to treatment and at the time of follow-up, as well as how much their condition had interfered with their activities prior to treatment and at follow-up. Some question might be raised about the reliability of such retrospective reports (some of which were made over 3 years following treatment). Since no controls were employed, we cannot conclude from this study that the results obtained were a function of the operant conditioning methods. It is possible that one or more of the occupational or physical therapy procedures or the counseling of the spouse may have contributed to the results. Such concerns as these make statements regarding the effectiveness of treatments with chronic-pain patients difficult, if not impossible, to make. These criticisms are not intended to suggest that the operant approach may not be a valuable approach to remediation of chronic pain but only to indicate that the hypothesis has not been substantiated by this one study.

Recently, Anderson, Cole, Gullickson, Hudgens, and Roberts (1977) reported on the efficacy of the operant model at a different hospital setting (University of Minnesota). The therapeutic strategy was essentially identical to the program conducted by the Fordyce group. Anderson *et al.* reported that 74% (25 patients) of the patients completing the program, when contacted at follow-up, reported "leading normal lives without drugs" when they are contacted from 6 months to 7 years following discharge. The Anderson *et al.* (1977) paper is a descriptive report with no data presented concerning pretraining or posttraining subjective pain ratings, occupational activity, physical activity, and so on.

Particularly noteworthy in the Anderson *et al.* (1977) report are the criteria employed for inclusion or exclusion from treatment. The factors considered included whether or not:

1. the patient had significant behavior associated with pain that could be identified and probably modified
2. the patient and family were significantly motivated to undergo the pain treatment program
3. litigation was pending
4. all reasonable treatment modalities had been tried and were found unsuccessful or were otherwise ruled out
5. there was reference to the degree to which the patient could perform activities in the program without doing physiological harm
6. the patient lived with one or more people who were willing to actively participate in the program
7. a psychotic or severe psychiatric disorder was present
8. the staff could identify possible reinforcers that would be effective
9. chemical dependency was a primary problem.

Employing these criteria, 46% (60) of 130 patients referred for the program were accepted for treatment. Unfortunately, no breakdown of the number of patients excluded for any of the criteria is provided. Of the 60 patients accepted for treatment in the program, only 37 (29% of the original 130 patients) chose to enter, with 3 of these dropping out prior to completion. Thus, when Anderson *et al.* report that 74% of the patients treated were "leading normal lives," they are actually speaking of only 26 (19%) of the original patients screened over a 7-year period. Although the syndromes treated usually have been resistant to amelioration by other conventional procedures, we are still concerned about the number of patients included. Is this subgroup atypical of the chronic pain group? This issue needs clarification if, for no other reason, than to help in screening which patients should be admitted into such extensive and expensive treatment (8-week inpatient program).

In a controlled study designed to examine the contribution of operant conditioning on pain behavior, Cairns and Pasino (1977) employed an ABA design with a sample of 9 chronic back-pain patients. They included a control group that received equivalent amounts of occupational and physical therapy as two experimental groups. One of the experimental groups received verbal reinforcement for exercise activity, and the second was composed of two conditions: (a) daily performance activities plotted on charts over the patients beds; and (b) charts were supplemented by verbal reinforcement. The data show significant increases in exercise (walking and bike riding) under the verbal reinforcement and chart-plus-verbal-reinforcement conditions (condition b), as compared to patients' own baselines and levels obtained by the control group. These two groups also produced significantly more "up time" (time out of bed) when compared to the control group. The demonstrated extinction of effects upon the removal of reinforcement underscores the necessity of efforts to promote generalization. Although treatment increased activity, it appears that the increase would be only temporary unless the proper reinforcement contingencies were available in the natural environment. Thus, the inclusion of spouse in treatment, as noted by Fordyce et al. (1973), may be a necessary component of any operant approach. This study does reveal that pain behavior can be directly controlled by environmental consequences. But we should emphasize again that this is a tentative conclusion bases on only one controlled group study that included a relatively small number of patients (three per group), with no attempt to generalize to the natural environment. Optimism for this expensive approach seems to outweigh the available evidence.

Several variants on the Fordyce approach have recently appeared in the literature, with promising results (Cairns, Thomas, Mooney, & Pace, 1976; Seres & Newman, 1976; Sternbach, 1974; Swanson, Swenson, Maruta, & McPhee, 1976).

Cairns et al. (1976) added weekly patient groups to the operant approach. These groups were designed to identify sources of stress related to pain complaints and to discuss alternatives to a life style based on habits of disability. One hundred consecutive patients received this treatment intervention. Ninety of these were followed from 1 to 12 months following discharge. The results indicate that 70% of the patients reported significant reductions of pain, with 58% reporting a significant reduction of analgesic medications consumed.

The three other variants of operant approaches combined a variety of therapeutic modalities (e.g., biofeedback, transcutaneous electrical stimulation) with the group treatment described by Cairns et al. (1976). Swanson et al. (1976) reported that 54% of an original group of 50 patients demonstrated marked to moderate improvement with the combined treatment, approximately one-third dropping out before completion of the program. At follow-up, 50% of the patients from the original group had maintained or had increased improvement. The patients selected for this program received minimal initial screening, which may account for the large dropout rate. Again, it seems critical that efforts be made to examine for whom such approaches are most effective.

The therapeutic program employed by Sternbach (1974) was quite similar to that of Swanson *et al.* (1976). Sternbach reported follow-up data on 61 patients (representing 67% of the total patients completing his program) examined 6 months subsequent to discharge. The group reported significantly less pain than at the time of hospital admission, with some increase following discharge. Activity levels increased following treatment, again with some decrease noted at follow-up. Analgesic medication was significantly reduced at discharge and was maintained at follow-up. These results indicate that treatment effects were maintained reasonably well at follow-up of 6 months, although Sternbach did not consider the large proportion (one-third) of nonresponders to the follow-up questionnaire that might have represented treatment failures.

Given the intractability of many of the pain syndromes manifested by these patients, the results are quite impressive. It is difficult to assess the addition of the group treatment and other therapeutic modalities with the operant approaches. Cairns *et al.* (1976) indicated that they found that the group sessions were essential for building unified concepts from the various facets of the program. Thus, although an operant approach teaches the patient to increase his performance ability in a variety of functional activities while in the hospital, he must learn to apply the newly gained skills in the natural environment. Group discussion and supportive counseling may foster the desired generalization.

In addition to the operant approach of Fordyce and to the variants discussed, a variety of cognitive–behavioral, combined therapeutic regimens have been employed with chronic pain patients and with a number of pain syndromes (e.g., phantom-limb pain, osteoarthritis, fibrositis). We will review some of the approaches employed in order to illustrate the variety (see Cautela, 1977; Draspa, 1959; Heinrich & Fuller, 1975; Levendusky & Pankratz, 1975; Rybstein-Blinchik & Grzesiak, 1977 for still other approaches). A general statement that can be made about each of these regimens is that they tend to address not only the current pain but also environmental factors that may contribute to the distress.

In one approach (Khatami & Rush, 1976), a combined treatment focused on symptom control (employing biofeedback or relaxation), stimulus control (employing cognitive modification techniques based on Beck's, 1976, model to modify events, both overt and covert, that might precipitate or exacerbate pain), and social-system intervention employing family counseling (to alter the interpersonal reinforcements for pain and for nonpain behaviors; Fordyce, 1976). This approach has been employed with a realtively small number of patients (five) and, thus, should be considered as a preliminary effort requiring larger-scale empirical investigation.

Gottlieb, Strite, Koller, Madorsky, Hockersmith, Kleeman, and Wagner (1977) employed a combined treatment with a much larger number of patients (72). The patients treated in this study suffered from chronic back pain and had poor demographics (i.e., complaint of back pain had persisted for 6 months or more, patient was unable to work and was supported by social security, welfare, or disability payments, and, despite previous surgery, continued to seek medical or surgical relief; Sternbach's [1974] "low-back pain losers").

The training developed by Gottlieb *et al.* (1977) included the following elements: (*a*) biofeedback training for teaching self-regulated muscle relaxation; (*b*) psychological counseling emphasizing self-control techniques for management of stress and anxiety; (*c*) patient-regulated medication program (this might be contrasted with the "pain cocktail" approach employed by Fordyce, 1976, in which analgesic medication is combined with a flavored liquid with a gradual reduction of the active medication over the course of the operant treatment.); (*d*) patient-involved case conferences; (*e*) physical therapy program emphasizing reconditioning of muscles; (*f*) comprehensive vocational rehabilitation services; (*g*) a series of educational lectures about the relationship between stress and back pain; (*h*) a therapeutic milieu designed for maximum relaxation, recreation, and socialization; and (*i*) individual, group, and/or family therapy. Obviously, this is quite a comprehensive and expensive inpatient treatment program (mean hospitalization 45 days), but, given the refractory nature of the problem, such a "total" program may be required.

The poor prognosis of the low-back-pain patients treated by Gottlieb *et al.* (1977) makes the results most encouraging. Gottlieb *et al.* (1977) report that 79% of the patients demonstrated unimpaired physical functioning levels and 82% were at success levels (employable or in training) at discharge. At 6 months' followup, 82% of the 23 patients contacted were employed or were in some training program. Unfortunately, little information is provided concerning the other 49 patients who were treated.

Both the Khatami and Rush (1976) and the Gottlieb *et al.* (1977) studies are limited by the omission of control groups, but the lack of effective prior medical intervention and the magnitude of the changes support the utility of such combined cognitive–behavioral control approaches. As noted previously, we cannot determine from these studies what ingredients of the regimens are necessary and sufficient. Component analyses would seem appropriate to address this question.

Biofeedback methodology has been employed to ameliorate chronic pain in a limited number of studies. Unsystematic case studies reporting on the efficacy of biofeedback have been reported by Coger and Werbach (1975) and by Gentry and Bernal (1977).

Two studies have considered the use of biofeedback with groups of chronic pain patients of various etiologies. Hendler, Derogatis, Avella, and Long (1977) made the supposition that EMG frontalis feedback would be useful in reducing chronic pain, since it should lead to a reduction of tension and anxiety. Thirteen patients suffering from a variety of pain syndromes were treated with five sessions of EMG frontalis feedback. They report that 6 of the 13 patients subjectively reported that they experienced a reduction of pain following treatment. At a 1-month follow-up all 6 patients reported that "they were getting some relief." From this report, we can note that no control procedures were employed. No specific information is provided regarding the length of baseline or the initial levels of EMG. For that matter, no specific information is reported regarding the posttreatment of follow-up levels of frontalis EMG. However, Hendler *et al.* did report that no correlation was established between muscle tension and reduction of pain. This mitigates the conclusion that the biofeedback training was the instrument of pain reduction. The authors concluded that "the beneficial effects of biofeedback for these responders may be explained in terms of an increased sense of mastery over their environment, which resulted in a reduction of obsessive concerns about their somatic problems, and improvement in their self-esteem as a result of their increased environmental control [p. 508]." Even though this might be the case, we can ask whether the biofeedback approach employed, focused solely on maladaptive physiological functioning, is the most effective approach for increasing the sense of self-mastery.

We might note, parenthetically, that the 6 patients who reported receiving some benefit from the feedback training each purchased individual biofeedback machines at a cost of $425. This raises the ethical issue of manufacturers of such equipment selling this hardware with essentially no data to support the efficacy of using such devices.

In the second study examining the efficacy of biofeedback in the reduction of pain, Melzack and Perry (1975) compared the relative effects of alpha biofeedback, hypnotic training, and a combination of both alpha and hypnotic training. The hypnotic training focused on increasing relaxation, energy levels, mental calmness, and a reduction in the level of worry required prior to the patient's becoming upset. Six patients received either the alpha or self-hypnosis training alone, and 12 received the combined training. All three groups increased their levels of alpha. The group receiving both the alpha and hypnosis training and the group receiving only the hypnotic training demonstrated substantial reductions in pain compared to baseline. Patients receiving the alpha training alone showed virtually no change in pain. This study suggests that the cognitive approach of hypnosis may be effective in reducing pain from unbearable to bearable levels but provides no support for the efficacy of EEG alpha biofeedback training. As Melzack (1975) suggested in the title of his review of biofeedback approaches to reduce chronic pain, "Don't hold the party yet."

The studies reviewed do not yield consistent results. One cannot conclude from them as an aggregate that any component is an indispensable part of the treatment or is always the most effective component. One can only conclude that (*a*) behavioral control strategies are effective for some patients in certain settings; (*b*) cognitive control strategies alone are effective for some; and (*c*) most often, a combination of cognitive and behavioral control is efficacious. Although in such cases the relative effects are unclear, studies to date have dealt with diverse populations, a variety of interventions, and a wide array of research designs. Consequently, generalizations must be tentative.

In summary, combined cognitive–behavioral interventions do appear to hold much promise for the prevention and remediation of both acute and chronic pain syndromes and warrant consideration by clinicians prior to more invasive procedures of questionable value (e.g., surgery). Approaches that are directed specifically toward altering maladaptive responding to stress and stressful life styles, as well as symptomatic behaviors, would appear to be the most efficacious approaches.

SUMMARY AND CONCLUDING OBSERVATIONS

This chapter has reviewed the relative efficacy of cognitive and behavioral interventions as preventative and remedial approaches for both chronic and acute pain. We have covered many different approaches with a variety of nociceptive situations and conditions. Let us summarize the data examined.

1. Although the data do not unequivocally support the utility of providing patients with sensory or procedural preparatory communications prior to nociceptive stimulation, combined approaches that incorporate both cognitive and behavioral control information seem useful for prevention of distress, reduction of pain perception, and modification of pain responses in acute situations (i.e., aversive diagnostic and therapeutic medical and surgical procedures).

2. No data was found regarding the use of cognitive and behavioral approaches as remedial techniques for acute pain and distress. The work of Fagerhaugh (1974) on a burn unit suggests that this might be an area that would benefit from some systematic cognitive–behavioral intervention.

3. A number of cognitive and behavioral interventions designed to prevent the onset of chronic headaches were examined. There does seem to be sufficient evidence for the applicability of cognitive–behavioral treatments in this area, but it remains unclear which components of the various treatments are necessary and sufficient.

The contribution of biofeedback training, which has generated great enthusiasm among practitioners and the lay press, is not unequivocally established as either necessary or sufficient for reducing the incidence of migraine or of muscle-contraction headaches. The cognitive–behavioral approaches that did not rely on any feedback training appear to be at least as effective and are less costly.

4. Successful remediation of chronic pain has been reported by investigators employing biofeedback methodology, operant conditioning (Fordyce et al., 1968), and a number of multifaceted cognitive–behavioral approaches. The literature examining the efficacy of biofeedback is rather meager, despite the widespread optimism for such approaches. The ''pure'' operant conditioning, operant variants, and combined cognitive–behavioral approaches, although encouraging, are based on a handful of empirical studies that have sacrificed methodological rigor for clinical relevancy. Question was raised as to how biased the selected patient groups were and as to the applicability of such approaches on a wider scale. The operant variants that included some form of cognitive restructuring and alteration in life style and other cognitive–behavioral approaches in addition to the operant procedures described previously (Fordyce, 1976) seem particularly promising. These multifaceted ap-

proaches emphasize generality and transfer of skills to the natural environment. The approaches await additional controlled investigations and replications with other clinical syndromes.

Taken together, these studies provide a strong, albeit somewhat presumtive, case for the relative efficacy of multifaceted cognitive–behavioral therapeutic regimens. The necessary and sufficient components of the complex packages have not been established, but, as Mahoney (1974) suggests, first we need to demonstrate a significant effect, then we can proceed to component analyses. It appears to us that the time has come for the conduct of such component analyses, as well as for comparisons of the various treatments with a diversity of patient populations.

Cognitive and behavioral-control interventions appear to be much more complex than many investigators have assumed. Simply providing a group of patients with procedural–sensory information, a suggestion to employ cognitive or behavioral coping strategies, or specific training in the control of physiological processes does not appear to be sufficient in all situations and with all patients. Important parameters, such as content of the information, the mode of presentation (e.g., audio- or videotape, modeled, written, one-to-one, group presentation), characteristics of the presentor, temporal factors (i.e., the most appropriate time and frequency of presentation), the degree of threat perceived by the patient, long- and short-term consequences (beneficial or harmful), the actual and perceived effectiveness of the information, training, or skills acquired (cf. Averill, O'Brien, & DeWitt, 1977), individual differences in coping style, feelings of self-efficacy (Bandura, 1977) or self-confidence, and involvement of significant others, each require careful attention.

What this suggests is that, when developing and presenting cognitive and behavioral control techniques, the investigator or trainer must become much more attuned to the individual's internal dialogue about the coping procedures being suggested, as well as to the particular noxious situation.

One explanation for the equivocal data noted is that such information has been presented in a didactic fashion, with little attention given to how the information may be perceived. When developing therapeutic regimens, we might maximize the effectiveness of our approach by not treating our patients as passive recipients of information. Rather, we should consider our patients as active information processors who are continually assessing the situation, the information available, and the coping resources available and required for adaptive mastery. The patient should be considered as a valuable resource and ally. We are suggesting a collaborative effort between trainer (therapist) and patient for the "tailoring" of the therapeutic regimen to the individual in a given situation.

In this model, different situations and individuals will require different approaches. Some individuals may require minimal cognitive and behavioral-control information (e.g., Cohen & Lazarus, 1973; DeLong, 1971), some more extensive information (e.g., Janis, 1958), some reinforcement of already established coping skills (e.g., Kendall *et al.*, 1979) and still others additional coping skills training (e.g., Mitchell & White, 1977). The ability of all patients to benefit from such information should be assessed. If required, the inclusion of cognitive–behavioral rehearsals of coping strategies can be considered (e.g., Fortin & Kirouac, 1976; Langer *et al.*, 1975; Meichenbaum & Turk, 1976) in order to consolidate coping skills and to enhance feelings of self-mastery.

In short, attempting to alter the individual's appraisal of a stressful or threatening situation is quite a complex process, depending upon the individual, the situation, and the person–situation–intervention strategy interaction. This statement may lead the reader to conclude discouragingly that the development of cognitive-control therapeutic regimens is a futile effort destined to fail. However, the studies employing multifaceted cognitive–behavioral control approaches mitigate this conclusion. Studies such as those of Kendall *et al.* (1979), Gottlieb *et al.* (1977), and Turk (1975, 1978a), in which situational analyses are conducted and, which have involved patients and subjects as collaborators in the reappraisal process, have attended to internal dialogues, and have provided some degree of decisional control, suggest that the problems, however formidable, are not insurmountable. Tailoring the therapeutic regimen, at least to some extent, appears to be a feasible and productive approach. As we conduct more careful analyses of situations, of effective coping strategies, and of our patients' thinking processes, it does not seem unreasonable to consider the development of standard sets of therapeutic packages to be implemented with consideration of each individual's needs and requirements.

An important criterion for all of the interventions discussed is that the skills obtained must be transferred from the clinic or laboratory to the natural environment. Following training, the patients must become observers of their own behaviors, both overt and covert, and come to recognize the situational cues that are highly correlated with the occurrence of maladaptive responding. Recognition of the relationship of environmental factors and subsequent responding must lead the patients to attend to situational cues and to use them as discriminative stimuli for the production of more adaptive responding, that is, signals for the patient to "talk to himself differently" (Meichenbaum, 1973, 1977).

Let us consider an example. Suppose a patient with chronic tension headaches receives a course of training in the reduction of fontalis EMG in a clinical setting. This acquisition of skills is but a prerequisite for clinical improvement. The patient must come to recognize the situations and stimuli that result in excessive contraction of the muscles and either change the situation or his maladaptive physiological responding prior to the onset of the headache. Only in this manner will the training in the clinic generalize to external situations. Skills training in reducing frontalis EMG may be necessary, but it does not appear to be sufficient. Providing feedback training to gain control over specific physiological systems in the hope that the symptom will subsequently remain under control or disappear seems rather naive. There is no a priori reason to expect that enhancing control of autonomic responding will in and of itself prove to be efficacious if the etiology and maintenance of the maladaptive responding involves individual differences and environmental stress. The addition of cognitive restructuring would seem to be an essential component of such training. Although we have presented an example of biofeedback training, the contribution of the patient's internal dialogues, appraisals, and attributions should be addressed in any of the treatment interventions described above.

To reiterate, the implicit assumption in many of the studies that employ simple cognitive or behavioral control techniques is that all individuals in the various threat and stress situations manifest a "skills deficit." That is, all patients exposed to nociceptive stimulation lack some information or demonstrate some deficiency in their self-regulatory repertoires. Many investigators assume that, if these patients are simply provided with appropriate information or skills, adaptive coping will ensue, with a reduction in perception of pain and distress. The presence of such information and training may be necessary, but not sufficient. Not only must the patient have the appropriate skills and information available; he must also be motivated to and capable of producing these skills when the situation requires. A failure to produce these skills when they are present is likely related to the individual's internal dialogue, what they say to themselves about the situation or stimuli, the adequacy of the coping repertoire, belief in the ability to master the situation, and the necessity of having to use some form of coping strategy.

When we examine the different components comprising the various therapeutic regimens reviewed previously, it becomes apparent that a number of factors contribute to the efficacy of the approaches. Some of these include a strong suggestion that the procedures will be effective and, in many cases, provide distraction of attention from a particular body-site or stressful situation.

Important questions still remain to be answered. For example, which treatments will be effective for which subjects in which situations, and what components of the treatment packages are necessary and sufficient.

The efficacy of combined cognitive–behavioral control regimens leaves little doubt that pain can be profitably viewed as a modifiable aspect of human behavior. Given the failure of conventional medical treatments to attenuate pain satisfactorily and consistently, cognitive–behavioral approaches appear to offer a most pragmatic addition to the pain management armamentarium as adjuncts or alternatives to conventional treatments.

REFERENCE NOTES

1. Chapman, C. R. *A behavioral perspective on chronic pain.* Paper presented at the Annual Convention of the American Psychological Association, Montreal, Canada, 1973.
2. Fuller, S. S., Endress, M. P., & Johnson, J. E. *Control and coping with an aversive health examination.* Paper presented at the annual meeting of the American Psychological Association, San Francisco, 1977.
3. Johnson, J. E., Rice, V. H., Fuller, S. S., & Endress, P. *Sensory information, behavioral instruction, and recovery from surgery.* Paper presented at annual meeting of the American Psychological Association, San Francisco, 1977.
4. Khatami, M., & Rush, A. J. *A pilot study of the treatment of out-patients with chronic pain: Symptom control, stimulus control, and social system intervention.* Paper presented at the annual meeting of the Association for the Advancement of Behavior Therapy, New York, 1976.

5. Heinrich, R., & Fuller, M. *Control and modulation of pain in selective pain patients by a guided affective imagery technique.* Paper presented at the First World Congress on Pain, Florence, Italy, 1975.
6. Rybstein-Blinchik, E., & Grzesiak, R. C. *Cognitive strategies in the treatment of chronic pain: A preliminary study.* Paper presented at the annual meeting of the Association for the Advancement of Behavior Therapy, Atlanta, 1977.

REFERENCES

Anderson, T. P., Cole, T. M., Gullickson, G., Hudgens, A., & Roberts, A. H. Behavior modification of chronic pain: A treatment program by a multidisciplinary team. *Journal of Clinical Orthopedics, 1977, 129,* 96-100.

Andrew, J. M. Recovery from surgery, with and without preparatory instruction, for three coping styles. *Journal of Personality and Social Psychology, 1970, 15,* 223-226.

Andreychuk, T., & Skriver, C. Hypnosis and biofeedback in the treatment of migraine headache. *International Journal of Clinical Experimental Hypnosis, 1975, 23,* 172-183.

Auerbach, S. M., Kendall, P. C., Cuttler, H. F., & Levitt, R. Anxiety, locus of control, type of preparatory information and adjustment to dental surgery. *Journal of Consulting and Clinical Psychology, 1976, 44,* 809-818.

Averill, J. R. Personal control over aversive stimuli and its relationship to stress. *Psychological Bulletin, 1973, 80,* 286-303.

Averill, J. R., O'Brien, L., & DeWitt, G. The influence of response effectiveness on the preference for warning and on psychophysical stress reaction. *Journal of Personality, 1977, 45,* 395-418.

Bandura, A. Self-efficacy: Toward a unified theory of behavioral change. *Psychological Review, 1977, 89,* 191-215.

Barber, T. X. Toward a theory of pain: Relief of chronic pain by prefrontal leucotomy, opiates, placebos, and hypnosis. *Psychological Bulletin, 1959, 56.* 430-460.

Beck, A. T. *Cognitive therapy and the emotional disorders.* New York: International University Press, Inc., 1976.

Beecher, H. K. *Measurement of subjective responses: Quantitative effects of drugs.* New York: Oxford University Press, 1959.

Beecher, H. K. Pain: One mystery solved. *Science, 1966, 151,* 840-841.

Bing, E. *Six practical lessons for an easier childbirth.* New York: Grosset and Dunlap, 1967.

Bonica, J. J. *The management of pain.* Philadelphia: Lea, 1953.

Bonica, J. J. Preface. In J. J. Bonica (Ed.), *Advances in neurology, Volume 4.* New York: Raven Press, 1974.

Budzynski, T. H., Stoyva, J. M., & Adler, C. S. Feedback-induced muscle relaxation: Application to tension headache. *Journal of Behavior Therapy and Experimental Psychiatry, 1970, 1,* 205-211.

Budzynski, T. H., Stoyva, J. M., Adler, C. S., & Mullaney, D. J. EMG biofeedback and tension headache: A controlled outcome study. *Psychosomatic Medicine, 1973, 6,* 509-514.

Cairns, D., & Pasino, J. A. Comparison of verbal reinforcement and feedback in the operant treatment of disability due to chronic low back pain. *Behavior Therapy, 1977, 8,* 621-630.

Cairns, D., Thomas, L., Mooney, V., & Pace, J. B. A comprehensive treatment approach to chronic low back pain. *Pain, 1976, 2,* 301-308.

Cattell, M. The action and use of analgesics. *Research Publication of the Association of Neurological and Mental Disease, 1943, 23,* 365-372.

Cautela, J. R. The use of covert conditioning in modifying pain behavior. *Journal of Behavior Therapy and Experimental Psychiatry, 1977, 8,* 45-52.

Chabon, I. *Awake and aware.* New York: Delacorte, 1966.

Chertok, L. *Psychosomatic methods in painless childbirth.* New York: Pergamon, 1959.

Chertok, L. *Motherhood and personality: Psychosomatic aspects of childbirth.* Philadelphia: Lippincott, 1969.

Coger, R., & Werbach, M. Attention, anxiety, and the effects of learned enhancement of EEG in chronic pain: A pilot study in biofeedback. In B. L. Crue, Jr., (Ed.), *Pain: Research and treatment.* New York: Academic Press, 1975.

Cohen, F., & Lazarus, R. S. Active coping processes, coping disposition, and recovery from surgery. *Psychosomatic Medicine,* 1973, *35,* 375–389.

Cox, D. J., Freundlich, A., & Meyer, R. G. Differential effectiveness of electromyograph feedback, verbal relaxation instructions, and medication placebo with tension headaches. *Journal of Consulting and Clinical Psychology,* 1975, *43,* 892–898.

Davenport-Slack, B., & Boylan, C. H. Psychological correlates of childbirth pain. *Psychosomatic Medicine,* 1974, *36,* 215–223.

DeLong, R. D. Individual differences in patterns of anxiety arousal, stress-relevant information, and recovery from surgery. *Dissertation Abstracts International,* 1971, *32*(3), 554.

Dick-Read, G. *Childbirth without fear: The principles and practices of natural childbirth.* (Second edition, revised) New York: Harper & Row, 1959.

Doering, S. G., & Entwisle, D. R. Preparation during pregnancy and ability to cope with labor and delivery. *American Journal of Orthopsychiatry,* 1975, *45,* 825–837.

Draspa, L. J. Psychological factors in muscular pain. *British Journal of Medical Psychology,* 1959, *32,* 106–116.

Egbert, L., Battit, G., Welch, C., & Bartletts, M. Reduction of postoperative pain by encouragement and instruction. *New England Journal of Medicine,* 1964, *270,* 825–827.

Enkin, M. W., Smith, S. L., Dermer, S. W., & Emmett, J. O. An adequately controlled study of the effectiveness of PPM training. In N. Morris (Ed.), *Psychosomatic medicine in obstetrics and gynecology.* Basel: Steiner, 1972.

Epstein, L. H., & Abel, G. G. An analysis of biofeedback training effects for tension headache patients. *Behavior Therapy,* 1977, *8,* 37–47.

Epstein, L. H., Hersen, M., & Hemphill, D. P. Music feedback in the treatment of tension headache: An experimental case study. *Journal of Behavior Therapy and Experimental Psychiatry,* 1974, *5,* 59–63.

Fagerhaugh, S. Y. Pain expression and control on a burn care unit. *Nursing Outlook,* 1974, *22,* 645–650.

Fiajalkowski, W. Current trends in psychoprophylaxis of pregnancy and labor. *Polish Medical Journal,* 1969, *8,* 768.

Fordyce, W. E. An operant conditioning method for managing chronic pain. *Postgraduate Medicine,* 1973, *53,* 123–128.

Fordyce, W. E. Chronic pain as learned behavior. In J. J. Bonica (Ed.), *Advances in Neurology, Volume 4.* New York: Raven Press, 1974.

Fordyce, W. E. Behavioral concepts in chronic pain and illness. In P. O. Davidson (Ed.), *The behavioral management of anxiety, depression, and pain.* New York: Brunner/Mazel, 1976.

Fordyce, W. E., Fowler, R., Lehmann, J., & DeLateur, B. Some implications of learning in problems of chronic pain. *Journal of Chronic Diseases,* 1968, *21,* 179–190.

Fordyce, W. E., Fowler, R., Lehmann, J., DeLateur, B., Sand, P., & Trieschmann, R. Operant conditioning in the treatment of chronic pain. *Archives of Physical Medicine,* 1973, *54,* 399–408.

Fortin, F., & Kirouac, S. A randomized controlled trial of preoperative patient education. *International Journal of Nursing Studies,* 1976, *13,* 11–24.

Gentry, W. D., & Bernal, G. A. Chronic pain. In R. B. Williams and W. D. Gentry (Eds.), *Behavioral approaches to medical treatment.* Cambridge, Massachusetts: Ballinger Publishing Company, 1977.

Gottlieb, H., Strite, L., Koller, R., Madorsky, A., Hockersmith, V., Kleeman, M., & Wagner, J. Comprehensive rehabilitation of patients having chronic low back pain. *Archives of Physical Medicine and Rehabilitation,* 1977, *58,* 101–108.

Haggard, H. W. *Devils, drugs, and doctors*. New York: Harper, 1929.

Haynes, S. N., Griffin, P., Mooney, B., & Parise, M. Electromyographic biofeedback and relaxation instructions in the treatment of muscle contraction headaches. *Behavior Therapy*, 1975, *6*, 672-678. (a)

Haynes, S. N., Moseley, D., & McGowen, W. T. Relaxation training and biofeedback in the reduction of frontalis muscle tension. *Psychophysiology*, 1975, *12*, 547-552. (b)

Hendler, N., Derogatis, L., Avella, J., & Long, D. EMG biofeedback in patients with chronic pain. *Diseases of the Nervous System*, 1977, *38*, 505-514.

Hilgard, E. K., & Hilgard, J. K. *Hypnosis in the relief of pain*. Los Altos, California: William Kaufman, Inc., 1975.

Hill, H., Kornetsky, C., Flanary, H., & Wikler, A. Effects of anxiety and morphine on discrimination of painful stimuli. *Journal of Clinical Investigation*, 1952, *31*, 473. (a)

Hill, H., Kornetsky, C., Flanary, H., & Wilker, A. Studies on anxiety associated with anticipation of pain. I. Effects of morphine. *Archives of Neurology and Psychiatry*, 1952, *67*, 612-619. (b)

Holroyd, K. A., Andrasik, F., & Westbrook, T. Cognitive control of tension headache. *Cognitive Therapy and Research*, 1977, *1*, 121-134.

Huttel, F. A., Mitchell, I., Fischer, W. M., & Meyer, A. E. A quantitative evaluation of psychoprophylaxis in childbirth. *Journal of Psychosomatic Research*, 1972, *16*, 81.

Janis, I. *Psychological stress*. New York: John Wiley & Sons, 1958.

Javert, C. T., & Hardy, J. D. Influence of analgesia on pain intensity during labor (''with a note on natural childbirth''). *Anesthesiology*, 1951, *12*, 189-215.

Johnson, J. E. Effects of accurate expectations about sensations on the sensory and distress components of pain. *Journal of Personality and Social Psychology*, 1973, *27*, 261-275.

Johnson, J. E. Stress reduction through sensation information. In I. G. Sarason & C. D. Spielberger (Eds.), *Stress and anxiety, Volume 2*. New York: John Wiley & Sons, 1975.

Johnson, J. E., & Leventhal, H. The effects of accurate expectations and behavioral instructions on reactions during noxious medical examination. *Journal of Personality and Social Psychology*, 1974, *29*, 710-718.

Johnson, J. E., Morrissey, J. F., & Leventhal, H. Psychological preparation for endoscopic examination. *Gastrointestinal Endoscopy*, 1973, *19*, 180-182.

Johnson, J. E., & Rice, V. H. Sensory and distress components of pain: Implications for the study of clinical pain. *Nursing Research*, 1974, *23*, 203-209.

Kendall, P., Williams, L., Pechacek, T. F., Graham, L. E., Shisslak, C., & Herzoff, N. The Palo Alto medical psychology project: Cognitive–behavioral patient education interventions in catheterization procedures. *Journal of Consulting and Clinical Psychology*, 1979, *47*, 49-58.

Kerr, F. W. L. Pain: A central inhibitory balance theory. *Mayo Clinic Proceedings*, 1975, *50*, 685-690.

Kewman, D. C. *Voluntary control of digital skin temperature for treatment of migraine headaches*. Unpublished doctoral dissertation, University of Texas, 1977.

Langer, E., Janis, I., & Wolfer, J. Reduction of psychological stress in surgical patients. *Journal of Experimental Social Psychology*, 1975, *1*, 155-166.

Lazarus, R. S. *Psychological stress and the coping process*. New York: McGraw-Hill, 1966.

Levendusky, P., & Pankratz, L. Self-control techniques as an alternative to pain medication. *Journal of Abnormal Psychology*, 1975, *84*, 165-169.

Leventhal, H., Singer, R. E., & Jones, S. Effects of fear and specificity of recommendations. *Journal of Personality and Social Psychology*, 1965, *2*, 20-29.

Leventhal, H., & Watts, J. C. Sources of resistance to fear arousing communications on smoking and lung cancer. *Journal of Personality*, 1966, *34*, 155-175.

Lindeman, C. A. Nursing intervention with the presurgical patient: The effectiveness and efficiency of group and individual preoperative teaching. *Nursing Research*, 1972, *21*, 196-209.

Lindeman, C. A.. & Van Aernam, B. Nursing intervention with the presurgical patient: The effects of structured and unstructured teaching. *Nursing Research*, 1971, *20*, 319-332.

Mahoney, M. J. *Cognition and behavior modification*. Cambridge, Massachusetts: Ballinger Publishing Company, 1974.

McKenzie, R. E., Ehrisman, W. J., Montgomery, P. S., & Barnes, R. H. The treatment of headache by means of electroencephalographic biofeedback. *Headache*, 1974, *13*, 164–172.

Meichenbaum, D. H. Cognitive factors in behavior modification: Modifying what clients say to themselves. In C. Franks & T. Wilson (Eds.), *Annual review of behavior therapy: Theory and practice*. New York: Brunner/Mazel, 1973.

Meichenbaum, D. H. Toward a cognitive theory of self-control. In G. Schwartz & D. Shapiro (Eds.), *Consciousness and self-regulation, Volume 1*. New York: Plenum Publishing Company, 1976.

Meichenbaum, D. H. *Cognition and behavior modification: An integrative approach*. New York: Plenum Publishing Company, 1977.

Meichenbaum, D. H., & Turk, D. C. The cognitive–behavioral management of anxiety, anger, and pain. In P. O. Davidson (Ed.), *The behavioral management of anxiety, depression and pain*. New York: Brunner/Mazel, 1976.

Melamed, B. G., & Siegel, L. J. Reduction of anxiety in children facing hospitalization and surgery by use of filmed modeling. *Journal of Consulting and Clinical Psychology*, 1975, *43*, 511–521.

Melzack, R. The promise of biofeedback: Don't hold the party yet. *Psychology Today*, 1975, *9*, 18–22.

Melzack, R., & Casey, K. L. Sensory, motivational, and central control determinants of pain: A new conceptual model. In D. K. Kenshalo (Ed.), *The skin senses*. Springfield, Illinois: Charles C. Thomas, 1968.

Melzack, R., & Perry, C. Self-regulation of pain: The use of alpha-feedback and hypnotic training for the control of chronic pain. *Experimental Neurology*, 1975, *46*, 452–464. '

Melzack, R., & Wall, P. D. Pain mechanisms: A new theory. *Science*, 1965, *150*, 971.

Melzack, R., & Wall, P. D. Psychophysiology of pain. *The International Anesthesiology Clinics*, 1970, *8*, 3–34.

Mitch, P. S., McGrady, A., & Iannone. A. Autogenic feedback training in migraine: A treatment report. *Headache*, 1976, *15*, 267–270.

Mitchell, K. R., & Mitchell, D. M. Migraine: An exploratory treatment application of programmed behavior therapy techniques. *Journal of Psychosomatic Research*, 1971, *15*, 137–157.

Mitchell, K. R., & White, R. G. Behavioral self-management: An application to the problem of migraine headaches. *Behavior Therapy*, 1977, *8*, 213–222.

Nathan, P. W. The gate-control theory of pain: A critical review. *Brain*, 1976, *99*, 123–158.

Romanczyk, R. G., Tracey, D. A., Wilson, G. T., & Thorpe, G. L. Behavioral techniques in the treatment of obesity. *Behavior Research and Therapy*, 1973, *22*, 629–640.

Rotter, J. B. Generalized expectancies for internal versus external control of reinforcement. *Psychological Monographs: General and Applied*, 1966, *80*(whole no. 609).

Sargent, J. D., Green, E. E., & Walters, E. D. Preliminary report on the use of autogenic feedback training in the treatment of migraine and tension headaches. *Psychosomatic Medicine*, 1973, *35*, 129–135.

Schmitt, F. E., & Wooldridge, P. J. Psychological preparation of surgical patients. *Nursing Research*, 1973, *22*, 108–116.

Schultz, J. H., & Luthe, W. *Autogenic therapy, Volume 1*. New York: Grune and Stratton, 1959.

Seres, J. L., & Newman, R. I. Results of treatment of chronic low-back pain at the Portland Pain Center. *Journal of Neurosurgery*, 1976, *45*, 32–36.

Shapiro, A. K. Psychological aspects of medication. In H. I. Lief, V. F. Lief, & N. R. Lief (Eds.), *The psychological basis of medical practice*. New York: Harper & Row, 1963.

Shor, R. Physiological effects of painful stimulation during hypnotic analgesia under conditions designed to minimize anxiety. *International Journal of Clinical and Experimental Hypnosis*, 1962, *10*, 183–202.

Skipper, J. R. Jr., & Leonard, R. C. Children, stress, and hospitalization: A field study experiment. *Journal of Health and Social Behavior*, 1968, *9*, 275–287.

Staub, E., & Kellett, D. Increasing pain tolerance by information about aversive stimuli. *Journal of Personality and Social Psychology*, 1972, *21*, 198–203.

Sternbach, R. *Pain patients: Traits and treatment*. New York: Academic Press, 1974.

Swanson, D. W., Swenson, W., Maruta, T., & McPhee, M. C. Program for managing pain. 1. Program descriptions and characteristics of patients. *Proceedings of the Mayo Clinic*, 1976, *51*, 401–408.

Tanzer, D. Natural childbirth: Pain or peak experience. *Psychology Today*, 1968, *2*, 17–21.

Tasto, D. L., & Hinkle, J. E. Muscle relaxation treatment for tension headaches. *Behavior Research and Therapy*, 1973, *11*, 347–349.

Toomey, T., Ghia, J. N., Mao, W., & Gregg, J. M. Acupuncture and chronic pain mechanisms: The moderating effects of affect, personality, and stress on response to treatment. *Pain*, 1977, *3*, 137–145.

Turin, A., & Johnson, W. G. Biofeedback therapy for migraine headache. *Archives of General Psychiatry*, 1976, *33*, 517–519.

Turk, D. C. *Cognitive control of pain: A skills-training approach*. Unpublished master's thesis, University of Waterloo, Waterloo, Ontario, Canada, 1975.

Turk, D. C. *A coping skills-training approach for the control of experimentally produced pain*. Unpublished doctoral dissertation, University of Waterloo, Waterloo, Ontario, Canada, 1978. (a)

Turk, D. C. Cognitive–behavioral techniques in the management of pain. In J. P. Foreyt & D. J. Rathgen (Eds.), *Cognitive behavior therapy: Research and application*. New York: Plenum Publishing Company, 1978. (b)

Turk, D. C. Coping with pain: A review of cognitive control techniques. In M. Feuerstein, L. B. Sachs, & I. D. Turkat (Eds.), *Psychological approaches to pain control*. New York: Wiley-Interscience, in press.

Tursky, B. Laboratory approaches to the study of pain. In D. I. Mostofsky (Ed.), *Behavioral control and modification of physiological activity*. Englewood Cliffs, New Jersey: Prentice-Hall, Inc., 1976.

Velvovsky, I., Platonov, K., Ploticher, V., & Shugon, E. *Painless childbirth through psychoprophylaxis*. Moscow: Foreign Langues Publishing House, 1960.

Vernon, D. T. A., & Bailey, W. C. The use of motion pictures in the psychological preparation of children for induction of anesthesia. *Anesthesiology*, 1972, *210*, 68–72.

Vernon, D. T. A., & Bigelow, D. A. The effect of information about a potentially stressful situation on responses to stress impact. *Journal of Personality and Social Psychology*, 1974, *29*, 50–59.

Williams, J. G. L., Jones, J. K., Workhoven, M. N., & Williams, B. The psychological control of preoperative anxiety. *Psychophysiology*, 1975, *12*, 50–54.

Wolfer, J. A., & Visintainer, M. A. Pediatric surgical patients' and parents' stress responses and adjustment as a function of psychologic preparation and stress-point nursing care. *Nursing Research*, 1975, *24*, 244–255.

Wolff, H. G. *Headache and other pain*. New York: Oxford University Press, 1943.

Wright, E. *The new childbirth*. London: Tandem Publishing Co., Ltd., 1964.

10

Alcohol Use and Problem Drinking: A Cognitive–Behavioral Analysis

G. ALAN MARLATT

THE GREAT ALCOHOLISM CONTROVERSY

According to recent surveys, approximately two-thirds (68%) of the adult American population consumes alcohol on at least some occasions. Survey statistics reveal that, of all individuals who drink, about 12% can be classified as heavy drinkers (21% of adult males and 5% of adult females). Heavy drinkers may be defined as those who drink on a daily basis or who consume relatively large amounts of alcohol on an intermittent basis. The remainder of the adult population can be classified as abstainers (32%) or as light to moderate social drinkers (56%). Among the heavy drinkers, a subset of individuals can be described as experiencing difficulties with their drinking, varying in degree of severity from *problem drinking* (drinking that is associated with one or more serious life problems) to *alcoholism* (compulsive, habitual, or addictive drinking that poses a serious threat to the individual's health and well-being). Estimates of the number of alcoholics in this country vary, with most figures falling somewhere between 5 and 15 million people. The statistics presented here are general ones, since drinking patterns vary considerably as a function of many other factors including age, sex, socioeconomic background, racial heritage, religious orientation, and place of residence. The interested reader is referred to recent surveys of American drinking practices (Cahalan, Cisin, & Crossley, 1969; Cahalan & Room, 1974) for further information. The federal government has also issued a series of reports that summarize ongoing research on patterns of drinking behavior, the effects of alcohol on health, and treatment approaches (National Institute on Alcohol Abuse and Alcoholism, 1971, 1974, 1978).

Cognitive–Behavioral Interventions:
Theory, Research, and Procedures

Considerable controversy exists concerning the development and nature of alcohol abuse problems. On the one hand, the prevailing contemporary view is that alcoholism is a disease and that alcoholics are individuals who are distinctly different from social drinkers in some way. Although the causes of alcoholism have yet to be specified on the basis of scientific research, those who favor the disease model assume that it is only a matter of time before research will uncover the constitutional or genetic factors that differentiate the alcoholic from the social drinker. Adherents of the disease theory (Jellinek, 1960; Keller, 1976) firmly believe that there is one and only one acceptable treatment goal for all alcoholics: total abstinence.

On the other hand, there is a small but increasingly vocal group of theorists who believe that alcohol consumption is a learned behavior and that a normally distributed continuum of drinking behavior exists in the population, ranging from light or infrequent consumption on the one end to heavy and problematic drinking on the other. Rather than defining excessive alcohol abuse as a disease "ism," adherents of this alternative model believe that drinking behaviors are acquired on the basis of social learning principles and that changes in drinking patterns can be brought about by the application of behavioral technology and procedures. Proponents of this view agree that there are legitimate alternatives to abstinence as a treatment goal, including the possibility of teaching problem drinkers skills that would enable them to become "controlled" drinkers. The very mention of controlled drinking as a viable alternative treatment goal for alcoholism is viewed as heresy by those who adopt the disease model. This controversy has become increasingly heated in recent years. In order to understand better the issues involved, let us examine the basic assumptions and treatment implications of these two opposing approaches in greater detail.

Alcoholism as a Disease

The concept of alcoholism as a disease was first advocated in its most detailed form by Jellinek (1960), one of the early pioneers of alcoholism studies in the United States. Prior to the introduction of the disease model, alcohol abuse was frequently viewed as a moral weakness, and attempts to deal with the problem were prompted by religious ideology that eventually led to the unsuccessful social experiment of prohibition. The disease model was successful in elevating the status of alcoholism from a moral issue to a medical problem, and individuals were encouraged to seek professional treatment for their drinking problems. Jellinek and others of similar persuasion provided convincing arguments that alcoholism was, indeed, an addictive disease, with its causes rooted deeply in the physiology of the body. Several physiological and biochemical theories have been advanced to account for the constitutional underpinnings of alcoholism, ranging from a physical allergic reaction to disorders in the brain's regulatory functions (Tarter & Sugerman, 1976), yet to date none of these theories has been clearly supported by empirical evidence or research (National Institute of Alcohol Abuse and Alcoholism, 1978). Advocates of the disease model firmly believe, however, that evidence will someday support the notion that the alcoholic is somehow "different" from his social drinking counterpart and that this difference is biochemical in nature. Recently, the idea that this biochemical factor may be determined on the basis of genetic differences has led to the notion that some people may be predisposed toward developing this disorder on the basis of their family backgrounds (cf. Goodwin, 1976).

Despite the lack of firm empirical evidence for the basic underlying cause of the disease, those who adopt the disease model are in strong agreement concerning the primary or pathognomonic symptom of alcoholism: loss of control drinking. Stated in its simplest form, loss of control drinking is said to occur whenever the alcoholic takes the first one or two drinks; the presence of alcohol in the bloodstream is thought to trigger off a physiological addictive mechanism that is experienced subjectively by the drinker as an irresistible craving for alcohol. Since the drinker is apparently powerless to control this intense craving or need for alcohol, he/she is driven to continue drinking until the point of intoxication is reached. In the words of Jellinek, "Loss of control means that as soon as a small quantity of alcohol enters the organism, a demand for more alcohol is set up which is felt as a physical demand by the drinker . . . the loss of control is effective after the individual has started drinking, but it does not give rise to the beginning of a new drinking bout [1952, p. 679]."

The symptom of loss of control drinking fulfills most of the criteria for a key "symptom" of an underlying "disease" entity: Just as a fever is often interpreted as a symptom of an underlying physiological disorder, loss of control drinking is viewed as an *involuntary* manifestation of an internal addictive disorder. The role of cognitive or other psychological factors is all but totally ignored in this analysis. The alcoholic cannot voluntarily control his or her consumption of alcohol, according to this position. Even the "dry" alcoholic is never free from this compulsive reaction: It is assumed that loss of control drinking will be triggered by the effects of alcohol even for those alcoholics who have been free from alcohol for periods of months or even years. Loss of control drinking is the behavioral manifestation that differentiates alcoholics and social drinkers, a predisposition that remains latent as long as the individual does not take a drink but that can become activated at any time through the triggering effects of alcohol. Loss of control is considered by Jellinek to be one of the defining characteristics of "gamma alcoholism" (binge or spree drinking), considered by him to be the predominant form of alcoholism in America.

According to this perspective, there is no such thing as the "cured" or recovered alcoholic: The disease is always waiting in the wings, ready to pounce on its victim as soon as any drinking is resumed. It is not difficult to see why total abstinence is considered to be the *sine qua non* of alcoholism treatment, given this theoretical framework. The slogans promoted by adherents of the disease approach strongly echo this sentiment: "Once an alcoholic, always an alcoholic"; "One drink away from a drunk"; etc. The fervent insistence upon abstinence as the only acceptable goal for the treatment of alcoholism persists, despite the fact that there is *no firm evidence* in support of the basic assumptions of the disease model. No physical crucial factor has yet been found to differentiate reliably the potential alcoholic from the social drinker. Thus, despite the arguments for the medical etiology of alcoholism, no reliably effective *medical* treatment program for alcoholism has yet been developed. It is ironic, therefore, that adherents of the disease model of alcoholism frequently rely upon a basically *moral* approach to treatment: Alcoholics Anonymous.

Alcoholics Anonymous (AA) is the oldest and most successful of all the self-help groups that have developed during this century. It is almost impossible to find a village or town in this country that does not have at least one local AA chapter. Founded by a physician and a layman friend (both former alcoholics) in the 1930s, AA has grown to the point today where its worldwide membership exceeds 650,000 (Norris, 1976). Like other self-help groups, AA is not a professional treatment program. Rather, it is an organization based on fellowship among alcoholics who maintain personal anonymity (no last names are used); there are no membership requirements (other than a concern with one's drinking), and no dues are paid. Members meet regularly and provide friendship and support for each other in their struggle to overcome their addiction. It is important to note that the basic tenets of AA are based on religious or moral principles, as embodied in the "Big Book" or "Bible" of AA principles (Alcoholics Anonymous, 1955). Members of AA devote themselves to a new lifestyle based on a series of moral imperatives or command-ments called the *"Twelve Steps."* The moral underpinnings of these principles are clearly evident in the following examples (Alcoholics Anonymous, 1955):

> We admitted we were powerless over alcohol—that our lives had become unmanageable. (Step 1)
> Admitted to God, to ourselves, and to another human being the exact nature of our wrongs. (Step 5)
> Made a list of all persons we had harmed, and became willing to make amends to them all. (Step 8)
>
> [p. 59]

Although no exact figures are available (AA does not provide research on the effectiveness of its methods), there is little doubt that AA has been a tremendously effective program for thousands of alcoholics. It seems to work best for those individuals who experience something similar to a religious conversion and who are willing to totally embrace the philosophy of the Twelve Steps. Perhaps the one belief that is inviolate among the AA membership is the insistence upon total abstinence as the only solution to the problem of alcoholism.

For those individuals who accept the disease model, AA may well be the best and most effective alternative to drinking. There are countless enthusiastic supporters of the AA approach, and there is no doubt that the organization has literally saved many lives. For many other problem drinkers, however, AA is not an acceptable system of beliefs. Although research on this distinction is incomplete and sketchy, it seems possible that many individuals are unwilling to accept the powerlessness and victimization that is implied by the disease model of alcoholism and by the surren-der of personal control required by the AA approach (cf. Nathan, Marlatt, & Loberg, 1978; Pattison, Sobell, & Sobell, 1977). For some persons, perhaps those with a more internal locus of control (Rohsenow & O'Leary, 1978), membership in AA is the equivalent to taking a course in learned helplessness (Seligman, 1975) in which every graduate receives the same letter grade: an A, standing for Alcoholic. For many members of AA, this letter grade takes the form of a new scarlet letter to be worn openly on the chest for the rest of their lives. Critics of this labeling process (Gove, 1975) take issue with the notion that a person's *behavior* (excessive drinking) should be taken as an indication of the person's entire *identity;* even if alcoholism is defined as a disease process, why is it necessary to label the whole person as a diseased individual—why do we call somebody an *alcoholic,* rather than simply say that he or she may suffer from a disorder called alcoholism? We don't label someone who has cancer as a "canceric"; why should we then label someone who drinks to excess as an alcoholic? As we shall see later, there is increasing evidence to suggest that this labeling process (and the underlying dogma that reinforces the notion that an alcoholic is a helpless victim of a disease), though it may help to convince the alcoholic never to take another drink, may lead to a backfire effect when and if the individual ever does take a drink after a commitment to total abstinence.

It is as if the entire model of alcoholism and the parallel AA philosophy is geared toward a single, unitary prohibition: if you are an alcoholic, *you must never take another drink!* But the reality is that the relapse rate among alcoholics is abysmally high despite the good intentions of AA and other treatment programs based on the disease model. In a recent comprehensive survey of representative treatment programs in the United States, based on a treatment evaluation project funded by the National Institute of Alcohol Abuse and Alcoholism (Armor, Polich, & Stambul, 1978), it was found that only 10% of alcoholics treated in abstinence-oriented programs remained abstinent during the 18-month follow-up period. This infamous report (tagged the *Rand Report,* since it was carried out under the auspices of the Rand Corporation in Santa Monica, California) infuriated members of the traditional alcoholism treatment community, since it also showed that about 26% of the alcoholics reported in the sample had returned to drinking in moderation for periods up to as long as 18 months following discharge from treatment. Since most previous treatment evaluation studies in the alcoholism field had relied only upon dichotomous outcome data for their patients (i.e., the patient was reported as either abstinent or relapsed, with little or no attention paid to the *amount* of drinking by those who had resumed drinking), the findings of the Rand Report directly contradicted the basic assumptions of the disease model, including the cornerstone notion of loss of control drinking as the inevitable outcome of any drinking behavior by former alcoholics. Although there was some attempt to redefine alcoholism as a *chronically relapsing disease* that sometimes is in remission, it is clear that some of the foundations of the disease model were beginning to crumble. The dust has yet to settle from this attack, however. The findings of the Rand Report continue to be criticized in the literature (Emrick & Stilson, 1977), despite the fact that over 74 documented accounts of controlled or moderate drinking by former alcoholics have now appeared in the research literature (for a review of these studies, see Pattison, Sobell, & Sobell, 1977).

Clearly, there is a need for an alternative to the disease model. Without such an alternative conceptualization and corresponding treatment procedures, many problem drinkers will never receive adequate attention or care. Given that, at most, less than 10% of the estimated number of alcoholics in this country are currently members of AA (Leach, 1973), what is available as an alternative source of help for the remaining 90%? Who will provide help for the many so-called "teenage alcoholics" (i.e., many adolescents and other young adults who are experiencing problems with drinking) who refuse to accept the requirement of total abstinence for the rest of their lives? Where can the individual who refuses to accept the semireligious dogma of AA or who cannot accept the image of oneself as a helpless victim of an incurable disease turn for guidance? Or what about the drinker who fits the "revolving door" pattern, who has been in treatment time and time again only to relapse within a few days of discharge from the hospital? Or the person who has been arrested for drunken driving or for other infractions of the law involving the use of alcohol? Must he or she be always sent to a local Alcohol Information and Referral Center to be lectured on the evils of alcohol and alerted to the potential dangers of alcoholism? Is someone who refuses to accept the label of being an alcoholic always guilty of "denial" and of other defense mechanisms that must be "broken through" before the individual can be a good candidate for treatment? Perhaps most importantly: Is there an alternative to the "learned-helplessness" model of alcoholism, an alternative that provides the problem drinker with awareness and skills and a sense of self-efficacy? Whether the goal of treatment is abstinence or controlled drinking is not the issue here, since abstinence may be the treatment of choice regardless of the theoretical model employed. In recent years, an alternative conceptualization of alcohol dependence has emerged, based on the assumptions of social learning theory. Some of the relevant research that has contributed to this new approach will be reviewed in the next section.

Drinking as a Learned Behavior: The Social Learning Model

In the past 15 years or so, an alternative approach to understanding alcohol problems has received increased attention. With its basis in data instead of dogma, the social learning approach makes a number of assumptions about the nature of drinking and about the development of drinking problems that differ markedly from the disease model. Problem drinking (a term that avoids defining drinking problems as indicative of an underlying alcoholism disease mechanism) is viewed as a learned behavioral disorder, one that can best be understood through the principles of social learning, cognitive psychology, and behavior modification. Excessive drinking is defined as but one element of a general class of *addictive behaviors,* a class that includes such other behaviors as smoking, substance abuse, overeating, and compulsive gambling. The focus of the social learning approach is on the observable aspects of drinking behavior, including the frequency and duration of drinking episodes, the amount of alcohol consumed, and the problems associated with excessive use. All drinking behavior, from social drinking to alcohol abuse, is assumed to be governed by similar principles of learning and reinforcement. As such, it is assumed that there is no crucial difference that distinguishes the social drinker and the problem drinker, other than the *amount* of alcohol consumed.

Adherents of the social learning approach are particularly interested in studying the *determinants* of drinking behavior, including situational and environmental antecedents, cognitive processes and expectations, and the individual's past learning history and prior experiences with alcohol. In addition, there is an equal interest in discovering the *consequences* of drinking, as a source of information about the reinforcing effects of alcohol that may contribute to increased drinking, as well as the negative consequences that serve to inhibit drinking rates. In addition to the effects of alcohol itself, attention is paid to the social and interpersonal reactions experienced by the drinker. In some cases, for example, it may be that the guilt and concern engendered in the problem drinker by the reactions of family and friends actually serve to increase consumption of alcohol.

If drinking is acquired and maintained on the basis of principles of learning, what are the reinforcing consequences of alcohol that make it such an attractive drug for many individuals? Until recently, social-learning theorists have evaluated the validity of the *tension-reduction hypothesis* as an explanation of alcohol's reinforcing properties. Based originally on research with animals (cf. Conger, 1956), this hypothesis states that drinking behavior is reinforced through the tension-reducing properties of alcohol. In this view, alcohol acts as a kind of liquid tranquilizer, producing a state of relaxation that has reinforcing effects (this hypothesis is similar to the drive-reduction component of Hullian learning theory). One prediction that is often made on the basis of this hypothesis is that individuals will drink more when they are tense or anxious. But does alcohol actually serve to reduce tension or anxiety? Do people drink more when they are nervous or tense?

Much of the available evidence bearing on the validity of the tension-reduction hypothesis has been contradictory and inconclusive. Unfortunately, many of the studies have been conducted with animal subjects (Cappell & Herman, 1972). Since this research ignores the contributing influences of cognitive factors as mediators of the reinforcement effect, the findings from the animal studies would seem to have little or no relevance to the understanding of drinking in humans (Marlatt, 1976a). Research with human subjects has produced some findings that contradict the tension-reduction model, however. Research with alcoholics whose drinking behavior has been observed over periods of days and weeks in an experimental ward setting, for example, has found that many subjects report an *increase* in tension, dysphoria, and depression over periods of prolonged drinking (e.g., Nathan & O'Brien, 1971). Another study showed that neither alcoholics nor social drinkers consumed more alcohol when they experienced a manipulated state of tension (anticipation of a painful electric shock), compared with low-tension control subjects (Higgins & Marlatt, 1973). In a follow-up study, however, male heavy social drinkers were found to consume signficantly more alcohol than did controls when they were exposed to a threat condition involving *social* tension (anticipation of evaluation by females), in contrast with the impersonal and asocial threat of electric shock used in the first study (Higgins & Marlatt, 1975). Social stress has also been found to be a determinant of drinking by Miller and his colleaques (Miller, Hersen, Eisler, & Hilsman, 1974). As we shall soon see, it is probably the drinker's *expectations* about the effects of alcohol that mediate the relationship between tension or stress and the consumption of alcohol. Whereas a drinker may not expect that alcohol will have an ameliorating effect on some sources of tension (e.g., apprehension of physical pain caused by an electric shock), he or she may expect that drinking will ease or reduce other forms of tension or arousal (e.g., alcohol as a "lubricant" to reduce social tension or evaluation threats).

Another important difficulty with the initial formulation of the tension-reduction hypothesis is that it is assumed that alcohol serves to reduce tension in a linear fashion: the higher the dose of alcohol, the lower the resultant tension level. Recent research suggests, however, that this assumption is basically incorrect. Experiments on the physiological effects of alcohol (on heart rate, galvanic skin response, etc.) strongly suggest that the body's response to alcohol may be essentially *biphasic* in nature (Docter, Naitoh, & Smith, 1966; Garfield & McBrearty, 1970; Mello, 1968). Taken as a group, these studies suggest that alcohol has not one but two effects on the body, one following the other, thus producing a biphasic reaction. The first effect, following a relatively low intake dose (approximately one or two ounces of whiskey, for example), is one of *increased arousal* (sympathetic activation). This initial increase in excitation is experienced by the drinker as a "high"—subjective feelings of excitement, increased energy, and perceptions of the self as more "powerful" (cf. McClelland, Davis, Kalin, & Wanner, 1972). These feelings of euphoria may parallel the rising level of alcohol in the bloodstream. As the dose level increases and time passes, however, the physical and affective effects begin to change and to swing in the opposite direction. The drinker then begins to experience a general state of dysphoria (increased feelings of fatigue, stupor, nausea, etc.), in marked contrast to the initial euphoric reaction. This second stage of the biphasic reaction may be parallel to the decreasing level of alcohol in the bloodstream that follows the cessation of drinking (cf. Jones & Vega, 1972). The dysphoric effects of alcohol are well known and have contributed to the general classification of alcohol as a depressant drug. Although much research needs to be done to specify the parameters of the biphasic response to alcohol and the theoretical implications of this reaction are still speculative, some authors have suggested that the biphasic response is a basic "opponent process" underlying reactions to many other psychoactive drugs and to affective dynamics in general (Solomon, 1977; Solomon & Corbit, 1974).

If the validity of the biphasic response is substantiated by future research, some of the apparent contradictions in our current knowledge about drinking behavior and alcohol dependence may be resolved. The principal reinforcing effects of drinking may be associated with the increased excitation or euphoria of the initial phase of the biphasic reaction, rather than the decrease in tension postulated by the tension-reduction hypothesis. Thus, the drinker may be correct in saying that he or she drinks to get "high"; alcohol's initial effects may be more in the form of an "upper," followed eventually by the "downer" of the second-stage depressant effects. In the analysis of alcohol's reinforcing properties, it is the immediate pleasurable effects that have the greatest impact on learning and on shaping the drinker's expectations about alcohol. The dysphoric effects of the second stage have less of an impact because of their delayed occurrence, a finding that is in line with previous research on the temporal gradient of reinforcement effect. Thus, although the eventual outcome of any excessive drinking episode is primarily negative (hangover, physical distress, social disapproval, etc.), it is the initial reinforcing "high" of the biphasic response that accounts most for the drinker's motivation to indulge.

In addition, it may be the case that the drinker expects to augment or to regain this "high" by further drinking, especially when the dysphoric effects of the second stage begin to increase in intensity. When this occurs, the problem drinker may try to "drink through" the dysphoric aftereffects by increasing intake over a longer period of time, in a vain attempt to escape or avoid the inevitable unpleasant consequences. Bouts of prolonged drinking or binges may result from this tendency. For those problem drinkers who have developed *tolerance* to alcohol (more and more alcohol is required to produce the desired initial "high"), the problem intensifies, since these individuals require high doses to begin with and frequently pass into the dysphoric stage (or pass out altogether) without experiencing much pleasure from their drinking.

One of the primary implications of the biphasic response just reviewed is that the problem drinker learns to expect the positive effects of drinking, despite the fact that the predominant quality of the experience is negative (McGuire, Mendelson, & Stein, 1966; Tamerin, Weiner, & Mendelson, 1970). Could it be the case, following this line of reasoning, that the so-called loss-of-control drinking problem described by Jellinek and other advocates of the disease model is mediated more by cognitive expectancies than by physiological addictive mechanisms? The answer to this question is of crucial importance, since a positive response would open the door to the possibility of controlled drinking as an alternative treatment goal to abstinence.

In order to put this question to an experimental test, we conducted a study of the determinants of drinking as an analogue to the loss of control phenomenon (Marlatt, Demming, & Reid, 1973). In this experiment, both male problem drinkers (previously diagnosed as alcoholic, but who had resumed drinking following treatment) and social drinkers (matched with the alcoholic group in terms of age and socioeconomic background) were asked to take part in a taste-rating task in which they were to sample and compare the taste qualities of either alcoholic or nonalcoholic beverages (see Marlatt, 1978a, for a complete description of the taste-rating task as an unobtrusive measure of alcohol consumption). In order to control for both the physiological effects of alcohol and the subject's expectancy or belief about the effects of alcohol, we employed a diacritical factorial design with subjects assigned to one of four independent conditions. Subjects in the expect alcohol conditions were led to believe that they would be sampling three brands of vodka (mixed with tonic), whereas subjects in the *expect no alcohol* conditions were instructed that they would be comparing three brands of tonic water. At the same time, we inde-

pendently varied the alcoholic content of the drinks in such a way that half the
subjects in each of the two expectation conditions actually received drinks containing vodka and half received drinks containing only tonic water. All subjects were
provided with three full decanters of each beverage and were asked to sample each
on an ad-lib basis while making the comparative taste ratings. The results showed
that the only significant determinant of the amount consumed (and of estimates of
the alcoholic content of the drinks) was the expectancy factor: Subjects who were
led to believe that they were drinking vodka and tonic consumed significantly more
in the task than did subjects who expected only tonic water, *regardless of the actual
alcohol content* of their drinks.

The results of this study provide strong experimental support for the contention
that cognitive mediational factors must be taken into account in any investigation of
the effects of alcohol on human behavior. Subsequent research has revealed that
expectancies override the pharmacological effects of alcohol for a variety of human
behaviors in which one's beliefs about the effects of alcohol play a paramount role,
including aggressive behavior (Lang, Goeckner, Adesso, & Marlatt, 1975), sexual
arousal (Wilson & Lawson, 1976), and anxiety (Wilson & Abrams, 1978). For
recent reviews of cognitive factors as they affect reactions to alcohol, the reader is
referred to the following sources: Marlatt (1976a, 1978b), Marlatt and Rohsenow
(1980), and Wilson (1978).

In addition to the importance of cognitive expectancies, our research and the
research of other social learning theorists has convinced us of the significance of
social and *situational factors* as determinants of drinking behavior. Like many other
learned behaviors, the consumption of alcohol appears to be influenced by environmental forces and social influences. Here again, the impact of physiological determinants, such as "craving" for alcohol and other addictive internal promptings
suggested by the disease model, seems to be minimal, at most.

Most people do not learn to drink by following any explicit instructions or other
formal guidelines. Instead, they acquire many of their drinking habits from observing others use alcohol, such as family members, friends, and media figures. In our
own research, we have investigated the role of peer *modeling* as a determinant of
drinking behavior in social drinkers. In an initial study, Caudill and Marlatt (1975)
asked male heavy drinkers to participate in a taste-rating task in the presence of a
peer partner. Unknown to the real subject, the other person was a confederate
subject acting as a drinking model. Both subjects were instructed to work on the
tasting-task independently, and each was required to make comparative taste-ratings
of three different wines. In two conditions in the experiment, the model played the
role of either a "heavy" or a "light" social drinker; the third condition was a
no-model control group. In the heavy-drinker modeling condition, the model consumed 700 ml. of wine (equivalent to a full bottle) during the 15-minute task,
compared to the light drinker who consumed only 100 ml. of wine. The results
showed that peer modeling exerts a powerful influence on drinking behavior: Subjects who observed the heavy drinking model drank twice as much wine as subjects
in the no-model control group, and the light drinking model produced a further drop

of 22% relative to the control condition. In a recent follow-up to this study, Lied and Marlatt (1979) found that the modeling effect is most pronounced in male heavy drinkers who are exposed to a heavy drinking model of the same sex. Female drinkers and males who are light drinkers do not show the same susceptibility to the modeling effect. It seems likely that many male problem drinkers have been influenced strongly by exposure to peers who drink heavily and by the cultural acceptance of drinking as a "macho" expression of masculinity.

Our research on modeling strongly suggests that social pressures exert considerable influence in shaping drinking habits, attitudes, and beliefs about alcohol. These findings are consistent with those reported by Higgins & Marlatt (1975), who found that impending social evaluation was a significant determinant of drinking by male social drinkers. In these examples, it could be argued that drinking serves as a means of *coping* with powerful external pressures. In this sense, drinking is an inadequate or inappropriate attempt to cope with a stressful situation, since it represents a form of giving in to external pressures. What happens if the drinker is given the opportunity to engage in constructive coping responses as an alternative to drinking?

In order to answer this question, Marlatt, Kosturn, and Lang (1975) designed a study in which heavy social drinkers were assigned to one of three experimental conditions. In two of the conditions, subjects were deliberately criticized and frustrated by a confederate subject prior to participating in a drinking task. A third group served as a nonangered control condition. In order to see what the effects of providing an alternative coping response would be, the subjects in one of the frustrated groups were allowed the opportunity to express their anger against the subject who had criticized them prior to the drinking task. The findings supported the notions described earlier. Subjects who were allowed to express their anger showed a significant *decrease* in alcohol consumption on the taste-rating task compared to those subjects who were not provided with an alternative coping response. Subjects who were frustrated and angry but who were deprived of the chance to express their anger consumed the most alcohol of all in this study, with subjects in the neutral control group falling between the two other conditions.

In most of the foregoing studies, the subjects consisted of social drinkers. Can we draw any parallel conclusions about the determinants of drinking with problem drinkers, or "alcoholics," from these data? We have been able to obtain data showing that there are striking similarities between the determinants of drinking in social drinkers and the determinants of relapse in individuals who have received treatment for alcohol dependence. Since most people who receive treatment for alcoholism are required to commit themselves to abstinence after leaving the treatment setting, we decided to follow up a large group of patients to see what factors were associated with the resumption of drinking in those individuals who had relapsed (Marlatt & Gordon, 1979). For those who had consumed at least one drink following termination of treatment, we gathered a wide range of information about the events immediately preceding the relapse, including questions concerning the individual's feelings and moods at the time, significant prior events, the setting, time, presence or absence of others, etc. In order to minimize problems of reliability associated with interpreting retrospective data of this type, we made every attempt to contact subjects as soon as possible following their relapses. These accounts of the relapse episode were carefully classified and assigned to categories descriptive of the precipitating circumstances. The results of this analysis provide clear support for the conceptualization of drinking as a coping response in stressful situations. Over three-quarters of our sample reported taking their first drink in situations in which they were faced with either unpleasant emotional states (e.g., anger and frustration stemming from an argument with someone) or social pressures to resume drinking (e.g., meeting an old drinking buddy who pressured the individual to resume drinking). It seems clear that many of the relapses we studied in this analysis could have been prevented if the individual had been able to execute an alternative coping response in the high-risk precipitating situation.

Our research with both social drinkers and problem drinkers has led us to a theoretical formulation of the factors that may determine excessive drinking. This theoretical model is the basis for an alternative to the disease model of alcoholism and provides a rationale for the treatment procedure to be described in the next section of this chapter. Although the model remains untested in its complete form, much of the aforementioned experimental evidence reviewed is consistent with predictions derived from the theory. The model is limited to drinking that is considered excessive or inappropriate in a given situation (e.g., drinking to the point of intoxication, precipitation of a binge or drinking spree, drinking beyond one's intended limits, or precipitation of a relapse or "slip" in the formerly abstinent drinker). Thus, the conditions specified in the following do not apply to appropriate social drinking (sometimes referred to as *recreational* drinking, as opposed to drinking as a means of coping with stress). In addition, the model applies only to the *immediate* precipitating factors or determinants of drinking in a particular situation. It should be noted, however, that the influence of more global or general factors (such as lifestyle, physical condition, past learning experiences, etc.) may serve to set the stage for the development of high-risk situations associated with drinking.

The model states that the probability of excessive drinking will vary in a particular situation as a function of the following factors:

1. The degree to which the drinker feels controlled by (or feels helpless relative to) the influence of another individual or group (e.g., social pressures to conform, modeling, evaluation or criticism by others, being frustrated or angered by others) or by external environmental events "beyond the control" of the individual (e.g., misfortune, financial loss, feeling bored or depressed). Any situational event that threatens the drinker's perception of control in this sense is defined as a *high-risk situation*.

2. The availability of an adequate *coping response* as an alternative to drinking in the high-risk situation. If the individual fails to perform an appropriate coping response, a sense of lowered *self-efficacy* develops. Based on Bandura's concept of self-efficacy (Bandura, 1977), a sense of low efficacy is associated with a decreased

expectancy of being able to perform adequately on a forthcoming task and is similar to a perceived sense of helplessness or loss of perceived control in a particular situation.

3. The drinker's *expectations* about the effects of alcohol as one means of attempting to cope with the situation. If the drinker believes that taking a drink will increase feelings of perceived control or personal "power" (e.g., thinking that, "If only I had a drink, I could get through this situation"), based on one's past experience with alcohol as a habitual means of coping with stress.

4. The availability of alcohol and the constraints upon drinking in a given situation.

COGNITIVE–BEHAVIORAL
INTERVENTION STRATEGIES

In the discussion to follow, a variety of assessment techniques and treatment procedures that we have found useful in working with people who have problems with alcohol will be discussed. Many of these principles and techniques have applications for treatment with other addictive behaviors, such as smoking, overeating, and substance-abuse problems. In this presentation, however, the discussion will be limited to alcohol abuse. The material to be described includes a wide variety of both cognitive and behavioral strategies, only some of which may be applied clinically in the treatment of an individual case. The selection of techniques for use with a particular client will depend on a variety of factors, including the client's age, educational background, drinking history, previous treatment history, and other extenuating circumstances. In using the pronoun "we" throughout this section of the chapter, I am including my wife (Dr. Judith R. Gordon, who often serves as my cotherapist in working with clients with drinking and/or smoking problems), along with many of my students and colleagues who have contributed important ideas and suggestions to the development of our overall approach to treatment.

General Approach to Clients

In most cases, the clients who come to us for help for their drinking problems are initially anxious and defensive. This defensiveness is particularly noticeable in clients who have been pressured into seeking help by others or who have reluctantly decided that it is time to do something about their drinking. Frequently, this defensive attitude stems from the guilt and fear associated with the big question in the client's mind: Am I an alcoholic? Or, will the therapist see me as an alcoholic? In response to this fear, we tell clients that we are not concerned with whether or not they deserve the label of alcoholic and, instead, provide them with a rationale for looking at their drinking behavior in an objective manner. We tell them about our attitude about drinking as a coping behavior and state that we would like to find out about any problems they might have associated with their drinking.

Contrary to the approach adopted by alcoholism counselors or other proponents of the disease model (who often begin by trying to break through the patient's denial system and force the client into accepting the diagnostic label of alcoholism), we try to foster a sense of objectivity or detachment in our clients' approach to their drinking. By employing the client as a kind of cotherapist or colleague, we hope to encourage a sense of cooperation and openness in which clients feel free to discuss *their drinking behavior* (as opposed to seeing their behavior as a symptom indicative of their status as an alcoholic). We also encourage clients to take an active role in treatment planning and decision making throughout the course of treatment. Rather than viewing the client as a passive victim of a disease, we try to encourage active participation and personal responsibility by the client in every stage of the program. Our overall goal is to increase our clients' awareness and choice concerning their drinking habits, to develop coping skills and self-control abilities, and, generally, to develop a greater sense of confidence, mastery, or self-efficacy in their lives.

Another significant aspect of our approach is the necessity to involve the client's spouse or significant other individuals in the treatment plans. Involving a significant other person is particularly important given the somewhat unorthodox techniques we use in the assessment and treatment of alcohol problems. In many instances, the client's wife or husband, for example, may expect the client to take a pledge of abstinence during the initial consultation session. One can imagine the reaction when the client comes home to announce that the therapist requires an ongoing written record of the client's drinking behavior for the next 2 weeks! For these reasons, it is important to involve both the client and a close relative or friend in the initial discussion of the rationale and the formulation of treatment goals.

The client's spouse, lover, or friend can provide considerable cooperation in the form of support and assistance during the course of treatment if that person can accept the basic assumptions of this novel approach to treatment. In many cases, however, the significant other may contribute to the client's sense of guilt and shame about drinking, particularly if the spouse or other family members suspect or fear that the client may be an alcoholic. Fear of being labeled as an alcoholic has led many of our clients to engage in denial about their drinking, to become secretive about their consumption of alcohol, and to resist seeking out help for their drinking problems. Guilt and anger are often the result of pressures from others over the client's drinking, and these emotional states have been found to act as significant determinants of drinking in their own right (Marlatt, Kosturn, & Lang, 1975). Clients sometimes sneak drinks and hide bottles because of the guilt and anger they experience as a result of the reactions of others, not because of an internal, insidious disease process. With the cooperation of family members and others who are willing to assume an objective, nonjudgmental attitude about the client's drinking during the treatment program, we have frequently observed in clinical practice that the client's drinking decreases significantly, even in the absence of any other intervention procedures.

Choice of Treatment Goal: Abstinence versus
Controlled Drinking

The possibility of controlled drinking as an alternative to abstinence is the single most controversial issue associated with treatment planning. Since this is a complex and difficult issue, a complete discussion of the controversy is beyond the scope of this chapter, and the reader is referred to a number of recent publications on the topic (Marlatt & Nathan, 1978; P. M. Miller, 1976; Miller & Caddy, 1977; Pattison, *et al.*, 1977; Sobell & Sobell, 1978). However, two important points that are often overlooked in the heat of this debate need to be made. First, despite claims to the contrary, behavioral psychologists and others who have explored the feasibility of controlled drinking as an alternative to abstinence do not advocate that an abstinent alcoholic should go out and try to drink like a social drinker or try to regulate drinking on the basis of willpower or of other similar maneuvers. Quite the opposite is true: Controlled drinking programs consist of precise *procedures* and technical *skills* that are designed to teach the drinker to moderate or to regulate consumption. Unlike the approach adopted by traditional supporters of the disease model, with their reliance upon advice, slogans, and faith as methods to induce abstinence, the controlled-drinking approach should be administered only by qualified professionals who are experienced in behavioral methodology and who are committed to an empirical, data-based evaluation of treatment effectiveness.

The second point to be made is that there is *no firm evidence* that abstinence is a superior goal to controlled drinking in terms of the client's overall level of functioning, personality, or psychosocial adjustment (Pattison, *et al.*, 1977). Certainly, abstinence is to be preferred to the continual, excessive abuse of alcohol that may lead to serious physical illness or even death. The real question to be addressed is the following one: How does controlled drinking compare to abstinence as a goal of treatment—for what clients, under what conditions, over what period of time, and in what ways? This is an empirical question, one that can only be answered in terms of well-designed outcome studies.

Evidence on the effectiveness of controlled drinking procedures continues to accumulate. In most cases, those who have investigated controlled drinking on an experimental basis have made use of a multifaceted or broad-spectrum approach to treatment intervention, integrating a wide variety of treatment procedures. Perhaps the most comprehensive program of this type has been developed by the Sobells (see Sobell & Sobell, 1978, for a complete review of this project). The Sobells evaluated the effectiveness of a controlled-drinking program as compared with conventional treatment; subjects were allowed to select either controlled drinking or abstinence as the treatment goal. The controlled-drinking component consisted of a number of intervention procedures, including behavioral self-analysis, self-management training, social skill training, aversive conditioning, and videotape feedback of both drunken and sober behavior. All subjects, consisting of chronic alcoholics, were carefully evaluated for a period of 2 years following completion of the inpatient treatment phase. For those alcoholics who selected the controlled drinking goal,

78.90% of those who received the behavioral treatment program were functioning well (either abstinent or drinking in a controlled manner on at least 80% of all days), compared to only 23.50% of the group receiving conventional treatment. For subjects who selected abstinence as the goal, 53.87% of the subjects receiving the behavioral program were doing well (as defined above), compared to only 31.43% of the control-group subjects who chose this goal. Although these results have created considerable controversy among supporters of the disease model of alcoholism, the viability of nonabstinence as a treatment goal can no longer be ignored (Miller & Caddy, 1977).

Based on the existing evidence and on our own clinical experience, we offer the following tentative guidelines concerning choice of treatment goals. A decision should rest on a careful, detailed assessment of the client's overall status, taking into consideration such factors as age, intelligence and educational background, degree of cognitive impairment, economic and family support systems, the duration of drinking problems (drinking history), as well as a full evaluation of the client's current drinking rates and patterns. As a general rule of thumb, selection of controlled drinking as a goal is *not* recommended for treatment with individuals who have a long-standing, chronic problem with alcohol abuse and who have developed serious life problems associated with their drinking. Many persons with chronic drinking problems have developed some form of brain dysfunction or other serious impairment that precludes them from benefiting from the educational, skills-acquisition approach demanded by controlled-drinking procedures. In addition, some clients may be well-suited for the type of experience offered by AA or by some of the traditional treatment programs stressing abstinence as the required goal. Clients with a moral orientation that would incline them toward embracing a semireligious conversion experience as a method of attaining abstinence might well be advised to seek out this form of help. Similarly, for those who need the type of constant group support offered by AA and by other self-help groups as a means of maintaining abstinence (as opposed to the more individualized self-control methods offered by the alternative approach), controlled drinking procedures are not recommended.

Controlled drinking may work best for those who are *beginning* to develop problems with their drinking, as a form of prevention, rather than as a remedial treatment program for individuals who have developed a long-term dependence upon alcohol. In our own clinical experience, the controlled-drinking approach seems to work well with younger drinkers who are open to learning new skills or with individuals who are unwilling to accept the goal of lifelong abstinence as the only alternative to problem drinking. Regardless of the expected outcome, however, we treat the issue of selection of treatment goal in the same way with all clients who request a controlled-drinking program. If we feel that a controlled-drinking program is a viable possibility, we ask that they try this approach for a trial period at first (usually about 6 weeks after completion of the training phase). If the program works, we ask the client to continue monitoring his or her progress on a more-or-less continuous basis (through the follow-up period and, afterward, on a spot-check basis). If the client continually fails to moderate drinking during this initial period, we suggest that he try abstinence as an alternative. In most cases, given that the client has tried the best techniques available for controlled drinking, he or she is much more willing to try an abstinence approach at this point.

Scope and Duration of the Intervention Program

All of our treatment to date has been applied in an outpatient setting. Occasionally, with severe cases, we have found it necessary to require a period of hospitalization to provide medical supervision for detoxification from alcohol. For most of our typical clients, however, drinking has not yet developed to the point of requiring this form of medical attention. Nonetheless, we usually require the client to undergo a complete physical examination, to rule out the possibility that continued drinking of any kind would seriously impair physical health. For those who are physically eligible to continue with the outpatient program, the following plan is used as a guide for the treatment program. This plan is not adhered to in a rigid fashion, however, and changes are made on an individual basis as circumstances dictate.

Following an initial consultation session and presentation of the treatment rationale (often with the spouse or a significant other present during the meeting), the first 2 or 3 weeks are devoted to an in-depth assessment of the client's drinking history and current drinking patterns. (The details of each component of the treatment program are described below.) For the second 2-week period, the client is asked to refrain entirely from all alcoholic beverages. Since the purpose of this assessment procedure is to gauge the clients' ability to regulate drinking on their own and to evaluate the intensity of situational, emotional, or other factors that may affect urges or other desires to drink during this period of abstinence, no special skills or techniques are imparted to the client during this stage. Often, clients are surprised to find how easy it is to stop drinking altogether for a short period, and they soon begin to realize that they can exert control over their use of alcohol—a realization that may run counter to their prior expectations that they cannot cope without alcohol. For those who are unable to adhere to the required period of abstinence, valuable information is gained concerning the forces or events that are most strongly associated with drinking (i.e., the determinants of relapse during this trial period of voluntary abstinence). For some clients, the knowledge that they cannot go for even a relatively short period of time without drinking may lead them to abandon controlled drinking as a treatment goal. For others, drinking during this 2-week period reveals a deficit in skills or other coping abilities (information gained from an analysis of the determinants of the relapse), providing knowledge that can be usefully applied during the treatment intervention phase of the program.

The treatment intervention phase usually lasts for a period of at least 6 weeks. If controlled drinking has been selected as a treatment goal, this period is devoted to the acquisition of skills and techniques designed to moderate the use of alcohol (described later). For those cases in which abstinence has been selected as the goal, this period is also designed to teach the client alternative coping skills and to learn to anticipate and to cope with the possibility of relapse (relapse prevention skills are described in the final section of this chapter). Regardless of the goal chosen, treatment continues until the client shows a stable level of performance and the therapist is relatively confident that the client can now serve as his or her own therapist (the ultimate aim of all self-control programs). Frequent follow-up meetings are scheduled during the remainder of the year (usually at intervals of 90 days or whenever the client wishes to come in for additional help). Long-term follow-up sessions are also recommended to the client during the following year. With the exception of the follow-up sessions, then, the active period of treatment continues for approximately 12 weeks. Considering that most inpatient treatment programs for alcoholics often last for a period of 30 days or longer and that a recent research report suggests that intensive long-term programs of this type may be no more effective than a single hour-long session consisting of little more than information and advice (Edwards, Orford, Egert, Guthrie, Hawker, Hensman, Mitcheson, Oppenheimer, & Taylor, 1977), the program described here represents a considerable savings in terms of time and money. Future research is needed, of course, to evaluate fully the effectiveness of these procedures in comparison with traditional treatment methods.

Assessment Procedures

The problem with traditional diagnostic questionnaires, such as the Alcadd Test (Manson, 1949) or the Michigan Alcoholism Screening Test (Selzer, 1971), is that these tests attempt to differentiate the alcoholic from the social drinker. This dichotomous, all-or-none approach to assessment is at odds with the social learning model assumption that views drinking behavior as falling along a continuous gradient of consumption rates and patterns. The National Council on Alcoholism (1972) has attempted to provide a list of differentiating criteria (many of them based on physiological test indicators) for the medical diagnosis of alcoholism, but these criteria have yet to prove reliable or valid on the basis of existing research (Jacobson, 1976). Although some questionnaires based on a factor analysis of alcohol use and of associated symptoms (such as the Alcohol Use Inventory developed by Wanberg, Horn, & Foster, 1977) may prove helpful in distinguishing among various types of alcohol abuse problems, the typology approach appears to have limited value for behaviorally oriented clinicians (W. R. Miller, 1976).

In our own work with problem drinkers, we use a variety of procedures designed to provide us with information about rates and patterns of drinking, antecedents and consequences of alcohol use, beliefs and expectations about the effects of alcohol, and the client's ability to cope with a variety of stressful situations and life problems. Assessment is viewed as a continual, ongoing, and integral part of our treatment program. We view assessment as a means of obtaining information necessary for treatment planning purposes, as a means of evaluating the effects of treatment interventions, and as a method of increasing the client's overall awareness of his or her drinking behavior. Assessment is not regarded as something that is "done" to the client but is presented as a set of procedures that clients can use to self-assess the status of their drinking behavior prior to, during, and following the treatment program. The procedures will be described in the order that we usually apply them during the treatment program.

One of the first homework assignments we ask our clients to complete following the initial intake interview is to write a brief autobiography, describing the history and development of their drinking problem. Points to be emphasized in such an account include the following: description of parents' drinking behavior during the client's childhood, the first drinking experience and the first "drunk," the role of drinking in the client's development as an adult (drinking during the school years, in the military, and as a part of important personal relationships), factors associated with the development of drinking problems, one's self-image as a drinker, and so forth. Since one's image of oneself as a drinker may have a profound influence on the course of treatment, information from the autobiography can provide valuable assistance to the therapist in treatment planning. An autobiography written by one of our clients was recently published in a text by Sarason (1976, pp. 540–542) and provides a good example of this assessment procedure.

Because of dissatisfaction with the traditional diagnostic questionnaires, we have developed our own questionnaire for the behavioral assessment of problem drinking. The Drinking Profile (Marlatt, 1976b) is a detailed, structured questionnaire designed to be administered on an individual basis by a trained interviewer. Sample items from the questionnaire are provided in Table 10.1. Since the Drinking Profile takes about an hour or so to administer, we usually schedule it for the second session with the client. In addition to a number of detailed demographic items, the instrument contains a variety of questions pertaining to drinking rates and patterns, problems associated with drinking, periods of abstinence, and typical drinking settings. Other items are designed to provide information about alcoholic beverage preferences and estimates of pretreatment drinking levels. A final section contains items in which the client is asked to specify his or her own reasons for drinking (both antecedents and consequences) and to respond to questions relating to motivations for past and present treatment and expectations of treatment outcome. Many of the items are quantifiable and can easily be coded for purposes of computer analysis. A scoring manual has also been developed for coding and categorizing responses to the open-ended questions. We have found the Drinking Profile to be a useful guide for treatment planning in both the outpatient and the inpatient treatment settings.

Since retrospective self-reports of drinking rates are frequently unreliable or invalid due to the combined influence of emotional reactions (especially guilt), memory lapses due to the effects of alcohol, and other sources of distortion, it is important for the therapist to obtain a reasonably accurate account of the client's current drinking behavior. Self-monitoring procedures (McFall, 1977) in which clients are asked to keep an ongoing record of their drinking behavior provide an invaluable source of information for treatment planning and evaluation. In our own practice, we ask clients to keep a daily record of every drink consumed. The Daily

TABLE 10.1
Sample Items from the Drinking Profile[a]

Reasons for drinking (antecedent events):
- In your own words, what is the main reason why you drink?
- Do you have any inner thoughts or emotional feelings or things within you as a person that ''trigger off'' your need or desire to take a drink at a particular moment in time?
- Are there any particular situations or set of events, things that happen to you in the outside world, that would be most likely to make you feel like having one or more drinks?
- Can you describe a situation or set of events that would be *least likely* to make you feel like drinking? In other words, when do you least feel like drinking?

Consequences for drinking:
- When you are actually drinking, what, for you, is the most positive or desirable effect of alcohol? Also, what, for you, is the most negative or undesirable effect of alcohol when you are actually drinking?

Periods of abstinence:
- Since drinking first became a real problem for you, what is the longest period of time during which you did not take a drink?
  _____ Days   _____ Weeks   _____ Months   _____ Years   _____ Never abstinent
- When did this period end?
  _____ Month   _____ Year
- What would you say was the main reason for stopping drinking at that time? What would you say was the main reason for starting to drink again after this period?

Motivation for treatment:
- What do you see as the most ideal outcome of treatment here for you? In your honest and realistic opinion, what do you estimate your chances are from 1 to 10 of obtaining this outcome?
- Some people have said that alcoholism is a disease or sickness, whereas others have said that it is not a disease, but, rather, it is more like a bad habit a person has learned. Do you see it more as a disease or as a bad habit? Would you say that you are an alcoholic?

[a]Marlatt, 1976b.

Drinking Diary is a special form (see Figure 10.1) that requires the client to record the exact amounts of alcohol consumed each day, the time-period for each drinking occasion, the social and situational setting in which drinking occurs, and the antecedents and consequences of each drinking act. A similar form, called the Alcohol Intake Sheet, has been developed by Sobell and Sobell (1973). When the validity of the client's self-monitoring is in doubt, the cooperation of a significant other who is asked to keep an independent record of the client's drinking (with the client's permission) may be needed.

Although self-monitoring may produce an initial reactive effect such that the client's drinking rate may be influenced by the act of continual recording, it has been our experience that most clients are able to provide us with reasonably accurate data when the therapist takes the time to explain the rationale and the instructions for this procedure. We also ask the client to prepare a bar graph showing the average amount of drinking each week in specific situations (e.g., before or after meals, social settings, etc.). The graph provides the therapist with information concerning the situational determinants of drinking that can be used in treatment planning

Time (When did drinking begin?):	Setting (Where? Who was present? Doing what?):	Antecedents (What was happening? How were you feeling prior to drinking?):	Amount consumed (Be specific—give exact ounces of beer, wine, or liquor consumed):	Consequences (What happened? How did you feel after drinking?):	Time (When did the drinking end?):

Daily summary

Total time spent drinking: _____ Minutes _____ Hours
Total ml of absolute alcohol consumed: _____ ml
Average blood-alcohol level for time spent drinking: _____ %
Peak blood-alcohol level obtained during day: _____ %

Figure 10.1. Daily drinking diary.

339

(development of alternatives to drinking, potential "high-risk" situations for relapse, etc.). In addition, preparation of the graph increases a sense of objectivity or detachment with regard to the client's drinking and helps foster the client's role as cotherapist when discussing the results of self-monitoring during the treatment sessions.

Another important area to assess is the client's ability to cope with a variety of situations associated with excessive drinking. The results of the self-monitoring may suggest, for example, that the client drinks more when feeling angry or when in social situations in which others are drinking heavily. In this case, we would need to know the extent to which the client is capable of coping with these situations by engaging in assertive behavior or by resisting social pressures to drink. The therapist must determine whether or not the client has learned the appropriate coping skills or whether the skills have been acquired but are inhibited through anxiety or some other blocking reaction (Bandura, 1969). This information is necessary in order to plan a skills-training program with the client, individually tailored to his or her own needs.

In a recent study evaluating the effectiveness of a skills-training approach with chronic male alcoholics, Chaney and other members of our research team (Chaney, O'Leary, & Marlatt, 1978) developed a coping-skill assessment procedure called the Situational Competency Test. In this procedure, the client is asked to respond verbally to a description of a stressful situation presented by a narrator on an audiotape. The client's response is recorded and is later scored along several dimensions (latency and duration of response, degree of compliance, and specification of alternative behaviors). A sample item from this test: "You are eating at a good restaurant on a special occasion with some friends. The waitress comes over and says, 'Drink before dinner?' Everyone orders one. All eyes seem to be on you. What would you do?" A variety of similar items is included on the test, drawn from a pool of high-risk situations developed on the basis of earlier research (Marlatt, 1978b). The Situational Competency Test is particularly useful for assessment of coping skills in a research setting.

A final focus for assessment is the client's general lifestyle. Our research findings (Marlatt & Gordon, 1979) and our clinical experience suggest that the degree of balance or imbalance in a person's daily activities strongly influences drinking behavior. Here, we are defining *balance* as the degree of equilibrium that exists in one's daily life between those activities perceived as external demands (the "shoulds") and those perceived as activities the person engages in for pleasure or self-fulfillment (the "wants"). Since drinking can be viewed in this context as a self-indulgent behavior (a "want"), we find that a lifestyle that is weighted down with a preponderance of "shoulds" is often associated with excessive drinking (or other forms of self-indulgence). It is as if the person who spends his or her whole day doing activities that are high in external demand (e.g., working on a dull or boring series of work tasks) attempts to balance this disequilibrium by engaging in an excessive "want" or self-indulgence at the end of the day (e.g., drinking to excess in the evening). The client may say, "I owe myself a drink—I deserve a break for myself." In order to assess the degree of balance in the client's lifestyle, we ask the client to keep a log of all discrete activities or tasks engaged in during the day and evening hours. Each activity is rated on a scale of from 0 to 100 points (based on the client's subjective perception), with scores above 50 indicating a greater proportion of "wants" and scores below 50 representing a greater proportion of "shoulds." Taking time off to go fishing may be assigned a high "want" score (close to 100), for example, whereas filling out one's income tax forms would usually receive a high "should" score (close to zero, unless one is expecting a big tax refund). The daily average score for all activities is called the want/should ratio and is taken as an index of the degree of balance.

There are a number of additional behavioral assessment procedures that have been described in recent years. Although most of these methods have been developed for purposes of research, some of them have direct application in the clinical setting. The direct observation of drinking behavior can provide valuable information to the therapist about the client's particular drinking style and habits (Reid, 1978). Direct observation can provide reliable and valid data concerning the client's drinking rate (e.g., whether the client sips a drink over a relatively long time period or gulps it down in a minute or two), degree of intoxication while drinking (e.g., by estimating blood-alcohol levels or by videotaping the client's behavior when intoxicated, etc.), and the client's susceptibility to social influence (e.g., whether the client's drinking increases when exposed to a heavy-drinking model). Drinking can be observed directly in the natural setting (with observers present in the bar or tavern) or can be monitored in an experimental bar (allowing greater experimental control over the independent variables).

One measure of drinking that we have used extensively in our own research is the *taste-rating task,* in which subjects are told that we are interested in their ability to discriminate taste qualities of various alcoholic beverages. In fact, however, we use the test as an unobtrusive measure of consumption, since subjects are provided with an ad-lib supply of beverages when making their ratings. The taste-rating task can be used as a pre- and posttreatment assessment procedure in treatment outcome evaluation. For further information concerning these additional behavioral assessment procedures, the reader is referred to recent reviews by Marlatt (1978a), Miller (1977), and Sobell and Sobell (1976).

Skill Training

The cornerstone of our approach to treatment is teaching the client coping skills. Unlike treatment deriving from the traditional medical model, the present approach attempts to foster a greater sense of efficacy or perceived control in clients by teaching them to cope more effectively with stress and with other problems in living. Responsible drinking skills are also included as part of the treatment package, both with those clients who have selected controlled drinking as a goal and with clients who have chosen to abstain (to prepare them to handle the occasional slip and to prevent a full-blown relapse from occurring). In our clinical work, skill training begins immediately following the assessment stage, after we have ascertained the client's current abilities and coping capacities. The particular skills to be taught are based on a thorough evaluation of the determinants of excessive drinking and on an analysis of the client's ability to cope with a variety of high-risk situations.

With each client, it is important to determine whether or not a particular skill has been acquired in the client's past learning history. For many clients, a skill may have been learned, but its performance is blocked by fear or anxiety. When this is the case, we attempt to disinhibit the skill by the use of an appropriate anxiety-reduction procedure, such as systematic desensitization. For those clients who are deficient in their initial skill repertory, we attempt to teach new skills in a systematic and structured manner. The approach we favor combines training in problem-solving skills with specific skill training. Adopting a problem-solving approach to stressful situations (D'Zurilla & Golfried, 1971) allows the client greater flexibility and adaptation to new problem situations, rather than having to rely on the rote learning of a number of specific skills that may or may not generalize across various settings and situations. Our skill-training methods are based on the work of McFall (1975), Goldstein (1973), and other behavioral investigators, and the method incorporates components of direct instruction, modeling, behavioral rehearsal and coaching (both of the actual response and of the cognitive processes used in generating the response), and feedback from the therapist. We have found the modeling of self-instructional statements (Meichenbaum, 1977) to be particularly helpful in teaching the clients adaptive self-statements to use in conjunction with execution of the behavior skills. The details of several skill training programs can be found in a number of recent behavior therapy texts (cf. Goldfried & Davison, 1976; Rimm & Masters, 1974). Miller and Mastria (1977) have reviewed a number of skill training procedures that have particular relevance for the treatment of problem drinkers.

We recently completed a controlled investigation of the effectiveness of a skill-training program applied to an inpatient population of chronic alcoholics (Chaney, O'Leary, & Marlatt, 1978). Male patients in the Seattle Veterans Administration Alcohol Treatment Program served as the subject pool for this study. Of the 40 subjects who participated in the program, the mean age was 45.6 years. Subjects were generally in the lower socioeconomic group, with an average of 12.3 years of formal education. The sample reported that they had experienced problems with their drinking for an average of 17.0 years prior to this treatment period, indicating that the group as a whole consisted of relatively chronic alcoholics (subjects reported an average consumption of 3250 ounces of 86-proof liquor or its equivalent during the 6 months prior to admission, with an average of 122 drinking days during this same period).

The subjects were randomly assigned to one of three groups: a skill training condition, a discussion-group control condition, and a no-treatment control. All subjects participated in the normal inpatient treatment program, lasting approximately 1 month and consisting of a standard series of individual and group counseling sessions. A variety of assessment procedures was administered to all subjects, both prior to and following the inpatient treatment phase, including the assessment of social skills using the Situational Competency Test. In addition to the evaluation of skill acquisition and performance, all subjects were followed up for assessment of their drinking status and other indices of adjustment in the outside world at 1, 3, 6, and 12 month intervals following discharge from the hospital.

The skill-training group received a series of 8 biweekly treatment sessions, each lasting approximately 90 minutes. Subjects met for sessions as a small group with two cotherapists, and each session was devoted to training skills in two problematic situations. The situations selected for coverage (16 situations in all) were chosen on the basis of their potential for triggering relapse in alcoholics. On the basis of an analysis of relapse situations with other alcoholic samples, we were able to determine that four categories of situations could be classified as high risk in terms of precipitating drinking in previously abstinent alcoholics. These categories include frustration and anger situations (e.g., your employer criticizes you unfairly after you have returned to work), interpersonal temptation situations (e.g., social pressure from old drinking buddies to resume drinking), negative emotional states (e.g., coping with boredom or depression), and intrapersonal temptation situations (e.g., attempting to test the effectiveness of treatment by trying an occasional drink).

In each treatment session, group members first were taught a general problem-solving orientation to deal with the specific high-risk situation under discussion. Subjects discussed the situation in detail and were encouraged to generate a variety of alternative coping strategies to deal with it. The likely consequences of each alternative were discussed, and, if necessary, the therapists proposed other alternatives. The therapist then modeled a constructive coping skill appropriate to that situation, using role-play procedures for all interpersonal situations. In the intrapersonal temptation situations, the therapist modeled an internal monologue of thoughts and self-statements designed to define explicitly the problem, to generate alternatives, to highlight the immediate and long-term consequences of each alternative, and to outline the steps involved to implement a constructive solution. After the modeling demonstration, each subject chose a particular response and rehearsed it, receiving feedback from other members of the group in the process. The therapist and members of the group provided instruction and coaching to each subject in turn, and subjects were required to repeat their performance until it met with the entire group's approval. After each subject had rehearsed and performed the skill involved (e.g., responding in an assertive way to an insult or other provocation), a member of the group was asked to summarize the method used to generate and to evaluate an adequate response to that situation.

Subjects in the discussion control group spent an equivalent amount of time in group meetings as did the skill training group. The focus in these sessions, however, was on eliciting and discussing emotions and feelings evoked by descriptions of the same high-risk situations covered in the skill-training group; no time was spent in teaching subjects coping skills. Discussion group procedures centered on eliciting the feelings that may be present in problematic situations, with the rationale that self-understanding and increased insight should result from these procedures. Finally, the no-treatment control group received all the assessment measures at the same time intervals as other subjects but participated only in the regular ward treatment program.

Several important findings were obtained in this study. Results comparing the pre- and posttreatment performance of subjects on the Situational Competency Test (the verbal role-playing measure of coping skills in high-risk situations) showed a significant improvement for skill training subjects as compared to the subjects in the two control groups. Of even greater importance, however, was the subjects' drinking status during the follow-up period. The data presented in Table 10.2 indicate some of these findings for the 1-year follow-up period. As is evident from inspection of these results, the skill-training group was significantly superior to the pooled findings for the two control groups (which did not differ significantly from each other) for the following measures: days drunk, total drinks consumed, and average number of days spent drinking. Thus, the skill-training approach was found to be more effective in the year following treatment; subjects in this group showed less overall drinking and fewer periods of intoxication than did control subjects. In general, the skills program seemed to be effective as a relapse prevention procedure; subjects receiving this training had an average number of days intoxicated one-sixth that of the combined control group, drank one-fourth as much when they did drink, and had an average drinking period less than one-eighth as long as did the control subjects. Clearly, the skill-training method shows considerable promise, even with the treatment of chronic drinking problems. Their application as a *prevention* method with a younger population of problem drinkers would seem to be of even greater potential.

For clients who select controlled drinking as a goal of treatment, skills specific to drinking behavior are an integral part of the program. These skills are also important

TABLE 10.2
Selected One-Year Follow-Up Data for Alcoholics Receiving Skill Training, Compared to Control Subjects[a]

Follow-up measure	Skill training group ($n = 14$)		Combined control group[b] ($n = 25$)		p level
	Mean	s.d.	Mean	s.d.	
Days drunk[c]	11.1	14.3	64.0	88.3	< .05
Days controlled drinking[d]	4.9	17.8	1.2	2.6	N.S.
Total drinks consumed[e]	399.8	507.8	1592.8	2218.4	< .05
Average days of drinking	5.1	6.9	44.0	62.2	< .05

[a] From Chaney, O'Leary, and Marlatt, 1978.

[b] Since no significant differences were obtained for these measures between the discussion-only control group and the no-additional-treatment control group, the data from these two groups were pooled for comparison purposes.

[c] Defined as any isolated day in which 10 or more drinks were consumed or as any day that was part of a period of 2 or more days during which 7 or 9 drinks were consumed.

[d] Defined as any day during which six or fewer drinks were consumed.

[e] A drink is defined as 1 ounce of 86-proof liquor or its equivalent in alcohol content for beer or wine.

for those who choose abstinence as a preventive measure to cope effectively with the possibility of relapse. Again, selection of specific skills to be imparted will depend on the outcome of behavioral assessment procedures with a particular client. In recent years, a variety of controlled-drinking skills have been described in the literature. Among the most promising of these methods are:

1. Blood-alcohol discrimination training, in which the client is taught to estimate his or her own level of intoxication by using a combination of internal cues (e.g., physical and subjective effects of alcohol) and external cues (estimating blood-alcohol levels based on the amount of alcohol consumed in a given time period). The client learns to estimate blood-alcohol levels in an actual drinking situation, with corrective feedback provided by means of a Breathalyzer or other breath-analysis instrument.

2. Setting limits on consumption by limiting drinking to particular safe situations (and avoiding drinking as a means of coping with stress) and by contracting upper limits of daily consumption (with fines for exceeding these limits).

3. Learning to exercise control over drinking patterns and habits (e.g., learning to order weaker or mixed drinks, spacing drinks out over a given time period, alternating nonalcoholic beverages with alcoholic beverages, etc.).

4. Learning to cope effectively with social pressures to drink beyond one's chosen limits (e.g., learning to refuse drinks).

5. Training the drinker to self-monitor consumption whenever drinking occurs, so as to increase awareness and to prevent drinking from dropping back to habitual (low awareness) levels.

Complete and detailed accounts of these controlled drinking skills and evaluation of their effectiveness with a variety of problem drinkers are provided in the following sources: Marlatt and Nathan (1978), Nathan, Marlatt, and Løberg (1978), P. M. Miller (1976), and Sobell and Sobell (1978). In our own work with clients, we have found a manual on drinking skills (written on a practical and nontechnical level) to be particularly helpful as a self-help guide (Miller & Muñoz, 1976).

Lifestyle Intervention

One of our clients recently disagreed with the traditional definition of loss-of-control drinking. Rather than referring to a loss of voluntary control over continued consumption of alcohol after having the first drink or two, she said that it was a good term to describe her own drinking when she felt "out of control" in the course of her daily life experiences. In a previous section, we suggested that the degree of balance in a person's lifestyle may have an important impact on one's overall consumption of alcohol. If one's daily lifestyle is out of balance (e.g., an imbalance of "wants" and "shoulds") or if the individual is under a great deal of stress, there is a perception of being "out of control"—of not feeling centered or in-touch with one's feelings and behavior (Tulku, 1976). Drinking is likely to increase when these feelings occur, enhanced by the need for self-indulgence or gratification (giving oneself a big "want" in response to an overload of "shoulds"). Similarly, the probability of drinking will increase, according to our theoretical model, whenever an individual's sense of perceived control is threatened or reduced by environmental events that are "beyond one's control."

By building the client's sense of self-efficacy or personal competence, we hope to counterbalance the feelings of helplessness or lack of perceived control that are associated with stress or with an unbalanced lifestyle. In the previous section, we described a number of specific skills that can be taught to help the client cope with a variety of high-risk situations. In this section, we would like to focus on a number of *global* intervention procedures that are likely to enhance one's self-efficacy. Life-style monitoring (the assessment of daily activities) serves as the basis for treatment planning, in which the therapist attempts to program in more adaptive forms of self-indulgence (e.g., jogging, meditation, relaxation training, etc.) as alternatives to drinking and as a means of lowering the subjective urge to overindulge. It is our hypothesis that a program of training that combines coping in specific high-risk situations with more global efficacy-enhancing procedures provides the most comprehensive approach to treatment with problem drinkers.

On one level, our underlying assumption for lifestyle intervention is to replace drinking with some form of "positive addiction" (Glasser, 1976). If a negative addiction (e.g., excessive use of drugs) can be defined as an activity that feels good at first but causes harm in the long run, a positive addiction (e.g., jogging or running) is an activity that feels bad at first but is very beneficial in terms of its delayed effects. Positive addictions soon become "wants," since the individual begins to look forward to engaging in the activity and misses the positive effects if the activity is not engaged in on a regular basis. Since the individual usually must acquire new skills in the development of positive addictions, self-efficacy increases as a result. Similarly, since the regular practice of these behaviors is associated with a greater sense of relaxation or improved physical well-being, one's overall coping capacity is increased—high-risk situations may be more easily dealt with, rather than serving as precipitating triggers for excessive drinking.

Glasser (1976) has stated that a positive addiction can be any activity or behavior that meets the following six criteria:

1. It is something noncompetitive that you choose to do and you can devote an hour (approximately) a day to it.
2. It is possible for you to do it easily and it doesn't take a great deal of mental effort to do it well.
3. You can do it alone or rarely with others but it does not depend upon others to do it.
4. You believe that it has some value (physical, mental, or spiritual) for you.
5. You believe that if you persist at it you will improve, but this is completely subjective—you need to be the only one who measures that improvement.
6. The activity *must* have the quality that you can do it *without criticizing yourself. If you can't accept yourself during this time, the activity will not be addicting* [p. 93].

In our own work with clients, we have found a number of activities that seem to enhance efficacy and to provide alternatives to drinking. Perhaps the easiest activity to learn in this regard is meditation. Meditation provides a deep relaxation experience and is often described as a "high" experience by those who engage in it on a regular basis. Research on meditation has shown that continued practice is associated with an increased capacity to cope with a variety of stressful situations (Carrington, 1977; Marlatt & Marques, 1977). Our clinical experience suggests that meditation is particularly helpful with clients who tend to conceptualize their fears and anxieties (e.g., by excessive worry and rumination or other obsessive thought patterns) and that deep muscle relaxation (e.g., Jacobson's technique) works best for those clients who somaticize their anxiety by becoming physically tense.

Other lifestyle-intervention procedures are recommended, depending on the client's individual needs and capacity. A regular program of exercise, such as running or jogging, is a potent antidote to excessive alcohol use—particularly if the client substitutes a run for the usual cocktails at the end of the workday. (Meditation and exercise provide experiences that are directly opposite in quality to those associated with programs such as AA, where members typically spend a good part of their meeting time drinking cup after cup of coffee, chain-smoking, and telling drinking stories.) Other activities include working on hobbies or on other creative tasks, gardening, reading, attending concerts or motion pictures, learning to play a musical instrument, and so forth. Learning to participate in "addictive" sports, such as skiing, sky-diving, sailing, hanggliding, and automobile racing may be recommended for the more adventurous client, since these activities provide an intense alternative "high" to the effects of alcohol (cf. Miller & Marlatt, 1977). Programming in periods of free time during the day, when the client can pursue his or her own interests (going shopping, having lunch with a friend, etc.), will help provide balance in an otherwise crowded schedule of "shoulds." Keeping an ongoing diary or journal also helps to develop a sense of perspective and choice over the flow of one's daily experiences. Lifestyle intervention may also involve therapeutic programs that have a major impact on the client's life (e.g., marital therapy, employment counseling, or changes in one's social or physical environment).

We have just begun to conduct research on the effectiveness of lifestyle intervention programs and on the development of global coping strategies as alternatives to drinking. In a recent study (Marlatt & Marques, 1977), we investigated the effects of participating in a daily program of relaxation on the ongoing drinking behavior of heavy social drinkers. Subjects who volunteered to participate in the study agreed to keep a daily record of their drinking behavior for a period of 15 weeks. After 2 weeks of pretreatment baseline recording, subjects were assigned randomly to one of four intervention programs: meditation training (Benson, 1975), progressive muscle relaxation, a bibliotherapy control group (in which subjects spent their daily relaxation periods quietly reading material of their own choosing), and a notreatment control group. After a 6-week training period, subjects were followed up for a period of 7 weeks, during which time they were free to continue or to discontinue practice of their techniques.

The results showed a significant reduction in alcohol use (approximately a 50% drop from pretreatment rates) for subjects in all three relaxation groups, in comparison with the no-treatment control condition. Subjects in the three treatment groups also showed a significant shift toward a greater internal locus of control (Rotter, 1966) during the treatment period—a finding that suggests either that the observed decrease in drinking may be mediated by an increase in perceived internal control over one's behavior or that drops in alcohol consumption are associated with increased perception of internal control. During the follow-up period, almost all of the subjects discontinued practice of the procedures, however, and drinking rates tended to increase toward baseline levels. Since the subjects in this study did not express any initial interest in decreasing their rates of drinking, their motivation to continue practicing the relaxation procedures would seem to be lower than it would be for clients who actively seek help with their drinking problems.

Relapse Prevention

In this final section, we will describe several procedures that are designed to prevent or to cope with the possibility of relapse. Although most of the comments apply specifically to the client who has chosen abstinence as the treatment goal, much of this material also applies to the controlled drinker for whom *relapse* is defined as a violation of self-imposed limits on drinking rates (e.g., a period of binge drinking). In a recent paper on determinants of relapse (Marlatt & Gordon, 1979), we have outlined a theoretical model of the relapse process based on cognitive–behavioral principles. In the paper, data are presented describing situational determinants of relapse for a large group of subjects who had attempted to abstain from the use of one of the following substances: alcohol, tobacco, or heroin. The results of this analysis of relapse showed that there were more similarities than differences involving these three substances, suggesting that there may be common elements involved in the determinants and reactions to relapse, regardless of the particular drug or behavior involved. Since the treatment implications deriving from this analysis are presented in detail in the Marlatt and Gordon (1979) paper, only the highlights of this program will be presented here.

In brief, the model proposes that the probability of relapse (defined as any use of a taboo substance) will increase in a high-risk situation if the individual fails to cope adequately with the problem. Failure to cope effectively leads to a decreased sense of self-efficacy wherein the individual feels less capable of handling forthcoming events or subsequent situations. If the succeeding situation involves the availability of the taboo substance (e.g., alcohol) and if the individual harbors positive expectancies for the effects of the substance (e.g., the initial "high" of the biphasic response to alcohol), the chances increase that a relapse will occur. Should the individual take a drink at this point, he or she is likely to experience a pronounced cognitive–affective reaction that we have called the *Abstinence Violation Effect* (AVE). There are two components of the AVE: (*a*) guilt or conflict similar to cognitive dissonance (in which the behavioral act associated with the first drink is in direct conflict with the individual's prior self-image as an abstainer); and (*b*) attribution of the cause of the "slip" or relapse to personal weakness or lack of willpower. The AVE is a powerful reaction that tends to elicit a sense of helplessness or victimization in the drinker, so that he or she feels a loss of personal control over subsequent intake of alcohol. Drinking becomes reinforced as a coping response in the face of a stressful situation, and the individual usually has considerable difficulty in going "back on the wagon" and regaining abstinence.

Most traditional treatment programs fail to prepare clients for the possibility of relapse. There seems to be a consensus among professional alcoholism counselors and other treatment personnel that talking about relapse is tantamount to giving one permission to go back to drinking. Since the disease model stresses physiological or internal addictive processes as determinants of relapse (e.g., craving experiences), it is little wonder that situational and social factors have been ignored from this perspective. In our view, teaching skills that may help an individual to cope successfully with a relapse, either in terms of preventing one from occurring altogether or of minimizing the extent of the relapse if it does occur, would seem to be a matter of common sense. In our society, we have adopted a number of precautionary measures to deal with the possibility of something going wrong, no matter how remote the possibility. We have procedures such as firedrills or lifeboat drills, for example, to cope with possible future accidents or catastrophes. In a sense, we are recommending a similar strategy: the use of relapse drills to teach our clients how to deal with a relapse. We also hope to train clients to recognize the early warning signals that often precede a relapse, so that they may take remedial action and perhaps prevent altogether a drinking episode.

Many of the components of the relapse prevention program have already been described earlier in this chapter. Behavioral assessment procedures (e.g., self-monitoring) are employed to identify potential high-risk situations that may trigger a relapse. The client's ability to cope with these situations is determined, and appropriate skill training programs are developed to increase coping capacity. Lifestyle engineering is planned to reduce the urge to indulge in alcohol and to increase the client's self-efficacy. Clients are given education about the biphasic effects of alcohol, to counter expectations about the initial "high" as the only effect of drinking. In addition to these procedures, however, there are several additional techniques that focus exclusively on the relapse process itself.

Cognitive intervention procedures can be used to heighten the client's awareness of the possibility of relapse. We need to train the client to foresee the factors that may lead up to a relapse so that adequate preventive steps can be taken. Clinical experience indicates that it is very difficult to prevent a relapse at the last moment, when the situation has already developed to the point of boiling over. It is our current hypothesis that a person who is headed for a relapse makes a number of minidecisions over time that bring one a little closer to the brink of the triggering situation. An example might be the abstinent drinker who buys a bottle of sherry to take home "just in case guests drop in." Another example might involve accepting an invitation to a New Year's Eve party where champagne is likely to be flowing in an atmosphere of unique celebration. It is as though the individual begins to slowly set the stage for a possible relapse, even though there may be little active awareness of this process. We have dubbed these minidecisions as AIDs—Apparently Irrelevant Decisions that precede a relapse.[1] The therapist can help the client to recognize and to articulate the development of these AIDs through the course of treatment. The emphasis here is on helping the client to recognize and to accept the role of personal responsibility in making decisions that may lead to a relapse and to take remedial action. Systematic application of decision-making theory, in which the client carefully works out the potential costs and benefits of making each decision, is a particularly useful strategy.

Another procedure that we recommend is called *relapse rehearsal*. Here, the client is asked to imagine the exact circumstances in which a relapse might occur. There are many cues that the client can use to construct a potential relapse scene. Abstinent individuals often entertain fantasies about drinking, and some report having dreams in which they "find themselves" drinking. Having the client elaborate upon these fantasies in order to develop a scenario for relapse enables the therapist to identify potential situational determinants for drinking and to develop alternative coping strategies. Asking the client to specify exactly what he or she would do to cope with the events associated with the potential relapse is an essential part of this prevention procedure. Repeated practice and rehearsal of the coping responses (both the behavioral and the cognitive components) will add to the client's preparation.

What if all the prevention procedures fail and the client takes a drink? We need to develop the client's abilities to cope with a single slip and to prevent the first drink or two from snowballing into a full-blown relapse. A combination of specific behavioral skills and cognitive restructuring is recommended to put the brakes on the client's drinking at this crucial juncture. First, we need to teach the client behavioral skills to moderate or to control the drinking once it has occurred. Here, the use of controlled drinking skills, as described earlier, would be the most useful intervention. In addition, if the controlled-use skills are to be effective, we must instruct the client to cope with the Abstinence Violation Effect by using cognitive restructuring procedures.

The client must be encouraged to view the first drink or slip as a discrete behavior, an event to be viewed as a learning experience, rather than as an act of transgression. Because abstinence is such an absolute requirement (there is no such thing as being "a little bit nonabstinent"), the client is likely to feel a tremendous sense of guilt and self-blame for breaking the abstinence rule (the reaction will vary as a function of the duration of the prior abstinence period and the degree of personal and public commitment one has made to abstain). Marlatt and Gordon (1979) have suggested presenting the following rationale as a means of cognitively restructuring the client's response to a relapse episode:

> A slip is not all that unusual. It does not mean that you have failed or that you have lost control over your behavior. You will probably feel guilty about what you have done, and

[1] I am indebted to a colleague at the University of Washington, Professor Lee Beach, who suggested this term to me.

will blame yourself for having slipped. This feeling is to be expected; it is part of what we call the Abstinence Violation Effect. There is no reason why you have to give in to this feeling and continue to drink. The feeling will pass in time. Look upon the slip as a learning experience. What were the elements of the high-risk situation which led to the slip? What coping response could you have used to get around the situation? Remember the old saying: One swallow doesn't make a summer? Well, one slip doesn't have to make a relapse, either. Just because you slipped once does not mean that you are a failure, that you have no will power, or that you are a hopeless addict. Look upon the slip as a single, independent event, something which can be avoided in the future with an alternative coping response.

In some situations, it may help actually to stage a supervised relapse with the client, particularly if the client is convinced that he or she is likely to go back to drinking in the near future. This technique, a procedure we call the *programmed relapse,* is recommended because the therapist programs or has control over the setting and events associated with the resumption of drinking. As such, it is less likely that the client will feel guilty and will attribute the cause of drinking to personal failings or to other internal weaknesses. The therapist can also help the client interpret the reactions to taking the first drink and be objective about the effects of alcohol (to counter the client's initial expectations).

The underlying philosophy that has guided my thoughts and that has influenced my research and clinical work in the past few years is not a popular one (to say the least) in the professional alcoholism field today. Throughout this work, I have tried to make my assumptions and definitions explicit, so that the predictions derived from our theoretical model can be subject to empirical verification. The implications of the social-learning model for assessment and treatment of alcohol problems is at complete variance with the traditional disease model. I think it all boils down to one basic choice. Either we are going to view addictions as diseases, as physiologically based and/or genetically predetermined illnesses in which the patient becomes the helpless victim of biological entities or forces beyond the individual's control (and for which absolute abstinence is the only salvation) *or* we are going to view addictions as habitual behavior patterns, as overlearned and relatively ineffective coping responses that are subject to modification through skill-training prodedures, modification of expectancies, and the overall increase in awareness and self-efficacy that follows from this approach. One key implication of this second alternative is that excessive behaviors are not always cured by insistence upon excessive restraints over these behaviors. The emphasis on the duality between abstinence and indulgence (or between control and loss of control) tends to reinforce the oscillation of addictive behaviors from one extreme to the other by forcing the individual to adopt one of two extreme roles. There may be, as an alternative, a middle way or position of balance between restraint and indulgence: moderation, based on awareness, skills, and responsible choice. Support for either of these opposing theoretical models must await the findings of future research. In the meantime, however, I think that my bias as an advocate of a cognitive–behavioral approach to addictive behaviors is clearly evident.

REFERENCES

Alcoholics Anonymous World Services, *Alcoholics Anonymous*. New York: A. A. World Services, Inc., 1955.

Armor, D. J., Polich, J. M., & Stambul, H. B. *Alcoholism and treatment*. New York: Wiley, 1978.

Bandura A. *Principles of behavior modification*. New York: Holt, Rinehart & Winston, 1969.

Bandura, A. Self-efficacy: Toward a unifying theory of behavioral change. *Psychological Review*, 1977, *84*, 191–215.

Benson, H. *The relaxation response*. New York: William Morrow & Company, 1975.

Cahalan, D., Cisin, I. H., & Crossley, H. *American drinking practices*. New Brunswick, New Jersey: Rutgers Center of Alcohol Studies, 1969.

Cahalan, D., & Room, R. *Problem drinking among American men*. New Brunswick, New Jersey: Rutgers Center of Alcohol Studies, 1974.

Cappell, H., & Herman, C. P. Alcohol and tension reduction: A review. *Quarterly Journal of Studies on Alcohol*, 1972, *33*, 33–64.

Carrington, P. *Freedom in meditation*. Garden City, New York: Anchor/Doubleday, 1977.

Caudill, B. D., & Marlatt, G. A. Modeling influences in social drinking: An experimental analogue. *Journal of Consulting and Clinical Psychology*, 1975, *43*, 405–415.

Chaney, E. F., O'Leary, M. R., & Marlatt, G. A. Skill training with alcoholics. *Journal of Consulting and Clinical Psychology*, 1978, *46*, 1092–1104.

Conger, J. J. Alcoholism: Theory, problem and challenge. II. Reinforcement theory and the dynamics of alcoholism. *Quarterly Journal of Studies on Alcohol*, 1956, *17*, 291–324.

Docter, R., Naitoh, P., & Smith, J. Electroencephalographic changes and vigilance behavior during experimentally induced intoxication with alcoholic subjects. *Psychosomatic Medicine*, 1966, *28*, 605–615.

D'Zurilla, T. J., & Goldfried, M. R. Problem solving and behavior modification. *Journal of Abnormal Psychology*, 1971, *78*, 107–126.

Edwards, G., Orford, J., Egert, S., Guthrie, S., Hawker, A.. Hensman, C., Mitcheson, M., Oppenheimer, E., & Taylor, C. Alcoholism: A controlled trial of "treatment" and "advice." *Journal of Studies on Alcohol*, 1977, *38*, 1004–1031.

Emrick, C. D., & Stilson, D. W. The "Rand Report": Some comments and a response. *Journal of Studies on Alcohol*, 1977, *38*, 152–193.

Garfield, Z., & McBrearty, J. Arousal level and stimulus response in alcoholics after drinking. *Quarterly Journal of Studies on Alcohol*, 1970, *31*, 832–838.

Glasser, W. *Postive addiction*. New York: Harper & Row, 1976.

Goldfried, M. R., & Davison, G. C. *Clinical behavior therapy*. New York: Holt, Rinehart, & Winston, 1976.

Goldstein, A. P. *Structured learning therapy*. New York: Academic Press, 1973.

Goodwin, D. *Is alcoholism hereditary?* New York: Oxford University Press, 1976.

Gove, W. (Ed.). *The labeling of deviance*. New York: Wiley, 1975.

Higgins, R. L., & Marlatt, G. A. The effects of anxiety arousal upon the consumption of alcohol by alcoholics and social drinkers. *Journal of Consulting and Clinical Psychology*, 1973, *41*, 426–433.

Higgins, R. L., & Marlatt, G. A. Fear of interpersonal evaluation as a determinant of alcohol consumption in male social drinkers. *Journal of Abnormal Psychology*, 1975, *84*, 644–651.

Jacobson, G. R. *The alcoholisms: Detection, assessment, and diagnosis*. New York: Human Sciences Press, 1976.

Jellinek, E. M. The phases of alcohol addiction. *Quarterly Journal of Studies on Alcohol*, 1952, *13*, 673–684.

Jellinek, E. M. *The disease concept of alcoholism*. New Brunswick, New Jersey: Hillhouse Press, 1960.

Jones, B. M., & Vega, A. Cognitive performance measured on the ascending and descending limb of the blood alcohol curve. *Psychopharmacologia*, 1972, *23*, 99–114.

Keller, M. The disease concept of alcoholism revisited. *Journal of Studies on Alcohol,* 1976, *37,* 1694–1717.

Lang, A. R., Goeckner, D. J., Adesso, V. J., & Marlatt, G. A. The effects of alcohol on aggression in male social drinkers. *Journal of Abnormal Psychology,* 1975, *84,* 508–518.

Leach, B. Does Alcoholics Anonymous really work? In P. G. Bourne & R. Fox (Eds.), *Alcoholism: Progress in research and treatment.* New York: Academic Press, 1973.

Lied, E. R., & Marlatt, G. A. Modeling as a determinant of alcohol consumption: Effects of subject sex and prior drinking history. *Addictive Behaviors,* 1979, *4,* 47–54.

Manson, M. P. A psychometric determination of alcoholic addiction. *American Journal of Psychiatry,* 1949, *106,* 199–205.

Marlatt, G. A. Alcohol, stress, and cognitive control. In I. G. Sarason & C. D. Spielberger (Eds.), *Stress and anxiety (Vol. 3).* Washington, D.C.: Hemisphere Publishing Co., 1976. (a)

Marlatt, G. A. The Drinking Profile: A questionnaire for the behavioral assessment of alcoholism. In E. J. Mash & L. G. Terdal (Eds.), *Behavior therapy assessment: Diagnosis, design, and evaluation.* New York: Springer, 1976. (b)

Marlatt, G. A. Behavioral assessment of social drinking and alcoholism. In G. A. Marlatt & P. E. Nathan (Eds.), *Behavioral approaches to alcoholism.* New Brunswick, New Jersey: Rutgers Center of Alcohol Studies, 1978. (a)

Marlatt, G. A. Craving for alcohol, loss of control, and relapse: A cognitive–behavioral analysis. In P. E. Nathan, G. A. Marlatt, & T. Løberg (Eds.), *Alcoholism: New directions in behavioral research and treatment.* New York: Plenum, 1978. (b)

Marlatt, G. A., Demming, B., & Reid, J. B. Loss of control drinking in alcoholics: An experimental analogue. *Journal of Abnormal Psychology,* 1973, *81,* 223–241.

Marlatt, G. A., & Gordon, J. R. Determinants of relapse: Implications for the maintenance of behavior change. In P. Davidson (Ed.), *Behavioral medicine: Changing health lifestyles.* New York: Brunner/Mazel, 1979.

Marlatt, G. A., Kosturn, C. F., & Lang, A. R. Provocation to anger and opportunity for retaliation as determinants of alcohol consumption in social drinkers. *Journal of Abnormal Psychology,* 1975, *84,* 652–659.

Marlatt, G. A., & Marques, J. K. Meditation, self-control, and alcohol use. In R. B. Stuart (Ed.), *Behavioral self-management: Strategies, techniques, and outcomes.* New York: Brunner/Mazel, 1977.

Marlatt, G. A., & Nathan, P. E. *Behavioral approaches to alcoholism.* New Brunswick, New Jersey: Rutgers Center of Alcohol Studies, 1978.

Marlatt, G. A., & Rohsenow, D. J. Cognitive processes in alcohol use: Expectancy and the balanced placebo design. In N. K. Mello (Ed.), *Advances in substance abuse.* Greenwich, Connecticut: JAI Press, 1980.

McClelland, D. C., Davis, W. M., Kalin, R., & Wanner, E. *The drinking man.* New York: Free Press, 1972.

McFall, R. M. Behavioral training: A skill-acquisition approach to clinical problems. In J. T. Spence, R. C. Carson, & J. W. Thibaut (Eds.), *Behavioral approaches to therapy.* Morristown, New Jersey: General Learning Press, 1975.

McFall, R. M. Parameters of self-monitoring. In R. B. Stuart (Ed.). *Behavioral self management: Strategies, techniques, and outcomes.* New York: Brunner/Mazel, 1977.

McGuire, M. T., Mendelson, J. H., & Stein, S. Comparative psychosocial studies of alcoholic and non-alcoholic subjects undergoing experimentally-induced ethanol intoxication. *Psychosomatic Medicine,* 1966, *28,* 13–25.

Meichenbaum, D. *Cognitive–behavior modification.* New York: Plenum, 1977.

Mello, N. K. Some aspects of the behavioral pharmacology of alcohol. In D. H. Efron (Ed.), *Psychopharmacology: A review of progress, 1957–1967.* Washington, D.C.: U.S. Government Printing Office, 1968 (Public Health Service Publication No. 1836).

Miller, P. M. *Behavioral treatment of alcoholism.* Oxford, U.K.: Pergamon, 1976.

Miller, P. M. Assessment of addictive behaviors. In A. R. Ciminero, K. S. Calhoun, & H. E. Adams (Eds.), *Handbook of behavioral assessment*. New York: Wiley, 1977.

Miller, P. M., Hersen, M., Eisler, R. M., & Hilsman, G. Effects of social stress on operant drinking of alcoholics and social drinkers. *Behaviour Research and Therapy*, 1974, *12*, 67–72.

Miller, P. M., & Mastria, M. A. *Alternatives to alcohol abuse: A social learning model*. Champaign, Illinois: Research Press, 1977.

Miller, W. R. Alcoholism scales and objective assessment methods: A review. *Psychological Bulletin*, 1976, *83*, 649–674.

Miller, W. R., & Caddy, G. R. Abstinence and controlled drinking in the treatment of problem drinkers. *Journal of Studies on Alcohol*, 1977, *38*, 986–1003.

Miller, W. R., & Marlatt, G. A. The Banff Skiism Screening Test: An instrument for assessing degree of addiction. *Addictive Behaviors*, 1977, *2*, 81–82.

Miller, W. R., & Muñoz, R. F. *How to control your drinking*. Englewood Cliffs, New Jersey: Prentice-Hall, 1976.

Nathan, P. E., Marlatt, G. A., & Løberg, T. (Eds.), *Alcoholism: New directions in behavioral research and treatment*. New York: Plenum, 1978.

Nathan, P. E., & O'Brien, J. S. An experimental analysis of the behavior of alcoholics and nonalcoholics during prolonged experimental drinking: A necessary precursor of behavior therapy? *Behavior Therapy*, 1971, *2*, 455–476.

National Council on Alcoholism. Criteria for the diagnosis of alcoholism. *American Journal of Psychiatry*, 1972, *129*, 127–135.

National Institute on Alcohol Abuse and Alcoholism. *Alcohol and health*. First, Second, and Third Reports to the U.S. Congress. Washington, D.C.: U.S. Government Printing Office, 1971, 1974, and 1978.

Norris, J. L. Alcoholics Anonymous and other self-help groups. In R. E. Tarter & A. A. Sugerman (Eds.), *Alcoholism: Interdisciplinary approaches to an enduring problem*. Reading, Massachusetts: Addison-Wesley, 1976.

Pattison, E. M., Sobell, M. B., & Sobell, L. C. *Emerging concepts of alcohol dependence*. New York: Springer, 1977.

Reid, J. B. The study of drinking in natural settings. In G. A. Marlatt & P. E. Nathan (Eds.), *Behavioral approaches to alcoholism*. New Brunswick, New Jersey: Rutgers Center of Alcohol Studies, 1978.

Rimm, D. C., & Master, J. C. *Behavior therapy: Techniques and empirical findings*. New York: Academic Press, 1974.

Rohsenow, D. J., & O'Leary, M. R. Locus of control research on alcoholic populations: A review. *International Journal of the Addictions*, 1978, *13*, 55–78, 213–226.

Rotter, J. B., Generalized expectancies for internal versus external control of reinforcement. *Psychological Monographs*, 1966, 80 (1; Whole No. 609).

Sarason, I. G. *Abnormal psychology: The problem of maladaptive behavior (2nd Ed.)*. Englewood Cliffs, New Jersey: Prentice-Hall, 1976.

Seligman, M. E. P. *Helplessness: On depression, development, and death*. San Francisco: W. H. Freeman, 1975.

Selzer, M. L. The Michigan Alcoholism Screening Test: The quest for a new diagnostic instrument. *American Journal of Psychiatry*, 1971, *127*, 89–94.

Sobell, L. C., & Sobell, M. B. A self-feedback technique to monitor drinking behavior in alcoholics. *Behaviour Research and Therapy*, 1973, *11*, 237–238.

Sobell, M. B., & Sobell, L. C. Assessment of addictive behavior. In M. Hersen & A. S. Bellack (Eds.), *Behavioral assessment: A practical handbook*. Oxford, U.K.: Pergamon, 1976.

Sobell, M. B., & Sobell, L. C. *Behavioral treatment of alcohol problems*. New York: Plenum, 1978.

Solomon, R. L. An opponent-process theory of acquired motivation: IV. The affective dynamics of addiction. In J. Maser & M. E. P. Seligman (Eds.), *Psychopathology: Experimental models*. San Francisco, California: W. H. Freeman, 1977.

Solomon, R. L., & Corbit, J. D. An opponent-process theory of motivation: I. Temporal dynamics of affect. *Psychological Review,* 1974, *81,* 119–145.

Tamerin, J. S., Weiner, S., & Mendelson, J. H. Alcoholics' expectancies and recall of experiences during intoxication. *American Journal of Psychiatry,* 1970, *126,* 1697–1704.

Tarter, R. E., & Sugerman, A. A. (Eds.) *Alcoholism: Interdisciplinary approaches to an enduring problem.* Reading, Massachusetts: Addison-Wesley, 1976.

Tulku, T. *Gesture of balance: A guide to awareness, self-healing and meditation.* Emeryville, California: Dharma Publications, 1976.

Wanberg, K. W., Horn, J. L., & Foster, F. M. A differential assessment model for alcoholism: The scales of the Alcohol Use Inventory. *Journal of Studies on Alcohol,* 1977, *38,* 512–543.

Wilson, G. T. Booze, beliefs, and behavior: Cognitive processes in alcohol use and abuse. In P. E. Nathan, G. A. Marlatt, & T. Løberg (Eds.), *Alcoholism: New directions in behavioral research and treatment.* New York: Plenum, 1978.

Wilson, G. T., & Abrams, D. Effects of alcohol on social anxiety and physioloical arousal: Cognitive versus pharmacological processes. *Cognitive Therapy and Research,* 1977, *1,* 195–210.

Wilson, G. T., & Lawson, D. M. Expectancies, alcohol, and sexual arousal in male social drinkers. *Journal of Abnormal Psychology,* 1976, *85,* 587–594.

11

Cognitive–Behavior Therapy for Eating Disturbances

GLORIA RAKITA LEON

INTRODUCTION

Over the past decade, there has been an increasing interest in formulating behavioral theories of the etiology of eating disturbances and in planning research activity in developing behavioral treatment procedures. For both obesity and anorexia nervosa, etiological theories and treatment strategies have moved from a primary emphasis on past history and psychodynamic pathology (Alexander & Flagg, 1965; Bruch, 1963) to a perspective that includes an analysis of behaviors and interaction patterns in the current environment. Many of the early behavioral treatment studies emphasized the modification of maladaptive habit patterns in response to food stimuli and the application of reinforcers contingent on the prescribed behavior changes. Recently, behavioral strategies for treating the eating disorders have been broadened to include cognitive processes among the stimuli targeted for modification. Thus, in addition to modifying overt maladaptive behavior patterns, treatment techniques also have been developed to deal with covert phenomena such as body image, self-control in response to maladaptive urges, and most recently, the decision-making process and issues of personal commitment. At the present time, one can, therefore, observe a synthesis of cognitive and behavioral variables in the continuing development of new and more effective intervention procedures for treating eating disturbances.

357

Cognitive–Behavioral Interventions:
Theory, Research, and Procedures

OBESITY

Behavioral Treatment Outcome Research

Initial Studies

The first significant step in the development of behavioral methods for weight reduction occurred when Stuart (1967, 1971) reported on the successful results of a treatment program based on learning principles that included both treatment and follow-up information. His approach was basically one of changing the environmental cues that signalled inappropriate eating behavior, monitoring food and drink consumption, and implementing material rewards for weight loss. Specific information was presented in Stuart and Davis (1972) on how to change the circumstances in which eating occurred and thus place food consumption under more appropriate stimulus-control conditions. Nutritional information also was presented, and the importance of eating balanced meals and engaging in daily exercise was stressed.

Other investigators (e.g., Harris, 1969; Penick, Filion, Fox, & Stunkard, 1971; Wollersheim, 1970) compared Stuart's procedure and their own modifications of his basic technique to other types of weight-reduction treatments. In all of these investigations, the behavioral techniques resulted in greater weight loss. Recently, Öst and Götestam (1976) reported that behavioral methods were more effective than the appetite suppressant fenfluramine in weight reduction and in weight-loss maintenance. The mean weight loss in the 1 year follow-up was 10.12 lb for the behavioral groups and 1.98 lb for the drug group. Wollersheim (1977) published information on a second, 16-week follow-up of her treatment groups and found that the focal therapy based on learning principles group and the social pressure group both reversed the trend toward weight loss attrition seen at the 8-week follow-up and manifested continued weight loss.

Other variations of behavior modification programs for weight reduction that developed and were systematically evaluated included group versus written manual instruction (Hagen, 1974), various types of therapist-provided and self-provided rewards for weight loss or eating pattern changes (e.g., Abrahms & Allen, 1974; Hall, 1972; Mahoney, Moura, & Wade, 1973), and contingency contracting (e.g., Harris & Bruner, 1971; Mann, 1972). Mahoney (1974) studied the relative effectiveness of self-monitoring, self-reward following weight loss, or self-reward following habit improvement and found that self-monitoring, in and of itself, did not produce significant weight loss. Relatively greater weight reduction occurred when persons self-rewarded for habit change rather than following weight reduction. (See Leon, 1976, for a more in-depth discussion and evaluation of these studies.)

Aversive procedures in the presence of preferred high calorie foods also have been evaluated. Particularly craved-for foods have been paired with an electric shock (Meyer & Crisp, 1964; Stollak, 1967), a noxious odor (Foreyt & Kennedy, 1971; Kennedy & Foreyt, 1968), and cigarette smoke (Morganstern, 1974). The studies generally indicate a greater effectiveness with behavior management procedures, since the aversive conditioning tends to be specific to a particular problem food and, therefore, does not generalize to a general monitoring and control of eating patterns.

The treatment outcome results evaluating behavior management techniques have been relatively promising. A survey of 11 studies in which follow-up information was available demonstrated a mean treatment period weight loss of 1.55 lb per week. The follow-up results (ranging from 4 to 52 weeks posttreatment) revealed that, in 8 of these 11 behavior management studies, the treatment-period weight loss was maintained or continued weight loss occurred (Leon, 1977). The follow-up information is important to consider because the true measure of any program's effectiveness should be long-term weight-loss maintenance. Many programs, including those involving special diets, fasting, jaw-wiring, and appetite suppressants, can produce rapid weight loss during treatment, but the weight is inevitably regained during the maintenance period following the treatment.

Recent Self-Management Studies

Current investigations show that the effectiveness of behavior management techniques may vary depending on the setting in which the procedures are taught and the amount of contact during the maintenance period. Kingsley and Wilson (1977) found that behavior management techniques taught to obese women in group settings resulted in significantly greater long-term maintenance of weight loss than occurred when these techniques were taught on an individual basis in an 8-week treatment program. There were 26 women in each of three different treatment conditions, with an overall attrition rate of 7.7%. The mean pretreatment to 1 year follow-up weight loss was 12.06 lb in the group behavioral condition that included periodic booster sessions during the maintenance period and 13.64 lb in the group behavioral–no booster condition. The individual behavioral–booster group exhibited a mean weight loss of 9.04 lb from pretreatment to 1 year follow-up. For the individual behavioral–no booster group, there was a mean weight gain of 0.26 lb over the same time period.

Kingsley and Shapiro (1977) adapted the Stuart and Davis program for use with 10–11-year olds and emphasized the daily-exercise and daily-recording-of-food-intake aspects of the program. They found no differences in weight loss in youngsters who were in a children-alone group, a mother-alone group (i.e., participation by just the mothers of the obese children), and a group in which both mothers and children were present. The mean weight loss of youngsters combined across treatment groups was 3.5 lb at the end of the 8-week treatment period. However, at the 20-week follow-up period, there was considerable attrition of the weight loss. The children-alone group showed a mean weight gain pretreatment to follow-up of 2.5 lb; the mothers-alone group, a 2.71 lb mean weight gain; and the mother–children group, a 0.29 lb mean weight loss.

Another recent study compared the weight reduction in a conventional self-management group, a programmed text with high therapist contact group, a programmed text with low therapist contact group, an attention-placebo group, and a no-treatment control group (Hanson, Borden, Hall, & Hall, 1976). Self-management for weight reduction taught through a programmed text was just as effective as the conventional type of self-management procedure that included lecture, group discussion, and assignments; all three groups showed significantly greater weight loss than did the control groups. The mean weight loss averaged across the three self-management groups was 6.28 lb at the end of the 10-week treatment program. However, the 1 year follow-up results indicated that only the persons in the programmed-text–low-therapist-contact group continued to lose weight.

McReynolds, Lutz, Paulsen, and Kohrs (1976) demonstrated that trained nutritionists were able to produce significant weight losses with behavioral self-control and stimulus-control behavior-modification groups over 15 weekly treatment sessions. There was no specific diet prescribed. The mean weight loss pre- to post-treatment was 18.6 lb for the self-control and 16.1 lb for the stimulus control group. From pretreatment to the 6-month follow-up, mean weight loss was 20.4 and 14.6 lb, respectively, for the two behavioral groups.

Successful weight loss through outpatient groups incorporating behavioral self-control programs and a diet of a specific number of calories per day has been reported by Marston, London, Cooper, and Lammas (1976). Musante (1976) also reported successful results with a behavioral program and a specific diet. However, no follow-up information was presented for either study.

Bellack, Schwartz, and Rozensky (1974) pointed out that the strategy common to self-control procedures for a variety of problem behaviors is the activity of the client in applying contingency management procedures to his or her own target behaviors. The investigators evaluated an external control group that self-monitored eating behavior, followed the other behavior management suggestions, and mailed the forms in to the experimenter. A no-contact group was also evaluated. The investigators found no additional treatment effect in the external-control group. Both self-control groups exhibited more weight loss than did the no-contact group.

It remains to be demonstrated that current self-control procedures, in comparison to other behavioral techniques, are relatively superior in producing long-term weight maintenance. Kelly and Curran (1976) found that a self-control group lost more weight during treatment than did an emotional coping group, a waiting-list control, and a placebo-control group, but there were no significant differences between the groups at follow-up. The need for continued treatment contact during the maintenance period was discussed and seems crucial to the long-term success of any program.

The treatment effectiveness of *in vivo* self-control training in the presence of high caloric preferred foods was evaluated by Murray, Davidoff, and Harrington (1975). One group received self-control training followed by the consumption of a low calorie food after self-control was exhibited. This group lost an average of 8.89 lb over the treatment period, but a mean of 7.33 lb was regained by the 24-week follow-up period. A self-control group without the subsequent low calorie food consumption and a control group did not manifest significant weight loss during treatment.

Eating Rates.   A number of studies have indicated that the eating style of obese individuals differs from that of nonobese persons, and some self-management strategies have emphasized the modification of eating rates. Observation of obese persons in natural settings demonstrates that obese adults, in comparison to persons of normal weight, perform fewer chews per bite, spend less time consuming their meals, and, thus, eat at a faster rate (Dodd, Birky, & Stalling, 1976; Gaul, Craig-head, & Mahoney, 1975; LeBow, Goldberg, & Collins, 1977; Wagner & Hewitt, 1975). Marston, London, and Cooper (1976) reported similar results in observing relatively fat or thin children in a school cafeteria. However, Gaul *et al.* found that obese subjects took more bites, Dodd *et al.* observed larger but not more frequent bites, and LeBow *et al.* reported fewer bites associated with less time spent in non-chewing activity. The consistent factor present in all of the studies reported is the obese person's more rapid pace of eating and the lesser time spent in chewing food. Therefore, it is likely that other family members will still be eating when the obese individual finishes the food on his or her plate. Unless that person then leaves the room, additional helpings of food available on the dining table will serve as cues for continued food consumption while passing time until others are through with the meal. Although there is some controversy about the importance of modifying eating rates for weight reduction (Mahoney, 1975), Epstein, Parker, McCoy, and McGee (1976) found that both obese and normal-weight children who were taught to control bite rate showed a significant reduction in the amount of food consumed. The technique of slowing down of the rate of eating, therefore, seems to be an appropriate self-management technique.

Imagery Studies

The use of imagery techniques in weight-reduction programs was stimulated by Homme's formulation (1965) of coverants as the operants of the mind. The application of coverant conditioning to weight reduction involves the systematic use of thoughts, images, and reflections to modify eating behavior. The coverant conditioning involves the elicitation of negative thoughts about being overweight, followed by positive coverants about weight reduction. The positive coverants are reinforced by engaging in predesignated highly probable positively reinforcing behaviors. Tyler and Straughan (1970) compared the weight loss of persons trained in coverant control, breath holding, or relaxation when tempted to eat high calorie foods. The results were unimpressive in all treatment conditions: a mean weight loss of less than 1 lb was observed in each of the three groups over a 9-week treatment period.

An investigation by Horan and Johnson (1971) evaluated the reinforcing function of the coverants through a comparison of a group in which the reinforced coverant procedure was used with a second group in which the coverants were elicited according to a preplanned schedule. The weight loss in the reinforced coverant control group was not significantly different from the weight loss obtained in the information and the scheduled coverant groups. The mean weight loss over the 8-week treatment period for the reinforced coverant group was 5.66 lb; for the scheduled coverants group, 2.72 lb; and for the information group, 3.13 lb. In the delayed-treatment control group, there was a mean weight gain of .02 lb. This investigation, as well as the one by Tyler and Straughan, suggests that the coverant control technique is a fairly ineffective weight-reduction procedure.

Horan, Baker, Hoffman, and Shute (1975) incorporated the coverant technique into a multiple-component treatment procedure. They found that positive coverants produced significantly more weight loss than did negative coverants in a treatment program that also included group or individual counseling conditions, stimulus control procedures, and an optional 1000 calorie per day diet. Seventy-five percent of the subjects in the positive coverants condition lost at least 1 lb per week in the 8-week treatment program, whereas only 35% of the negative coverants subjects manifested at least 1 lb per week weight loss. However, it is not clear which aspect of the program produced the differential treatment results. Furthermore, the investigators pointed out that coverant control should be considered as a highly reactive short-term component of a more comprehensive treatment program. This conclusion is based on Horan and Johnson's earlier study indicating a decrease in the frequency with which clients used the coverant procedure over the course of the treatment program.

Another imagery procedure that has been used alone or in combination with behavioral management procedures is covert sensitization. This technique was described by Cautela (1967) as a method for treating maladaptive behavior, including overeating. The client is placed in a state of relaxation and then, according to Cautela's formulation, develops a conditioned avoidance response to the problem behavior through imagining the undesirable stimulus (eating) paired with an extremely aversive stimulus.

The treatment outcome studies assessing the covert sensitization procedure have generally demonstrated a minimal treatment influence. Harris (1969) found no additional weight loss effect when she added a covert sensitization condition to the behavioral management procedures already employed. Janda and Rimm (1972), in a 6-week treatment program, found no statistically significant differences in weight loss between a covert sensitization, realistic attention control, and a no-treatment control group. However, at the 6-week follow-up, the mean pretreatment to follow-up weight loss of the covert sensitization group was significantly greater than that of the other two groups (11.7 lb).

A comparison of the efficacy of covert sensitization and covert reinforcement in weight reduction was carried out by Manno and Marston (1972). Both treatment groups exhibited significantly greater weight loss over the eight treatment sessions than did the control group, but the covert imagery groups were not significantly different from each other. The mean weight loss in the covert sensitization group was 4.13 lb and, in the covert reinforcement group, 5.1 lb. The mean pretreatment to

3-month follow-up weight loss was 8.9 lb for both groups. Foreyt and Hagen (1973) compared a covert sensitization group with a placebo group instructed to imagine pleasant scenes associated with food and eating and with a no-treatment control group. There were no significant differences in weight loss among the three groups; all groups lost some weight. Similarly, Elliott and Denney (1975) found no differences in weight loss in a covert sensitization, a covert sensitization augmented by false feedback, and an attention placebo group. All groups showed a weight loss with no differences between groups at the 4-week follow-up. These studies indicate that covert sensitization is not more effective than other imaginal and placebo procedures.

Diament and Wilson (1975) also questioned the efficacy of covert sensitization as an aversive conditioning procedure on the basis of their findings comparing a covert sensitization, attention-placebo, and a no-treatment control group. There were no differences between the groups in weight loss, in quantity of food consumed in an analogue eating situation, and in the palatability of a target food as measured by salivary response. Both the covert sensitization and the attention-placebo groups reported a significantly decreased liking for the target food, implying suggestion or demand characteristics rather than aversive conditioning effects in the reported treatment results.

Cautela developed a covert conditioning technique termed *covert response cost,* and this procedure was evaluated in a treatment study with two overweight females (Tondo, Lane, & Gill, 1975). The technique consists of covert conditioning trials pairing scenes in which there is a response-cost or loss of a positive reinforcer contingent on the imagination of scenes in which a maladaptive eating response is about to occur. After the covert conditioning trials, the clients are instructed to imagine response-cost scenes contingent on both imaginary and real-life situations in which a maladaptive eating response is about to take place. Tondo, Lane, and Gill reported that carrying out the covert response cost treatment procedure led to a reduction in the consumption of target foods when the client used this imagery technique. However, the treatment effect was quite specific, and there was no generalization to nontarget foods and beverages. On the theoretical side, it is unclear whether the covert response cost is a conditioning procedure or merely serves as a cue to remind one not to eat.

The incorporation of covert imagery in self-control groups was reported by Bellack, Glanz, and Simon (1976). The influence of positive imagery (self-reinforcement) applied when resisting the temptation to eat and negative imagery (self-punishment) applied after inappropriate eating was investigated. Clients lost similar amounts of weight irrespective of whether the self-reward or the self-punishment conditions occurred first. In addition, the clients lost more weight in the first 3 weeks than in the last 3 weeks of treatment. However, since the investigators did not separately evaluate self-control and imagery, it is difficult to judge the additional contribution that covert imagery makes to the self-control treatment program.

The "Personal Scientist" System

The "personal scientist" weight reduction treatment program described by Mahoney and Mahoney (1976) relies heavily on cognitive variables, self-monitoring, and environmental programming in order to achieve self-control over eating behavior. Self-control is learned through extensive self-monitoring of the time, place, and amount of food eaten, the monitoring of food-related thoughts, and the development of social support systems. The client is advised to experiment with particular behavior changes and to graph and evaluate the effect of these changes on a particular problem behavior related to inappropriate eating.

Clients also are instructed to specify maladaptive cognitions associated with eating and to replace these cognitions with more adaptive thoughts and images. The Mahoney and Mahoney cognitive-restructuring approach for modifying behavior and feelings emphasizes behavior-oriented self-statements aimed at changing problem eating patterns. Some of the procedures suggested are: replacing negative self-defeating subverbal monologues with more appropriate self-talk and setting reasonable goals for behavior change that are flexible enough so they can be modified if the individual has difficulty meeting these particular goals. Thus, a three-step sequence is suggested for modifying maladaptive monologues: identification of maladaptive self-statements, evaluation of the reality of their message, and self-encouragement to change behavior in a more positive direction.

One method suggested for evaluating the impact of one's cognitions on eating behavior is to monitor food-related thoughts through recording the content of these thoughts and the time of day that they occurred. Next, one evaluates whether these thoughts are maladaptive and self-defeating or are appropriate for the situation. Options can then be specified for changing the maladaptive thoughts, and these options can be tried out and data collected about the effectiveness of these changes on one's self-talk. Mahoney and Mahoney also suggest that the client place a stamp on the face of his or her watch, clock, mirror, scale, wall, etc. and then stop upon seeing a stamp cue and record and evaluate one's thoughts for the preceding few minutes. The individual is instructed to write down an encouraging replacement thought and, finally, to praise oneself for completing this sequence.

Some of the environmental programming, behavioral management, and self-monitoring of eating-pattern techniques suggested by Mahoney and Mahoney have been subjected to experimental testing, and the treatment efficacy of these procedures has been demonstrated (Mahoney, 1974; Mahoney et al., 1973). However, at the present time it is unclear whether the self-monitoring and modification of maladaptive self-statements and personal goals in relation to eating behavior influences treatment efficacy. Until these procedures are systematically evaluated, the importance of their addition to the "treatment package" is unknown.

It also seems relevant to investigate the possibility of individual differences in the effectiveness of the procedures involving cognitive self-monitoring and the graphing of experiments in changing eating patterns. The motivation to carry out the extensive record-keeping suggested by Mahoney and Mahoney may be related to the educational level of the individual, the degree of obsessive–compulsive behavior patterns he/she exhibits, and the sex of the client. (It has been my personal experience that male clients and research subjects are on the whole less likely to keep extensive, detailed records than are female clients and research subjects.) Furthermore, Weisenberg and Fray (1974) reported ethnic and racial differences in the effectiveness of behavior modification as compared to more standard diet treatments. The differences seemed based in part on a differential willingness to take an active role in point-keeping and self-reinforcement procedures.

A Cognitive–Behavioral Treatment Program

Self-Control and Commitment to Change

The early behavioral programs for weight reduction (e.g., Stuart, 1967) stressed environmental programming techniques such as eating at the same time and place each day, placing portions of food on the plate prior to sitting down at the table, and making the consumption of excess foods as difficult as possible. Thus, self-management occurred through changing the environmental cues that signaled eating behavior and applying self-reward and self-punishment for behavior change. The assumption was that manipulating the environment would shape eating behavior and that these changes would be maintained through the contingent application of reward and/or punishment by the self and others.

However, the behavior-therapy field in general and weight-reduction programs in particular have moved from a primary emphasis on management of the environment to a greater interest and recognition of the importance of cognitive factors in behavior change. The development of self-control is assuming greater importance as a significant variable in the treatment process. It seems that self-control in large measure is based on the procedures through which an individual makes a decision that he or she will not perform a particular problem behavior. Specific cognitions, images, and overt behaviors are then systematically engaged in in order that the individual may refrain from performing the problem behavior.

It should be recognized that, irrespective of how well the person has learned to manage the environment in order to reduce the number of cues for eating behavior, a decision may still have to be made many times during the day about whether to engage in the problem behavior or to refrain from doing so. No matter how many weight-reduction treatment-sessions a person has attended, there still will be occasions when he/she is standing in front of the refrigerator door or looking at some food on a cupboard shelf, and a decision has to be made whether or not to consume the food that one has the urge to eat. Techniques such as positive and negative imagery, covert sensitization, and coverant control, rather than functioning as conditioning procedures, could serve as tools that influence the decision-making process. These procedures may be helpful to some persons as part of a more comprehensive decision-influencing strategy.

Factors that may positively influence treatment outcome are those that highlight individual responsibility for change in treatment. Individual responsibility for managing one's internal and external environment may be crucial for the long-term maintenance of the weight loss. It has been my experience that the specifics of the behavior-modification procedures are not difficult for either children or adults to learn. However, the probability that the person will follow the procedures he/she has learned is another matter. With my own clients, I have been spending increasing amounts of time discussing the factor of personal responsibility for behavior change and making a decision that one is willing to modify one's eating patterns. I have found it helpful to point out to the client that virtually all adults with an obesity problem will answer "yes" when asked whether they would like to lose weight. An entirely different question, however, is whether the client is willing to change the way that he/she eats. When pressed on this point, some clients will state that at the present time they are not ready to change their eating patterns.

Highlighting the fact that a decision is involved in the process of behavior change is helpful in making some persons aware of their ambivalence about changing eating patterns and in expediting the decision-making process. For some individuals, confronting their ambivalence may result in the decision not to continue with a program requiring active effort on their part and in a recognition that they are not prepared at the present time to make a commitment to changing their eating behavior. However, subsequent personal events such as illness, social rebuff, or the loss of a promotion opportunity may result in the individual at a future time making a commitment to change and following through with a weight-reduction program.

The Decision-Making Process

Janis and Mann (1977) recently formalized the issues involved in the decision-making process and have presented a theory about how to help an individual reach a decision that he/she will be committed to follow. Their suggestions on the implementation of the decision-making process have important implications for helping persons to change their maladaptive eating patterns.

The authors present a list of seven criteria necessary for decision-making procedures to be of high quality. The criteria are as follows: a thorough canvassing of a wide range of alternative courses of action, an evaluation of the full range of the objectives and values fulfilled by a particular course of action, an evaluation of the costs and risks of negative consequences as well as the benefits of positive consequences associated with each alternative, a search for new information relevant to each alternative, the correct assimilation of the new information one is exposed to, reexamination of the consequences of all possible courses of action before making a final choice, and the making of detailed provisions for implementing the chosen course of action, including contingency plans for dealing with the possibility that potential known risks might materialize.

Janis and Mann reported some success in using a balance-sheet procedure to help persons make health-related decisions and adhere to these decisions. The counselor and client work together in filling out a sheet in which alternative courses of action are listed. Each of these decision–choice cells is filled in from the perspective of

anticipated utilitarian consequences for self and for significant others and anticipated approval or disapproval from self and from significant others. The balance-
sheet procedure, therefore, calls attention to the consequences of various decisional
choices and may aid in the process of commitment to a particular course of action.
The commitment process is conceived as beginning at the point of making a decision and continuing with the implementation of the decided course of action despite
negative feedback. Decision counselors can, therefore, function to help the individual through the decision-making and commitment processes.

Cognitive–Behavioral Treatment Specifics

Persons that I treat for weight reduction generally attend weekly sessions for a
period of approximately 3 months and are weighed before each session. The weekly
weight-loss goal that I feel is realistic and nonstressful is about 1.5 lb per week. The
weight loss is not as rapid as with some appetite suppressant programs, but the
behavioral program is oriented toward maintaining the weight loss through realistic
habit changes. It is also extremely important to have periodic maintenance sessions
to deal with possible weight-loss erosion and to review again the behavioral principles for changing one's eating patterns.

The weight-loss program begins with a self-monitoring period to ascertain the
client's eating patterns and the type of food eaten. Then, the client is given reading
materials about environmental management (Leon, 1974) and is encouraged to think
of methods for changing the environmental cues for eating behavior that are specific
to that person's home and work situation. Eating patterns are monitored on a daily
basis by means of a form (Fig. 11.1) with categories for checking off whether one
has eaten a balanced breakfast, lunch, and dinner. Additional categories record
whether or not snacks were eaten in the morning, afternoon, and evening. The form
also has categories for recording the consumption of reduced portion sizes and for
recording daily exercise.

Throughout the sessions with the client, the relationship between environmental
management to reduce the number of cues that are discriminative stimuli for eating
behavior and self-management is stressed. Environmental management refers to the
process of changing eating behavior through procedures such as eating at the same
time and place each day, removing food from places other than the kitchen, locking
up excess foods, and buying only those foods at the grocery store that were designated ahead of time on a shopping list. Self-management can be viewed as a broader
aspect of environmental management and can involve such activities as planning
ahead what to order at a restaurant, what one will eat or drink at a cocktail party, or
the amount of food that one will consume at a Thanksgiving or Christmas dinner.
Encouraging the client to take the responsibility for self-managing his/her environment is extremely important in order to instill the attitude that the choices and
decisions in relation to food consumption are under the control of the client. This
attitude is crucial because specific techniques taught to the client will be ineffective
if the person does not carry out the procedures suggested.

When I first started using the program just described, I actively urged if not

Point system for _____ Date: _____

	Balanced breakfast	No or low-calorie snack, morning	Balanced lunch	No or low-calorie snack, afternoon	Balanced dinner	No or low-calorie snack, evening	Reduced portion sizes	Daily exercise		Daily total
Monday										
Tuesday										
Wednesday										
Thursday										
Friday										
Saturday										
Sunday										

Number of daily points needed _____

   Daily reward _____

Weekly point total _____

   Weekly rewards (choice) _____

Number of points needed _____ (first week)

_____ (second week)

_____ (third week)

FIGURE 11.1. Eating patterns point form.

cajoled clients into specifying some sort of daily reward and/or punishment system as well as a weekly reward for earning a designated amount of points. However, I have dropped this aspect of the treatment program except for the children I see. Virtually every adult client indicated that the feedback about weight loss was reward enough, and the notion of earning points or material rewards along the way seemed rather childish.

Consultation sessions with a dietician have been quite helpful for those persons whose nutritional information is quite poor. I have refrained from suggesting specific diets because most persons view a diet as something temporary and artificial that almost by definition they will follow only for a limited period of time. If the person eats balanced meals, refrains from snacking between meals or makes low-calorie choices for these snacks, reduces portion sizes below customary levels, and engages in some sort of sustained exercise activity on a daily basis, then weight reduction should occur, since the individual is burning more calories than he/she is taking in. The significant role of snacking in regaining the weight that one has previously lost was demonstrated in a study comparing weight-loss regainers and weight-loss maintainers (Leon & Chamberlain, 1973b).

It is important to bear in mind, however, that some obese persons may actually consume fewer calories per day than persons of normal weight but may engage in markedly less physical activity. This phenomenon was clearly demonstrated by Mayer and his colleagues in studies of adolescents and adults (Bullen, Reed, & Mayer, 1964; Mayer, 1965; Stefanik, Heald, & Mayer, 1959). Therefore, it should be recognized that not all obese persons are overweight for the same reasons, and, for some persons, marked increases in physical activity with a relatively lesser emphasis on reducing caloric intake may be the most appropriate strategy for weight reduction.

The management of emotional arousal through means other than eating is for some obese persons crucial to successful weight reduction and its long-term maintenance. Although anxiety reduction may not occur with food intake (Leon & Roth, 1977), the consumption of food may be a response that is incompatible with anxiety or merely a learned response to the cue of emotional arousal. (Weight regainers reported eating in response to a greater number of emotional and other stimuli inappropriate to cues of hunger than did weight maintainers [Leon & Chamberlain, 1973a].) It is important to explore with the client the situations, if any, in which eating is a response to states of emotional arousal. After these situations have been identified, it may be necessary to focus on the development of alternative behaviors for dealing with emotions than through food consumption. A general exploration of interpersonal interaction styles may be relevant, as well as training in social skills, assertion, and relaxation.

Counseling the person to get involved in activities outside of the house may also alleviate the boredom that often serves as a cue for aimless snacking. This strategy is particularly helpful with obese children. Furthermore, for both youngsters and adults, daily exercise activities are not only important in terms of burning calories but also enable the person to be away from the large variety of stimuli in the home that signal eating behavior. Also, exercise activities may increase the opportunity for social contact with others. The informed social support of the spouse in changing eating patterns would also seem to be quite important.

Some individuals have reported that the decision to refrain from eating in a specific situation was facilitated by visualizing how he/she looks right now, particularly the image of oneself unclothed in front of the mirror. Conversely, for some the image of how one would like to look in a bathing suit has also been helpful at temptation points. However, I feel that the efficacy of the various imagery and planning procedures will vary from one individual to another. Therefore, it is important to teach the client an array of environmental management and imagery procedures and to encourage the person to experiment with and use the procedures that he/she has found most helpful. This attitude of experimentation should help to engender in the client an expectancy of self-management as the means of gaining self-control.

Related Research Issues

An investigation of the behaviors involved in the process of self-control was carried out by asking persons on a diet to record the behaviors they engaged in to avoid eating when they had the urge to eat (Leon, Roth, & Hewitt, 1977). Persons just starting on a weight-reduction program were asked to record the occasions when they were tempted to eat and whether they had eaten or had refrained from eating at that time. The subjects were also asked to indicate how they had restrained themselves from eating. The methods that the subjects reported as successful for them fell into two general categories: active behavior and covert activities. The persons reported that they had engaged in a variety of behaviors that served as a distraction from eating, such as doing the laundry, scrubbing the floor, and starting to sew. Many of these activities physically removed them from the place that was associated with the urge to eat (e.g., going into another room or out for a walk). Sometimes, persons increased the pace of activities they were already involved in, such as scrubbing the floor even harder than before they had the urge to eat. The covert activities involved the visualization of positive or negative self-images or subvocal self-instruction, such as statements like, "Don't," "No," "You're on a diet," and "That's fattening." The subjects generally used a variety of these self-control procedures along with the environmental programming procedures typically taught in behavior-management programs. Furthermore, normal-weight persons also reported the use of similar covert and overt self-control procedures when tempted to eat but refraining from doing so.

In terms of covert imagery, a particularly intriguing phenomenon has been the experience of having several clients ask me "When is my body image going to change? Even though I've lost weight, I still think of myself and picture myself as a fat person." This cognitive and kinesthetic image of oneself as fat occurs even though research evidence suggests that, on a semantic level, there is a change in the adjective ratings of one's body with weight loss. Semantic differential evaluations of body image indicate that obese persons with a longstanding obesity problem who were successful in losing weight show a realistic adjustment in their image of themselves at the moment and are able to distinguish semantically between their present image and their more obese image before weight loss (Leon, 1975; Leon & Chamberlain, 1973a). Furthermore, massively obese persons who had undergone bypass surgery and lost a dramatic amount of weight over a 1-year period (mean weight loss = 98 lb) showed an accurate adjustment of their body dimensions on perceptual estimations of various body parts (Leon, Eckert, & Buchwald, 1977). Nonetheless, many formerly obese persons continue to report that the subjective picture they have of their bodies is still that of a fat person.

I have occasionally speculated that one of the factors involved in the difficulty many obese persons have in maintaining a weight loss might be a feeling of discomfort because the subjective image of oneself (as a fat person) does not fit with the realistic physical image at the present time. Since the subjective image probably developed over many years' experience as a fat person, this obese body-state is part of their self-image. Although weight loss may elicit the social approval of other persons, the discrepancy between the objective and subjective images of oneself is a dissonant condition that can be resolved by regaining the lost weight. This hypothesis, however, clearly needs evaluation in a treatment-outcome study specifically dealing with modifying one's subjective body image.

Conclusions

It may strike some readers as a paradox that, on the one hand, excessive food consumption leading to obesity is viewed by some cognitive–behaviorists as a highly overlearned behavior that has been generalized to a variety of environmental stimuli. On the other hand, part of the treatment process is devoted to issues of a decision to change one's problem behaviors and personal commitment. However, it does not seem that the cognitive aspect of the treatment process emphasizing commitment, decision making, and self-control negates the influence of operant and classical conditioning processes in learning. The emphasis on self-control suggests that human beings, as thinking organisms, can be taught to modify their own environments and, thus, to shape new learned responses and extinguish maladaptive ones. The motivation to make these changes and thus gain self-reinforcement for self-initiated behavior change is what I have termed *commitment*. The delineation of this process and of the procedures necessary to help persons achieve this commitment is one of the as yet unanswered questions in therapy.

My own experience in using cognitive–behavioral techniques for weight reduction has been mixed. Some adults and children have benefited from learning the self-management and imagery techniques, whereas others have not. Although these procedures are relatively more effective than other types of treatment, I do not feel that we have yet found the answer to the treatment of obesity. Many have pointed out that the early studies demonstrating the efficacy of behavioral procedures were essentially demonstration studies on mildly overweight college students. It should be noted that these persons showed a trend toward weight regain even in the relatively short 6–8-week follow-up periods of the early studies.

Stunkard (Note 1) recently stated that behavior modification treatments for obesity have not progressed beyond the effectiveness of the earlier treatment outcome studies and that no one has been able to replicate Stuart's (1967, 1971) dramatic weight loss and weight maintenance results. Stunkard suggested that current efforts at combining behavior modification programs with spouse involvement, exercise regimens, and appetite suppressants may prove more effective than any of these programs used alone. My personal judgment is that the problem of how to shape self-control behavior has yet to be solved and that this process must be better understood and further studied before it can be effectively implemented in a treatment program.

Recent Nonbehavioral Treatment Developments

Liquid Diets and Hormone Injections

Many types of commercial and self-help weight-reduction groups have incorporated instruction in behavior management techniques into their ongoing group processes. There also has been a great deal of current interest in the use of various types of liquid diets and hormone treatments for weight reduction. The recent marketing of the low-calorie, protein-sparing, modified-fast liquid diet has created a flurry of excitement because of the rapid weight loss that occurs with this regimen. However, the Food and Drug Administration has issued warnings due to a number of reported deaths from cardiac arrythmias associated with the use of this liquid diet. Furthermore, comprehensive long-term follow-up results on persons who lost weight on the diet have not as yet been published.

Some physicians have treated obesity through the use of daily injections of human chorionic gonadotrophin (HCG) obtained from the urine of pregnant women, in combination with a 500 calorie per day diet. The assumption is that HCG selectively mobilizes "abnormal" or reserve fat rather than normal fat. Simeons (1956) asserted that persons receiving the HCG injections and the 500 calorie diet feel better, are less hungry, and are more likely to remain in treatment than are those persons who are just on the diet. Asher and Harper (1973) evaluated these statements in a double-blind study with 40 female patients over a 6-week period. Both groups were placed on a 500–550 calorie diet. The HCG group lost significantly more weight, reported less hunger, and felt better than the persons in the placebo-injection group. The mean weight loss in the HCG group was 19.96 lb and, in the placebo group, 11.05 lb. However, a comprehensive study was reported by Young, Fuchs, and Woltjen (1976) that involved 202 persons in a double-blind random crossover design. The injections and 500-calorie diet were evaluated through a 6-week injection period, 6-week maintenance period, 6-week crossover injection period, and then a second 6-week maintenance period. The overall mean weight loss while receiving HCG was 14.96 lb and, with the placebo injection, 15.4 lb. The results clearly indicated that there were no significant differences in weight, skinfold thickness, dropout rates, reasons for dropping out, and patient subjective response in the HCG versus placebo conditions of the study. Furthermore, Ballin and White (1974) concluded that there is no scientific evidence whatsoever that HCG causes preferential mobilization of reserve fat.

The difficulty with specific diets or other types of restricted food regimens is that many persons are able to maintain the program as long as they are not faced with making food choices in the natural environment. Thus, as long as the individual has no choice about what to eat, the dieting procedures are relatively effective if the person stays on the program. However, during the maintenance period, when the individual is faced with decisions about whether to eat or not, the person may gradually revert back to his/her problem eating patterns.

Prolonged Fasting or Starvation

One way out of the dilemma of making food choices is just not to eat at all. Persons undergoing prolonged starvation for weight reduction generally do not experience hunger sensations after the first 2–4 days on the program (Drenick, Swendseid, Blahd, & Tuttle, 1964). In contrast, many persons continue to experience hunger even with the extended use of low-calorie diets (Weight Loss without Hunger, 1964), possibly because the food intake stimulates hunger without satisfying it. Stunkard and Rush (1974) concluded that short-term fasting (lasting no longer than 2 weeks) on an in-patient basis did not result in depression or in other severe emotional disturbances; nor were there medical complications. They therefore recommended the short-term fast on an in-patient basis as a benign method for beginning an obesity treatment program.

For persons who are severely overweight, the consequence of the 1.5–2 lb per week weight-loss goal of behavior modification programs is that there is a long period of time in which there is little reinforcement from visible feedback of weight loss. Furthermore, the individual may feel overwhelmed by the large amount of weight yet to be lost in order to reach the goal weight. This situation of ratio strain may be alleviated by allowing the severely obese person immediate progress in weight reduction through a short-term fast. Then, that person can continue to progress in weight reduction on an out-patient basis through learning and implementing self-management and other behavioral methods for modifying eating patterns. At the present time, however, there are no outcome studies evaluating this treatment combination. The ineffectiveness of prolonged fasting or starvation when used alone is demonstrated by the fact that, in virtually every single investigation of this procedure, the persons eventually regained the weight they had lost in the hospital (Leon, 1976).

Bypass Surgery

Because of the extremely difficult problem that the treatment of obesity represents, there has been a recent interest in the intestinal and gastric bypass surgical procedures for treating massive obesity. These procedures have elicited a great deal of attention because of the often dramatic weight loss that can occur during the first year after surgery. Reports indicate a 35% average weight loss over time with the jejunoileal bypass procedure (Buchwald, Schwartz, & Varco, 1973), and this weight loss is in the majority of cases, quite permanent, apparently irrespective of what the person eats. However, there are extensive physical side effects and complications of the operation, including diarrhea, electrolyte imbalance, abdominal bloating, hair loss, and liver damage. These physical problems point to the need to use this surgical procedure only as a last resort for morbidly obese persons who have tried all other recommended weight reduction methods and have failed and for whom the medical and psychological complications of obesity are greater than the possible physical complications of the surgical procedure.

The gastric bypass procedure involves stapling shut approximately three-fourths of the stomach, thus making it physically impossible for the stomach to retain more than a small amount of food at a time. The mean weight loss with the gastric bypass procedure is somewhat less than that observed with intestinal bypass surgery. Maini, Blackburn, Reinhold, Bistrian, and Maletskos (1977) reported an average rate of weight loss of 7.48 lb per month over a period of 16 months. Because there are a lesser number of physical complications reported to date with the gastric bypass than with the intestinal bypass, many surgeons are turning to the gastric bypass procedure for treating massive obesity.

From a cognitive point of view, an intriguing aspect of this procedure is the effect of the fairly dramatic weight loss on body-image perception. In a study just completed, a total group of 67 persons were evaluated who had undergone jejunoileal bypass surgery for massive obesity (Leon *et al.*, 1977). One group of patients was initially evaluated 6 months prior to surgery, and all patients were periodically evaluated until they had reached the 1-year postsurgery point. The psychological findings are quite dramatic in demonstrating a marked overall improvement in mood, decrease in tension, anxiety, and depression, and increased activity level. There also was an enhancement in subjective feelings of physical attractiveness, a more positive evaluation of one's body and one's personality (as measured by semantic differential ratings), and increased feelings of personal competence. However, these findings should be tempered by the fact that other investigators have reported severe postsurgery psychiatric problems in some bypass patients (Espmarck, 1975), as well as minor emotional distress necessitated by adjustments in life-style due to the patient's changed physical appearance (Castelnuovo-Tedesco & Schiebel, 1976). The more positive long-term results in our study may be due to the fact that persons with severe psychiatric problems were not recommended for the procedure. However, we also found a number of cases in which interpersonal stress and disruptions in preexisting interaction patterns occurred after surgery. The stress seems to have been associated with the greater independence and assertiveness of the persons who had undergone the operation, concomitant with their markedly changed physical appearance. Several individuals reported that they were in the midst of marriage counseling or had separated from their spouses. In two cases, problems with their children requiring professional intervention apparently were precipitated by the change in family homeostasis due to the mother's more independent functioning.

Arnold Lazarus (1971), in a discussion of the necessity of looking at the total interaction patterns and not treating just a single symptom, pointed out that changes in the functioning of one individual can have a profound influence on the behavior of other persons in the family milieu. These changed patterns may lead to emotional and interpersonal difficulties if other members of the family are unwilling to change their customary behavioral patterns. This problem may be relevant to any type of treatment program and should be dealt with as one of the processes likely to occur in weight reduction and weight-loss maintenance. I have observed on many occasions the phenomenon of family members in some way sabotaging the client's weight-loss efforts. These maladaptive interactions further point to the need to deal with the problem-eating behavior in the context of the total social milieu.

ADIPOSE CELLULARITY AND EARLY LEARNING

The work of Hirsch and his colleagues at Rockefeller University on the differences in adipose cellularity in obese and normal weight organisms (e.g., Hirsch, 1971; Hirsch & Han, 1969; Hirsch & Knittle, 1970) indicates that the period from infancy to puberty may be extremely important in the development of a tissue structure that places one at high risk for a lifelong obesity problem. Excessive weight gain up to the adolescent period results in the laying down of excessive numbers of adipocytes (hyperplastic obesity), which is, apparently, a permanent morphological change in the individual, even with subsequent weight reduction. Adult-onset obesity results primarily in an increase in the size rather than the number of adipocytes (hypertrophic obesity). Although a specific relationship has not as yet been demonstrated between the number and the size of adipocytes and the ease of weight reduction and weight-loss maintenance, it is possible that there may be a physiological influence on the difficulty that persons with juvenile-onset obesity have in maintaining a weight loss.

However, it is all too early to call obesity an incurable disease and to lay all the blame for this condition on fat cells that one is born with or that have been laid down in early childhood. Analysis of the overfeeding practices resulting in the proliferation of adipocytes during childhood suggests that the behavior toward food of persons in the child's environment is extremely important. The parents and other family members may model the consumption of large quantities of food and also the consumption of food as a means of dealing with positive and negative emotional arousal and boredom. The parents may reinforce the youngster for eating large portions of food and punish or make the youngster feel guilty for eating less than what the parents feel is appropriate. Thus, the child grows up with a particular cognitive image of the quantity of food on one's plate that is an appropriate amount to eat. Furthermore, he/she may develop the expectation that a second or third helping is part of the mealtime requirements, regardless of how much one has already eaten. Thus, over time a complex interaction occurs among constitutional, reinforcement, and modeling processes. All may be influential in the development of an obesity problem, and modification of eating patterns may still be the most effective way to deal with this problem.

ANOREXIA NERVOSA

Definition and Symptoms

Anorexia nervosa is an eating disturbance that occurs primarily in adolescent and young adult females. The term refers to a lack of appetite due to "nervous" reasons. Among psychodynamically oriented theorists, there has been the assumption that the supposed lack of appetite is emotionally mediated. However, there is no clear evidence to support this assumption. Many anorexics can be characterized as desiring an extremely thin appearance, and this strong need for thinness, rather than a diminishment or cessation of hunger, appears to be an important aspect of the eating disorder. Persons meeting the criteria for the diagnosis of anorexia nervosa often maintain an avid interest in food and may not experience a true loss of hunger and appetite (Bemis, 1978). Therefore, a phobia of gaining weight or of taking in food seems to best describe this condition.

The conception of anorexia nervosa as a weight phobia is strengthened by the findings of Garfinkel (1974), who studied the perception of hunger and satiety in 11 anorexics aged 16–23 and 11 normal-weight matched controls. The subjects were required to fast for 12 hours and then eat a standard meal. A questionnaire assessing the sensations of hunger was filled out prior to the meal, and another questionnaire assessing satiety was completed after food consumption. There were no significant differences between groups in the reports of hunger; almost all subjects reported hunger as a feeling of gastric emptiness. However, a significantly greater number of the anorexics indicated an association between hunger and negative mood (nervous, irritable, tense, and depressed). Furthermore, a significantly greater proportion of the anorexics reported a strong urge to eat when hungry and a strong preoccupation with thoughts of food. In terms of satiety, the control subjects indicated that they tended to eat until they had experienced gastric fullness, whereas the anorexic group reported that they stopped eating because they had set a self-imposed limit on food intake. Significantly fewer in the anorexic group reported that they experienced gastric fullness at the end of the meal. Therefore, the anorexic subjects in this study experienced hunger associated with negative mood and indicated a strong urge to eat. Food consumption was terminated after reaching an arbitrarily set limit, despite a lack of a feeling of gastric fullness. Hunger and appetite were clearly present, but the fear of gaining weight seems to have been the mediator resulting in the termination of the eating behavior.

Once the dieting pattern has started, persons who become anorexic may exhibit an unsatisfied striving for the loss of still another few pounds to bring one closer yet to the ever-decreasing weight-loss ideal. The food intake of anorexics may average only 200–500 calories per day, although some persons may alternate between restricted food intake and uncontrolled eating binges in which excessive eating without satisfaction occurs (bulimia). Self-induced vomiting may follow these binge episodes and may also occur after what the anorexic considers to be excessive food consumption. Persons who periodically engage in binge overeating and self-induced vomiting appear to have a poorer prognosis than those who do not engage in this eating–vomiting cycle.

The refusal of food, per se, is a behavior that is associated with a number of types of deviant behavior such as hysteria, hypochondriasis, schizophrenia, and depression. The specific criteria for the diagnosis of anorexia nervosa were designated by Halmi and Sherman (1975), based on adaptations of symptom lists reported by other investigators. These criteria are: onset between the ages of 10 and 30 years; weight loss of at least 25% of original body weight, resulting in the individual's being at least 15% below normal weight; and a distorted, implacable attitude and behavior toward eating, food, and weight. An additional sign designated by Feighner, Robins, Guze, Woodruff, Winokur, and Muñoz (1972) is no known psychiatric or medical illness. For females, the criteria also include amenorrhea of at least 3 months' duration unless the symptoms occur before the onset of menses, with no known medical illness that could account for the amenorrhea. Some clinicians have argued that anorexia nervosa is a disorder found exclusively in females, but reports of the incidence of this disorder in males place it at between 3 and 10% (Bemis, 1978). The death rate has been estimated at 10–20%.

The clinical literature is reasonably consistent in describing the behavior of anorexic persons before the onset of severe weight loss as obsessive–compulsive, intelligent, conscientious, shy, and reserved. Anorexics have been characterized as extremely crafty and manipulative in relation to their eating behavior. They often exert a tremendous amount of control over their families and over hospital personnel as others become entangled in efforts to prepare foods the anorexic says that he or she would like to eat or to try to persuade that person to eat food that has already been prepared. Anorexic individuals may actively avoid gaining weight by engaging in strenuous, ritualized, daily exercise programs, concealing the fact that they have not eaten and engaging in self-induced vomiting to rid themselves of food they might have been pressured to eat.

Hilde Bruch (1970a,b), writing from a psychodynamic perspective, has stated that anorexics and obese persons are unable to discriminate between the signals of various body urges and suffer from a disturbance in body identity, including the lack of a sense of ownership of one's body. These difficulties were posited to be due to an early severe disturbance in mother–child interactions. Since the onset of the anorexic symptoms commonly occurs at puberty, traditional psychoanalytic writers (e.g., Waller, Kaufman, & Deutsch, 1964) have suggested that the refusal to take in food is associated with conflicts about sexuality, specifically, a symbolic denial of the fantasy of oral impregnation by the father.

A number of the symptoms of anorexia, such as tension, irritability, emotional lability, sexual disinterest, and preoccupation with and dreams of food, are similar to the symptoms observed in persons evaluated during states of semistarvation (Schiele & Brozek, 1948). Therefore, instead of positing some type of psychodynamic explanation for the behavioral symptoms, the behaviors could be accounted for by the severe state of nutritional deprivation the person is in. For example, cessation of menstruation can also occur during semistarvation. However, it may not be tenable at the present time to posit a physiological explanation for the cessation or arrested onset of menses in anorexia nervosa, since amenorrhea often occurs in the early stages of weight loss or even before weight loss has begun (Halmi, 1974). At present, the specific relationship between anorexia nervosa and amenorrhea is unclear and has not been fully explained by either psychological or physiological theories. Furthermore, it is unknown whether there is some physiological factor contributing to the overwhelming incidence of anorexia nervosa in females.

Behavioral Treatment Methods

Behavioral formulations of anorexia nervosa have focused on an analysis of environmental reinforcement patterns and have considered the eating disturbance as a manifestation of avoidance behavior (Blinder, Freeman, & Stunkard, 1970; Leitenberg, Agras, & Thomson, 1968). However, the behavioral literature generally has not been oriented toward theoretical explanations of the onset and course of the anorexic behavior pattern and, instead, has emphasized the development of effective treatment programs.

The first case-descriptions employing behavior-therapy techniques in the treatment of anorexia nervosa were published in 1965. Lang (1965) described the use of relaxation techniques to desensitize a 23-year-old woman who abstained from eating and vomited whenever she was in a new situation or did something opposed to someone else's wishes. The description of her symptoms suggests, however, that she did not meet the criteria commonly designated for anorexia nervosa. Deep muscle relaxation was used to countercondition specific anxiety responses to hierarchies based on travel, criticism, and being the center of attention in a classroom. Her eating behavior improved with treatment, and her weight gain was maintained at a 1-year follow-up. Hallsten (1965) presented a single case-report of a 12-year-old anorexic girl in which systematic desensitization was employed with scene visualizations of actual eating situations. A final weight of 80 lb was achieved, and it was reported that her general improvement was maintained at a 5-month follow-up. Schnurer, Rubin, and Roy (1973) also described the use of systematic desensitization with one patient in combination with supportive therapy. An average weight gain of 1.09 lb per week was reported.

Bachrach, Erwin, and Mohr (1965) presented a case history of a 37-year-old, 47 lb anorexic woman whose eating behavior was modified through the systematic use of operant procedures. Upon admission to the hospital, the patient was isolated in a barren room and was not permitted to have visitors or to engage in any recreational activities. All meals were served in her room, with one of the experimenters present; the experimenters provided verbal reinforcement on a variable schedule aimed at shaping eating behavior. Reinforcement was first applied to movements associated with eating, and, eventually, the required response for reinforcement was the consumption of given amounts of food. After there was an increase in the caloric intake at meals, privileges outside of the room were made contingent on the amount of food eaten. Later, reinforcement occurred in relation to weight gain, rather than the quantity of food consumed. The program resulted in a reversal of an anorexic pattern that had existed for approximately 17 years. The patient was discharged from the hospital 2 months after admission at a weight of 64 lb. Three years posthospitalization, she reported that her weight was 72 pounds, and she also indicated that she had continued to maintain a high rate of eating behavior.

A similar operant program was instituted by Leitenberg *et al*, (1968) with two girls aged 14 and 17. Reinforcers were contingent on weight gain. Contrary to expectation, the reversal phase of the treatment study did not result in the extinction of the increased food consumption, suggesting the importance of intrinsic reinforcement factors. Both youngsters were discharged from the hospital at nearly normal weight, which was maintained at a 4- and 9-month follow-up, respectively.

A case study using a token reinforcement system without isolation in treating a 13-year-old anorexic female was reported by Azerrad and Stafford (1969). Tokens for weight gain could be earned on a daily basis and exchanged for a variety of reinforcers. Contrary to many of the other operant treatment studies in the literature, reinforcement for weight gain did not result in changes in eating behavior or in weight gain. However, reinforcement for the amount of food eaten at each meal did prove effective in increasing both weight and the amount of food eaten. Garfinkel, Kline, and Stancer (1973) used an operant-treatment program based on weight gain and reported an average weekly weight increase of 3.36 lb.

Blinder *et al.* (1970) made use of the anorexics' often noted high degree of physical activity by making the opportunity for physical activity a reinforcer for weight gain. Five patients were evaluated, with some variations on this procedure in each individual case. All were on some type of medication as well. In a sixth patient, the reinforcer for weight gain was a reduction in dosage level for a sedative drug. The data for the first three patients indicated an average rise in weight of 3.9 lb per week for the entire treatment period of approximately 40 days. Although weight gain generally was maintained at the follow-up, interpersonal problems still existed. The first patient eventually committed suicide, and the third patient continued the practice of periodic severe purging with laxatives.

Bianco (1972) reported on the successful use of operant techniques in combination with chlorpromazine and family therapy with two anorexic girls who were required to gain .5 lb per day in order to earn specified reinforcers. The average weight gain was 5.9 lb per week, but the combination of treatments prevents one from evaluating the contributions of the various components to treatment outcome. Bhanji and Thompson (1974), with a relatively larger sample, treated 11 girls aged 13–21 with operant conditioning procedures in combination with psychoactive medication. The patients were isolated in their rooms at bed rest and allowed up only to be weighed. Each was asked to draw up a seven-item hierarchy of rewards, and the least-preferred reward was obtained after the consumption of eight consecutive meals eaten within 60 minutes of presentation. The reward criteria were made successively more stringent, until a normal eating pattern was established. The rate of weight gain for the groups as a whole varied between 1.98 to 7.26 lb per week. The follow-up information is difficult to evaluate, since only 3 of the 11 patients reported their current weights. However, global ratings of status at follow-up suggest mild to moderate improvement. The investigators pointed out that, although operant techniques may be valuable for rapid weight gain in the hospital, these procedures may be inadequate for the long-term maintenance of the behavior change.

Halmi, Powers, and Cunningham (1975) evaluated a behavior modification program with eight patients that also included systematic contact with the family during the maintenance period. The patients were hospitalized in a barren room and were placed on a liquid diet that was later replaced by balanced meals. The reinforcers for weight gain were social activities, increased physical activities, and visiting privileges. The program resulted in mean weekly weight gains of 3.1 lb over an average length of hospitalization of 6.25 weeks. At follow-up (mean = 7.2 months), four of the eight patients were rated as manifesting "good" adjustment, three "fair" adjustment, and one "poor" adjustment. Contact with the family was maintained during the follow-up period with instructions to have the patient rehospitalized for tube feeding if a weight loss of more than 2.2 lb occurred at any follow-up visit. Individualized reinforcements were given by the family for a 1.1 lb weight gain per week until the individual reached normal weight. The involvement of the family during the maintenance period may have contributed to the relatively better long-term results than those found in the investigation by Bhaji and Thompson.

The operant treatment programs are fairly consistent in demonstrating success in producing short-term weight gain. However, it is difficult to formulate conclusions about the treatment efficacy of the specific variations of the operant procedures because of the small number of persons evaluated in the various treatment outcome studies. Other problems in generalizing from these investigations stem from the lack of consistency in the criteria for diagnosing anorexia nervosa, the differences in the target behaviors that were reinforced (pounds gained, amount of food eaten, normal eating patterns), and the variability in the use of medications and in the lengths of the follow-up periods. Furthermore, Van Buskirk (1977) pointed out that treatment outcome should be evaluated from a short-term perspective of rapid weight gain and from a long-term perspective emphasizing psychological adjustment and normal weight maintenance. It is possible that there are differences in the treatment procedures that are most effective at these various points in restoring and maintaining normal eating patterns. The maintenance of a more adaptive eating pattern would seem ultimately to depend on learning how to monitor and regulate one's food intake around the number of calories at which normal weight can be maintained, rather than learning and being reinforced for the consumption of large amounts of food.

Family therapy oriented around teaching family members how to provide social support for positive behavior change in relation to food and other interpersonal areas would seem to be a crucial factor in the generalization and maintenance of the progress achieved during the hospital treatment program. Beginning the treatment process with the anorexic patient to promote weight gain and then generalizing treatment to include intervention in the family system seems quite important.

Theoretical Formulation

Some anorexics begin a dieting or food restriction program during adolescence because of being told by their family or friends that they are slightly overweight or because of their own self-evaluation of their weight status (Bemis, 1978). Frequently, what begins as a typical dieting program becomes an eating disturbance because the youngster is unable to stop the dieting process and to resume normal eating habits even though stating that he or she would like to. In essence, the strict self-control over food consumption that was so effective in weight reduction becomes extremely difficult to modify. The food-restrictive behavior may have become so overlearned and difficult to extinguish because of the association between extremely negative thoughts and images about weight gain and the behavioral act of food consumption. Over time, the strength of the conditioning process increases because aversive affect such as feelings of revulsion and disgust also becomes conditioned to the thought of food intake. As the subjects in the Garfinkel (1974) study indicated, the anorexic experiences feelings of hunger, a preoccupation with food, and a strong urge to eat. However, during the steps in the process of taking in food, there is a conditioned aversion to eating, along with a cognitive appraisal that eating will lead to weight gain. Therefore, food consumption is terminated, or else the person engages in self-induced vomiting. At the point where the person verbally states a desire to resume more normal eating patterns, the conditioning process may be too strong to extinguish without some type of external incentive.

Given the severity of this eating disturbance and its frequent intractability during outpatient treatment, it seems remarkable that simply placing the individual in a barren room and making various types of reinforcers contingent on weight gain should fairly consistently result in a rapid treatment effect. I feel that a decision-making process is in operation similar to the process postulated for treatment success in weight reduction. The hospitalized anorexic embarking on the operant treatment program learns very quickly that the reinforcers that one has learned to value in the social milieu will not be provided unless there is a change in eating behavior or a weight gain of a designated amount per day. Furthermore, these reinforcers assume greater potency the longer the individual is restricted to a barren room with nothing to do. Despite the aversive conditioning factors hypothesized to be associated with food intake, it seems that the individual makes a conscious decision to eat and then does so in order to gain access to the now extremely reinforcing environment outside of the hospital room. The association of food intake and positive reinforcement increases the frequency of eating behavior, and, consequently, weight gain occurs. The more frequent food intake may result in the counterconditioning or the extinction of the classically conditioned aversive aspects of food consumption. The positive reinforcement of physical activity and access to the social environment becomes, for the time being, more salient than the fear of weight gain.

Cognitive–Behavioral Treatment Possibilities

The systematic desensitization case studies described in the Behavioral Treatment Methods section are, apparently, the only imagery treatment procedures that have been evaluated with anorexia nervosa. The formulation of the anorexia nervosa syndrome as a weight phobia maintained by a conditioned aversion to the image of food intake may provide some clues as to how systematic desensitization hierarchies can be constructed more effectively and incorporated into a more general treatment program.

Several investigations have indicated that anorexics have a severe body image disturbance (Bruch, 1970a; Crisp & Kalucy, 1974). However, psychological and psychiatric test results suggest relatively normal psychological functioning and no distortions of reality. As weight loss progresses, the anorexic patient, when confronted with his/her emaciated appearance in a mirror, may accurately perceive one's physical image but find this body state rewarding because it confirms the fact that one has strong self-control over the urge to eat. Therefore, cognitive procedures may be helpful if focused on changing the anorexic's irrational beliefs about the advisability of total self-control. Recognizing the reality image of oneself as thin and unhealthy and dealing with the issue of self-control may be a viable means of treating those persons who manifest this distortion in their *interpretation* of the favorableness of their body state. Thus, systematic desensitization or covert reinforcement procedures might not be effective without dealing with the anorexic's distorted judgment of body image and associated weight phobia.

It should be emphasized, however, that some anorexics are eventually concerned with their emaciated state but still are unable to resume normal eating habits without treatment. Therefore, the specific treatment procedures must be tailored to the individual case. However, active intervention during the early stages of the anorexic behavior pattern when the maladaptive behaviors possibly can be reversed more easily is of extreme importance.

Although operant programs have been relatively successful in short-term weight gain, a further issue is the maintenance of a normal weight level after the person has been discharged from the hospital. Hospital programs consisting of group therapy, social skills training, and family therapy seem to be important components of the treatment program. Eventually, the family and other persons in the environment can provide the social support needed to maintain a regulated eating pattern. Family and peer interpersonal difficulties can be dealt with through periodic therapy sessions conducted on an outpatient basis after the person is back in the usual social milieu. With the social reinforcement provided by others for the change in eating behavior and the healthful change in physical appearance, the fear of weight gain may extinguish over time.

The life-threatening nature of this eating disturbance often requires immediate and fairly drastic steps to prevent death from physical debilitation and starvation. The use of tube feeding and enforced bed rest during the initial stages of nutritional rehabilitation was the most effective procedure for saving the life of the patient prior to the development of the operant behavior-modification programs. Tube feeding must still be used initially in cases of severe emaciation, until the patient gains enough weight so that the immediate threat to life is reduced (Halmi *et al.*, 1975).

Ethical issues concerning the use of operant procedures developed to modify the eating behavior of the anorexic have been raised. It is clearly mandatory to obtain the consent of both the patient and the parents before engaging in a deprivation program of this nature. The justification for using these techniques, of course, is the extreme severity of this disorder, its associated threat to life, and the fact that the published studies indicate that patients generally begin gaining weight and earning reinforcers fairly rapidly. Any aversive program, however, should be under the supervision of an objective review committee in order to prevent possible abuses.

The treatment suggestions just presented have tended to focus on in-hospital procedures, reflecting in part the difficulty in changing the food restriction patterns of many individuals who become anorexic. As long as the person is losing weight and is not markedly emaciated, there is a great deal of reinforcement in this dieting pattern and little motivation to change. An area in need of extensive research is the development of effective procedures for intervention in the anorexic pattern before the eating disturbance becomes so severe that hospitalization is required. Emphasis in therapy on the concept of prolonged dieting as an extreme of the self-control process, along with rational–emotive techniques for changing the commitment to continue dieting, may be particularly helpful in the early stages of the anorexic syndrome.

GENERAL CONCLUSIONS

The treatment outcome studies in the area of obesity suggest that an emphasis on self-control procedures and on the process of making a decision and a commitment to behavior change may be significant treatment variables requiring more research.

Presently used behavior management procedures have had limited success in terms of the long-term maintenance of the weight change. Cognitive–imaginal procedures have been relatively ineffective.

Anorexia nervosa is an eating disturbance characterized by a fear of weight gain and, possibly, a conditioned aversion to food. This disorder does not seem to involve a lack of appetite, and the eating disturbance appears to be maintained by an excess of self-control in relation to food consumption. Operant treatment procedures that have made the consumption of food and subsequent weight gain more reinforcing than the contingencies associated with the restriction of food intake have proven relatively effective on a short-term basis. However, the procedures that are effective in the long-term maintenance of a more adaptive eating pattern may be different from the treatment procedures that are effective in short-term weight gain. The maintenance of the change in eating behavior may be aided by the addition of social skills training and family therapy to promote more satisfying interpersonal relationships. Cognitive procedures aimed at reversing irrational beliefs about the advisability of total self-control over one's body and dealing with the distortion in the interpretation of one's body state may be helpful in reversing the eating disturbance.

REFERENCE NOTE

1. Stunkard, A. J. *Behavioral treatment of obesity: A 1977 perspective.* Paper presented at the Second International Congress on Obesity, Washington, D.C., October, 1977.

REFERENCES

Abrahms, J. L., & Allen, G. J. Comparative effectiveness of situational programming, financial payoffs and group pressure in weight reduction. *Behavior Therapy,* 1974, *5,* 391–400.

Alexander, F., & Flagg, G. W. The psychosomatic approach. In B. J. Wolman (Ed.), *Handbook of clinical psychology.* New York: McGraw-Hill, 1965. Pp. 855–947.

Asher, W. L., & Harper, H. W. Effect of human chorionic gonadotrophin on weight loss, hunger, and feeling of well-being. *The American Journal of Clinical Nutrition,* 1973, *26,* 211–218.

Azerrad, J., & Stafford, R. Restoration of eating behavior in anorexia nervosa through operant conditioning and environmental manipulation. *Behavior Research and Therapy,* 1969, *7,* 165–171.

Bachrach, A. J., Erwin, W., & Mohr, J. P. The control of eating behavior in an anorexic by operant conditioning techniques. In L. P. Ullman & L. Krasner (Eds.), *Case studies in behavior modification.* New York: Holt, Rinehart, & Winston, 1965. Pp. 153–163.

Ballin, J. C., & White, P. L. Fallacy and hazard. Human chorionic gonaotropin/500-calorie diet and weight reduction. *Journal of the American Medical Association,* 1974, *230,* 693–694.

Bellack, A. S., Glanz, L. M., & Simon, R. Self-reinforcement style and covert imagery in the treatment of obesity. *Journal of Consulting and Clinical Psychology,* 1976, *44,* 490–491.

Bellack, A. S., Schwartz, J., & Rozensky, R. H. The contribution of external control to self-control in a weight reduction program. *Journal of Behavior Therapy and Experimental Psychiatry,* 1974, *5,* 245–249.

Bemis, K. M. Anorexia nervosa. *Psychological Bulletin,* 1978, *85,* 593–617.

Bhanji, S., & Thompson, J. Operant conditioning in the treatment of anorexia nervosa: A review and retrospective study of 11 cases. *British Journal of Psychiatry,* 1974, *124,* 166–172.

Bianco, F. J. Rapid treatment of two cases of anorexia nervosa. *Journal of Behavioral Therapy & Experimental Psychiatry,* 1972, *3,* 223–224.

Blinder, B. J., Freeman, D., & Stunkard, A. J. Behavior therapy of anorexia nervosa: Effectiveness of activity as a reinforcer of weight gain. *American Journal of Psychiatry,* 1970, *126,* 1093–1098.

Bruch, H. Disturbed communication in eating disorders. *American Journal of Orthopsychiatry,* 1963, *33,* 99–104.

Bruch, H. Eating disorders in adolescence. *Proceedings of the American Psychopathology Association,* 1970, *59,* 181–202. (a)

Bruch, H. Instinct and interpersonal experience. *Comprehensive Psychiatry,* 1970, *11,* 495–506. (b)

Buchwald, H., Schwartz, M. Z., & Varco, R. L. Surgical treatment of obesity. *Advances in Surgery,* 1973, *7,* 235–255.

Bullen, B. A., Reed, R. B., & Mayer, J. Physical activity of obese and nonobese adolescent girls appraised by motion picture sampling. *American Journal of Clinical Nutrition,* 1964, *14,* 211–223.

Castelnuovo-Tedesco, P., & Schiebel, D. Studies of superobesity: II. Psychiatric appraisal of jejuno-ileal bypass surgery. *American Journal of Psychiatry,* 1976, *133,* 26–31.

Cautela, J. R. Covert sensitization. *Psychological Reports,* 1967, *20,* 459–468.

Crisp, A. H., & Kalucy, R. S. Aspects of the perceptual disorder in anorexia nervosa. *British Journal of Medical Psychology,* 1974, *47,* 349–361.

Diament, C., & Wilson, G. T. An experimental investigation of the effects of covert sensitization in an analogue eating situation. *Behavior Therapy,* 1975, *6,* 499–509.

Dodd, D. K., Birky, H. J., & Stalling, R. B. Eating behavior of obese and normal-weight females in a natural setting. *Addictive Behaviors,* 1976, *1,* 321–325.

Drenick, E. J., Swendseid, M. E., Blahd, W. H., & Tuttle, S. G. Prolonged starvation as treatment for severe obesity. *Journal of the American Medical Association,* 1964, *187,* 100–105.

Elliott, C. H., & Denney, D. R. Weight control through covert sensitization and false feedback. *Journal of Consulting and Clinical Psychology,* 1975, *43,* 842–850.

Epstein, L. H., Parker, L., McCoy, J. F., & McGee, G. Descriptive analysis of eating regulation in obese and nonobese children, *Journal of Applied Behavior Analysis,* 1976, *9,* 407–415.

Espmark, S. Psychological adjustment before and after bypass surgery for extreme obesity - A preliminary report. In A. Howard (Ed.), *Proceedings of the First International Congress on Obesity.* London, England: Newman Publishing, 1975. Pp. 242–243.

Feighner, J. P., Robins, E., Guze, S. B., Woodruff, R. A., Winokur, G., & Muñoz, R. Diagnostic criteria for use in psychiatric research. *Archives of General Psychiatry,* 1972, *26,* 57–63.

Foreyt, J. P., & Hagen, R. L. Covert sensitization: Conditioning or suggestion? *Journal of Abnormal Psychology,* 1973, *82,* 17–23.

Foreyt, J. P., & Kennedy, W. A. Treatment of overweight by aversion therapy. *Behavior Research and Therapy,* 1971, *9,* 29–34.

Garfinkel, P. E. Perception of hunger and satiety in anorexia nervosa. *Psychological Medicine,* 1974, *4,* 309–315.

Garfinkel, P., Kline, S., & Stancer, H. Treatment of anorexia using operant conditioning techniques. *Journal of Nervous and Mental Disease,* 1973, *157,* 428–433.

Gaul, D. J., Craighead, W. E., & Mahoney, M. J. Relationship between eating rates and obesity. *Journal of Consulting and Clinical Psychology,* 1975, *43,* 123–125.

Hagen, R. L. Group therapy versus bibliotherapy in weight reduction. *Behavior Therapy,* 1974, *5,* 222–234.

Hall, S. M. Self-control and therapist control in the behavioral treatment of over-weight women. *Behavior Research and Therapy,* 1972, *10,* 59–68.

Hallsten, E. A. Adolescent anorexia nervosa treated by desensitization. *Behavior Research and Therapy,* 1965, *3,* 87–91.

Halmi, K. A. Anorexia nervosa: Demographic and clinical features in 94 cases. *Psychosomatic Medicine,* 1974, *36,* 18–26.

Halmi, K. A., Powers, P., & Cunningham, S. Treatment of anorexia nervosa with behavior modification. *Archives of General Psychiatry,* 1975, *32,* 93–96.

Halmi, K. A., & Sherman, B. M. Gonadotrophin response to LHRH in anorexia nervosa. *Archives of General Psychiatry,* 1975, *32,* 875–878.

Hanson, R. W., Borden, B. L., Hall, S. M., & Hall, R. G. Use of programmed instruction in teaching self-management skills to overweight adults. *Behavior Therapy,* 1976, *7,* 366–373.

Harris, M. B. Self-directed program for weight control. *Journal of Abnormal Psychology,* 1969, *74,* 263–270.

Harris, M. B., and Bruner, C. G. A comparison of a self-control and a contract procedure for weight control. *Behavior Research and Therapy,* 1971, *9,* 347–354.

Hirsch, J. Adipose cellularity in relation to human obesity. *Advances in Internal Medicine,* 1971, *17,* 289–330.

Hirsch, H., & Han, P. W. Cellularity of rat adipose tissue: Effects of growth, starvation, and obesity. *Journal of Lipid Research,* 1969, *10,* 77–82.

Hirsch, J., & Knittle, J. L. Cellularity of obese and non-obese human adipose tissue. *Federation Proceedings,* 1970, *29,* 1516–1521.

Homme, L. E. Perspectives in psychology: XXIV. Control of coverants, the operants of the mind. *Psychological Record,* 1965, *15,* 501–511.

Horan, J. J., Baker, S. B., Hoffman, A. M., & Shute, R. E. Weight loss through variations in the coverant control paradigm. *Journal of Consulting and Clinical Psychology,* 1975, *43,* 68–72.

Horan, J. J., & Johnson, R. G. Coverant conditioning through a self-management application of the Premack principle: Its effect on weight reduction. *Journal of Behavior Therapy and Experimental Psychiatry,* 1971, *2,* 243–249.

Janda, L. H., & Rimm, D. C. Covert sensitization in the treatment of obesity. *Journal of Abnormal Psychology,* 1972, *80,* 37–42.

Janis, I. L., & Mann, L. *Decision making: A psychological analysis of conflict, choice, and commitment.* New York: The Free Press, 1977.

Kelly, A. H., & Curran, J. P. Comparison of a self-control approach and an emotional coping approach to the treatment of obesity. *Journal of Consulting and Clinical Psychology,* 1976, *44,* 683.

Kennedy, W. A., & Foreyt, J. P. Control of eating behavior in an obese patient by avoidance conditioning. *Psychological Reports,* 1968, *22,* 571–576.

Kingsley, R. G., & Shapiro, J. A comparison of three behavioral programs for the control of obesity in children. *Behavior Therapy,* 1977, *8,* 30–36.

Kingsley, R. G., & Wilson, G. T. Behavior therapy for obesity: A comparative investigation of long-term efficacy. *Journal of Consulting and Clinical Psychology,* 1977, *45,* 288–298.

Lang, P. J. Behavior therapy with a case of anorexia nervosa. In L. P. Ullman & L. Krasner (Eds.), *Case studies in behavior modification.* New York: Holt, Rinehart, & Winston, 1965. Pp. 217–221.

Lazarus, A. A. *Behavior therapy and beyond.* New York: McGraw-Hill, 1971.

LeBow, M. D., Goldberg, P. S., & Collins, A. Eating behavior of overweight and nonoverweight persons in the natural environment. *Journal of Consulting and Clinical Psychology,* 1977, *45,* 1204–1205.

Leitenberg, H., Agras, W. S., & Thomson, L. E. A sequential analysis of the effect of positive reinforcement in modifying anorexia nervosa. *Behavior Research and Therapy,* 1968, *6,* 211–218.

Leon, G. R. A behavior modification approach to the treatment of obesity. *Minnesota Medicine,* 1974, *57,* 977–980.

Leon, G. R. Personality, body image, and eating pattern changes in overweight persons after weight loss. *Journal of Clinical Psychology,* 1975, *31,* 618–623.

Leon, G. R. Current directions in the treatment of obesity. *Psychological Bulletin,* 1976, *83,* 557–578.

Leon, G. R. A behavioral approach to obesity. *American Journal of Clinical Nutrition,* 1977, *30,* 785–794.

Leon, G. R., & Chamberlain, K. Emotional arousal, eating patterns, and body image as differential factors associated with varying success in maintaining a weight loss. *Journal of Consulting and Clinical Psychology,* 1973, *40,* 474–480. (a)

Leon, G. R., & Chamberlain, K. A. Comparison of daily eating habits and emotional states of persons successful or unsuccessful in maintaining a weight loss. *Journal of Consulting and Clinical Psychology,* 1973, *41,* 108–115. (b)

Leon, G. R., Eckert, E., & Buchwald, H. Psychological concomitants of jejuno-ileal bypass surgery for morbid obesity. *Proceedings of the Second International Congress on Obesity.* Washington, D.C., October, 1977 (Abstract).

Leon, G. R., & Roth, L. Obesity: Psychological causes, correlations, and speculations. *Psychological Bulletin,* 1977, *84,* 117–139.

Leon, G. R., Roth, L., & Hewitt, M. I. Eating patterns, satiety, and self-control behavior of obese persons during weight reduction. *Obesity and Bariatric Medicine,* 1977, *6,* 172–181.

McReynolds, W. T., Lutz, R. N., Paulsen, B. K., & Kohrs, M. B. Weight loss resulting from two behavior modification procedures with nutritionists as therapists. *Behavior Therapy,* 1976, *7,* 283–291.

Mahoney, M. J. Self-reward and self-monitoring techniques for weight control. *Behavior Therapy,* 1974, *5,* 48–57.

Mahoney, M. J. Fat fiction. *Behavior Therapy,* 1975, *6,* 416–418.

Mahoney, M. J., & Mahoney, K. *Permanent weight control. A total solution to the dieter's dilemma.* New York: W. W. Norton, 1976.

Mahoney, M. J., Moura, N. G., & Wade, T. C. Relative efficacy of self-reward, self-punishment, and self-monitoring techniques for weight loss. *Journal of Consulting and Clinical Psychology,* 1973, *40,* 404–407.

Maini, B. S., Blackburn, G. L., Reinhold, R., Bistrian, B. R., & Maletskos, C. Body composition after gastric bypass for morbid obesity. *Proceedings of the Second International Congress on Obesity.* Washington, D.C., October, 1977 (Abstract).

Mann, R. A. The behavior-therapeutic use of contingency contracting to control an adult behavior problem: Weight control. *Journal of Applied Behavior Analysis,* 1972, *5,* 99–109.

Manno, B. & Marston, A. R. Weight reduction as a function of negative covert reinforcement (sensitization) versus positive covert reinforcement. *Behavior Research and Therapy,* 1972, *10,* 201–207.

Marston, A. R., London, P., & Cooper, L. M. A note on the eating behavior of children varying in weight. *Journal of Child Psychology and Psychiatry,* 1976, *17,* 1–4.

Marston, A. R., London, P., Cooper, L. M., & Lammas, S. E. Lifestyle: A behavioral program for weight reduction and obesity research. *Obesity and Bariatric Medicine,* 1976, *5,* 96–100.

Mayer, J. Obesity in adolescence. *The Medical Clinics of North America,* 1965, *49,* 421–432.

Meyer, V., & Crisp, A. H. Aversion therapy in two cases of obesity. *Behavior Research and Therapy,* 1964, *2,* 143–147.

Morganstern, K. P. Cigarette smoke as a noxious stimulus in self-managed aversion therapy for compulsive eating: Technique and case illustration. *Behavior Therapy,* 1974, *5,* 255–260.

Murray, D. C., Davidoff, L., & Harrington, L. G. II. *In vivo* self-control training. *Psychological Reports,* 1975, *37,* 249–258.

Musante, G. J. The dietary rehabilitation clinic: Evaluative report of a behavioral and dietary treatment of obesity. *Behavior Therapy,* 1976, *7,* 198–204.

Öst, L. G., & Götestam, K. G. Behavioral and pharmacological treatments for obesity: An experimental comparison. *Addictive Behaviors,* 1976, *1,* 331–338.

Penick, S. B., Filion, R., Fox, S., & Stunkard, A. J. Behavior modification in the treatment of obesity. *Psychosomatic Medicine,* 1971, *33,* 49–55.

Schiele, B. C., & Brozek, J. Experimental neurosis resulting from semistarvation in man. *Psychosomatic Medicine,* 1948, *10,* 31–50.

Schnurer, A., Rubin, R., & Roy, A. Systematic desensitization of anorexia nervosa seen as a weight phobia. *Journal of Behavioral Therapy & Experimental Psychiatry,* 1973, *4,* 149–153.

Simeons, A. T. Chorionic gonadotrophin in geriatrics. *Journal of the American Geriatric Society,* 1956, *4,* 36-40.

Stefanik, P. A., Heald, F. P., & Mayer, J. Caloric intake in relation to energy output of obese and nonobese adolescent boys. *American Journal of Clinical Nutrition,* 1959, *7,* 55-62.

Stollak, G. E. Weight loss obtained under different experimental procedures. *Psychotherapy: Theory, Research, and Practice,* 1967, *4,* 61-64.

Stuart, R. B. Behavioral control of overeating. *Behavior Research and Therapy,* 1967, *5,* 357-365.

Stuart, R. B. A three-dimensional program for the treatment of obesity. *Behavior Research and Therapy,* 1971, *9,* 177-186.

Stuart, R. B., & Davis, B. *Slim chance in a fat world: Behavioral control of obesity.* Champaign, Illinois: Research Press, Inc., 1972.

Stunkard, A. J., & Rush, J. Dieting and depression reexamined. A critical review of reports of untoward responses during weight reduction for obesity. *Annals of Internal Medicine,* 1974, *81,* 526-533.

Tondo, T. R., Lane, J. R., & Gill, K. Jr. Suppression of specific eating behaviors by covert response cost: An experimental analysis. *Psychological Record,* 1975, *25,* 187-196.

Tyler, V. O., & Straughan, J. H. Coverant control and breath holding as techniques for the treatment of obesity. *Psychological Record,* 1970, *20,* 473-478.

Van Buskirk, S. S. A two-phase perspective on the treatment of anorexia nervosa. *Psychological Bulletin,* 1977, *84,* 529-538.

Wagner, M., & Hewitt, M. I. Oral satiety in the obese and nonobese. *Journal of the American Dietetic Association,* 1975, *67,* 344-346.

Waller, J., Kaufman, M. R., & Deutsch, F. Anorexia nervosa: A psychosomatic entity. In M. R. Kaufman & M. Heiman (Eds.), *Evolution of psychosomatic concepts.* New York: International Universities Press, 1964. Pp 245-273.

Weight loss without hunger. *Connecticut Medicine,* 1964, *28,* 265-266.

Weisenberg, M., & Fray, E. What's missing in the treatment of obesity by behavior modification? *Journal of the American Dietetic Association,* 1974, *65,* 410-414.

Wollersheim, J. P. Effectiveness of group therapy based upon learning principles in the treatment of overweight women. *Journal of Abnormal Psychology,* 1970, *76,* 462-474.

Wollersheim, J. P. Follow-up of behavioral group therapy for obesity. *Behavior Therapy,* 1977, *8,* 996-998.

Young, R. L., Fuchs, R. J., & Woltjen, M. J. Chorionic gonadotropin in weight control. *Journal of the American Medical Association,* 1976, *236,* 2495-2497.

12

How and Why People Quit Smoking:
A Cognitive–Behavioral Analysis

TERRY F. PECHACEK
BRIAN G. DANAHER

INTRODUCTION

Only one aspect of cigarette smoking is understood with some clarity—the long-term health consequences. From an intervention perspective, we have only begun to clarify how or why the average person succeeds or fails in attempts to become an ex-smoker. Bernstein (1969) concluded in his excellent review that, based on the current research, "very little in the way of useful knowledge has been contributed beyond the rather elementary observations that smoking behavior is widespread and becoming more so . . . and that it is incredibly resistant to long-term modification [p. 437]."

Unfortunately, the research and model-building of the last 9 years is only beginning to illuminate meaningfully the unique phenomena called smoking. Yet, despite frustrating results, the social relevance of the topic and the fact that it is an objectively measurable target behavior have helped maintain considerable interest in smoking behavior. Unfortunately, the models of smoking behavior have tended to be long on theory but short on heuristic value (Lichtenstein & Danaher, 1976). Consequently, the mildly optimistic outcome data from recent intervention strategies have continued to be trapped in self-perpetuating cycles that attempt to refine unvalidated or only moderately useful strategies (Bernstein & McAlister, 1976). Although the literature on procedures adopting a social learning approach appears most promising (Bernstein & McAlister, 1976; Lichtenstein & Danaher, 1976; Pechacek & McAlister, 1979), nonreplications and inconsistent results in this literature still can be found.

389

Cognitive–Behavioral Interventions:
Theory, Research, and Procedures

The focus in this chapter will be an appraisal of some major trends in both smoking behavior and research from a cognitive–behavioral perspective. This perspective should offer the reader some new insights into reasons why some treatments work whereas others fail. Since the intervention literature has been comprehensively reviewed elsewhere (Bernstein, 1969; Bernstein & McAlister, 1976; Best & Bloch, 1979; Lichtenstein & Danaher, 1976; Pechacek & McAlister, 1979; Schwartz, 1969; Schwartz & Rider, 1977), this report will highlight only those aspects of the literature that elucidate important trends or have produced noteworthy effectiveness. Finally, if this chapter is to serve any purpose, it will encourage both the novice and the seasoned researcher to spend more time analyzing the smoking problem from a more integrative perspective rather than forging ahead with theoretically attractive but unproven interventions. Such concentration on the complexity of the problem may help break the now classic pattern of significantly reduced smoking behavior during initial intervention, followed by rapid relapse during follow-up (Hunt & Bespalec, 1974).

SMOKING—THE NUMBER ONE PUBLIC HEALTH PROBLEM

Health Consequences

The magnitude of the health consequences of cigarette smoking is staggering. It has been estimated that over 37 million Americans, at a rate of over 300,000 per year, will die years prematurely due to smoking (Pollin, 1977; USPHS, 1977a, 1978). These excess deaths will occur primarily due to the direct, etiological role of smoking on cardiovascular diseases (CVD), chronic bronchopulmonary diseases (COPD), and various cancers (USPHS, 1978). Elimination of smoking would likely produce approximately one-third fewer middle-age (35–59) male deaths, 85% fewer COPD deaths, one-third fewer CVD deaths, 50% fewer deaths from cancer of the bladder, and 90% fewer deaths from cancer of the trachea and lungs (Pollin, 1977; USPHS, 1977a, 1978).

The corresponding economic impact of smoking in terms of premature deaths, illness, and disability is similarly large in magnitude, with an estimated loss of 26 billion dollars per year, or about 11.3% of the economic cost of all disease (Luce, 1977). It comes as no surprise, then, that smoking has been labeled as one of the major causes of the current health care crisis (Abelson, 1976; Kristein, 1977; Luce, 1977; Pollin, 1977).

Current Trends in Smoking

Within the preface of the latest *Health Consequences of Smoking* (USPHS, 1978), Cooper stated that the medical consequences are well-established and rather clearly understood. He further argued that the "task now is to convert this knowledge into programs for reducing and eliminating the preventable death and disability related to the smoking habit [p. iii].'' This knowledge about the long-term consequences of smoking, unfortunately, only provides indirect assistance in developing programs either to prevent the onset of smoking or to aid in adult cessation.

Most of the positive effects of this increased knowledge have occurred as a part of the vast public health education campaign against smoking. This effort appears to have had several effects, including the blunting of the escalating smoking consumption pattern of the 1940s and 1950s (Warner, 1977) and the encouragement of the trend toward use of filtered and lower tar–nicotine cigarettes (USPHS, 1976a). The campaign has been most successful in providing risk information: Both smokers and the general public are now almost uniformly aware of at least the general health consequences of smoking (USPHS, 1976a).

It is unfortunate that many people believe that such increased risk awareness will be sufficient to produce widespread smoking cessation. This simplistic perspective is encouraged by the fact that recent surveys of U.S. adults have documented a pattern of steady decline in the proportion of smokers at almost all age levels (USPHS, 1969, 1973, 1976a). Moreover, among males, for whom health risks like heart disease are more widely known, the decline has been even more dramatic (i.e., from 52.4% smokers in 1964 to 39.3% in 1975; USPHS, 1976a). Finally, faced with rising concerns from families and friends about the effects of smoking on health, an estimated 90% of current adult smokers have tried or want to quit smoking completely (USPHS, 1976a).

Unfortunately, the problem and its solution are not as simple as the data may initially suggest. First, although American's youth are almost uniformly aware of the long-term risks of smoking, the proportion of young women (aged 12–18) who smoke has nearly doubled since 1968, eliminating earlier differences between males and females (USPHS, 1976b, 1977b). And, even though the number of ex-smokers has swelled to over 30 million, active ''recruitment'' of new smokers and increases in the general population have kept the *number* of smokers at about 52 million since the late 1960s (Reeder, 1977). Moreover, since fewer women than men are quitting and more are starting, the *number* of female smokers has steadily *increased* (Reeder, 1977). Almost all smokers express a desire to quit, but the 1975 survey revealed the ominous fact that 64% of the males and 59.5% of the females had already tried unsuccessfully to quit on their own (USPHS, 1976a). As a result, the almost 47 million adult smokers have seemingly become a ''troubled minority,'' aware of the health consequences of their behavior but unable to give up their habit easily (USPHS, 1977a).

UNDERSTANDING THE PROBLEM

Need for a Behavioral Perspective

The clearer understanding of the medical and pathological aspects of smoking has produced only moderate improvements in the smoking problem, leaving to the behavioral sciences the task of converting this knowledge into effective treatments to modify smoking behavior. A notable effort has been made to gain an understanding of the pharmacology of tobacco smoking; however, results continue to be frustrating (Jarvik, 1977) and only equivocally support a nicotine-dependency hypothesis (Editorial, 1977; Kumar, Cooke, Lader, & Russell, 1977). Nevertheless, smoking can easily be labeled as "probably the most addictive and dependence producing form of object-specific self-administered gratification known to man (Russell, 1976)."

The lack of a specific pharmacological mechanism, plus the obvious tenacity of the habit, has traditionally resulted in the conclusion that "the habitual use of tobacco is related primarily to psychological and social drives (USPHS, 1964, p. 354)." Thus, the need for the input of the behavioral sciences in the solution of the problem has long been recognized. The emerging emphasis on the role of personal health behavior in health care has only strengthened this awareness (Schwartz & Weiss, 1977; Weiss, 1976). Unfortunately, the smoking problem is very complex and does not lend itself to simple theoretical solutions (Bernstein, 1969; Lichtenstein & Danaher, 1976).

Models of Smoking Behavior

The emphasis on the behavioral aspects of smoking has produced a plethora of theoretical notions and models. Unfortunately, these have been "long on theory but short on data (Lichtenstein & Danaher, 1976)." Too often, they appear to conceptualize smoking within the framework of general psychological theories, with the belief that valid treatments will be derived. But most theories lack the specificity to generate hypotheses and treatments that can be validated through empirical tests (Bernstein, 1969). Nevertheless, a brief excursion through some of the models of smoking behavior may clarify both the complexity of the problem and the need for a broader perspective.

As was evident in the 1964 Surgeon General's Report on Smoking and Health (USPHS, 1964), early models focused on internal "needs" and "drives" that were discussed in fairly general terms (Bernstein, 1969). However, the Tomkins (1968) model offered a more specific delineation of the possible psychosocial mechanisms controlling smoking. Tomkins proposed that smoking is maintained by its role in managing affect (enhancing the positive and reducing the negative), to the point that the behavior becomes so entrenched that other addictive patterns also develop.

Horn used the Tomkins model in developing a questionnaire for the classification of smokers (Ikard, Green, & Horn, 1969). The resulting instrument was found via factor analysis to have six scales: habitual, addictive, negative affect, pleasurable, stimulation, and sensory motor, which defined different patterns or supports for smoking. The Tomkins model and the questionnaire have become widely known and used; however, only tentative validity data is available (Ikard & Tomkins, 1973). Moreover, its primary use has been in aiding smokers to gain insight about their behavior, rather than in guiding the development of specific interventions.

Horn (1968) continued his attempts to clarify aspects of the habit that inhibit cessation. Initially, he focused on the rewarding aspects of smoking (Horn, 1968, 1970), but more recently a broader model has been drawn emphasizing the decision-making process involved in a cost–benefit appraisal (Horn, 1976). In this latter conceptualization, he characterized smoking during the initiation, establishment, maintenance, and cessation phases. Utilizing primarily general psychosocial and self-appraisal variables along with environmental factors, the model offers only general suggestions regarding the process through which successful ex-smokers need to progress.

As Bernstein (1969) and Keutzer, Lichtenstein, and Mees (1968) predicted, learning theory conceptualizations gained in popularity during the 1970s because of their more concise definations and general heuristic nature. Persuasive arguments were presented defining smoking as an overlearned pattern of behaviors (Hunt & Matarazzo, 1970, 1973; Logan, 1970, 1973). Viewing the smoking response as learned during mass trials in diverse stimulus conditions and under partial reinforcement schedules, the tenacity and resistance to extinction of the behavior were easy to predict from existing theories of learning. Consonant with the learning formulations, cognitive and affective variables were minimized in these models.

A variety of research resulted from these models, but the derived treatments generally have failed to fulfill their promise of enhanced efficacy (Lichtenstein, 1971; McFall & Hammen, 1971; Yates, 1975). Nevertheless, the resulting research was conducted within a basically sound theoretical and methodological framework, so that slow but steady progress was possible (Bernstein & McAlister, 1976; Lichtenstein & Danaher, 1976). As a result, the successful programs based on this model offer some of the best guidance for additional reconceptualizations.

Independent of the learning theory research, a variety of social psychological research was relevant to smoking. Working basically within a cognitive model, basic attitude structures involved in both the maintenance and the cessation of smoking were experimentally evaluated. Leventhal (1967, 1968) summarized the major early trends in this research. More recently, he has succinctly elaborated the sequence of steps leading to change, including: exposure to new information, understanding and acceptance of the message, change in attitude, and change in smoking behavior (Leventhal, 1971, 1973). Following along a similar vein, other concepts have been presented by Mettlin (1973), Foss (1973), and Rogers (1975). Unfortunately, the research derived from these types of models has tended to answer theoretical questions rather than generate specific intervention strategies. Except for exposure to sensory deprivation, treatments based upon these models have primarily resulted in changes in verbal rather than in smoking behaviors (Bernstein & McAlister, 1976; Best & Bloch, 1979).

As the preceding models failed to produce definitive and generalizable treatments, interest in the role of pharmacological factors was increasing (Dunn, 1973; Russell, 1976). Unfortunately, the biochemistry of nicotine and other tobacco derivatives is such that pharmacological researchers have not been able to unravel the possible mechanisms of chemical dependency (Jarvik, 1977). Nicotine is the chemical most likely involved, but traditional methods of drug research have been unable to define exactly how it may be reinforcing (Jarvik, 1977). The most persuasive argument supporting the role of nicotine in tobacco dependency was presented by Russell (1976). Schachter and associates (Schachter, 1978; Schachter, Silverstein, Kozlowski, Perlick, Herman, & Liebling, 1977) provided some initial and provocative data suggesting that variations in smoking rate customarily interpreted in psychological terms could be better understood as attempts to regulate nicotine. Despite the comprehensiveness of Russell's (1976) review and the implications of Schachter's work (Schachter *et al.*, 1977), experimental attempts to evaluate the effects of intravenously presented nicotine on *ad libitum* smoking still raise doubts about the role of nicotine in tobacco dependency (Editorial, 1977; Kumar *et al.*, 1977).

In their diversity, all of the preceding models have helped to clarify various aspects of the dependency phenomena, namely, (*a*) the general psychosocial aspects; (*b*) behavioral or habit mechanisms; (*c*) cognitive or attitudinal factors; and (*d*) pharmacological relationships. This complexity of the problem has been long recognized (Bernstein, 1969), and some models have attempted to integrate two or more of these broad categories. The work of Mausner and Platt (1971) illustrates this integration to some degree. Working primarily from a subjective expected utility and decision theory type model, physical and habit mechanisms were considered. Supports for smoking were conceptualized along the Tomkins (1968) framework and were evaluated by means of questionnaires. The model accurately predicted that behavior change was preceded by a higher pretreatment level of subjective expected utility (benefits) for stopping. However, based on the authors' social psychological background, the intervention focused primarily upon emotional role-playing and produced only limited changes in actual smoking behavior (Mausner & Platt, 1971). Some additional validation data and discussion were offered by Mausner (1973), yet the model has resulted in only limited practical demonstrations.

Russell (1971a; 1974) also offered a comprehensive theory of smoking based on learning-theory, pharmacological, and psychosocial aspects. As noted earlier, Russell has been a strong advocate of the dependency-producing power of nicotine (Russell, 1976); however, within his model he also concisely discussed the learning-theory determinants of habit strength and the social and psychological motives for smoking. These latter were based largely upon the work of McKennell (1968, 1970) and the Tomkins model (1968). Additionally, Russell (1971a,b, 1974) has outlined how these various factors may account for smoking at the development and maintenance stages of the habit. However, neither the resulting behavioral nor the pharmacological research has adequately validated his model.

An interesting and integrative model was outlined by Glad, Tyre, and Adesso (1976). They conceptualized smoking behavior within a multidimensional model, integrating a diversity of theoretical and applied research under components: cognitive, behavioral, and affective. The cognitive component considered the role of self-concepts, socialized attitudes, and functional attributions. Operant, respondent, and modelling aspects of smoking are discussed within the behavioral component. Finally, the affective properties of smoking included both the physiologically reinforcing and the stimulating aspects of nicotine, as well as the subjective pleasurable experiences associated with smoking. Although the authors recognized that their brief presentation was only a prototype, they seem quite accurate in concluding "that a multidimensional behavior such as smoking must be treated with a multifaceted approach [Glad et al., 1976, p. 87]." As attractive as the model is, its recency has not made research validation of their treatment recommendations possible.

As should be obvious from this excursion through existing theories and models, the area tends to be characterized by diversity and a lack of specificity. Moreover, this state of affairs helps to demonstrate that smoking is a complex, multidefined behavior that does not lend itself to simple or to theoretically narrow models. However, before drawing conclusions regarding smoking, another data base is worthy of consideration, namely, the intriguing evidence for smoking cessation that occurs outside of formal programs.

Smoking: An Opportunity for Self-Control

Cigarette smoking behavior has been commonly offered as a classic example of the opportunity to use self-control mechanisms (Bandura, 1969; Thoresen & Coates, 1975; Thoresen & Mahoney, 1974). As with other consummatory behavioral excesses, the response cues offer immediate positive (pleasurable experiences) and negative (reduction in craving or negative affect) reinforcement, to the exclusion of delayed aversive consequences (long-term health consequences). This set of cues and consequences has encouraged a variety of behavioral self-control and learning-theory-based treatments. However, as Premack (1970) sagely noted, the inconsistent results of such behavioral treatment programs for smokers seem paradoxical, given the large numbers of smokers who apparently quit successfully on their own. Survey data on U.S. adult smokers (USPHS, 1969, 1973, 1976a) and retrospective analyses of ex-smokers document this trend. As noted earlier, there are over 30 million ex-smokers in the U.S. today (Reeder, 1977), and it has been estimated that about 95% of them quit outside formal programs (USPHS, 1977a). Unfortunately, the unaided quitter is a relatively unstudied social phenomena.

Social Trends in Quitting

Surveys of the smoking behavior of Americans provide a wealth of descriptive evidence on the sociology of tobacco use (Gordon, Kannel, Dawber, & McGee, 1975; Srole & Fischer, 1973; Sterling & Weinkam, 1976; USPHS, 1969, 1973, 1976a). One clear trend that is consistently supported is that quit rates increase with age, especially among males. Table 12.1 shows cumulative quit rates to demonstrate how striking this phenomena has become with a majority of male smokers

TABLE 12.1
Cumulative Quit Rates by Age and Sex (1964, 1966, 1970, and 1975)[a]

Ages	Males				Females			
	1964	1966	1970	1975	1964	1966	1970	1975
21–24	12%[b]	10%	29%	28%	15%	14%	29%	23%
25–34	23%	25%	37%	34%	19%	21%	32%	32%
35–44	28%	27%	39%	35%	19%	21%	29%	33%
45–54	32%	33%	44%	47%	16%	19%	30%	32%
55–64	33%	39%	53%	54%	25%	34%	40%	37%
65+	47%	51%	66%	60%	30%	41%	44%	51%
Total	30%	31%	44%	43%	19%	22%	33%	33%

[a]*Source:* USPHS. *Use of Tobacco: Practices, Attitudes, Knowledge, and Beliefs, Fall 1964 and Spring 1966; Adult Use of Tobacco, 1970;* and *Adult Use of Tobacco, 1975.*

[b]Quit Rates are computed by dividing the number of former smokers by the number of ever smokers in each cohort (see original references for definitions of categories). Due to the higher death rates among smokers, this method may slightly underestimate the actual quit rates in older age cohorts.

having quit by middle-age. The longitudinal data from both the Framingham (Gordon *et al.,* 1975) and the Midtown Manhattan (Srole & Fischer, 1973) studies add credence to the cross-sectional data presented in Table 12.1.

The marked gender difference in quit rates at all survey points is also striking. Other interesting interrelationships between smoking and broad demographic variables are presented in Table 12.2. Persons currently divorced or separated were a small minority of the sample (5.7% of males and 7.7% of females) with the 1975 survey (USPHS, 1976a), but their smoking rates were markedly higher than those of other groups (See Table 12.2). Likewise, their cumulative quit rates were much lower: married males, 45.6%; divorced or separated males, 24.8%; married females, 35.13%; divorced or separated females, 22.6%. Additionally, the surveys suggest that the more educated smokers are leading the trend toward cessation. However, among the women, the patterns become mixed, with the more affluent women and those in white-collar professions tending to maintain smoking parity with their male counterparts. The comprehensive occupational survey of smoking by Sterling and Weinkam (1976) confirmed these patterns.

Certain occupational groups have demonstrated even more dramatic changes in their smoking behavior. Health-care professionals, especially physicians, have led in this trend, with doctors decreasing from 30% smokers in 1967 to 21% in 1975, to produce an estimated cumulative quit rate of about 67% (USPHS, 1977c). Pharmacists and dentists have shown similar dramatic decreases; however, nurses, 98% of whom were females, showed a slight increase in the proportion of smokers from 37% in 1968 to 39% in 1975 (USPHS, 1977c). A longitudinal survey from 1959 to 1972 revealed comparable changes in the health professionals (Garfinkel, 1976). Finally, a recent survey of academic psychologists showed similar trends, with males having a cumulative quit rate of 55% versus 33% for the females (Dicken &

TABLE 12.2
Smoking Rates by Gender, Marital Status, Education, Income, and Occupation among Adults in 1970 and 1975[a]

	Males		Females	
Categories	1970	1975	1970	1975
All persons	42.2%	39.3%	30.5%	28.9%
By marital status				
Single (never married)	56%	38%	36%	31%
Married (currently)	40%	38%	32%	28%
Divorced or separated (currently)	76%	60%	44%	50%
By education				
High school only	49%	46%	33%	32%
Some college	37%	36%	36%	32%
College graduates	31%	28%	26%	21%
By annual family income				
Less than $10,000	43.2%	45.6%	27.9%	27.3%
$10,000 to $19,999	43.9%	39.1%	37.3%	31.3%
More than $20,000	31.2%	35.0%	39.4%	34.0%
By occupation				
Blue collar	51%	47%	38%	32% ⎫ 40% of
White collar	37%	36%	36%	34% ⎬ women
Housewives			27%	27% ⎭

[a]*Source:* USPHS, 1973, 1976a.

Bryson, 1978). Thus, there has been a vast social trend toward smoking cessation that is being led by the more educated and affluent members of the society, with the males being the most obvious.

Smokers versus Ex-Smokers

Data on differences between continuing smokers and ex-smokers aid in the interpretation of the social trends noted earlier. Much of the specific data are from retrospective analyses (Burns, 1969; Graham & Gibson, 1971; Hammond & Percy, 1958; Jones, 1977; Lindenthal, Myers, & Pepper, 1972; Pederson & Lefcoe, 1976; USPHS, 1976a), but some is prospective and longitudinal (Eisinger, 1971; Srole & Fischer, 1973; Straits, 1967, 1970). One consistent finding to help explain increased cessation with age is that a specific condition (e.g., cough) made worse by cigarettes seems the most commonly noted factor precipitating cessation (Burns, 1969; Graham & Gibson, 1971; Hammond & Percy, 1958; Jones, 1977; Pederson & Lefcoe, 1976; Srole & Fischer, 1973; Straits, 1967, 1970). Given the retrospective nature of the assessment, it is difficult to tell the difference between precipitating factors and motivations to quit (USPHS, 1977a). However, it would seem valid to conclude that "quitting cigarettes is not generally to be regarded as a triumph in reason but as a symptom of illness [Jones, 1977, p. 287]."

As would be predicted by both fear-arousal research (Leventhal, 1968, 1971, 1973) and social-learning theory (Bandura, 1969, 1977a), the ultimate consequences become relevant when attached to immediate, personal health effects such as coughing, breathlessness, hoarseness, and/or chest pains. Data on males who have survived a heart attack further confirm this pattern. Follow-up results on hundreds of patients indicate that 30–50% of the smokers will immediately quit following only conventional medical advice and will display only minor relapse over many years (Croog & Richards, 1977; Weinblatt, Shapiro, & Frank, 1971). More active counseling and follow-up procedures have produced even more dramatic results (Burt, Thornley, Illingworth, White, Shaw, & Turner, 1974). Additionally, the smokers who did not quit tended to reduce their intake drastically (Burt *et al.,* 1974; Croog & Richards, 1977; Weinblatt *et al.,* 1971).

Retrospectively, the majority of ex-smokers report being successful on the first attempt to quit. Graham and Gibson (1971) found that quitting was not easy for many but that 84.4% of the successful quitters reported needing only one attempt. The 1975 survey of U.S. adult smokers (USPHS, 1976a) revealed a slightly more conservative figure, with 43% of the ex-smokers reporting being successful on the first try and 13% more on the second attempt; only 14.7% of the males and 9.1% of the females stated that six or more attempts were needed. However, other data suggest that multiple attempts (Pederson & Lefcoe, 1976) and more perseverance (Perri, Richards, & Schultheis, 1977) may be the norm.

When these successful quitters are compared with recidivists, we find the successes reporting fewer withdrawal symptoms, lighter smoking habits, and more clearly defined and multiple reasons for quitting (Graham & Gibson, 1971; Pederson & Lefcoe, 1976; Straits, 1967, 1970). The successful ex-smoker appeared to have used multiple techniques and alternative behaviors (Baer, Foreyt, & Wright, 1977; Graham & Gibson, 1971; Pederson & Lefcoe, 1976), as well as more self-reinforcement strategies (Newman, 1977; Perri *et al.,* 1977). Additionally, continuing smokers and recidivists tend to have less stable interpersonal environments and somewhat more impaired psychological functioning (Srole & Fisher, 1973; Straits, 1967, 1970) and may be more likely to increase smoking during stressful life-events (Lindenthal, Myers, & Pepper, 1972).

Finally, continuing smokers believe that it will be difficult for them to quit. They tend to believe that they will gain weight if they quit (in 1975, 47% of the male and 60% of the female smokers thought this; USPHS, 1976a) and that smoking helps them relax (76% of the smokers agreed in 1970; USPHS, 1973). In fact, almost 60% of the smokers conclude that they probably still will be smoking in 5 years (USPHS, 1976a).

Thus, we have only slim data, much of it retrospective and subjective, upon which to make our interpretations of the dramatic behavioral changes noted in adult smoking cessation outside formal programs. It does appear, however, that there is a consistent relationship between increased symptoms related to smoking and successful cessation. This finding would strongly argue for the importance of immediate negative contingencies, either physiologically or cognitively presented, to counter the immediate attractions of smoking (Bandura, 1969, 1977a; Leventhal, 1967, 1968, 1971, 1973; Premack, 1970). Smokers seem to quit when the health consequences or other negative aspects of the habit become immediate and inescapably obvious. However, many smokers do not quit, even in the face of these obvious cues. Although this type of smoker tends to be in the minority, they highlight the tenacity of the behavior.

THE PROCESS OF SMOKING CESSATION

Cognitive–Behavioral Analysis

Reasons for a Cognitive–Behavioral Analysis

Learning-theory-based therapies for a variety of disorders and problems besides smoking flourished during the late 1960s and early 1970s (Franks, 1969; Franks & Wilson, 1973). Yet, despite the improved experimentation and specificity of the approaches, early successes gave way to less supportive results (Yates, 1975). Based upon their own applied research, major theorists in this area have continued to elaborate and expand their models along cognitive–behavioral lines (Bandura, 1977a,b; Mahoney, 1974; Mahoney & Arnkoff, 1978; Meichenbaum, 1977). Since the behavioral strategies for smoking developed from the earlier social learning models have shown encouraging though somewhat inconsistent results (Bernstein & McAlister, 1976; Best and Bloch, 1979; Pechacek & McAlister, 1979), the analysis of smoking relative to more recent theoretical formulations may offer additional ideas about strategies to modify smoking behavior. Additionally, the cognitive-behavioral perspective provides a framework for integrating the best elements of the diverse smoking models surveyed earlier (see pp. 392–395).

The learning theory and conditioning aspects of smoking that are relevant to both the maintenance and the cessation of the behavior have been very adequately presented in past reviews (Hunt, 1970, 1973; Lichtenstein & Danaher, 1976) and briefly summarized (see p. 393). Smoking conforms to the model of an overlearned behavior, and the behavioral perspective provides the most straightforward analysis of factors maintaining smoking. However, as the issue of cessation is considered, the cognitive and pharmacological factors offer additional insights into the problem. Fortunately, the cognitive–behavioral perspective provides the framework to integrate both the role of attitude change (Leventhal, 1973) and the decision-making model (Horn, 1976; Mausner, 1973; Mausner & Platt, 1971). Finally, the inconsistencies of the pharmacology area (Jarvik, 1977) may be clarified by an attributional analysis (Bem, 1972; Kopel & Arkowitz, 1975).

Understanding How and Why People Quit Smoking

The cessation of smoking is a dramatic behavioral change that some individuals are not capable of achieving even when constantly confronted with the most traumatic consequences of their behavior (e.g., heart disease, emphysema, or cancer). Eiser and Sutton (1977) have suggested that such behavior may involve quite rational choices. They point out that previous work in both America (Mausner & Platt,

1971) and England (McKennell, 1968, 1970) has found a large number of smokers who report stronger motivations for stopping than for continuing smoking, yet they continue to smoke. Eiser and Sutton (1977) sought to clarify the paradox of these seemingly dissonant smokers by suggesting that the decision to keep smoking may be a "cautious" alternative when one is faced with the risks of failing in the attempt to quit.

Bandura's (1977a,b) recent conceptualization of self-efficacy expectations offers a specific framework for understanding the situation presented by Eiser and Sutton (1977). The self-efficacy model suggests that two types of expectations mediate behavior change. First, the more commonly discussed response–outcome expectancies involving probabilistic estimates that a given course of action (e.g., quitting smoking) will lead to a certain outcome (e.g., improved health and well-being). This type of conditional expectancy has been discussed and measured as subjective expected utility (Mausner & Platt, 1971) or as general motivations for quitting (Horn, 1968, 1976; Ikard *et al.*, 1969). Within any model of behavior change, these expectancies (or, more operationally, the forecasted contingencies upon which behavior change occurs) must be favorable if behavior modification is to be obtained. However, salient response–outcome expectancies may be insufficient to motivate cessation.

The second type of expectancy involves one's perception of personal ability to reach the goal or outcome. To clarify this type of situation, Bandura (1977a,b) suggested that procedures that positively alter the level and strength of self-efficacy expectations are needed when persons already have significant motivation for change. The outcome and efficacy expectations are separate in that individuals can believe that a certain course of action will result in desired outcomes but question whether they can perform the behaviors necessary to attain that goal. Bringing the discussion back to smoking control, the strength of the smoker's convictions in his or her ability to produce the habit changes and coping responses necessary to quit smoking determines whether or not an attempt will be made. Furthermore, expectations can have a major bearing both on the degree of persistence in efforts to quit and on the long-term success of the effort. Finally, given high enough levels of outcome expectancies (valuing cessation highly) combined with low levels of self-efficacy (complete lack of confidence in ability to quit), the smoker may adopt a learned helplessness pattern of responding (i.e., no attempt to quit even when given the opportunity) to even obvious cues of negative effects (Leventhal, 1971; Seligman, 1975).

These concepts can be incorporated into a cognitive–behavioral model of smoking that offers an explanation of various stages through which smokers may proceed from initiation through successful cessation or continuing smoking despite obvious health consequences. Figure 12.1 provides a flowchart outlining major decision points in this process. The more detailed description of each of these stages from a cognitive–behavioral perspective should clarify the process of smoking cessation both within and outside formal treatment.

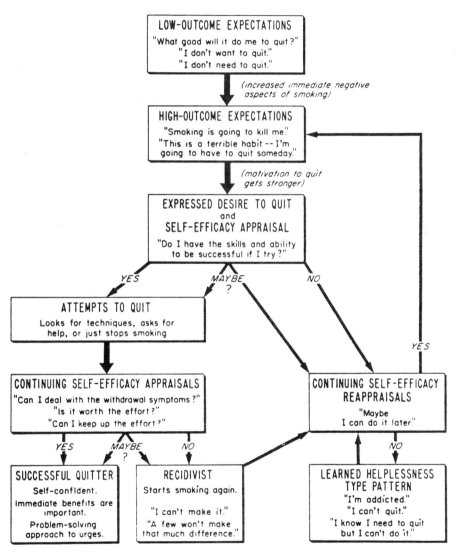

Figure 12.1 The process of quitting smoking.

Adoption.   At the onset of smoking, psychosocial factors appear to be the most influential (Dekker, 1977; USPHS, 1976b, 1977b), with the adoption of smoking being one means of expressing rebelliousness, a liberated or self-confident self-image, and social or sexual maturity. By the time the novice becomes a regular smoker, the pharmacological (Russell, 1976) and habit (Hunt & Matarazzo, 1970) mechanisms become more critical. In these initial stages of the habit, psychosocial benefits outweigh the long-term health consequences (Leventhal, 1973), and personally convincing rationales are formed. These may include various rationalizations and attributions regarding the potential benefits of tobacco, uses such as arousal control, avoidance of weight gain, and/or enhancement of personal experiences. Actual long-term effects are minimized so that outcome expectancies are easily outweighed by the perceived immediate benefits. Hence, there is very little motivation to discontinue the behavior.

Decision to Quit.   Consistent with the concept of attitude change, the cost-benefit appraisal appears to change when immediate and salient health effects are presented to the smoker. Unfortunately, this does not occur for most smokers until the social benefits from smoking begin to decrease and negative physical symptoms appear. The balance between immediate positive and negative reinforcements for smoking and immediate and long-term consequences begins to favor cessation, and smokers start expressing an interest in quitting. And yet, the *decision* to quit or not is not exclusively based upon the cost–benefit analysis, as some models have suggested. Instead, this appraisal is also influenced by the perceived likelihood of success in making the change (Bandura, 1977a,b; Eiser & Sutton, 1977).

First, the person must believe that there is an effective set of behavioral changes that will produce the desired outcomes; that is, the smoker must believe that stopping smoking will enable him/her to avoid the long-term consequences of smoking. Specifically, the smoker must believe that attaining a nonsmoking status will mean an escape from the feared diseases and premature death (Leventhal, 1971). This first appraisal can be termed *response efficacy*.

Second, given that the smoker believes that smoking cessation would produce the desired results, then he/she must also be confident in his/her ability to perform the behaviors necessary to become and remain abstinent. These latter self-efficacy "expectations determine how much effort people will expend and how long they will persist in the face of obstacles and aversive experiences [Bandura, 1977b]."

Even when the outcome expectancies and response efficacy appraisal clearly favor quitting, self-efficacy appraisals may be quite variable (Bandura, 1977a,b). Factors that may strongly influence the critical estimates of success in quitting are: fear of withdrawal symptoms (based on personal or vicarious learning), generalizations from experiences with similar self-managed changes, appraisals of psychological or emotional stability, and expectations regarding environmental supports (Bandura, 1977b).

Quitting.   If the self-efficacy expectations are sufficiently positive (on a negative to positive continuum), an effort will be made to quit. Based on the model, the first attempt at behavior change would likely be without formal assistance or pro-grams, since the perception of strong self-confidence would negate the need for outside help. Data suggest that most successful ex-smokers have quit through inde-pendent efforts (see pp. 395–399). Moreover, only about a third of the smokers who are motivated to quit express a willingness to attempt a formal program (Gallup, 1974); most just want some form of do-it-yourself aid (Schwartz & Dubitzky, 1967). Given positive self-efficacy appraisal, the smoker would make the necessary changes, such as throwing away cigarettes, declaring oneself as an ex-smoker and utilizing available alternative behavior based on personal knowledge or readily available information. Self-efficacy reappraisals would focus more and more on the ability to sustain nonsmoking in the face of problems and urges during the days and weeks after initial cessation or after periodic lapses of smoking. Individual skills in dealing with withdrawal symptoms such as nervousness, irritability, or weight gains or especially strong smoking urges would be influential in these reappraisals.

Additional assistance would be sought by the person who perceives deficits in personal skills or environmental supports. Similarly, some individuals may feel able to quit fairly easily alone but, based on personal or vicarious learning, believe that personal efforts without special techniques will be more painful and difficult. Thus, confidence in the ability to quit may be adequately strong, but expectations regard-ing the response efficacy of different methods may vary.

Continued success at performing the nonsmoking behaviors would enhance self-efficacy appraisals to the point that the pattern would persist until attainment of positive response-outcome expectancies would be able to reinforce the new life-style. Expectation of mastery based upon performance accomplishments, vicarious experiences, verbal persuasion, and physiological feedback are, theoretically, the critical elements in producing enhanced self-efficacy (Bandura, 1977a,b). Thus, feedback from significant others regarding these expectations would also be very influential.

Relapse can, of course, occur at any point where either the self-efficacy reap-praisals became less positive or attainment of initial response-outcome expectancies were insufficient to reinforce the new behaviors. Dependence upon cigarettes to cope with negative affect states seems to be generally predictive of relapse (Jacobs, Spilken, Norman, Wohlberg, & Knapp, 1971; Pechacek, Note 1; Pomerleau, Ad-kins, & Pertschuk, 1978; Schwartz & Dubitzky, 1968), suggesting that, when life crises arise, the difficulty in finding new coping strategies could lead to lower self-efficacy reappraisals and a return to smoking. Similarly, heavier smoking or a more overlearned pattern would require more persistence and greater effort, which would predict lower self-efficacy appraisals. When such problems or demands result in decreased expectations of mastery and lowered self-efficacy, a single cigarette could cause a collapse in self-confidence and a reverting back to the overlearned pattern of baseline smoking—a phenomena all too common in the smoking area.

The smoker who tries to quit and relapses or who initially feels unable to quit would be predicted to reappraise the situation further. Such smokers would be faced with the decision to defer an attempt until some later time, seek more formal outside assistance, or give up and not try to quit. When the choice is to seek a more formal treatment, the perceived efficacy of the program appears to be very important (Hynd, Stratton, & Severson, 1978). The actual efficacy of the treatment would depend upon how well the program is able to provide the skills and support to foster enough initial success so that expectations of mastery and self-efficacy would be enhanced (Bandura, 1977b). Smokers who have tried various self-initiated techniques (such as changing brands, smoking in fewer situations, or eliminating un- necessary cigarettes) without success may seek more extreme therapies because of their perceived need for something "stronger" to "break" their tenacious habit. But, once the treatment is initiated, it must be able to provide personally relevant informations and skills regarding the participants' ability to cope with the problems of cessation and of long-term maintenance of nonsmoking. Performance accomplishments, successful peer models, persuasive communications from peers or therapist, and mastery of physiological or emotional arousal levels are all important (Bandura, 1977b).

"Helpless" Smokers.   The cycling of smokers through attempts to quit selectively separates persons who are able to quit either alone or with assistance from less successful smokers, who presumably have lower self-efficacy appraisals based on their negative experiences. With advancing age, when the obvious and traumatic signs of smoking appear, these individuals with perceived minimal self-efficacy increasingly function in a learned helplessness pattern (Seligman, 1975). They can clearly and emotionally identify *why* they should quit, but the excessive fear of being without available coping strategies makes them feel totally unable to take the actions necessary to quit successfully (Leventhal, 1971). With each failure at cessation, they have experienced a number of problems (irritability, cravings, weight gains, depression, problems in concentration, and the like) that have been attributionally enhanced and now function as rationales to perceive themselves as addicted. The reality of the pharmacology of smoking tends to become secondary to the self-fulfilling prophecy of these attributions. Hence, the low self-efficacy and attributionally enhanced withdrawal problems insure a low probability of success in any cessation effort—no matter how clear and imminent the consequences of continued smoking may be.

This summary of the process of cessation from a cognitive–behavioral perspective is truly a speculative interpretation. However, it provides a framework that incorporates much of the diversity of previous models (see pp. 393–395) and it suggests possible explanations for some of the observed paradoxes of smoking behavior. Equally important, the self-efficacy model (Bandura, 1977a,b) provides guidelines regarding intervention design and selection. This perspective can also guide the appraisal of existing treatment strategies and may enhance future treatment. To this end, effective treatments will be surveyed from this perspective, and intervention recommendations will be made consistent with both the outcome literature and the implications of the cognitive–behavioral model.

An Appraisal of Interventions

General Perspective

The smoking intervention literature has been characterized by a diversity of strategies evaluated with varying degrees of rigor but generally producing a fairly consistent pattern of unoptimistic results. Hunt and Bespalec (1974), in a review of 89 controlled studies representing all manner of approaches, found that, in general, abstinence rates declined sharply during the first 1–5 weeks posttreatment and asymptoted with only 20–30% abstinence at 3–12 months of follow-up among the subjects not smoking at treatment termination. Evaluations of a small subgroup of behavioral interventions found that only from 9 to 17% (mean of 13%) of all subjects were abstinent at 3–6 months of follow-up (McFall & Hammen, 1971). Evaluations of programs in general continue to suggest that few treatments consistently exceeded this pattern (Bernstein, 1969; Bernstein & McAlister, 1976; Best & Bloch, 1979; Lichtenstein & Danaher, 1976; Pechacek & McAlister, 1979; Schwartz, 1969; Schwartz & Rider, 1977).

However, some efforts have been relatively more successful. Treatments adopting a social-learning approach appear to be more optimistic, especially when presented in multicomponent formats (Bernstein & McAlister, 1976; Best & Bloch, 1979; Lichtenstein & Danaher, 1976; Pechacek & McAlister, 1979). Several lines of research that seem to offer the most promise and seem to produce success rates notably superior to the unoptimistic pattern of results discussed earlier will be considered in greater detail. However, for more complete reviews of the development of these techniques or their relative standing versus other treatments, one of the recent reviews cited in the preceding should be consulted.

Treatment Strategies

Behavior modification or social-learning-based strategies for the modification of smoking can be categorized into two broad but not mutually exclusive classes: (*a*) those using aversive conditioning procedures, usually presented in laboratory settings; and (*b*) those employing homework assignments and stimulus-control procedures, commonly labeled as behavioral self-control techniques (Lichtenstein & Danaher, 1976). However, programs demonstrating impressive long-term results when compared to the general trend (Hunt & Bespalec, 1974) are more accurately considered as a combination of aversion and self-control procedures.

Additionally, treatments based on different models or theoretical perspectives will be briefly reviewed. Important highlights of such treatments will be considered with the outcome data that does exist. Finally, proprietary and public-service clinic results will be briefly discussed.

Aversion Treatments.   Based on learning theory models of smoking behavior, a variety of aversion strategies have been evaluated. These have commonly been discussed according to the major aversive stimuli used: electric shock, covert sensitization, or cigarette smoke (Lichtenstein & Danaher, 1976). Highlights of the research in each area will be briefly reviewed.

The data from controlled research on electric shock had provided only minimal evidence for permanent effectiveness (Bernstein & McAlister, 1976; Lichtenstein & Danaher, 1976). A controlled study by Russell, Armstrong, and Patel (1976) is representative of the general failure of the technique to produce differential results compared to nonshock and attention-placebo controls. However, a recent study (Dericco, Brigham, & Garlington, 1977) did produce a clear treatment effect for faradic shock therapy. Sixteen of 20, or 80%, of the subjects receiving shock were abstinent at 6-month follow-up, but the treatment involved sessions 5 days per week for several weeks, with higher-than-normal shock intensities and the additive influence of other treatment factors. Thus, shock augmented by other procedures may produce an effective treatment package, but as a sole treatment it fails because subjects can too easily discriminate between shock and no-shock situations, such that generalization outside therapy usually does not occur (Lichtenstein & Danaher, 1976).

The literature on covert sensitization—the imaginal pairing of smoking with the experience of nausea or vomiting (Cautela, 1970)—has failed to support its long-term efficacy or superiority relative to placebo controls (Bernstein & McAlister, 1976; Lichtenstein & Danaher, 1976). These findings are in agreement with Mahoney's (1974) negative appraisal of covert conditioning therapies in general.

The literature dealing with cigarette smoke as the main aversive stimulus has been much more impressive, especially the results of the rapid-smoking procedure (Bernstein & McAlister, 1976; Best & Bloch, 1979; Danaher, 1977b; Lichtenstein & Danaher, 1976; Pechacek & McAlister, 1979). The logic of the procedure is straightforward in that the aversion is tied in with many of the endogenous cues that characterize smoking (Danaher & Lichtenstein, 1974; Lichtenstein & Danaher, 1976). In their comprehensive review of behavioral cessation strategies, Lichtenstein and Danaher (1976) discussed the development and logic of aversive smoking procedures, and Danaher (1977b) reviewed the outcome literature on rapid smoking. Therefore, only the highlights of this research history will be presented.

Requiring subjects to smoke rapidly (inhaling every 6 seconds) and continually while blowing warm, stale smoke into their faces had been only marginally effective until refined by Lichtenstein and his colleagues (Lichtenstein, Harris, Birchler, Wahl, and Schmahl, 1973; Schmahl, Lichtenstein, & Harris, 1972). The smoke-aversion strategies were found to be significantly more effective than a normal-paced-smoking attention placebo control, and almost 100% abstinence at treatment termination and 60% abstinence at 6-month follow-up was attained by rapid smoking with or without exposure to smoke blown in the face (Lichtenstein et al., 1973). Thus, later research has focused almost exclusively on the more convenient rapid-smoking-only condition (Danaher, 1977b; Lichtenstein & Danaher, 1976). Two unpublished analyses of the rapid smoking procedure clarified that a warm, contingently persuasive interpersonal context during treatment is an important element of the procedure (Harris & Lichtenstein, Note 2) and that elimination of smoking urges as the termination criterion enhances the treatment effect (Weinrobe & Lichtenstein, Note 3). A multiyear follow-up of these early studies has shown some relapse, but the absolute findings are still encouraging (Lichtenstein & Rodrigues, 1977).

The procedure has been extensively investigated in over 30 studies (Danaher, 1977b). Although some recent evaluations reported minimal results (e.g., Sutherland, Amit, Golden, & Rosenberger, 1975), the overall pattern shows rapid smoking to have relatively superior effects. Moreover, a careful appraisal suggests that a number of procedural variations may have accounted for the findings in many recent studies (Danaher, 1977b). Finally, the data now strongly suggest that the early successful procedure involved a number of active variables, including flexible sessions-to-cessation format, warm persuasive social context, induction of positive expectations, and active cognitive revivification of the aversive experiences (Bernstein & McAlister, 1976; Danaher, 1977b; Lichtenstein & Danaher, 1976) and thus can be classed more accurately as a multicomponent therapy than as a simple aversion procedure (Bernstein & McAlister, 1976; Pechacek & McAlister, 1979).

Concern has been focused on the medical safety of rapid smoking (Hall, Sachs, Hall, 1979; Lichtenstein & Glasgow, 1977; Miller, Schilling, Logan, & Johnson, 1977; Sachs, Hall, & Hall, 1978) and has encouraged interest in other forms of smoke-aversion therapy. One technique that has been receiving continued attention is known as *satiation* and involves instructions to increase daily smoking consumption as much as 200 to 300% for a period of days prior to cessation. The basic logic of the procedure is similar to that described for rapid smoking. A major procedural difference is that satiation usually involves regular paced smoking without any specific instructions regarding when to smoke the extra cigarettes and has been primarily carried out by the subjects in their natural environments (Lichtenstein & Danaher, 1976). Early reserach on the technique was promising, but subsequent studies failed even to demonstrate superiority relative to placebo controls (Bernstein & McAlister, 1976; Lichtenstein & Danaher, 1976). More recently, however, several studies (Best, Bass, & Owen, 1977; Best, Owen, & Trentadue, 1978; Delahunt & Curran, 1976; Lando, 1977; Lando & McCullough, 1978) have reported impressive results with the satiation procedure when combined with a general package of self-control training.

Thus, the satiation procedure alone appears less effective than rapid smoking despite their functional similarities, but it may be a very useful element of a *multicomponent* treatment. Also, the doubling or tripling of normal smoking rates could produce medical risks much like rapid smoking and, hence, require similar medical screening and subject-selection criteria (Hall, Sachs, Hall, 1979; Lichtenstein & Glasgow, 1977; Sachs, Hall, & Hall, 1978).

Aversion treatments in general have produced encouraging results, but nonreplications have been common. More recent successful studies suggest that a number of active variables beyond a simple conditioning effect are involved. Therefore, the treatments that maximize the social and cognitive aspects of the techniques and incorporate other behavioral strategies seem to be most effective.

Self-Control Treatments. The social learning perspective has produced a variety of treatments that can be loosely categorized under the self-control label. These forms of treatment commonly have the client or subject more actively involved in defining and applying the treatment program. Stimulus-control procedures, based on the assumption that smoking is prompted by environmental cues and that the variety and number of cues lead to difficulty in quitting, have attempted a gradual elimination of smoking by narrowing the range of controlling cues. Interventions focusing increasing stimulus intervals and hierarchical reductions and/or narrowing smoking situations have produced limited and usually only case-study demonstrations of effectiveness (Bernstein & McAlister, 1976; Best and Bloch, 1979; Lichtenstein & Danaher, 1976). Studies by Shapiro and associates (Levinson, Shapiro, Schwartz, & Tursky, 1971; Shapiro, Tursky, Schwartz, & Schnidman, 1971) demonstrated the general pattern of these studies, namely, a clear reduction in smoking that stabilized around 10–12 cigarettes per day and produced minimal long-term abstinence.

Other learning-theory-based strategies have attempted to eliminate smoking behavior more indirectly by either reinforcing nonsmoking or fostering behaviors incompatible with smoking. Except for occasional case studies (e.g., Danaher, 1976), these types of strategies have generally produced minimal clinical effectiveness (Bernstein & McAlister, 1976; Lichtenstein & Danaher, 1976; Mahoney, 1974).

Results with direct contingency contracting to reinforce nonsmoking appear to be more promising but still mixed. Several studies have demonstrated that contingency contracting may directly initiate changes in smoking behavior when the valued consequences were made contingent upon progressively longer periods of abstinence or gradually more stringent reduction goals (Axelrod, Hall, Weis, & Rohrer, 1974; Brengelmann & Sedlmayr, 1977; Tighe & Elliott, 1968; Winett, 1973). Based on the overall positive and negative pattern of results with the procedure, it has been commonly included as one element in more elaborate treatment programs, rather than as a sole treatment (Bernstein & McAlister, 1976; Best & Bloch, 1979; Lichtenstein & Danaher, 1976; Pechacek & McAlister, 1979).

Both Brengelmann (Brengelmann & Sedlmayr, 1977) and Pomerleau (Pomerleau *et al.*, 1978) have reported notable success with such a multicomponent self-control program involving stimulus control, the modification of covert behaviors, and the development of alternatives to smoking. Each package was developed based on clinical experience and continuing refinement. The Pomerleau program (Pomerleau & Pomerleau, 1977) produced 61% abstinence at posttreatment and 32% abstinence at 1-year follow-up. Brengelmann has reported similarly encouraging data (Brengelmann & Sedlmayr, 1977).

Other empirical tests combining self-control and aversion procedures have also shown impressive results. Chapman, Smith, and Layden (1971) combined daily electric-shock sessions and self-management training to produce abstinence in 6 of 11 subjects (54%) at 12-month follow-up. Similarly, several more recent studies have obtained very impressive long-term results combining satiation within a multicomponent self-control treatment with abstinence rates of 47% (Best *et al.*, 1977, 1978), 55% (Delahunt & Curran, 1976), 75% (Lando & McCullough, 1978), and 76% (Lando, 1977) at 6-month follow-ups. Morrow, Sachs, Gmeinder, and Burgess (1973) had similar results when combining rapid smoking with self-control procedures, but other studies have produced mixed or inconclusive results with similar combinations (Danaher, 1977a; Flaxman, 1978; Glasgow, 1978;

Pechacek, 1977). Additionally, Brockway, Kleinmann, Edelson, & Gruenewald (1977) and McGrath & Hall (1976) found no significant difference at follow-up between a comprehensive self-control package and control conditions.

Thus, as had been stated at the start of this section, the general conclusion has been that some of the most conclusive results have been produced by multicomponent treatments. Well-developed self-control programs (e.g., Pomerleau *et al.*, 1978) or combinations of aversion and self-control strategies (Best *et al.*, 1977, 1978; Delahunt & Curran, 1976; Lando, 1977; Lando & McCullough, 1978) appear encouraging. However, the failure of other multicomponent treatments points out that the manner in which the techniques are administered or other only partially defined process variables could be important in the failure of some programs.

Diverse Treatment Strategies. Schwartz & Rider (1977) recently reviewed the variety of smoking interventions currently in use. Besides the behavioral techniques reviewed earlier, a variety of public service and proprietary programs have been utilized widely, with limited evaluation data collected. Hypnosis has produced numerous clinical demonstrations but little experimentally evaluated outcome data. Therefore, the objective data on such interventions will be briefly reviewed.

The majority of smokers exposed to formal cessation programs have been treated by public service programs, especially the 5-Day Plan and the American Cancer Society programs (McAlister, 1975). Unfortunately, these clinics are rarely evaluated in an objective fashion. Schwartz & Rider (1977) surveyed existing published and unpublished data and concluded that in most cases they do not exceed the general trends noted by Hunt & Bespalec (1974). The analysis of 20 American Cancer Society groups by Pyszka, Ruggels, and Janowicz (Note 4) found that about 40% of the participants quit but only 20% remained abstinent beyond 12–18 months of follow-up. Similarly, no recent published data have contradicted the 20–25% long-term abstinence rates reported for the 5-Day Plan (Guilford, 1972; Thompson & Wilson, 1966). Thus, the public service programs appear to produce the same minimal to moderate results verified in research programs involving general types of group treatments (Schwartz & Dubitzky, 1968; Shewchuk, 1976; Shewchuk, Dubren, Burton, Forman, Clark, & Jaffin, 1977).

Proprietary groups commonly report very impressive results, but little objective evaluation data are available (McAlister, 1975; Schwartz & Rider, 1977). The high cost of some programs could enhance their efficacy, but their impressive claims may be due more to selective follow-up procedures (Lichtenstein & Danaher, 1976; McAlister, 1975). Published data on the SmokEnders method (Kanzler, Jaffe, & Zeidenberg, 1976) indicated a 39% 4-year success rate, but this was based on an extrapolation from 167 out of 553 subjects and highlights the common pattern of reporting data on subjects easily located (Schwartz & Rider, 1977). Nevertheless, some programs continue to incorporate techniques produced within behavioral research and may thus package programs with meaningful effectiveness.

Hypnosis has been another procedure with outstanding clinical claims of success but little objective or comparative testings. The technique has been utilized as a part of antismoking treatments for over 30 years, but almost all outcome data remain in the form of clinical reports (Johnson & Donoghue, 1971; Orne, 1977). Thus, the controversy over the effectiveness of the technique continues (Schwartz & Rider, 1977). Until the as yet unidentified unique component of hypnosis is found to be critical to producing cessation, the procedure can best be conceptualized as a combination of existing behavioral interventions, such as directed imagery, relaxation training, and contractual management (Danaher & Lichtenstein, 1978). Moreover, the mystique of hypnosis continues to exert what appears to be a general placebo response that may lead to some less-traumatic initial cessation (Orne, 1977).

Preventing Relapse

Even though all the major reviews have stressed the importance of maintaining nonsmoking beyond the point of temporary cessation, the limited success of cessation efforts still appears to distract researchers back toward the issues of initial change. The results from booster sessions or follow-up contacts with therapists have generally been inconclusive (Bernstein, 1970; Best *et al.,* 1977; Kopel, 1975; Relinger, Bornstein, Bugge, Carmody, & Zohn, 1977; Schmahl *et al.,* 1972). In general, subjects tend not to use such assistance (Best, 1975; Shewchuk, 1976).

Positive results for maintenance programming were reported by Lando (1977; Lando & McCullough, 1978). Maintenance groups involving aversive smoking booster sessions and contingency contracting significantly enhanced the long-term results of the cessation package. Similar results were reported by Gordon and Katz (Note 5). General self-management techniques may also be effective in promoting greater maintenance of treatment effects (Best & Bloch, 1979).

Results from providing treatment elements specifically designed to fulfill individualized needs of subjects have also been encouraging (Best, 1975; Pechacek, Note 1). Hence, maintenance effects may be enhanced by special posttreatment programming (Lando, 1977) or by providing the skills to overcome special deficits (Best & Bloch, 1979; Pechacek, Note 1). It has been suggested that a subject's ability to make self-attributions of the continuing abstinence rather than an attribution to some treatment variable that will be shortly withdrawn may be a critical element in maintenance success (Best & Bloch, 1979; Kopel & Arkowitz, 1975).

Successful Cessation in Treatment

Within the model of smoking cessation that has been presented, participation in formal cessation programs is only a small part of the overall cessation process. First, smokers must be motivated to change their behavior before they will seek out a treatment. Additionally, the smoker must perceive the need for external assistance in the attempt. The smoker comes to treatment seeking specific assistance for special problems or general support to overcome low self-efficacy appraisals.

During the initial period of participation in a treatment, the smoker is appraising the response-efficacy of the program. Several aspects of treatment would seem to be important at this stage. First, the treatment must have a persuasive rationale presented by a credible therapist. Second, the smoker forms expectations of success based on vicarious data (e.g., how well friends have done in similar programs) or on the therapist's persuasive communication regarding expected outcomes. Finally, the smoker will appraise the availability and inclusion of treatment components for self-perceived deficits or needs.

Treatments based on social learning theory seem to have a generally persuasive rationale and are presented by therapists with confidence in the procedures. However, many techniques elicit varying degrees of confidence both from smokers (Hynd, Stratton, & Severson, 1978) and from nonsmoking significant others whose opinions may effect the smokers' treatment choice (Hynd, Chambers, Stratton, & Moan, 1977). Some behavioral self-control techniques have become so widely known that they may have been applied inappropriately already and may have lost their aura of uniqueness or potency. Thus, the presentation of techniques may have to restore their perceived response-efficacy.

Aversive smoking procedures may especially be able to induce perceived response-efficacy when the complete logic of the techniques is presented. The fact that they are more extreme may attract persons who feel that such dramatic techniques will make quitting easier. However, with only minimal explanations such procedures were rated as less credible than relaxation alone (Hynd *et al.*, 1977, 1978).

Once treatment is initiated, the critical issue is the enhancement of expectations of mastery and self-efficacy. Performance accomplishments are most important, but vicarious experiences via group treatments can also be important. Powerful induction procedures (such as aversive smoking) may be necessary to produce initial abstinence. As self-efficacy is bolstered by initial periods of 24 or 48 hours of abstinence, self-attributions regarding maintenance need to be instilled. The therapist's ability to provide effective solutions to initial problems and needs enables the participant to gain confidence in being able to learn the new skills needed to maintain nonsmoking. The long-term maintenance of nonsmoking would be predicted when the numbers of successes experienced during initial cessation were sufficient to enhance self-efficacy, when the magnitude, generality, and strength of this self-efficacy has been made strong enough to persevere through minor relapses, and when the participant is able to attribute the success to ability rather than to effort (Bandura, 1977b).

Therefore, in conclusion, successful cessation is produced when

1. the smoker perceives the treatment as credible and as having high response efficacy;
2. the treatment produces rapid enhancement of self-efficacy by performance accomplishments, vicarious learning, and/or by persuasive communications;
3. the participant gains the specific new skills needed to cope with special personal problems during both early and later maintenance;
4. the positive changes in smoking behavior are attributed to existing or learned abilities and skills rather than to effort or to the external aspects of treatment;

5. all of these result in strong and generalizable personal efficacy that will not be extinguished by disconfirming smoking relapses.

TREATMENT RECOMMENDATIONS

The first sections of this chapter have summarized both the smoking problem and attempts at effective intervention. As part of this evaluation of the problem, a cognitive–behavioral model has been applied to smoking control. As noted, this model should have heuristic implications for intervention strategies.

Recent analyses of treatment planning have generally categorized intervention into three stages: preparation, cessation, and maintenance (Best & Bloch, 1979; Danaher & Lichtenstein, 1978). Goals and possible techniques are reviewed for each stage. Table 12.3 provides a brief outline of these recommendations; however, the specific techniques are only suggestions of procedures generally supported by the outcome literature and consistent with the treatment goals derived from the cognitive–behavioral model.

TABLE 12.3
Treatment Strategies at the Three Stages of Smoking Cessation

Stage One: Preparation
    Goals: 1. Provide a clear and persuasive rationale for the treatment program
              2. Clarify immediate and long-term expectations regarding program effectiveness
              3. Identify special problems of participants
              4. Encourage self-attribution of changes to be made
    Strategies: 1. Cognitive–behavioral rationale
              2. Self-monitoring of normal smoking
              3. Behavioral Self-control model

Stage Two: Cessation
    Goals: 1. Rapid induction of behavior change and production of performance accomplishments
              2. Reattribution or minimization of withdrawal fears or expectations
              3. Enhancement of attribution of change to ability rather than effort
    Strategies: 1. Aversive smoking (satiation, rapid smoking, electric shock, or other), target quit dates, behavioral contracting, or complex self-control packages
              2. Massed or daily treatment sessions
              3. Persuasive counseling sessions

Stage Three: Maintenance
    Goals: 1. Establish effective coping skills and alternatives to smoking
              2. Clarify benefits of cessation
              3. Develop self-perception of self as nonsmoker
    Strategies: 1. Skills Training—relaxation, positive self-verbalizations, self-contracting, self-reinforcement, problem solving
              2. Behavioral rehearsal of alternatives
              3. Persuasive counseling sessions
              4. Space treatment sessions

Stage One—Preparation

In the preparation phase, the smokers must gain confidence that the program can be successful in aiding them to overcome the problems that they think make it difficult or impossible for them to quit. A cognitive–behavioral rationale focusing on smoking as a learned behavior that can be modified through specific and systematic techniques is one way of enhancing the perceived efficacy of the program. The confidence, authority, and prestige of the therapist can enhance this message (Goldstein, 1975). Self-monitoring can aid in the acceptance of this rationale and help the smoker to clarify perceptions of special needs. The interpretation of the self-monitoring data as an introduction to the individualized nature of the program can also enhance appraisals of the program's efficacy for the individual's unique needs. Moreover, presentation of the behavioral self-control model can establish the foundation for self-attributions of success and facilitate appraisals of personal efficacy. Finally, immediate and long-term expectations regarding both the treatment and the nonsmoking lifestyle should be explicitly considered.

Stage Two—Cessation

Both the cognitive–behavioral model and the outcome literature seem to favor rapid cessation of the behavior. The model strongly suggests that powerful induction methods should be used initially and then removed to foster self-mastery experiences. The outcome literature suggests that aversive smoking techniques (especially rapid smoking and satiation) are particularly effective in producing rapid cessation. However, a variety of other techniques, including target quit dates (Flaxman, 1978), behavioral contracting (Brengelmann & Sedlmayr, 1977), and complex self-control programs (Brengelmann & Sedlmayr, 1977; Pomerleau *et al.,* 1978), can also be used.

The outcome literature also seems to favor high frequency contacts during the initial withdrawal period. Aversive-smoking programs with impressive cessation rates (e.g., Dericco *et al.,* 1977; Lando, 1977; Lando & McCullough, 1978; Lichtenstein *et al.,* 1973) have utilized daily sessions with reported success. Persuasive counseling, either individual or group, can be used to focus participants' attention on the positive perceptions of self-efficacy, reattribution of withdrawal symptoms (McAlister, 1975), and the attribution of success to the use of techniques (i.e., enhanced personal skills) rather than effort (i.e., "will power"). The rapid-smoking procedure appears to be a very powerful tool to aid in this persuasive communication, since the participant is told that the satiation will eliminate almost all urges until the next session and the next session will wipe out any lingering nicotine cravings. Furthermore, the posttrial counseling focuses on cognitive re-vivification to formalize this expectation (Lichtenstein & Danaher, 1976). The daily satiation sessions used by Lando (1977; Lando & McCullough, 1978) and the almost daily shock sessions used by Dericco and associates (1977) may also work in the same fashion.

Stage Three—Maintenance

Maintenance should be viewed as a gradual transition away from cessation. As withdrawal fears and problems are diminished by the successful accomplishment of the cessation strategies, the focus should be shifted toward skill training to enhance the participants' ability to cope with special problems identified during the preparation stage or in using cessation strategies. The behavioral self-control model and the problem-solving techniques inherent in it can be effective guides for developing the cognitive and behavioral coping strategies. One additional focus of the sessions can be to provide specific information on the immediate benefits of cessation (i.e., rapid clearance of carbon monoxide from the blood, reduced risks of sudden death, clearance of the lungs) that can then be used to develop effective self-verbalizations incompatible with smoking (Danaher, 1976; Pomerleau et al., 1978). Furthermore, having produced the initial behaviors to escape the health consequences of smoking, the participants will generally be much more receptive to specific information about the health consequences of their old habit (Leventhal, 1971; Pomerleau et al., 1978). This information can also be used to form therapeutically relevant self-verbalizations.

However, effective maintenance usually requires more than attitudinal shifts or persuasive communication interventions. As one would predict, strong and generalizable self-efficacy appraisals regarding the ability to maintain nonsmoking require performance accomplishments relevant to specific problem areas. Skills need to be learned to help the ex-smoker resist commonly troublesome cues, such as alcohol drinking situations, negative affect cues, and other times when general self-management or coping skills decrease. If the behavioral self-management philosophy can be instilled and reinforced with new skills such as relaxation, smoking-incompatible self-verbalizations, and self-reinforcement, then persuasive counseling should be able to strengthen the sense of personal efficacy regarding future situations that may have especially strong cue strengths for smoking. In this process, the participant will begin to accept the new self-perceptions (Bem, 1972) of "self" as an ex-smoker. Hence, the participant will attain the ability to endure challenges to perceived self-efficacy (e.g., one or two cigarettes at a party) without the collapse of the perseverance to cope with smoking cues and the utilization of the new nonsmoking alternatives.

CONCLUDING COMMENTS

An effort has been made to provide a new theoretical and practical perspective to the smoking problem. The outcome literature on strategies to modify smoking behavior clearly reflects the need to avoid what Bernstein (1969) called the directionless and circular course of research. The diverse data surveyed within this chapter may help both the novice and the seasoned researcher conceptualize the smoking problem more clearly. The magnitude of the problem demands that research energies find answers to more than attractive theoretical questions.

This appraisal of the intensive intervention situation should help to clarify further the cognitive–behavioral model of smoking. However, until tested by appropriate research, the guidelines presented are, at best, suggestive. Nevertheless, the research on strategies to modify smoking behavior seem to support the basic tenets of this model. The reviews of the literature all consistently conclude that the most effective programs tend to be multidimensional, individualized, and based on a sound rationale. Additionally, rapid behavioral change with massed sessions or strong induction techniques also seems to be generally more effective. Finally, the unoptimistic and frustrating results from cessation strategies should not cloud the inescapable need for effective maintenance strategies. Even though specific recommendations have been made, the inconsistency and almost paradoxical nature of some data in this area make the recommendations even more tentative until additional empirical tests have been concluded.

REFERENCE NOTES

1. Pechacek, T. F. *Specialized treatments for high anxious smokers.* Paper presented at the meeting of the Association for Advancement of Behavior Therapy, New York, December, 1976.
2. Harris, D. E., & Lichtenstein, E. *The contribution of nonspecific social variables to a successful behavioral treatment of smoking.* Paper presented at the meeting of the Western Psychological Association, San Francisco, April, 1971.
3. Weinrobe, P. A., & Lichtenstein, E. *The use of urges as termination criterion in a rapid smoking program for habitual smokers.* Paper presented at the meeting of the Western Psychological Association, Sacramento, April 1973.
4. Pyszka, R. H., Ruggels, W. L., & Janowicz, L. M. *Health Behavior Change: Smoking Cessation.* Menlo Park, California: Stanford Research Institute, December, 1973.
5. Gordon, S. P., & Katz, R. C. *A comparison of three maintenance procedures following treatment by rapid smoking.* Paper presented at the meeting of the Western Psychological Association, Seattle, April, 1977.

REFERENCES

Abelson, P. Cost-effective health care: Editorial. *Science,* 1976, *192,* 862.

Axelrod, S., Hall, R. V., Weis, L., & Rohrer, S. Use of self-imposed contingencies to reduce the frequency of smoking behavior. In M. J. Mahoney & C. E. Thoresen (Eds.), *Self-control: Power to the person.* Monterey, California: Brooks/Cole, 1974.

Baer, P. E., Foreyt, J. P., & Wright, S. Self-directed termination of excessive cigarette use among untreated smokers. *Journal of Behavior Therapy and Experimental Psychiatry,* 1977,*8,* 71–74.

Bandura, A. *Principles of behavior modification.* New York: Holt, Rinehart & Winston, 1969.

Bandura, A. *Social learning theory.* Englewood Cliffs, New Jersey: Prentice-Hall, 1977. (a)

Bandura, A. Self-efficacy: Toward a unifying theory of behavior change. *Psychological Review,* 1977, *84,* 191–215. (b)

Bem, D. J. Self-perception theory. In L. Berkowitz (Ed.), *Advances in experimental social psychology (Vol. 6).* New York: Academic Press, 1972. Pp. 1–62.

Bernstein, D. A. Modification of smoking behavior: An evaluative review. *Psychological Bulletin,* 1969, *71,* 418–440.

Bernstein, D. A. The modification of smoking behavior: A search for effective variables. *Behavior Research & Therapy,* 1970, *8,* 133–146.

Bernstein, D. A., & McAlister, A. The modification of smoking behavior: Progress and problems. *Addictive Behaviors,* 1976, *1,* 89–102.

Best, J. A. Tailoring smoking withdrawal procedures to personality and motivational differences. *Journal of Consulting and Clinical Psychology,* 1975, *43,* 1–8.

Best, J. A., Bass, F., & Owen, L. E. Mode of service delivery in a smoking cessation programme. *Canadian Journal of Public Health,* 1977, *68,* 469–473.

Best, J. A., & Bloch, M. On improving compliance: Cigarette smoking. In R. B. Haynes & D. L. Sackett (Eds.), *Compliance.* Baltimore: Johns Hopkins University Press, 1979.

Best, J. A., Owen, L. E., & Trentadue, L. Comparison of satiation and rapid smoking. *Addictive Behaviors,* 1978, *3,* 71–78.

Best, J. A., & Steffy, R. A. Smoking modification procedures for internal and external locus of control clients. *Canadian Journal of Behavior Science,* 1975, *7,* 155–165.

Brengelmann, J. C., & Sedlmayr, E. Experiments in the reduction of smoking behavior. In J. Steinfeld, W. Griffiths, K. Ball, & R. M. Taylor (Eds.), *Proceedings of the 3rd World Conference on Smoking and Health.* Washington, D.C.: USDHEW, 1977. DHEW Publication No. (NIH) 77–1413.

Brockway, B. S., Kleinmann, K., Edleson, J., & Gruenewald, K. Non-aversive procedures and their effect on cigarette smoking. *Addictive Behaviors,* 1977, *2,* 121–128.

Burns, B. H. Chronic chest disease, personality, and success in stopping cigarette smoking. *British Journal of Preventive and Social Medicine,* 1969, *23,* 23–27.

Burt, A., Thornley, P., Illingworth, D., White, P., Shaw, T. R. D., & Turner, R. Stopping smoking after myocardial infarction. *Lancet,* 1974, *i,* 304–306.

Cautela, J. R. Treatment of smoking by covert sensitization. *Psychological Reports,* 1970, *26,* 415–420.

Chapman, R. F., Smith, J. W., & Layden, T. A. Elimination of cigarette smoking by punishment and self-management training. *Behavior Research and Therapy,* 1971, *9,* 255–264.

Croog, S. H., & Richards, N. P. Health beliefs and smoking patterns in heart patients and their wives: A longitudinal study. *American Journal of Public Health,* 1977, *67,* 921–929.

Danaher, B. G. Coverant control of cigarette smoking. In J. D. Krumboltz & C. E. Thoresen (Eds.), *Counseling methods.* New York: Holt, Rinehart and Winston, 1976.

Danaher, B. G. Rapid smoking and self-control in the modification of smoking behavior. *Journal of Consulting and Clinical Psychology,* 1977, *45,* 1068–1075. (a)

Danaher, B. G. Research on rapid smoking: Interim summary and recommendations. *Addictive Behaviors,* 1977, *2,* 151–166. (b)

Danaher, B. G., & Lichtenstein, E. Aversion therapy issues: A note of clarification. *Behavior Therapy,* 1974, *5,* 112–116.

Danaher, B. G., & Lichtenstein, E. *Become an ex-smoker.* Englewood Cliffs, New Jersey: Prentice-Hall, 1978.

Dekker, E. Youth culture and influences on the smoking behavior of young people. In J. Steinfeld, W. Griffiths, K. Ball, & R. M. Taylor (Eds.), *Proceedings of the 3rd World Conference on Smoking and Health.* Washington, D.C.: USDHEW, 1977. DHEW Publication No. (NIH) 77–1413.

Delahunt, J., & Curran, J. P. Effectiveness of negative practice and self-control techniques in the reduction of smoking behavior. *Journal of Consulting and Clinical Psychology,* 1976, *44,* 1002–1007.

Dericco, D. A., Brigham, T. A., & Garlington, W. K. Development and evaluation of treatment paradigms for the suppression of smoking behavior. *Journal of Applied Behavior Analysis,* 1977, *10,* 173–181.

Dicken, C., & Bryson, R. Psychology in action: The smoking of psychology. *American Psychologist,* 1978, *33,* 504–507.

Dunn, W. L. (Ed.) *Smoking behavior: Motives and incentives.* Washington, D.C.: Winston & Sons, 1973.

Editorial: Do people smoke for nicotine? *British Medical Journal,* 1977, *ii,* 1041–1042.

Eiser, J. R., & Sutton, S. R. Smoking as a subjectively rational choice. *Addictive Behaviors,* 1977, *2,* 129–134.

Eisinger, R. A. Psychosocial predictors of smoking recidivism. *Journal of Health and Social Behavior,* 1971, *12,* 355–362.

Flaxman, J. Quitting smoking now or later: Gradual, abrupt, immediate, and delayed quitting. *Behavior Therapy,* 1978, *9,* 260–270.

Foss, R. Personality, social influence and cigarette smoking. *Journal of Health and Social Behavior,* 1973, *14,* 279–286.

Franks, C. M. (Ed.) *Behavior therapy: Appraisal and status.* New York: McGraw-Hill, 1969.

Franks, C. M., & Wilson, G. T. (Eds.) *Annual review of behavior therapy: Theory and practice.* New York: Brunner/Mazel, 1973.

Gallup Opinion Index. Report #108, June, 1974. Pp. 20–21.

Garfinkel, L. Cigarette smoking among physicians and other health professionals, 1959–1972. *CA—A Cancer Journal for Clinicians,* 1976, *26,* 373–375.

Glad, W. R., Tyre, T. W., & Adesso, V. J. A multidimensional model of cigarette smoking. *American Journal of Clinical Hypnosis,* 1976, *19,* 82–90.

Glasgow, R. E. Effects of a self-control manual, rapid smoking, and amount of therapist contact on smoking reduction (Doctoral dissertation, University of Oregon, 1977). *Dissertation Abstracts International,* 1978, *38,* 5014B. (University Microfilms No. 78-02521)

Goldstein, A. P. Relationship-enhancement methods. In F. H. Kanfer & A. P. Goldstein (Eds.), *Helping people change: A textbook of methods.* New York: Pergamon Press, 1975. Pp. 15–49.

Gordon, T., Kannel, W. B., Dawber, T. R., & McGee, D. Changes associated with quitting cigarette smoking: The Framingham study. *American Heart Journal,* 1975, *90,* 322–328.

Graham, S., & Gibson, R. W. Cessation of patterned behavior: Withdrawal from smoking. *Social Science and Medicine,* 1971, *5,* 319–337.

Guilford, J. S. Group treatment versus individual initiative in the cessation of smoking. *Journal of Applied Psychology,* 1972, *56,* 162–167.

Hall, R. G., Sachs, D. P. L., & Hall, S. M. Medical risk and therapeutic effectiveness of rapid smoking. *Behavior Therapy,* 1979, in press.

Hammond, E. C., & Percy, C. Ex-smokers. *New York State Journal of Medicine,* 1958, *58,* 2956–2959.

Horn, D. Some factors in smoking and its cessation. In E. F. Borgatta & R. R. Evans (Eds.), *Smoking, health, and behavior.* Chicago: Aldine, 1968.

Horn, D. Man, cigarettes, and the abuse of gratification. *Archives of Environmental Health,* 1970, *20,* 88–92.

Horn, D. A model for the study of personal choice health behavior. *International Journal of Health Education,* 1976, *19,* 89–98.

Hunt, W. A. (Ed.) *Learning mechanism in smoking.* Chicago: Aldine, 1970.

Hunt, W. A. (Ed.), Special issue: New approaches to behavioral research on smoking. *Journal of Abnormal Psychology,* 1973, *81,* 107–198.

Hunt, W. A., & Bespalec, D. A. An evaluation of current methods of modifying smoking behavior. *Journal of Clinical Psychology,* 1974, *30,* 431–438.

Hunt, W. A., & Matarazzo, J. D. Habit mechanisms in smoking. In W. A. Hunt (Ed.), *Habit mechanisms in smoking.* Chicago: Aldine, 1970. Pp. 65–106.

Hunt, W. A., & Matarazzo, J. D. Three years later: Recent developments in the experimental modification of smoking behavior. *Journal of Abnormal Psychology,* 1973, *81,* 107–115.

Hynd, G. W., Chambers, C., Stratton, T. T., & Moan, E. Credibility of smoking control strategies in non-smokers: Implications for clinicians. *Psychological Reports,* 1977, *41,* 503–506.

Hynd, G. W., Stratton, T. T., & Severson, H. H. Smoking treatment strategies, expectancy outcomes, and credibility in attention-placebo control conditions. *Journal of Clinical Psychology,* 1978, *34,* 182–186.

Ikard, F. F., Green, D. E., & Horn, D. A scale to differentiate between types of smoking as related to the management of affect. *International Journal of Addictions,* 1969, *4,* 649–659.

Ikard, F. F., & Tomkins, S. The experience of affect as a determinant of smoking behavior: A series of validity studies. *Journal of Abnormal Psychology,* 1973, *81,* 172–181.

Jacobs, M. A., Spilken, A. Z., Norman, M. M., Wohlberg, G. W., & Knapp, P. H. Interaction of personality and treatment conditions associated with success in a smoking control program. *Psychosomatic Medicine,* 1971, *33,* 545–556.

Jarvik, M. E. Biological factors underlying the smoking habit. In M. E. Jarvik, J. W. Cullen, E. R. Gritz, T. M. Vogt, & L. J. West (Eds.), *Research on smoking behavior.* Washington, D.C.: USDHEW, 1977. DHEW Publication No. (ADM) 78-581. Pp. 122–146.

Johnson, E., & Donoghue, J. R. Hypnosis and smoking: A review of the literature. *American Journal of Clinical Hypnosis,* 1971, *13,* 265–272.

Jones, J. S. Cigarette abandonment: Its significance. *British Journal of Diseases of the Chest,* 1977, *71,* 285–288.

Kanzler, M., Jaffe, J. H., & Zeidenberg, P. Long- and short-term effectiveness of a large-scale proprietary smoking cessation program—A 4-year follow-up of SmokEnders participants. *Journal of Clinical Psychology,* 1976, *32,* 661–669.

Keutzer, C. S., Lichtenstein, E., & Mees, H. L. Modification of smoking behavior: A review. *Psychological Bulletin,* 1968, *70,* 520–533.

Kopel, S. A. The effects of self-control, booster sessions, and cognitive factors on the maintenance of smoking reduction (Doctoral dissertation, University of Oregon, 1974). *Dissertation Abstracts International,* 1975, *35,* 4182B–4183B. (University Microfilms No. 75-3895)

Kopel, S. A., & Arkowitz, H. The role of attribution and self-perception in behavior change: Implications for behavior therapy. *Genetic Psychology Monographs,* 1975, *92,* 175–212.

Kristein, M. M. Economic issues in prevention. *Preventive Medicine,* 1977, *6,* 252–264.

Kumar, R., Cooke, E. C., Lader, M. H., & Russell, M. A. H. Is nicotine important in tobacco smoking? *Clinical Pharmacology and Therapeutics,* 1977, *21,* 520–529.

Lando, H. A. Successful treatment of smokers with a broad-spectrum behavioral approach. *Journal of Consulting and Clinical Psychology,* 1977, *45,* 361–366.

Lando, H. A. Toward a clinically effective paradigm for the maintenance of nonsmoking. *Behavior Therapy,* 1978, *9,* 666–668.

Lando, H. A., & McCullough, J. A. Clinical application of a broad-spectrum behavioral approach to chronic smokers. *Journal of Consulting and Clinical Psychology,* 1978, *46,* 583–585.

Leventhal, H. Effect of fear communication in the acceptance of preventive health practices. In S. V. Zagona (Ed.), *Studies and issues in smoking behavior.* Tucson, Arizona: University of Arizona Press, 1967.

Leventhal, H. Experimental studies of anti-smoking communication. In E. F. Borgatta & R. R. Evans (Eds.), *Smoking, health, and behavior.* Chicago: Aldine, 1968.

Leventhal, H. Fear appeals and persuasion: The differentiation of a motivational construct. *American Journal of Public Health,* 1971, *61,* 1208–1224.

Leventhal, H. Changing attitudes and habits to reduce risk factors in chronic disease. *American Journal of Cardiology,* 1973, *31,* 571–580.

Levinson, B. L., Shapiro, D., Schwartz, G. E., & Tursky, B. Smoking elimination by gradual reduction. *Behavior Therapy,* 1971, *2,* 477–487.

Lichtenstein, E. Modification of smoking behavior: Good designs—Ineffective treatments. *Journal of Consulting and Clinical Psychology,* 1971, *36,* 163–166.

Lichtenstein, E., & Danaher, B. G. Modification of smoking behavior: A critical analysis of theory, research, and practice. In M. Hersen, R. M. Eisler, & P. M. Miller (Eds.), *Advances in behavior modification, Vol. 3.* New York: Academic Press, 1976. Pp. 79–132.

Lichtenstein, E., Harris, D. E., Birchler, G. R., Wahl, J. M., & Schmahl, D. P. Comparison of rapid smoking, warm, smoky air, and attention placebo in the modification of smoking behavior. *Journal of Consulting and Clinical Psychology,* 1973, *40,* 92–98.

Lichtenstein, E., & Glasgow, R. E. Rapid smoking: Side effects and safeguards. *Journal of Consulting and Clinical Psychology,* 1977, *45,* 815–821.

Lichtenstein, E., & Rodrigues, M. R. P. Long-term effects of rapid smoking treatment for dependent cigarette smokers. *Addictive Behaviors,* 1977, *2,* 109–112.

Lindenthal, J. J., Myers, J. K., & Pepper, M. P. Smoking, psychological status, and stress. *Social Science and Medicine,* 1972, *6,* 583–591.

Logan, F. A. The smoking habit. In W. A. Hunt (Ed.), *Learning mechanisms in smoking.* Chicago: Aldine, 1970. Pp. 131–154.

Logan, R. A. Self-control as habit, drive, and incentive. *Journal of Abnormal Psychology,* 1973, *81,* 127–136.

Luce, B. R. The economic costs of smoking-induced illness. In M. E. Jarvik *et al.* (Eds.), *Research on smoking behavior.* Washington, D.C.: USDHEW, 1977. DHEW Publication No. (ADM) 78-581.

Mahoney, M. J. *Cognition and behavior modification.* Cambridge, Massachusetts: Ballinger Press, 1974.

Mahoney, M. J., & Arnkoff, D. Cognitive and self-control therapies. In S. L. Garfield & A. E. Bergin (Eds.), *Handbook of psychotherapy and behavior change (2nd ed).* New York: Wiley, 1978.

Mausner, B. An ecological view of cigarette smoking. *Journal of Abnormal Psychology,* 1973, *81,* 115–126.

Mausner, B., & Platt, E. S. *Smoking: A behavioral analysis.* New York: Pergamon Press, 1971.

McAlister, A. Helping people quit smoking: Current progress. In A. J. Enelow & J. B. Henderson (Eds.), *Applying behavioral science to cardiovascular risk.* New York: American Heart Association, 1975. Pp. 147–165.

McFall, R. M., & Hammen, C. Motivation, structure, and self-monitoring: Role of nonspecific factors in smoking reduction. *Journal of Consulting and Clinical Psychology,* 1971, *37,* 80–86.

McGrath, M. J., & Hall, S. M. Self-management treatment of smoking behavior. *Addictive Behaviors,* 1976, *1,* 287–292.

McKennell, A. C. British research into smoking behavior. In E. F. Borgatta & R. R. Evans (Eds.), *Smoking, health, and behavior.* Chicago: Aldine, 1968.

McKennell, A. C. Smoking motivation factors. *British Journal of Social and Clinical Psychology,* 1970, *9,* 8–20.

Meichenbaum, D. *Cognitive–behavior modification: An integrative approach.* New York: Plenum Press, 1977.

Mettlin, C. Smoking as behavior: Applying a social psychological theory. *Journal of Health and Social Behavior,* 1973, *14,* 144–152.

Miller, L. C., Schilling, A. F., Logan, D. L., & Johnson, R. L. Potential hazards of rapid smoking as a technique for the modification of smoking behavior. *New England Journal of Medicine,* 1977, *297,* 590–592.

Morrow, J. E., Sachs, C. B., Gmeinder, S., & Burgess, H. Elimination of cigarette smoking behavior by stimulus satiation, self-control techniques, and group therapy. Paper presented at the meeting of the Western Psychological Association, Anaheim, California, April, 1973.

Newman, A. The effect of reinforcement of intention statements and/or execution of self-control in smokers and ex-smokers. *Addictive Behaviors,* 1977, *2,* 15–20.

Orne, M. T. Hypnosis in the treatment of smoking. In Steinfeld *et al.* (Eds.), *Proceedings of the 3rd World Conference on Smoking and Health.* Washington, D.C.: USDHEW, 1977. DHEW Publication No. (NIH) 77-1413.

Pechacek, T. F. An evaluation of cessation and maintenance strategies in the modification of smoking behavior (Doctoral dissertation, University of Texas at Austin, 1977). *Dissertation Abstracts International,* 1977, *38,* 2380B. (University Microfilm No. 77-23, 013)

Pechacek, T. F., & McAlister, A. Strategies for the modification of smoking behavior: Treatment and prevention. In J. Ferguson & B. Taylor (Eds.), *A comprehensive handbook of behavior medicine*. New York: Spectrum Publications, 1979.

Pederson, L. L., & Lefcoe, N. M. A psychological and behavioral comparison of ex-smokers and smokers. *Journal of Chronic Disease*, 1976, *29*, 431–434.

Perri, M. G., Richards, S., & Schultheis, K. R. Behavioral self-control and smoking reduction: A study of self-initiated attempts to reduce smoking. *Behavior Therapy*, 1977, *8*, 360–365.

Pollin, W. Forward. In M. E. Jarvik *et al.* (Eds.), *Research on smoking behavior*. Washington, D.C.: USDHEW, 1977. DHEW Publication No. (ADM) 78-581. Pp. V–VI.

Pomerleau, O. F., Adkins, D. M., & Pertschuk, M. Predictors of outcome and recidivism in smoking cessation treatment. *Addictive Behaviors*, 1978, *3*, 65–70.

Pomerleau, O. F., & Pomerleau, C. S. *Break the smoking habit: A behavioral program for giving up cigarettes*. Champaign, Illinois: Research Press Company, 1977.

Premack, D. Mechanisms of self-control. In W. A. Hunt (Ed.), *Learning mechanisms in smoking*. Chicago: Aldine, 1970. Pp. 107–130.

Reeder, L. G. Sociocultural factors in the etiology of smoking behavior: An assessment. In M. E. Jarvik *et al.* (Eds.), *Research on smoking behavior*. Washington, D.C.: USDHEW, 1977. DHEW Publication No. (ADM) 78-581. Pp. 126–201.

Relinger, H., Bornstein, P. H., Bugge, I. D., Carmody, T. P., & Zohn, C. J. Utilization of adverse rapid smoking in groups: Efficacy of treatment and maintenance procedures. *Journal of Consulting and Clinical Psychology*, 1977, *45*, 245–249.

Rogers, R. W. A protection motivation theory of fear appeals and attitude change. *Journal of Psychology*, 1975, *91*, 93–114.

Russell, M. A. H. Cigarette smoking: Natural history of a dependence disorder. *British Journal of Medical Psychology*, 1971, *44*, 1–44. (a)

Russell, M. A. H. Cigarette dependence: I—Nature and classification. *British Medical Journal*, 1971, *2*, 330–331. (b)

Russell, M. A. H. The smoking habit and its classification. *Practitioner*, 1974, *212*, 791–800.

Russell, M. A. H. Tobacco smoking and nicotine dependence. In R. J. Gibbins *et al.* (Eds.), *Research advances in alcohol and drug problems (Vol. 3)*. New York: Wiley, 1976.

Russell, M. A. H., Armstrong, E., & Patel, U. A. Temporal contiguity in electric aversion therapy for cigarette smoking. *Behavior Research & Therapy*, 1976, *14*, 103–123.

Sachs, D. P. L., Hall, R. G., & Hall, S. M. Effects of rapid smoking: Physiologic evaluation of a smoking-cessation therapy. *Annals of Internal Medicine*, 1978, *88*, 639–641.

Schachter, S. Pharmacological and psychological determinants of smoking. *Annals of Internal Medicine*, 1978, *88*, 104–114.

Schachter, S., Silverstein, B., Kozlowski, L. T., Perlick, D., Herman, C. P., & Liebling, B. Studies of the interaction of psychological and pharmacological determinants of smoking. *Journal of Experimental Psychology—General*, 1977, *106*, 3–40.

Schmahl, D. P., Lichtenstein, E., & Harris, D. E. Successful treatment of habitual smokers with warm, smoky air and rapid smoking. *Journal of Consulting and Clinical Psychology*, 1972, *38*, 105–111.

Schwartz, G. E., & Weiss, S. M. What is behavioral medicine? *Psychosomatic Medicine*, 1977, *39*, 377–379.

Schwartz, J. E. A critical review and evaluation of smoking control methods. *Public Health Reports*, 1969, *84*, 483–506.

Schwartz, J. E., & Dubitzky, M. Expressed willingness of smokers to try 10 smoking withdrawal methods. *Public Health Reports*, 1967, *82*, 855–861.

Schwartz, J. E., & Dubitzky, M. One-year follow-up results of a smoking cessation program. *Canadian Journal of Public Health*, 1968, *59*, 161–165.

Schwartz, J. E., & Rider, G. Smoking cessation methods in the United States and Canada: 1969–1974.

In J. Steinfeld *et al.* (Eds.), *Proceedings of the 3rd World Conference on Smoking and Health.* Washington, D.C.: USDHEW, 1977. DHEW Publication No. (NIH) 77-1413. Pp. 695-752.

Seligman, M. E. P. *Helplessness.* San Francisco: Freeman, 1975.

Shapiro, D., Tursky, B., Schwartz, G. E., & Schnidman, S. L. Smoking on cue: A behavioral approach to smoking reduction. *Journal of Health and Social Behavior,* 1971, *12,* 108-113.

Shewchuck, L. A. Problems of high-risk populations and high-risk nonresponders: Smoking behavior. In J. W. Cullen, B. H. Fox, & R. N. Isom (Eds.), *Cancer: The behavioral dimensions.* New York: Raven Press, 1976. Pp. 93-99.

Shewchuck, L. A., Dubren, R., Burton, D., Forman, M., Clark, R. R., & Jaffin, A. R. Preliminary observations on an intervention program for heavy smokers. *International Journal of the Addiction,* 1977, *12,* 323-336.

Srole, L., & Fischer, A. L. Smoking behavior 1953 and 1970: The midtown Manhattan study. In W. L. Dunn (Ed.), *Smoking behavior: Motives and incentives.* Washington, D.C.: Winston & Sons, 1973. Pp. 255-266.

Straits, B. C. Social and psycho-physiological correlates of smoking withdrawal. *Social Science Quarterly,* 1970, *51,* 82-96.

Straits, B. C. The discontinuation of cigarette smoking: a multiple discriminant analysis. In S. V. Zagona (Ed.), *Studies and issues in smoking behavior.* Tucson, Arizona: University of Arizona Press, 1967.

Sterling, T. D., & Weinkam, J. J. Smoking characteristics by type of employment. *Journal of Occupational Medicine,* 1976, *18,* 743-754.

Sutherland, A., Amit, A., Golden, M., & Rosenberger, Z. Comparison of three behavioral techniques in the modification of smoking behavior. *Journal of Consulting and Clinical Psychology,* 1975, *43,* 443-447.

Thompson, D. S., & Wilson, T. R. Discontinuance of cigarette smoking: "Natural" and with "therapy." *Journal of the American Medical Association,* 1966, *196,* 1048-1052.

Thoresen, C. E., & Coates, T. J. Behavioral self-control: Some clinical concerns. In M. Hersen, R. M. Eisler, & P. M. Miller (Eds.), *Advances in behavior modification (Vol. 3).* New York: Academic Press, 1975.

Thoresen, C. E., & Mahoney, M. J. *Behavioral self-control.* New York: Holt, Rinehart and Winston, 1974.

Tighe, T. J., & Elliott, R. Breaking the cigarette habit: Effects of a technique involving threatened loss of money. *Psychological Record,* 1968, *18,* 503-513.

Tomkins, S. S. Psychological model for smoking behavior. In E. F. Borgatta & R. R. Evans (Eds.), *Smoking, health, and behavior.* Chicago: Aldine, 1968.

United States Public Health Service. *Smoking and Health. Report of the Advisory Committee to the Surgeon General of the Public Health Service.* Public Health Service Bulletin 1103. 1964.

United States Public Health Service, *Uses of Tobacco: Practices, attitudes, knowledge, and beliefs, U.S. Fall 1964 and Spring 1966.* USDHEW, PHS, NCSH, July, 1969.

United States Public Health Service. *Adult Use of Tobacco—1970.* Atlanta: CDC, NCSH, June, 1973. DHEW Publication No. (HSM) 73-8727.

United States Public Health Service. *Adult Use of Tobacco—1975.* Atlanta: CDC, June, 1976. (a)

United States Public Health Service. *Teenage Smoking: National patterns of cigarette smoking, ages 12 through 18, in 1972 and 1974.* Atlanta: CDC, 1976. DHEW Publication No. (NIH) 76-931. (b)

United States Public Health Service. *The smoking digest: Progress report on a nation kicking the habit.* Bethesda, Maryland: National Institutes of Health, National Cancer Institute, Office of Cancer Communications, October, 1977. (a)

United States Public Health Service. *Cigarette smoking among teen-agers and young women.* Washington, D.C.: National Institutes of Health, 1977. DHEW Publication No. (NIH) 77-1203. (b)

United States Public Health Service. *Smoking behavior and attitudes: Physicians, dentists, nurses, pharmacists.* Atlanta: CDC, NCSH, 1977. (c)

United States Public Health Service. *The health consequences of smoking: A reference edition.* Atlanta, Georgia: CDC, 1978. HEW Publication No. (CDC) 78-8357.

Warner, K. E. The effects of the anti-smoking campaign on cigarette consumption. *American Journal of Public Health,* 1977, *67,* 645-650.

Weinblatt, E., Shapiro, S., & Frank, C. W. Changes in personal characteristics of men, over five years, following first diagnosis of coronary heart disease. *American Journal of Public Health,* 1971, *61,* 831-842.

Weiss, S. M. *Proceedings of the NHLI working conference on health behavior.* Basye, Virginia, May 12-15, 1975. Washington, D.C.: National Heart and Lung Institute, 1976. DHEW Publication No. (NIH) 76-868.

Winett, R. A. Parameters of deposit contracts in the modification of smoking. *Psychological Records,* 1973, *23,* 49-60.

Yates, A. J. *Theory and practice in behavior therapy.* New York: Wiley, 1975.

13

Cognitive Skills and Athletic Performance[1]

MICHAEL J. MAHONEY

INTRODUCTION

Although its development is very recent, sport psychology is perhaps one of the most diverse and complicated specialties in the field. It includes, for example, subspecialties that range from cellular biology to social facilitation (cf. Christina & Landers, 1976; Cratty, 1973; Edwards, 1973; Fisher, 1976a; Landers, 1976; Landers, Harris, & Christina, 1975; Martens, 1975a; Morgan, 1970, 1972). Investigators have studied the biomechanics of various skills, the parameters of skill acquisition, and even the cellular substrate of some athletic abilities. As with any area of science, these inquiries have often produced more questions than answers, but their progress is clearly discernible. Studies of carbohydrate loading, electrolyte balance, and negative resistance exercise are examples of the growing research in this area (as well as the wealth of persistent questions).

Besides the advances that have been made in our understanding of the biochemistry and biomechanics of athletic performance, researchers have begun to unravel some of the psychological and social aspects of sports (cf. Fisher, 1976a; Morgan, 1970, 1972). The topic of social facilitation, for example, has generated dozens of studies (cf. Landers, Harris, & Christina, 1975; Landers & McCullagh, 1976; Martens, 1975a; Singer, 1972; Zajonc, 1965). Does an audience facilitate athletic performance? This simple question has defied a simple answer. Judging from the

---

[1]This chapter was based, in part, on a paper presented at the eleventh annual meeting of the Association for the Advancement of Behavior Therapy, Atlanta, December, 1977. For his comments on an earlier draft, I am grateful to Daniel M. Landers.

Cognitive–Behavioral Interventions:
Theory, Research, and Procedures

available evidence, it would appear that an audience is facilitative when the performer is skilled and self-confident. During the initial stages of learning, however, an audience may detract from performance. But even this generalization is simplistic. A more accurate summary of the literature would require qualifying statements about task difference, team-versus-individual performance, and a wide range of person variables.

But biology and social psychology are relatively recent developments in the field of sport psychology. Both historically and quantitatively, research in this area has been dominated by personology—the study of the personality traits of athletes. Scores of studies have been enlisted in the search for a global "athletic personality," and more than one investigator has claimed to have found it. Bruce Ogilvie (1968), for example, has argued that the data "strongly support the tendency for certain personality traits to receive greater reinforcement within the competitive world of athletics. . . . We can state with some certitude that . . . [athletes] . . . have most of the following personality traits: ambition, organization, deference, dominance, endurance, and aggression [p. 786; material in brackets added]." Confident in their understanding of the athletic personality, personologists have rendered sweeping pronouncements about the best ways to select and train an athlete (cf. Ogilvie & Tutko, 1966; Vanek & Cratty, 1970). Ogilvie and Tutko have developed a psychometric instrument called the Athletic Motivation Inventory (AMI), which has received increasing use by coaches and physical educators. The widespread use of this instrument in making critical sports decisions has recently been challenged by other sport researchers. Martens (1975a), for example, has minced few words in his evaluation of this popular instrument:

> Besides Ogilvie and Tutko's failure to provide the scientific community with experimental evidence to support their claims, in perspective to current scientific research in personality, their assertions are extraordinary, particularly when based on the outmoded "trait psychology" approach. . . . Indeed, if their unavailable research can substantiate their sale of personality assessment and diagnoses, their discovery will doubtless be considered the most remarkable advance in all of the social sciences in the twentieth century [p. 155].

Martens' reservations are not restricted to the work of Ogilvie and Tutko, however. He and Rushall (1972) have been vocal critics of the trait approach to sport psychology. In an extensive review of the sport personality literature from 1950 through 1973, Martens (1975b) identified 202 references to the relationship between sports and personality. Of these, 79% were data-based and 21% lacked original data. More telling, perhaps, was the fact that only 10% of the data-based studies involved an experimental manipulation. The remaining 90% were restricted to correlational and interview studies that often drew sweeping generalizations and causal inferences. Other critics have also noted the dismal state of affairs in sport personality research:

> The research in this area has largely been of the "shot gun" variety. By that I mean the investigators grabbed the nearest and most convenient personality test, and the closest sports groups and with little or no theoretical basis for their selection fired into the air to see what they could bring down. It isn't surprising that firing into the air at different times and at different places, and using different ammunition, should result in different findings. In fact it would be surprising if the results weren't contradictory and somewhat confusing [Ryan, 1968, p. 71].

Rushall, one of the few behavior modifiers in the field, has emphasized the need for a functional analysis of factors affecting athletic performance (e.g., McKenzie & Rushall, 1974; Rushall & Siedentop, 1972). Although these analyses have been heavily weighted toward environmental variables, they may represent a promising shift from the exclusive organismic focus of the personologists.

This introduces a familiar topic of debate among psychologists—the age-old battle between internalists and externalists. Internalists have been typically stereotyped as persons who are preoccupied with factors *inside* the person. More often than not, these factors have been reified into static dispositions, such as traits. The externalists, on the other hand, have been stereotyped as being narrowly preoccupied with factors *outside* the person. The operant behavior modifier is a popular prototype and is often portrayed (by critics, at least) as a dogmatic environmentalist who is enamored with mechanistic input–output analyses of a functionally empty organism. The misrepresentativeness of these stereotypes is obvious, and the shortcomings of extreme internalism and externalism have already received extensive discussion (cf. Bandura, 1974; Endler & Magnusson, 1976; Mahoney, 1974; Mischel, 1968). The increasing popularity of integrated perspectives that recognize both internal and external influences is, perhaps, reassuring. Many of these have involved a combination of cognitive and behavioral emphases (cf. Bandura, 1977a; Beck, 1976; Mahoney, 1977; Mahoney & Arnkoff, 1978; Meichenbaum, 1977). Unfortunately, however, there are also signs of possible polarization between the more extreme proponents of internal and external influence.

It is my opinion that at least some of the dissension between these two groups may stem from their failure to separate issues of *procedure* from those of *process*. This distinction has been cogently defended by Bandura (1977a,b) who argues an interesting conceptual compromise, namely, that, although human behavior is governed by cognitive processes, these processes are most effectively activated by procedures that involve environmental manipulations. Understanding the cognitive processes may help us to refine our procedures. It is worth noting here that the internal factors invoked by Bandura and others are not static traits but malleable skills that can be learned and modified. Bringing all of this back into the realm of sport psychology, we must be careful not to throw out all internal variables simply because of the dismal performance of prior trait approaches. In the pages that follow I would like to illustrate how a cognitive-skills approach might be promising in both the understanding and the improvement of athletic performance. For purposes of exposition, I shall divide my remarks into four broad categories: (*a*) self-efficacy; (*b*) imagery; (*c*) arousal regulation; and (*d*) attentional variables.

SELF-EFFICACY IN THE ATHLETE

Theory and Research

Bandura (1977b) has recently outlined a theory of *self-efficacy* which, among other things, argues that

> expectations of personal mastery affect both initiation and persistence of coping behavior. The strength of people's convictions in their own effectiveness is likely to affect whether they will even try to cope with given situations. . . . Not only can perceived self-efficacy have directive influence on choice of activities and settings, but, through expectations of eventual success, it can affect coping efforts once they are initiated. Efficacy expectations determine how much effort people will expend and how long they will persist in the fact of obstacles and aversive experiences. The stronger the perceived self-efficacy, the more active the efforts [pp. 193–194].

Preliminary studies have been consistently corroborative of these assertions. It should be noted that self-efficacy theory does not discount the importance of skill level and incentives. Assuming that a person is capable of a response and that there are appropriate incentives for performance, the theory asserts that actual performance will be predicted by the person's beliefs in their personal competence. Likewise, although self-efficacy increments may generalize to new tasks, Bandura does not view self-efficacy as a global personality trait. A person's self-efficacy expectations may vary from moment to moment and across various tasks.

Although self-efficacy theory is primarily derived from research and theory on avoidance patterns, I would argue that it has relevance for a much broader realm of human functioning. In drawing it into these wider vistas, of course, it must be compared to such notions as *competence* and *self-confidence*. The latter often connote a transsituational trait that is invoked to explain overall performance optimism. Self-efficacy, on the other hand, would appear to be a more specific variable. An athlete's self-efficacy expectations may vary across events, as well as in response to other factors. The competitive wrestler, for example, may feel optimistic about beating some opponents and pessimistic about beating others. Such outspoken athletes as Muhammad Ali and Joe Namath exemplify the extreme in publicly claimed self-efficacy.

Several years ago I was speaking with a super heavyweight power lifter who was publicly boasting that he would win the upcoming world championships ''with brute strength and sheer sex appeal.'' When I commented on his apparent self-confidence, he looked at me in a rather condescending fashion and said, ''Look, shorty—you show me a humble athlete and I'll show you a loser.'' His words were noteworthy, and I often recalled them as I interviewed other athletes. I have yet to interview a national champion who was not very confident about his/her ability. Indeed, when I talked to the finalists for the 1976 U.S. Men's Olympic team in gymnastics, I was impressed with the generally high level of self-efficacy expectations. Interestingly, those who reported experiencing occasional doubts about their abilities tended to perform more poorly during the qualifying meet. Among the 12 finalists, actual performance was moderately correlated with premeet self-confidence ($r = .57$, Mahoney & Avener, 1977).

But these are primarily anecdotes. Is there any experimental evidence that self-efficacy expectations can affect athletic performance? Given the recency of Bandura's (1977b) theory, it would be surprising if this term were employed. There are, however, a handful of studies suggesting that perceived ability may influence actual performance. Nelson and Furst (1972), for example, tested subjects for arm strength and asked them to rate themselves relative to their peers. Subjects were then paired off such that one was clearly stronger, but *both* subjects believed the stronger subject to be weaker. Twelve such pairs arm-wrestled. In 10 of those contests (83%), the results favored the expectation factor over physical strength. That is, the objectively weaker athlete won. Since this study failed to isolate several experimental components, it is difficult to conclude much from it other than the possibility of an expectation effect.

Other studies have explored expectancy effects in the guise of placebos. In the areas of sports nutrition and drugs, for example, there are dozens of studies suggesting that an athlete's performance may be influenced by his/her belief in the power of a chemical factor (cf. Golding, 1972). The generality of such effects is noted by Horstman (1972) after an extensive review of the literature on sports nutrition: "Investigators who have studied the effects of diet on athletic performance agree that if an athlete is deprived of a nutrient which he considers essential for successful performance the chances are very good that he will not perform successfully [p. 345]." In these instances, it is apparent that at least some of the athlete's expectancy of success is coming from a belief in the power of some chemical aid.

Another factor in self-efficacy expectations is the perceived difficulty of the athletic challenge. Some weightlifters, for example, develop a mental block and cannot surpass a certain barrier despite their consistent success with weights that are only slightly below that level. Informal reports suggest that American lifters tend to develop barriers in terms of poundage (e.g., 200, 300, 400 lb), whereas European lifters more often develop barriers in kilograms (100, 200 kg). This is analogous to the "psychological barriers" formerly posed by the 4-minute mile, the 7-ft-high jump, and the 18-ft pole vault. Among weightlifters, one strategy used to help a person overcome a psychological barrier involves outright deception. Without his awareness, the barbell is loaded with the "magic" poundage, but the lifter is told that it is actually slightly less (i.e., a poundage he has already mastered). When he then successfully lifts the weight (which is not uncommon), he is told about the deception, and the barrier is thereafter surpassed.

In an attempt to study the effectiveness of this deceptive strategy, Bob De-Monbreun and I conducted a pilot study in which we asked weightlifters to perform under two conditions—aware and blind (to the poundage). We were only able to run a few subjects, but the results were interesting. A couple of the lifters felt that their lack of awareness aided their lifting, but another felt that it was detrimental. Unfortunately, they knew that we were trying to deceive them in terms of poundage, and they did a lot of guessing. In a later attempt to explore this phenomenon, Fred Heide and I used a strength task with women and tried to deceive them about actual poundage. Our manipulation was again unsuccessful, however, in that participants did not believe us when we tried to convince them that they were lifting a lower poundage. A recent report by Ness and Patton (in press) has, apparently, succeeded in this regard. Forty-eight male volunteers were asked to perform the bench press under conditions in which (*a*) they were unaware of the poundage; (*b*) they believed to be greater than its actual value; or (*c*) they believed it to be less than its actual value. Overall, subjects lifted significantly more weight when they believed it to be less than its actual value.

Intervention Possibilities

To say that treatment implications are as yet vague and premature is a sizable understatement. In learning from the mistakes of earlier personology researchers, it is imperative that a cognitive-skills advocate remain both cautious and accountable in making assertions about what the athlete or coach "should" do to improve performance. Thus, the remarks that follow and those that appear in subsequent sections should be viewed as intervention possibilities, rather than as direct or confident recommendations. They hardly exhaust the list of possible cognitive-skills strategies that might assist athletic performance, and it goes without saying that they are in need of controlled experimental evaluation. It is hoped that their partial enumeration, however, will assist in speeding and facilitating that evaluation.

With regard to self-efficacy in the athlete, one must first determine whether he/she may be deficient in perceived ability to perform some skill that is within their repertoire. In other words, the self-efficacy literature is probably most relevant when one has reason to believe that (a) the athlete is physically capable of the task or skill in question but (b) is not confident about that ability. At the present time, we have no standardized assessment devices for assessing self-efficacy and must therefore rely on the accuracy and honesty of direct self-report. Since Bandura conceptualizes self-efficacy as a cognitive process that may be affected by specific contextual circumstances, a general test of self-efficacy may be difficult to provide. On the other hand, one can use several assessment strategies to evaluate the athlete's expectancies about his/her performance of the task in question. Among these assessment possibilities are the following:

1. Retrospective report—asking the athlete to recall his/her expectations just prior to recent attempts at the task
2. Imaginal rehearsal—asking the athlete to imagine (mentally rehearse) preparation for performance and then inquiring directly about self-efficacy expectations at the point of task initiation
3. Direct inquiry—asking the athlete to report self-efficacy expectations just before the crucial performance (either in training or in actual competition)
4. Dream report—asking the athlete to record and report all dreams relevant to the target performance

There are problems with each of these, not the least of which may be the athlete's inclination to report more self-confidence than may be present. This misrepresentation may be most likely when the coach or consultant has emphasized the importance of self-confidence and/or has been critical of the athlete's lack thereof. Although it has yet to be adequately evaluated, athletic dream content may be a particularly promising assessment tool. Some athletes report a dramatic increase in performance-related dreams just before competition, and their success in those dreams may reflect on their self-efficacy expectations. This speculation merits empirical appraisal, and it has yet to be determined whether the athlete's dream content is closely related to any of the other self-efficacy measures.

For the athlete who appears to be less confident than seems to be warranted by his/her current abilities, a variety of intervention strategies are worth consideration. It is important to remember, however, that self-efficacy is viewed as a moderator of performance *when the prerequisite athletic skills are present*—it is not here suggested as a solution or alternative to skill development. The "over-confident" athlete, although perhaps rare, may be just as impaired by his/her inappropriate expectations as is one lacking in confidence. This is not to say that positive expectations may not help the athlete strive for a personal gain, but the point should be reiterated that he/she must be capable of much more than just "thinking positive" if an improved performance is desired.

Drawing heavily on current research in self-efficacy and on the few relevant inquiries with athletes, it would appear that the following strategies could be helpful in augmenting the self-efficacy expectations of an athlete:

1. Response induction aids—special equipment that may reduce dangers and/or reduce the perceived size of the discrepancy between the athlete's current and desired performance
2. Imaginal rehearsal—asking the athlete to practice mentally the desired performance
3. Direct reassurance—simple and sincere encouragement from a respected authority (e.g., a coach), with emphasis on confidence in the athlete's ability
4. Modeling—asking the athlete to observe closely another person successfully perform the desired response
5. Self-statement modification—asking the athlete to practice self-efficious monologues prior to the performance
6. False performance feedback—such that the athlete (*a*) believes he/she has passed a personal "best" when in fact it has only been approximated; or (*b*) believes he/she is attempting a task near their personal best when in fact it surpass that level

This last strategy obviously invokes some ethical as well as practical considerations. Excessive reliance on deceptive feedback could undermine the effectiveness of the strategy by creating generalized distrust. The occasional use of this strategy, on the other hand, might help athletes past momentary psychological barriers.

One of the most important considerations in all of the foregoing strategies may be the size of the gap between present and desired performance. As in motor-skill development, it would appear that small gradual increments are preferable to large and drastic ones. Asking for slight improvements may also create fewer self-efficacy problems in that the athlete may develop increased self-confidence as these gradual improvements are realized. At the present time, it would appear that self-perceived success is one of the more important factors in self-efficacy increments (Bandura, 1977b). Thus, the coach or consultant may be well advised to ask for small, reasonable improvements and to employ response induction aids as a means of "convincing" the athlete that he/she is very near the desired skill level. As these aids are gradually withdrawn, the athlete will hopefully attribute more and more of his or her success to "internal" (skill-related) factors.

IMAGERY IN THE ATHLETE

It is no surprise to anyone that athletes often engage in imaginal rehearsal of their performance. Individuals like Dick Fosbury, for example, have often frustrated both the crowd and officials by insisting on this "mental practice." Fosbury, who revolutionized the style of high jumping, used to spend several minutes at the runway. He reported that he was "jumping in his head" and that he sometimes missed. When his imaginal rehearsal resulted in failure, he picked himself up out of the pit and—still in imagery—made another fantasized attempt. Fosbury refused to make an actual approach to the bar until he had successfully cleared it in his head.

Theory and Research

There are numerous other anecdotes of this variety, as well as scattered reports of successful training in imaginal rehearsal (e.g., Suinn, 1972, 1977). But this is one area where anecdotes can be supplemented by experimental evidence. At the present time, there have been over 50 experimental analyses of mental practice with athletes (cf. Corbin, 1972; Richardson, 1967a,b). Unfortunately, the results of those experiments are far from consistent. A cautious interpretation of this literature is offered by Corbin (1972): "There seems to be little doubt that mental practice can positively affect skilled motor performance, especially when practice conditions are 'optimal.' It is equally clear, however, that mental practice is not always an aid to performance [p. 115]." A number of factors have been suggested as possible moderators of this influence. The athlete's familiarity with the task, for example, can influence the effects of imaginal rehearsal. In general, some prior familiarity with the skill seems to enhance the effects of imaginal rehearsal. Likewise, the timing of the mental practice may be an important variable. If one can extrapolate from recent analyses of vicarious learning in sports, imaginal rehearsal may be most effective when it is interspersed throughout skill acquisition (cf. Landers, 1975).

The kind of imagery employed may also be a factor. Early researchers have noted that the vividness and controllability of the image may be significant variables. *Controllability* here refers to whether the image changes according to the athlete's intentions. In one study with basketball players, for example, several athletes reported that their images seemed almost noncooperative. Thus, in dribbling before a free throw, one player reported that his imagined basketball simply would not bounce (Corbin, 1972). To date, the evidence on imagery vividness and controllability are too preliminary and mixed to warrant a confident conclusion.

Another parameter of imagery that has received some recent attention is that of its "orientation." In our exploratory work with Olympic gymnasts (Mahoney & Avener, 1977), the successful finalists (those who qualified for the team) often reported the use of internal (phenomenological) imagery, as contrasted with external (third-person) imagery ($r = .51$). Internal imagery involves a fantasized experiencing of something from the performer's perspective. It is sometimes nonvisual and often includes proprioceptive rehearsal of the performance. In external imagery, on the other hand, a person views himself or herself from an external perspective (much like in home movies). One Olympian reported that he could not "see" himself in his images—all he could "see" was the gymnasium as it would appear to him in normal vision. In recent interviews with a former national champion and the 1977 women's gymnastics champion, both reported use of internal imagery. Karen Schuckman, for example, said, "I see what I would see if I was doing it. Like, I try to remember what I see. . . . I don't have the actual feeling right then, but I have the memory of what it feels like." Likewise, national champion Ann Carr reported very phenomenological imagery. At first, she said she used no imagery at all. When it was clarified that an image need not be visual, her remarks were interesting: "I kind of just feel the motion of exactly what I'm going to do, but I don't see myself doing it. (I can feel it in my muscles) I don't know how to describe it . . . but I feel like (there is body sensation but not too much of a visual thing)." (Both of the preceding quotations come from person-to-person interviews with the author.)

When I later discussed this with another sports researcher, I learned of the "clock test" sometimes used by coaches to assess this phenomenon. The athlete is asked to close his/her eyes while the face of a clock is traced on their forehead. The clock hands are traced to read 3 o'clock from the perspective of an external observer. When asked to report the time, a response of "3 o'clock" is interpreted as reflecting external imagery; a response of "9 o'clock" is thought to indicate internal imagery. Needless to say, there are problems with this crude test of imagery perspective. An athlete's response may be influenced, for example, by whether he/she thinks you want the time read from the experimenter's perspective. Likewise, it is not clear whether the internal–external dimension is reliably associated with superior athletic performance. If this is replicated with gymnasts, we should not be surprised that it may not apply to other sports. Whether people can be trained in phenomenological imagery—and whether it consistently affects some athletic performances—are questions that await further research.

One other dimension that bears on imaginal rehearsal is that called "coping–mastery." In cognitive–behavioral research, a coping model is one who makes mistakes and experiences difficulty or distress in executing some performance. The mastery model, on the other hand, performs perfectly and without any obvious signs of discomfort. In research on avoidance patterns, the coping model appears to be more therapeutic than the mastery model (Mahoney & Arnkoff, 1978). Is this also the case with athletics? In three recent studies, Martens and his colleagues have found that demonstrations by a "correct" model were about as effective as demonstrations by a model who was gradually learning a motor skill (Martens, Burwitz, & Zuckerman, 1976). Both of these conditions were superior to an "incorrect" model and to no model at all. This report is hardly definitive, however, and there is a clear need for more extensive scrutiny. Of particular interest may be the issue of differential cost–benefits to the athlete. A coping orientation may sensitize the athlete to the possibility of mistakes but simultaneously prepare him/her to recover from competitive failures. Mastery training, on the other hand, may encourage perfectionistic expectations but may leave the athlete less prepared to cope with mistakes. These are conjectures that may warrant future experimental scrutiny.

Intervention Possibilities

Once again, we must realize that intervention strategies in the realm of athletic imagery remain poorly evaluated. Despite the extensive research reviewed by Richardson (1967a,b) and Corbin (1972), the effectiveness and crucial parameters of mental practice remain equivocal. Although it seems to aid some athletes, its power has not been consistent. Thus, the following remarks should be read as a partial list of research-worthy speculations, rather than firmly established recommendations:

1. Mental practice may be more effective when (*a*) the athlete has already attempted the target performance (i.e., is familiar with the task) and (*b*) the mental practice is itself alternated or interspersed with actual motoric practice.
2. Mental practice may be more effective if the athlete is encouraged to use phenomenological and proprioceptive imagery rather than external or exclusively visual imagery.
3. A coping model—one who makes mistakes but recovers from them—may help to develop recovery skills in the athlete, but it is still unclear as to whether it might also increase the likelihood of actual performance errors.

Until further evidence is available, it may be safer to use coping imagery only with athletes who have already demonstrated problems in recovering from performance errors.

Generalizing from the psychological literature on imagery techniques (e.g., Singer, 1974), mental practice may be facilitated by prior training in muscular relaxation. A supine position in a quiet and undistracting location may also be helpful, along with encouragement to make the imagery as vivid as possible (e.g., to hear the crowd, to feel the ball, and so on). Finally, the skills rehearsed during mental practice should probably be only slightly above those actually performed, and the difficulty of the rehearsed performance should be gradually elevated so that it overlaps with and slightly improves upon current performance.

AROUSAL REGULATION

Theory and Research

The role of arousal in athletic performance is a topic that has received considerable attention (cf. Fisher, 1976b; Morgan, 1972; Nideffer, 1976a). A dominating theme in this area has been the Yerkes–Dodson inverted-U law that asserts that performance is impaired by extremely low and extremely high levels of arousal. This hypothesized curvilinear relationship is clearly illustrated in a recent study by Ahart (Note 1), who studied free-throw accuracy in basketball players. Ahart inferred that a player was under more stress when the game was very close and that stress would be minimal when the score differential was large. He therefore predicted that free-throw accuracy would be best where there was a modest discrepancy in team scores and that it would be worst when the scores were either very close or very disparate. As shown in Fig. 13.1, these predictions were clearly corroborated by the data.

Other studies have also yielded data consistent with the Yerkes–Dodson law. Unfortunately, however, the evidence in this area is anything but consensual. After an extensive review of the role of arousal in athletic endeavors, Martens (1972) offered the following comments:

> With respect to the inverted-U hypothesis, many, if not most, believe that this relationship is firmly established. The evidence reviewed for varying levels of trait anxiety, induced muscular tension, and psychological stress showed no clear support for this relationship for motor responses. . . . No clear relationships between either trait or state anxiety and muscular performance were elucidated [p. 61].

Does this mean that arousal is an irrelevant factor in athletic performance? Not necessarily. It does appear that the effects of arousal may vary, however. Different sports may demand different levels of optimal arousal.

This conjecture is voiced by Fisher (1976b) in his discussion of sport "psyching" strategies: "The *nature of the task* must be considered before one can even attempt

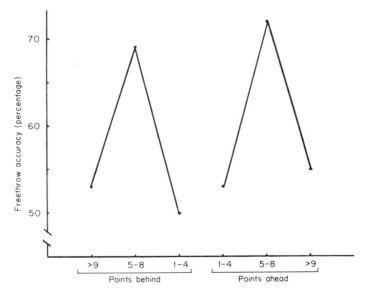

Figure 13.1 Basketball players' freethrow accuracy as a function of score differential. (From the data of Ahart, 1973.)

to understand the relationship of arousal to sport performance [p. 137]." This point is also emphasized by Oxendine (1970):

> On the basis of research evidence, scientific literature, and empirical observation the following generalizations are offered on the arousal–performance topic:
> 1. A high level of arousal is essential for optimal performance in gross motor activities involving strength, endurance, and speed.
> 2. A high level of arousal interferes with performances involving complex skills, fine muscle movements, coordination, steadiness, and general concentration.
> 3. A slightly-above-average level of arousal is preferable to a normal or subnormal arousal state for all motor tasks.

The accuracy of these generalizations has recently been examined by Landers (1977), who offers several refinements of Oxendine's remarks. The relevance of such generalizations is illustrated by the fact that athletes in different sports appear to use somewhat different psyching strategies. Golfers, for example, often report using "calming" strategies prior to putting. Weightlifters, on the other hand, often employ adrenalizing images and self-statements, especially when they are preparing to execute a "power" lift (i.e., bench press, squat, or deadlift). When the lift requires precise timing and balance, however (e.g., the snatch), they often report using a mixture of strategies designed to produce controlled arousal.

The ability to control arousal may be an important factor in successful athletic performance. The competitive weightlifter, for example, must lift six to nine times during a meet. Despite the fact that these lifts usually take less than 20 seconds, the meet itself may last 4–6 hours. Successful lifters must, therefore, develop the ability to turn themselves "on" and "off." Informal observations during competition suggest that the experienced lifter can go from a normal resting pulse to a heightened state of arousal in just a few seconds. Between lifts, many competitors meditate or distract so they can conserve their arousal for later competition.

Tony Shelton and I recently completed a study involving 30 Olympic-style weightlifters (Shelton & Mahoney, 1978). We were interested in two things: (a) the content of their "psyching" strategies; and (b) the effects of those strategies. Using a hand dynamometer, we measured grip strength on a baseline trial. All lifters were then asked to count backwards by 7s from a four-digit number. This distraction task was intended to impose a standard cognitive exercise during a second experimental trial. It did not significantly alter their performance. Finally, we asked half of the weightlifters to "psych" themselves up prior to a third trial. Control subjects were instructed to repeat the backward-counting strategy. As shown in Figure 13.2, those lifters who were told to psych themselves showed dramatic increases in performance. In a postexperimental interview, they related that their psyching strategies were often a combination of self-efficacy statements, imaginal rehearsal, self-generated arousal, and attentional focus. The latter was the most popular strategy.

The optimal psyching strategy may vary across persons, as well as across athletic events. Fisher (1976b) points out that the common use of "Knute Rockne pep talks" among football coaches prior to a game may help some players but harm others. All-star hockey player Glenn Hall, for example, "reportedly 'lost his lunch' before every contest he ever played and sometimes even before practice [p. 138]."

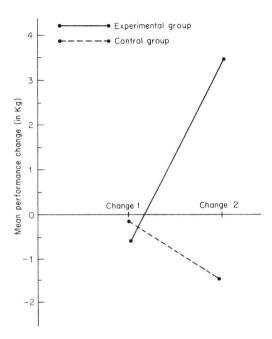

Figure 13.2 Groups' mean performance change scores.

Fisher argues that athletes like Hall may respond more favorably to "psyching down" strategies, rather than to pregame arousal tactics. Relaxation training, hypnosis, and transcendental meditation have been applied in some coaching situations, but there are relatively few controlled studies of their effects (cf. Benson, Beary, & Carol, 1974; Fisher, 1976a; Morgan, 1972; Nideffer & Deckner, 1970).

Related to the issue of an athlete's ability to control arousal is his/her ability to utilize that arousal in an adaptive fashion. The same physiological cues may be interpreted as signs of impending disaster or cues to prepare for optimal performance. This is illustrated in the extensive work of Walter Fenz and his colleagues with skydivers (Fenz, 1973, 1975). In studying the developmental sequence of coping with stress, Fenz and co-workers noted that mastery experience often brought changes in arousal patterns. Where an athlete originally showed monotonically increasing arousal as he prepared to perform, this pattern later resemble an inverted U curve. That is, the skydiver's arousal began to peak before the actual jump itself. As a person became more experienced and confident, their arousal did not necessarily decrease. Instead, it became more anticipatory and specific. As they began their jump sequence, these athletes showed an early increase in arousal, followed by a decline prior to the actual jump. When they actually left the plane, many of them were experiencing near-normal levels of arousal.

Experience does not always produce confidence, however. In their later research, Fenz *et al.* began to investigate differences in the arousal patterns of athletes who were at equivalent levels of experience but at different levels of competence. They were particularly interested in the coping strategies used by these two groups. In one study, they measured the heart rate of experienced skydivers at various points in their hierarchy of performance. The data suggested that the good performers peaked in their anxiety halfway through the sequence. Poor performers, on the other hand, seemed to escalate in arousal throughout most of the hierarchy. Other studies have replicated the tendency of poor performers to show an abrupt increase in arousal at the beginning of performance, whereas good performers are usually already past their peak arousal at this point (Fenz, 1975).

What is going through the minds of these athletes at various points in the approach sequence? Unfortunately, Fenz *et al.* have not reported interviews that revealed cognitive content. They have, however, administered projective tests (a modified Thematic Apperception Test) in which skydivers were asked to speculate on the thought patterns of parachutists in various stages of performance preparation:

> Responses to our thematic apperception test give us some insight into what may be going on in the mind of parachutists about to make a jump. . . . It seems clear that the experienced jumper becomes increasingly more externally task oriented, whereas the novice jumper ruminates on his own fears or expends much of his energy definding against them [1975, p. 331].

In response to pictures of a parachutist standing in the open doorway of an airplane, for example, experienced athletes suggested that he was checking the wind, calculating his fall, and preparing to jump. The conjectures of inexperienced jumpers were intriguingly different. They suggested that the parachutist was frightened, doubting his nerve, and probably thinking about the dangers involved.

In our own work with gymnasts (Mahoney & Avener, 1977), a pattern similar to that reported by Fenz was observed. When the Olympic finalists were asked to rate their anxiety at various points during the competition, some interesting patterns were apparent. Two points are worth noting—(*a*) all of the athletes were very anxious; and (*b*) the Olympic qualifiers tended to show a decrease in self-reported arousal during actual performance. Interviews with these athletes suggested very different coping skills among those who were successful as compared with those who did not make the Olympic team. The remarks of one nonqualifier are representative: "When I start chalking up, I feel all queasy and I think to myself, 'Oh shit, am I scared! Six thousand people watching! What if I make a mistake? What if I fall off?' I hear myself talking like that and I know I'm not ready [original interview]." Although the Olympic qualifiers were hardly a picture of tranquility, their last-second self-talk tended to be very different in focus: "I get out there and they're waiting for me and all I can think is how scared I am. Twelve years I've worked to lay my life on the line for 30 seconds. Then I try to concentrate—'O.K. This is it; it's now or never. Let's pay attention to your tuck, stay strong on the press out, and be ready for that dismount.' I just start coaching myself [original interview]." It seems apparent that absolute level of arousal may be only one factor in athletic performance. The person's reactions to that arousal may be a significant determinant of its course—and its effects on performance.

Intervention Possibilities

In rendering any speculations about arousal regulation strategies, an earlier point bears reemphasis: One must evaluate each athlete's needs on the basis of the athletic skills involved and of their own individual patterns of arousal. The coach or consultant must judge whether the athlete's arousal is excessive or deficient and must decide whether it is detracting from optimal performance. Since this may vary from one athlete to the next, total team strategies may be less advisable than individualized training. Likewise, it may be important to bear in mind that heightened arousal may be facilitative in sports that emphasize strength or speed, whereas lesser levels may be appropriate for sports involving fine motor coordination and complex skills.

Within the limitations of our current knowledge, the following strategies may be helpful in arousal regulation:

1. For the athlete who desires heightened arousal, focused concentration and adrenalizing imagery or self-statements may be beneficial.
2. For the athlete who desires lowered arousal, it may be helpful to offer training in (*a*) muscular relaxation; (*b*) calming self-statements; and (*c*) special breathing exercises.

Some sports may require the athlete to alternate between periods of high and low arousal, in which case it may be helpful to practice both strategies. For the athlete who seems to "clutch" under performance pressure, the coach or consultant might suggest that he/she monitor private monologues and imagery during these periods. In my own work with athletes, it has been common for these situations to arise when the athlete perseverates on a mistake and/or engages in self-critical or self-defeating cognitions (e.g., self-denigration and/or images of "blowing it" for the remainder of the competition). One possible strategy for this problem is to have the athlete practice (*a*) monitoring such cognitions and (*b*) switching to task-relevant self-statements after performance errors. Concentrating on the athletic task (rather than on one's past mistakes) appears to be an important element in optimal performance.

ATTENTIONAL FOCUS

Theory and Research

The role of attentional factors in athletic performance has long been appreciated by coaches and physical educators. *Concentration* has been a popular term in locker rooms and athletic workshops. Only recently, however, have researchers begun to come to grips with some of the complexities that abound in the domain of "attention." Exploratory studies have examined the nature of athletes' concentration prior to a key performance. Figure 13.3, for example, shows the duration of preparatory concentration exhibited by the Russian weightlifter Zhabotinski during the 1965

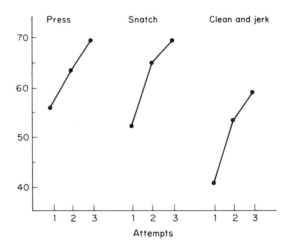

Figure 13.3 Psyching up (concentration) time taken by world champion L. Zhabotinski (USSR) at the 1965 World Championships. (Successive attempts in each lift are heavier.) (Redrawn from Genov, 1970.)

world championships (Genov, 1970). This was before the press was dropped from Olympic lifting. It is noteworthy that Zhabotinski's concentration time increased with each attempt at heavier weights. Likewise he spent more time preparing for the press and snatch—lifts that are considered more difficult than the clean and jerk.

Other inquiries have included Morgan's series of studies with elite athletes (cf. Morgan & Pollock, 1977). Given the role of pain in long distance running, Morgan was interested in the ability of marathon runners to overcome the "pain barrier." A popular strategy for achieving this is distraction—"distancing" oneself from the pain by concentrating on other topics:

> One of the first marathoners interviewed . . . rehearsed or reconstructed his entire educational experience during each marathon. . . . Another runner always builds a house when he marathons; another writes letters to everyone he owes a letter; another listens to a stack of Beethoven records; another participates in extremely complex mathematical exercises; another steps on the imaginary faces of two co-workers she detests throughout the marathon; another repeatedly sings the Star Spangled Banner in crescendo fashion; another age regresses and becomes a steam locomotive at the base of heartbreak hill; and so on. The various rehearsal themes are rather different, but they all seem to be directed toward the same end—dissociating the painful sensory input [Morgan & Pollock, 1977, pp. 10–11].

Many of the Boston marathoners reported having used this strategy. The top finishers, however, and world-ranked runners said that they used the very *opposite* strategy and often focused on the pain—almost as if it were a barometer of their work efficiency. Experts are now beginning to speculate that, although it may make things more pleasant, distraction from pain may also detract from concentration on the task at hand—namely, running at peak efficiency. It is interesting that weightlifters in the Shelton and Mahoney (1978) study also reported that attentional-focus strategies were the most popular methods of preparing for competition.

Nideffer (1976b) has offered a stimulating analysis of attentional processes in the regulation of human behavior in general and sports in particular. He begins with a subtly significant observation: "It is hard to imagine a variable more central to performance than the ability to direct and control one's attention [p. 395]." Nideffer goes on to suggest that attention can be conceptualized on at least two dimensions— direction and breadth of focus. A person may attent to either external or internal cues, and this attention may be either broad or narrow in its focus. Crossing these two dimensions, Nideffer develops a matrix of attentional styles. He has developed a Test of Attentional and Interpersonal Style (TAIS) and reports data on its test-retest reliability and construct validity. More relevant to the present topic, he has examined the predictive validity of this test in a study with competitive swimmers (Nideffer, in press). Athletes who scored high on a TAIS scale measuring funneled attention:

> were rated by the coach (a) as choking under pressure ($r = .75$), (b) as falling apart if they make early performance errors ($r = .59$), (c) as having to work hard for everything they obtain ($r = .66$), and (d) as becoming worried about one particular thing and being unable to think of anything else ($r = .80$). In addition, swimmers the coach described as being "very inconsistent" . . . tended to become overloaded with external ($r = .60$) and internal stimuli ($r = .67$), to be unable to integrate thoughts and ideas ($r = .63$), and to be unable to effectively narrow attention ($r = .63$).

Related to this last point, it is noteworthy that the Olympic gymnasts consistently reported confidence in their ability to focus their attention (Mahoney & Avener, 1977).

Intervention Possibilities

It is tempting to speculate on the possibility of a complex relationship among the phenomena of arousal, attention, and athletic performance. Assuming that the latter is our primary concern, where do we focus our intervention efforts? The athlete's arousal may be reduced to expand his/her breadth of attention, but this may have no effect on its direction. Likewise, we may not want to increase arousal as a means of focusing attention, since the heightened arousal may detract from fine motor coordination. Why not intervene on attentional skills themselves? Indeed, redirection of attention may help to reduce the athlete's arousal. It is noteworthy in this regard that almost all relaxation strategies involve attentional redirection (cf. Benson *et al.,* 1974) and that Fenz's (1975) research suggests a shift toward external focusing as the athlete becomes more competent. Likewise, a recent study by Borkovec and O'Brien (1977) suggests that physiological, behavioral, and self-report measures of fear may be reduced by manipulation of attention. In their study, attention to external stimuli was more stress-reducing than attention to internal physiological cues. The athlete must usually divide his/her attention between these two realms. However, the optimal balance for each task–person combination may present a formidable assessment challenge. Likewise, we may need to examine techniques for refining attentional skills. Would it be possible to train athletes on signal detection tasks and gradually increase stress levels as they develop better attentional skills?

At present, we are left to conjecture on the most efficacious methods and goals for attentional regulation in the athlete. Among the possibilities are the following:

1. The athlete may be well advised to practice concentrating on the immediate task and to avoid thoughts about evaluation (from audience or coach).
2. The optimal focus of attention may depend on the performance demands (e.g., broad focusing by a quarterback, narrow focusing by a golfer).
3. It may be the case that attention should be concentrated on the ''here and now'' rather than on earlier or forthcoming aspects of the competition.
4. The athlete's ability to concentrate may be facilitated by prior training in which intentional distractions are gradually introduced into practice and accelerated as the athlete becomes progressively more proficient in attention regulation.
5. Practice in attention-related skills such as meditation may be useful.

Needless to say, exploration of attention-manipulation skills and effective training methods may well be one of the most promising directions in future sports research.

CONCLUDING REMARKS

This review has, admittedly, ranged from personal anecdotes and athlete interviews to a few exploratory studies in the realm of sport psychology. It is hardly my contention that we are well on our way toward understanding the parameters of athletic performance. Not only are we poorly supplied with data-based ''answers,'' but we must also acknowledge the probable naivete of some of our current questions. This is not to say that sports psychology is an unfertile area of research, but only to comment on our delinquency in the empirical cultivation of this field. Likewise, I have argued that a cognitive-skills approach may offer promising directions and an ideological compromise between the extremes of personology and environmentalism. Until we lend further experimental scrutiny to this approach, however, its promise will remain unevaluated.

As a clinical psychologist, I would like to close with a comment on the priority and relevance of sports psychology. When our clinics and mental health centers are overflowing with severely distressed persons, is it either reasonable or ethical to devote our professional energies to sports performance? Is not the pain of a suicidal depressive more humanistically compelling than the batting average of a baseball player? These are questions that should not be taken lightly. Given our limited energy and work force, I think that we must give some thought to the question of priorities. At the same time, however, I would defend the priority of research in sports psychology. My views here are based on several considerations. First, sports are a pervasive aspect of our culture (Michener, 1976). They play an integral role in the socialization of our youth and are much too important an element to escape our concern as mental health professionals. Second, sports are well-suited to quantitative research because of their outcome measures. Speed, distance, and height are common examples that offer considerable improvement over the precision of popular psychometric indices. Third, I agree with Dorothy Harris (1973) and others who argue that physical activity may be a facilitator of psychological adjustment. The relationship here is far from simple, but there is some evidence to suggest that—although physical fitness and activity may not be *essential* for psychological well-being—they may facilitate a person's efforts toward self-valuation and growth. Finally, competitive athletics offer many parallels to the demands and stresses of everyday life. As such, they may represent an invaluable microcosm within which we may test and refine our understanding of human adaptation. The athlete must learn to cope with a wide range of stressors—performance standards, the experience of failure, aging, and so on. In evaluating our theories and developing new treatment techniques, the athlete may, therefore, be an able and willing ally. My own recent attempts to bridge the gap between clinical and sports psychology have convinced me that we can learn much about the former from the latter. It may be the case, then, that the athlete is not only a willing ally, but also a welcome one.

REFERENCE NOTE

1. Ahart, F. C. *The effect of score differential on basketball free throw shooting efficiency.* Unpublished master's thesis, Ithaca College, 1973.

REFERENCES

Bandura, A. Behavior theory and the models of man. *American Psychologist,* 1974, *29,* 859–869.

Bandura, A. *Social learning theory.* Englewood Cliffs, New Jersey: Prentice-Hall, 1977. (a)

Bandura, A. Self-efficacy: Toward a unifying theory of behavioral change. *Psychological Review,* 1977, *84,* 191–215. (b)

Beck, A. T. *Cognitive therapy and the emotional disorders.* New York: International Universities Press, 1976.

Benson, H., Beary, J. F., & Carol, M. P. The relaxation response. *Psychiatry,* 1974, *37,* 37–46.

Borkovec, T. D., & O'Brien, G. T. Relation of autonomic perception and its manipulation to the maintenance and reduction of fear. *Journal of Abnormal Psychology,* 1977, *86,* 163–171.

Christina, R. W., & Landers, D. M. (Ed.) *Psychology of motor behavior and sport (2 vols).* Champaign, Illinois: Human Kinetics Publishers, 1976.

Corbin, C. B. Mental practice. In W. P. Morgan (Ed.), *Ergogenic aids and muscular performance.* New York: Academic Press, 1972. Pp. 93–118.

Cratty, B. J. *Psychology in contemporary sport: Guidelines for coaches and athletes.* Englewood Cliffs, New Jersey: Prentice-Hall, 1973.

Edwards, H. *Sociology of sport.* Homewood, Illinois: Dorsey Press, 1973.

Endler, N. S., & Magnusson, D. (Eds.) *Interactional psychology and personality.* New York: Wiley, 1976.

Fenz, W. D. Stress and its mastery: Predicting from laboratory to real life. *Canadian Journal of Behavioural Sciences,* 1973, *5,* 332–346.

Fenz, W. D. Strategies for coping with stress. In I. G. Sarason & C. D. Spielburger (Eds.), *Stress and anxiety, Vol. 2.* New York: Wiley, 1975. Pp. 305–336.

Fisher, A. C. (Ed.) *Psychology of sport*. Palo Alto, California: Mayfield Publishing Co., 1976. (a)

Fisher, A. C. Psych up, psych down, psych out: Relationship of arousal to sport performance. In A. C. Fisher (Ed.), *Psychology of sport*. Palo Alto, California: Mayfield Publishing Co., 1976. Pp. 136–144. (b)

Genov, F. The nature of the mobilization readiness of the sportsman and the influence of different factors upon its formation. In G. S. Kenyon (Ed.), *Contemporary psychology of sport*. Chicago: Athletic Institute, 1970.

Golding, L. A. Drugs and hormones. In W. P. Morgan (Ed.), *Erogenic aids and muscular performance*. New York: Academic Press, 1972. Pp. 367–397.

Harris, D. V. *Involvement in sport: A somatopsychic rationale for physical activity*. Philadelphia, Pennsylvania: Lea & Febiger, 1973.

Horstman, D. H. Nutrition. In W. P. Morgan (Ed.), *Ergogenic aids and muscular performance*. New York: Academic Press, 1972. Pp. 343–365.

Landers, D. M. Observational learning of a motor skill: Temporal spacing of demonstrations and audience presence. *Journal of Motor Behavior*, 1975, *7*, 281–287.

Landers, D. M. (Ed.) *Social problems in athletics*. Urbana, Illinois: University of Illinois Press, 1976.

Landers, D. M. Motivative and performance. The role of arousal and attentional factors. *NCPEAM–NAPECW Proceedings*, 1977, 216–218.

Landers, D. M., Harris, D. V., & Christina, R. W. (Eds.) *Psychology of sport and motor behavior: II*. University Park, Pennsylvania: College of HPER Monograph Series No. 10, 1975.

Landers, D. M., & McCullagh, P. D. Social facilitation of motor performance. *Exercise and Sport Science Reviews*, 1976, *4*, 125–162.

Mahoney, M. J. *Cognition and behavior modification*. Cambridge, Massachusetts: Ballinger, 1974.

Mahoney, M. J. Reflections on the cognitive learning trend in psychotherapy. *American Psychologist*, 1977, *32*, 5–13.

Mahoney, M. J., & Arnkoff, D. B. Cognitive and self-control therapies. In S. L. Garfield & A. E. Bergin (Eds.), *Handbook of psychotherapy and behavior change*. New York: Wiley, 1978.

Mahoney, M. J., & Avener, M. Psychology of the elite athlete: An exploratory study. *Cognitive Therapy and Research*, 1977, *1*, 135–141.

Martens, R. *Social psychology and physical activity*. New York: Harper & Row, 1975. (a)

Martens, R. The paradigmatic crises in American sport personology. *Sportwissenschaft*, 1975, *5*, 9–24. (b)

Martens, R. Trait and state anxiety. In W. P. Morgan (Ed.), *Ergogenic aids and muscular performance*. New York: Academic Press, 1972. Pp. 35–66.

Martens, R., Burwitz, L., & Zuckerman, J. Modeling effects of motor performance. *Research Quarterly*, 1976, *47*, 277–291.

McKenzie, T. L., & Rushall, B. S. Effects of self-recording on attendance and performance in a competitive swimming training environment. *Journal of Applied Behavior Analysis*, 1974, *7*, 199–206.

Meichenbaum, D. *Cognitive–behavior modification*. New York: Plenum, 1977.

Michener, J. A. *Sports in America*. New York: Random House, 1976.

Mischel, W. *Personality and assessment*. New York: Wiley, 1968.

Morgan, W. P. (Ed.) *Contemporary readings in sport psychology*. Springfield, Illinois: Charles C. Thomas, 1970.

Morgan, W. P. (Ed.) *Ergogenic aids and muscular performance*. New York: Academic Press, 1972.

Morgan, W. P., & Pollock, M. L. Psychological characterization of the elite distance runner. In P. V. Milvy (Ed.), *Annals of the New York Academy of Science*. New York: New York Academy of Science, 1977.

Nelson, L. R., & Furst, M. L. An objective study of the effects of expectation on competitive performance. *Journal of Psychology*, 1972, *81*, 69–72.

Ness, R. G., & Patton, R. W. The effect of beliefs on maximum weight lifting performance. *Cognitive Therapy and Research*, in press.

Nideffer, R. M. The inner athlete. New York: Thomas Crowell, 1976. (a)

Nideffer, R. M. Test of attentional and interpersonal style. *Journal of Personality and Social Psychology,* 1976, *34,* 394–404. (b)

Nideffer, R. M. The relationship of attention and anxiety to performance. *Coach and Athlete,* in press.

Nideffer, R. M., & Deckner, C. W. A case study of improved athletic performance following use of relaxation procedures. *Perceptual and Motor Skills,* 1970, *30,* 821–822.

Ogilvie, B. C. Psychological consistencies within the personality of high level competitors. *Journal of the American Medical Association,* 1968, *205,* 780–786.

Ogilvie, B. C., & Tutko, T. A. *Problem athletes and how to handle them.* London: Pelham, 1966.

Oxendine, J. B. Emotional arousal and motor performance. *Quest,* 1970, *13,* 23–30.

Richardson, A. Mental practice: A review and discussion. Part I. *Research Quarterly,* 1967, *38,* 95–107. (a)

Richardson, A. Mental practice: A review and discussion. Part II. *Research Quarterly,* 1967, *38,* 263–273. (b)

Rushall, B. S. Three studies relating personality variables to football performance. *International Journal of Sport Psychology,* 1972, *3,* 12–24.

Rushall, B. S., & Siedentop, D. *The development and control of behavior in sport and physical education.* Philadelphia, Pennsylvania: Lea & Febiger, 1972.

Ryan, E. D. Reaction to ''Sport and Personality Dynamics.'' *Proceedings of the National College Physical Education Association for Men,* 1968, 70–75.

Shelton, T. O., & Mahoney, M. J. The content and effect of ''psyching up'' strategies in weight lifters. *Cognitive Therapy and Research,* 1978, *2,* 275–284.

Singer, J. L. *Imagery and daydream methods in psychotherapy and behavior modification.* New York: Academic Press, 1974.

Singer, R. N. Social facilitation. In W. P. Morgan (Ed.), *Ergogenic aids and muscular performance.* New York: Academic Press, 1972. Pp. 263–289.

Suinn, R. M. Behavior rehearsal training for ski racers. *Behavior Therapy,* 1972, *3,* 519–520.

Suinn, R. M. Behavioral methods at the Winter Olympic Games. *Behavior Therapy,* 1977, *8,* 283–284.

Vanek, M., & Cratty, B. J. *Psychology and the superior athlete.* New York: Macmillan, 1970.

Zajonc, R. B. Social facilitation. *Science,* 1965, *149,* 269–274.

14

Cognitive–Behavioral Interventions: Theory and Procedure

STEVEN D. HOLLON
PHILIP C. KENDALL

INTRODUCTION

All three behavioral modalities—motor, autonomic, and cognitive—participate in most human behavior, in parallel and in sequence.

—Wolpe, 1978, p. 440

The authors in this volume have addressed themselves to a delineation of the role of the specific interrelationships between the various organismic-response modalities. The primary emphasis has been on intervention: What procedures, targeted at what processes, provide maximum change (defined in terms of magnitude, stability, and generality) in the phenomena of interest? Though considerable variability exists regarding both theory and procedure, interventions designated as cognitive–behavioral (with respect to either target or procedure) appear to be relatively consistent in their outperformance of alternative approaches.

OUTCOME EFFICACY

At present, it would appear that many of the various cognitive–behavioral interventions have met the principal requirement for judging the adequacy of any systematic intervention: They do what they are designed to do with respect to their target phenomena. However, Ledwidge (1978) has recently argued that cognitive–behavioral approaches ought to be labeled *cognitive therapy,* since they (*a*) did not

445

Cognitive–Behavioral Interventions:
Theory, Research, and Procedures

attempt to modify behavior directly; and (*b*) had, in Ledwidge's judgment, not yet been shown to be any more effective than traditional semantic or strictly behavioral therapies with *clinical* populations.

Ledwidge's review has been criticized by Meichenbaum (Note 1), among others, for what Meichenbaum regards as a selective review of studies, a misrepresentation and erroneous categorization of several studies, an inadequate conceptualization of cognitive–behavioral interventions, and a less than critical endorsement of behavior therapy techniques. Independent of any considerations of the accuracy of Ledwidge's initial critique, it is evident that both of his major concerns have been amply answered during the 3 years that have elapsed since the end of the period covered in his review. For instance, several of the authors in this volume explicitly incorporate traditional behavioral techniques within their cognitive–behavioral interventions: Linehan's use of motor skills training as a component of her structured assertion therapy (Chapter 7); Goldfried's use of progressive relaxation in reducing anxiety (Chapter 5); and Leon's use of stimulus-control procedures in obesity (Chapter 11). Others explicitly use behavioral techniques to enhance learning of cognitive skills: Kendall and Finch's use of response-cost contingencies as an incentive manipulation with impulsive children (Chapter 3); and Meichenbaum and Asarnow's use of modeling as a technique to enhance metacognitive development (Chapter 2). Still others employ cognitive techniques to enhance engagement in behavioral procedures: Hollon and Beck's use of cognitive restructuring to facilitate engagement in assigned "pleasant" activities for depressives (Chapter 6); and Novaco's use of cognitive preparation to facilitate nonaggressive responding in a potentially provocative situation (Chapter 8). In each of these procedures, behavior change is directly approached, albeit behavior change is, presumably, facilitated by attention to cognitive factors.

Ledwidge's second concern, that of comparative treatment efficacy in clinical populations, also seems to have been adequately addressed. Cognitive–behavioral interventions have been shown to be effective in populations with clinically relevant drinking problems (Marlatt, Chapter 10), chronic or transitory pain (Turk & Genest, Chapter 9), assertion problems (Linehan, Chapter 7), anxiety (Goldfried, Chapter 5), and impulsivity (Kendall & Finch, Chapter 3). With regard to depression, cognitive–behavioral interventions have proven superior to strictly behavioral or strictly cognitive interventions across a range of populations, including clinical populations (Fuchs & Rehm, 1977; Shaw, 1977; Taylor & Marshall, 1977), while a comparison with pharmacotherapy favoring a cognitive–behavioral approach (Rush, Beck, Kovacs, & Hollon, 1977) has been criticized as involving a sample that was *too* chronically and severely depressed to be representative of clinical depressives in general (Becker & Schuckit, 1978). In addition to clinical populations, cognitive–behavioral interventions have been applied to populations with problem phenomena in the actual environment. Novaco (Chapter 8) has described a successful intervention for anger and stress-related problems among police, clearly a nonclinical, but very important, population of interest. Although cognitive–behavioral interventions cannot be said to have generated strong support for claims of efficacy for obesity (Leon, Chapter 11), smoking cessation (Pechacek & Danaher, Chapter 12), or delinquency (Little & Kendall, Chapter 4), neither can other available modalities. Problems in *maintaining* treatment-related changes appear central to these areas, problems that have yet to be resolved by any of the alternative interventions. Mahoney's review of cognitive-behavioral factors in athletics (Chapter 13) is admittedly speculative; efforts to develop theoretically based interventions of any kind are just beginning. Nevertheless, the issue with respect to clinical efficacy seems no longer to be one of demonstration; rather, it has become one of replication and extension. Increasingly, attention can be turned away from questions involving "Does it work?" to questions involving "What are the necessary and sufficient procedures?" and "What are the mechanisms through which these procedures operate?"

PROCEDURAL VARIABILITY

As noted previously, there remains considerable variability in terms of the actual operations utilized and the targets at which they are directed. Cognitive–behavior therapy appears to include any combination of cognitive or behavioral techniques directed at any combination of cognitive or behavioral targets. Table 14.1, similar to Table 1.1 from Chapter 1, restates this point and expands the comparison to

TABLE 14.1
Theories, Goals, and Procedures of Intervention

	Theory	Goal	Procedure
Dynamic–Traditional	Unconscious fantasy, actively repressed ideation	Redistribution of inferred energies and insight into unconscious motives	Semantic–symbolic techniques: Free association, interpretation, catharsis, analysis of transference
Cognitive–Semantic	Reportable ideation affecting behavior and emotion	Change in ideation	Semantic–symbolic techniques: Reason, persuasion, logic
Behavioral	Consequent events control behavior; antecedent conditioned stimuli control emotion	Change in behavior	Enactive techniques: Manipulation of antecedent and consequent events
Cognitive–Behavioral	Reportable ideation involved in processing effects of external events, both antecedent and consequent	Change in ideation and change in behavior, each enhancing the other	Both semantic–symbolic and enactive techniques applied to either target independently (combination), or jointly to either (partially integrative), or both (fully integrative) targets

include the theory, goals, and procedures of the various intervention strategies. Cognitive, behavioral, and cognitive–behavioral interventions can all be distinguished from traditional approaches by virtue of being ahistorical, structured, concerned with limiting the range of inference, and, generally, wedded to the principles of methodological behaviorism (Beck, 1970). Cognitive approaches have tended to emphasize semantic intervention procedures (e.g., reason and persuasion) to effect cognitive goals. Behavioral approaches have typically employed enactive procedures or direct environmental manipulations to effect changes in behavioral phenomena. Cognitive–behavioral interventions, albeit apparent in the label, focus upon both. Cognitive–behavioral interventions achieve the dual edge by being (a) a combination, as when two sets of discrete techniques are applied to two sets of discrete phenomena (e.g., using contingency management procedures to alter eating behavior while using cognitive restructuring to alter ideation about food); (b) partially integrative, using both sets of techniques to modify targets in either single domain; or (c) fully integrative, when both sets of techniques are utilized to modify components of both sets of phenomena. Examples would include the use of response-cost incentive manipulations to facilitate self-instructional training designed to alter cognitive tempo and classroom behavior (Kendall & Finch, Chapter 3) or the use of cognitive restructuring techniques with depressives to alter the negative self-statements (automatic thoughts) that interfere with carrying out enactive procedures (Hollon & Beck, Chapter 6). In general, the various programs presented in this text have been either partially or fully integrative.

CONCEPTUAL HETEROGENEITY

The notion that cognitive–behavioral interventions are generally integrative requires a theoretical model that is also integrative. Issues of treatment efficacy and treatment process rest, in part, on the utility of the underlying theoretical models involved. To what extent can cognitive processes be treated as covert behavioral phenomena? To what extent will their incorporation require new models and procedures?

We would suggest that at least one distinction is of particular importance, the distinction between elicited processes, largely under antecedent stimulus control, and emitted processes, largely under consequent stimulus control.[1] Figure 14.1 presents two traditional paradigms, classical and operant S–R models, and a third,

---

[1]Our use of the terms *antecedent stimulus control* and *consequent stimulus control* requires some explanation. In contradistinction to traditional, classical, or operant theories, we are not implying any necessary automaticity in learning processes as a function of mere exposure to contingent events (conditioning). Recent reanalyses and extensions of the learning literatures have emphasized the role of cognitive factors in the acquisition and performance of both classes of responses (cf. Bandura, 1977b; Bolles, 1972; Brewer, 1974; Grings, 1973). *Antecedent stimulus control* might more accurately be termed *the influence of predictive information regarding subsequent events,* whereas *consequent stimulus control* might read *the influences of predictive information regarding differential subsequent events more or less likely to occur as a function of differential motoric activities.*

CLASSICAL

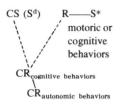

Stimuli (CS's) that predict (precede) biologically significant stimuli (UCS's) come to elicit organismic processes (CR's) similar to the organismic processes (UCR's) elicited by those biologically significant stimuli.

OPERANT

$S^d \cdots R\text{———}S^*$

Organismic processes (R) can be modified by the nature of the events that follow them (S^*), and various stimuli (S^d) that reliably precede those R–S^* events can come to serve as cues for R emission.

COGNITIVE-BEHAVIORAL

CS (S^d)   R———S^*
                 motoric or
                 cognitive
                 behaviors

$CR_{\text{cognitive behaviors}}$

$CR_{\text{autonomic behaviors}}$

Cognitive processes can mediate motoric events and/or subsequent cognitive events and can elicit autonomic events: Cognitive (like behavioral) processes may be either respondents (under stimulus control) or operants (under consequent control).

Figure 14.1. Theoretical models for intervention.

cognitive-mediated, or S-O-R, paradigm. In the classical paradigm, initially neutral stimuli (CSs) paired with biologically relevant stimuli (UCSs) that elicit organismic responses (UCRs) come to elicit similar organismic processes (CRs). These conditioned or organismic processes are generally assumed to occur largely as a function of the antecedent stimuli; that is, they occur independently of their consequences for the organism. The various autonomic and motoric components of syndrome anxiety—sweating, increased heartbeat, change in respiration rate, etc.— represent examples. Classical conditioning represents the core mechanism in Wolpe's model of neurosis (1958).

In the traditional operant paradigm, various antecedent stimuli (S^d's) may serve as cues for response–outcome contingencies, but maintenance and modification of organismic responses are generally considered to be largely a function of consequent stimuli (S^*'s) be they reinforcing or punishing. It is the nature of the consequent event and its relationship to the preceding organismic response that determines the subsequent probabilities of response emission. The modification of response probability by the differential application of various consequent stimuli forms the core of an operant approach (Skinner, 1953).

Our cognitive–behavioral model is essentially two-process, combining both classical and operant components within an S-O-R framework. Along the vertical dimension, antecedent stimuli (labeled either CS or S^d) elicit organismic processes, labeled CRs, in a manner largely independent of the hedonic or adaptive consequences of those processes for the organism. A basic cognitive theory (Beck, 1964; Ellis, 1962) would assert that cognitive mediational processes play a major role in determining the nature of subsequent autonomic processes. Thus, the vertical dimension approximates Ellis's *A–B–C* cognitive model, in which the nature of beliefs at point *B,* perhaps triggered by various stimuli at point *A,* lead irrevocably to automomic (emotional) processes at point *C.* An individual about to step into an airplane (*A*), who thinks that the plane is potentially dangerous (*B*), experiences fear (*C*) and will continue doing so each time he/she is confronted by the initial stimulus. Note that the experience of fear at (*C*) reduces the probability of getting on the plane, not of evaluating the plane as dangerous (*B*).

Across the horizontal dimension, antecedent stimuli (CS or S^d) are similarly thought to be potential elicitors of cognitive processes that deal with either response emission (R) or response–outcome probabilities (R–S*). Continuing with our example from before, the individual approaching the airplane (CS–S^d), thinking about possible danger (CR), steps toward the plane (R), and experiences an increase in fear (CR automomic). Subsequent response probabilities (Rs) in similar situations may largely depend on consequent events, for example, safely arriving at the destination as a consequence of boarding the plane versus staying safely on the ground and experiencing a reduction of unpleasant automomic arousal as a consequence of not boarding the plane.

Although cognitive processes can be seen as elicited organismic responses to stimuli, meaning that their occurrence will be relatively independent of their consequences (e.g., aversive physiological states), some cognitive processes may also function as organismic processes (Rs) in the horizontal (operant) dimension. Thus, processes such as attention, memory search, and reasoning may be somewhat more under consequent control, hence modifiable on the basis of the nature of events that follow. Such a notion is hardly novel with respect to motoric behavior; breathing typically functions without attention to its regulation, and yet it can be brought under consequent control, in the operant sense, within certain parameters. What this suggests is that some cognitive processes may be maintained despite their autonomic (emotional) consequences, whereas others may well be amenable to modification on the basis of the alteration of contingent outcomes.

Both Table 14.1 in this chapter and Table 1.1 in Chapter 1 refer to cognitive and behavioral excesses and deficits. Basic distinctions between some of the phenomena of interest may be highlighted by focusing on the excess–deficit dimension and by contrasting depression and impulsivity. Hollon and Beck (Chapter 6) ascribe to a cognitive theory of depression that focuses on the presumed occurrence of specific cognitions that both elicit negative affect (CR autonomic) and undermine adaptive responding (R motoric). Many of the therapeutic procedures described are targeted at altering the nature of those cognitions. In essence, this represents a cognitive *excess* model. Kendall and Finch (Chapter 3) focus on the apparent absence of task-facilitating cognition in impulsive children, *deficits* that result in an absence of problem solving and verbal mediation, inaccurate responding in various task situations, and excessive behavioral switching (R motoric). Therapeutic techniques are largely geared toward the training of mediating cognitions. Both models emphasize the role of cognitive mediation, but in the first case the emphasis is on the alteration of presumably existing cognitive activity, whereas in the second case the emphasis is on the introduction of cognitive processes where they presumably do not occur.

Ultimately, reliance on stimulus–response paradigms (or, in this case, a cognitively mediated, or S–O–R, paradigm) may prove to be outmoded. Meichenbaum (Note 2) has argued that reliance on stimulus–response terminology may misrepresent current developments and retard further progress in the field. The danger lies in uncritically accepting concepts and assumptions long associated with such terminology. Meichenbaum notes that phenomena such as the development of metacognitive skills (see Meichenbaum & Asarnow, Chapter 2) would be difficult to encompass within an S–O–R framework. He suggests that what is needed is a new language system, one that goes beyond simple stimulus–response terminology.

Certainly, no matter what terminology is utilized, hypotheses regarding causal relationships between the various phenomena of interest require careful attention. Our use of stimulus–response terminology in this chapter was not intended to imply an adherence to any simple deterministic model, especially not a model that necessarily attributes all variation in motoric, cognitive, or affective processes to external environmental events. Bandura's notion of reciprocal determinism may prove to be particularly useful in conceptualizing the nature of causality across classes of events (Bandura, 1978). Bandura notes that various classes of phenomena (e.g., environmental, person, or behavioral variables) may act on, and interact with, one another over time. That is, though external events influence subsequent behaviors or cognitions and affects, behaviors can similarly influence subsequent external events. Person variables, such as cognitive systems or affective propensities, can, similarly, by influencing subsequent motoric acts, influence subsequent external events. Although people are, to some extent, influenced by their environments or their perceptions of their environments, they also play a major role in the shaping of those environments. Models, such as the reciprocal interaction model, do not so much ask which classes of phenomena "cause" which other classes; rather, they start from the premise that each class may be influenced by variations in any other class over time. The issue, then, becomes one of specifying the nature of the various relationships over time and determining the stochastic weight accorded any given variable in the functional relationship.

In this context, one intriguing possibility is that the nature of the development of these various phenomena for any given individual or groups of individuals may influence the very nature of those relative stochastic lines of influence from one class of phenomena to another. For example, Beck (Note 3) has argued that, in some instances, ongoing trains of rumination appear largely autonomous from outside stimuli and that it is the progression of content in the ruminations that is most consistent across situations, not the greater interaction between environment, person, and behavior that more typically holds. It is this predominance of idiosyncratic cognitive sets that Beck regards as central to some types of psychopathology, such as depression (Beck, 1976). Bower (1978) has discussed information-processing models in which hierarchial organizations may facilitate prediction of subsequent cognitive productions. Although cognitions can be considered as stimuli for subsequent cognitions, it remains unclear to what extent preexisting cognitive organization mediates such processes. Mahoney (1977) has suggested that a weighted combination of phenomenological and situational factors provides the best predictor of subsequent behavior. It may well prove that the weights given these respective factors may vary meaningfully as a function of preexisting cognitive organization.

At this time, we know too little about the parameters of information processing, attention, perception, inference, memory organization and retrieval, expectancy formation, attribution, etc., despite their obvious implications for cognitive-behavioral models, but increasing attention is being paid to these phenomena. Efforts by several of the authors in this text, as well as notable contributions by theorists such as Bandura (1977a), with his articulation of self-efficacy theory or Kanfer's articulation of self-control theory (Kanfer, 1970), provide beginning examples.

Central to such research endeavors that seek to clarify the conceptual heterogeneity is the accurate assessment of cognitive phenomena. Current cognitions that may be stimuli for subsequent thought (e.g., Klinger, 1975) or cognitive "styles" (e.g., Kagan, 1966) that may represent preexisting cognitive organizations must be assessed with methodological rigor if questions of prediction are to include cognitive variables. In addition, cognitive assessment is essential for the investigation of the role of cognition in psychopathology and for the confirmation of treatment mechanisms (Kendall & Korgeski, 1979). Although the efforts to develop new cognitive–behavioral interventions and to modify and improve existing treatments are highly valued, there is a similar need to develop further cognitive–behavioral assessment instruments (e.g., Hollon & Kendall, Note 4; Kendall & Wilcox, Note 5).

If, indeed, various cognitive processes may take on either respondent or operant properties, then several propositions follow:

1. Motivational factors, for example, differential consequences, cannot be inferred to exist simply on the basis of reported occurrence of cognitions.
2. Efforts at cognitive–behavior modification may need to follow careful functional analyses of relationships to antecedent and consequent events.
3. Efforts to modify cognitions and behaviors should be closely tied to the results of those functional analyses; different intervention strategies may be required to alter different cognitive processes, just as different strategies appear differentially effective in altering various motoric and autonomic processes.

Our effort is but one step in trying to identify the interactional function of cognition and of other classes of behavior in psychopathology and psychotherapy. At this time, none of the current models can be considered to be entirely satisfactory, but it is clear that some useful gains have been made in this endeavor.

AFTERWORD

There can be little doubt that cognitive-behavioral theories and interventions have reached a point of youthful maturity. The statements of initial promise heard over the last decade have developed into a first generation of studies demonstrating clinical efficacy. Models are becoming increasingly diversified, and intervention strategies are multiplying. Efforts to draw on experimental cognitive psychology are increasing and efforts to integrate cognitive and behavioral theories have become increasingly sophisticated (Bandura, 1977a; Beck, 1976; Kanfer, 1970; Mahoney, 1974, 1977; Meichenbaum, 1977); yet, more work is needed in the area of cognitive–behavioral assessment (Kendall & Korgeski, 1979). The goal remains to increase the breadth and power of explanatory concepts and therapeutic interventions without sacrificing methodological rigor.

REFERENCE NOTES

1. Meichenbaum, D. *Cognitive behavior modification: The need for a fairer assessment.* Unpublished manuscript, University of Waterloo, Ontario, 1978.
2. Meichenbaum, D. Personal communication, September, 1978.
3. Beck, A. T. Personal communication, August, 1978.
4. Hollon, S. D., & Kendall, P. C. *Self-statements in depression: Development of an automatic thoughts questionnaire.* Manuscript submitted for publication, 1979.
5. Kendall, P. C., & Wilcox, L. E. *Self-control in children: The development of a rating scale.* Manuscript submitted for publication, 1979.

REFERENCES

Bandura, A. Self-efficacy: Toward a unifying theory of behavioral change. *Psychological Review*, 1977, *84*, 191–215. (a)

Bandura, A. *Social learning theory.* Englewood Cliffs, New Jersey: Prentice-Hall, 1977. (b)

Bandura, A. The self system in reciprocal determinism. *American Psychologist*, 1978, *33*, 344–358.

Beck, A. T. Thinking and depression: II. Theory and therapy. *Archives of General Psychiatry*, 1964, *10*, 561–571.

Beck, A. T. Cognitive therapy: Nature and relation to behavior therapy. *Behavior Therapy*, 1970, *1*, 184–200.

Beck, A. T. *Cognitive therapy and the emotional disorders.* New York: International Universities Press, 1976.

Becker, J., & Schuckit, M. A. The comparative efficacy of cognitive therapy and pharmacotherapy in the treatment of depressions. *Cognitive Therapy and Research*, 1978, *2*, 193–198.

Bolles, R. C. Reinforcement, expectancy, and learning. *Psychological Review*, 1972, *79*, 394–409.

Bower, G. H. Contacts of cognitive psychology with social learning theory. *Cognitive Therapy and Research*, 1978, *2*, 123–146.

Brewer, W. F. There is no convincing evidence for operant or classical conditioning in adult humans. In W. B. Weimer & D. S. Palermo (Eds.), *Cognition and the symbolic processes.* Hillsdale, New Jersey: Erlbaum, 1974.

Ellis, A. *Reason and emotion in psychotherapy.* New York: Stuart, 1962.

Fuchs, C. Z., & Rehm, L. P. A self-control behavior therapy program for depression. *Journal of Consulting and Clinical Psychology*, 1977, *45*, 206–215.

Grings, W. W. The role of consciousness and cognition in autonomic behavior change. In F. J. McGuigan & R. A. Schoonover (Eds.), *The psychophysiology of thinking.* New York: Academic Press, 1973.

Kagan, J. Reflection–impulsivity: The generality and dynamics of conceptual tempo. *Journal of Abnormal Psychology*, 1966, *71*, 17–24.

Kanfer, F. H. Self-regulation: Research, issues, and speculations. In C. Neuringer & J. L. Michael

(Eds.), *Behavior modification in clinical psychology*. New York: Appelton-Century-Crofts, 1970.

Kendall, P. C., & Korgeski, G. P. Assessment and cognitive–behavioral interventions. *Cognitive Therapy and Research*, 1979, *3*, 1-21.

Klinger, E. Consequences of commitment to and disengagement from incentives. *Psychological Review*, 1975, *82*, 1-25.

Ledwidge, B. Cognitive behavior modification: A step in the wrong direction? *Psychological Bulletin*, 1978, *85*, 353-375.

Mahoney, M. J. *Cognition and behavior modification*. Cambridge, Massachusetts: Ballinger, 1974.

Mahoney, M. J. Reflections on the cognitive-learning trend in psychotherapy. *American Psychologist*, 1977, *32*, 5-13.

Meichenbaum, D. *Cognitive–behavior modification: An integrative approach*. New York: Plenum, 1977.

Rush, A. J., Beck, A. T., Kovacs, M., & Hollon, S. D. Comparative efficacy of cognitive therapy versus pharmacotherapy in outpatient depressives. *Cognitive Therapy and Research*, 1977, *1*, 17-37.

Shaw, B. F. Comparison of cognitive therapy and behavior therapy in the treatment of depression. *Journal of Consulting and Clinical Psychology*, 1977, *45*, 543-551.

Skinner, B. F. *Science and human behavior*. New York: Macmillan, 1953.

Taylor, F. G., & Marshall, W. L. Experimental analysis of a cognitive–behavioral therapy for depression. *Cognitive Therapy and Research*, 1977, *1*, 59-72.

Wolpe, J. *Psychotherapy by reciprocal inhibition*. Stanford, California: Stanford University Press, 1958.

Wolpe, J. Cognition and causation in human behavior and its therapy. *American Psychologist*, 1978, *33*, 437-446.

Author Index

Subject Index